# SOUTHERN CALIFORNIA

LIZ HAMILL SCOTT

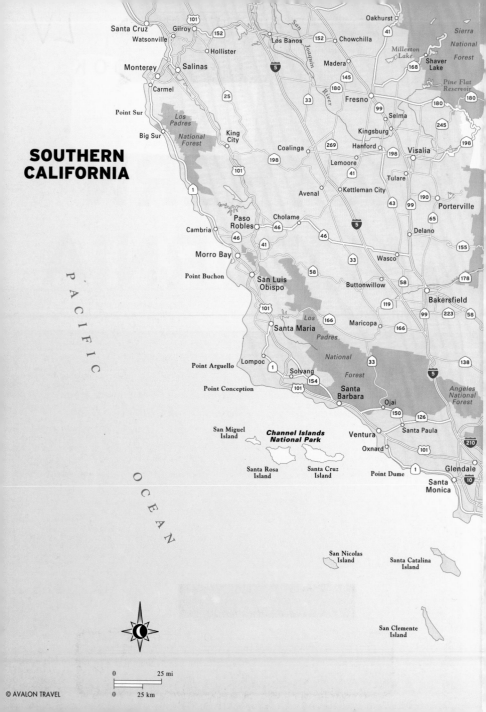

# Contents

# Discover
# Southern California

Southern California is a land of extremes. The urban metropolis of Los Angeles gives way to endless acres of empty desert wilderness. San Diego's smooth, sugar-sand beaches transform into the rocky coves and frigid, crashing surf of Big Sur. The region is home to both the intense heat of the Mojave Desert and the icy coolness of the Eastern Sierra. It harbors Mount Whitney, the highest point in the lower 48 – which sits less than 200 miles from Badwater in Death Valley, the lowest elevation in the United States.

To many, Los Angeles's broad beaches, colorful cityscapes, myriad museums, and multitudes of movie stars *is* Southern California – the epitome of fame and fortune. Yet this sophistication is only an hour from Disneyland, *the* destination for kids of any age. Further still, a laid-back urban getaway lies in San Diego, with picture-perfect beaches and a relaxed vibe.

A few hours east of these big, coastal cities, the austere and forbidding Southern California deserts lure visitors to their sun-drenched reaches. Palm Springs manages to combine cosmopolitan luxury and desert wildness, with a wonderful melting pot of gays and straights, locals and visitors, retired golfers and youthful hipsters.

Yet only a few miles further east lies the vast desert landscapes of Joshua Tree, Anza-Borrego, the Mojave, and Death Valley. Strange yucca

plants, abandoned mines, sculpted sand dunes, relentless temperatures, and acres of solitude are your companions in this remote desert.

These deep, desert valleys stretch north into the jagged, granite peaks of Yosemite, Sequoia, and Kings Canyon National Parks. "Tall" defines this region, with plunging waterfalls, massive boulders, towering redwoods, and mountains that scrape the sky. Waterfalls flow at their peak in spring, leaves color the valley in fall, and skiers swoop down Badger Pass in winter, while summer-only Tioga Pass connects these two sides of the Sierras.

As Southern California stretches north from Los Angeles along the gorgeous Central Coast, a new land emerges. Big Sur's craggy cliffs and dew-soaked redwoods, Cambria's rocky beaches strewn with gemstones, San Simeon's legendary Hearst Castle, and Monterey's basking sea lions – the twisting coast takes in some of the most beautiful scenery in the state.

Whether you want the ultimate urban getaway or total silence and solitude, you can find it all in Southern California.

# Planning Your Trip

## ▶ WHERE TO GO

### Los Angeles and Orange County

For an iconic visit to Southern California, you can't beat a trip to Los Angeles. From the glitz and glamour of **Hollywood** and **Beverly Hills** to the camp and kitsch of **Santa Monica's** Pier, L.A. is all California culture, all the time. Kids of all ages come to visit Walt's original **Disneyland** while sun and surf worshippers ride the waves or relax on the coastal beaches of **Orange County.**

### San Diego

For the sun-drenched, sugar-sand California beach experience portrayed in endless films and TV shows, come to **San Diego.** Maritime museums ring the **Downtown** harbor while across the bay, **Coronado's** vibrant and historic Hotel del Coronado creates a center-piece for visitors to the city. Gorgeous beaches stretch from **Point Loma** north to **La Jolla** and the **North County** coast, begging for surfers, swimmers, strollers, and sunbathers to ply their sands.

### The Deserts

A different kind of beauty makes the Southern California deserts legendary and popular attractions. **Palm Springs** takes the cake as the biggest and coolest desert city. **Joshua Tree**—named for its funky namesake plant—straddles the two major

**IF YOU HAVE. . .**

- **A WEEKEND:** Visit Los Angeles
- **ONE WEEK:** Add San Diego
- **TWO WEEKS:** Add the Deserts and Yosemite
- **A MONTH:** Add the Central Coast

coyote, Joshua Tree

## Yosemite

The work of Ansel Adams and John Muir have helped make **Yosemite National Park** a worldwide icon. Thousands crowd into Yosemite Valley to view the much-photographed Half Dome, Yosemite Falls, and El Capitan. On the other side of the Sierras, **Mono Lake, Mammoth Lakes,** and the **Sequoia and Kings Canyon National Parks** provide a wealth of recreation and wilderness to explore.

## Central Coast

Some of the most beautiful coast in all of California sits right in the middle of the state. Ogle gray whales and sea lions off the rugged **Monterey** bay. Camp and hike the unspoiled wilderness of **Big Sur.** Check out the views from Hearst Castle, **San Simeon's** grandiose mansion, or go wine-tasting in the rolling hills of nearby **Paso Robles.** Further south, **Santa Barbara** beaches await.

desert ecosystems. **Death Valley** boasts both the lowest *and* the hottest spot in the Western Hemisphere. Far south, **Anza-Borrego Desert State Park** is California's biggest state park and one of its most intriguing regions.

## ▶ WHEN TO GO

Believe it or not, summer is *not* the de facto best time to visit Southern California. Sure, it's warm—in fact it can get blisteringly hot and even downright deadly in the deserts—but Southern California is truly a year-round destination.

To catch the central coast at its best, plan a **fall** driving tour. The summer fog lightens up, but temperatures stay reasonably warm and winter storms aren't yet pounding the shores.

Desert rats know **winter** is the best time to hike, bike, and climb the Southern California deserts. This is also a popular time on the golf courses of Palm Springs. (Many courses close in summer, for the sake of both the courses and the players.) To take advantage of the desert's wondrous wildflower blooms, plan your trip for February, March, or early April, and check park websites for annual bloom forecasts and reports. Winter sports enthusiasts should plan a trip to Mammoth Lakes or Badger Pass.

Yosemite is amazing year-round and a trip here will be fabulous whether it's sun-drenched summer or snow-frosted winter. For peak waterfall views, come in **spring** as soon as the snow melts start swelling the rivers.

Sun-worshippers should definitely come in **summer** to ply the San Diego and Orange County beaches. To miss the worst of the crowds, visit the big beaches on a mid-September weekday; it will still be nice and hot, but with school in session, much less crowded.

California wildflowers

# ► BEFORE YOU GO

Southern California is easily reached by **flying** into Los Angeles International Airport, or one of its five subsidiary airports, and San Diego International. Both major cities boast significant **train** stations with daily Amtrak service. Numerous freeways crisscross the region, providing easy driving access.

If planning a trip to the deserts, the central coast, or the Eastern Sierra, rent a **car** or drive your own; you'll find little in the way of public transit. Death Valley visitors will find the nearest major airport in Las Vegas, Nevada rather than in California.

If staying in Los Angeles or along the Orange County corridor, skip the car rental and use public transit. Driving in L.A. can be the slowest, most frustrating exercise you will ever encounter. If you must drive, expect to pay a premium for parking.

Coming to Southern California from abroad? You'll need your **passport** and possibly a **visa**.

Make **reservations** and **buy tickets** in advance, especially if you're visiting the beaches or Yosemite during July and August or on a holiday weekend. It's also a good idea to make early reservations at popular hotels and inns.

Bring seasonal **clothing** based on the specific locales you will visit. Beaches tend to be warm in summer—bikinis are okay, especially in San Diego! Winter in the deserts means long pants and sweatshirts. For snowy winter destinations, dress in warm, weather-resistant layers. Sunglasses and a wide-brimmed hat are also almost always a good idea and no matter what, don't forget sunscreen!

# Explore Southern California

## ▶ THE BEST OF SOUTHERN CALIFORNIA

While the options for travel in Southern California are limitless, first-timers can take this trip to check out some of the best and brightest spots in the region.

### Day 1

Begin in **Los Angeles.** Take a drive along **Wilshire Boulevard,** winding through L.A.'s urban jungle. Stop at a few of the coolest spots—the **La Brea Tar Pits** delight both kids and adults, while **LACMA** offers a more cultural respite—before stopping in Hollywood for lunch. Spend the afternoon walking the **Hollywood Walk of Fame** and checking out the handprints of the stars in front of **Grauman's Chinese Theatre.**

### Day 2

Go to **Disneyland!** Spend the day riding rides, rambling through crowds, and watching parades at the most lovingly created theme park in the state. For a full on Disney-riffic experience, spend the night at the Disneyland Hotel.

### Day 3

Point the car south and follow the Pacific Coast Highway to **San Diego.** Stop often along the North County coast to drink in the surfers, sunsets, and sugar-sand beaches. Arrive in San Diego in time for dinner and spend the evening taking a ghost tour of the **Gaslamp District.**

### Day 4

Spend a sunny day at **Balboa Park** and visit the legendary **San Diego Zoo.** The park plays host to a wealth of museums—art, culture,

## BEST BEACHES

Santa Monica State Beach

- **Best for Biking:** Will Rogers State Beach (L.A.); Natural Bridges State Park (Santa Cruz)

- **Best for Beach Games:** Malibu Lagoon State Beach (L.A.); Huntington City Beach and Dana Point (Orange County); Santa Cruz Beach Boardwalk (Santa Cruz)

- **Best for Dogs:** Ocean Beach (San Diego); Carmel Beach (Carmel); Arroyo Burro Beach (Santa Barbara)

- **Best for Sunbathing:** Santa Monica State Beach (L.A.); Coronado Main Beach (San Diego); East and West Beaches (Santa Barbara); Seabright Beach (Santa Cruz)

- **Best for Wildlife:** Avalon (Catalina Island); La Jolla Cove (San Diego); Santa Barbara Harbor (Santa Barbara); Point Lobos State Reserve (Carmel); Natural Bridges State Park (Santa Cruz)

panda, San Diego Zoo

history, science—and the trails in shady Palm Canyon offer a tranquil respite.

## Day 5

Get an early start on I-15 north. You'll be returning to the L.A. basin to head east on I-10 toward the desert enclave of **Palm Springs.**

Botanical Garden at Balboa Park, San Diego

Ride the **Palm Springs Aerial Tramway,** ascending 8,000 feet for epic vistas of the surrounding desert. Spend an hour or two napping beside the pool or indulging in a spa, then gather your energy for a hot night out at the popular clubs, like Mixi's Boy Bar, that cluster in downtown Palm Springs.

## Day 6

In just an hour, the Twentynine Palms Highway cruises quickly to **Joshua Tree National Park.** Stop at the **Oasis of Mara** visitors center and stroll along the lush nature trail for a quick introduction to the park's natural features. For epic views, take the park road to **Keys View** for a panorama of the Coachella Valley. The tiny town of Twentynine Palms offers a few accommodations, or return to the nightlife of Palm Springs.

## Day 7

Gas up the car and prepare for one of the great desert drives—where civilization ends and the clear air makes rock edges knife-sharp and distant mountains loom close. You'll be hopping on I-15 north, connecting with Highway 395 to CA-190 into remote **Death Valley.** Spend the night at Panamint Springs or push on to Furnace Creek for closer access to the area's amenities and attractions.

In summer, skip Death Valley and take a quick side trip out to **Devil's Postpile National Monument,** possibly the weirdest natural geological feature you'll ever see.

## Day 8

Spend the day driving Death Valley's major sights—**Artist's Palette, Badwater Basin,** and **Scotty's Castle.** At sunset, hop out of the car for a quick hike to the **Sand Dunes** when the setting sun colors the shifting sands.

## Day 9

Return to Highway 395 and head north into the Eastern Sierra Nevada. Stop near Lee Vining to explore the unique tufa formations at **Mono Lake Tufa Preserve.**

In summer, check out the historic ghost town of **Bodie State Historic Park,** an abandoned Gold Rush–era town left in a state of "arrested decay." Then wind along the famed Tioga Pass, stopping at Tuolumne Meadows to stretch your legs and enjoy the gorgeous grasses and trickling streams. (Reserve campsites in advance to stay the night.)

In winter, play in the snow at **Mammoth Lakes,** an upscale skier's paradise filled with fabulous lodges and rental condos thick on the ground.

## Day 10

Continue west along Tioga Pass Road into breathtaking **Yosemite Valley.** A drive along the Valley floor passes gushing waterfalls,

Mirror Lake, Yosemite

# MISSIONS TO MID-CENTURY MODERN

The early Spanish Catholic missionaries inadvertently started a fad for distinctive architecture that endures to this day. Architecture buffs come to Southern California to tour Missions both historic and in the Mission Revival-style, as well as Craftsman and Mid-Century Modern homes, mansions, and buildings. For living examples of these styles, visit the following architecturally significant locales.

## MISSIONS

To get a taste for the oldest permanent architecture in Southern California, follow the historic Mission Trail. The trail begins at **Mission San Diego de Alcala** and progresses north along the El Camino Real (the old Mission road, marked by a series of raised bells), showcasing the 17th century Mission style of crosses, arches, light stucco facades, and red-clay tile roofs. Along the way, you'll find Span-

Carmel Mission

ish Missions in all stages of restoration, from the gorgeously refurbished facade of **Carmel Mission** to the fourth incarnation of **Mission Santa Cruz.**

## MISSION REVIVAL

At the end of the 19th century, long after most Missions were secularized (and often abandoned), California builders rediscovered the lost architecture of these original structures. The Mission Revival style flowered from 1890 through 1915 and remains a popular style for homes and public buildings in Southern California. The lush coastal town of **Santa Barbara** is a great place to see firsthand how the iconic **Santa Barbara Mission** influenced the town's architecture.

## CRAFTSMAN

As the popularity of the Mission Revival style began to fade, the American Arts and Crafts movement started sweeping the nation from the late 19th to early 20th centuries. Many of these fabulous Craftsman homes can be found in the wealthy residential sections of the Los Angeles basin. The **Gamble House** in Pasadena is one of the most famous Craftsman homes in California. After touring this Greene & Greene masterpiece, take a walking tour of the other Craftsman mansions in this quiet, shady neighborhood.

## MID-CENTURY MODERN

Perhaps the most recognizable architecture of Southern California, the Mid-Century Modern style — sweeping curves and angles, frosted glass blocks, crazily tilted flat roofs — often graces the silver screen. Many Mid-Century Modern homes and buildings dot the landscape of Los Angeles and a great way to see these funky '50s exteriors is a drive along famed **Mulholland Drive.** For a better look at the style that defined Hollywood, tour the homes and hotels of **Palm Springs.** Out in the desert retreat of Hollywood's famous stars, you can even stay in several of these architectural gems, including the William F. Cody designed **Del Marcos Hotel** or the **Triangle Inn.**

amazing rock formations, sweeping meadows, and historic structures. Book (in advance!) a luxurious suite or a rustic tent cabin and dine at the legendary **Ahwahnee Hotel.**

### Day 11

The best way to experience Yosemite is on foot. Hike the relatively flat **Mirror Lake** loop or the more challenging **Mist Trail,** which passes not one but *two* waterfalls. End the day with a casual dinner in **Wawona.**

### Day 12

Make the long drive back to Los Angeles (down Highway 41 to CA-99 and I-5), ending your whirlwind SoCal tour!

## ▶ FAMILY FUN IN THE SUN

Woohoo! There's no place quite like Southern California to spend a fun family vacation. Whether your brood prefers the exotic animals of the San Diego Zoo, splashing in the surf of a sandy beach, or the carefully sculpted kitsch of Disneyland, the fun is just waiting for you to find it.

### Amusement Parks

Everyone should visit Uncle Walt's original **Disneyland** at least once in their life. (Think of it as Mecca for secular Americans.) With scads of hotels, motels, and theme resorts packed into a multiple-mile radius of the Happiest Place on Earth, planning your family's trip to worship at the altar of the Mouse is a no-brain proposition.

Even curmudgeonly adults find themselves getting into the spirit of the place as they read the tombstones outside of the Haunted Mansion and suck on hard candies while promenading down Main Street, USA.

Competing with Disneyland is nearby **Knott's Berry Farm.** Knott's boasts a wide array of thrill-heavy roller coasters, making it a worthy alternative for families whose teenagers are just too cool for the "kiddie" rides at the House of Mouse. **Magic Mountain,** well outside of L.A. proper but still accessible via car, is another thrill-rider's favorite, with G-force coasters and rides.

### Beaches

If your family wants to spend their vacation playing in the sand and surf of Southern California beaches, you've got plenty of options to choose from. On the L.A. coast, the **Santa Monica Pier** has a big, flat, sandy beach, an amusement park, and plenty of food and service options within walking distance of the prime beach-blanket spots.

The beach adjacent to the **Venice Boardwalk** will appeal to teens. With close proximity to the carnival sideshow that *is* the Boardwalk, as well as the sand and surf, the entertainment options are endless. Down on the Orange County coast, **Huntington Beach** is a great place for families to play.

Almost any San Diego beach will suit

Ferris wheel and pier, Santa Monica

# FOLLOWING THE FOOTSTEPS OF THE STARS

the historic Grauman's Chinese Theatre in Hollywood

Perhaps the best known aspect of Southern California is its rarified position as the legendary home of the film industry. From the production houses in the San Fernando Valley to film locations scattered like leaves all over the area, movie buffs can follow in the paths of their favorite actors, directors, and films.

## HOLLYWOOD

Where to start? Why, Hollywood, of course! Sure, it's a cliché, but it's a cliché for a reason. Pound the star-studded sidewalks of the **Hollywood Walk of Fame,** see your favorite "stars" in the **Hollywood Wax Museum,** then join the crowd oohing and aahing in the courtyard of **Grauman's Chinese Theatre.** Overlooking Hollywood sits grand **Griffith Park,** whose Observatory hid James Dean and Natalie Wood in *Rebel Without a Cause.*

A variety of major studios offer tours of back lots, sets, and other spiffy "behind the scenes" aspects of movie and TV production. Book reservations in advance for tours of **Universal, Warner Bros.,** and **NBC Studios.**

## PALM SPRINGS

In the golden 1940s and 50s, beleaguered movie stars retreated from Los Angeles to get their relax on in the desert haven of Palm Springs. The amazingly clear dry air also drew plenty of directors, who used the city and its surrounding countryside as a prime film location.

Lay your head in the same bed as Liz Taylor at **A Place in the Sun.** The stylish motel once housed the cast and crew of the 1950s Elizabeth Taylor-Montgomery Clift vehicle of the same name. **Desert Memorial Park** is the final resting place of 'Ol Blue Eyes and several members of the Sinatra family also reside here. To fully explore the area's celebrity residents and their fabulous abodes, take a **Celebrity Tour** through the town.

## CORONADO

Filmmakers and TV producers realized early on that Southern California featured screenworthy gems. The **Hotel del Coronado,** on the island of Coronado in San Diego, may look familiar at first sight. The grandiose "Del" has starred in a number of films, most famously *Some Like It Hot* with Marilyn Monroe.

a family's wants and needs; **Del Mar City Beach** is a favorite.

Along the central coast, the beaches of Big Sur, Carmel, and Monterey tend to be cold, rocky, and less kid-friendly. This changes in Santa Cruz, where the **Santa Cruz Beach Boardwalk** appeals to kids of every age and temperament.

## Water Parks

Some refreshing, easy-to-find family fun can be found at numerous water parks scattered across Southern California. It gets hot (and I do mean *hot*) in the summertime. Inland Orange County responds with two water parks—**Knott's Soak City** and **Wild Rivers Water Park**—to cool off the kids (and adults) with dozens of slides and pools. **Knott's Soak City USA** offers Palm Springs denizens a welcome respite from the desert heat.

## Zoos

A trip to the **San Diego Zoo** or the **San Diego Wild Animal Park** makes for a different kind of theme park vacation. With rides to satisfy the kids and informative animal exhibits to enchant the adults, both the San Diego Zoo and the Wild Animal Park offer something special and unique—there's nothing else quite like them in California. Plus, the San Diego Zoo is centrally located in lovely Balboa Park, making it easy to get a bite to eat and even explore the art museum or botanical garden as part of a zoo-based vacation.

**SeaWorld San Diego** has a winning combination of wild animals, sea life, fun rides, and upbeat shows for the whole family. Meet killer whales and cool off overworked kiddies afterwards with a river ride or splash-down roller coaster.

# ▶ ROMANTIC COASTAL GETAWAYS

If three (or more) is a crowd, head to one of Southern California's charming seaside cities where you can choose from a near-infinite array of romantic inns, luxury spa resorts, gourmet restaurants, and secluded beaches for the perfect romantic getaway.

## Catalina Island

For a more Mediterranean feel to your holiday, without the jet-lag of a flight to Italy, you can't go wrong with a trip to Catalina Island. Ferries depart daily from several Orange Counties ports and Avalon, Catalina's sole town, is rife with charming Riviera-style villas that climb up the steep hillside from the semicircular beach.

Go **snorkeling** amid schools of bright-orange garibaldi fish, anemones, and swarms of other sea creatures. For the ultimate adventure in romantic seclusion, kayak to one of Catalina's **boat-in campsites,** where you may have the beach—and your lover—all to yourself on a warm summer's night.

## San Diego

At Southern California's tip, the San Diego beach scene offers almost unlimited romance potential. The pounding surf serenades guests in the beachfront rooms at historic **Hotel del Coronado** while the more risqué **Black's Beach** provides clothing-optional sands. At night, sail around the bay on a **dinner cruise** or book a candlelight table at one of the **Gaslamp District's** excellent restaurants.

## Carmel

Carmel is particularly well set up to accommodate travelers à deux, with quaint streets perfect for strolling, inns overlooking the ocean, delightfully upscale California cuisine,

# WHERE TO GET YOUR KICKS

The epicenter of the car culture explosion in America sits right in the midst of Southern California. So make like a native: Get in a car, and take a road trip!

## ROUTE 66

Sometimes, it's the road itself that's the "sight to see." No strip of Southern California asphalt has been so adored in legend and song than the desert Route 66. Fans of historic kitsch still get their kicks on the Great American Highway, which starts in **Santa Monica,** wends through **Los Angeles,** then flows out to San Bernardino, Barstow, and Needles before continuing on into the Arizona desert.

## PACIFIC COAST HIGHWAY (PCH)

A prettier – but more crowded – road is the Pacific Coast Highway, or PCH. Beginning in **San Diego,** the PCH clings to the coastline as it winds up through **Orange County, Los Angeles,** and **Santa Barbara.** As it rolls further north along the rocky central

State Highway 1

coast, the PCH becomes State Highway 1, slowing waaaaay down near the soaring cliffs of **Big Sur** before speeding up again through bucolic **Carmel,** historic **Monterey,** and sun-loving **Santa Cruz.**

## HIGHWAY 395

To check out the fabulous mountain reaches of the Eastern Sierra Nevada, roll north up I-15, then pick up Highway 395 outside Barstow. The one-time trading route wends up through the popular **Mammoth Lakes** ski area, **Mono Lake's** unique tufa towers, **Bodie's** historic ghost town, and (in summer) into the high sierra of **Yosemite National Park.**

and at least one perfect B&B just waiting for lovers to come along.

Wander the chamomile labyrinth at **Earthbound Farms,** or just pick up supplies for a picnic at one of the many beaches along scenic **17-Mile Drive.** Couples preferring the performing arts can get seats for plays and classical music performances almost year-round.

## Big Sur

Honeymooners who want to be (or at least feel) all alone in the world can find their hearts' solitude in Big Sur. The luxurious accommodations at **Ventana** and **Post Ranch** cost more than just a pretty penny. But when sitting in your own private outdoor hot tub, feasting on homemade pastries and watching birds and butterflies play in a wildflower meadow that stretches out toward the distant sea, you'll never feel happier or more serene.

Budget lovers can forego the luxury resorts in favor of a secluded wooded campsite or a riverside cabin for two in **Pfieffer Big Sur State Park,** one of the coast's lush redwood parks. Spend your days hiking in forests, combing the rocky mineral-strewn beaches, or meditating on cliffs facing the endless Pacific.

## Santa Barbara

In Santa Barbara, the only hitch you may find in your romantic plans is competing with locals who've been taking their anniversary getaways to this legendary seaside town for years.

Stroll hand-in-hand through the **Santa Barbara Botanic Gardens** or opt for romance by the glass at one of the region's intimate **wineries.** Browse for gifts for your sweetie along **State Street**—Santa Barbara's main drag does double duty as an enormous mall. Spend the evening gazing at the setting sun from your room in one of the town's many oceanfront resorts.

# ▶ SURF'S UP!

Among Southern California's major attractions, the endless opportunities to surf, scuba, and swim draw visitors by the thousands. Whatever your favorite water activity, Southern California has plenty of places to just dive in!

## Kayaking

Southern California offers endless opportunities for both ocean and river kayaking. Sedate harbor and lagoon tours are perfect for the whole family, even if they've never kayaked before.

Kayaking around **Santa Barbara** is one of the best ways to experience these rich ocean waters—filled with dolphins, seals, and even whales—firsthand. Sign up for lessons, a tour, or simply rent your own and get out on the water!

Many unreachable parts of **Catalina Island** open up to exploration on a kayak. A variety of tours accommodate everyone from small children and beginners to rescue-certified sea kayakers.

North of **San Diego,** you can tour the sea caves of the La Jolla Cove Ecological Reserve in sit-on-top kayaks. Or stick to the central coast and explore the chilly waters of **Monterey.** The surrounding bay is a popular kayaking spot, with plenty of local outfitters and rental shops ready to hook you up.

## Snorkeling and Scuba

To explore the undersea ecology of the California coast, head to **Catalina Island,** where a number of outfitters offer snorkel and scuba tours of the island's pristine and life-filled waters. Explore shipwrecks, kelp forests, and even swim with dolphins at this sunny ocean retreat.

The sparkling clear waters of **La Jolla Cove,** north of San Diego, provide a calm surface for beginning snorkelers. More adventurous travelers can sign up for an exciting night dive.

The frigid waters of **Monterey** may not seem inviting at first, but there's no better place to get certified in scuba diving. Draw on a dry-suit and brave the seriously cold water, or head instead to the **Monterey Bay Aquarium** for a sense of the local undersea environment in more comfortable surroundings.

## Surfing

Prefer to ride the waves rather than dive beneath them? Take your first surfing lesson at one of the San Diego or Orange County beaches. **Huntington City Beach** and **Del Mar City Beach** feature low, even waves that make for an easy first ride, but still have plenty to offer experienced surfers. Santa Barbara's **Leadbetter Point** is another great surf spot for beginners.

Adrenaline junkies can head to the surfing Mecca of Santa Cruz where the longboard paradises of **Pleasure Point** or famous—and dangerous—**Steamer Lane** beckon.

Even if you don't quite have the coordination to rise to your feet on the waves, you can still get a thrill out of a good Pacific roller. Many surf beaches, such as Huntington City Beach and Zuma Beach near Malibu, are also good spots for **boogie boarding.**

SoCal surfer

# ON THE TRAIL

While better known for its car culture, Southern California also offers an endless array of foot paths and hiking trails to tempt locals and visitors alike.

## LOS ANGELES

Pick up one of the L.A. coast's many flat, paved pedestrian paths and friendly streets. The peaceful waterways of the **Venice Canals,** where locals walk their dogs, are perfect for a sedate stroll. **Griffith Park** is filled with great hiking trails; pick a short nature walk or a more strenuous hike into the undeveloped mountains.

## SAN DIEGO

Beautiful wilderness trails at **Torrey Pines State Reserve** lead from forest to ocean and back.

## THE DESERTS

If you love a walk out into the desert, come in winter to check out any of the stunning waterless landscapes. The Black Rock Campground at **Joshua Tree** accesses a number of trails offering scenic vistas of the eponymous plants. In **Death Valley,** the constantly shifting Sand Dunes near Stovepipe Wells provide an ever-changing desert beauty. Explore ancient grinding rocks used by Native Americans on the quick and easy Trail to the Morteros in **Anza-Borrego Desert State Park.**

Upper Yosemite Fall, Yosemite National Park

## YOSEMITE

From the flat meadow loop trail on the **Yosemite Valley** floor to the hardcore climb up the back of Half Dome to the miles of backcountry tracks off **Tioga Pass,** Yosemite National Park has a perfect hike for any traveler.

## BIG SUR

The lush landscapes of the Central Coast offer redwood forest hikes and spectacular on-the-beach walks. Stroll to waterfalls in **Julia Pfeiffer Burns State Park** or wander among the coast redwoods in **Pfeiffer Big Sur State Park.**

## Swimming

Second only to *laying* on the beach, swimming is one of the most popular ways to get into Southern California's rivers, lakes, and ocean.

The Los Angeles coast is a prime beach destination, with plenty of places to dive into the cool Pacific waters. **Zuma Beach, Malibu State Lagoon State Beach,** and **Redondo State Beach** all get the nod of approval as perfect spots to frolic in the surf. The 70°F waters of lovely **Catalina Island** are perfect for a lazy beach day.

Warmer waters beckon further south along the coast. Dip into crystal-clear **La Jolla Cove** north of San Diego or stay in the city proper and head toward mile-long **Ocean Beach.**

The water at **New Brighton State Beach** may be cold, but the scenery can't be beat. This sandy spot near Santa Cruz offers cold-water swimming and even campgrounds, if you just can't bare to leave the lovely surf. Want to bring your four-legged friend with you? Head to **Carmel Beach** where canines and their people are welcome to wade and splash around in the windy surf.

# LOS ANGELES AND ORANGE COUNTY

With icons like Hollywood, Disneyland, and Malibu, Los Angeles and Orange County together form the California that rest of the world envisions. It's true that palm trees line sunny boulevards and the Pacific Ocean starts to warm to a swimmable temperature here—and that traffic is always a mess. But celebrities don't crowd every sidewalk signing autographs and movies aren't filming on every corner.

Instead, L.A. combines the glitz, crowds, and speed of the big city with an easier, friendlier feel in its suburbs. A soft haze often envelops the warm beaches, which draw lightly clad crowds vying to see and be seen while children play in the water. Power shoppers pound the sparkling pavement lining the ultra-urban city streets. Tourists can catch a premiere at Grauman's Chinese Theatre, try their feet on a surfboard at Huntington Beach, and ogle the relics of the La Brea Tar Pits.

For visitors who want a deeper look into the Los Angeles Basin, excellent museums dot the landscape, as do theaters, comedy clubs, and live music venues. L.A. boasts the best nightlife in California, with options that appeal to starwatchers, hard-core dancers, and cutting-edge music lovers alike.

Out in the O.C., as Orange County is referred to, lies the single most recognizable tourist attraction in California: Disneyland. Even the most jaded native residents tend to soften at the bright colors, cheerful music, sweet smells, and sense of fun that permeate the House of Mouse. Orange County visitors also find scenic,

# HIGHLIGHTS

**◖ La Brea Tar Pits:** It's worth braving the smell for a glimpse at the fossilized remains of everything from mammoths to mice. The accompanying museums allows visitors a peek at museum's paleontologists at work (page 28).

**◖ LACMA:** LACMA's seven buildings house a diverse and extaordinary array of art in a variety of mediums. Time your visit to coincide with one of their prestigous exhibitions (page 28).

**◖ Hollywood Walk of Fame:** Since 1968, entertainment legends have wished for a star on this three-mile walk of fame (page 31).

**◖ Grauman's Chinese Theatre:** This Hollywood icon opened in 1927 and has played host to hand and footprints of the stars, along with premieres of their movies (page 33).

**◖ Griffith Park:** A welcome expanse of greenery, "L.A.'s Central Park" includes the Griffith Observatory, the L.A. Zoo, and the Hollywood sign, as well as several film locations (page 33).

**◖ Santa Monica Pier:** On a sunny Southern California day, nothing beats a day at the pier. Rides the rides, gorge at the midway-style stands, or simply spread a blanket on the beach (page 38).

**◖ Venice Boardwalk:** From the freaky to the fantastic, the Venice Boardwalk has it all. Park yourself for people-watching of fantastic proportions or even participate a bit yourself (page 38).

**◖ The Gamble House:** Take a tour of the Gamble House, a (potentially haunted!) masterpiece of 20th century Craftsmen architecture (page 40).

**◖ California Adventure:** Disneyland may have the mouse, but it's California Adventure – the Golden State–themed park that acompanies it – that has all the rides (page 74).

**◖ The *Queen Mary*:** This famous former pleasure cruiser is now a famously haunted and historic hotel, musem, and entertainment center. Be sure to book the Paranormal Ship Walk for a highlight of the ship's "most haunted" spots (page 83).

LOOK FOR ◖ TO FIND RECOMMENDED SIGHTS, ACTIVITIES, DINING, AND LODGING.

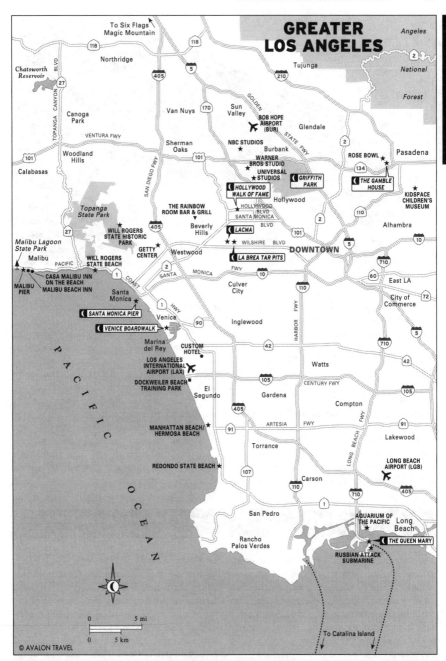

# GREATER LOS ANGELES

To Six Flags Magic Mountain

Chatsworth Reservoir

Northridge

Tujunga

Angeles

National

Forest

Canoga Park

Van Nuys

Sun Valley

BOB HOPE AIRPORT (BUR)

Glendale

VENTURA FWY

Sherman Oaks

NBC STUDIOS ★

Burbank

Rose Bowl ★

Pasadena

Woodland Hills

WARNER BROS STUDIO ★

UNIVERSAL ★ STUDIOS

Calabasas

HOLLYWOOD WALK OF FAME

GRIFFITH PARK

THE GAMBLE HOUSE

Topanga State Park

THE RAINBOW ROOM BAR & GRILL

Hollywood

KIDSPACE CHILDREN'S MUSEUM

HOLLYWOOD BLVD
SANTA MONICA BLVD

Alhambra

WILL ROGERS STATE HISTORIC PARK

Beverly Hills

LACMA

Malibu Lagoon State Park

GETTY CENTER

Westwood

WILSHIRE BLVD

DOWNTOWN

Malibu

WILL ROGERS STATE BEACH

LA BREA TAR PITS

PACIFIC

SANTA MONICA

CASA MALIBU INN ON THE BEACH
MALIBU BEACH INN

MALIBU PIER

COAST

Santa Monica

FWY

SANTA MONICA PIER

Culver City

East LA

City of Commerce

VENICE BOARDWALK

Venice

Inglewood

HWY

Marina del Rey

CUSTOM HOTEL

Watts

LOS ANGELES INTERNATIONAL AIRPORT (LAX)

HARBOR FWY

DOCKWEILER BEACH TRAINING PARK

El Segundo

Gardena

CENTURY FWY

Compton

MANHATTAN BEACH/ HERMOSA BEACH ★

ARTESIA FWY

Lakewood

Torrance

LONG BEACH AIRPORT (LGB)

REDONDO STATE BEACH ★

Carson

San Pedro

AQUARIUM OF THE PACIFIC

Long Beach

Rancho Palos Verdes

THE QUEEN MARY

RUSSIAN ATTACK SUBMARINE

PACIFIC OCEAN

0          5 mi
0          5 km

© AVALON TRAVEL

To Catalina Island

Malibu Pier

© LANCE SCOTT

sun-swept beaches with lots of great activities, state and national parks, and Knott's Berry Farm (the other O.C. amusement park).

## PLANNING YOUR TIME

When you get into Los Angeles, you'll understand quickly that you'll need to pick and choose your itinerary. The vast urban sprawl is just too big to take in unless you've got several weeks in the area. Your best bet is to follow your own heart to whatever types of activities are your favorites. If you're a first-timer to the Los Angeles area, a great initial tour is a drive down Wilshire Boulevard from end to end, stopping to check out all the many and various sights along the 15-mile way.

If you're planning a trip to Disneyland with your family or a group of friends, stick with the Mouse as your main plan. Many people spend several days exploring the parks, never leaving the Anaheim area. Plenty of restaurants and hotels circle the theme park area, making staying and eating a breeze.

Sun-worshippers and surfers will want to stick with the coastline. It's possible to drive from Malibu to San Juan Capistrano over a weekend, stopping at beachside towns for meals and to spend the night.

# Sights

The only problem you'll have with the sights of Los Angeles and its surrounding towns is finding a way to see enough of them to satisfy yourself. You'll find everything from museums to streets, cheese to class, ancient art to modern production studios ready to welcome you throughout the sprawling cityscape.

## DOWNTOWN AND VICINITY

Downtown L.A. has its tall, glass-coated skyscrapers creating an urban skyline, its sports arenas, its rich neighborhoods, its poor neighborhoods, and its endless shopping opportunities. But most of all, it has some of the best and most unique cultural icons in all of L.A. County. Even kids get a kick out of the museums and parkland of Exposition Park, and adults enjoy the kitsch, shopping, and restaurants of Chinatown. Koreatown is thriving in the 21st century. Downtown makes a great start for any trip to Los Angeles.

## Natural History Museum

If you'd like to get your kids some fun with educational purpose, take them to the Natural History Museum (900 Exposition Blvd., 213/763-3466, www.nhm.org, Mon.–Fri. 9:30 A.M.–5 P.M., Sat.–Sun. 10 A.M.–5 P.M., adults $9, teens/seniors $6.50, children $2, parking $6). This huge museum features many amazing galleries; some are transformed into examples of mammal habitats, others display artifacts of various peoples indigenous to the Western Hemisphere. The Discovery Center welcomes children with a wide array of live animals and insects, plus hands-on displays that let kids learn by touching as well as looking. The chaparral exhibit is a favorite, and it provides a multisensory experience that includes smell as well as sight and sound. Dinosaur lovers can spend a whole day examining the museum's collection of fossils and models, which include a tyrannosaur skull. Be sure to visit the Megamouth as you walk through; it's one of only 17 examples of this species of shark ever discovered by humans. Rock nuts flock to the Natural History Museum to see the fabulous gem and mineral display, complete with gold and a vault filled with rare precious stones. If you're interested in the natural history and culture of California, be sure to spend some time in the Lando Hall of California History.

The Natural History Museum sits within the larger Exposition Park complex. The museum café is open daily 10 A.M.–4 P.M. All exhibits are both wheelchair- and stroller-accessible, but ask at the ticket booths if you need special assistance to tour the museum. Do be aware that the surrounding neighborhood can be dicey, so don't plan to explore the area around the museum on foot.

## California Science Center

Another gem of Exposition Park, the exhibits at the California Science Center (39th and Figueroa St., 323/724-3623, www.californiasciencecenter .org, daily 10 A.M.–5 P.M., admission free, parking $6) focus on the notable achievements and gathered knowledge of humankind. Some of the best traveling scientific exhibits come here. Permanent exhibits start before you even enter the building with the outdoor Science Plaza. Once inside, you'll find galleries dedicated to air and space technology, life as we know it, and human creativity. The central Science Court delights both children and adults with exhibits they can get involved with. Visitors can ride a bike on a three-story-high wire, climb a cliff, or check out a motion-based simulator. The Science Court attractions are *not* part of the free admission to the center.

Many people come to the California Science Center for the IMAX theater, which is open daily and shows educational films on its tremendous seven-story screen. Adult tickets cost $8, while teens, seniors, and students pay $5.75, and tickets for younger children cost $4.75. Your IMAX tickets also get you onto the ride-able attractions of the Science Court.

## Fashion Institute of Design and Marketing

Have you come to L.A. for the fabulous designer clothes, but your credit cards are screaming in agony? Is your all-time favorite TV show *Project Runway?* Then L.A.'s got the perfect museum for you. The FIDM Museum & Galleries (919 S. Grand Ave., 800/624-1200, www.fidm.com, Mon.–Sat. 10 A.M.–5 P.M., hours vary by exhibit, free) are open free to the public, giving costume buffs and clotheshorses a window into high fashion, Hollywood costume design, and the world of fashion design school. Check the website for current and coming exhibitions at the museum. Each winter around award season, the museum shows off a collection of costumes from the previous year's movies, highlighting the film honored with the Oscar for Best Costume Design. Through the rest of the year, the FIDM pulls from its collection of more than 10,000 costumes and textiles to create exhibits based on style, era, movie genre, and whatever else the curators dream up. Parking is available in the underground garage for a fee. When you enter the building, tell the folks at the security desk that you're headed for the museum. A small but fun museum shop offers student work, unique accessories, and more.

Also housed in the FIDM building is the **Annette Greene Perfume Museum** (Mon.–Fri. 9 A.M.–5 P.M., Sat. 9 A.M.–4 P.M.). This museum is dedicated to scent and the role of perfume in society.

## Japanese American National Museum

The Japanese American National Museum (369 E. 1st St., 213/625-0414, www.janm .org, Tues.–Sun. 11 A.M.–5 P.M., Thurs. until 8 P.M., adults $8, children $4) focuses on the experience of Japanese people coming to and living in America. Japanese immigrants came by the thousands to California—one of the easiest and most pleasant places in America to get to from Japan. From the first, they had a hard time of it, facing unending prejudice, exclusion, fear, and outright hatred. Despite this, the tenacious immigrants persisted, even after the horrific acts of the U.S. government upon the Japanese American population during World War II. Japanese culture has folded into the bizarre mix that is the United States. It is especially influential in California, where sushi bars are almost as common as diners in urban centers, and whole nurseries devoted to bonsai gardening thrive. This museum shows the Japanese American experience in vivid detail, with photos and artifacts telling much of the story. You'll also find galleries sheltering temporary exhibitions, from astonishing displays of ikebana floral art to a show devoted to the *Giant Robot* comic book.

## MOCA

The Museum of Contemporary Art, Los Angeles (250 S. Grand Ave., 213/626-6222, www.moca.org, Mon. and Fri. 11 A.M.–5 P.M., Thurs. 11 A.M.–8 P.M., Sat.–Sun. 11 A.M.–6 P.M., adults $8, students $5,

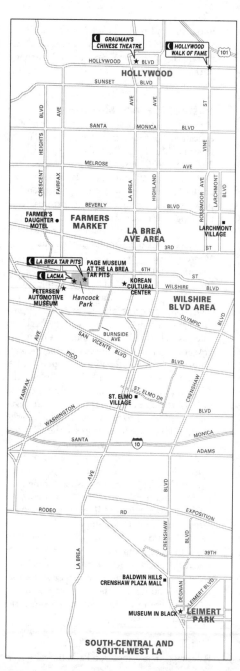

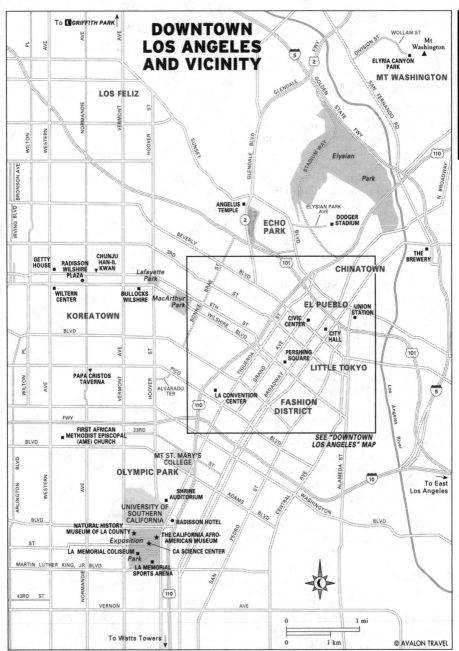

# DOWNTOWN LOS ANGELES AND VICINITY

To **GRIFFITH PARK**

WOLLAM ST

Mt Washington

ELYRIA CANYON PARK

**MT WASHINGTON**

DIVISION ST

SAN FERNANDO RD

**LOS FELIZ**

NORMANDIE

VERMONT ST

HOOVER ST

WILTON

WESTERN

BRONSON AVE

IRVING BLVD

SUNSET

GLENDALE BLVD

GOLDEN STATE FWY

STADIUM WAY

Elysian Park

N BROADWAY

ELYSIAN PARK AVE

ANGELUS TEMPLE

**ECHO PARK**

BEVERLY

3RD

DODGER STADIUM

THE BREWERY

GETTY HOUSE

RADISSON WILSHIRE PLAZA

CHUNJU HAN-IL KWAN

Lafayette Park

BRAE ST

BLVD

**CHINATOWN**

WILTERN CENTER

BULLOCKS WILSHIRE

MacArthur Park

6TH ST

**EL PUEBLO**

UNION STATION

CIVIC CENTER

CITY HALL

**KOREATOWN**

BLVD

BONNIE

VERMONT ST

WILSHIRE BLVD

FIGUEROA

GRAND

AVE

PERSHING SQUARE

**LITTLE TOKYO**

101

PL

WILTON AVE

PAPA CRISTOS TAVERNA

PICO

HOOVER

ALVARADO TER

110

LA CONVENTION CENTER

BROADWAY

**FASHION DISTRICT**

Los Angeles River

5

FWY

FIRST AFRICAN METHODIST EPISCOPAL (AME) CHURCH

23RD

BLVD

*SEE "DOWNTOWN LOS ANGELES" MAP*

ARLINGTON BLVD

WESTERN AVE

BLVD

ST

MT. ST. MARY'S COLLEGE

**OLYMPIC PARK**

ADAMS

ST

BLVD

CENTRAL AVE

WASHINGTON

ALAMEDA ST

10

To East Los Angeles

SHRINE AUDITORIUM

UNIVERSITY OF SOUTHERN CALIFORNIA

RADISSON HOTEL

NATURAL HISTORY MUSEUM OF LA COUNTY

*Exposition Park*

THE CALIFORNIA AFRO-AMERICAN MUSEUM

CA SCIENCE CENTER

LA MEMORIAL COLISEUM

PEDRO

SAN

BLVD

LA MEMORIAL SPORTS ARENA

MARTIN LUTHER KING, JR BLVD

NORMANDIE

110

43RD ST

VERNON

AVE

To Watts Towers

0 _____ 1 mi

0 _____ 1 km

© AVALON TRAVEL

children under 12 free) is better known to its friends as MOCA. Here you'll see an array of artwork created between 1940 and yesterday afternoon. Highlights of the permanent collections include pop art and abstract expressionism from Europe and America.

### C La Brea Tar Pits

Even if you've never been within a thousand miles of California before, you've probably heard of the La Brea Tar Pits and the wonders found within them. But where once tour groups made their stinky way around crude fences protecting them from the pits, now paved paths lead around the most accessible pits, and others (mostly those that are in active excavation) are accessible by guided tour only. Nothing can stop the smell of the tar, or the slow bubbling of the shallow miasma of water that covers the tar.

If what interests you most are the fossilized contents of the tar pits, head for the beautiful **Page Museum** (5801 Wilshire Blvd., 323/934-7243, www.tarpits.org, Mon.–Fri. 9 A.M.–5 P.M., Sat.–Sun. 10 A.M.–5 P.M., adults $7, children $4.50, parking $6–8 in lot). The Page contains the bones of many of the untold thousands of animals that became trapped in the sticky tar and met their fate there. The museum's reasonably small size and easy-to-understand interpretive signs make it great for kids, and good for a shorter stop for grown-ups. You'll see some amazing skeletal remains—like sloths the size of Clydesdale horses. Genuine mammoths died and were fossilized in the tar pits, as were the tiniest of mice and about a zillion dire wolves. One of the coolest things for science geeks is the big windowed cage housing the paleontologists at work. You can watch them cleaning, examining, sorting, and cataloging bones from the most recent excavations.

### C LACMA

Travelers who desperately need a break from the endless, shiny, and mindless entertainments of L.A. can find respite and solace in the Los Angeles County Museum of Art (5905 Wilshire Blvd., 323/857-6000, www.lacma

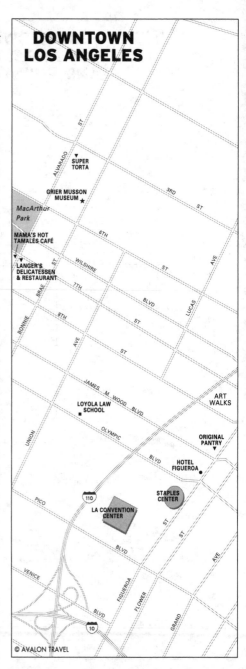

**DOWNTOWN LOS ANGELES**

© AVALON TRAVEL

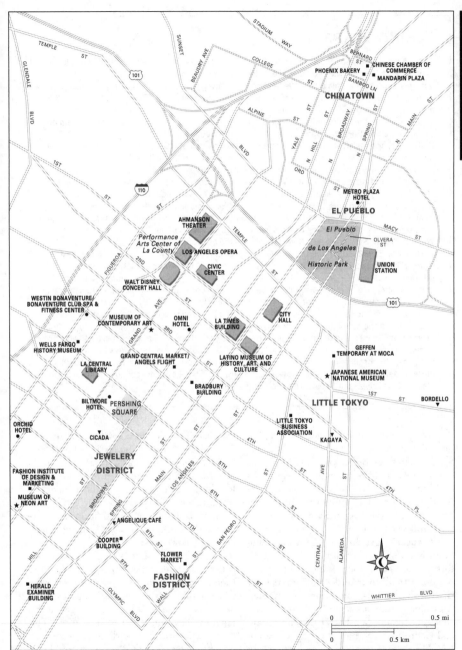

TEMPLE ST
GLENDALE BLVD
101
STADIUM WAY
SUNSET
BEAUDRY AVE
COLLEGE
BERNARD ST

PHOENIX BAKERY ■
■ CHINESE CHAMBER OF COMMERCE
■ MANDARIN PLAZA
BAMBOO LN

**CHINATOWN**

1ST ST
110
ST
ALPINE ST
BLVD
ORD ST
YALE ST
N HILL ST
BROADWAY
SPRING ST
N ST
MAIN ST

■ METRO PLAZA HOTEL

**EL PUEBLO**

FIGUEROA ST
AHMANSON THEATER
Performance Arts Center of La County
2ND ST
LOS ANGELES OPERA
TEMPLE ST
CIVIC CENTER
WALT DISNEY CONCERT HALL

MACY ST
El Pueblo de Los Angeles Historic Park
OLVERA ST
UNION STATION

WESTIN BONAVENTURE/ BONAVENTURE CLUB SPA & FITNESS CENTER ■
GRAND AVE
3RD ST
MUSEUM OF CONTEMPORARY ART ★
OMNI HOTEL ●
LA TIMES BUILDING
CITY HALL
101

WELLS FARGO HISTORY MUSEUM ■
GRAND CENTRAL MARKET/ ANGELS FLIGHT
LATINO MUSEUM OF HISTORY, ART, AND CULTURE
GEFFEN TEMPORARY AT MOCA ■

LA CENTRAL LIBRARY
BRADBURY BUILDING ■
JAPANESE AMERICAN NATIONAL MUSEUM ★

**LITTLE TOKYO**
1ST ST
BORDELLO ▼

BILTMORE HOTEL ●
PERSHING SQUARE
LITTLE TOKYO BUSINESS ASSOCIATION ■
KAGAYA

ORCHID HOTEL ■
CICADA ▼
4TH ST
AVE ST
4TH PL

**JEWELERY DISTRICT**
MAIN ST
LOS ANGELES ST
5TH ST
SAN PEDRO ST
CENTRAL AVE
ALAMEDA ST

FASHION INSTITUTE OF DESIGN & MARKETING ■
BROADWAY
SPRING ST
6TH ST
MUSEUM OF NEON ART ★
7TH ST

ANGELIQUE CAFÉ ▼
8TH ST
COOPER BUILDING ■
FLOWER MARKET ■
9TH ST

**FASHION DISTRICT**
HILL ST
OLYMPIC BLVD
WALL ST

HERALD EXAMINER BUILDING ■
WHITTIER BLVD

0                    0.5 mi

0          0.5 km

# SEEING STARS

When you hear local SoCal denizens talk about "The Valley," they're always talking about the San Fernando Valley. This is the true home of many of the major TV and movie studios. (It's also the reputed origin of valley girls, valley speak, and the teen shopping mall culture.) Suburbs include Burbank, Sun Valley, North Hollywood, and the strangely underwhelming San Fernando.

One of the biggest draws of The Valley is the plethora of major movie and TV studios studding the landscape. Many of these offer tours to visitors who long to see the sets and behind-the-scenes actions of their favorite films and shows. A great place to start is the **Warner Bros. Studio** (3400 Riverside Dr, Burbank, 818/972-8687, www.wbstudiotour.com, VIP Tour $45/person). The tour lasts a little over two hours – you'll ride in carts as you go from place to place through the vast spaces of the studio and back lot. Making both movies and TV shows, the WB tour takes you backstage to the sets and scenes of current productions. You'll also get to tour an array of historic sets, and you'll wind up at the Warner Bros. Memorabilia Museum. For an even more in-depth look at the inner workings of Warner Bros., check out the $150 Deluxe Tour,

which lasts five full hours and includes lunch in the Commissary Fine Dining Room. If you're lucky, you might catch a glimpse of one of your favorite stars from ER or Cold Case! The WB recommends that you purchase your tour tickets in advance – you can call or buy them on the website.

The tour at **NBC Studios** (3000 W. Alameda Ave., Burbank, 818/840-3537, tours Mon.-Fri. 9 A.M.-3 P.M., adults $8.50, children $5) takes you into the wide and often obscure world of network television. Unlike the movie studios, NBC films live and daily shows every day – you'll get to see the working sets of Days of Our Lives and The Tonight Show. In addition, the network has preserved the legendary sets of classic TV shows for your viewing pleasure. Check out the tour-available areas for wardrobe, makeup, and set design. You'll visit the real props and set construction departments. The NBC studio tour lasts just over an hour and requires you to walk for the bulk of the time.

If you want to be part of the action, show up early to stand in line for free tickets to The Tonight Show. Giveaways begin at 8 A.M. daily, or you can send away via snail mail six or more weeks in advance to guarantee yourself seats.

.org, Mon.–Tues. and Thurs. noon–8 P.M., Fri. noon–9 P.M., Sat.–Sun. 11 A.M.–8 P.M., adults $9, children free). Better known to its friends as LACMA, this large museum complex prides itself on a diverse array of collections and exhibitions of art from around the world, from the ancient to the most ultra-modern. With seven full-sized buildings filled with galleries, don't expect to get through the whole thing in an hour, or even a full day. You'll see all forms of art here, from classic painting and sculpture to all sorts of decorative arts (that is, ceramics, jewels, metalwork, and more). All major cultures are represented, so you can check out Islamic, Southeast Asian, European, and Californian art, plus more. Specialties of LACMA include Japanese art and artifacts in

the beautifully designed Pavilion for Japanese Art and the costumes and textiles of the Doris Stein Research Center. Several galleries of LACMA West are dedicated to art and craft for children. Perhaps best of all, some of the world's most prestigious traveling exhibitions come to LACMA; past exhibitions have included the works of Salvador Dali and a new take on Tutankhamen.

You'll do a lot of walking from gallery to gallery and building to building at LACMA. Inquire at one of the two welcome centers for wheelchairs. Not all the buildings are connected; you must walk outside to get to the Japanese Pavilion and LACMA West. The complex is equipped with two full-service museum cafés, an ATM, and a gift and book shop. And finally, if you're in need of some fine rental artwork, LACMA can hook you up.

If you prefer automotive artistry to more conventional forms, head across the street from LACMA to the **Petersen Automotive Museum** (6060 Wilshire Blvd., 323/930-2277, www .petersen.org, Tues.–Sun. 10 A.M.–6 P.M., adults $10, children $3, students $5, parking $8).

# HOLLYWOOD

You won't find any movie studios in Hollywood, and few stars walk its streets except on premiere evenings. It's an odd irony that what the world perceives to be the epicenter of the film industry has little left of that industry beyond its tourist destinations. The only "real" movie business remaining are the blockbuster premieres at the major movie theaters here. Most of the other destinations range from the oversold to the downright kitschy. But still, if you've ever had a soft spot for Hollywood glamour or American camp, come check out the crowds and bustle of downtown Tinseltown. (And be aware that no local would *ever* call it that.) Hollywood is also famous for its street corners. While the most stuff sits at Hollywood and Highland, the best-known named corner is certainly Hollywood and Vine.

## ◖ Hollywood Walk of Fame

One of the most recognizable facets of Hollywood is its star-studded Walk of Fame (Hollywood Blvd. and Vine St.). This area, portrayed in countless movies, contains more than 2,000 five-pointed stars honoring both real people and fictional characters who have contributed significantly to the entertainment industry and the legend that is Hollywood. Each pink star is set into a charcoal square, and has its honoree's name in bronze. The little symbols—movie camera, TV set, record, radio microphone, and tragedy/comedy masks—designate which part of the entertainment industry the honoree is recognized for. The Walk opened in 1968, with its very first star going to Joanne Woodward. Gene Autry has five stars on the walk, one for each industry (film, TV, radio, recording, and live theater)

Hollywood Walk of Fame

he contributed to. At the corner of Hollywood and Vine, check out the four moons that honor the Apollo XI astronauts. Also look for your favorite cartoon characters; Kermit the Frog, Mickey Mouse, and Bugs Bunny are all honored on the Walk of Fame.

You don't need to pay to get into anything, just get out on the sidewalk and start to stroll; the complete walk is about 3.5 miles. You'll be looking down at the stars, so watch out for other walkers crowding the sidewalks in this tourist-dense area. At the edges of the Walk of Fame, you'll find blank stars waiting to be filled by up-and-comers making their mark on Tinseltown. If you desperately need to find a specific star and want help doing so, you can take a guided tour of the Walk. (But really, it's a waste of money.) Careful reading and an online map (www.gocalifornia.about.com/ od/calamenu/a/walkfame.htm) will find you everyone's star you need to see.

## Hollywood Wax Museum

It immortalizes your favorite stars, all right. If

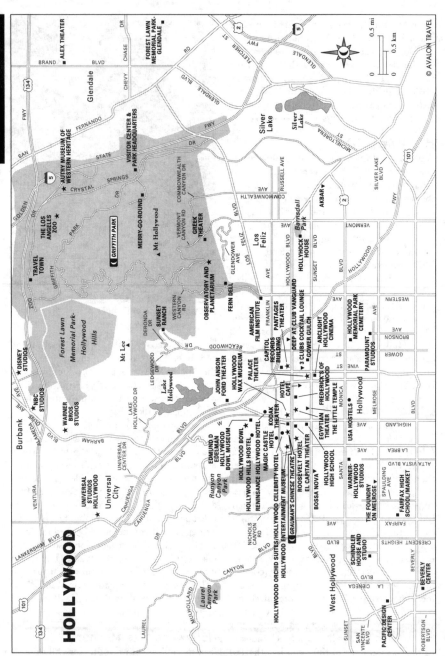

you want to see the Hollywood heavyweights all dressed up in costume and completely unable to run away, visit the Hollywood Wax Museum (6767 Hollywood Blvd., 323/462-8860, www .hollywoodwax.com, daily 10 A.M.–midnight, adults $16, children $7). You can't miss it, since the brilliant sign lights up a good chunk of Hollywood Boulevard, especially at night. Inside, you'll see everyone from Lucille Ball to Captain Jack Sparrow. The shtick of this wax museum is, of course, movies. The exhibits are re-creations of sets of all sorts of films, and as you pass through you'll be right in the action (if staring at eerie, life-sized wax likenesses of real people can be called action). You can even get a glimpse of stars on the red carpet at an awards show–style set.

The Hollywood Wax Museum first opened to amazed crowds in 1966. To this day, it remains inexplicably popular with tourists and locals alike.

If you need yet another cotton-candy museum experience, right across the street you can visit the **Guinness World of Records Museum** (6764 Hollywood Blvd., 323/463-6433). Here you'll find exhibits describing the records related in the book of the same name.

## ◖ Grauman's Chinese Theatre

You can't miss Grauman's Chinese Theatre (6925 Hollywood Blvd., 323/464-8111, www .manntheatres.com/chinese) on Hollywood Boulevard. With its elaborate 90-foot-tall Chinese temple gateway and unending crowd of tourists, Grauman's Chinese may be the most visited and recognizable movie theater in the world. Inside the courtyard, you'll find handprints and footprints of legendary Hollywood stars. Be sure to stop and admire the bells, dogs, and other Chinese artifacts in the courtyard—most are the genuine article, imported from China by special permit in the 1920s. The theater in all its splendor opened on May 18, 1927, with the premiere of *The King of Kings* and all the stars swanning up the red carpet to the cheers (and eventual riot) of the throng of thousands of fans gathered outside. The next day, the public was allowed into the hallowed theater.

The studios put up premieres at Grauman's all the time. Check the website for showtimes and ticket information. The Chinese Theatre has only one screen, but seats over 1,000 people per showing. While you're welcome to crowd the sidewalk to try to catch a glimpse of the stars at a premiere, be aware that most of these are private events.

## Egyptian Theater

Even before the Grauman's Chinese, Hollywood had the Egyptian Theater (6712 Hollywood Blvd., 323/466-3456, www .americancinematheque.com/egyptian/egypt. htm, tickets $10). Built by the auspices of the legendary Sid Grauman, the Egyptian was the first of the grandiose movie houses build in Hollywood proper and a follower of those in downtown Los Angeles. King Tut's tomb had been discovered in 1922, and the glorified Egyptian stylings of the theater followed the trend for all things Egyptian that followed that discovery. The massive courtyard and the stage both boasted columns, sphinxes, and other Egyptian-esque decor. The first movie to premiere at the Egyptian was *Robin Hood,* soon followed by *The Ten Commandments.* In the 1920s, the showing of a film was preceded by an elaborate live "prologue" featuring real actors in costume on a stage before the screen (the early ancestry of the *Rocky Horror Picture Show*). The Egyptian's stage was second to none, and the prologue of *The Ten Commandments* was billed as the most elaborate to date.

After a haul through the 1950s as a reserved-seat, long-run movie house, the Egyptian fell into disrepair and eventually closed. A massive renovation completed in 1998 restored it to its former glory. Today, you can get tickets to an array of old-time films. Or take a morning tour to get a glimpse at the history of this magnificent old theater. Expect to pay $5–20 for parking in one of the nearby lots.

## ◖ Griffith Park

Technically, Griffith Park (Los Feliz Blvd., Zoo Blvd., or Forest Lawn Dr., 213/485-5501, daily 6 A.M.–10 P.M.) is part of the city of Los Angeles, not of Hollywood. This huge park, sometimes called "L.A.'s Central Park" has an endless array of attractions and amenities to suit every style of visitor. If you love the stars, visit the recently renovated **Griffith Observatory** (4730 Crystal Springs Dr.). Golfers can choose between two 18-hole courses and one 9-hole course located on the parklands. A swimming pool cools visitors in the summer. You'll find a baseball field, basketball and tennis courts, and endless miles of hiking and horseback riding trails that thread their way far into the backcountry of the park.

If you prefer a more structured park experience, try the **L.A. Zoo** (5333 Zoo Dr., 323/644-4200, www.lazoo.org, daily 10 A.M.–4 P.M., adults $12, children $7). If the weather is poor (yes, it does rain in L.A.), step inside the **Museum of the American West** (4700 Western Heritage Way, 323/667-2000, www.autry-museum.org, Tues.–Sun. 10 A.M.–5 P.M., adults $9, children $5). Kids love riding the trains of the

operating miniature railroad in the **Travel Town Museum** (5200 Zoo Dr., 323/668-0104, http://traveltown.org, Mon.–Fri. 10 A.M.–4 P.M., Sat.–Sun. 10 A.M.–5 P.M.) and taking a spin on the park's carousel.

Griffith Park has played host to many production companies over the years, with its land and buildings providing backdrops for many major films. Scenes from *Rebel Without a Cause* were filmed here, as were parts of the first two *Back to the Future* movies. Its use is appropriate to the park's rich history. The land was donated by miner and Colonel Griffith J. Griffith (really). It has changed much over the years, but remains one of Los Angeles' great prizes.

The **Hollywood Sign** sits on Mount Lee, which is part of the park and indelibly part of the mystique of Hollywood.

## Mulholland Drive

As you drive north out of downtown Hollywood into the residential section of Hollywood Boulevard, you will find folks on

## ALTERNATIVES TO THE MOUSE

The longtime Hollywood-centric alternative to Disneyland is the **Universal Studios Hollywood** (100 Universal City Plaza, Los Angeles, www.universalstudios.com, daily 10 A.M.–6 P.M., adults $64, children under 48 inches $54, parking $11) theme park. Kids adore this park, which puts them right into the action of their old favorite movies. Flee the carnivorous dinosaurs of *Jurassic Park*, take a rafting adventure on the pseudo-set of *Waterworld*, or quiver in terror of an ancient curse in *Revenge of the Mummy*. If you're the parent rather than the child, you may find some of the effects on the rides pretty cheesy. On the other hand, you may be thrown back to your childhood with memories of your favorite shows and movies. KIT from *Knight Rider* still talks to visitors, and one of the major rides re-creates the nightmare world of *Terminator 2: Judgment Day*.

If you're more interested in how the movies

are made than the rides made from them, take the Studio Tour. You'll get an extreme close-up of the sets of major blockbuster films like *War of the Worlds*, though the *King Kong* set (along with the famed New York set and a number of others) was destroyed in an accidental fire in 2008. Better yet, you can get tickets to be part of the studio audience of TV shows currently taping at the Audiences Unlimited Ticket Booth. If you're a serious movie buff, consider getting a VIP pass – you'll get a 6-hour tour that takes you onto working sound stages, into the current prop warehouse, and through a variety of working prop build shops that service films and programs currently filming.

You can enjoy a meal, store your heavier things in a locker, and buy a near-infinite number of souvenirs at Universal Studios. If you need a little help getting yourself or your child around, rent a wheelchair or stroller. Pretty much every ride and show is wheelchair street corners hawking maps of stars' homes on Mulholland Drive and its surrounding neighborhoods. Whether you choose to pay up to $10 for a photocopied sheet of dubious information is up to you. What's certain is that you can drive the famed drive yourself. When you reach the ridge, you'll see why so many of the intensely wealthy in the L.A. Basin choose to make their homes here. From the ridgeline, on clear days you can see down to Los Angeles and the coast to the west, and the fertile land of the San Fernando Valley to the east. Whether you care about movie star homes or not, the view by itself is worth the trip, especially if it's rained recently and the smog is down. You won't see the facade of Britney Spears' multimillion-dollar hideaway facing the street, but a few homes do face the drive—most boasting mid-century modern architecture. If you can see them, they probably don't belong to movie stars who guard their privacy from the endless intrusion of paparazzi and fans.

# BEVERLY HILLS AND WEST HOLLYWOOD

Although the truly wealthy live above Hollywood on Mulholland Drive, in Bel-Air, or on the beach at Malibu, there's still plenty of money floating around in Beverly Hills. Some of the world's best and most expensive shops sit on the streets of Beverly Hills. You'll also find more than adequate high-end culture in the area, which bleeds into West L.A. The division seems almost seamless now, compared to the tremendous class gash that used to exist between Beverly Hills and the infamous Sunset Strip.

## Getty Center

Even more famous for art and culture in Los Angeles is The Getty Center (1200 Getty Center Dr., 310/440-7300, www.getty.edu, Tues.–Thurs. and Sun. 10 A.M.–6 P.M., Fri.–Sat. 10 A.M.–9 P.M., admission free, parking $8). Donated by the family of J. Paul Getty to the people of Los Angeles, this museum features European art, sculpture, manuscripts,

accessible – ask at the ticket booth for more information about how to get around easily or if you need assisted listening devices and TTD phones.

For yet another amusement park adventure, hit **Six Flags Magic Mountain** (Magic Mountain Parkway, Valencia, www.sixflags.com/magicmountain). This park provides good fun for the *whole* family – even the snarky teenagers who hate almost everything. Magic Mountain has long been the extreme alternative to The Mouse, offering a wide array of thrill rides. You'll need a strong stomach to deal with the G-forces of the major-league roller coasters, the death-defying drops, and the whirling spinners. For the younger set, plenty of "family" style rides offer a less intense but equally fun amusement park experience. Both littler and bigger kids enjoy interacting with the classic Warner Brothers characters, especially in *Bugs Bunny World*, and a kids' show features

Bugs, Donald, and others. Other than that, Magic Mountain has little in the way of staged entertainment – this park is all about the rides. The park is divided into areas, just like most other major theme parks – get a map at the entrance to help maneuver around and pick your favorite rides.

You'll find services, souvenirs, and snacks galore throughout the park. The food offerings run to burgers, pizza, and ethnic fast food. The highest concentration of snack shacks sits in the Colossus County Fair area-others are evenly distributed throughout the other areas. You can also by tchochkes in any area, but most of the shopping centers around Cyclone Bay. All major services can be found at the park, including many ATM machines, a First Aid station, ample restrooms, and disability assistance. The Guest Relations office at Six Flags Plaza can help you with just about anything you need.

and European and American photos. The magnificent works are set in a fabulous modern building with soaring architecture and you're guaranteed to find something beautiful to catch your eye and feed your imagination. The spacious galleries have comfy sofas to let you sit back and take in the paintings and drawings on the walls. Be sure to take a stroll outdoors to admire the sculpture collections on the lawns, as well as the exterior architectural itself.

## Wilshire Boulevard

Though the most famous stretch of Wilshire Boulevard runs through Beverly Hills, in truth this major artery reaches from Downtown L.A. all the way out to the coastline (almost) of Santa Monica. If you drive the whole thing, you'll travel 16 slow miles along the densely populated, totally developed strip. Along the way, you'll travel the **Miracle Mile,** pass the **Regent Beverly Wilshire Hotel** and the **La Brea Tar Pits,** see the main drag in **Koreatown,** and whiz past **MacArthur Park.** You can spend more than a day touring L.A. just by making your way from one end of Wilshire to the other, stopping at the dozens of sights and landmarks as you go.

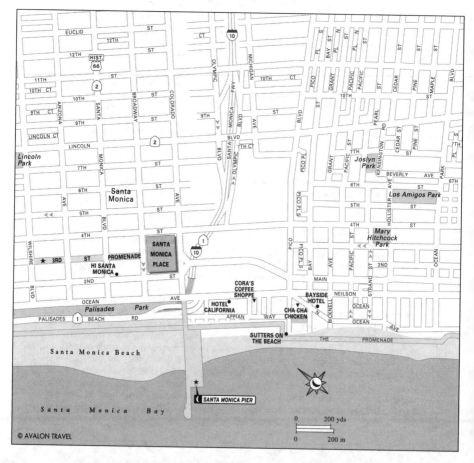

© AVALON TRAVEL

## Sunset Strip

A much shorter but equally famous stretch of road, the Sunset Strip really is part of Sunset Boulevard—specifically the part that runs through West Hollywood from the Hollywood border to the Beverly Hills city limits. The Strip exemplifies all that's grandiose and tacky about the L.A. entertainment industry. Few other places, even in California, boast about the number and glaring overstatement of their billboards. You'll also find many of the Sunset's legendary rock clubs, such as the **Roxy** and the **Whisky** and the infamous after-hours hangout **The Rainbow Bar & Grill.** Decades worth of up-and-coming rock acts first made their names on the Strip, and lived at the "Riot Hyatt."

If you last visited the Strip more than a decade ago, you might fear bringing your children to what was once a distinctly seedy neck of the woods. Then again, old-timers might be horrified *now* by the gentrification of the Strip. Today, a woman alone can stroll the street in comfort in daylight. At night, especially on weekends, no one's alone on the Strip. Don't plan to drive quickly or park on the street after dark; the crowds get big, complete with celebrity hounds hoping for a glimpse of their favorite star out for a night on the town.

## SANTA MONICA, VENICE, AND MALIBU

When many people from around the world think of "L.A.," what they're really picturing are the beach communities skirting the coastline to the west and Los Angeles proper to the east. Some of the most famous (and most expensive) real estate in the world sits on this stretch of sand and earth. Of the communities that call the northern coast of L.A. County home, the focal points are Malibu to the north, Santa Monica, then Venice to the south.

Malibu doesn't look like a town or a city in the conventional sense. If you're searching for the historic downtown or the town center, give up. There isn't one. Instead, the "town" of Malibu stretches for more than 20 miles, hugging the beach the whole way. A few huge homes perch precariously on the mountains rising up over the coastline, also part of Malibu. Many beach-loving superstars make their homes here, and the price of a beach house can easily exceed $20 million.

A few more liberal and social stars prefer to purchase from among the closely packed dwellings of Venice Beach. A bastion of true California liberal-mindedness and the home of several famous landmarks, Venice might be the perfect (if expensive) place to take a movie-style L.A. beach vacation.

Santa Monica comes as close to a community of moderate means as you'll find in this region. With its fun-but-not-fancy pier, its inexpensive off-beach motels, and a huge variety of delicious inexpensive dining options, Santa Monica is a great choice for a family vacation.

### ( Santa Monica Pier

For the ultimate in SoCal beach kitsch, you can't miss the Santa Monica Pier (Ocean Ave. at Colorado Ave.). As you walk the rather long stretch of concrete out over the water, you'll see an amazing array of carnival-style food stands, an arcade, a small amusement park, the smallest miniature golf course ever paid for by tourists, and restaurants leading out to the fishing area at the tip of the pier. The main attraction is **Pacific Park** (310/260-8744, www.pacpark.com, free).

This park features a roller coaster, a scrambler, and the world's first solar-powered Ferris wheel. Several rides are geared for the younger set, and a 20-game midway provides fun for all ages. Beneath the pier lies a sandy beach with a decent surf break—one of the major attractions of the area in the summertime.

You can drive onto the first half of the pier. Parking lots sit both on and beneath it, though your chances aren't great if you're trying for a spot on a summer weekend. Many hotels and restaurants are within walking distance of the pier, as is the Third Street Promenade. Admission to Pacific Park is free, but the rides aren't; you can pay per-ride or buy an all-ride wristband.

### ( Venice Boardwalk

If the Santa Monica Pier doesn't provide you with enough chaos and kitsch, head on down to the Venice Boardwalk (Ocean Front Walk at Venice Blvd.) for a nearly unlimited supply of both all year-round. Locals refer to the Boardwalk as "The Zoo" and tend to shun the area, especially in the frantic summer months. As you shamble down the tourist-laden path, you'll pass an astonishing array of tacky souvenir stores, tattoo and piercing parlors, walk-up food stands, and more. An honest-to-goodness carnival freak show sits near the middle of the Boardwalk, and a surprisingly good bookstore is tucked in beside a large sidewalk café. On the beach side of the path, dozens of artists create sculptures and hawk their wares. You can watch sculptors creating amazing works of art out of sand, or purchase a piece of locally made jewelry. The dude with the roller skates, the turban, and the guitar is pretty much always there—if you talk to him, he may follow you around until you pay him to leave you alone. (He's harmless.) The beach side includes the infamous **Muscle Beach** (two blocks north of Venice Blvd.), an easily distinguished chunk of sand filled with modern workout equipment and encircled by a barrier.

The wide, flat beach adjacent to the Boardwalk gets incredibly crowded in the summer. Parking can be nightmarish in this land of car-free walk streets. Expect to park far from the beach and the Boardwalk and to pay for the privilege. The beach at Venice is lifeguard-protected and has restroom and shower facilities built on the sand. You can get all the junk food you can stomach from the Boardwalk stands.

## Venice Canals

If you've grown tired of the frenzied Boardwalk (or the idea of those crowds just flat make you break out in hives), consider taking a much more sedate walk along the paths of the Venice Canals (btwn. Washington Blvd., Strongs Dr., S. Venice Blvd., and Ocean Ave.). Venice locals seek out the canals when they want to take a stroll or walk their dogs (Venice is a very dog-oriented town), and enjoy the serenity and peace of the quiet waterways. The home gardens and city-maintained landscaping add a lush layer of greenery to the narrow canals. Taking these paths gets you deep into the neighborhood and close to the impressive 20th-century Southern California architecture of Venice. Many of the people who own homes

on the canals launch small boats, and put on an annual boat parade for the holidays. As you wander this area, marvel at the history of the canals, modeled after those in this beach town's European namesake city. Also, admire the tenacity with which the city saved these last few from the landfill that removed their brethren from the landscape.

## Will Rogers State Historic Park

Did you grow up loving the films and culture of the early Hollywood western? If so, one of the best sights in Santa Monica for you is the Will Rogers State Historic Park (1501 Will Rogers State Park Rd., Pacific Palisades, 310/454-8212, www.parks.ca.gov, tours Tues.–Sun. 11 A.M., 1 P.M., 2 P.M., free). This 186-acre ranch with its 31-room sprawling home was the home and retreat of Will Rogers and his family. The Rogers family raised their brood here, and Mrs. Rogers donated the property to the state after her death in 1944. Today, you can tour the large home and check out some of the facilities of the active working

© LANCE SCOTT

Venice Canals

ranch that still exists on the property. Or take a walk around the regulation-sized polo field that was Will's joy. If you share Will's love of horses, visit the stables to take a lesson or go out for a ride out on the local range. Travelers who prefer their own two feet can take a three-mile hike to Inspiration Point, or a longer trek on the Backbone Trail out into the Santa Monica Mountains.

## Malibu Pier

There are few true "sights" along the long thin stretch of sand that is Malibu. One of those worth checking out is the Malibu Pier (23000 Pacific Coast Hwy., www.malibupiersport fishing.com). The pier gets busy in the summertime and lonely in the winter, though the die-hard surfers plying the adjacent three-point break stick around year-round. A few pier fishermen also brave the so-called chilly weather of the Malibu off-season, but you'll feel a sense of some solitude when you walk out across the planks. Some attractions out on the pier include interpretive signs describing the history of Malibu, sport-fishing and whale-watching charters, restaurants and food stands. If you'd prefer to ride the waves yourself, you can rent surf and boogie boards as well as other beach toys on the pier.

## PASADENA

If Venice Beach is the liberal haven of L.A., rockers love the Sunset Strip, and the gay community flocks to West Hollywood, Pasadena is the elder statesman of the Los Angeles neighborhoods and towns. Once a resort-like haven for the very wealthy, Pasadena gently decayed, then was re-created as a charming upper-middle-class residential town. Dotted throughout Pasadena, you can still see fabulous examples of the Craftsman architecture that was prevalent throughout Southern California in the early 20th century. This older city also lays claim to one of the best known and most attended parades (and ensuing college football games) in the United States. Finally, Pasadena has the distinction of being the town in which my dad was born and raised.

## Huntington Gardens

Some of the most beautiful botanical gardens in the world grow in Pasadena. The Huntington Gardens (1151 Oxford Ave., San Marino, 626/405-2100, www.huntington.org, Wed.– Mon. noon–4:30 P.M., Sat.–Sun. 10:30 A.M.– close, adults $20, students $10, children $6) also includes an amazing library filled with rare and ancient books and manuscripts. Literary travelers and locals come to the Huntington to view (and worship) the Gutenberg Bible and a manuscript of the *Canterbury Tales.* Art lovers come to view works by van der Weyden, Gainsborough, Hopper, and more. And everyone comes to explore the 120 acres of gardens, the most popular part of the complex.

More than a dozen different gardens beckon, including the Desert Garden, the Japanese Garden, and the Rose Garden. It takes more than one tour to get a real sense of all that grows here; pick your favorite area and enjoy a peaceful respite from the endless chaos of the L.A. Basin. Admission to the center includes a docent-led garden tour. Check the website for a look at what will be in bloom when you're in town.

Some of the best museum café food in the state can be had at the **Rose Garden Tea Room.** You can get a scrumptious buffet-style high tea for as long as the museum is open. For a more traditional snack or light lunch, the walk-up café offers salads, sandwiches, and hot soups.

## ◖ The Gamble House

Where Northern California prides itself on its Victorian architecture, major construction didn't get underway quite as fast in the southern part of the state. Here many of the rich residents, such as the Gambles (of "Procter &" fame), built homes in the early 20th century. The Gamble House (4 Westmoreland Pl., 626/793-3334, www.gamblehouse.org, Thurs.–Sun. noon–3 P.M., adults $10, children under 12 free) was designed and decorated by legendary SoCal architects Greene & Greene in the Craftsman style. The only way to get inside is to take a tour (schedules vary based on

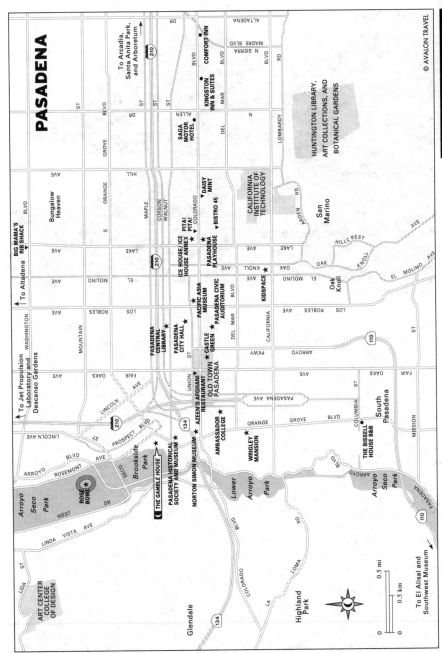

# PASADENA

© AVALON TRAVEL

To Arcadia, Santa Anita Park, and Arboretum

To Altadena

To Jet Propulsion Laboratory and Descanso Gardens

ALTADENA

COMFORT INN

KINGSTON INN & SUITES

SAGA MOTOR HOTEL

BIG MAMA'S RIB SHACK

Bungalow Heaven

DAISY MINT

BISTRO 45

PITA! PITA!

PASADENA PLAYHOUSE

ICE HOUSE/ICE HOUSE ANNEX

CALIFORNIA INSTITUTE OF TECHNOLOGY

San Marino

HUNTINGTON LIBRARY, ART COLLECTIONS, AND BOTANICAL GARDENS

KIDSPACE

Oak Knoll

PACIFIC ASIA MUSEUM

PASADENA CENTRAL LIBRARY

PASADENA CITY HALL

CASTLE GREEN

PASADENA CIVIC AUDITORIUM

AZEEM'S AFGHANI RESTAURANT

OLD TOWN PASADENA

Brookside Park

AMBASSADOR COLLEGE

WRIGLEY MANSION

THE GAMBLE HOUSE

PASADENA HISTORICAL SOCIETY AND MUSEUM

NORTON SIMON MUSEUM

ROSE BOWL

Arroyo Seco Park

Lower Arroyo Park

South Pasadena

THE BISSELL HOUSE B&B

Arroyo Seco Park

ART CENTER COLLEGE OF DESIGN

Glendale

Highland Park

To El Alisal and Southwest Museum

0        0.5 mi

0        0.5 km

© LANCE SCOTT

**The Gamble House**

the season). To buy tickets, go to the side of the main mansion and into the garage. The garage, built in the same style as the house, now acts as the house's bookstore and ticket office.

Inside the house, you'll be led from room to room as the docent describes the construction and decor in detail. The Craftsman aesthetic attempted to "answer" the overly ornate and precious Victorian style with long, clean lines and botanical motifs. The Greenes took this philosophy to heart in the construction of the Gamble house—you'll learn how they created this masterpiece as you view each unique room. You'll also see how the Gambles lived inside the house and hear some of their stories, even that of the house's possible haunting by the Gambles' Aunt Julia. The only place in the mansion that you won't see are two upstairs servants' rooms, now the home of two lucky architecture students who live in the house each school year.

## Norton Simon Museum

Believe it or not, the two millennia of art displayed at the Norton Simon Museum (411 W. Colorado Blvd., 626/449-6840, www.norton simon.org, Wed.–Mon. noon–6 P.M., Fri. until

9 P.M., adults $8, seniors $4, students free) were once part of a private collection. Wealthy industrialist Norton Simon collected the thousands of works of art over 30 years. He particularly loved the European Renaissance, the works of South and Southeast Asia, and 20th-century sculpture. Several of his most famous Rodins decorate the walkway up to the main entrance to the museum. You can visit the lovely modern building housing large, airy galleries to study the beautiful works of fine art here. Be sure to head outside to walk through the sculpture gardens in the courtyards behind the building. You can purchase books and reproductions in the museum store or grab a bite to eat at the simple, walk-up Garden Café.

## Rose Bowl

The Rose Bowl Stadium (1001 Rose Bowl Dr., 626/577-3101, www.rosebowlstadium.com), true to its name, is the home to the famed "Granddaddy" of the Bowl Games and to the UCLA college football team. Built in 1922, this huge elliptical bowl began with an open side. It was closed only a few years later, and now seats almost (but not quite) 100,000 people—perfect for the Super Bowl, as well as the flea markets and endless parade of college games! In addition to the endless vista of seats, you'll find plenty of restrooms and concessions scattered throughout the stadium—far more than the average college football team's home.

You can visit the Rose Bowl anytime, though you might need a ticket during an event, and you'll definitely need to plan in advance to attend the Rose Bowl game. Check the online calendar to find a fun event to attend for the best sense of this National Historic Landmark.

# Entertainment and Events

## NIGHTLIFE
### Bars and Clubs

Want to know which of the many dance and nightclubs in the L.A. area is the hottest or hippest or most popular with the stars this week? You'll need to ask the locals or read the alt-weeklies when you arrive, since these things change almost weekly. What was hot when this guide was written will no doubt be out by the time it's published. So check out the scene when you arrive, or pick one of these reasonably reliable standards.

Know that clubs in L.A. get crowded (and overcrowded) on weekend nights, and that bouncers take joy in selecting only the most chic hipsters in line to allow into the sacred spaces beyond the doors. Women have a slight edge, but in the top L.A. clubs, this can mean little to nothing. Being young and beautiful helps, of course, as does being dressed in the latest designer fashions and knowing a celebrity or the club's owner. So put on your finest and fanciest clubbing outfit, head out, and go for it!

For a good time dancing into the wee hours on a usually sedate Sunday night, head for **Deep at Club Vanguard** (6021 Hollywood Blvd., Hollywood, 323/463-3331, www .deep-la.com, Sun. only 9:30 P.M.–4 A.M., cover $20). This one-night-only monument to the freshest house music was opened in 1999 and has been growing in popularity ever since. Expect top-shelf house DJs from New York, L.A., and anywhere else the best are spinning these days. In addition to the crowded dance floor, you'll find a full bar and a back patio done up in the finest Asian style.

For the rest of the week, this space is simply **Club Vanguard** (www.vanguardla.com), hosting DJs in various styles, VIP nights, lingerie fashion shows, and other events that draw in the young and hip on the Hollywood scene.

For serious rockers looking for something a little bit heavier, there's the **Key Club** (9039 W. Sunset Blvd., West Hollywood, 310/274-5800, www.keyclub.com, daily 7 P.M.–2 A.M., cover $20). The Key Club caters to the heavy metal-and-dining crowd (yes, there is definitely such a thing in L.A.), with a full stage that hosts live bands and a full-service restaurant. This club feels like a warren, what with the stage and dance room, the casual and (in theory) quieter room down the hall, and the plush VIP suite upstairs. Of course you'll find more than one full bar inside this multi-purpose club.

For an ever-so-slightly more laid-back L.A. clubbing experience, head on down to **The Little Temple** (4519 Santa Monica Blvd., 323/660-4540, www.littletemple.com, Mon. midnight–2 A.M., Tue.–Thurs. 8 P.M.–2 A.M., Fri.–Sat. 9 P.M.–2 A.M., Sun 9 P.M.–midnight, cover $5). This funky, hip space mixes Buddhist Asian decor with deep house, hip-hop, and Latin music for a sometimes dance-heavy, sometimes lounge-centric evening of fun and flirtation. You can get your groove on down on the dance floor, then flop onto the huge communal bed to rest and relax with your oldest and newest friends. Decor mixes the sacred with the profane, and the full bar lubricates an already friendly evening with beer, wine, and cocktails.

Sometimes, a place doesn't need a huge description or build-up to illuminate its atmosphere and theme. **Bordello** (901 E. First St.,

213/687-3766, www.bordellobar.com, daily 7 P.M.–2 A.M., cover $10), with its provocative name and plush red interior, exemplifies such an establishment. Sitting at the former location of Little Pedros, the first bar opened in L.A. with a notorious reputation for its "other" business as a brothel, Bordello strives to be worthy of its historic locale. The interior feels almost cluttered to a modern sensibility; it's crammed with antique glass light fixtures, ornately painted and leafed geegaws, and velvet lounging couches. Musical offerings are deliberately eclectic. You might hear jazz one night, ska the next, and indie rock the night after that. Bordello also hosts regular burlesque shows. The full bar offers beers on tap as well as club-appropriate pink cocktails. Come in and be seduced.

The **3 Clubs Cocktail Lounge** (1123 Vine St., Hollywood, 323/462-6441, www.three clubs.com, Mon. midnight–2 A.M., Tue.–Sat. 6 P.M.–2 A.M., Sun. 6 P.M.–midnight, no cover) acts at once as a locals' watering hole and a reasonably priced nightclub catering mostly to the collegiate set. Expect to find the dance floor of the rear club crowded and sweaty, with fairly generic modern dance mixes blaring out over the crush of writhing bodies. Two bars serve up drinks to the masses, and drinks are a bit cheaper here than in the "hotter" spots. But if you're a lone female, do be aware that 3 Clubs has no decent parking and you may have to walk several blocks along Hollywood Boulevard long after dark. Consider brining a friend or two along with you to up your safety quotient.

## Gay and Lesbian

An alternative to glammed-up West Hollywood gay bars, **Akbar** (4356 Sunset Blvd., 323/665-6810, www.akbarsilverlake .com, Mon.–Sun. 7 P.M.–2 A.M.) pulls in a gay-friendly crowd with its cozy, Moroccan-themed decor, neighborhood vibe, and friendly, unpretentious bartenders.

Sleek, glamorous, and candlelit, the **Abbey Food and Bar** (692 N. Robertson Blvd., West Hollywood, 310/289-8410, daily 8 A.M.–2 A.M.) is a popular gay bar with a great outdoor patio

and pillow-strewn private cabanas—all of which are usually jam-packed. Savvy bartenders mix 40 different specialty martinis.

## Live Music

Los Angeles has long been one of the biggest destinations for struggling young rockers to come out, live cheap, and struggle to grab a spot on stage to take their shot at that all-important record contract. The clubs in the Sunset district, particularly those on the Sunset Strip, incubated some of the biggest rock acts of all time long before anybody knew who they were. The top three clubs drip rock history from their very walls. You might want to hold your nose when you first walk into the **Whisky A Go Go** (8901 Sunset Blvd., West Hollywood, 310/652-4202, www.whiskyagogo.com, cover $10). Despite a stench almost as memorable as its sound, throngs of music fans pack into the Whisky every night of the week. Most nights you'll get a lineup of new bands—sometimes as many as seven in one evening. For those shows, you can pay about $10 in advance or $12 at the door to see groups that might (or might not) be the Next Big Thing. The Whisky also hosts many cover and tribute bands that pay homage to the elder statesmen that once played here, such as Led Zeppelin and The Doors. And once in a great while, the Whisky hosts a major event like The Police reunion tours, or a performance by a current star.

Almost next door to the Whisky you'll find **The Roxy Theatre** (9009 Sunset Blvd., West Hollywood, http://theroxyonsunset.com). A comparative newcomer to the scene, The Roxy opened in 1973 with Neil Young performing. The second(ish) generation of heavy-duty rock acts made their name here (think Guns & Roses, Jane's Addiction, and Pearl Jam). Today you'll find the newest acts gracing the stage. Most shows feature three to five bands. The Roxy also puts up non-musical shows, from standup comedy to full-on theatrical productions to performance art. The big black-box theater has an open dance floor, comfy-ish booths (if you can get one), and bare-bones food service during shows. Nearby parking is nearly non-existent, so think about taking public transit or a cab to the show. You'll find the performance calendar on the website, and tickets available through major ticket agents. For one of the best after-hours parties on the strip, try to get into **On the Rox,** located directly above The Roxy. Or stagger next door to the **Rainbow Bar & Grill** (9015 Sunset Blvd., West Hollywood, 310/278-4232, daily 11 A.M.–2 A.M.).

It's not on the Strip, but its reputation is just as big and bad as its brethren. **The Troubadour** (9081 Santa Monica Blvd., West Hollywood, www.troubadour.com) opened its doors in 1957. Over its more than 50 years, Bob Dylan jammed, total unknown comic Steve Martin sang, Tom Waits was discovered, Billy Joel opened for somebody else, Metallica headlined for the very first time, and countless A-list bands have recorded in and even about The Troubadour (and my husband, also this guidebook's photographer, once played the Troubadour!). Today, you'll find everyone from Coldplay to Fiona Apple to the newest amateur acts at The Troubadour. If you're in town past the weekend, come on down for a fabulous "Free Monday" and save your money for drinks. You can check the events calendar in advance to find your favorite bands, then buy tickets online or via fax. If you've decided on a whim to hit tonight's show, you can buy tickets at the on-site box office on the day of the show only, so long as the show isn't sold out.

If you're looking for something smaller in the way of a semi-underground club, your best bet is to ask around once you're on the ground in L.A. Hot spots turn to cold spots quickly here, and the locals usually know what's up.

## Comedy

Not far behind the live music scene, L.A.'s live comedy scene is second only to Manhattan's as a way to see the brightest current stars and the most impressive young new talent. More than a dozen major live comedy clubs make their home in the smog belt. Pick your favorite, sit back, and laugh (or groan) the night away.

Located in the former Ciro's Nightclub on the Strip, **The Comedy Store** (8433 Sunset Blvd., West Hollywood, 323/656-6225, www.the comedystore.com, $10, 21 and older) is owned by 1980s comedian Pauly Shore's mother. With three separate rooms, you'll find a show going on at The Store every night of the week; most start at 9 P.M. or later, but you can check the website's calendar for both early and late shows. In all three rooms you'll often find a showcase featuring more than a dozen stand-up comics all performing one after another (and leaving space for possible celebrity drop-ins). Local sketch and improv groups also have regular gigs at The Store. Once upon a time, legendary comics got their starts here, often on Monday Amateur Nights. Imagine being among the first people ever to see Yakov Smirnoff perform, or getting to see Steve Martin or Whoopi Goldberg 10 feet from your table for less than $20. That's the level of talent you'll find performing here on a nightly basis. You can buy tickets online for bigger shows, and at the door for non-sellouts and The Belly Room. Most shows have a two-drink minimum in addition to the cover; no-cover acts in The Belly Room are your best bet for a bargain.

It seems unlikely that a major comedy club would make its home in peaceful, suburban Pasadena, but that's where the **Ice House** (24 N. Mentor Ave. off Colorado Blvd., 626/577-1894, www.icehousecomedy.com, Tues.–Sun., cover $5–20) sits. With shows running nightly and a double-header most Saturday nights, anyone who wants a laugh will enjoy an evening at the Ice House. Comedians who've performed here recently include Jeff Garcia, Bill Dwyer, and Gabriel Iglesias. You'll also find a focus on female comics and a regular Latino comedy showcase here. The $5 newcomers-heavy showcase on Wednesday nights makes for one of the best bargains in the L.A. entertainment scene, and you never know who you'll see. That bouncing hobbit-shaped guy named Daymon Ferguson or the lanky pseudo-depressive comic songster Phil Johnson might be the next ones to hit it big, and you can say you saw them when! If you actually favor a lower-budget, newer-comic evening, hit the Ice House **Annex,** the smaller ancillary room sitting right next door to the main club.

# THE ARTS
## Theater

Even with all the hoopla over film in L.A., there's still plenty of room for live theatrical entertainment in and around Tinseltown. The **Kodak Theater** (6801 Hollywood Blvd., 323/308-6300, www.kodaktheatre.com) has as its most notable annual event the Academy Awards, often called The Oscars. But for the rest of the year, the Kodak hosts live shows of various types. Many other awards shows make their homes here, and the stage is often graced by major performers such as Eddie Izzard and Ricky Gervais. Also look for classical music concerts and vocal music performances.

Some theatergoers prefer outdoor entertainment to indoor, and the **Ford Theater** (2580 Cahuenga Blvd. E., 323/461-3673, www.ford amphitheater.org) certainly takes advantage of Hollywood's temperate climate to bring the shows outdoors. Every sort of theatrical event imaginable can find a stage at the Ford, from classical ballet to experimental theater to postmodern circus acts. Lots of musical acts play the Ford—think jazz, folk, world music, and beyond. Children's shows come to the Ford, and the theater even puts up the occasional film-based multimedia production. Check the monthly events calendar to see what's up during your visit.

The **Ahmanson Theater** (135 N. Grand Ave., 213/628-2772, www.centertheatregroup .org, $86–220) specializes in big Broadway-style productions. You might see a grandiose musical, heart-wrenching drama, or gut-busting comedy here. Expect to find the names of many familiar shows on the annual schedule, from *A Chorus Line* to *Death of a Salesman* to *Who's Afraid of Virginia Woolf?* With hundreds of seats (all of them expensive), there's usually enough room to provide entertainment even for the most last-minute of visitors.

## Classical Music

Though L.A. is better known for its rock than its classical music offerings, you can still find plenty of high cultural concerts as well. If you love the grandiose, get a ticket for a show at the **Los Angeles Opera** (135 N. Grand Ave., 213/972-7219, www.losangelesopera .com, $20–238). The L.A. Opera has only existed since 1986, but in that time it has grown to be one of the largest opera companies in the United States, gaining national recognition for the quality of its work. The dazzling performances held at the Dorothy Chandler Pavilion in the Music Center of L.A. County have included such masterworks of the genre as *Don Giovanni, La Bohème,* and *Tristan and Isolde.* If you're in town in 2009, you might catch *The Magic Flute* or *La Traviata.* Each season includes about 10 different operas. The company gets recognition for its amazing production values, which include at least a couple of shows with truly fantastical costumes that in themselves are worth the price of the ticket.

If you prefer your musicians in black and white, take in a show by the **Los Angeles Philharmonic** (323/850-2000, www.laphil.com, $35–150), better known to its friends as the L.A. Phil. The philharmonic performs primarily at the **Walt Disney Concert Hall** (111 S. Grand Ave., 323/850-2000, www.disneyconcert hall.com). Concerts can range from classics by famed composers like Tchaikovsky, Bach, and Beethoven to the world music of Asha Bhosle to jazz by Bobby McFerrin. Guest performers can be the modern virtuosi of classical music—Midori plays here on occasion. Whatever style of music you choose to listen to, conductor Esa-Pekka Salonen or one of his guests will lead you on a wonderful aural journey.

With its art deco band shell set against canyon chaparral, the **Hollywood Bowl** (2301 N. Highland Ave., 323/436-2827 or 323/850-2000, www.hollywoodbowl.com) has long been a romantic setting for outdoor summer concerts by the L.A. Philharmonic and other artists.

If you're interested in supporting the work of amateur musician or just seeing a chamber concert in a more intimate setting, consider getting tickets to the **Los Angeles Doctors Symphony** (www.ladso.org, $10). This lovely community orchestra has been performing regularly since its inception in 1953. Many, though by no means all, of the musicians you'll hear are members of the medical community. They play everything from Mozart and Schubert to traditional music of various cultures, depending on the concert venue and the event. Check the website for the annual schedule, programs, and ticket information. If they're playing when you're in town, it's definitely worth your time to support the musical culture of the Los Angeles community!

## Cinema

Movie premieres are a big deal in L.A. and Hollywood for the obvious reasons. Crowds throng the streets outside of Grauman's Chinese Theatre and the Egyptian, where the stars tromp down the red carpets to enjoy the sight of themselves on the big screen. Even the standard AMC and Century theaters get packed on opening nights, so come early or buy tickets online to assure yourself of seats to your favorite star's latest release.

The current favorite movie house for star sightings is the **ArcLight Hollywood Cinema** (6360 W. Sunset Blvd., Hollywood, 323/464-1478, www.arclightcinemas.com, tickets $12–14). Perhaps this is due to the ArcLight's 21-and-older-only screenings of major blockbuster movies, which allow patrons to purchase beer and wine at the Café and bring their drinks into the theater with them. But most of all, the ArcLight complex offers the best visual and sound technologies, all-reserved seating, and the updated geodesic Cinemarama Dome theater. Do be sure to make reservations in advance (you can buy tickets online or at kiosks at the theater) if you want great seats to the latest films. The ArcLight also shows a few art house flicks and even the occasional "retrospective" (code for old) movie in its hallowed theaters. Ask for parking validation for a discount on the adjacent parking structure. You'll need it, since due to the ArcLight's status as a Hollywood favorite, you'll pay above even the usual high L.A. movie theater rates to see a show here.

# Shopping

In Los Angeles, shopping qualifies as a major source of entertainment for locals and visitors alike. Don't worry about being materialistic or a spendthrift here—that's what you're *supposed* to be. If it exists anywhere on earth, you can probably buy it somewhere in L.A., whether "it" is a Smart Car, a bunch of flowers, an indie CD, or a pair of pants that cost as much as a Smart Car. Different areas and towns have their own unique shopping feel, so decide what kind of retail experience you want and then pick the right spot to find it.

## DOWNTOWN AND VICINITY
### Flower District

If you have even the slightest love of plants and flowers, you can't miss the world-famous Los Angeles Flower District (766 Wall St., 213/622-1966, www.laflowerdistrict.com, Mon.–Sat. mornings). Sometimes called "America's Flower Market," this vast sea of color and beauty is a triumph of American multicultural entrepreneurial spirit. The first flower cultivators in Los Angeles were Japanese Americans, and today many growers are of Hispanic descent—perhaps especially fitting for an industry that creates products in all colors of the rainbow. When you visit this vast sea of beauty, you'll find a fun cacophony of different languages being spoken as floral retailers vie for the best products available on any given day. But never fear: Anyone can come and stroll the narrow aisles of the various markets, and you'll find plenty of pre-made bouquets with which to impress your sweetie. Or better yet, find someone who can create a custom arrangement for you, since just about every kind of cut flower, potted plant, and exotic species can be purchased here. You can take away a bouquet filled with flowers you've never even seen before!

Among other major events, the Flower District supplies the unbelievable needs of the Rose Parade each New Year's. Literally millions of flowers go into the creation of the stunning floats (which *must* incorporate flowers to qualify for most of the awards in the parade). It's hard to image the work necessary to fill the orders for the floats, but the denizens of the flower market do it every year.

One caution: while the flower market itself is safe for visitors, the area to the south is not. Get good directions before you come, and don't plan to wander the neighborhood on foot.

## Jewelry District

If you're looking for the bleeding edge of style when you shop for jewelry, you can't do much better than the Los Angeles Jewelry District (bordered by 5th St., 8th St., Broadway, and Olive St., www.lajd.net). With more than 3,000 wholesalers, even the most avid lover of sparkly stones and glittering gold will get her (or his) fill here. Do be a little bit careful if you're a woman alone, especially at dusk or later, as this isn't the squeakiest clean part of downtown L.A. But you can shop in reasonable peace here, and even in some confidence that you won't get ripped off so long as you do some preliminary research. The district website provides information on vendor ratings and a map to help you get around more easily. From wholesale dealers of unset gems, to professional gem setters who'll create a beautiful piece from the stones you've bought, you can find just about anything you ever dreamed of here.

## BEVERLY HILLS AND WEST HOLLYWOOD
### Rodeo Drive

If you're reading this book, you probably don't have enough money to go on a serious spree in the shops of Rodeo Drive. The hottest stars and other big-spenders come here to purchase the best and most expensive goods the world has to offer.

Have you ever seen a $1,500 pair of pants? Walk into the **Chanel** (400 N. Rodeo Dr., Beverly Hills, 310/278-5500, www.chanel. com) store and you'll be able to. You'll see original artwork, catalogs, the very edgiest high-end clothes in existence, and salespeople who will look down their noses at you if your outfit cost you less than four figures. Head upstairs for racks of on-sale clothing from last season, though you'll quickly learn that "on sale" is a relative concept. If you're lucky, you might even get dissed by one or more of the über-rich women wearing fur hats and carrying little yippy dogs (they're unaware of the irony). Hunt the racks for the classic tweedy Coco Chanel dress—you will find it. Or if you prefer another designer, head outside and find one; all the big leaguers, from Dior to Michael Kors, maintain storefronts on Rodeo.

Though Rodeo Drive is most famous for its designer apparel, many other retailers offer a vast array of expensive things, from sunglasses to jewelry to housewares. If you're looking for (or just want to look at) the perfect diamond ring, walk past the guards into the huge hallowed halls of **Tiffany's** (210 N. Rodeo Dr., Beverly Hills, 310/273-8880, www.tiffany.com, Mon.–Fri. 10 A.M.–7 P.M., Sat.–Sun. 10 A.M.–6 P.M.). The store has three floors of the most exquisite necklaces, bracelets, rings, watches, and accessories you'll ever find anywhere. This storefront compares easily to its sister store in Manhattan. You'll find the sales help here a bit friendlier here than in the clothing stores, since even the middle-class of L.A. come to Tiffany's to purchase special-occasion jewelry.

The wealthy who want to fall asleep with their skin soothed by the softest sheets around go to **Frette** (459 N. Rodeo Dr., Beverly Hills, 310/273-8540, www.frette.com, Mon.–Sat. 10 A.M.–6 P.M., Sun. 12–5 P.M.) to make their purchases. This store doesn't get as crowded as many others on Rodeo and much of Frette's business goes to high-end hotels. But the doors of this open, airy retail store remain defiantly open, beckoning shoppers who love luxury more than life itself. Salespeople encourage you to pet the merchandise, comparing one set of sheets to another and imagining the feel of the plushy bath sheets after your next shower.

## Melrose Avenue

Melrose Avenue (btwn. San Vicente and La Brea Aves.) is really two shopping districts. High-end fashion and design showrooms dominate the western end, near La Cienega Boulevard; head east past Fairfax Avenue for tattoo parlors and used clothing.

If you miss 1960s mod, 1970s grooviness, 1980s power-dressing, or even last year's haute couture, drop by **Decades** (8214½ Melrose Ave., 323/655-0223, www.decadesinc.com, Mon.–Sat. 11:30 A.M.–6 P.M.) and browse among the prime, vintage Courrèges, Hermès, and Pucci castoffs.

If you adore the clothes from *Sex and the City* and *Friends,* stop in at **Fred Segal** (81118 Melrose Ave., 323/651-1935, Mon.–Sat. 10 A.M.–7 P.M., Sun. 12–6 P.M.), a deluxe department store, which has everything from the ridiculously trendy to the severely tasteful.

Futuristic specs from **l.a.Eyeworks** (7407 Melrose Ave., 323/653-8255, www.laeyeworks.com, Mon.–Fri. 10 A.M.–7 P.M., Sat. 10 A.M.–6 P.M.) have appeared in films like *The Matrix* and *Blade Runner,* and celebs like Jennifer Aniston and Wesley Snipes are fans of the store's lightweight, trend-defining frames.

The buyers at **Wasteland** (7428 Melrose Ave., 323/653-3028, www.thewasteland.com) carefully pick out merchandise for their club-hopping clientele, so everything at this secondhand store has style. The selection covers a wide range, from Gucci to Gap.

## SANTA MONICA, VENICE, AND MALIBU

Shopping down by the beaches can be as much fun as anyplace else in the L.A. area. Santa Monica offers your best bet for an entertaining retail experience, since Venice Beach and Malibu tend more toward strip malls.

### Third Street Promenade

Looking for the place where middle-class locals come to shop in the L.A. area? Head for the Third Street Promenade (Third St., Santa Monica, http://thirdstreetpromenade.org). Much of Third Street in Santa Monica is closed to auto traffic to make it easier to walk along the Promenade. This long vertical outdoor mall features all your favorite chain stores for clothing, shoes, jewelry, housewares, computers, and just about anything else you can think of. You'll find people plying the Promenade day and night, seven days a week. If your goal is a serious retail spree, come out to the Promenade on a weekday during daylight hours to avoid the bigger crushes of people that pile into the area on weekends. On the other hand, if you're looking for a fun social outing, the Promenade gets popular with a younger crowd at night. You can hit one of the movie theaters, stop in at a bar, or just stroll the pedestrian walks enjoying the mild night air and the street performers who work the area. The Promenade is within easy walking distance of the Santa Monica Pier and adjacent beach as well.

The Promenade's shops tend toward the classic mall fare. You'll find a tremendous three-story Gap offering classic clothes to the masses. The high-end Anthropologie and Armani Exchange can get you looking fine for the remainder of your L.A. vacation and beyond. If you need a new computer or a shiny iPod or iPhone to get you back home in style and entertained, a huge Apple Store can hook you up. If you're looking to catch the latest flick, choose from three different movie theaters, including a Mann Theater. On weekends, you can get the freshest and tastiest fruits and vegetables from the legendary farmers market at the Promenade.

## PASADENA
### Old Town Pasadena

Old Town Pasadena (Colorado Blvd., www.oldpasadena.com) was once a quaint downtown area serving a small but wealthy resort community. Today, Old Town essentially acts as a street-based shopping mall, with upscale chain stores inhabiting classic deco and mid-century modern buildings.

# Sports and Recreation

You'll find an endless array of ways to get outside and have fun in the L.A. Basin. Among the most popular recreation options are those that get you out onto the beach or into the Pacific Ocean.

## BEACHES

If you're in SoCal for the first time, it's almost a given that one of your destinations is a genuine California beach. You've got plenty to choose from in the L.A. area. From north of Malibu down to Manhattan and Hermosa Beach, you'll find a seemingly endless stretch of public beaches. Most of these have lots of visitor amenities (unlike their Northern California brethren), such as snack bars, boardwalks, showers, beach toy rental shacks, surf schools, and permanent sports courts. Believe it or not, those listed here are just a drop in the bucket; if none of these beaches do it for you, you can choose from dozens of others that stretch in a nearly unbroken line from one end of the county to the other.

Not all L.A. beaches are created equal. With a very few exceptions, you won't find clean, clear water to swim in, since pollution is a major issue on the L.A. coast. Also keep in mind that Los Angeles County is not a tropical zone. The water does warm up in the summer, but not into the 80s like you find in Hawaii. (Happily, it's also not in the icy 50s and 60s, as in the northern reaches of the state.) Expect to cool off significantly when you dive into the surf, and if you plan to be out in the water for an extended period, get yourself a wetsuit to prevent chills that can turn into hypothermia.

## Zuma Beach

If you've ever seen the cult classic film *Earth Girls Are Easy,* you've heard of legendary Zuma Beach (Pacific Coast Highway, 19 miles north of Malibu). This popular surf and boogie-boarding break, complete with a nice, big stretch of clean, white sand, fills up fast on summer weekends but isn't as crowded on weekdays. Grab a spot on the west side of the Pacific Coast Highway for free parking, or pay a little for one of the more than 2,000 spots in the beach parking lot. Zuma has all the amenities you need for a full day out at the beach, from restrooms and showers to a kid-friendly snack bar and a beachside boardwalk.

Water lovers can ride the waves or just take a swim in the cool and (unusual for the L.A. area) crystal-clear Pacific waters. Zuma has lifeguards during daylight hours, and for landlubbers, it's got beach volleyball courts set up and a playground for the kids. Perhaps best of all, this beach doesn't fill up with litter-happy tourists. It's actually a locals' favorite for weekend R&R.

## Malibu Lagoon State Beach

In a sea of private beaches fronting mansions, Malibu Lagoon State Beach (23200 Pacific Coast Hwy., 818/880-0363, www.parks.ca.gov, daily 8 A.M.–sunset) and its ancillary **Malibu Surfriders Beach** offer public access to a great northern L.A. location. Running alongside the Malibu Pier, this pretty stretch of sugar-like sand offers a wealth of activities as well as pure California relaxation. This beach offers a number of unusual attractions, including both the **Adamson House** (310/456-8432, www.adamson house.org) and the **Malibu Lagoon Museum.** You can take a guided tour that goes through the museum and out to the wetlands, butterfly trees, tidepools, and flower gardens. Malibu Creek runs into the ocean here, creating a unique wetlands ecosystem that's well worth exploring. If a beach party is more your style, you can rent beach toys at the pier and stake your spot on the sand. Surfers man the break here year-round; please be careful of your fellow riders.

At the intersection that leads to the museum, you can also drive down to the main parking lot. It's likely to fill up fast in the summer, so get there early for a spot.

## Will Rogers State Beach

If you're a film buff and a beach bum, you must take a day out of your travel schedule to hang out on the Will Rogers State Beach (17700 Pacific Coast Hwy., Pacific Palisades, beaches.co.la.ca.us/bandh/beaches/willrogers. htm). Yet another fabulous full-service L.A. beach, a number of movies have been filmed at Will Rogers. Even if you don't care about that, you'll love the nearly two miles of sandy beach, easy to get to from the parking lot, studded with volleyball courts, playground equipment, restrooms, and picnic tables. The bike path running along the land side of the sand runs for 19 miles all the way down to Redondo State Beach. Out in the water, you can swim, skin dive, and surf. A mild right point break offers a good learning ground for beginners. Lifeguards protect the shores during the day in summer, and the locals think their guards are some of the best-looking in the county. Just be sure to pay attention to the flags and signs, since pollution can be a big problem at Will Rogers due to storm drains emptying out into the ocean.

Bring cash to pay for parking, but be happy that with more than 1,750 spots, you'll probably find one that's legal and reasonably secure.

### Santa Monica State Beach

If you're looking for "The Beach" in Santa Monica, well it's hard to miss. The waterside edge of town is encompassed by Santa Monica State Beach (Pacific Coast Hwy., www.santa monica.com/index.php/beach.html). For 3.5 miles, the fine sand gets raked daily beneath the sun that shines over the beach more than 300 days each year. Flop down in the sand to enjoy the warm sunshine, take a dip in the endless waves of the Pacific, stroll along the boardwalk, or stand at the edge of the of the water and peer out to see if you can catch sight of a pod of dolphins frolicking in the surf. If you don't mind crowds, hang out on the sand right near the pier. The best people-watching runs south of the pier area and on towards Venice Beach. For a bit more elbow room, head north of the pier to the less populated end of the beach.

Due to its location right "in" town and adjacent to and beneath the Santa Monica Pier,

you'll find a near-endless array of services at the beach. On the pier and just across from the beach, you can get snacks and meals, rent surf and boogie boards, hit the arcade, and go shopping. Parking varies, depending on which part of the beach you head for. The north end has spotty parking, the pier area can get really crowded but has more options, and the south probably has the best bet for a good spot.

## SURFING

If you ask anyone the around what the defining sport in California is, they'll tell you it's surfing. And the craze for wave riding began in Los Angeles. The mystical athletic endeavor stars in movies and TV shows, yet it's something lots of folks can learn to do. Whether you've been riding waves for decades or you've never before touched a surfboard, going surfing will add a touch of real California culture to your L.A. visit.

You'll find a fabulous array of surf breaks in the L.A. area, with waves of all sizes beckoning to riders of every ability level. Most folks come out to the beach at Venice to check out the zoolike boardwalk, but you can ride the waves here on the lifeguard-protected beach too. A great break for all levels, the breakwater at Venice Beach is a favorite spot for locals.

### Surf Lessons

If you've never surfed before, your best bet is to sign up for a lesson (or two) with a reputable surf school. Most schools can get you standing up on your longboard on the very first lesson! One of these, **Learn to Surf LA** (641 Westminster Ave., #5, Venice, 310/663-2479, www.learntosurfla.com, $60–120), operates on Venice Beach. You can take a private lesson, a semi-private lesson with friends, or join a regularly scheduled group. Each lesson lasts almost two hours and includes all equipment (you'll get a full wetsuit in addition to a board), shore instruction and practice, and plenty of time in the water. No, the brightly colored foam longboards you'll learn on aren't the coolest or most stylish, but they're perfect for new surfers looking for a stable ride on smaller waves. Learn to

Venice Beach swimmers

Surf LA offers lessons for both kids and adults-, and this can be a great activity for the whole family to tackle together. Intermediate and advanced surfers can also find great fun with this school, which has advanced instructors capable of helping you improve your skills.

## HANG GLIDING

You can pick the kind of ground you want to soar over in L.A.: the ocean or the inland mountains and valleys. If you prefer to see the water slipping past beneath you, head for **Dockweiler Beach Training Park** (12000 Vista del Mar, Playa del Rey, Wed.–Sun. 11 A.M.–sunset). For a higher-altitude adventure, head to the San Fernando Valley and up to **Sylmar Flight Park** (daily 10 A.M.–sunset). For a good school and rental facility, call **Windsports Soaring Center** (818/367-2430, http://windsports.com, prices vary). You can go tandem with an instructor at Sylmar Flight Park (recommended for first-time gliders) or get bold and try a solo ride (which starts at an altitude of five feet out on the beach at Dockweiler). Windsports

provides all the equipment and training you need, so all you have to bring are a good pair of athletic shoes, a bottle of water, and, of course, a camera.

## SPAS

Inside the Westin Bonaventure Hotel downtown, enjoy some good pampering at the **Bonaventure Club Spa & Fitness Center** (404 S. Figueroa St., 888/629-0900, http://bonaventureclub.com, daily 11 A.M.–11 P.M., $20–225). With a focus on beauty as well as health and relaxation, the Bonaventure Club features a number of heavy-duty facials, as well as dermabrasion and collagen treatments. You'll also find a full nail and waxing salon, and an array of massages and body scrubs. The Bonaventure isn't the poshest spa around, but you'll get decent service. The locker rooms, sauna, and other facilities are clean, and the spa is open later than most to accommodate busy travelers. Book in advance if you want a specific treatment at a specific time of day, but you're likely to find a same-day appointment if you aren't too picky about exactly which treatment you want.

## SPECTATOR SPORTS

Befitting a major American city, Los Angeles boasts a nearly full complement of professional sports teams. (L.A. no longer has an NFL team in town, but once it had two. Oops!)

The **L.A. Kings** (213/742-7100, http://kings.nhl.com) play lightning-fast NHL hockey downtown at the Staples Center (1111 S. Figueroa St., www.staplescenter.com). Well, they try to play lightning-fast, anyway. The Kings are more famous for their failures than their successes, but going out to the games is still fun, particularly if your home team is playing the Kings while you're in town.

As great legends of the NBA, the individual players and the organization as a whole of the **Los Angeles Lakers** (www.nba.com/lakers) have well and truly earned their places. Though Magic no longer dunks for the Lakers, Kobe Bryant carries on the star torch for the still-winning team.

As for the MLB, baseball takes advantage

of the perfect climate in L.A. to host some of the most beautiful outdoor summer games anywhere in the country. The **Los Angeles Dodgers** (http://losangeles.dodgers.mlb.com) make their home in this hospitable climate, playing often and well throughout the long baseball season. Just one thing: Don't refer to Dodger Stadium (1000 Elysian Park Ave.) as "Chavez Ravine" unless you really mean it. (That old field designation has become a derogatory term used primarily by San Francisco Giants fans.)

# Accommodations

From the cheapest roach-ridden shack motels to the most chi-chi Beverly Hills hotel, Los Angeles has an endless variety of lodgings to suit every taste and budget.

## DOWNTOWN AND VICINITY

If you want to stay overnight in Downtown L.A., plan to pay for the privilege. As expected, most hostelries here run to high-rise towers catering more to the business than the leisure set. Still, if you need a room near the heart of L.A. for less than a month's mortgage, you can find one if you look hard enough. But be aware that once you get into the Jewelry District and farther towards the Flower Market, the neighborhood goes from high-end to sketchy to downright terrifying. If you need a truly cheap room, avoid these areas and head instead for Pasadena or The Valley.

### Under $100

You won't miss the sign for the **Metro Plaza Hotel** (711 N. Main St., 213/680-0200, $88). The low-rise hotel with its white facade and big oddly constructed front marquee sits near Union Station, convenient for train travelers and public transit riders. You can also get transport to and from LAX for about $5, a genuine bargain. Inside, you'll find your room to look like any average, reasonably clean motel room. The bedspreads are floral, the carpets light blue, and the space ample. A complimentary continental breakfast comes with your room, and the Metro Plaza has an on-site fitness center. But the true gems here are the location, central to transportation to all the major L.A. attractions, and the lower-than-average price point for the region.

### $100-150

Can you image staying at a cute B&B only a mile from the towering skyscrapers of downtown Los Angeles? You can, at the **Inn at 657** (657 W. 23rd St., 213/741-2200, www .patsysinn657.com, $145–225). The lovely home has one-bedroom guest accommodations and two-bedroom suites, each individually decorated. You'll find a comfortable antique bed in a room scattered with lovely fabrics and pretty antiques. Each morning, you'll head downstairs to the long, dark table set with fine china for a full breakfast complete with fruit, hot food, great coffee, and fresh juice. The inn has a massage therapist on retainer, a nail salon they love just down the street, Wi-Fi, and a moderate-charge laundry service. You're within easy distance of the Staples Center, the downtown shopping areas, and the rest of the attractions of Los Angeles.

### $150-250

You'd expect plenty of urban, modern hotels in Downtown L.A. What comes as a surprise is the (for what it is) reasonably priced and fantastically fun **( Custom Hotel** (8639 Lincoln Blvd., 877/287-8601, www.customhotel.com, $175–300). From the herd of sheep in the lobby to the dog-print bedspreads, a sense of whimsy pervades this otherwise ultra-stylish hotel. Your room might not be the biggest in town, but it will be clean and pristine, with snowy-white linens, comfortable beds, and an attractively appointed bathroom. On the counter you'll find a basket full of fun favors (for a price, of course); we'll leave it to you to figure out why you'd want to purchase a packet of radish seeds from a high-end hotel. The in-room Wi-Fi is free, as are the views of Los Angeles. You'll find the staff incredibly friendly and helpful, ready to help with anything from valet parking to dinner reservations. If you prefer to eat in the hotel, the hip if preciously named Bistrotek can feed you either in the restaurant or in your room. Or if you're in a more casual mood, hit the Hopscotch Pool Bar & Grill, which sits adjacent to the sparkling swimming pool. For a drink in the evening, take the elevators with the slightly scary giant faces down to the Lobby Lounge to enjoy a cocktail and possibly even a local DJ spinning into the evening.

The **Orchid Hotel** (819 S. Flower St., 213/623-9904, www.ohotelgroup.com, $180) is better known as The O to its friends and devoted returning guests. This upscale property takes the modern urban chic hotel concept and does it L.A. style. True to its name, orchids are a major theme of this hotel, and you'll find plants both in the common areas and inside your room. Guest rooms are done in a modern style, with platform beds, sparkling white linens, and black-and-white bathrooms. A boutique establishment, The O has only 68 rooms. You'll find tapas and Mediterranean-inspired cuisine at the on-site restaurant, plus a full bar. The health spa offers both fitness facilities and massage and other spa services. Perhaps best of all for those travelers who come to L.A. for its retail possibilities, you won't need the services of the 24-hour concierge desk to find the Macy's Plaza center just across the street from the hotel.

## Over $250

If you're longing for a taste of true L.A. style, get a room at the **Omni Los Angeles at California Plaza** (251 S. Olive St., 213/617-3300, www.omnihotels.com, $266). From the grand exterior to the elegant lobby and on up to your room, the light colors, live plants, and lovely accents will make you feel rich, even if just for one night. Your room or suite will have plush mattresses and your choice of pillows, stylish decor, plushy towels and robes, and all the right amenities to make your stay perfect. If you're in town for business, you can get a room complete with a fax machine, copier, and office supplies. On the other hand, if you're on vacation with your family you can get a suite decorated especially to delight your children—with a closing door to an adult bedroom to delight you. You can dine at this magnificent hotel, choosing between the Noe Restaurant and the Grand Cafe. Take a swim in the lap pool or a run on the exercise equipment in the large fitness room. Relax with a massage, hot river rock treatment, or facial at the Spa at Omni. Whatever your pleasure, you'll find it at the Omni.

If you're yearning to stay someplace with a movie history, book a room at the **Westin Bonaventure** (404 S. Figueroa, 213/624-1000, www.starwoodhotels.com, $250). The climactic scene of the Clint Eastwood thriller *In the Line of Fire* was filmed in one of the unusual elevators in the glass-enclosed, four-leaf-clover-shaped high-rise building. This hotel complex has every single thing you'd ever need: shops, restaurants, a day spa, a concierge, and plenty of nice guest rooms. You'll find your rooms comfortable and convenient, complete with fancy beds and clean spacious bathrooms. Views range from fairly innocuous streets of L.A. to panoramic cityscapes. The most fun restaurant and lounge to visit at the Bonaventure is without doubt the Bona Vista Lounge, which revolves slowly 360° at the top of the building.

## HOLLYWOOD

If you're star-struck, a serious partier, or a rock music aficionado, you'll want to do more than just visit Hollywood. You'll want to stay the night within staggering distance of the hottest clubs or the hippest music venues. Heck, you might even luck out and find yourself sleeping in the same room where Axl Rose once vomited or David Lee Roth broke all the (hopefully replaced) furniture!

### Under $100

Reputed to be one of the best hostels in the state, the **USA Hostels - Hollywood** (1624

Schrader Blvd., 800/524-6783, www.usa hostels.com, $26 dorm bed, $70 private room) still offers the same great prices you'll find at seedier, more bare-bones hostels. Okay, so the exterior doesn't look like much. But in this case, it's what's inside that counts. You can choose between dorm rooms and private rooms, but even the larger dorm rooms have baths attached—a nice convenience that's unusual in the hostel world. (You'll also find several common bathrooms in the hallways, helping to diminish the morning shower rush.) Another great boon is the daily all-you-can-make pancake breakfast, which comes free with your room along with all the coffee or tea you can drink. Add that to the $5 barbecue nights on Monday, Wednesdays, and Fridays, and you've got a great start on seriously diminished food costs for this trip! This smaller hostel also goes a long way to fostering a sense of community among its visitors, offering a standard array of area walking tours and beach shuttle, plus two free comedy nights per week (Wed. and Sun.). If you need to make contact with friends back home, hook up to the free Wi-Fi with your own laptop or use one of the complimentary Internet kiosks.

## $100-150

For a nice modestly priced room in the Hollywood vicinity, stay at the **Hollywood Orchid Suites** (1753 Orchid Ave., 323/874-9678, www.orchidsuites.com, $110–350). The Orchid's location couldn't be better; it's in the Hollywood & Highland Center, right behind Grauman's Chinese Theatre, next door to the Kodak Theater, and around the corner from Hollywood Boulevard and the Walk of Fame. If you're a film lover or star seeker on a moderate budget, it's tough to do better than this—especially with the free parking and proximity to public transit. Guest rooms are actually suites, with plenty of space and an eye toward sleeping your large family or several friends all in the same suite. All suites but the Juniors have full kitchens. Don't expect tons of luxury in the furnishings or the decor; it all looks like last decade's motel stuff, though you'll get a coffee maker, free Wi-Fi, and other better-

than-average perks. The rectangular pool offers cooling refreshment in the summertime, perfect after a long day of stalking Brad or Britney!

Only a few steps away, you can get a room at the **Hollywood Celebrity Hotel** (1775 Orchid Ave., 323/850-6464, www.hotelcelebrity.com, $135–200). This nice budget motel aspires to Hollywood's famed luxury. Guest rooms have satin comforters, Hollywood-flavored black-and-white artwork, and a modern aesthetic in the furnishings and accents. Amenities include free, wired high-speed Internet, a valet laundry service, a fitness room, and steam rooms. In the morning, come down to the lobby for a complimentary continental breakfast, and in the evenings take advantage of otherwise hard-to-come-by passes to the **Magic Castle Club** (www.magiccastle.com). Leave your car in the gated, off-street parking lot.

## $150-250

If you've got a little bit more cash, you'll find more lodging options in Hollywood. One good spot is the **Hollywood Hills Hotel** (1999 N. Sycamore Ave., 323/874-5089, www.holly woodhillshotel.com, $175–275, parking $8/day), not to be confused with the Best Western Hollywood Hills. The Hollywood Hills Hotel offers truth in advertising, set up in the Hollywood Hills offering lovely views of the L.A. skyline on rare smog-free days. The view of the resort itself can be almost as grand, with its Chinese stylings and attractive greenery. All rooms here, even the studios, have fully equipped kitchens for travelers seeking to save money on meals. These suites land somewhere between a standard motel and a more upscale resort in their style. You'll find floral comforters, warm-toned painted walls, and attractive if sparse artistic touches. Best of all, the rooms facing out over the city of Los Angeles have huge windows to help you enjoy the view from the comfort of your bed. On-site, you'll find a cool Chinese pagoda, a prettily landscaped swimming pool, and a grand California-Asian restaurant, Yamashiro.

Named for the world renowned magic club

next door, the **Magic Castle Hotel** (7025 Franklin Ave., 323/851-0800, www.magiccastle hotel.com, $180–350) boasts the best customer service of any L.A. area hostelry. You'll have to make that judgment for yourself, but if one of your goals for your visit to the area is to find a way into the exclusive **Magic Castle Club** (www.magiccastle.com), their ancillary hotel has your ticket waiting at the desk. If you're just looking for a nice place to relax between days filled with touring, you'll definitely get that here. Sparkling light rooms with cushy white comforters and spare, clean decor offer a haven of tranquility. A courtyard pool invites lounging day and night, and you can even enjoy a midnight swim here without breaking the hotel rules (so long as you don't wake the other guests). Many rooms at the Magic Castle have their own kitchens. But be sure to enjoy the little luxurious touches, such as high-end coffee, baked goodies in the free continental breakfast, plushy robes, and nightly turn-down service.

### Over $250

A lovely upscale hotel is the **Renaissance Hollywood Hotel** (1755 N. Highland Ave., 323/856-1200, www.renaissancehollywood .com, $313). Right at the corner of Hollywood and Highland, you'll be in the thick of all the action here. This hotel has taken the SoCal mid-century modern style and given it some new millennium touches to create a colorful, high-end property that appeals to well-heeled travelers of many tastes. With more than 600 rooms, you'll probably find one to suit you. Expect eye-piercingly bright blue, yellow, and red bedspreads and upholstered chairs in sizeable rooms, some with nice city views. Kids are welcome here, and the hotel offers childcare for parents looking a few hours' respite or more adult attractions. If you're not up for the Walk of Fame or the Wax Museum, grab a chaise lounge on the rooftop pool or just order room service. To dine in true style, try **Twist,** the on-site California cuisine restaurant that features small bites to let diners try as many menu items as they can stand. If you're staying at the Renaissance to admire the modern artistic

touches, get a brochure from the desk and take a tour of the common spaces, which display more than 70 works of colorful modern art for your admiration (many by local artists).

## BEVERLY HILLS AND WEST HOLLYWOOD

Most travelers don't come to Beverly Hills looking to stay in a youth hostel. In a town whose name equals wealth, the point is to dive headfirst into the lap of luxury. Though you might have to save up to get a room near Rodeo Drive, if you choose wisely you might just get a sense of how the other .001 percent live for just one or two nights.

For budget accommodations in the general vicinity, look to the chain motels in the West Hollywood region. This upscale area, which serves as L.A.'s gay mecca, divides its lodgings between the Ramada and the equal-to-Beverly-Hills upscale unique hotels.

### Over $250

A newcomer to the Beverly Hills luxury hotel scene, **The Mosaic Hotel** (125 Spalding Dr., 800/463-4466, www.mosaichotel.com, $390–710) offers a laid-back, urban vibe in both its chill common areas and its comfortable guest accommodations. Rooms are furnished in contemporary fabrics, with soothing light colors blending into attractive wall art and fluffy white down comforters. Mattresses are topped with feather beds, and the bathrooms sparkle and sooth with Frette towels and BVLGARI bath products. If you've got the cash to spring for a suite, you'll be treated to something that feels like your own elegant apartment, with a living room with 42-inch plasma TV, sofa, and armchair. Downstairs, a hip bar and small dining room offer top-shelf cocktails and tasty California cuisine. Friendly, helpful staff will serve you tidbits in the bar, and can help with any travel or room needs.

The most famous of all the grand hotels of Beverly Hills, the **Beverly Wilshire** (9500 Wilshire Blvd., 310/275-5200, www.fourseasons .com/beverlywilshire, $500) is now a Four Seasons property. But never fear: The recent multimillion-dollar renovation didn't scour away all the classic charm of this historic hotel. Nor did it lower the price of the privilege of sleeping inside these hallowed walls. Even the plainest of guest rooms here feature exquisite appointments such as 42-inch plasma TVs, elegant linens, attractive artwork, and even live plants. Of course, guests with all the money in the world can rent a suite; the Presidential suite resembles nothing so much as a European palace, complete with Corinthian columns. With an in-house spa, a dining room, room service, and every other service you could want, folks who can afford it consider a stay at the Beverly Wilshire well worth the expense.

In West Hollywood, the **Sunset Tower Hotel** (8358 Sunset Blvd., West Hollwyood, 323/654-7100, www.sunsettowerhotel.com, $330) might look familiar to recent visitors of Disney's California Adventure. Indeed, its architecture inspired the "Tower of Terror" ride at the amusement park. But there's no terror in the Sunset Tower today. Instead, you'll find a gorgeous deco exterior paired with a fully renovated modern interior. Guest accommodations range from smallish standard queen guest rooms with smooth linens and attractive appointments up to luxurious suites with panoramic views and limestone bathrooms. All rooms include flat-screen TVs, 24-hour room service, and free Wi-Fi.

The **Le Montrose Suite** (900 Hammond St., West Hollywood, 310/855-1115, www.le montrose.com, $270) will give you a taste of the kind of luxury celebrities expect in their accommodations, especially in trendy, gay-friendly West Hollywood. The atmosphere and decor are almost desperately modern, from the silver discs behind the front desk to the neo-patchwork bedspreads in the guest rooms. Happily, you'll find lots of plush comfort in amongst the primary colors and plain geometric shapes in your room. A Berber carpet snuggles your feet, a high-end entertainment system sees to your every audio-visual and gaming need, and a gas fireplace provides just the right romantic atmosphere for an evening spent indoors. Outside of your posh suite, you can take a dip in the rooftop saltwater swimming pool and whirlpool, play a set on the lighted tennis courts, or get in a good workout inside the fitness center. Hotel guests alone can enjoy the gourmet delicacies of the private dining room or order from 24-hour room service. If you're dying for some great clubbing or a seat at a show while you're in town, just ask the concierge, who can provide all the assistance you need.

## SANTA MONICA, VENICE, AND MALIBU

Arguably, the best place to stay in Los Angeles is down by the beach. It seems ironic that you can camp in a park for $25 a night in exclusive Malibu, and you can pay over $1,000 for a resort room in so-called "working class" Santa Monica. But whether you choose either of those or a spot in Venice Beach, you'll get some of the best atmosphere

### Under $100

For a bed indoors for cheap, your options near the beach run to youth hostels. The huge **HI-Santa Monica** (1436 2nd St., Santa Monica, 310/393-9913, www.hilosangeles.org, $29) offers 260 beds in a building constructed specifically to house the hostel. You'll be right in the thick of downtown Santa Monica in a good neighborhood, within walking distance of the Santa Monica Pier, the Third Street Promenade, and the beach. Plenty of great, cheap restaurants cluster in the area, or you can make use of the hostel's open kitchen. This ritzy hostel offers tons of amenities for the price, including a computer room, game room, TV room, movie room, excursions, wheelchair access, sheets with the bed price, and even a complimentary continental breakfast every morning. If you prefer to find your own way around L.A., the local public transit system runs right outside the door.

The **Venice Beach Cotel** (25 Windward Ave., Venice Beach, 888/718-8287, www.venice beachcotel.com, $24–77) claims to be "a hostel with hotel standards." You can make your own judgments on its amenities, which include women's-only and co-ed dorms with and without in-room bath, private rooms, and private rooms with baths. Rooms get maid service daily (a rarity in the hostelling world), and a computer room and kick-back lounge welcome guests and encourage them to socialize. But the best part of the Cotel is undoubtedly its location *on* the Boardwalk right across from Muscle Beach. Fall out of your bunk and into the warm sands of Venice's beach every morning. The fabulous restaurants of Washington Street are reached by an easy walk, and the canals sit just a block or two away. Book well in advance for summer.

## $100-150

If you're looking for a moderate-priced motel near the beach, look to the 1950s-era motor inns of Santa Monica. One of these that manages to be cute and kitschy despite a desperate need for a remodel is the **Bayside Hotel** (2001 Ocean Ave., Santa Monica, 310/396-6000, www.baysidehotel.com, $110–225). The hotel's not right on the beach, but you can walk there in about two minutes. Inside your room, you'll find the 1950s, from the Pepto-pink tile in the bathroom to the odd arrangement of older furniture in the bedroom to the utterly retro kitchens in the suites. If you crave elegance, speedy check-in and check-out, or even spotless cleanliness, the Bayside isn't for you. But if you're seeking a fun stay in a place that looks like it ought to be in a Gidget movie, the Bayside's just right for you.

## $150-250

The **Venice Beach Suites & Hotel** (1305 Ocean Front Walk, 888/877-7602, www.venicebeachsuites.com, $155–250) is a surprisingly lovely and affordable little Venice hotel. It sits right on the beach, but it's far enough from the Boardwalk to acquire a touch of peace and quiet. You can also stroll over to Washington Street to grab a meal or a cup of coffee, or just wander out of the lobby and straight onto the beach. Inside, the rooms and suites all have full kitchens so you can cook for yourself—perfect for budget-conscious travelers and folks staying in Venice for several days. The kitchen's also

great for simply coming in from the beach for a quick lunch with ice-cold drinks! The guest room decor is cuter than that of an average motel; you might find exposed brick walls and polished hardwood floors stocked with rattan furniture and cute accessories. Check the website for weeklong rental deals.

For a charming hotel experience only a block from the ever-energetic Boardwalk, stay at the **Inn at Venice Beach** (327 Washington Blvd., 800/828-0688, www.innatvenicebeach.com, $165–275, parking $5/day). The charming yellow-and-blue exterior, complete with a lovely bricked interior courtyard-cum-café, makes all guests feel welcome. Inside, you might be surprised by the brightly colored modern furniture and decor. Common spaces are done in a postmodern, blocky style, while the guest rooms pop with brilliant yellows and vibrant accents. The two-story boutique hotel offers only about 20 rooms, and its location on Washington Street makes it a perfect base from which to enjoy the best restaurants and beaches of Venice. Start each day with a complimentary continental breakfast, either in the dining room or outside in the Courtyard Café. If you need to stay connected while you're in Venice, the inn has complimentary Wi-Fi throughout the hotel.

If you want to bring your family to stay in legendary Malibu, one of the best hotels going is the **Casa Malibu Inn on the Beach** (22752 Pacific Coast Hwy., 800/831-0858, $150–250). This pleasant and kid-friendly property sits right out on the beach. Many of the rooms have ocean views; some also have gas fireplaces for cozy cool winter evenings. White bedsteads match the paint and draperies in the smallish rooms, while colorful bedspreads add visual appeal to the European styling of each unique guest room. Some of the gleaming white bathrooms have oversized bathtubs, perfect for a relaxing soak after a long day out on the beach. Head down to the lobby of this unpretentious 1950s-era building for a genuinely fresh continental breakfast each morning. From there, you can stagger right out onto the sand to pick out a prime spot before the crowds descend. You don't even have to worry about parking!

Yes, you really can stay at the **Hotel California** (1670 Ocean Ave., Santa Monica, 310/393-2363, $197–310). Appropriately decorated with classic longboards and electric guitars, this moderate hotel sits a short block from the beach and next to the Santa Monica Pier. You'll be in the perfect spot to enjoy all the best of Santa Monica without ever having to get into a car or worry about finding parking. Inside the hotel, you'll find hardwood floors and matching bedsteads, calming pale yellow walls, and white comforters and linens. Choose between a classic guest room, a Jacuzzi suite with the obvious amenity, and one- and two-bedroom suites. Outside, enjoy the lush greenery of the oddly named Spanish Courtyard, which looks more like something from the tropics than from Europe. Other perks include free Wi-Fi, a mini-fridge, and a smoke-free hotel experience.

## Over $250

In Malibu, if you've got silly amounts of cash to spare, stay at the **Malibu Beach Inn** (22878 Pacific Coast Hwy., Malibu, 310/456-6444, www.malibubeachinn.com, $350). This oceanside villa offers all the very best furnishings and amenities. Every room has a view of the ocean, and the boutique hotel sits on "Billionaire's Beach," a private and exclusive stretch of sand you can't access unless you're a guest of one of its properties. Your guest room will be done in rare woods, gleaming stone, and the most stylish modern linens and accents. A plasma TV, plush robes, and comfy beds tempt some visitors to stay inside, but equally tempting are the balconies with their own entertainment in the form of endless surf, glorious sunsets, and balmy breezes. The more affordable rooms are a bit small but just as attractively turned out as the over-the-top suites. When lunch and dinnertime come, go downstairs to the airy, elegant, on-site Carbon Beach Club to enjoy delicious cuisine in an upscale beach atmosphere.

One of the best-known resort hotels in the L.A. beach community has long been **Shutters on the Beach** (1 Pico Blvd., Santa Monica, 310/458-0030, www.shuttersonthebeach.com,

$475). Make no mistake: You'll pay handsomely for the privilege of laying your head on one of Shutters' hallowed pillows. On the other hand, the gorgeous airy rooms will make you feel like you're home, or at least staying at the home you'd have if you could hire a famous designer to decorate for you. Even the most modest guest rooms have not only the comfortable beds, white linens, plasma TVs, and oversized bathtubs of a luxury hotel, you'll also find a comfortable clutter of pretty ornaments on tables and shelves. If you can pry yourself out of your private space, head down to the famed lobby for a drink and a people-watching session. Get a reservation for the elegant white-tablecloth One Pico or grab a more casual sandwich or salad at beachside Coast.

The impressive multi-level resort edifice sits right on the beach, so there's no need to find a premium parking spot to enjoy a day in the sand. If you long for more formal relaxation, book a massage at the **ONE Spa.** Art lovers can spend hours just wandering the halls of the hotel, examining the works of many famous modern photographers and painters.

## PASADENA

Pasadena lodgings run to the old standard national chains, plus a few funky 1950s-era motor lodges and the occasional upscale B&B. If you're planning to stay in Pasadena over the New Year, book early! The town fills up for the legendary Rose Parade. If your aim is to get yourself a room from which you can watch the Rose Parade, book earlier still; while you can get the perfect view from a room of your own, such places are at a premium during parade season.

### Under $100

The **Kingston Inn & Suites** (2156 E. Colorado Blvd., 626/793-9339, www.kingstonpasadena.com, $80–350) provides good clean rooms right along the Rose Parade route for reasonable nightly rates (which go way up for the Parade). You're also nice and close to Old Town, restaurants, and museums. The guest rooms have standard dark floral bedspreads and matching deep red carpets, enough room to walk around your two queens or king bed, and average motel bathrooms. A sizeable balcony outside each room offers the perfect Parade vantage point, and a sparkling pool with hot tub beckon travelers outside. Modern in-room amenities include Wi-Fi, iPod docking stations, coffee makers, fridges, and more.

## $100-200

The top pick of the quaint motor inns is the **Saga Motor Hotel** (1633 E. Colorado Blvd., 626/795-0431, www.thesagamotorhotel.com, $113). Outside it's all 1950s, from the structure of the low buildings to the Astroturf around the swimming pool. The ambiance extends to the door of your room, which includes a doorknob and an actual metal key to open it with. But inside your room, the decor gets a lot more contemporary. The big space has either a king or two double beds, clean if worn carpeting and linens, and a nice bathroom with a surprisingly good bathtub and nice hot showers. Locationwise, the Saga is right on the Rose Parade route on broad Colorado Boulevard, but it's not right downtown or in Old Town. Sadly, the service is spotty at best, but few people expect concierges at motor hotels.

Of the main chain motels, the best inexpensive one might be the **Comfort Inn** (2462 E. Colorado Blvd., 626/405-0811, www .comfortinn.com, $93). You'll find comfortable amenities in pleasant standard motel rooms here, along with yet another good set of views of the Rose Parade. Expect room prices to skyrocket for the Parade.

## Over $250

Once upon a time, Pasadena was the resort haven of wealthy East Coasters. To revisit this wealthy past, stay at **The Bissell House Bed & Breakfast** (201 Orange Grove Ave. S., 626/441-3535, www.bissellhouse.com, $225–400) on "Millionaire's Row." The tall mint-green Victorian surrounded by the deeper green of lush mature landscaping opens its doors to well-heeled travelers who want a luxurious place to stay while they're in the L.A. area. It is named for one of its residents, Anna Bissell McCay, heiress to the original Bissell vacuum cleaner fortune. Each of the five rooms has a unique decorating scheme, yet each shares a European floral theme that binds the inn together into a coherent whole. Guest rooms have comfy beds, a luxurious bathroom (most have clawfoot tubs), and lots of wonderful amenities, and the property has a swimming pool with a hot tub and lots of lovely plants scattered about. Your room includes a full breakfast each morning, served at the long table in the downstairs dining room.

# Food

You'll find a wide variety of cuisine all over Los Angeles and its surrounding towns. Whatever kind of food you prefer, from fresh sushi to Armenian, you can probably find it in a cool little hole-in-the-wall somewhere in L.A. Local recommendations often make for the best dining experiences, but even just walking down the right street can yield a tasty meal.

## DOWNTOWN AND VICINITY

Sure, you can find plenty of bland, tourist-friendly restaurants serving American and Americanized food in the Downtown area—but why would you, when one of Downtown L.A.'s greatest strengths is its ethnic diversity and the great range of cuisine that goes along with it? An endless array of fabulous holes-in-walls awaits you. Getting local recommendations is the best way to find the current hot spots, or you can choose from among this tiny sampling of what's available.

## American

If you're just looking for a good pastrami sandwich, you can get it at **Langer's Delicatessen and Restaurant** (704 S. Alvarado St., 213/483-

8050, www.langersdeli.com, Mon.–Sat. 8 A.M.–4 P.M., $10–20). Operating continuously since 1947, the house specialty at Langer's is a hot pastrami sandwich that some say is the best in the world (yes, they're including New York). Whether you're willing to go that far or not, Langer's serves both hot and cold dishes in the traditional Jewish deli style to satisfy any appetite level or specific craving. Granted, it's still California, so you can get fresh avocado on your tongue sandwich if you really want to. You'll also find a vast breakfast menu and plenty of desserts (noodle kugel, anyone?). If you don't have time to sit down for lunch, order in advance and pick up your meal curbside. If you can dine in, be sure to take a few minutes to gaze at the photos on the walls; the family you'll see has run this deli since its opening in the post-war era.

## Asian

One of the largest Asian areas in Los Angeles is Koreatown. It's only fitting that a city with such a large Korean population has plenty of good Korean restaurants. One of these is **Chunju Han-il Kwan** (3450 W. Sixth St. 213/480-1799, $10). Beware: This is an authentic Korean restaurant that caters primarily to the expat Korean community. You won't find English menus here, but you will find helpful waitresses who can guide you through the process of ordering. If your server tells you a dish is very spicy, she means it, but that doesn't mean you won't love it anyway. The menu is eclectic to say the least—you can get a hot dog, octopus, fish soup, Korean stew (thickened with American cheese), kimchi, and much more. Many patrons crave the veggie side dishes that come with the entrées here. Don't worry about your standard of dress when you dine here, since this casual restaurant resides in a strip mall and has gas burners on the tables.

For a serious authentic Japanese cuisine experience, visit **Kagaya** (418 E. Second St., 213/617-1016, http://kagaya.dla.menuclub. com, Tues.–Sat. 6–10:30 P.M. Sun. 6–10 P.M., $40–60). Even L.A. denizens who've eaten at shabu shabu places in Japan proper come back to Kagaya again and again. They make

reservations in advance, because the dining room is small and the quality of the food makes it popular even on weeknights. The term "shabu shabu" refers to paper-thin slices of beef and vegetable that you dip and swish into a pot of boiling *daishi* (broth), then dunk in *ponzu* or other house-made sauces before eating. The shabu shabu is but one course in the meal you'll get at Kagaya, since all meals include several appetizers (varieties change daily), shabu shabu with beef and seafood, udon, and dessert. You can pay a premium for Wagyu beef if you choose, but the king crab legs in season are part of the regular price of dinner. Even the regular beef here isn't cheap, but the quality makes it worth the price. Sit at the counter if you want to watch all your food being prepared before your very eyes.

## French

A surprisingly cute little brick-fronted café, the **Angelique Café** (840 S. Spring St., 213/623-8698, www.angeliquecafe.com, Mon.–Fri. 8 A.M.–3:30 P.M., Sat.–Sun. 8 A.M.–4 P.M., $7–20) offers a relaxed French atmosphere and good French-styled food. The original chef-owner came from France and brought his recipes and his dining aesthetic with him. The large menu has an array of both French and American dishes, going heavy on the salads and more traditional hot fare. If you come for breakfast, you can choose from a list of omelets and crepes plus a few American egg dishes, or the more traditional continental breakfast of pastry and coffee. Angelique's small green-and-yellow dining room is open for breakfast and lunch only. If it's a nice day, grab a table outside on the wrought-iron fenced patio, which has almost as many tables as the inside dining room does.

## Greek

Originally a Greek import company in the 1960s, the **Papa Cristos Taverna** (2771 W. Pico Blvd., 323/737-2970, www.papa cristo.com, Tues.–Sat. 9 A.M.–8 P.M., Sun. 9 A.M.–4 P.M., $10) restaurant opened in the 1990s. The import shop still supplies the local Greek community with hard-to-come-by delicacies, which also become ingredients in the cuisine at the Taverna. Dishes are traditionally Greek, from the salads to the kebabs to the baba ghanouj. After you're finished with your meal, wander the aisles of the store to pick up a few unusual Greek delicacies to take with you.

## Italian

It seems odd to name a high-end restaurant after a decidedly low-end bug, but that's what the owners of **Cicada Restaurant** (617 S. Olive St., 213/488-9488, www.cicadarestaurant .com, Mon.–Sat. 5:30–9 P.M., $40–80) did. Set in the 1920s Oviatt building decorated in high French art deco style, the beautiful restaurant glitters with some of its original Lalique glass panels—be sure to check out the elevator doors on your way in or out. The palatial dining room features huge round tables for large parties, and balcony seating for intimate groups of two. The immense space lets Cicada space its tables farther apart than in most restaurants, giving diners a sense of privacy and romance that can be hard to come by.

As for the food, calling it "Italian" isn't quite right, since the cuisine here fuses Italian concepts with California ingredients, techniques, and presentations. Expect a varied seasonal menu of inventive dishes, including pastas and meats after the Italian style with distinct California flavors. Be sure to save room for Cicada's beloved desserts, which many diners declare to be their favorite part of the meal.

## Mexican

Everyone in L.A. (and most of the rest of California for that matter) knows that the best tamales come from the kitchens of Mexican grandmothers, and get sold on the streets from carts or trucks. If you're not a local and don't feel able to find the best little sidewalk tamale cart, your best option is **Mama's Hot Tamales Café** (2124 W. Seventh St., 213/487-7474, www.iurd. org/mamashottamales, Mon.–Sat. 11 A.M.– 3:30 P.M., Sun. 9 A.M.–3:30 P.M., $6–10). You'll even get a little social justice with your lunch, as Mama's operates as a training ground for "informal" food purveyors to develop the skills

they need to become higher-paid employees of the formal food service world. Open pretty much for lunch only, Mama's serves salads, appetizers, burritos, tostadas, and other simple Latin American dishes. But if you know what's right, you'll order the house namesake: a homemade tamale.

## HOLLYWOOD

Hollywood's got just as many tasty treats tucked away in strip malls as other areas of Los Angeles. If you want to rub elbows with rock stars, you're likely to find yourself at a big, slightly raunchy bar and grill. For a chance at glimpsing stars of the silver screen, look for upscale California cuisine or perhaps a high-end sushi bar. If all you need is tasty sustenance, you can choose from a range of restaurants.

## American

If you've ever owned a rock album—any rock album—it's worth your time to stop in for a meal at ❿ **The Rainbow Bar & Grill** (9015 W. Sunset Blvd., 310/278-4232, www.rainbow barandgrill.com, lunch Mon.–Fri. 11 A.M.–4 P.M., dinner daily 4 P.M.–2 A.M., $13– 30). You'll find a lack of fancy sauces, and an amazing myriad of rock and roll memorabilia in this dark (but no longer smoky) restaurant. To the surprise of some intrepid diners, the hallowed haven, in which countless rockers have been serviced by innumerable groupies, does serve a darn tasty cheeseburger. If you show up for lunch on a weekday, you're likely to have the cavernous space almost to yourself to enjoy your salad and make your slow way along the walls checking out the endless parade of photos, guitars, newspaper snippets, and other cool stuff. In the even dimmer bar area, you can play a for-real game of authentic table Ms. Pac-Man as you sip your favorite cocktail or quaff a beer.

Nighttime is a whole different story. The crowds start trickling into the Rainbow as the sun goes down. By the time the shows let out at the Roxy and the Whisky, your chances of finding a booth diminish significantly. The good news is that the rockers still gather here after playing shows in the neighborhood. You never know who you'll bump into as you weave your way through the main dining room and outdoor patio to get your next drink. The back rooms also open up late, and you'll find dancing, drinking, smoking (shhh!), and fun upstairs in a warren-like space that includes either two or three separate bar-and-club spaces on any given night, depending on whose tales you believe.

As for amenities, expect woefully inadequate and difficult-to-access bathrooms, particularly if you happen to be female. Wait staff runs to cute and buxom young women. You can take your cigarettes just outside of the exits to be legal.

If you prefer to combine your love of live acts and your need for food, head for the **Hotel Café** (1623½ N. Cahuenga Blvd., 323/461-2040, www.hotelcafe.com, daily 7 P.M.–close, $10–30, 21 and over). Food choices run to the casual here—paninis, salads, and desserts, but the restaurant has a beer list, a wine list, and a full bar. The restaurant opens early; it's easiest to secure a table if you show up before the show starts. After 7 P.M., prepare for things to get loud. If you do love yourself some new-to-the-scene music, stick around.

## Brazilian

Need food really, really, *really* late? **Bossa Nova** (7181 W. Sunset Blvd., 323/436-7999, www.bossafood.com, daily 11 A.M.–4 A.M., $10–20) can hook you up. A big menu of inexpensive entrées can satisfy any appetite from lunch to way past dinnertime at Bossa. Some of the dishes bear the spicy flavors of the owners' home country of Brazil, but you'll also find a ton of pastas, plenty of salads, and classic Italian-American build-your-own pizzas. Check out the desserts for some South American specialties if you need sweets after a long night out at the clubs. Not near the Sunset Strip? Bossa Nova has three other L.A. locations: one on Robertson Boulevard, one in Beverly Hills, and one in West L.A. If you've made it back to your hotel room and aren't inclined to leave again, Bossa delivers!

## California

It seems right somehow that the spot in L.A.

that combines live music with upscale cuisine sits on Melrose Avenue. At **The Foundry on Melrose** (7463 Melrose Ave., 323/651-0915, www.thefoundryonmelrose.com, Tues.–Wed. 6–10 P.M., Thurs. 6 P.M.–midnight, Fri.–Sat. 6 P.M.–2 A.M., Sun. 2–9 P.M., $25–30), expect to find elegance and art in a style that improbably marries Arts and Crafts, art deco, and modern industrial. The art extends to the plates, where the chef creates elaborate presentations of an array of ingredients. The dinner menu is small, seasonal, and utterly haute California. You might even see an occasional celebrity dining here, though you'll also remark on the refreshing lack of oh-so-trendy 'tude at this restaurant. At the big curving black bar, you can get a lighter (and less pricey) meal from the bar menu. If you prefer an al fresco dining experience, ask for a table out on the patio. (Yes, that's an olive tree dangling its streamers in your soup.) The third room at the Foundry shelters a small piano bar, where a trio called CD3 plays until late into the nights Thursday through Sunday. And for the strong of ear and stomach, a Sunday "Be-Bop Brunch" helps hangovers with a little hair of the dog and some zippy live jazz.

## BEVERLY HILLS AND WEST HOLLYWOOD

Between Beverly Hills and West L.A., you'll find an eclectic choice of restaurants. Unsurprisingly, Beverly Hills tends toward high-end eateries serving European and haute California cuisine. On the other hand, West L.A. boasts a wide array of ethnic restaurants. You'll have to try a few to pick your favorites, since every local has their own take on the area's best eats.

## Asian

For a genuine, locally beloved, and cheap sushi spot, try **Sushi Mac** (2222 Sawtelle, 310/481-9954, daily 11:30 A.M.–9 P.M., $2.50/plate, cash only). Before you order, read the laminated signs on the walls to learn the rules of engagement. Every plate of sushi costs precisely $2.50, whether it's two pieces of nigiri or eight slices of a freshly made roll. The

# A BEGINNER'S GUIDE TO SUSHI

Your first time dining in a sushi restaurant can be an intimidating experience. What to do with the slabs of raw fish, the tentacles, the eggs, the eels, the seaweed — did I mention the raw fish? It's tough to know what's good for a first-timer: The *ebi* or the *unagi?* The *toro* or the *maguro?* Do they cook anything in here??

What follows is a by-no-means-complete beginner's guide to ordering and eating sushi:

**Maki (Rolls).** When most folks think of sushi, they think of seaweed-wrapped circles of rice with fish and vegetables in the middle. This form is called a roll, or *maki*. Almost every sushi place in California will offer certain common rolls, for example the (duh) California Roll. This newcomer-friendly roll contains no raw fish; instead, it has cooked crab or crab salad, avocado, and cucumber wrapped in sushi rice and *nori* (seaweed). There are also plain cucumber rolls, Philadelphia rolls (smoked salmon, cream cheese, and avocado), shrimp salad rolls, and tempura rolls at most sushi bars. On the other hand, adventurous diners often eat rolls with raw fish or barbecued eel inside and out, perhaps dusted with flying fish eggs for a touch of salty crunch or a raw quail egg for smoothness.

**Nigiri (Sushi).** *Nigiri*, sometimes called simply "sushi" on restaurant menus, consists of a slice of (usually) raw fish lying on top of a glob of sticky sushi rice, usually with a dab of wasabi paste in between the fish and the rice. *Nigiri* are almost always sold in pairs per order. Order *nigiri* with a rectangle of scrambled egg instead of fish, with a whole cooked shrimp, or with smoked salmon to ease yourself into the fishiness of it all. Hardcore sushi-ites munch on seasonal fish, sweet shrimp, and even octopus.

**Sashimi.** Sashimi refer to slices of raw fish pared to perfection, often arranged in beautiful patterns and designs by the sushi chef. Don't like raw fish? Then don't bother with sashimi. If you want raw fish almost exclusively, then ask for the chef's selection of sashimi.

**Wasabi.** Important safety tip: That little glob of green stuff on the edge of your plate is *not* the avocado! It's wasabi — a hot Japanese horseradish that's been grated or ground then mixed into a paste. (In truth, most California wasabi is actually regular ol' western horseradish mixed with green food coloring.) Take a tiny dab of wasabi and put it into the little empty dish the server brought. Add soy sauce and mix the wasabi in until it dissolves. If you're unaccustomed to spicy foods, use only a tiny fleck of wasabi to start with, and ignore the Japanese diners creating a thick sludge with more wasabi in it than soy sauce. They're professionals.

**Common Raw Fish.** If you've never had raw fish before and are hesitant to start now, ask for smoked salmon. It's not raw (it's like lox) and it's a good stepping stone into a world without fire.

Next, consider ordering a couple of common and easy-to-eat fish. *Maguro* is red tuna. It can be served as *nigiri*, but it's often diced fine and mixed with arcane ingredients to create "spicy tuna," which is often more palatable for sushi newcomers who don't mind spicy food. *Sake* is raw salmon. It's often served as *nigiri*, and used to decorate the outside of rolls. If you prefer a delicate flavored white fish, try some *hamachi* (yellowtail, a firm white fish) or *tai* (red snapper). To take the next step, order some *unagi*. Hey, it's cooked! In fact, it's barbecued eel.

**How to Order Sushi.** While you can order your own plate of rolls and *nigiri*, most sushi fans will tell you that sushi tastes best when shared family-style. Each diner orders a few of their favorite items, all the food comes out on platters, and you and your friends dig in with fingers or chopsticks to try at least one piece of everything.

**How to Eat Sushi.** Contrary to popular American belief, it is acceptable to pick up both *nigiri* and roll slices with your fingers. You can then dip your sushi into your dish of wasabi and soy sauce. Be gentle — don't soak your *nigiri* rice in the sauce, or you'll completely cover up the taste of the fish. Next, eat! Chase with hot green tea, sake, or Japanese beer. Repeat until plate or wooden serving tray empties.

decor is nothing to write home about, but the ever-frantic chefs will slice and dice their way right in front of you. It might not be the biggest or most creative sushi, but you can get your fill for about half the cost of most other sushi spots. Be aware that Sushi Mac can get crowded with locals on weekdays at lunchtime. However, they've got another location at 8474 West Third Street.

## Italian

If you're looking for upscale Italian cuisine in a classy environment, enjoy lunch or dinner at **Il Pastaio Restaurant** (400 N. Canon Dr., Beverly Hills, 310/205-5444, www .giacominodrago.com/pastaio.htm, Mon.–Sat. 11:30 A.M.–11 P.M., Sun. 5–10 P.M., $15–30). The bright dining room offers a sunny luncheon experience, and the white tablecloths and shiny glassware lend an elegance to dinner, which is served reasonably late into the evening even on weekdays. Boasting a large menu for a high-end restaurant, Il Pastaio offers a wide variety of salads, risotto, and pasta dishes, as well as some overpriced antipasti and a smaller list of entrées. Preparations and dishes evoke authentic Italy, so you might see osso bucco or fettuccine Bolognese on the menu. The blue-painted bar offers a tasteful selection of California and Italian vintages, and serious wine lovers will be pleased to see the Italian selections broken out by region.

Happily located right on the Strip, the **Vivoli Cafe & Trattoria** (7994 Sunset Blvd., West Hollywood, 323/656-5050, www.vivolicafe .com, Mon.–Thurs. and Sun. 11:30 A.M.–10 P.M., Fri.–Sat. 11:30 A.M.–11 P.M., $15–30) offers a copious menu of Italian cuisine. Expect white tablecloths, wooden chairs, and friendly service at this locals' favorite. The broad menu focuses on seafood and a surprising variety of salads. But you can also get your favorite cheese-heavy pasta dishes or hearty, meaty entrées. Don't forget dessert—leave the guns, take the cannolli!

## Steak

There's nothing like a good steak dinner, Brazilian style. At **Fogo de Chao** (133 N. La Cienega Blvd., Beverly Hills, 310/289-7755, http://fogo dechao.com, Mon.–Fri. 11 A.M.–2 P.M. and 5–10 P.M., Fri. until 10:30 P.M., Sat. 4:30–10:30 P.M., Sun. 4–9:30 P.M., $40–80), be prepared for an interactive dining experience. The meat is slow roasted, then skewered and cut right onto your plate by ever-moving servers. Be sure to use the red-and-green token on your table; if you don't turn it over to the red side occasionally, you will be continuously bombarded with the 15 different kinds of meat the restaurant offers. The fixed-price meal includes endless trips to the salad bar, fresh-cut veggies, and traditional Brazilian side dishes (fried bananas are a starch here, not a dessert). The extensive wine list includes plenty of both California and European vintages, plus a wider-than-average selection of ports and dessert wines. While the food is fabulous, you'll get the most out a meal here with a lively group that will enjoy the service as much as the spicy flavors.

## Coffee and Tea

A grand afternoon tea in stately Beverly Hills just seems like the right thing to do at least once. You can get some of the best tea in L.A. at ◖ **The Living Room in The Peninsula Hotel** (9882 Santa Monica Blvd., Beverly Hills, 310/975-2736, www.peninsula.com, seatings at 2:30 P.M. and 5 P.M., $18–45). The Peninsula has three restaurants, but for tea head to the elegant Living Room and grab a comfy chair near the fireplace. Sit back and enjoy the delicate harp music while admiring the elegant and tasteful furnishings in this posh space. If you skipped lunch or plan to miss dinner, go with the heartier Royal Tea or Imperial Tea. Lighter eaters prefer the Full Tea or the Light Tea. All come with tea sandwiches, scones, pastries, and, of course, a pot of tea. The loose-leaf teas are Peninsula originals; many are flavored. For an extra fee, you can add a glass of champagne to complete your high tea experience.

Dress properly for the occasion: Jackets are required even for tea. Ladies have more latitude, but shouldn't show up in jeans and a T-shirt.

## SANTA MONICA, VENICE, AND MALIBU

Yes, there's lots of junky beach food to be found in Santa Monica and Venice Beach. But there are also an amazing number of gems hiding in these towns.

### American

**Cora's Coffee Shoppe** (1802 Ocean Ave., Santa Monica, 310/451-9562, Tues.–Fri. 6:30 A.M.–3 P.M., Sat.–Sun. 7 A.M.–3 P.M., $10) doesn't look like much; it's a tiny building with a smallish sign. But don't be fooled by the unpretentious exterior. The small, exquisite restaurant inside is something of a locals' secret hiding in plain sight, serving breakfast and lunch to diners who are more than willing to pack into the tiny spaces that Cora's calls dining rooms. In addition to the two tiny, marble-topped tables and miniature marble counter inside, a small patio area off to one side, screened by latticework and venerable bougainvillea vines, offers a warm and pleasant atmosphere.

What's best about Cora's is simply the food. The chefs crammed into the eensie kitchen use high-end and sometimes organic ingredients to create breakfast and lunch dishes that don't seem like anything fancy on the menu, but will make you rethink your opinion of humble scrambled eggs or lowly oatmeal when they get to your table. The espresso drinks are reminiscent of European coffees—dark, bitter, and served in cups the size of bowls. Perhaps it's the coffee that keeps the staff moving so fast, endlessly serving and busing and serving some more to keep up with the steady flow of diners, many of whom the waiters seem to know quite well.

### Asian

If your tastes run to the exotically spicy and romantic, walk across Pacific Avenue from Venice Beach into Marina Del Ray and to the **Siamese Garden** (301 Washington Blvd., Marina Del Rey, 310/821-0098, www.siamese garden.com, Mon.–Thurs. 11 A.M.–10 P.M., Fri. 11 A.M.–11 P.M., Sat. 5–11 P.M., Sun. 5–10 P.M., $10–30). A favorite of local couples both straight and otherwise looking for a romantic evening out, Siamese Garden boasts outdoor tables set in an overhanging lantern-lit garden, complete

Cora's Coffee Shoppe

© LANCE SCOTT

with glimpses of the Venice Canals through the foliage and fencing. In the kitchen, Siamese Garden prides itself on creating delightful dishes created with only the freshest and best produce and ingredients available. The wide menu offers all of your favorite Thai classics, such as coconut soup, pad thai, and a rainbow of curries. Mint, lemongrass, peanut sauce, basil, and hot chiles crowd the menu with their strong and distinct flavors. Vegetarians have a great selection of tasty dishes, while carnivores can enjoy plenty of good beef, poultry, and seafood. For dessert, try one of the fun sticky rice and fruit dishes. To accompany your meal, you can get a rich Thai iced tea (ask to see one before you order if you've never had it before) or a light Thai beer.

## Barbecue

As is right and proper in California, you have to go to the seedier part of town to get the best authentic Southern barbecue. **Baby Blues BBQ** (444 Lincoln Blvd., Venice, 310/396-7675, www.babybluesbarbq.com, Mon.–Thurs. 11:30 A.M.–10 P.M., Sat. 11:30 A.M.–11 P.M., Sun. noon–10 P.M., $10–30) disobeys the haute Venice rule of AWOL (Always West of Lincoln), sitting right on Lincoln Boulevard with its grubby sidewalks and elderly strip malls. This disreputable street corner location (really, it's not that bad) does not dissuade locals, who line up at lunchtime to grab a plate of ribs or chicken. The menu pays little attention to cholesterol or carb counters. Choose from sausages, pulled pork, beer-braised brisket, barbecued chicken, and pork or beef ribs, all covered in homemade sauces and spice rubs. The cooks know their business, and regional specialties from different parts of the South are created with specific intent and understanding of the cuisine. Fixin's (side dishes) include Baby Blues' famed hot cornbread, baked beans, slaw, mac and cheese, and other appropriate stuff.

## Caribbean

How can you not love a restaurant called **Cha Cha Chicken** (1906 Ocean Ave., Santa Monica, 310/581-1684, www.chachachicken .com, Mon.–Fri. 11 A.M.–10 P.M. Sat.–Sun.

10 A.M.–10 P.M., $10)? It looks just like it sounds—a slightly decrepit but brightly painted shack only a short walk from the Santa Monica Pier and the Third Street Promenade. You can't miss it even if you're driving quickly down Ocean Avenue. The best place to get a table is definitely the palm tree–strewn patio area outdoors. It's the perfect atmosphere to enjoy the wonderful and inexpensive Caribbean dishes that come from the fragrant kitchen. The jerk dishes bring a tangy sweetness to the table, while the *ropa vieja* heats up the plate, and the funky enchiladas put a whole new spin on a Mexican classic. Salads, sandwiches, and wraps are popular with lighter eaters and the lunch crowd. Quaff an imported Jamaican soda or a seasonal *agua fresca* with your meal, since Cha Cha Chicken doesn't have a liquor license.

## Italian

A Venice institution, the **C&O Trattoria** (31 Washington Blvd., Venice Beach, 310/823-9491, www.cotrattoria.com, Mon.–Thurs. 11:30 A.M.–10 P.M., Fri. 11:30 A.M.–11 P.M., Sat. 8 A.M.–11 P.M., Sun. 8 A.M.–10 P.M., $13–18) manages to live up to its hype, and then some. Pick a seat in the dimly lit indoor dining room with rustic wood furniture and red-checked tablecloths, or sit outside in the big outdoor dining room, enjoying the mild weather and the soft pastel frescoes on the exterior walls surrounding the courtyard. C&O is known for its self-described gargantuan portions, which are best shared family-style among a group of diners. Be sure to start off with the addictive little garlic rolls. Next, seriously consider the pasta list, which includes some truly creative and delectable preparations. If you need help deciding on dishes, be sure to ask your friendly, knowledgeable server, who will be attentive but not overzealous. While C&O has a nice wine list, it's worth trying a jug of the surprisingly tasty house Chianti.

## Mexican

Looking for good cheap tacos in an unfamiliar town can be a scary proposition, but you have no need to fear **El Tarasco** (109 Washington

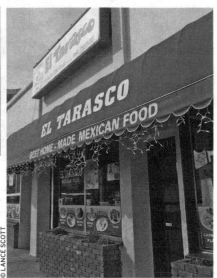

© LANCE SCOTT

El Tarasco

Blvd., Marina Del Rey, 310/306-8552, www
.eltarascoburritos.com, daily 9 A.M.–11 P.M.,
$5–10). This walk-up dive taqueria has the lo-
cals' stamp of approval, and boasts of the fresh-
ness of its food. Specialties of the house are the
burritos and tostadas, which are big and cheap
and yummy. Even the full-fledged dinners that
come with rice and beans and a combination
of items please budget diners, since nothing
on the menu costs more than $10. You can eat
at El Tarasco in the decidedly down-rent but
charming dining room, or get your food to go,
perhaps for a quick walk down Washington to
chow down on your burritos at the beach.

### Seafood
**Neptune's Net** (42505 Pacific Coast Hwy.,
Malibu, 310/457-3095, www.neptunesnet
.com, Mon.–Thurs. 10:30 A.M.–7 P.M., Fri.
10:30 A.M.–8 P.M., Sat.–Sun. 10 A.M.–7:30 P.M.,
$10–20) in Malibu catches all kinds of sea-
food to serve to hungry diners. Locals call it
The Net and usually order the fish and chips.
Situated on the Malibu coastline adjacent to
the County Line surf break, you'll often find
sandy and salt-encrusted local surfers satisfying

their enormous appetites after hours out on the
waves. Even Midwestern visitors who are put
off by the endless raw and rare fish eaten in
California will feel comfortable dining in this
casual palace of fried seafood. The large menu
includes a seemingly endless variety of combinations, à la carte options, and side dishes.

## PASADENA
### Afghan
For a delicious and upscale dining experience,
have lunch or dinner at **Azeen's Afghani
Restaurant** (110 E. Union St., 626/683-3310,
www.azeensafghanirestaurant.com, Mon.–Fri.
11:30 A.M.–2 P.M., 5:30–9:30 P.M., $20–30).
Inside, you'll find white tablecloths, black furniture, and unusual paintings. On the menu,
the offerings take you into another world—
one largely mysterious to denizens of the West.
Trade routes, invasions, religion, tribal culture,
and lots and lots of sand all contribute to the
way Afghanistan and its cuisine have evolved.
Vegetarians, be aware that while you will find
some limited options, Afghani food tends
heavily toward meat. Kabobs of all kinds are
a regional specialty, and the country's proximity to India brings with it a love for truly spicy
(and incredibly flavorful) dishes. At Azeen's,
you can get kabobs, spicy lamb dishes, dump-
lings, and traditional desserts.

### Asian
If you're just dying for Thai or Vietnamese
food, one of the better spots in Pasadena
is **Daisy Mint** (1218 E. Colorado Blvd.
626/792-2999, www.daisymint.com, Mon.–
Fri. 11 A.M.–9 P.M., Sat.–Sun. noon–9 P.M.,
$10–30). The tiny green dining room's ex-
posed brick and original artwork speak of
SoCal, while the menu items tend to come
from Southeast Asia and beyond. You'll find
the aforementioned Thai and Vietnamese, plus
Korean and uniquely Californian Asian-fusion
dishes here. Some of the fun special touches of
the house include a variety of steamed rice that
you can choose to accompany your meal, and
a large selection of unusual and fragrant teas.
Pick whatever you think will go best with your

satay, curry, seafood, or soup. Reservations are recommened on weekend evenings.

## Barbecue

If you're looking for some down-home Southern food, head straight for **Big Mama's Rib Shack** (1453 N. Lake Ave., 626/797-1792, www.bigmamas-ribshack.com, Tues.–Thurs. 11:30 A.M.–9 P.M., Fri.–Sat. 11:30 A.M.–10 P.M., Sun. noon–8 P.M., $10–30). While Big Mama never brewed up the sauce at this Pasadena kitchen, she was a Southern restaurateur who made her way from Georgia across the country to California over her long life. Today, her legacy lives on in the big ol' menu at Big Mama's, which boasts traditional Southern cuisine plus a number of Creole and Cajun dishes that speak to a strong New Orleans influence. Whether your poison is a po' boy or good gumbo, you can get it (in good hearty portions) at Big Mama's. Fish lovers will find oysters and catfish, but strict vegetarians will find their dining options limited here. And Big Mama's isn't a diet-friendly establishment since few salads balance out the weight of the fried chicken, smothered ribs, and velvet cake.

## California

For an upscale meal without having to fight the crowds in Westside or Downtown, check out **Bistro 45** (45 S. Mentor Ave., 626/795-2478, www.bistro45.com, lunch Tues.–Fri. 11:30 A.M.–2 P.M., dinner Tues.–Thurs. 6–9 P.M., Fri.–Sat. 6–9:30 P.M., Sun. 5–9 P.M., $40–80). This nationally lauded restaurant has beautiful dining rooms: one light and bright with hardwood floors and peach walls with beautiful glass lantern fixtures, and one semi-outdoor space done in gray-blues with distinctive woven chairs and classic French prints. The cuisine is grounded in the French tradition, but includes a hearty twist of California in the preparation. Menus change seasonally (or more often), and offer lots of fresh seafood as well as high-end meat and veggie-based dishes. For lunch, lighter appetites can be satisfied with fancy salads, but don't expect much of a midday price break on the bigger entrées. The wine list shifts seasonally to complement the food, and Bistro 45 boasts a full bar with a list of signature martini-esque cocktails.

## Greek

For a quick and reasonably healthy lunch in downtown Pasadena, try **Pita! Pita!** (927 E. Colorado Blvd., #101, 626/356-3099, $8–10). This walk-up Greek place offers tasty meals with lots of fresh veggies that fill you up without emptying your wallet in the process. If you eat in, you can find your own seat on the uncovered tables in the narrow dining room with its worn tile floor. Fill up your own cup with soda or water while you wait for your pita wrap or falafel and hummus plate to be made up. If you're in a hurry, order your food to-go; the pita wrap sandwiches are big and a bit juicy, but properly wrapped they can be reasonably sidewalk-friendly.

# Information and Services

## INFORMATION
### Tourist Information

New to L.A.? Make one of your first stops one of the two visitors centers. The Los Angeles Convention and Visitors Bureau (www .discoverlosangeles.com) maintains Visitor Information Centers adjacent to two METRO stations. One of these sits up in Hollywood at **Hollywood and Highland Visitors Center** (6801 Hollywood Blvd., 323/467-6412) and the other **Downtown Visitors Center** (685 S. Figueroa St., 213/689-8822). L.A. has also created a Mobile Visitors Center, so just look to the streets for the brightly decorated Honda Element. The denizens of this van can give you maps, brochures, information, and advice about visiting the greater Los Angeles area.

If you're an advance planner, you can take

advantage of the Visitors Bureau website to grab half-price tickets to all sorts of shows all around L.A. Just visit the website on Tuesday, about a week in advance of the date you want to see a show. You'll see all available tickets posted here. These tickets are also offered at the bricks-and-mortar Visitor Information Centers in town.

## Media and Communications

Los Angeles publishes one of the country's major daily newspapers, the **Los Angeles Times** (www.latimes.com). Pick one up at any newsstand anywhere in the L.A. Basin for a healthy dose of national news, regional current events, and even some good up-to-the-minute restaurant and nightlife information. The Food section comes out once per week, and the Travel section and glossy magazine are included with the Sunday edition.

You'll find Wi-Fi at nearly every hotel, an Internet café on nearly every corner, and a need to pay a fee for that access in most places. Expect to pay $10–20 per day to hook your laptop to the Internet.

All those Hollywood agents would probably spontaneously combust if they ever lost signal on their cell phones. You'll get coverage pretty much everywhere in L.A., regardless of your provider, with the possible exception of a few minutes going over a mountain pass.

## SERVICES
## Post Offices

Each separate municipality in the L.A. Basin has at least one post office. You can find them at: 750 West Seventh Street, at 1122 East Seventh Street, and 8383 Wilshire Boulevard, #106.

## Medical Services

The greater L.A. area offers some of the best medical care in the world. People come from all over to get novel treatments and plastic surgery in the hospitals frequented by the stars. If you need immediate assistance, **L.A. County General Hospital** (1200 N. State St., 323/226-2622, www.ladhs.org/wps/porta) can fix you up, no matter what's wrong with you.

# Getting There and Around

## GETTING THERE
## Air

L.A. is one of the most commercial airport–dense metropolitan areas in the country. Wherever you're coming from and whichever part of L.A. you're headed for, you can get there by air. **Los Angeles International Airport** (1 World Way, Los Angeles, www.airport-la.com), known as LAX, has the most flights to and from the most destinations of any area airport. LAX is also the most crowded of the L.A. airports, with the worst security and check-in lines. If you can find a way around flying into LAX, do so. One option is to fly into Other airports in the area include the **Bob Hope Airport** (2627 N. Hollywod Way, Burbank, 818/840-8840, www.burbankairport.com). It may provide a slightly longer drive to your final destination

but can be well worth the hassle. If you must use LAX, be sure to arrive a *minimum* of two hours in advance of your domestic flight time for your flight out, and consider three hours on busy holidays.

## Train

**Amtrak** (800/872-7245, www.amtrak.com) has an active rail hub in Los Angeles. Most trains come in to **Union Station** (800 N. Alameda St., 213/683-6875, www.westworld.com). From Union Station, you can get to the Bay Area, Redding, and eventually Seattle on the Coast Starlight train, or you can take the Surfliner down the coast to San Diego. The San Joaquin runs out to Sacramento via the Bay Area. To get to and from L.A. from the east, the Southwest Chief comes in from Chicago, Kansas City, and Albuquerque. The famed Sunset Limited runs from Jacksonville, Florida, out to New Orleans, on to El Paso, and then into California.

From Union Station, which also acts as a Metro hub, you can take the Metro Rail to various spots in Los Angeles.

## Car

Los Angeles is crisscrossed with freeways, providing numerous yet congested access points into the city. From the north and south, I-5 provides the most direct access to downtown L.A. From I-5, Highway 101 south leads directly into Hollywood; from here, Santa Monica Boulevard can take you west to Beverly Hills. Connecting from I-5 to I-210 will take you east to Pasadena. The best way to reach Santa Monica, Venice, and Malibu is via Highway 1, also known as the Pacific Coast Highway. I-10 can get you there from the east, but it will be a long, tedious, and trafficked drive.

## GETTING AROUND
### Car

Think you're up to the challenge of driving the world-infamous L.A. freeway system? Consider carefully. It's not as much fun as you might think. Traffic can be awful all the time. (If you believe you'll miss the jam on I-405 just because it's 8 P.M., you're flat wrong. I-405 often stays jammed up.) Local drivers accustomed to the conditions don't bother being polite, so expect to be cut off constantly and to deal with drivers paying attention to everything in the world but the road. And finally, if you're planning to use the traffic reports or local advice, there's a catch. Most road signs use numbers. But locals, including the radio traffic reporters, use names. There's no visible name-to-number translation on most maps, and just to make things even more fun, the names change (sometimes into one another) depending on where you are. Public transit is an increasingly viable and definitely preferable alternative.

Parking in Los Angeles can be as much of a bear as driving. And it can cost you quite a lot of money. You will find parking lots and

structures included with many hotel rooms—L.A. is actually better than San Francisco about that. But parking on the street can be difficult or impossible, parking lots in sketchy areas (like the Flower and Jewelry Districts) can be dangerous, and parking structures at popular attractions can be expensive.

## Metro

Against fairly significant odds in the region that invented car culture, Los Angeles has created a functional and useful public transit system. The Metro (www.metro.net, cash fare $1.25, day pass $5) runs both the subway Metro Rail system and a network of buses throughout the L.A. metropolitan area. You can pay on board a bus if you have exact change. Otherwise, purchase a ticket or a day pass from the ticket vending machines present in all Metro Rail Stations.

Some buses run for 24 hours. The Metro Rail lines can start running as early at 4:30 A.M. and don't stop until as late as 1:30 A.M. See the website for route maps, timetables, and fare details.

## Taxis

Taxis aren't cheap, but they're quick, easy, and numerous. And in some cases, when you add up gas and parking fees, you'll find that the cab ride isn't that much more expensive than driving yourself.

To call a cab, try: **Yellow Cab** (800/200-1085, L.A., LAX, Beverly Hills, Hollywood) and **City Cab** (800/750-4400, San Fernando Valley, Hollywood, and LAX). Or check out www.taxicabsla.org for a complete list of providers and phone numbers.

## Tours

If you don't feel up to driving around Los Angeles on your own (and no one will blame you if you don't), dozens of tour operators would love to do the driving for you and let you sit back and enjoy the sights and sounds of Southern California. You can choose between driving tours, walking tours, and even helicopter tours that take you up to get a bird's-eye view of the city, beaches, and the wide Pacific Ocean.

## WALKING TOURS

In amongst the dozens of cheesy "walking tour" operators who will charge you to walk you over the stars on Hollywood Boulevard (which you can do yourself for free), one organization can give you a better, more in-depth look into the true history of the Los Angeles area. The **Los Angeles Conservancy** (www.laconservancy .org, tours Sat. 10 A.M., adults $10, children $5) offers more than a dozen different walking tours that explore the architectural history of different parts of Los Angeles in depth. You can pick a style-themed tour, such as Art Deco or Evolving Skyline or a specific street, area, or major structure such as Union Station, the Broadway Theaters, or the Biltmore Hotel. Check the website for tour schedules, and for a few self-guided tours you can take on your own if you can't make your chosen guided tour. While children are welcome on Conservancy tours, the nature of the entertainment focuses much more on adult visitors; consider leaving the kids elsewhere so they are not bored to bits by all the talk of moldings and archways.

## BUS TOURS

For bus tours, you can't beat the weight of history provided by **Starline Tours** (800/959-3131, www.starlinetours.com, adults $40–65, children $20–45), which has been in the business of showing L.A. and Hollywood to the tourists since 1935. Take a tour of Movie Stars Homes (which actually covers many famous star-studded spots around the region), Hollywood, or try the Grand Tour of Los Angeles (can be narrated in many languages) for a start. Starline can pick you up at almost any hotel in the L.A. Basin. Your tour vehicle will be either an air-conditioned mini-bus, full-sized bus, or topless "Fun Bus" with a second open-air deck that lets visitors breathe the native smog of L.A. unhindered. Fun Tours also allow passengers to jump on and off at various sights and attractions as they please. Expect your tour to last 2–6 hours, depending on which route you choose. Once you're on board, sit back, relax, and enjoy the sights and stories of Los Angeles.

# Disneyland

The "Happiest Place on Earth" lures millions of visitors of all ages each year with promises of fun and fantasy. During high seasons, waves of humanity flow through Disneyland (1313 S. Disneyland Dr., Anaheim, 714/781-4565, http://disneyland. disney.go.com, daily 8 A.M.–midnight), moving slowly from Land to Land and ride to ride. The park is well set up to handle the often-immense crowds. Everything from foot-traffic control to ample restrooms make even a Christmastime trip to Disneyland a happy time for the whole family. Despite the undeniable cheese factor, even the most cynical and jaded resident Californians can't quite keep their cantankerous scowls set once they're ensconced inside Uncle Walt's dream. It really *is* a happy place.

Disney's rides, put together by the park's "Imagineers," are better than those at any other amusement park in the state—perhaps better than any in the world. The technology of the rides isn't more advanced than other parks, but it's the attention to detail that makes a Disneyland ride experience so enthralling. Even the spaces where you stand in line match the theme of the ride you're waiting for, from the archaeological relics of Indiana Jones to the tombstones of the Haunted Mansion. If you've got several days in the park, try them all! But if you don't, pick from the best of the best in each Land.

## SIGHTS

Your first stop inside the park should be one of the information kiosks near the front entrance gates. Here you can get a map, a schedule of the day's events, and the inside scoop on what's going on in the park during your visit.

In California Adventure, you'll find two information booths just inside the main park entrance, one off to the left as you walk through the turnstile and one at the opening to Sunshine Plaza. Here's where you'll get your park guide, Time Guide, and more information about what's going on in the park that day.

## Downtown Disney

You don't need an admission ticket to take a stroll through the shops of Downtown Disney. In addition to the mammoth World of Disney Store, you'll find an Anne Geddes gallery, a Build-a-Bear workshop, and a LEGO Imagination Center. For a more adult audience, the Illuminations candle shop, Sephora, and the Sunglass Icon boutique beckon. If you need reading material, the small but adequate Compass Books & Café has the most recent bestsellers, travel books, and a few more interesting tomes and titles. You can also have a bite to eat or take in some jazz or a new release movie at Downtown Disney.

## New Orleans Square

In New Orleans Square, the unquestioned favorite ride for the 21st century is the newly revamped **Pirates of the Caribbean.** If you haven't visited Disneyland in a few years, you'll notice some major changes to this old favorite. Beginning in the dim swamp overlooked by the Blue Bayou restaurant, inside the ride's classic scenes have been revamped to more closely tie to the movies. Look for Jack Sparrow to pop up among your other favorite disreputable characters engaged in all sorts of debauchery. Lines for Pirates can get long, so consider grabbing a FastPass for this one if you don't want to wait. Even if you don't FastPass, the line for Pirates moves fast. Pirates is suitable for younger children as well as teens and adults.

For a taste of truly classic Disney, line up in the graveyard for a tour of the **Haunted Mansion.** Next to Pirates, this ride hasn't changed much in the last 40 years. It hasn't needed to. The

sedate motion makes the Haunted Mansion suitable for younger children, but beware! The ghosties and ghoulies that amuse adults can be intense for little kids.

## Adventureland

Adventureland sits next to the New Orleans Square area. **Indiana Jones** is arguably one of the best rides in all of Disneyland, and the details make it stunning. As you stand in the queue, check out the signs, equipment, and artifacts in mock-dusty tunnels winding toward the ride. The ride itself, in a roller-coaster style variant of an all-terrain vehicle, jostles and jolts you through a landscape that Indy himself might dash through, pursued by booby-traps and villains. Hang on to your hat—literally! Use the pouches provided in your seat to secure your unattached things or they will get jostled out of this exciting ride. This one isn't the best for tiny tots, but the big kids love it and everyone might want a FastPass for the endlessly popular attraction.

On the other end of the spectrum, you'll either love the **Tiki Room** or you'll hate it. Up a tree, literally, you'll take a seat and enjoy some classic pseudo-Polynesian tiki entertainment. Even the smallest children love the bright colors and cheerful songs in the Tiki Room, though some adults can't quite hack the cheesiness here.

## Frontierland

Take a ride on a Wild West train on the **Big Thunder Mountain Railroad.** This older roller coaster whisks away passengers on a brief but fun thrill-ride through a "dangerous, decrepit" mountain's mine shafts. As you stand in line, be sure to read the names of the locomotives as the trains come rushing by.

## Fantasyland

The favorite of many Disneyland visitors, Fantasyland rides tend to cater to the younger set. And for many Disneyphiles, the ultimate expression of Uncle Walt's dream is the **Small World.** Toddlers adore this ride, which introduces their favorite Disney characters and the famous (some would say infamous) song. You can almost feel the fairy dust sprinkling down on you as you tour this magical miniature kingdom. (Warning: If ultra-cutesiness makes you gag, you might want to skip this one.)

Kids who are just a little bit older might prefer the crazy fun of **Mr. Toad's Wild Ride.** Even though it's not really a roller coaster, this ride makes for big fun for children and adults alike. What's cool about Mr. Toad's is the wacky scenery you'll get to see along the ride, from a sedate library to the gates of hell.

If it's a faster thrill you're seeking, head for one of the most recognizable landmarks at Disneyland. The **Matterhorn** roller coaster looks like a miniature version from its namesake in the Swiss Alps. Inside it, you'll board a sled-style coaster car and plunge down the mountain on a twisted track that takes you past rivers, glaciers, and the Abominable Snowman.

## Tomorrowland

In order to keep up with the realities of the future, many of the rides in this section of the 50-year-old park have been updated or even replaced over the years. Completely revamped after being down for years, the microscope-style ride is now named **"Honey, I Shrunk the Audience."** Now associated with the Disney movie with a similar title, this ride shrinks the audience down to a miniscule size. You'll be surrounded by immense shapes—familiar objects blown up to help make you feel little.

Another classic that's been given a makeover to connect it to a recent Disney blockbuster movie is the **Finding Nemo Submarine.** On this ride, you and fellow guests board a submarine and descend into a manmade pool. Under water, you'll find yourself in the brightly colored world of Nemo and his frantic father, filled with an astonishing array of sea life. Help your kids count the number of familiar fish!

Finally, for the bigger visitors, the best thrill ride of the main park sits inside a space-aged building. **Space Mountain** is a fast roller coaster that whizzes through an almost entirely darkened world. All you'll see are the stars overhead. You will hear your screams, and those of your fellow passengers, as your "spaceship" swerves and plunges along tracks you cannot see. Despite its age, Space Mountain remains one of the more popular rides in the park. Consider getting a FastPass to keep out of sometimes-long lines.

## ◖ CALIFORNIA ADVENTURE

Disney's California Adventure (daily 10 A.M.–9 P.M.) celebrates much of what makes California special. If Disney is your only stop on this trip but you'd like to get a sense of the state as a whole, California Adventure can give you a little taste. (Though for my money, you'll do better to extend your vacation and spend some time exploring California in all its real non-Disneyfied glory.)

Like Disneyland proper, California Adventure is divided into themed areas. Rides in California Adventure tend toward the thrills of other major amusement parks, but include the great Disney touches that make the Mouse special.

### Hollywood Pictures Backlot

Celebrating SoCal's famed film industry, the Backlot holds the ultimate thrill ride inside: **The Twilight Zone Tower of Terror.** Enter the creepy "old hotel," go through the "service area," and take your place inside an elevator straight out of your worst nightmares. This ride aims for teens and adults rather than little kids, and it's not a good one for folks who fear heights or don't do well with free-fall rides.

Less extreme but also fun, **Monsters, Inc. Mike & Sully to the Rescue!** invites guests into the action of the movie of the same name. You'll help the heroes as they chase the intrepid Boo. This ride jostles you around a bit, but can be suitable for smaller kids as well as bigger ones.

### a bug's land

Wanna live like a bug? Get a sample of the world of tiny insects on **It's Tough to Be a Bug!** This big-group, 3-D, multi-sensory ride offers fun for little kids and adults alike. You'll fly through the air, scuttle through the grass, and get a good idea of what life is like on six little legs. But beware:When they say this ride engages *all your senses,* they mean it.

For the littlest California Adventurers, **Flik's Fun Fair** offers almost half a dozen rides geared toward toddlers and little children. They can ride pint-sized hot-air balloons, climb aboard a bug-themed train, or run around under a gigantic faucet to cool down after hours of hot fun.

## Paradise Pier

Paradise Pier mimics the Santa Monica Pier and other waterfront attractions like it, with thrill rides and an old-fashioned midway. Most of the extreme rides cluster in the Paradise Pier area. It seems reasonable that along with everything else, Disney does the best roller coasters in the business. They prove it with **California Screamin'**, a high-tech roller coaster designed after the classic wooden coasters of carnivals past. This extra-long ride includes drops, twists, a full loop, and plenty of time and screaming fun. California Screamin' has a four-foot height requirement and is just as popular with nostalgic adults as with kids. Get a ride on a big-kid swing inside an improbable gigantic orange on the **Orange Stinger.** The Stinger requires riders to be at least four feet tall and in good health, and it's probably a good idea to have a strong stomach as well.

## Golden State

For a glimpse into other parts of the state, with attractions styled after the Bay Area, Wine Country, and Cannery Row, head to the aptly named Golden State. Want a bird's-eye view of California? Get on board **Soarin' Over California.** This combination ride and show puts you and dozens of other guests on the world's biggest "glider" and sets you off over the hills and valleys of California. You'll feel the wind in your hair as you see the vineyards, mountains, and beaches of this diverse state. If you prefer water to wind, take a ride down the **Grizzly River Run,** a Disney version of one of the many wild California rivers that rafters love to run.

Smaller visitors can get some exercise and fun in the **Redwood Creek Challenge Trail.** This adventure course mimics the ropes courses adults love, but it's sized small enough for kids. Parents can join in on some of the course, but must wait and watch for their charges to swing on the ropes.

## Parades and Shows

Do you remember the brilliant, colorful **Electric Light Parade** of years past? While bright lights are no longer the biggest or most advanced thing, thousands of people still love the kitsch and fun of this classic parade. So it moved from the main Disney parade route, where newer shows run, to California Adventure where you can relive your childhood joys most evenings. Check the park's Times Guide for the schedule during your visit.

Other regular shows in California Adventure are **High School Musical 2: School's Out!** and **Disney's Aladdin – A Musical Spectacular.** Both of these shows hearken back to favorite children's movies. Your kids can sing along with favorite songs and characters while you take a load off your feet and relax for a while. Check your park guide and Time Guide for more information about these and other live shows throughout California Adventure.

## ACCOMMODATIONS

The best way to get fully Disneyfied is to stay at one of the park's hotels. Several sit just beside or across the street from the park.

### Disney Hotels

For the most iconic Disney resort experience, you must stay at the **Disneyland Hotel** (1150 Magic Way, 714/956-6425 or 714/778-6600, http://disneyland.disney.go.com, $350). This nearly 1,000-room high-rise monument to brand-specific family entertainment has everything a vacationing Brady-esque bunch could want: themed swimming pools, themed play areas, and even character-themed guest rooms that allow the kids to fully immerse themselves in the Mouse experience. Adults and families on a budget can also get rooms with either a king or two queen beds and more traditional motel fabrics and appointments. The monorail stops inside the hotel, offering guests the easiest way into the park proper without having to deal with parking or even walking.

It's easy to find the **Paradise Pier Hotel** (1717 S. Disneyland Dr., 714/956-6425 or 714/999-0990, http://disneyland.disney.go.com, $450); it's that high-rise thing just outside of the parks on the California Adventure side. This hotel boasts what passes for affordable lodgings within walking distance of California Adventure, Downtown Disney, and Disneyland's main gate. Rooms are cute, colorful, and clean; many have two double or queen beds to accommodate families or couples traveling together on a tighter budget. You'll find a (possibly refreshing) lack of Mickeys in the standard guest accommodations at the Paradise, which has the feel of a beach resort motel.

The **Grand Californian** (1600 S. Disneyland Dr., 714/956-6425 or 714/635-2300, http://disneyland.disney.go.com, $200–450) lies inside California Adventure, attempting to mimic the famous Ahwahnee Lodge in Yosemite. While it doesn't quite succeed (much of what makes the Ahwahnee so great is its views), the big-beam construction and soaring common spaces do feel reminiscent of a great luxury lodge. The hotel is surrounded by gardens and has restaurants, a day spa, and shops attached on the ground floors; it can also get you right out into Downtown Disney and thence to the parks proper. Guest rooms at the Californian offer more luxury than the other Disney resorts, with dark woods and faux-Craftsman detailing creating an attractive atmosphere. You can get anything from a standard room that sleeps two up to spacious family suites with bunk beds that can easily handle six people. As with all Disney resorts, you can purchase tickets and a meal plan along with your hotel room (in fact, if you book via the website they'll try to force you to do it that way).

## Outside the Parks

The massive park complex is ringed with motels, both popular chains and more interesting independents. **The Anabella** (1030 W. Katella Ave., Anaheim, 714/905-1050, www.anabellahotel.com, $94–119) offers a touch of class along with a three-block walk to the parks. The elegant marble-clad lobby seems like it belongs closer to Downtown L.A. than Downtown Disney. Guest rooms are furnished with an eye toward modern, stylish decor (occasionally at the expense of practicality). Adults looking for an overnight escape from the endless parade of kid-oriented entertainment and attractions will find a welcome respite at the Anabella. A decent restaurant, nail salon, and mini-mart sit on the hotel property, and a fairly lousy diner is right next door. You can get limited room service at the Anabella, and you can leave your car in their parking lot to avoid the expense of parking at Disneyland.

Another nice out-of-park hotel, in walking distance of Disneyland, is the **Desert Palms Hotel & Suites** (631 W. Katella Ave., 714/535-1133, www.desertpalmshotel.com, $180–550). Its spacious and elegant lobby welcomes visitors, the pool and spa provide fun for children and adults alike, and the many amenities make travelers comfortable. Regular rooms have one king or two queen beds, a TV, a phone, Internet access, and not a ton of room to walk around after all your luggage is crowded in with the furniture. Bedspreads catch the eye with their bright, multicolored palm design; the rest of the decor is neutral by comparison. Guests with more discretionary income can choose from a number of suites, some designed to delight children and others aimed at couples on a romantic getaway.

## FOOD
### Disneyland

One of the few things the Mouse doesn't do too well is haute cuisine. For a truly good or healthy meal, get a hand stamp and go outside the park. But if you're stuck inside and you absolutely need sustenance, you can get it. The best areas of the park to grab a bite are Main Street, New Orleans, and Frontierland—they offer the most variety in concessions—but you can find at least a snack almost anywhere in the park.

For a sit-down restaurant meal inside the park, make reservations in advance for a table at the **Blue Bayou Restaurant** (New Orleans Square, 714/781-3463, $20–30). The best part about this restaurant is its setting in the dimly lit swamp overlooking the Pirates of the Caribbean ride. Appropriately, the Bayou has a reputation for being haunted. The Cajun-ish cuisine matches the jungle-like setting, though if you're looking for authenticity you'd do better looking elsewhere. You will get large portions, and tasty sweet desserts make a fine finish to your meal. Watch your silverware, though—the alleged ghosts in this restaurant like to mess around with diners' tableware.

If you need to grab a quicker bite, *don't* do it at the French Market restaurant in the New Orleans area. It sells what appears to be day-old (or more) food from the Bayou that's been sitting under heat lamps for a good long time. You're better off finding one of the McDonalds Fries carts and getting some greasy food that at least tastes good.

### California Adventure

If you need a snack break in California Adventure, you'll find most of the food clustered in the Golden State area. Take a tour of the **Mission Tortilla Factory** or the **Boudin Bakery,** then taste the delectable products of these places in the nearby restaurants. For a Mexican feast, try **Cocina Cucamonga Mexican Grill,** which uses the products of the tortilla factory. For more traditional American fare, enjoy the food at the **Pacific Wharf Cafe** or the **Taste Pilots' Grill.**

Unlike Disneyland proper, in California Adventure responsible adults can quaff their thirst with a variety of alcoholic beverages. If you're just dying for a cold beer, get one at the **Pacific Wharf Distribution Co.** Or if your love is for the endless variety of high-quality wines produced in the Golden State, head

for the **Golden Vine Winery,** where you can learn the basics of wine creation and production. Have a glass and a pseudo-Italian meal at the sit-down **Wine Country Trattoria at the Golden Vine Winery.**

## PRACTICALITIES
### Tickets

There are as many varying ticket prices and plans as there are themes in the park. A single-day theme park ticket will run you $66 ($56 for children age 3–9). A variety of other combinations and passes are available online (http://disneyland.disney.go.com).

To buy tickets, go to one of the many kiosks

# HERE AT DISNEY, WE HAVE A FEW RULES

Think that anything goes at the Happiest Place on Earth? Think again. Uncle Walt had distinct ideas about what his dream theme park would look like, and that vision extended to the dress and manner of his guests. When the park opened in 1955, among the many other restrictions, no man sporting facial hair was allowed into Disneyland. The rules on dress and coiffure have relaxed a bit since the opening, but you still need to mind your manners when you enter the Magic Kingdom.

- Adults may not wear costumes of any kind except on Halloween.
- No shirt, no shoes, no Disneyland.
- If you must use the "F-word," do it quietly. If staff catches you cussing or cursing in a way that disturbs others, you can be asked to desist. Or leave.
- The happiest of happiness is strictly prohibited inside the Magic Kingdom. If you're caught having sex on park grounds, not only will you be thrown out, you'll be banned from Disneyland for life. (At least that's the rumor.)
- Ditto for any illicit substances.

in the central gathering spot that serves as the main entrance to both Disneyland proper and California Adventure. Bring your credit card, since a day at Disney is not cheap. After you've got tickets in hand (or if you've bought them online ahead of time), proceed to the turnstiles for the main park. You'll see the Disneyland Railroad terminal and the large grassy hill with the flowers planted to resemble Mickey's famous face. Pass through, and head under the railroad trestle to get to Main Street and the park center.

Horrifyingly, the already expensive regular one-day Disneyland ticket doesn't include California Adventure. If you're interested in checking out California Adventure as well as Disneyland proper, your best bet is to buy a **Park Hopper** pass ($81–91 single day, $112–132 two days), which lets you move back and forth between the two parks at will for a slight discount. If you're planning to spend several days touring the Houses of Mouse, buy multi-day passes in advance online to save a few more bucks per day. It'll help you feel a little bit better about the wads of cash you'll undoubtedly drop on junk food, giant silly hats, stuffed animals, and an endless array of Disney apparel.

The magical **FastPasses** are free with park admission and might seem like magic after awhile. The newest and most popular rides offer FastPass kiosks near the entrances. Feed your ticket into one of the machines, and it will spit out both your ticket and a FastPass with your specified time to take the ride. Come back during your window and enter the always-much-shorter FastPass line, designated by a sign at the entrance. If you're with a crowd, be sure you all get your FastPasses at the same time, so you all get the same time window to ride the ride.

## Services

Check your park map or look for signs to the restrooms available in each Land of the park. Restrooms have ample space, so you'll rarely find lines even on the most crowded days.

If mobility is a problem for you or for a small child in your family, consider renting (no, they're not free) a stroller, wheelchair, or scooter. Ask for directions to the rental counter when you enter the park.

Cell phones work inside Disneyland, which is actually a fabulous thing. It's already loud and raucous in the parks, and the ability to use cell phones to connect up with lost family or party members at Disneyland is one of *the* finest advances in modern technology in a long, long time.

Disneyland offers its own minor medical facilities, which can dispense first aid for scrapes, cuts, and mild heat exhaustion. They can also call an ambulance if something nastier has occurred.

If you need to stow your bags or hit the restroom before plunging into the fray, banks of lockers and restrooms sit in the main entrance area.

## Getting There

Disneyland is located on Disneyland Drive in Anaheim and is most accessible from I-5 south where it crosses Ball Rd. (stay in the left three lanes for parking). The parking lot is located at 1313 S. Disneyland Drive and costs $12.

If you're coming to the park from elsewhere in the O.C., consider bailing on the car (avoiding the parking fees) and taking public transit instead. Shuttles from LAX and John Wayne airport take you directly to the park or the hotels. **Anaheim Resort Transit** (ART, www.rideart.org) can take you to and from the Amtrak station and all around central Anaheim for $3 per ride.

## Getting Around

Disney's California Adventure sits across the main Disney entry plaza from Disneyland. You can enter from the main parking lots, from Downtown Disney, or you can hop over from Disneyland. Need a tram for the long-distance walk in or out of the park? The **Lion King Tram Route** can get you to and from the main parking areas. The **Mickey & Friends Tram Route** takes you toward Downtown Disney and the resort hotels.

## INLAND ORANGE COUNTY

The lure of the inland O.C., a primarily residential area, tends to be dominated by the Mouse. But if you just have to get away from the overwhelming cutesy happiness for a while, a few other entertaining attractions lurk in the shadows.

### Knott's Berry Farm

Believe it or not, other amusement parks make their home in Orange County. For a taste of history along with some ultra-modern thrill rides and plenty of cooling waterslides, head for Knott's Berry Farm (8039 Beach Blvd., Buena Park, 714/220-5200, http://knotts. com, Mon.–Fri. 10 A.M.–6 P.M., Sat. 10 A.M.– 10 P.M., Sun. 10 A.M.–7 P.M., adults $43, seniors and children $20). This park's unusual name stems from its agricultural past. The fertile land beneath the roller coasters really was a berry farm decades ago. The Knott family grew strawberries, raspberries, boysenberries, and more here, then made the fruits of their labors into preserves. Knott's jams retain

© AVALON TRAVEL

their popularity in supermarkets across the country to this day.

Today, instead of berry vines you'll find twisting tracks at this thrill-oriented park. From the tall landmark GhostRider wooden coaster to the 30-story vertical drop ride to the screaming Silver Bullet suspended coaster, even the most hard-core ride lover will get excited by Knott's. For the younger crowd, Camp Snoopy offers an array of pint-sized rides and attractions, plus Snoopy and all the characters they love from the Peanuts comics and TV shows.

In the heat of the summer, many park visitors adjourn from the coasters to **Knott's Soak City** (daily Memorial Day–Labor Day, weekends May–Sept., adults $24, seniors and children $18). The full-sized water park has 22 rides, a kid pool and water playground, and plenty of space to spread out and enjoy the O.C. sunshine after cooling off on the waterslides.

## Wild Rivers Water Park

If you've been to the O.C. in July, you know why the county can support two large water parks. Out in Irvine, head for Wild Rivers Water Park (8770 Irvine Center Dr., 949/788-0808, www.wildrivers.com, adults $32, children $20). One of the biggest parks of its kind in the state, Wild Rivers has not one but two wave pools, more than 40 slides and rides, and areas geared for both kids and adults. You can't bring your own food into the park, but two restaurants, a coffee kiosk, and a sweet shop serve all comers all day long.

## Discovery Science Center

If you'd like your kids to spend at least one day in the O.C. doing something educational, take them to the Discovery Science Center (2500 N. Main St., Santa Ana, 714/542-2823, www.discoverycube.org, daily 10 A.M.–5 P.M., adults $13, children $10). The star attraction, the interactive DinoQuest, lets kids get inside the lost world of dinosaurs. Way inside! You can also take a quick nap on a bed of nails, create your own clouds and tornadoes, and experience the buffeting of a hurricane inside a wind tunnel. The Discovery Science Center combines interactive play with scientific learning to create a fun day that's not wasted.

## Ripley's Believe It or Not

For a totally education and enlightenment-free trip to a sort of museum, walk one block up from Knott's to Ripley's Believe It or Not (7850 Beach Blvd., 714/522-7045, www.ripleysbp.com, Mon.–Fri. 10 A.M.–6 P.M., Sat.–Sun. 9 A.M.–7 P.M.). Here you'll see the wild and wacky artifacts said to be "collected" by Robert Ripley on his travels around the globe. In fine old sideshow style, see exhibits such as the eight-legged pig, the world's tallest man, the bearded lady, and the human unicorn. Wild tattoos and body modifications figure large into this "museum's" cache of oddities, so be prepared for small children to get a little bit freaked out by some of the weirdness here.

## Crystal Cathedral

Looking to see a modern cathedral, O.C. style? Visit the shiny and immense Crystal Cathedral (12141 Lewis St., Garden Grove, 714/971-4000, www.crystalcathedral.org). You may already have seen it from the road or the air during your travels around the O.C.! This modern-day megachurch offers free tours daily; stop by the Welcome Center for information and tour times. On a tour or wandering by yourself, you'll see the 2,800-seat auditorium that acts as both congregational seating and a TV studio, beautiful religious sculptures, and the magnificent glass walls of the interior. The Crystal Cathedral hosts the taping of the *Hour of Power* each Sunday, and you can be a part of this national and international inspirational telecast. Or just show up on Sunday morning or evening for the regular services, which include music from the outstanding organ, the 20-piece church orchestra, and the 80-member choir.

© ROBERT HOLMES / CALTOUR

Crystal Cathedral

## Accommodations

Away from the Disney resorts, the accommodations in inland Orange County run to chain motels. The good news is that you can find a decent room for a reasonable price almost everywhere you go in the O.C. The less-good news is that you won't find much of anything in the way of character or distinction in any of them.

The **Red Roof Inn Buena Park** (7121 Beach Blvd., Buena Park, 714/522-7280, www.red roof.com, $74) offers a clean bed and bathroom near Knott's and Disney. Amenities include a heated pool and a spa, free Wi-Fi, and a fitness center. Medium-sized motel rooms feature a standard motel setup with a variety of bed configurations, dark carpets, and floral bedspreads.

At the **Best Western Orange County Airport** (2700 Hotel Terrace, Santa Ana, 714/432-8888, www.bestwestern-oc.com, $110) you'll find everything you expect of the popular national chain, including floral and wine-colored édecor in your comfortable guest room, a pool and hot tub, and a free shuttle to and from John Wayne Airport. Down in the lobby, you'll find a complimentary "cook-to-serve" breakfast each morning (that is, pre-packaged heat-and-eat items plus cold cereals, bagels, and coffee).

In Garden Grove, stay at the **Hyatt Regency Orange County** (11999 Harbor Boulevard Garden Grove, 714/750-1234, http://orange-county.hyatt.com/hyatt/hotels/index.jsp, $165). The attractive rooms are decorated in the latest style inside a tall glass-fronted tower. White linens emphasize the cleanliness of beds and bathrooms, while bright yellows and deep blues provide classy artistic touches. In the sun-drenched atrium, enjoy a cocktail or sit back and read a good book in the attractive atmosphere. Grab a chaise lounge by the pool or take a refreshing dip. If you're bringing your family, consider renting one of the "family-friendly suites" that have separate bedrooms with bunk beds and fun decor geared toward younger guests.

If your major destination is Knott's Berry

Farm, consider staying at the **Knott's Berry Farm Resort Hotel** (7675 Crescent Ave., Buena Park, 714/995-1111, $175–250). This high-rise resort includes all the extras and amenities you'd expect from a corporate hotel. You can lounge by the pool and spa, work out at the fitness center, and have dinner in one of the on-site restaurants, the **Amber Waves** dining room or the **Citrus Café**. Get a drink at the **Sports Bar** after a long day out at the park or seeing the sights of O.C. Your comfortable room will greet you each night; choose one queen, two queens, or a king bed. Check the Internet for a variety of specials and discount rates.

## Food

Want to keep the kids—and yourself—entertained during dinner? Check out one of the dinner-and-a-show restaurants, both near Disney and Knott's Berry Farm at Buena Park. At the famous **Medieval Times** (7662 Beach Blvd., Buena Park, 888/935-6878, http://medievaltimes.com, adults $52, children 12 and under $35), you'll enter a castle-shaped building, take your seat, and watch as gallant knights battle for the title of First Knight. You'll see live jousts (there's a big courtyard in this restaurant!), swordfights, and ladies in gowns parading for your pleasure. Your meal, served on a pewter-styled plate, provides hearty if not particularly healthy or high-quality sustenance. Vegetarian and kids' meal options are available upon request.

If you prefer pirates to knights, the O.C. can hook you up. Practically next door to the castle, buckle your swash at the **Pirate's Dinner Adventure** (7600 Beach Blvd., 714/690-1497, www.piratesdinneradventure.com, adults $55, children 3–11 $36). Combining dinner theater, the current pirate craze, and a touch of Cirque du Soleil, everyone in your family will find something to watch at dinner with the Pirates. Even if the cheesy acting and the swordfights don't do it for you, the aerobatics that form an integral part of this show can be great fun to marvel at. A four-course meal includes both chicken and meat (or fish), plus salad and dessert. It's not the best food, but hopefully you'll

be too busy enjoying the show to care. Check for special holiday shows in season.

If you're looking for a bite to eat sans pirates and knights **Casa De Soto Restaurant** (8562 Garden Grove Blvd., Garden Grove, 714/530-4200, www.casadesoto.com, Sun.–Thurs. 11:30 A.M.–9 P.M., Fri.–Sat. 11:30 A.M.–10 P.M., $10) offers standard Mexican fare in three festive rooms. **Whole Pita Greek Island Grill** (3940 S. Bristol St., Santa Ana, 714/708-3000, www.greekisland grille.com, Sun.–Thurs. 11 A.M.–9 P.M., Fri.–Sat. 11 A.M.–9:30 P.M., $10) serves Mediterranean specialties including soulvlaki. gyros, and moussaka.

## Information and Services

For information, visit the **Anaheim Visitor and Postal Center** (640 W. Katella Ave., 714/991-4636, www.anaheim411.com, daily 8 A.M.–7 P.M.). As the name implies, not only does this facility have the 411 on the O.C., you can also mail a letter or a package here. The office lies inside the Jolly Roger Hotel at the corner of Katella and Harbor.

Need a dose of hard news? Get in a copy of the *Los Angeles Times* (www.latimes.com), Orange County Edition.

The O.C. has plenty of Internet access, though you'll find few people crouched over laptops inside Disneyland. Look to your hotel, or find a Starbucks outside the park to hook up to the world. The **West Anaheim Medical Center** (3033 W. Orange Ave., Anaheim, 714/827-3000, wamc.phcs.us) is a full-service hospital with an emergency room.

## Getting There and Around

The nearest airport to Disneyland, serving all of Orange County is **John Wayne Airport** (18601 Airport Way, Santa Ana, 949/252-5200, www.ocair.com). It's much easier to fly into and out of John Wayne than LAX, though it can be more expensive. John Wayne's terminal has plenty of rental car agencies, and many shuttle services that can get you where you need to go—especially to the House of Mouse.

If you have to fly into LAX for scheduling or

budget reasons, you can catch a shuttle straight from the airport to your Disneyland hotel. Among the many companies offering and arranging such transportation, the one with the best name is **MouseSavers** (www.mouse savers.com). Working with various shuttle and van companies, MouseSavers can get you a ride in a van or a bus from LAX or John Wayne to your destination at or near Disneyland.

To get around the O.C., your major free-way will be I-5. See the *Getting Around* section for Los Angeles for information about driving here.

If you prefer to use public transit rather than drive, see the the *L.A. and O.C. Coasts* section of this chapter for information about OCTA bus services.

# The L.A. and O.C. Coasts

If you're looking for the famed surf beaches of SoCal, look no further than the coast of Orange County. Sadly, when you look out over the pretty white sands of Huntington and Laguna, you're likely to see the lighted towers of the local oil rigs. Echoing rigs dot the shoreline of Newport and Huntington as well, and as you drive up the legendary Pacific Coast Highway you'll see honest-to-goodness oil fields that will make you wonder if you took a wrong turn into Texas somehow. In truth, the Southern California oil industry has been thriving for many a decade now.

And so you'll surf, sun yourself, bike, in-line skate, eat, drink, and be merry in the sight of the rigs. Despite their unsightliness, the beaches of the O.C. and their surrounding resort-oriented towns offer great vacationing potential to all comers.

## LONG BEACH AND THE L.A. COAST

The L.A. coast passes the Palos Verde Penninsula, stretching further south to Redondo Beach and Long Beach, where haunted ships and sunny coasts await.

### ◖ The *Queen Mary*

The major tourist attraction of Long Beach is the *Queen Mary* (1126 Queens Highway, Long Beach, 562/435-3511, www.queenmary.com, daily 10 A.M.–6 P.M.), one of the most famous ships ever to ply the high seas. This great ship, once a magnificent pleasure cruise liner, now sits at permanent anchor (it's been gutted and is no longer seaworthy) in Long Beach Harbor. The *Queen Mary* acts as a hotel, a museum, an entertainment center with several restaurants and bars, and a gathering place for both locals and visitors. You can book a stateroom and stay aboard, come for dinner, or just buy a regular ticket and take a self-guided tour. The museum exhibits describe the history of the ship, with special emphasis on its tour of duty as a troop transport during World War II. You can explore many of the decks at the bow, including the engine room that still boasts much of its massive machinery, the art gallery, and the various upper exterior decks where vacationers once relaxed on their way to Europe.

But it's not just the extensive museum and the attractive hotel that make the *Queen Mary* famous today. The ship is also one of the most famously haunted places in California. Over its decades of service, a number of unfortunate souls lost their lives aboard the *Queen Mary,* and it is rumored that several of them have stuck with the ship ever since their tragic deaths. If you're most interested in the ghost stories of the *Queen Mary,* book a spot on one of the "Attractions at Night," which include the Paranormal Ship Walk (562/499-1666, Thurs.–Sat. 8 P.M.) that takes you to the hottest haunted spots and Dining With the Spirits (Sat. 7 P.M.), a combination of dinner and haunted tour. For more serious ghost hunters, Paranormal Investigation tours happen on the first and third Fridays of each month. Appropriately, the investigations begin at midnight.

The *Queen Mary* offers a large pay parking lot near the ship's berth. You'll walk from the parking area up to a square with a ticket booth and several shops and a snack bar. Purchase your general admission ticket to get on board the ship. It's also a good idea to buy any guided tour tickets now. Night tours can fill up in advance, so consider calling ahead to reserve a spot.

## Russian Attack Submarine

Berthed right next to the luxurious *Queen Mary* you'll find a much smaller and more lethal little boat, The Russian Attack Submarine (562/432-0424, daily 10 A.M.–6 P.M., adults $11, children $10), code-named the Scorpion, helped the Soviet Union spy on the United States for more than 20 years during the Cold War. Your admission includes a brief history film and the opportunity to explore the innards of the submarine. Squeeze through the tiny spaces and learn how members of the Soviet Navy lived and worked aboard this attack submarine, which has a history that's still shrouded in secrecy.

## Aquarium of the Pacific

Even the locals enjoy the exhibits at Aquarium of the Pacific (100 Aquarium Way, 562/590-3100, www.aquariumofpacific.org, daily 9 A.M.–6 P.M., adults $21, children $12). The large aquarium hosts animal and plant life native to the Pacific Ocean, from the local residents of SoCal's sea up to the North Pacific and down to the tropics. While the big modern building isn't much to look at from the outside, it's what's inside that's beautiful. Aquarium of the Pacific has far more than the average number of touch-friendly tanks. Kids and adults all love the unusual feel of sea stars, urchins, and rays. More exciting, you can dip your fingers into the Shark Lagoon and "pet" a few of the more than 150 sharks the Aquarium cares for. If you prefer tamer and more colorful denizens of the air, spend time in the loud Lorikeet Forest. For visitors who are just too cool for fish, there's the Catch a Wave exhibit, which

displays the history and culture of surfing, the science of waves, and the species that inhabit this turbulent small part of the ocean.

## Redondo State Beach

At the other end of the 20-mile bike and pedestrian path from Will Rogers State Beach, you'll find Redondo State Beach (400–1700 Esplanade, http://beaches.co.la.ca.us). Sitting next to the Redondo Beach Pier, this sand stretch gets really crowded in the summertime, so if rubbing elbows with your fellow sun worshippers doesn't work for you, Redondo isn't your best bet. On the other hand, the lack of surfers makes swimming a prime activity here, complete with lifeguards during the daytime. You'll also find the usual volleyball and other beach games, the bike path (which is lit at night), and the restaurants of the pier. The beach features restrooms and showers, and a large multilevel pay parking structure at the pier offers ample space to stow your car for the day.

## Entertainment and Events

For a low-key good time, grab a table and a drink at the **Starboard Attitude** (202 The Pier, Redondo Beach, 310/379-5144, www.starboardattitude.com, no cover) on the Redondo Beach Pier. This cool little local's joint features live music four nights a week and karaoke on the off nights. Pro acts tend towards talented classic rock cover bands and soulful blues groups. Expect folks to get up and dance to their favorite songs, and be prepared to be asked to dance if you're a woman on your own. However, the atmosphere here is more friendly than scary, with a mix of younger to middle-aged patrons who all seem to know each other and the servers. Talk up your bartender, and you'll get the whole scoop on the local scene as well as any drink you can imagine and probably one or two you've never heard of. The staff takes good care of the patrons too, so you'll find yourself drinking as much water as liquor as the evening wears on. There's no cover, but you will get hit with a two-drink minimum that's easy to meet, because it's easy to sit down, enjoy the mellow vibe, and stay a good long while at the Attitude.

## Accommodations

Rooms down in this stretch of beach towns don't come cheap, but you'll find some attractive independent inns and B&Bs in this area.

### $100-150

For a quiet, private inn experience in the midst of the big city, try the **The Turret House** (556 Chestnut, Long Beach, 562/624-1991, www .turrethouse.com, $130–160). This cute late-Victorian home sits on a street corner in the densely packed residential section of Long Beach. Each of the five guest rooms has its own decorative theme, an antique bedstead, a clawfoot tub, plenty of knick-knacks, and a few pieces of high-end original art—all for a surprisingly reasonable rate. After your breakfast, stroll out into town for more coffee or perhaps a brief downtown shopping spree.

For a cute near-the-sand motel in Manhattan Beach, stay at the **Sea View Inn at the Beach** (3400 Highland Ave., Manhattan Beach, 310/545-1504, www.seaview-inn.com, $143–250). With only a block to the sands of the beach, this is a great place to hole up if you're in town for some surfing, volleyball, or sunbathing along the shore. (You'll avoid the traditional summer beach parking nightmare by leaving your car at the motel.) Just grab a boogie board and some beach chairs from the lobby and head on out. Inside, the guest room appointments are prettier and more coordinated than those of most moderate motels. Rooms are done in light blues and whites, with matching prints on the walls and possibly even a live plant to add a homelike touch. The complex of blocky, mid-century modern buildings has its own small swimming pool as well, set in a small, plant-strewn courtyard. Just around the corner, you'll find an array of restaurants, shops, bars, and clubs.

Of the three Best Westerns that comprise much of Redondo Beach's hospitality, the **Best Western Sunrise** (400 North Harbor Dr., Redondo Beach, www.bestwestern-sunrise .com, $148) is the best of the lot, with rooms overlooking Redondo's King Harbor and the location within walking distance of the pier and its restaurants and bars. Rooms are clean and comfortable, and the decor is cute and modern, with plaid bedspreads and light wood furniture. You'll get all the standard amenities you'd expect at a Best Western, plus a nice pool and spa, a gym, free Wi-Fi, and a complimentary breakfast.

### $150-250

Looking for something completely different? Check in to the **Dockside Boat and Bed** (316 East Shoreline Dr., Dock 5A, Rainbow Harbor, Long Beach, 562/436-3111, www .boatandbed.com, $235–330). You won't get a regular old hotel room—instead, you'll get one of four yachts. The yachts run 38–54 feet and can sleep four or more people apiece. The amenities include TVs with DVD players, stereos, kitchen facilities, wet bars, and ample seating. No, you can't actually take your floating accommodations out for a spin; these yachts are permanent residents of Rainbow Harbor.

### OVER $250

For a fabulous high-end hotel stay on the beach, go to the **Beach House at Hermosa Beach** (1300 The Strand, Hermosa Beach, 310/374-3001, www.beach-house.com, $275–400). It might be the tiniest bit pretentious, but it's hard not to love this larger boutique hotel that looks right out over the water. The "loft suite" has a cushy king bed with Frette sheets, a big bathroom with separate tub and shower, two TVs and a stereo, and a real wood-burning fireplace. The casual, upscale decor makes visitors feel at home, but you'll probably want to spend more time out on the porch or balcony on sunny days. Guests get a free continental breakfast, the use of the outdoor spa, and access to the on-site gym. If you prefer an outdoor workout, enjoy The Strand for a walk, run, or bike ride. Head downstairs to The Strand Café for a bite and a tasty view from the outside tables, or to the spa for a delightful massage or facial.

## Food

Combining elegance, fine Continental-

California cuisine, and great ghost stories, **Sir Winston's** (1126 Queens Hwy., Long Beach, 562/499-1657, www.queenmary.com, Mon.–Thurs. and Sat.–Sun. 11 A.M.–11 P.M., $30) floats gently onboard the *Queen Mary*. For the most beautiful dining experience, request a window table and make reservations for sunset. And dress in your finest; Sir Winston's requests that diners adhere to their semi-formal dress code.

Have you come to Los Angeles to seek genuine homestyle Mexican food? You can find it at **Sion's Mexican Restaurant** (235 N. Sepulveda Blvd., Manhattan Beach, 310/372-4504, Sun.–Mon. 8 A.M.–2 P.M., Tues.–Sat. 8 A.M.–9 P.M., $10). Expect nothing fancy, but everything fresh—from tacos to salsa—in this utterly casual and family owned hole in the wall.

A local's favorite down where the shops and cafes cluster, **Natraj Cuisine of India** (5262 E. 2nd St., Long Beach, 562/930-0930, Mon.–Thurs. 11 A.M.–2:30 P.M. and 5–10 P.M., Fri. 11 A.M.–2:30 P.M. and 5–11 P.M., Sat.–Sun. 11 A.M.–11 P.M., $10–30) offers good food for reasonable (by L.A. standards) prices. Come by for the all-you-can-eat lunch buffet to sample a variety of properly spiced meat and vegetarian dishes created in classic Indian tradition.

The **Green Temple Vegetarian Restaurant** (1700 S. Catalina Ave., Redondo Beach, 310/944-4525, www.greentemple.net, Mon. 12–4 P.M., Tues.–Thurs. 11 A.M.–4 P.M. and 5–9 P.M., Fri.–Sat. 11 A.M.–4 P.M. and 5–10 P.M., Sun. 9 A.M.–12 P.M., $10–20) strives for a Southern California zen in both its cuisine and its dining room. All the vegetarian cuisine comes from sustainable and (whenever possible) organic sources, including Trader Joes and Whole Foods stores.

## Practicalities

For information, maps, brochures, and advice about Long Beach and the surrounding areas, visit the **Long Beach Convention and Visitors Bureau** (1 World Trade Center, 3rd Fl., 562/436-3645, www.visitlongbeach.com). There is a **post office** in Long Beach (300 Long Beach Blvd., 562/628-1303).

For medical attention, visit the emergency room at the **Long Beach Memorial Medical Center** (2801 Atlantic Ave., Long Beach, 562/933-2000, www.memorialcare.org).

While you can get to the coast easily enough from LAX, the **Long Beach International Airport** (4100 Donald Douglas Dr., 562/570-2600, www.longbeach.gov/airport) is both closer to the beach and less crowded than the LAX.

I-710, which runs north–south, is known as the Long Beach Freeway. Along the coast, the Pacific Coast Highway can get you from one beach town to the next.

Parking in Long Beach and the other beach towns is just bad as parking anywhere else in L.A. Prepare to pay for the privilege of stuffing your car someplace for the day. Beach parking on summer weekends is the worst, but on weekdays and in the off-season you can occasionally find a decent space down near the beach for reasonable rates.

## ORANGE COUNTY COAST

The Orange County coast begins at Huntington Beach and stretches south across a collection of sunny scenic beaches until ending at San Juan Capistrano. Along the way, Newport Beach, Huntington Beach, Laguna Beach, and Dana Point provide surf, sun, and sand galore.

### Newport Beach

Most of the activity in Newport Beach (www.visitnewportbeach.com) centers around Newport Pier (McFadden Pl.) and Main Street on the Balboa Peninsula. Some folks like to hearken back to the old days of individual beach houses and long, lazy summer vacations. The **Crystal Cove Beach Cottages** (35 Crystal Cove, Newport Beach, 949/497-0900, www.crystalcovebeachcottages.org, dorm rooms $30, cabins $180) can help recreate the feeling of another time. Right out on the sands of historic Crystal Cove south of downtown Newport Beach, this collection of 14 cabins offers a delightful and serene beach vacation experience to all who stay here. Eleven of the cabins are individual rentals where you get the whole house to yourself. The other three "dorm cottages" offer by-the-room accommodations (linens included, room doors lock) that let even solo budget travelers the opportunity to experience life on a Southern California beach. Cottages include a common refrigerator and microwave, but no full kitchen so you'll need to make plans to eat out—perhaps at the adjacent **Beachcomber Restaurant** or concession-style **Shake Shack.** Maid service is minimal, with towels changed every four days and trash taken out daily. None of the cottages have TVs or any type of digital entertainment.

The **Island Hotel Newport Beach** (690 Newport Center Dr., Newport Beach, 949/759-0808, www.theislandhotel.com, $400) offers perhaps the ultimate O.C. experience. It's a luxury, high-rise hotel situated in a giant shopping mall, within a few minutes' drive of the beach. No, really. On the bright side, the tropical-themed rooms really do have both luxury and comfort in abundance. Expect cushy beds with white linens, attractive private bathrooms, big TVs, views over the mall (and if you're lucky, out to the ocean beyond the city), and all the best amenities. Perhaps the most innovative of these goodies rests within the room service menu; it's called the "In-Flight Menu" and it's a selection of gourmet box lunches. The idea is to allow airline travelers to carry on their own food.

The hotel's **Palm Terrace** (690 Newport Center Dr., Newport Beach, 949/760-4920, www.theislandhotel.com, daily 6:30 A.M.–10:30 P.M., $10–35) offers stylish small bites and sophisticated entrées in a picturesque setting. For something French, colorful **Pescadou Bistro** (3325 Newport Blvd., Newport Beach, 949/675-6990, www.pescadoubistro.com, Tues.–Sun. 5:30–close, $20–35) will fill the bill.

## Huntington Beach

The main reason to come to the west edge of Orange County is to hit the beach. The good news is that the coast of the O.C. is rife with wide, flat, sandy beaches. The bad news is that the beaches still get crowded in the summer. If you want a prime spot, come early in the morning and try to avoid having to park a car if you possibly can.

**Huntington City Beach** (Pacific Coast Hwy. from Beach Blvd. to Seapoint St., daily 5 A.M.–10 P.M.) runs the length of the south end of town, petering out as the oil industry gets going at the north end. This famous beach hosts major sporting events such as the X Games and the U.S. Open of Surfing & Beach Games. But even the average beachgoer can enjoy all sorts of activities on a daily basis, since Huntington City Beach includes a cement walkway for biking, inline skating, jogging, and walking. On the sand, get up a game of Frisbee or take advantage of the beach volleyball courts. Out in the water, catch a wave at the famous Huntington surf break or make use of prevailing winds for a thrilling kite-surfing run. Non-riders can boogie-board, bodysurf, and skim board closer to the shore. Anglers and lovers prefer the Huntington Beach Pier, which leads out over the water. While dogs aren't allowed on the main portion of Huntington City Beach, the beach offers a dog-friendly section at the north end where dogs can be let off-leash, and you'll even see the occasional surfer riding tandem with a four-legged friend.

This beach offers plenty of services and amenities. In high season, lifeguards keep watch over surfers and swimmers. A number of concessions stands make their homes along Huntington City Beach, so you can buy drinks and snacks, or rent a wetsuit and surfboard. Buildings with restrooms and outdoor showers also rise from the sand at regular intervals, though lines do form during the most crowded summer weekends and holidays.

Most visitors to the O.C. coast want to stay as close to the beaches as they can. You can have your beachfront room at the **Sun 'N Sands Motel** (1102 Pacific Coast Hwy., Huntington Beach, 714/536-2543, www.sunnsands.com, $143–300). At this tiny place (17 rooms total) you can expect standard motel room decor in your king or double-queen guest room, plus an adequate private bathroom, a TV with movie channels, and Wi-Fi access. But the main attraction lies across the treacherous Pacific Coast Highway: long, sweet Huntington Beach. Please *be careful* crossing the highway to get to the sand. Find a traffic light and a crosswalk rather than risking life and limb for the minor convenience of jaywalking.

For a quick bite to eat, stop off at the **Bodhi Tree Café** (501 Main St., Huntington Beach, 714/969-9500, daily 10 A.M.–9 P.M., $5–15) for vegetarian soups, salads, and sandwiches. **Sugar Shack Café** (213 Main St., Huntington Beach, 714/536-0355, Thurs.–Tues. 6 A.M.–4 P.M., Wed. 6 A.M.–8 P.M., $20) is a great place for breakfast.

## Laguna Beach

Farther south, the town of Laguna Beach has some of the nicest sands in the county. You'll find more than a dozen separate beaches here, though many connect to one another—you'll just have to choose your favorite. **Heisler Park** and the **Main Beach Park** (Pacific Coast Hwy.) offer protected waterways, with tidepools and plenty of water-based playground equipment. The two parks are connected, so you can walk from one to the other. Both display works of local art in the form of benches and sculptures. Hang out on a bench, pick a spot on the sand to lounge about, or take a swim in the cool Pacific. If you're into scuba diving, you can dive several reefs right off the beach.

You'll find all the facilities and amenities you need at Heisler and Main Beach Parks, from picnic tables to lawns to restrooms. Please use the provided charcoal grills rather than bringing your own. You can park on the street if you find a spot, but be aware that the meters get checked all the time, so feed them well!

## Dana Point

At the southern tip of the O.C., Dana Point (www.danapoint.org) has a harbor-turned-recreation-marina that draws visitors and locals from all around. It also has several beaches nearby. One of the prettiest of these is **Capistrano Beach** (35005 Beach Blvd., www

.capistranobeach.com, daily 6 A.M.–10 P.M.). You can relax on the soft sand or paddle out and catch a wave here. Paths make biking, inline skating, and walking popular pastimes here, while others prefer a rousing game of volleyball out on the sand. You'll find a metered parking lot adjacent to the beach, plus showers and restrooms available.

For travelers looking to escape the endless crowds of the Newport/Huntington Beach scene, options beckon from farther south on the O.C. coast. The **Blue Lantern Inn** (34343 Blue Lantern St., Dana Point, 949/661-1304, www.bluelanterninn.com, $190–550) sits south of San Juan Capistrano, making access to the small mission town easy. This attractive contemporary inn offers beachfront elegance, from the exterior to the downstairs restaurant to the guest rooms. Each of the 29 rooms boasts soothing colors, charming appointments, and lush amenities, including a spa tub in every bathroom and honest-to-goodness free drinks in the mini-fridge. All beds come with their own teddy bear, and many of the rooms have private patios facing the sea and sunsets.

## Mission San Juan Capistrano

One of the most famous and beloved of all the California missions is Mission San Juan Capistrano (26801 Oretga Hwy., 949/234-1300, http://missionsjc.com, daily 8:30 A.M.–5 P.M., adults $9, children $8). The lovely little town of San Juan Capistrano hosts flocks of swallows, which return every year at about the same time in the spring to fanfare and celebration by the whole town. These celebrations began during the mission's heyday in the 18th century, and may have been started by Native Americans centuries before that. (Swallows are really, really loyal to their nesting grounds!)

Today, thanks in part to the famous birds, this mission has a beautiful new Catholic church on-site, extensive gardens and land, and an audio tour of the museum, which was created from the old mission church and buildings. In late fall and early spring, monarch butterflies flutter about in the flower gardens and out by the fountain in the courtyard.

Mission San Juan Capistrano

history and use over the years. In names and decor, the swallow is a major theme in San Juan Capistrano, which nestles in a tiny valley only minutes from the sea.

## Information and Services

Need assistance upon arriving on the O.C. coast? A good place to get it is the **Huntington Beach Convention and Visitors Bureau** (301 Main St., Ste 208, 800/729-6232, www .surfcityusa.com, Mon.–Fri. 9 A.M.–5 P.M.).

The major newspaper on the O.C. coast is the Orange County edition of the *Los Angeles Times*, which you can pick up at any newsstand.

Each town on the coast has at least one **post office.** In Huntington Beach, head for the post office at 6671 Warner Avenue (714/843-4200). In Newport Beach, choose between the post office on the inland tip of the bay at 1133 Camelback Street, or pick the one down by the ocean at 204 Main Street, Newport Beach.

If you need medical care while you're visiting the beach, **Hoag Hospital** (1 Hoag Dr., Newport Beach, 949/764-4624, www.hoag hospital.org) can probably fix whatever's broken.

## Getting There and Around

Two airports serve the O.C. coast region. On the coast side, the **Long Beach Airport** (4100 Donald Douglas Dr., 562/570-2600, www.longbeach.gov/airport) serves as one of L.A.'s metropolitan satellite airports. Lots of commercial flights go in and out of Long Beach, making it a good alternative to LAX for the coast-bound. The other regional airport is John Wayne International; see the *Disneyland* section of this chapter for more information.

The Orange County Transportation Authority, **OCTA** (www.octa.net) runs buses along the O.C. coast. The appropriately numbered Route 1 Bus runs right along the Pacific Coast Highway from Long Beach down to San Clemente and back. Other routes can get you to and from inland O.C. destinations,

Inside the original church, artifacts from the early time of the mission tell the story of its rise and fall. This was the only mission church where Father Serra presided over Sunday services. The graveyard outside continues that narrative, as do the bells and other buildings of the compound. If you love stories of times past, you could spend hours wandering Mission San Juan Capistrano, with or without the audio tour. The complex includes adequate restrooms for visitors, plus plenty of garden and courtyard benches for rest, relaxation, and quiet meditation and reflection.

Regrettably, when you exit the mission into the charming town of San Juan Capistrano and stroll back to look at the historic buildings, you'll be standing next to a Starbucks. But if you turn the corner, you'll find yourself on the town's main street, which positively drips Spanish Colonial history. Each old adobe building boasts a brass plaque describing its including Anaheim. Regular bus fares run $1.25 per ride, payable in cash on the bus with exact change. You can also buy a day pass from the bus driver for $3.

The one true highway on the O.C. coast is the Pacific Coast Highway, often called the PCH for short and officially designated as Highway 1. You can get to the PCH from I-405 near Seal Beach, or catch I-710 to Long Beach and then drive south from there. From Disneyland, you'll take I-5 to Route 55, which takes you into Newport Beach. If you stay on I-5 going south, you'll eventually find yourself in San Juan Capistrano.

Parking along the beaches of the O.C. on a sunny summer day has been compared to one of Dante's circles of Hell. You're far better off staying near the beach and walking out to your perfect spot in the sand. Other options include public transit and pay parking, which means "up to $40 per day and still six blocks to the beach."

# Catalina Island

For a slice of Greece in Southern California, take a ferry or a helicopter out to Catalina Island (www.catalina.com). You can see Catalina from the shore of Long Beach on a clear day, but for a better view you've got to get out onto the island. The port town of Avalon welcomes visitors with plenty of European-inspired hotels, restaurants, and shops. But the main draw of Catalina lies outside the walls of its buildings. With its Mediterranean summer climate, Catalina draws hikers, horseback riders, and ecotourists. Most of all, it beckons to water-lovers of all kinds, from scuba divers and snorkelers to kayakers and anglers.

The climate on Catalina tends toward the temperate, with beautiful, warm, sunny summer days that make getting out into the ocean a pleasure. Even in the winter, you'll find pleasantly warmish days and cool nights. But every once in a while, when the Santa Ana winds come billowing down from the mainland, life in Avalon harbor gets exciting. Storms and winds can whip up the seas, which then come crashing up onto and over the beaches and walkways of Avalon. When you see the yellow sandbags, be aware that the locals are serious. Even on a non-flooding morning, the Pacific can completely engulf the harborside beaches, hit the retaining walls, and spray dozens of feet into the air. If you're lucky enough to be around, take a walk down toward the waterside and enjoy the show!

## SIGHTS
### The Casino
No, it's not that kind of casino. The Casino Building at Avalon harkens back to the older Italian meaning of the word ("place of entertainment"). The round, white, Art Deco building acts as a community gathering place and

the Via Casino arch

© LANCE SCOTT

© LANCE SCOTT

the Casino door

home for all sorts of different activities. The Avalon Theatre, home to a Page organ, is located on the main level. Be sure to check out the murals by John Gabriel Beckman, he of Grauman's Chinese Theatre fame, inside.

## Wrigley Memorial and Botanical Garden

Upcountry, the coolest place to visit may be the Wrigley Memorial and Botanical Garden (Avalon Canyon Rd., 1.5 miles west of town, 310/510-2595, daily 8 A.M.–5 P.M., adults $5, children free). Stroll through serene gardens planted with flowers, trees, and shrubs that are native to the California or even to Catalina specifically. You'll see a number of endangered species among the unique plants that grow nowhere else in the world. The temperate climate on Catalina lends itself to hardy, drought-tolerant species that still manage to produce beautiful colors and fragrances. Just don't eat (or let your kids eat) the wild tomatoes—they're incredibly poisonous! Also don't bother with

the Catalina cherries. They're not deadly, but they don't taste too good.

At the center of the garden you can't miss the Wrigley Memorial, an edifice dedicated to the memory of chewing-gum magnate William Wrigley, Jr. Wrigley adored Santa Catalina Island, and used his sticky fortune to make many improvements to it; most notably, he funded the building of the Avalon Casino. The monument is made and decorated with mostly local materials; the crushed stone on the facade comes from the island, as do the blue flagstones, the red roof tiles, and the brightly colored decorative ceramic tiles. All the local-centric construction makes a perfect centerpiece to the gardens.

For a more thorough look at the history, culture, and diverse natural abundance of Catalina, visit the **Interpretive Center** (Avalon Canyon Rd.) just down the road from the botanical garden. Here you can learn more about the native plants, indigenous people, and the ocean channel and its islands (of which Catalina is the most visited).

## Catalina Island Museum

Another take on the history of Catalina is displayed at the Catalina Island Museum (The Casino, Avalon, 310/510-2414, www.catalina museum.org, daily 10 A.M.–4 P.M., closed Thurs. Jan.–Mar., adults $4, children $1). Located on the top floor of the landmark Casino, this small museum makes for a great 15–30 minute culture stop in the midst of a beach vacation. Learn about the history of the Chicago Cubs' spring training camp on the island, the short but famed production of Catalina tile and ceramics, the World War II history of Catalina, and more. You'll find a good-sized collection of Native American artifacts from the island's original inhabitants, plus a huge collection of historic photos. Look for Hollywood stars enjoying Catalina's natural beauty and luxurious resort amenities among the photographic history of the island. Purchase reproductions of tiles, photos, and more in the museum store, and check the website for museum activities geared to kids and adults.

## SPORTS AND RECREATION

Outdoor recreation is the main reason most people venture across the channel to Catalina. On land or in the water, you'll find the activities that are right for you.

### Scuba and Snorkeling

If you want to get out into the water on your own, you'll find plenty of places to kick off from shore. The most popular spot is the **Avalon Underwater Park** (Casino Point). This protected area at the north end of town has buoys and markers to help you find your way around the reefs and keep safe. Not only will you see the famous bright-orange garibaldi fish, you'll get the opportunity to meet jellyfish, anemones, spiny lobsters, and plenty of other sealife. Out at the deeper edge of the park, nearly half a dozen wrecked ships await your examination. Snorkeling and scuba tours groups come here, as do locals and visitors who rent equipment from local shops and shacks or bring their own. Expect big crowds on summer weekends.

If you prefer to take a guided tour, a number of companies offer snorkeling, scuba, kayaking, and combinations all around the island. **Catalina Snorkel & Scuba** (877/766-7535, www.divecatalina.com) offers guided snorkel tours of the Lover's Cove Marine Reserve that include all equipment with the fees. This clear-water preserve sits just southeast of the boat terminal, and includes a life-filled kelp forest. If you're a certified scuba diver, you can book a two-hour guided tour of Avalon Underwater Park. If you want to become a scuba diver, Catalina Snorkel & Scuba offers certification classes as well as intro tours that give you a taste of the world underwater. Catalina Snorkel & Scuba also offers equipment rental for snorkelers and divers who want to take off on their own.

Another company to try is **Snorkel Catalina** (877/218-9156, www.snorkelingcatalina.com). This company specializes in deeper water excursions farther away from shore, taking guests out on a custom pontoon boat all year long. If your purpose in coming to Catalina is to swim with the dolphins, Snorkel Catalina can make it happen for you. Standard tours run 2–4 hours, and let you check out the prettiest fish, sleekest seals, and friendliest dolphins around the island.

If it's hardcore scuba you're interested in, take a walk out onto the Avalon pier to **Catalina Divers Supply** (800/353-0330, www.catalinadiverssupply.com). The little blue shack out toward the end of the pier offers everything from certification and referral classes to guided shore dives at the Avalon Marine Preserves to charter trips on the 46-foot *Scuba Cat*. You'll see things that just aren't visible from the surface with a snorkel. The company highly recommends making reservations for any of their tours and trips.

### Kayaking

Kayaking is one of the most popular ways to see otherwise unreachable parts of Catalina. Rent a kayak, or if you're not confident in your own navigation abilities, take a tour with a reputable company. **Descanso Beach Ocean Sports/ Catalina Island Kayak & Snorkel** (310/510-1226, www.kayakcatalinaisland.com, $40–80) offers several kayak tours to different parts of the island. You don't need previous river or sea kayaking experience to take these tours, since double-sized, sit-on-top kayaks make the trip easy and safe even for total beginners and small kids. But if you are a rescue-certified sea kayaker, the folks at Descanso Beach also have an array of lean, sleek, enclosed ocean kayaks for advanced paddlers. This company offers regular, year-round trips to Frog Rock (2 hours), Fox Canyon (3 hours, includes a nature walk), and Willow Cove (half-day excursion with snorkeling and hiking). All trips start north of Avalon and the Casino at Descanso Beach Club.

Another kayak tour provider, **Wet Spot Rentals** (310/510-2229, www.catalinakayaks.com, $40–150) specializes in a full-day land and sea tour that includes both kayaking and an auto tour into the Catalina backcountry. After a van trip and nature tour at the airport on top of the hill, you'll travel down to the less-traveled windward side of the island. You'll get a rare opportunity to kayak on the other side of the island from Avalon, exploring the coves and cliffs around Little Harbor. A brief portage and hike takes you to a waterfall. This fabulous, nearly whole-island tour takes all day, and lunch, water, and all equipment (including sit-on-top beginner kayaks) are provided. Wet Spot also offers several shorter kayak expeditions; they're a great operator if you want to combine kayaking with snorkeling the reefs of the leeward (Avalon) side of the island.

These operators also rent kayaks to individuals (you'll have to prove yourself capable to rent an enclosed sea kayak). They also have an array of snorkel equipment, and you can take a kayak out for some fabulous fish-watching and even skin-diving.

## Rafting

For an adventurous ocean tour, head out with **Catalina Ocean Rafting** (103 Pebbly Beach Rd., 800/990-7238, www.catalinaoceanrafting .com, $41). From the Avalon harbor, you'll head out on a two-hour, half-day, or full-day trip on a small, powered, inflatable raft. The small maneuverable craft can take you right up to cliffs and into sea caves, around Eagle Rock and Ribbon Rock, and into reef areas perfect for snorkeling (equipment is provided with your tour). You'll get to harbors beyond Avalon, and enjoy lunch, drinks, and snacks as part of your trip. A raft tour is a great way for adventurous newcomers to get the lay of the land and sea before striking off on their own.

## Swimming

In the summertime, the waters of Catalina can reach the more than 70°F—perfect for taking a long, lazy swim in the salty waters of the Pacific! Bring your family out to any one of the charming beaches in the sunny coves for a lazy day on the beach and in the water. The most crowded spots will be at the Avalon Underwater Park, the harbor, and other coves near Avalon. For a more deserted beach, try the windward side of the island; just be aware that it may be, well, windy. Keep a close eye on your children and even adult friends wherever you swim. Catalina's beaches, like most of the

California coastline, are subject to dangerous rip currents.

## Wildlife-Watching

If you're not keen on swimming in the ocean, but you want a peek at the famous Catalina garibaldi (a bright-orange fish), take a semi-submersible or glass-bottom boat tour. The **Undersea Tour** (310/510-8687, www.visitcatalinaisland.com, adults $28–35.50, children $14–17.75) takes you a few feet underwater in a comfy cabin to watch the abundant array of aquatic life around Avalon. For a special (and budget-conscious) treat, book a nighttime Undersea Tour to check out a whole different variety of sea species. Every seat on the boat has a great view of the water, and kids love the colorful fish and mysterious bat rays that glide gracefully by.

In the summertime, take another boat trip out to see one of the legends of Catalina. A **Flying Fish Boat Trip** (800/626-1496, www .visitcatalinaisland.com, adults $19.50, children $9.75) lights up the air just over the waterline, making visible the famous Catalina flying fish as they leap out, putting on a unique show.

## Horseback Riding

Perhaps the best and most ecologically sound way to explore the backcountry of inland Catalina, with all its diverse wildlife, is on a horseback ride. **Catalina Stables** (600 Avalon Canyon Rd., Avalon, 310/510-0478, catalinas-tables@catalinaisp.com, $42–82 for standard rides, more for custom tours) offers guided rides up into the hills above Avalon. Walk a sedate, well-behaved horse along trails used by Native Americans for thousands of years, viewing buffalo, bald eagles, and other wildlife. Enjoy knowing that the likes of John Wayne and Tom Mixx have ridden the trails on this island, taking in the immediate wildlife and distant glorious views of the ocean surrounding the island (plus the regrettable but usual smog-smear that is the L.A. coastline). Choose from half-hour, one-hour, or two-hour rides that go out every day (weather permitting). If you're a serious equestrian, call in advance to arrange a half-day, full-day, or even overnight horseback riding adventure. Catalina Stables can arrange exactly the trip you've always wanted to take. Even if you only want a 30-minute standard trail ride, call in advance for a reservation to guarantee yourself a horse, especially in high season.

## Biking

Even most of the locals on Catalina eschew cars in favor of smaller, lighter forms of transportation. A great way to get around and beyond Avalon is on a bicycle. You can bring your own aboard the ferries that travel to and from the airport. If you don't have one, you can rent a bicycle right on the island at **Brown's Bikes** (underneath Holly Hill House, 100 yards from the ferry dock, 310/510-0986, www.catalinabiking.com, $5–15/hour, $12–40/day). If you're looking for a simple, one-speed cruiser to putter around downtown Avalon and down to the beach, you can get one for $5 per hour or $12 per day. With no gas to buy, it's the ultimate in affordable transportation! Brown's also has six- and 21-speeds, tandems, and an array of mountain bikes. You'll also get a map of the bikeable roads and trails in Avalon and around the island.

Mountain bikers, this island's for you! An array of trails from easy to steep and difficult take you up into the hills, providing views and thrills galore. Street bikers will find that Avalon is bike-friendly; the road that runs along the shore on either side of the town is paved, mostly level, and zoned for bicycles. If you've got the legs for it, you can obtain a permit from the Catalina Conservancy to ride farther afield. Call or email Brown's Bikes for more information on biking outside of Avalon.

## Golf

As most of Catalina Island is devoted to wildlife preservation, you won't find a wealth of golf courses here. But if just can't abide the notion of going for a trip without exercising your clubs, get yourself a tee time at the nine-hole **Catalina Island Golf Course** (1 Country Club Rd., Avalon, 310/510-0530, www.visit catalinaisland.com, $30–85). You'll be walking on greens built in 1892, used for the Bobby

Jones Tournament from the 1930s through the 1950s, and more recently played on by up-and-coming SoCal junior players like Craig Stadler and Tiger Woods as they built their skills. Heck, even if you don't play, it's worth walking the course on a sunny day just to enjoy the unbelievable views out to the Casino, the town of Avalon, and the clutch of sailboats bobbing in the harbor. The full-service pro shop provides rental equipment and golf carts, as well as a set of **tennis courts** you can rent by the hour.

If your taste in golf runs a little less serious, head for **Golf Gardens** (Sumner Ave., 1 block inland from the fountain, 310/510-1200), a miniature golf course. This is a great break for kids tired of sightseeing and eco-touring. This cute, 18-hole course has a tropical feel, complete with palm trees, and good putting challenges.

## Yoga

After hours or days of recreating outdoors on Catalina, you might really appreciate a good massage or a nice relaxing hour of yoga.

For yoga, go to **Pisces Yoga** (310/510-1803 or 310/510-1666) takes place at the Seaport Village Inn (119 Maiden Ln., Avalon) on Mondays and Wednesdays at 8 A.M. and Tuesdays and Thursdays at 6 P.M.

## Spas

You've got a surprising number of massage and spa options right in and around Avalon. If you prefer your massage in the privacy of your hotel room or condo, call **In-Room Massage by Michelle** (310/510-8920, www.catalina massagebymichelle.net, $85–95 massage, $120–300 spa treatments). Michelle loves to work with couples looking for a relaxing day or evening of romance, and she is trained in a variety of massage techniques and spa therapies, including heated stones and Thai massage. Book a simple Swedish massage or a full spa package with facials, body scrubs, and massages for one or two people. Check the website for a full list of available treatments. Be sure to book in advance to get the date and time you want. Studio sessions are also available.

Whether you're looking for a divine romantic

experience with your sweetie or a solo day of spa-induced respite from your busy life, you'll find it at **The Spa at Catalina** (888 Country Club Rd., Avalon, 310/510-9255, www.catalina spa.com, $60–325). This full-service day spa offers all sorts of massage and treatment packages, from a simple half-hour of bodywork up to nearly three hours of head-to-toe bliss. The spa has dual rooms (many complete with private baths for two) to serve couples or pairs of friends who want to enjoy their treatments together. Choose from the many packages that focus on facials and scalp treatments using lavender, peppermint, and other delicious essential oils. You can also breathe deep and detox with a body wrap or heated stone massage. The spa sits in Falls Canyon outside of downtown Avalon; ask about getting a free shuttle from your hotel to the spa at the Best Western Canyon Hotel when you book your treatments. It's best to make reservations at least a couple of days in advance; even in wintertime, same-day appointment availability is rare.

Decide for yourself whether the treatments you receive in downtown Avalon live up to the name **A Touch of Heaven** (205 Crescent Ave., 310/510-1633, daily 9 A.M.–5 P.M., $45–200). This day spa echoes the European flavor of the town surrounding it; you'll find an extensive menu of Euro-styled facials, from the intense relaxation of a LaStone Facial to the aesthetically focused glycolic/lactic acid peel and facial. Also look for a few unusual treatments including raindrop therapy and ear candling, as well as practitioners of both Eastern and Western massage modalities. The spa also offers massage for children, and well-behaved young people are welcome to enjoy the the treatments here.

## ACCOMMODATIONS

You'll find plenty of charming inns and hotels on Catalina; most sit in or near Avalon. You can also camp on Catalina, and eco-tourists often prefer to immerse themselves in the natural world of the island by sleeping and eating outdoors.

### Camping

Camping is the best way to get away from Avalon and stay on other parts of the island. It's also a great way to get to know the precious Catalina wilderness in an up close and personal way. Check the island's visitor website (www .visitcatalinaisland.com) for a list and descriptions of all the major campgrounds around the island. Also be sure to read the regulations, which are more stringent than at some other camping areas and are strictly enforced. Permits are required for all campsites. Also check out the equipment rentals; if you don't want to bring your own tent and gear, you can rent it at the Two Harbors ranger station.

You have a choice of more than half a dozen campgrounds, some on the coast and some up the mountains in the interior. One of the largest and most developed campgrounds sits just outside the tiny town of **Two Harbors** (adults $12, children $6). You can bring your own tent and equipment, rent it, or book one of the tent cabins at this site. The tent cabins come with cots and mattresses, sunshades, and a camp stove and lantern in addition to the usual barbecue grill, fire ring, and picnic table. All campers have access to showers, restroom facilities, and lockers to keep valuables safe while you're out exploring the area.

If you're looking to camp on the beach, check out the **Little Harbor** (adults $12, children $6) campground. Located seven miles away from the town of Little Harbor, the sandy campsites make a perfect place to sleep if your aim is snorkeling, kayaking, and playing out away from all the casual tourists. You'll find potable water, showers, and toilets here. The best way to get to the Little Harbor campground is to take the Safari Bus, so be sure to book seats and space for your gear when you book your campsite.

Perhaps the coolest way to stay on Catalina is to bring or rent a kayak and paddle into one of the **boat-in campsites** (adults $12, children $6). These nine primitive campsites can't be accessed by land at all—you must bring and moor your own boat. You'll get a wholly natural experience at any of these beautiful remote locations, with no running water, shower or toilet facilities, or shade structures. Whatever you want and need, you must pack into your boat with you. A ranger checks each campsite daily, so you're not completely cut off from the outside world. However, take precautions such as bringing a two-way radio and an above-average first-aid kit just in case an emergency crops up.

## $100-150

For inexpensive indoor accommodations, your best bet is the **Hermosa Hotel & Cottages** (131 Metropole St., 877/453-1313, www.hermosa hotel.com, $75–155). This simple budget hotel has rooms with shared bathrooms in the main building—in the way-off season, some of these clean rooms are dirt cheap if you're willing to walk down the hall to the shower. Even in the summer, you can get a decent room for under $100. (Be aware of a two-night minimum for stays involving a Saturday night in the high season.) The cottages have private baths, and some have kitchens and TVs. "Family units" can sleep up to six people in the main building and have kitchens—perfect for larger families or groups of friends traveling together on a budget. The 100-plus-year-old building sits only about a block from the harbor beaches and a short walk from the Casino, shops, and restaurants.

The **Hotel Atwater** (125 Sumner Ave., 800/626-1496, www.visitcatalinaisland.com, $107–219) also has bright cheerful rooms for reasonable rates. Take in the history of a budget hotel that's been hosting guests since the 1920s. Clean, light-colored economy rooms provide the best value for your buck, while the more posh suites cost more and offer prettier decor and better amenities. Whichever type of room you book, you'll have a TV, coffee maker, air conditioning, and more. You'll find storage for your diving gear and bikes, and a rinse-off area outside for divers, snorkelers, and swimmers. The Atwater closes each winter; call ahead to confirm their availability.

## $150-250

Want to stay right on the waterfront? Book a room at the bright yellow **Hotel Mac Rae** (409 Crescent Ave., 800/698-2266, www

.hotelmacrae.com, $239–259). This bit of Catalina history has been in the Mac Rae family for four generations, and they've been running the hostelry since 1920. The Mediterranean flavor of Avalon follows you into the rooms and common spaces of the Mac Rae. Relax with a drink in the bright brick courtyard. You can choose one of the premium rooms that looks right out into the harbor, or a more economical courtyard-view room. Grab a complimentary continental breakfast downstairs, and either eat in the courtyard or take your coffee and your pastries back to your pretty Côte d'Azur–styled room for more privacy. Catching the afternoon ferry but want to enjoy one last morning in the warm Catalina water? The Mac Rae has luggage storage and even a public shower for use after you check out.

For a European hotel experience in Avalon, stay at the **Hotel Metropole** (205 Crescent Ave., 310/510-1884, www.hotel-metropole .com, $175–550). The comfortably cluttered and warmly decorated rooms feel like home almost immediately. You'll find gas fireplaces in some rooms and oversized two-person whirl-pool bathtubs in a few pretty, tiled bathrooms. The beds feel great after a long day of ocean swimming or the ferry ride over from Long Beach. The little extras are nice too from the nightly turn-down service to the L'Occitane toiletries. You can also use the Wi-Fi service in your room and grab a snack from the honor bar. The Metropole is built in a modern style with a pretty gray paint job. On the roof you'll find a whirlpool tub with glass walls enclosing its deck, letting you look out over the rooftops into the harbor. The lower-end rooms don't have much in the way of ocean views, so for a window on the water you'll need to pay premium rates for an oceanfront suites. You can walk half a block down the street to the ocean-side. For extra pampering, make an appointment at the day spa located on the bottom floor of the hotel. Just outside by the back elevator, start a shopping jaunt in the little Metropole center, where you can grab a cup of coffee, or walk down Crescent Avenue for a meal.

The **Villa Portofino** (111 Crescent Ave.,

888/510-0555, www.hotelvillaportofino.com, $215) offers Mediterranean elegance on the Avalon waterfront. The bright-white exterior with red tile roofs invites you inside this 34-room boutique hotel. Guest rooms range from small standard rooms up through immense, lush, individually named suites with fireplaces, soaking tubs, and richly colored furnishings. Amenities include a complimentary continental breakfast, free Wi-Fi, free beach chairs and towels, and an on-site restaurant. The Portofino's location is perfect—right on the main drag running along the harborside beach.

## FOOD

To be honest, the culinary presence on Catalina isn't much to write home about. While there's certainly no lack of restaurants in Avalon, the trend toward delicious cuisine at both the high and low ends hasn't made it across the island to the channel yet. You might consider getting a room or a condo with a kitchen and cooking a few of your own meals to save a bit of cash while you're here. Still, a tourist's gotta go out to eat sometimes! Here are a few places to try.

### American

So where do the locals go? Many of them crowd into **El Galleon** (411 Crescent Ave., 310/510-1188, daily 11 A.M.–9 P.M., $10–30). It's easy to get to since it's part of the walk-only area on Crescent Avenue, and the porch has a fabulous view out to the harbor. The large menu speaks to hearty American diners with lots of aged steaks, chicken dishes, and fresh fish. Lighter eaters can peruse the selection of salads, soups, and seafood appetizers. For a major feast, take a look at the prix-fixe menu, which offers a hearty four-course dinner for about $70 per person. The dessert menu offers a few unusual treats, plus a wide array of sweet and strong coffee drinks to round off your evening. El Galleon boasts a full bar and a fun vibe, and live karaoke runs into the night. If you prefer an earlier evening, happy hour is 3–6 P.M. each evening.

For a more serious upscale dining experience,

get a table in the dining room at the **Catalina Country Club** (310/510-7404, www.visitcatalina island.com, $30). You don't need to be a member to enjoy a refined dinner here, or at one of the Country Club's two more casual dining venues. Unlike most of the rest of the island's restaurants, here you'll be served some high-end California cuisine, complete with a focus on organic and sustainable ingredients.

### Italian

The **Ristorante Villa Portofino** (101 Crescent Ave., 310/510-2009, www.ristorantevilla portofino.com, $15–35), attached to the Villa Portofino hotel, serves tasty pasta and protein dishes with a distinct Italian flare—and you'll get a fabulous harbor view with your cannelloni or calamari. In homage to the locale, the menu here runs to seafood, with some classic and a few inventive preparations. The pastas bring homey comfort food to Catalina, and the hot appetizer menu is well worth a look. For dessert, the Ristorante offers a goodly selection of Italian favorites such as cannoli and panna cotta. In the summertime, see if you can get a table out on the patio to enjoy the balmy island breezes—you'll feel almost as though you're really on the Mediterranean coast of Italy.

### Mexican

Looking for an unpretentious taco? You can get one at the **Catalina Cantina** (313 Crescent Ave., 310/510-0100, $7–15) or its fast-food walk-up neighbor, the **Topless Taco.** Serving a mix of American diner (think burgers and fries, wings, and fish and chips) and Americanized Mexican staples (burritos, fajitas, combo plates), the Catalina Cantina offers tasty food for decent prices. Better still, if you come in the evening, cool off with one of the Cantina's buckets o' liquor. Rum punch, margaritas, something called the Blue Shark, and more come in either normal human-sized glasses or in a 28-ounce bowl that they really hope you'll share with friends!

### Seafood

If all you want is a slab of really fresh fish, you can get it down on the Pleasure Pier at **Avalon**

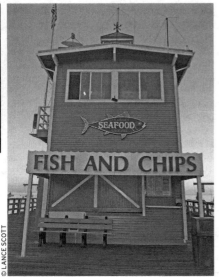

© LANCE SCOTT

Avalon Seafood

**Seafood** (Pleasure Pier, 310/510-0197). That's the cute blue building at the end of the pier bearing a sign that says "Fish and Chips." It's part fish-and-chips stand, part fresh seafood market, and you can get a casual eat-at-the-picnic-table lunch or barbecued fish dinner here. Or if you've got kitchen or barbecue access, pick up the catch of the day and make a fresh fish dinner for yourself and your family or friends.

### Steak
All the locals recommend that tourists try **Steve's Steakhouse** (417 Crescent Ave., 310/510-0333, www.stevessteakhouse.com, daily lunch 11:30 A.M.–2 P.M., dinner from 5 P.M., $10–33). It's possible that the locals are trying to keep the tourists away from their favorite spots by sending them here. Sure, Steve's offers a wide array of classic steakhouse fare with plenty of seafood options thrown in as a nod to the water lapping the harbor beach just outside. Generous portions of meat or fish are accompanied by traditional steakhouse sides, and the desserts up the ante with some tasty sweetness. (The mud pie's not half bad.) But compared to the lush cuisine you can get on the mainland, the quality of the ingredients and the preparations seem a bit lackluster at Steve's, and the tourist-high prices can be a bit painful.

### Coffee
Looking for a cup of coffee and maybe a quick pastry down by the Casino? Stop by **El Encanto Courtyard Coffee** ($1.50–5). In the wintertime, the hot lattes and chais offer steamy warmth, while the summertime sees customers ordering refreshingly icy smoothies and frappes. Courtyard Coffee sits in the El Encanto marketplace, across from the Via Casino Arch.

## INFORMATION AND SERVICES
If you are camping in a remote location, talk to the rangers at the Two Harbors station before leaving to learn how best to contact them or the police in an emergency. Bring a two-way radio, since cell signal may be unreliable or nonexistent.

For medical assistance, go to the **Avalon Municipal Hospital** (100 Falls Canyon Rd., 310/510-0700).

Your major local daily newspaper on Catalina is the *Los Angeles Times.* Your hotel might have copies. A good website for visitors is www.visitcatalinaisland.com.

Catalina isn't one of Orange County's major shopping destinations; if you're hoping to put a serious dent in your credit cards, you'll want to head back to the mainland. But if you're looking for kitschy souvenirs and reproduction ceramic tiles, you can find them in downtown Avalon in the area sometimes called the **South Coast Plaza.**

## GETTING THERE AND AROUND
There are two ways to get to Catalina: by boat and by air.

### Boat
Most folks take the ferry over from the mainland coast. The **Catalina Express** (310/519-1212, www.catalinaexpress.com, adults $60–62/round-trip, children $46–48) serves

© LANCE SCOTT

Catalina seaside

as the major carrier, with multiple departures every day, even in the off-season. During high season, you can choose to leave from two docks in Long Beach, one dock in San Pedro, and another in Dana Point. Most ferries dock at Avalon, but you can arrange to travel directly to Two Harbors if you prefer. You can bring your bike, your luggage, and your camping gear aboard for a comfortable hour-long ride on one of eight ferries. Bars on both levels offer snacks and drinks, and TVs help make the cruise go by a little bit faster. Though on the way it's worth looking out the window—you might spot seals or sea lions, different varieties of pelicans, or even a pod of dolphins playing in the swells. Catalina Express also offers plenty of return cruises to the mainland each day.

An alternate ferry service, the **Catalina Flyer** (400 Main St., Newport Beach, 949/673-5245, www.catalinainfo.com, adults $61/round-trip, children $46) offers one trip out and one trip back each day. The Flyer operates primarily from March through November.

## Air

You can also get to Catalina by air. A helicopter pad sits just northwest of Avalon harbor. **Island**

**Express Helicopter Service** (1175 Queens Highway S., Long Beach, 310/510-2525, www.islandexpress.com, $160/round trip) can fly you from Long Beach or San Pedro to Catalina in about 15 minutes. You can get a cab into town from the helipad. Island Express also offers aerial tours of the island and various travel packages. Or if you prefer to fly your own small plane into Catalina, the **Airport-in-the-Sky** (310/510-2196, Apr.–Oct. daily 8 A.M.–7 P.M., Nov.–Mar. daily 8 A.M.–5 P.M.) offers general aviators a 3,000-plus-foot runway and $5 tie-downs—no gas, though, so fuel up for a round-trip before you head out.

## Car

On Catalina, cars just aren't the fashionable way to get around. Even the locals tend to eschew full cars since they aren't practical in the tiny town of Avalon. Instead, locals and visitors in the know prefer to drive golf carts. Walk from the ferry dock down toward town, and you'll see any number of rental services, complete with herds of carts out and ready for use. The cost runs about $40 per hour for a 4–6 passenger cart. A couple of easy-to-find companies include **Island Rentals** (125 Pebbly Beach

Rd., 310/510-1456) underneath the Holly Hill House near the ferry dock and **Cartopia** (615 Crescent Ave., 310/510-2493).

You can also grab a taxi if you need to get somewhere in a hurry, especially with your luggage. Taxis hover near the ferry dock when the ferries are due in each day, and it's customary to share your ride with as many people as can fit into the car (which is often a minivan). To get a cab back to the ferry or the helipad when it's time to leave, call 310/510-0025. It only takes about 10 minutes for a taxi to get to just about anywhere in town.

## Bus

Public transit on Catalina includes the **Safari Bus** (310/510-2800, adults $4–26 depending on distance, children $2.75–20), which runs from Avalon to Two Harbors each day. The bus stops at the southeast corner of Island Plaza in Avalon. You can buy tickets at visitors services and the Discovery Tours booth on the Pleasure Pier. Alternately, the **Avalon Trolley** (310/510-0342, June 15–Sept. 15 Fri.–Sat. 9 A.M.–10 P.M., Sun.–Thurs. 9 A.M.–6 P.M., Sept. 16–June 14 daily 9 A.M.–5 P.M., $2–6) runs in and around Avalon, hitting most of the major sightseeing and outdoor adventuring spots near town. With two lines that converge inland, you can get where you need to go for a reasonable fare without having to hoof it. The trolley runs approximately every 30–40 minutes.

## Tours

One of the main forms of entertainment on the island is touring. You can take a bus tour, Jeep tour, glass-bottom boat tour, and more. The Catalina Island Conservancy offers **Jeep Eco-Tours** (310/510-2595, www.catalina conservancy.org, $495/half-day, $795/full day, up to 6 people) for either a half-day or a full day out in the wilds of Catalina. You can go much farther on these tours than you can by yourself—out into the wilderness to see the bison, the wild horses, plant species unique to

this one island, and more. Be sure to bring your camera, both for close-ups and for views out toward the sea. On the full-day trips, you'll get lunch, drinks, and snacks, while on the half-day trip you'll get snacks and drinks.

For a sedate view of Catalina's more settled areas as well as it's road-viewable wilderness, try a **Classic Inland Motor Tour** (310/510-8687, www.visitcatalinaisland.com, adults $69, children $34.50). This four-hour tour aboard a restored 1950s cruising bus takes you away from the coastline and into the island's interior via old stagecoach routes. Along the way you'll see Middle Ranch, the magnificent Arabian horses and Old West mementos of El Rancho Escondido, and the Airport-in-the-Sky Nature Center. A shorter version of this tour is the **Skyline Drive** (adults $34, children $17), a two-hour trip that takes you up from Avalon to the Airport-in-the-Sky Nature Center along a route cluttered with spectacular vistas of island and ocean.

If you want a guided walking tour of Avalon, consider taking an **Avalon Walk-About Tour with Chuck Liddell** (310/510-1356 or 310/510-8401, avalonwalkabout@yahoo.com, adults $10/hour, children $7/hour). Pick a one-hour tour of downtown Avalon ending at the Casino for an easy walk. The two-hour tour can include a variety of routes, most of which require that you climb some moderately steep hills. Or try an evening tour that takes you past the nighttime hot spots of Avalon. Wear comfy shoes for any tour you take, bring a camera, and be prepared to enjoy the narration. Chuck Liddell can tell you all about the places you're passing as you stroll along.

Another company that offers both land and sea tours of Catalina is **Catalina Adventure Tours** (877/510-2888, www.catalinaadventure tours.com). Whether you want to board the semi-submersible Nautilus, take a 1–2 hour adventure drive around the island, or get a guided walking view of the botanical garden or the Casino, Catalina Adventure Tours can hook you up.

# SAN DIEGO

San Diego is the ideal destination for anyone whose idea of the perfect California vacation is a day (or a week, or a month) lying on a white sand beach, sipping cocktails, and looking out over the Pacific Ocean. Resort hotels and restaurants perch along the seaside, beckoning visitors to what is often thought to be the friendliest big city in California.

Even though San Diego's physical area seems small compared to other parts of California, it can't be beat for density of things to see. From a world-famous zoo to dozens of museums to the thick layer of military and mission history, San Diego offers education, enlightenment, and fun to visitors with all different interests.

Animal lovers flock to the San Diego Zoo and SeaWorld, while water spirits dive into the Pacific Ocean to catch a wave or examine a variety of sea life in their natural habitat. Travelers who want a little more of the trappings of city life will enjoy the bar and club scene, as well as a thriving theater community.

Across the bay, the long, blue Coronado Bridge connects San Diegans to Coronado, an island-like encalve that beckons beach bums and film aficionados alike to the grandly historic (and reputedly haunted) Hotel del Coronado, where the Marilyn Monroe film *Some Like It Hot* was filmed.

North of San Diego proper, the towns of La Jolla, Del Mar, and North County offer a more relaxed pace for exploring. Snorkel the azure water of La Jolla Cove or vye for a piece of that

# HIGHLIGHTS

◖ **Gaslamp Quarter:** This former red-light district is now the re-imagined epicenter of downtown San Diego's restaurants, shops, and nightlife (page 103).

◖ **San Diego Zoo:** The San Diego Zoo is world renowned for a reason. The 80-acre park and botanical garden is home to a vast array of plants and animals both exotic and ordinary, from elephants and tigers to meerkats and pythons (page 106).

◖ **Whaley House:** The most haunted house in the United States can be found in Old Town San Diego. Built in 1857, this historic Greek Revival mansion housed members of the Whaley family – and is reputed to house their ghosts as well (page 110).

◖ **Mission San Diego del Alcala:** California's first mission is still a working Catholic church, as well as a museum, with insights into mission life for both the Franciscan monks and native Kumeyaay people (page 111).

◖ **California Surf Museum:** Southern California is synonymous with surfing, and this museum explores the sport's California origins with a wealth of exhibits and events (page 119).

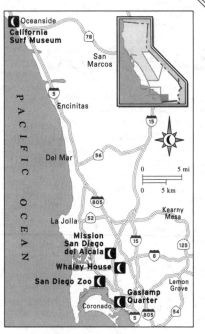

LOOK FOR ◖ TO FIND RECOMMENDED SIGHTS, ACTIVITIES, DINING, AND LODGING.

pristine sand with the beach crowd. Splurge some of that vacation cash on a horse race at the Del Mar Racetrack, or get up-close and personal interaction with the exotic animals at the Wild Animal Park.

## PLANNING YOUR TIME

Compared to other parts of California, San Diego's major attractions sit relatively close together, and it's easy to get from one place to another in a reasonable amount of time. San Diego County has arguably the best beaches in the state. If your travel goals are focused on sand and surf, consider staying in Mission Bay or Point Loma, or farther afield

in the North County coastal area. On the other hand, if you're in town to see the zoo or take in some museums, you'll be spending time in Balboa Park, which abuts the Old Town and downtown areas. If you're starting a tour of California Missions, head for Old Town first. Military history and Navy buffs will be content to spend their whole trip within the city limits of San Diego, dividing their time between the Harbor and Point Loma. If you've got an extra couple of hours and you haven't been out there yet, take the bridge over to Coronado to gawk at the ridiculous exuberance of the Hotel del Coronado.

# Sights

## DOWNTOWN

The downtown area of San Diego isn't as big and intimidating as its cousins in San Francisco and Los Angeles. Instead, you'll find a smaller, homier area that feels safe to walk in—even if you're a lone woman after dark. The Gaslamp Quarter highlights downtown, offering hundreds of restaurants, dozens of bars and clubs, and a rich history. The area near the airport has a range of hotels and skirts the harbor of San Diego Bay with its museums and ships and ship-museums. The rest of downtown stretches out toward Old Town and Balboa Park.

## ◖ Gaslamp Quarter

Perhaps the best known area of downtown San Diego, the Gaslamp Quarter (Fourth, Fifth, and Sixth Sts. and Broadway) exudes atmosphere, whether you visit during the day or night. Of course, the Gaslamp Quarter has exuded atmosphere since its earliest inception in the 19th century. The Fifth Street Pier led sailors right to the area, where saloons and brothels flourished. Ida Bailey—a famous lady of the evening—moved in and cemented the area (then called Stingaree) as a red-light district. After decades of thriving debauchery, a police raid in 1912 heralded the end of the Gaslamp Quarter's popularity. Throughout the first two-thirds of the 1900s, the area decayed, becoming a low-rent district filled with porn theaters and liquor stores. In the mid-1970s, the Gaslamp Quarter Association came to be, and the renewal of this downtown area began.

Today, the Gaslamp Quarter bustles with foot traffic, both locals and tourists. People crowd into the popular and sometimes quirky restaurants, dance like mad at the many bars and clubs, and spend their cash in the shops and boutiques. (But only tourists insist on taking photos under the Gaslamp Quarter sign.) Ghosts reputedly haunt several buildings here; check into a ghost tour or explore on your own to try to see or feel a spook. In general, the Gaslamp Quarter is quite safe, though you will see a scattering of homeless people wandering and sometimes sleeping on the sidewalks. In the evenings, the gaslamp-shaped streetlights illuminate the sidewalks and the historic architecture of some of the structures, especially along Fifth Street.

## Maritime Museum of San Diego

Once you're on the downtown waterfront, it's easy to spot the Maritime Museum of San Diego (1492 N. Harbor Dr., 619/234-9153, www.sdmaritime.org, daily 9 A.M.–8 P.M., adults $12, seniors $9, children $8): Just look for the tall masts with sails. This museum features a collection of floating historic ships, many of which still sail on a regular basis. The gem of the collection, the famous *Star of India* has been plying the high seas for almost 150 years. Other genuine historic ships include the *Medea,* the *Berkeley,* and the *Pilot.* Another ship that makes regular passenger cruises is the *Californian*—the state's Official Tall Ship. (Yes, California has such a thing!)

Come any day to tour the various ships at dock—onboard you'll find a wealth of exhibits depicting the maritime history of San Diego, war at sea in centuries past, the story of the ship you're on, and more. This museum makes a perfect outing for anyone who loves naval history, sailing, ships in general, or even just being out on the water. The museum recommends that you make reservations in advance for their historic ship cruises.

## USS *Midway*

Need more naval history? Visit the USS *Midway* (910 N. Harbor Dr., 619/544-9600, www.midway.org, daily 10 A.M.–4 P.M., adults $15, seniors/students $10, children $8). This carrier, which dates to the period just after World War II, served as an active part of the U.S. Navy through Desert Storm in 1991. Onboard, you'll get to roam throughout the ship, checking out everything from fighter planes to the enlisted mess to the dreaded brig as you climb narrow

SAN DIEGO

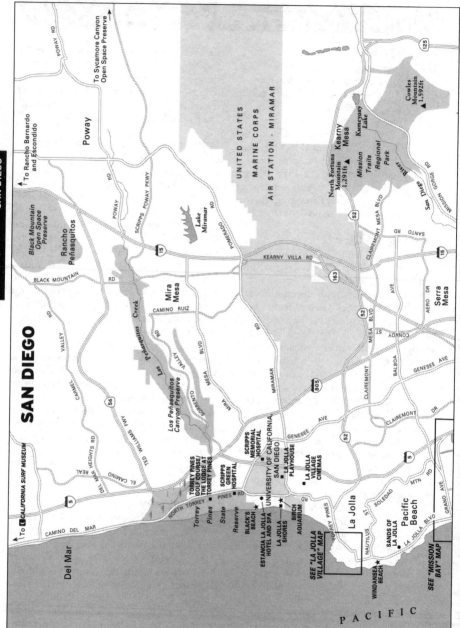

# SAN DIEGO

To Rancho Bernardo and Escondido

To Sycamore Canyon Open Space Preserve

Poway

Black Mountain Open Space Preserve

Rancho Peñasquitos

UNITED STATES MARINE CORPS AIR STATION - MIRAMAR

Cowles Mountain 1,592ft

Kumeyaay Lake

Mission Trails Regional Park

North Fortuna Mountain 1,291ft

Kearny Mesa

San Diego River

Lake Miramar

KEARNY VILLA RD

Mira Mesa

CAMINO RUIZ

Serra Mesa

AERO DR

CONNOY ST

BLACK MOUNTAIN RD

Los Peñasquitos Canyon Preserve

Las Peñasquitos Creek

GENESEE AVE

BALBOA

CLAIREMONT

CLAIREMONT DR

Del Mar

CALIFORNIA SURF MUSEUM

CAMINO DEL MAR

TORREY PINES GOLF COURSE / THE LODGE AT TORREY PINES

SCRIPPS GREEN HOSPITAL

SCRIPPS MEMORIAL HOSPITAL

UNIVERSITY OF CALIFORNIA, SAN DIEGO

LA JOLLA PLAYHOUSE

LA JOLLA VILLAGE CINEMAS

BLACK'S BEACH

ESTANCIA LA JOLLA HOTEL AND SPA

LA JOLLA SHORES

BIRCH AQUARIUM

La Jolla

Pacific Beach

SANDS OF LA JOLLA

WINDANSEA BEACH

SEE "LA JOLLA VILLAGE" MAP

SEE "MISSION BAY" MAP

PACIFIC

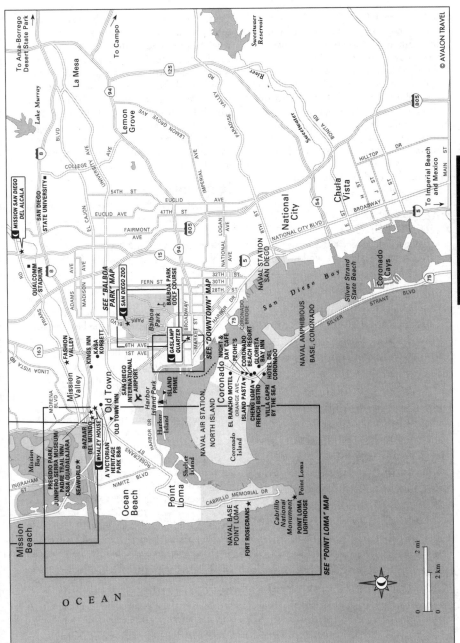

SAN DIEGO

© AVALON TRAVEL

metal steps from deck to deck. One of the best parts of a trip to the *Midway* is the opportunity to talk to the docents, many of whom are veterans who served aboard the ship during the Cold War, Vietnam, or Desert Storm. Consider taking one of the docent-guided tours if you're interested in the realities of life aboard an aircraft carrier. The self-guided audio tour also makes a good introduction to the ship, after which you can check out the flight simulators, linger near the exciting aircraft, or head to the café and gift shop at the stern. Parts of the ship are wheelchair accessible and there are restrooms onboard.

## BALBOA PARK AND HILLCREST

The Balboa Park you see today was created for the 1915 Panama-California World Exposition. The Spanish Revival architecture is set amid immense, almost tropical, greenery and welcomes visitors with a wealth of museums, halls, exhibitions, gardens, and open spaces. Stop at the **Balboa Park Visitors Center** (1549 El

Gaslamp Quarter architecture

Prado, 619/239-0512, www.balboapark.org) for a park map and to plan your visit—there won't be time to see it all!

Hillcrest, immediately northwest of the park, was once a gentrified residential area. Today, a touch of shabbiness has met with hip urban renewal to create a mixed neighborhood that still shelters many older residents, while providing entertainment and energy to a younger crowd. Hillcrest beckons to the San Diego gay community as well, with clubs and bars creating a hip queer nightlife scene.

## ◖ San Diego Zoo

The jewel of San Diego's vast interconnected wildlife park system, the San Diego Zoo (2920 Zoo Dr., 619/234-1515, www.sandiego zoo.org, summer daily 9 A.M.–8 P.M., rest of the year daily 9 A.M.–4 P.M., adults $34, children $24) lives up to its reputation and then some. The 80-acre zoo actually doubles as the state's largest botanical garden. The zoo grows lovely plants from around the globe that serve as shelter, hiding places, and food for the hundreds of exotic animals that inhabit state-of-the-art enclosures. You'll see perennial zoo favorites including elephants, lions, polar bears, and you'll also meet a host of other famous and exotic species, such as meerkats, one-foot-tall deer, pythons, and parrots. For the comfort of the human visitors, ample restrooms, benches, concessions, and gift shops scatter through the zoo.

To get the best zoo experience possible, stroll its meandering paved walkways, stopping whenever and wherever you feel a need to watch the birds and beasts as they sleep, eat, and play. Some of the paths can be steep— if you're visiting with kids or folks who have trouble walking, keep that in mind when you plan. The map provided by the zoo can help with good walking routes for your party's endurance levels. If you can't do it all, pick the paths that take you to your primary points of interest—be those pandas, birds, or big kittycats. For another great way to enhance your experience, pick up one or more of the fliers that describe the park's extensive flora in

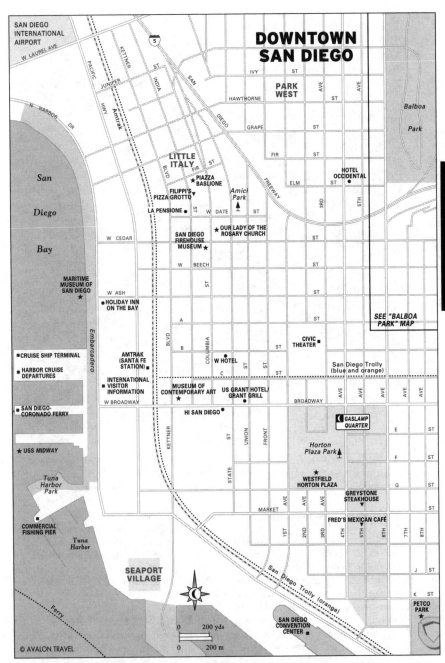

SAN DIEGO INTERNATIONAL AIRPORT

W LAUREL AVE

KETTNER ST
INDIA ST
PACIFIC HWY
JUNIPER
Amtrak
N HARBOR DR

# DOWNTOWN SAN DIEGO

IVY ST
**PARK WEST** AVE ST AVE
HAWTHORNE ST
GRAPE ST
Balboa Park

*San Diego Bay*

FIR ST
**LITTLE ITALY** FIR ST
ELM ST
HOTEL OCCIDENTAL
★ PIAZZA BASLIONE
*Amici Park*
FILIPPI'S PIZZA GROTTO ▼
LA PENSIONE ● ST W DATE ST
3RD
5TH

MARITIME MUSEUM OF SAN DIEGO ★

W CEDAR
SAN DIEGO FIREHOUSE MUSEUM ★
★ OUR LADY OF THE ROSARY CHURCH
ST

W BEECH
ST

W ASH
● HOLIDAY INN ON THE BAY
ST

*Embarcadero*

A
BLVD
COLUMBIA ST
B
CIVIC THEATER ■
SEE "BALBOA PARK" MAP

■ CRUISE SHIP TERMINAL
■ HARBOR CRUISE DEPARTURES
AMTRAK (SANTA FE STATION) ■
W HOTEL
C ST ST ST
San Diego Trolly (blue and orange)

■ SAN DIEGO-CORONADO FERRY
■ INTERNATIONAL VISITOR INFORMATION
MUSEUM OF CONTEMPORARY ART ★
US GRANT HOTEL/ GRANT GRILL
AVE AVE AVE AVE AVE
W BROADWAY BROADWAY

★ USS MIDWAY
HI SAN DIEGO ●
KETTNER ST
UNION ST
FRONT ST
GASLAMP QUARTER
E ST
F ST

*Tuna Harbor Park*
*Horton Plaza Park* ▲
STATE ST
★ WESTFIELD HORTON PLAZA
G ST

● COMMERCIAL FISHING PIER
*Tuna Harbor*
GREYSTONE STEAKHOUSE ▼
ST

MARKET AVE AVE
1ST 2ND 3RD 4TH 5TH 6TH 7TH 8TH
FRED'S MEXICAN CAFÉ ▼
J ST

**SEAPORT VILLAGE**
San Diego Trolly (orange)
K ST
PETCO PARK ★

*Ferry*

0   200 yds
0   200 m

SAN DIEGO CONVENTION CENTER ■

© AVALON TRAVEL

SAN DIEGO

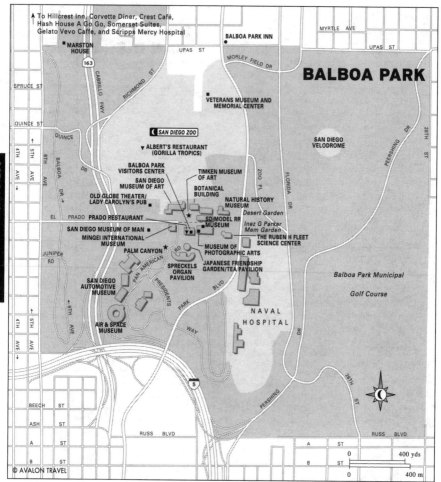

detail. Plant lovers love playing Spot the Acacia as they enjoy the animals.

If walking the whole zoo just isn't for you, consider one of the bus rides. The Guided Bus Tour takes you to many of the highlights of the zoo, letting dozens of animals show off for you as you snap photos from the coveted upper deck of the two-story bus. Friendly and knowledgeable docents drive the buses and describe each of the animals and their habitats as you pass. If you just want to get from one section of the zoo to another, jump on an Express Bus. For a special treat, take the Skyfari from the front of the park to the rear, where the polar bears play in their pond. You'll get a lovely view of the whole of Balboa Park out to the sea as you traverse the length of the zoo in less than 10 minutes.

## San Diego Museum of Art

The San Diego Museum of Art (1450 El Prado, www.sdmart.org, Tues.–Sun. 10 A.M.–6 P.M.,

© LIZ HAMILL SCOTT

flamingos, San Diego Zoo

they planned to take with them to the next world, while in the Maya exhibit you'll see reproductions and relics of South American daily life. The museum also features exhibits on the daily life and times of the Kumeyaay, the native people of the San Diego region. Further exhibits describe the process of human evolution and physiology. A tour through these galleries teaches kids and adults alike about their own history, growth, development, and lifestyles. The museum website highlights special events and traveling exhibitions. (In 2007, the Museum of Man hosted the Dead Sea Scrolls!)

## Palm Canyon
For a peaceful break from the endless educational opportunities of Balboa Park, take a walk through Palm Canyon (location 34 on the Balboa Park map, daily). The canyon offers visitors an intense look at various varieties of that ubiquitous California icon: the palm tree. With 58 species of palms creating a cool, shady space, the Canyon is a perfect place to slow down and enjoy a break on a hot summer day. The Mexican fan palms at the center of the garden have lived here almost 100 years. The groomed paths connect the canyon to the Old Cactus Garden; the Alcazar Garden also sits adjacent to the palms, and a tram stop nearby makes access a breeze.

## Japanese Friendship Garden
Cultural centers form an important element of Balboa Park. The Japanese Friendship Garden (2125 Park Blvd., 619/232-2721, www.niwa .org, Tues.–Sun. 10 A.M.–4 P.M.) began as a teahouse during the 1915–1916 Exposition, and grew over the years to include many elements of a traditional Japanese formal garden. You can enjoy the tranquility of the Zen garden, koi pond, and wisteria arbor, or take tea and sushi at the Tea Pavilion. This is the perfect place to enjoy a quiet walk hand-in-hand with your sweetie. For variety, the garden displays temporary exhibitions that mesh with the Japanese cultural traditions exemplified here. Check the website

Thurs. till 9 P.M., adults $10, seniors $8, students $7, children $4) is a highlight, even among the 15 incredible museums of Balboa Park. The collections and exhibitions at the Museum of Art range from Old Masters to Asian art to modern American painting and sculpture. From photography to painting in unusual media to modern sculpture, you'll see many media as you stroll through the galleries admiring the art of centuries. For a deeper experience, take one of docent tours that run a few times each day. Check the website for the latest special exhibitions and upcoming fun museum events.

## San Diego Museum of Man
Rather than focusing solely on the arts and achievements of humankind, the San Diego Museum of Man (1350 El Prado, 619/239-2001, www.museumofman.org, daily 10 A.M.–4:30 P.M., adults $10, youth 13–17 $7.50, children 3–12 $12) hones in on Man himself and herself. In the Egyptian collection, you'll find mummified humans and the possessions

for one-day classes in Japanese arts, usually held on weekends.

## Other Museums and Gardens

Balboa Park is filled with a number of other worthy museums, and meandering paths lead to even more botanical areas and gardens. It's impossible to see everything in one day, but a repeat visit could include the **Air and Space Museum** (2001 Pan American Plaza, 619/234-8291, www.aerospacemuseum.org, $15) for a history through human flight; the **Reuben H. Fleet Science Center** (1875 El Prado, 619/238-1233, www.rhfleet.org, Mon.–Thurs. 9:30 A.M.–5 P.M., Fri. 9:30 A.M.–9 P.M., Sat. 9:30 A.M.–8 P.M., Sun. 9:30 A.M.–6 P.M., $8), where young ones can explore the interactive science exhibits; and the **Natural History Museum** (1788 El Prado, 619/232-3821, www.sdnhm.org, Mon.–Thurs. 10 A.M.–6:30 P.M., Fri. 10 A.M.–7:30 P.M., Sat.–Sun. 9 A.M.–8:30 P.M., $9), which houses a vast collection of fossils and other artifacts presenting San Diego's geologic history.

The **Botanical Building** (El Prado, Fri.–Wed. 10 A.M.–4 P.M., free) is a lovely centerpiece to the Prado and a perfect way to relax in the Zen-like atmosphere its thousands of exotic plants provide.

## OLD TOWN

San Diego is the oldest European-settled "town" in California. The Old Town area encompasses the first Spanish settlements of what would eventually become California, 19th-century homes and businesses, parks, and modern shops and restaurants. Old Town is the perfect place to get started on a historic tour of California, a ghost-hunting visit to San Diego, or a good sightseeing trip.

### ◀ Whaley House

Billed as the most haunted house in all of the United States, the Whaley House (2476 San Diego Ave., 619/297-7511, www.whaleyhouse.org, Mon.–Tues. 10 A.M.–5 P.M., Thurs.–Sun. 10 A.M.–10 P.M., summer daily 10 A.M.–10 P.M., adults $6, seniors $5, children $4) was built by Thomas Whaley in 1857—and over the century it was inhabited, many members of the Whaley family lived and died inside the brick-constructed Greek Revival mansion. The house was also leased out as a home, and used as a courthouse, general store, and billiards hall, among other things. Before Whaley built the house on the corner of San Diego Avenue and Harney Street, the spot was used for at least one public hanging on record.

Reportedly, the haunting of the Whaley House began almost as soon as the Whaleys first moved in. Thomas Whaley believed that the specter of a criminal hanged on the land was the source of loud, ominous footfalls that rattled the floorboards of his new home late at night. More recently, visitors have spotted many different ghosts inside the house, which has been featured on *America's Most Haunted*. Children and adults have seen male shades, female spirits, and even the vision of a spaniel dog that matches the description of Thomas Whaley's family pet. If you love a good ghost story and long to see the spirits of the Whaley House yourself, consider coming to visit at night, or even calling ahead and booking a private tour (two people minimum) after 10 P.M.

Even if you don't believe all the ghost stories, the Whaley House Museum contains enough concrete lore pertaining to the house and its various incarnations to entertain history buffs for hours. Self-guided tours are enhanced by the wandering docents, who can answer questions about the artifacts inside the house as well as the house itself. And should you feel an unexpected chill or see an inexplicable shadow as you wander through a room, well, the staff is used to that sort of thing and will be happy to help you out with the experience!

### Old Town State Historic Park

The Old Town San Diego State Historic Park (corner of San Diego Ave. and Twigg St., 619/291-4903, www.parks.ca.gov, daily 10 A.M.–5 P.M., free) makes a great place to start exploring the history of California's first town. The visitors center sits in a house first built in 1853 as a family home and set of local offices by attorney James Robinson. Another major home, the McCoy House, was built in 1869, excavated and reconstructed over the years 1995–2000. Move on to the early 19th-century Mexican pueblos, including La Casa de Machado y Stewart; this adobe structure contains many artifacts that would have been part of the daily life of San Diego citizens in 1821–1872. Out and about in the park, you can enjoy period music, pet the burros, and observe the park staff engaging in activities folks might have done 150 years ago. Wednesdays are living history days, and the park hosts many events over the course of each year. If you're more into the afterlife of the residents of Old San Diego, you can visit the El Campo Santo Cemetery—the oldest cemetery in the city. The park also includes a number of known haunted sites, including the Robinson-Rose House, Casa de Bandini, and La Casa de Estudillo.

## Presidio Park

One of the early Mexican settlements in San Diego was a military installation, now Presidio Park (2811 Jackson St., 619/692-4918). The **Junípero Serra Museum** (2727 Presidio Dr., 619/297-3258, daily 10 A.M.–4:30 P.M., adults $5, seniors $4, children $2) sits inside the park, on the spot where Father Junipero Serra and Captain Gaspar de Portola established the Presidio fort. Its collections include housewares, artifacts, and a cannon from the Mexican occupation through the early California period of San Diego through 1929. If you prefer nature with your history, take a stroll along the more than two miles of trails winding through the acres of gardens and wild areas of the park. Palm Canyon features lawns surrounded by stately old palm trees. The Arbor has a more formal garden feel, complete with pillars and flowers. It's hard to believe as you wander the charming parkland that you're on the site of a former military base.

## ◖ Mission San Diego del Alcala

The first mission erected in California was

Mission San Diego del Alcala

© ROBERT HOLMES / CALTOUR

SAN DIEGO

Mission San Diego del Alcala (10818 San Diego Mission Rd., www.missionsandiego .com, daily 9 A.M.–4:45 P.M.). It was blessed by Father Junipero Serra in 1769, making it the first Christian church in California. Ironically, it was also the poorest Mission for most of its hey-dey. Native Americans raided and burned it, the harsh soil resisted cultivation, and eventually the Mexican independence from Spain rendered the church a secular building. Time and renovation came to the Mission, and it was re-established as a sacred space. It still operates as an active Catholic church today; if you visit, please respect the Mission as a house of worship even as you appreciate its significance as a museum. The church you see is actually the fifth church built on this site, erected and fortified against California's infamous earthquakes. One of the bells in the tower is original (dating to 1801). Inside, you'll see evidence of the life of the Franciscan monks who operated the Mission until 1834, and of the native Kumeyaay people who lived here before the Europeans came and whose lives were changed forever by their arrival.

## POINT LOMA

Point Loma is at once one of the most beautiful and one of the most important pieces of land in the San Diego region. From the tip of the point, you can see everywhere, from the Cuyamaca Mountains to the land and seas of Mexico, and down into the safe harbor of the San Diego Bay. This fabulous view also meant a perfect place to build a defense for the harbor and the settlements beyond. Accordingly, Point Loma has served more than 200 years as a military installation. From owl limpets to soldiers' graves, there are innumerable unique items to see in the area.

### Fort Rosecrans Military Reserve

San Diego has historically maintained an extensive military presence, regardless of whose rule the land fell under. Even today, a large U.S. Navy installation remains here, guarding the Pacific shores. Fort Rosecrans

began as a Spanish Presidio that was fortified against imminent British threat in the late 1700s. Then called Fort Guijarro, it lasted as an active Spanish military base only 40 years, after which it began to decay. After the creation of California as a state, the U.S. government refurbished the fort to protect the San Diego harbor once more. It was rechristened Fort Rosecrans, and parts of it are still used to this day for Army Reserve activities.

Today, when you visit the parklands of Cabrillo National Monument, you can see remnants of old buildings belonging to the fort, many used during the two World Wars. But the highlight of any visit to the fort is the **Fort Rosecrans National Cemetery** (1880 Cabrillo Memorial Dr., 619/553-2084). In addition to the haunting rows of stark white tombstones marching in dressed line across green lawns, you'll find graves here from combatants who fought wars of the California Republic. Wander the grounds to view graves old and recent, as well as monuments to fallen soldiers from little-known battles long past.

### Cabrillo National Monument

Cabrillo National Monument (1800 Cabrillo Memorial Dr., 619/557-5450, www.nps.gov/ cabr) celebrates the initial discovery of San Diego Bay by Spanish Explorer Juan Rodriguez Cabrillo in the mid-16th century. This was the first landing of the Spanish—indeed of any Europeans—on the West Coast of North America. Today, a large statue of Cabrillo stands within the monument lands, overlooking the San Diego Bay. At the visitors center, you can learn more about the history of Cabrillo's life and explorations.

The wildlife and the scenery are other great reasons to visit the national monument. Views from the high places here are second to none. Turning around, you can see the harbor, the San Diego cityscape, the Pacific Ocean, and all the way south to Mexico. Be sure to bring your camera! For a micro-view of San Diego's seas, check the tide tables and head down to the tide pools on the west side of Point Loma. Here you'll find a myriad of sea

SAN DIEGO

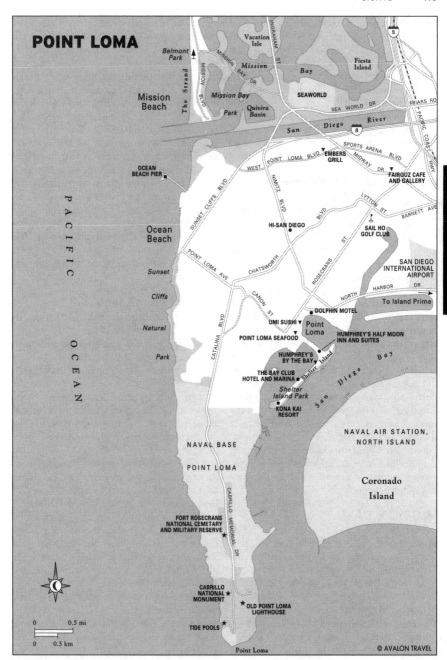

**POINT LOMA**

Belmont Park

Vacation Isle

Mission Bay

Fiesta Island

Mission Beach

INGRAHAM ST

MISSION BLVD

MISSION BAY DR

Mission Bay

The Strand

MISSION BLVD

Mission Bay Park

Quivira Basin

SEAWORLD

SEA WORLD DR

FRIARS RD

PACIFIC COAST HWY

5

San Diego River

8

OCEAN BEACH PIER

WEST POINT LOMA BLVD

SUNSET CLIFFS BLVD

NIMITZ BLVD

SPORTS ARENA BLVD

EMBERS GRILL ▼

MIDWAY DR

FAIROUZ CAFE AND GALLERY ▼

PACIFIC OCEAN

Ocean Beach

HI-SAN DIEGO ●

POINT LOMA AVE

CHATSWORTH

CANON ST

BLVD

ROSECRANS ST

LYTTON ST

BARNETT AVE

SAIL HO GOLF CLUB

SAN DIEGO INTERNATIONAL AIRPORT

Sunset

Cliffs

Natural

Park

CATALINA BLVD

NORTH HARBOR DR

To Island Prime

DOLPHIN MOTEL ●

UMI SUSHI ▼

POINT LOMA SEAFOOD ▼

Point Loma

HUMPHREY'S HALF MOON INN AND SUITES ●

HUMPHREY'S BY THE BAY ▼

THE BAY CLUB HOTEL AND MARINA ●

Shelter Island

San Diego Bay

Shelter Island Park

KONA KAI RESORT ●

NAVAL BASE

POINT LOMA

NAVAL AIR STATION, NORTH ISLAND

Coronado Island

CABRILLO MEMORIAL DR

FORT ROSECRANS NATIONAL CEMETARY AND MILITARY RESERVE ★

CABRILLO NATIONAL MONUMENT ★

OLD POINT LOMA LIGHTHOUSE ★

TIDE POOLS ★

0        0.5 mi

0        0.5 km

Point Loma

© AVALON TRAVEL

life waiting for discovery. Just be sure that you and your children look with your eyes, not your fingers—many tide pool creatures can be injured or even killed by a mere touch from a human.

The parkland of Cabrillo offers hiking trails through the southern coastal scrub ecosystem so precious and unique to this part of the state. Enjoy the wildlife and lovely plants, and come in spring for the best profusion of wildflowers.

## Old Point Loma Lighthouse

Among the oldest lighthouses in California, the Old Point Loma Lighthouse (1800 Cabrillo Memorial Dr., daily 9 A.M.–5 P.M.) began its watch over the San Diego Bay in 1855. Unfortunately, the light was often dimmed by pernicious fog, and a new lighthouse went into operation in a better location in 1891. Luckily for visitors today, the old lighthouse remained unmolested. Come in to peruse the exhibits, or sign up for a ranger-led tour and talk that goes into detail about the history of the lighthouse. You'll see the restoration of the lighthouse by the National Park Service to its original mid-19th-century glory. Perhaps the most interesting stories you'll hear during your visit are of the lighthouse-keepers and their families. Several descendents of the original keepers have provided family stories to round out the human history of the lighthouse. Old Point Loma Lighthouse is part of the Cabrillo National Monument, perfectly located for a day out exploring the early history of California's statehood.

## MISSION BAY

Mission Bay offers serene waters untroubled by the sometimes pounding Pacific surf. It's a perfect place to center your family vacation, take in the natural wonders of Mission Bay Park, or head for the colorful fun of SeaWorld.

### Mission Bay Park

The acres of Mission Bay Park (Mission Blvd.) are not a natural wonder. In fact, the land and sea of the popular recreation area were once a tidal marsh—the primary outlet of the San Diego River. In the 1940s, the marsh was dredged and the beaches and land formations you see today were created. Among them are 19 miles of charming sandy beach perfect for sunbathing, sandcastle-making, beach volleyball, and more—and 14 miles of bike paths. Half of the designated parkland is actually off the shore, in the abundant calm waterways. Swim in one of the eight designated, lifeguard-protected areas throughout the park, or take a deeper dive out into the channel to windsurf or water-ski. In the non-swimming, non-skiing areas, you can string out a line and go fishing. Despite the manmade nature of this park, it has several areas that have become significant wildlife preserves. You can go birding at Perez Cove, Telecote Creek, Fiesta Island, or a number of other spots throughout the park.

### SeaWorld San Diego

With a charming mix of rides and sea-life attraction, SeaWorld San Diego (500 SeaWorld Dr., 800/257-4268, www.seaworld.com, hours vary, adults $60, children $50) makes a fun destination for families. SeaWorld is navigable in half a day, even when taking the time to include some rides and shows. Kids love meeting Shamu and his brothers and sisters in the killer whale pool just inside the park entrance. Also in SeaWorld you'll meet sea lions, endangered sea turtles, dolphins, and other denizens of the deep. On hot days, the river ride and splash-down roller coaster cool off overheated park visitors. Plenty of food concessions (including a coffee stand) revive weary families, getting them ready for more animal shows and action-packed rides. If you want to have breakfast or dinner with Shamu at the restaurant looking out into the killer whale tank, advance reservations are recommended.

While SeaWorld offers great fun for small children, the laboriously cute decor, rollercoaster-style rides, and trained animal acts can get a bit tiresome for more sophisticated or outdoor-oriented adult travelers. The food

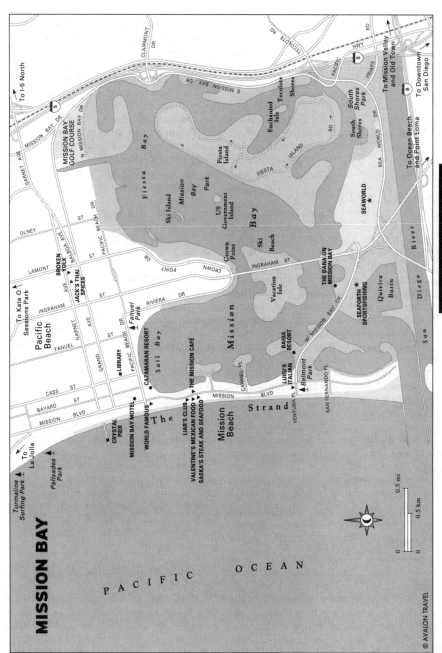

SAN DIEGO

# MISSION BAY

PACIFIC OCEAN

0.5 mi
0.5 km

© AVALON TRAVEL

in the park also caters to the younger set, and tends to be higher on fat content than quality. Frankly, better adult-oriented wild animal experiences are available in the San Diego area at both the zoo and the Wild Animal Park.

## LA JOLLA
North of San Diego, La Jolla (which means "The Jewel") is a well-to-do neighborhood filled with high-end boutiques, exemplary restaurants, and a coastline awash in scenic beauty.

### Sunny Jim's Cave
Of the seven sea caves in the La Jolla cliffs, Sunny Jim's Cave (1325 Cave St., daily 9 A.M.–5 P.M., adults $4, children $3) is unique. You don't need a kayak or scuba gear to get down into this cave; a manmade tunnel created 100 years ago lets visitors into the cavern via a reliable land route. You'll purchase admission at the weathered, shingle-fronted Cave Store, then climb carefully down the 145 steps to the cavern proper. You'll see a sizeable sea cave of sandstone, carved over the millennia by the Pacific into the cliffside. You can look from inside the cave out towards the ocean—an interesting and perhaps just a little bit eerie view.

But how did the tunnel get built? Gustav Schultz, a retiree and painter, hired laborers to hand-dig the tunnel in 1903 as a tourist attraction. The cave was later named "Sunny Jim's" after a cartoon breakfast cereal mascot by the author of *The Wizard of Oz*. (No, I am not making this up.) Schultz painted local landscapes in the Cave Store until his death in 1912.

### La Jolla Cove and Scripps Park
One of the most photographed beaches in the state, La Jolla Cove (1100 Coast Rd.) differs from other San Diego beaches. The small cove sits sandwiched between two sandstone cliffs, and the coarse sand feels more like the rough pebbles of the northern part of the state than the silky-soft stretches of the south. Visitors snap pictures of the picturesque scenery, swim in the warm water, and trek up to Ellen Browning Scripps Park (Coast Blvd., 4–8 P.M.) for a picnic or a game of soccer on the manicured lawn. La Jolla Cove is famous for its sparkling clear water, and at low tide scuba divers and snorkelers enjoy the local marine life. Lifeguards stay on duty year-round from 9 A.M. until sunset during the high season and from 10 A.M. in wintertime. Up at Scripps Park, land-lovers enjoy walking on the boardwalk along the cliffs overlooking the vast Pacific, playing on the lawns, and admiring the oddly grown trees scattered around providing shade. The park has restrooms and showers. Parking for either the beach or the park can be tough, especially in the summer. Consider parking in a pay lot downtown and hoofing it down to the beach.

### Birch Aquarium
The Birch Aquarium at Scripps (2300 Expedition Way, 858/534-3474, http://aquarium.ucsd.edu, daily 9 A.M.–5 P.M., adults $11, seniors $9, youth 3–17 $7.50) is run by the University of California at San Diego. Both children and adults love the Scripps Institute's research and displays in this state-of-the-art aquarium complex. For a classic beginning, view sea life from oceans the world over along the Hall of Fishes. This area includes coral reef displays from Mexico and the Caribbean, a kelp forest similar to the ones right off the La Jolla coast, and the fabulous and fascinating Shark Reef. The Art of Deception display allows visitors to see the amazing camouflaging defenses of sea creatures from various marine environments. Kids love to splash in the Wonders of Water exhibit, and playing here is not only allowed, it's encouraged!

### Museum of Contemporary Art San Diego–La Jolla
The MCASD La Jolla (700 Prospect St., 858/454-3541, www.mcasd.org, Fri.–Tues. 11 A.M.–5 P.M., Thurs. 11 A.M.–7 P.M., general admission $10, free for those 25 and under) is one of two MCASD campuses in the area.

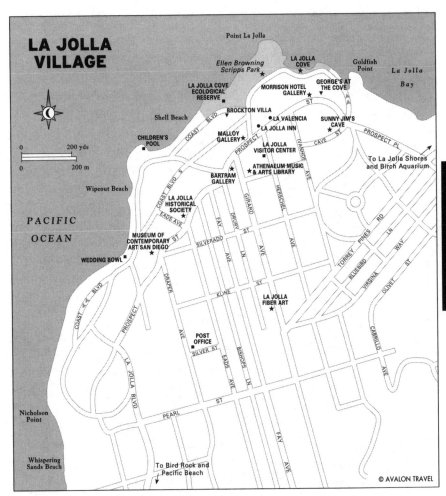

# LA JOLLA VILLAGE

Point La Jolla

Ellen Browning
Scripps Park

LA JOLLA
COVE

Goldfish
Point

La Jolla
Bay

LA JOLLA COVE
ECOLOGICAL
RESERVE

MORRISON HOTEL
GALLERY ★

GEORGE'S AT
THE COVE

Shell Beach

BROCKTON VILLA ▼

★ LA VALENCIA

SUNNY JIM'S
CAVE ★

CHILDREN'S
POOL

MALLOY
GALLERY ★

● LA JOLLA INN

LA JOLLA
VISITOR CENTER ■

PROSPECT PL.

To La Jolla Shores
and Birch Aquarium

Wipeout Beach

ATHENAEUM MUSIC
★ & ARTS LIBRARY

BARTRAM
GALLERY ■

PACIFIC

LA JOLLA
HISTORICAL
SOCIETY
★

OCEAN

MUSEUM OF
CONTEMPORARY
ART SAN DIEGO ★

SILVERADO

WEDDING BOWL ■

KLINE

LA JOLLA
FIBER ART
★

POST
OFFICE ■

SILVER ST.

Nicholson
Point

PEARL

Whispering
Sands Beach

To Bird Rock and
Pacific Beach

0    200 yds

0    200 m

© AVALON TRAVEL

(The other is in downtown San Diego.) At the La Jolla site, perfectly located on Prospect Street for easy access, you'll see works of art in all media created from 1950 to the present. MCASD takes particular pride in its collections of Pop and Minimalist art from the 1960s and '70s, as well as a selection of pieces from artists working in the San Diego and Tijuana areas. If you love the new, unique, and misunderstood arts of the modern era, the MCASD La Jolla is a must-see. And if all that art makes you hungry, be sure to stop at the museum café for a quick bite.

## NORTH COUNTY

As you drive north up the Pacific Coast Highway from downtown San Diego, you begin to see where all the legends about California beaches and surfing came from. The sun shines down over desert plants, pale sands, cute little towns, the mountains to the east, and the glittering blue sea to the west. If

SAN DIEGO

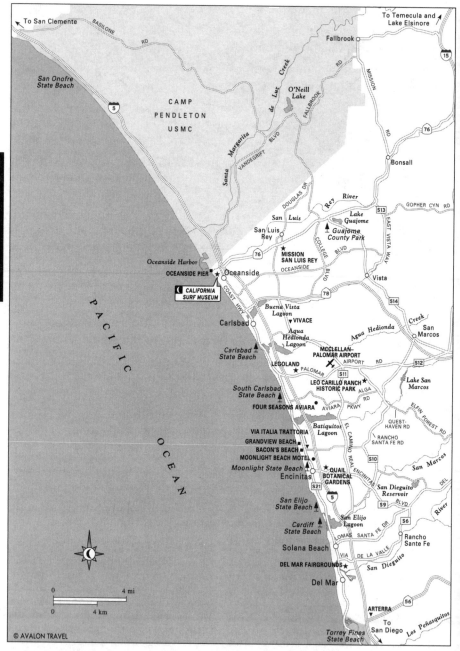

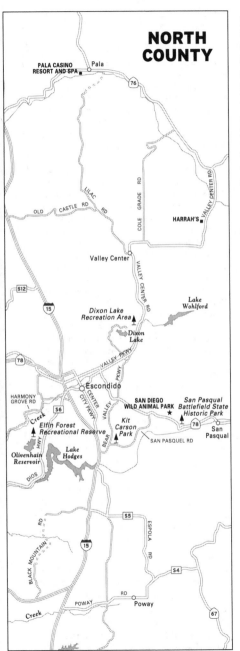

**NORTH COUNTY**

you want a movie-style California beach vacation, you can't do better than a weekend (or a whole week or two!) in Encinitas, Del Mar, or Solano Beach. At the same time, the north end of San Diego County offers some great sights and activities, from the Wild Animal Park to Mission San Luis Rey.

## ◖ California Surf Museum

Nothing says "California" quite like the image of a lithe young man (or woman) standing tall on an impossibly small slab of wood (or fiberglass), riding a wild wave in to shore. And at the legendary California Surf Museum (223 N. Coast Hwy., Oceanside, 760/721-6876, www .surfmuseum.org, daily 10 A.M.–4 P.M., free), you can admire, appreciate, and learn about the ancient sport and art of surfing. While surfing's origins may be in the South Pacific islands, the unusual sport began to catch on at the warm beaches of Southern California, catching on big once surf movies began to appear in theaters. From the silly Frankie Avalon and bongo drum fluff pieces to the semi-documentary *Endless Summer,* surf movies inspired thousands of boys and young men to get out and try to catch a wave. With the novel *Gidget* and subsequent movies, what had been an almost all-male endeavor caught on with girls, too. Surfing became a part of the California version of the 1960s and '70s hippie movement—earning the respect of the young and the animosity of the older generation. Today, there's no such thing as an "average" surfer. You might find a 10-year-old out tearing it up and a 70-year-old hanging ten, both at the same break.

At the Surf Museum, you'll see and pay homage to all that has gone into the California surf scene over its many decades. From exhibits on board-shaping to photo essays by and about legendary surfers, you'll see all there is to see about the history and current events of the unique world of surfing. Check the website for current exhibitions and events at the museum. (And yes, if you're in town especially to ride the waves, ask around at the museum for the latest "secret" local breaks.)

# TEMECULA WINERIES

Wine? In San Diego? Yes, indeed! It's not Napa or Sonoma, but if you're in California to sample all the best wine the state has to offer, don't miss out on the terrific SoCal vintages available in the San Diego region.

The major wine-producing region of San Diego is the Temecula Valley. An hour north of San Diego proper, off I-15, this small, hot valley plays home to well over a dozen wineries. Most of the tasting rooms cluster along the main wine drag, Rancho California Road, but it's also worth your time to explore farther into the valley for hidden gems off the beaten path. The Temecula Valley Winegrowers Association (www.temeculawines.org) offers a tasting map and brochure highlighting the wineries and other attractions of the area.

To check out an early example of a quality-heavy boutique winery, visit the **Hart Family Winery** (41300 Avenida Biona, 951/676-6300, www.thehartfamilywinery.com, daily 9 A.M.-4:30 P.M., $5). With vineyards first planted by the Hart family in 1974, this small vintner produces only 5,000 cases of wine, total, each year. This low production allows for intense attention to detail and quality of every single bottle of wine. And despite the small total case number, you can try a number of varietals suited perfectly to the hot climate of the high-altitude Temecula Valley. The grapes used and wines released vary from year to year, but if you can, be sure to try the fruity white Viognier, the stunning Syrah, and

several less famous varietals such as Barbera and Tempranillo.

**Churon Winery** (33233 Rancho California Rd., 951/694-9070, www.innatchuronwinery.com, daily 10 A.M.-4:30 P.M., $10) brings a taste of classic French wine country to the Temecula Valley. This winery, built on an 11-acre estate in the style of a French chateau, also operates as a high-end inn — so you can stay and enjoy the wines all night long! But even if you're not an overnight guest, you can sip the many Churon vintages in the tasting room each day. With a list that encompasses many French-styled reds and classic California whites plus a few select dessert sweets (including an unusual-to-California sherry), Churon offers something for everyone — even folks who usually shun the heavy Cabs and buttery Chards of California's wine regions.

A relative newcomer to the area, the **Falkner Winery** (40620 Calle Contento, 951/676-8231, www.falknerwinery.com, daily 10 A.M.-5 P.M., $8) fits perfectly into the casual elegance of the Temecula Valley. The elegant half-circular main building houses the tasting room, gift shop, and a Mediterranean lunch-only restaurant, Pinnacles. Inside the tasting room, sip from a wide range of wines; Falkner takes particular pride in some different styles from the average California vintner. Here, be sure to try at least two or three of the wonderful blended reds — made in the traditions of Tuscany and Bordeaux. For wine drinkers who like

## San Diego Wild Animal Park

The San Diego Zoo doesn't keep too many large animals in the confines of its limited site. To see and experience the life and times of giraffes, lions, elephants, and other natives of spacious grasslands in Africa and Asia, visit the wildly popular San Diego Wild Animal Park (15500 San Pasqual Valley Rd., Escondido, www.sandiegozoo.org/wap, daily 9 A.M.-4 P.M. or later, $28.50 adults, $17.50 children, parking $8). Deliberately set well away from the center of urban San Diego, this huge park gives a variety of animals the

space they crave to live more naturally. You could spend days in the Wild Animal Park and not see all the diverse species that live here. Walking trails offer miles of adventure through different areas of the park, such as Condor Ridge, Lion Camp, Lorikeet Landing, and the Heart of Africa. If you're not up for a day of hardcore hiking, consider paying extra for one of the "Safari" tours that take guests out into different areas of the park in colorful vehicles. On Safaris, docents tell their groups about the wildlife (both animal and vegetable) as they come upon it. You can experience a little sweet with their savory, Falkner offers a number of not-quite-dry wines that are *not* as syrupy as a standard dessert wine. For added fun, take a tour of the winery any day of the week 11 A.M.-2 P.M. for $3 per person.

Even if you're not into wine, the **South Coast Winery & Resort** (34843 Rancho California Rd., 951/587-9463, www.wineresort.com, daily 10 A.M.-6 P.M., $10) will make a stop worth your while. From the colorful frescoes decorating the tasting room to the posh GrapeSeed Spa, South Coast caters to the most luxury-loving travelers. For the full South Coast experience, book one of their private villas for your stay and reserve a table at the Tuscan-style Vineyard Rose restaurant. Back in the beautiful tasting room, you can try wines under the four different South Coast labels. From the splashy and moderately priced Elevation wines to the elegant Wild Horse Peak Mountain vintages, you'll find a wine for every taste and every budget level. For a special experience, take the inclusive $20 estate tour, which includes the vineyards as well as the production facilities and barrel rooms, and concludes with a private wine-and-cheese tasting.

A large extended family owns and runs most every aspect of the **Wilson Creek Winery & Vineyards** (35960 Rancho California Rd., 951/699-9463, www.wilsoncreekwinery .com, daily 10 A.M.-5 P.M., $10). You might even catch a Wilson when you visit the light, bright tasting room. You'll find some different wines here – one of the Wilson mainstays is Almond

Champagne, a truly special occasion beverage. Other sweet wines might include Muscat Canelli, Angelica cream sherry, chocolate port, and luscious late-harvest red wines. (You might want to avoid the "white" wines made from red grape varietals, though. They can be a little bit strange.) More traditional wine lovers will enjoy the hefty Cabernet, Zinfandel, and Petit Sirah. On the other hand, if jazz is your favorite vice, check the website for the annual calendar of concerts held on the purpose-built stage.

At **Palumbo Family Vineyards & Winery** (40150 Barksdale Circle, 951/676-7900, www .palumbofamilyvineyards.com, Fri. noon-5 P.M., Sat.-Sun. 10 A.M.-5 P.M.), you won't find the immense tasting room complex and thousands of cases of wines available at other local wineries. A tiny family operation, Palumbo takes pride in growing every grape that goes into each bottle of wine. With 12 acres of vineyards, the winery produces 1,500 cases of wine each year. A season's release might include five wines – mostly reds with a token Viognier or other hot-weather white for variety. Though they're only open regularly on the weekends, you can call the winery for a private tasting appointment during the week. Or better yet, offer to bring 7-15 of your friends down to the winery for a private winemaker's dinner! Nicholas Palumbo is a chef as well as viticulturalist and winemaker, and has been known to entertain private parties who express an interest in his fabulous food and wine.

---

the thrill of seeing a cheetah run full-speed, the simple pleasure of the grazers enjoying an afternoon munching grasses and leaves, or the vista of the full park from the air on the Balloon Safari.

The Wild Animal Park caters both to families and to adults without children seeking a more grown-up experience. Check your map for the location of playgrounds and family-themed attractions. On the website, you can find out which tours and dates are best for an adults-only day at the park. Ample food, restrooms, and concessions cluster around the

entrance area, but services get thinner as you get farther out into the park.

## Mission San Luis Rey

Sometimes referred to as the "King of the Missions," Mission San Luis Rey (4050 Mission Ave., Oceanside, 760/757-3651, www.sanluis rey.org, tours daily 10 A.M.–4 P.M., adults $6, children $4) certainly is the biggest of the California missions. It is also one of the most lavishly restored. You can visit the stately formal gardens, complete with manicured lawns, roses, antique sculptures, and ruins of structural elements of the mission buildings. Or take a tour of the museum and church, both of which contain the history of Mission San Luis Rey through interpretive panels and many artifacts. Out in front of the mission, a unique experience awaits as you explore the ruins of the Lavanderia. This large open space contains the remains of the area where Native Americans washed their clothes and themselves outside of the mission grounds. Take the stairs down to seek out the remains of the gargoyles that once sprayed water for laundry. The cemetery is one of the largest and best maintained in the mission system, with memorials dating from the earliest days of this 1798-founded Franciscan church.

### Quail Botanical Gardens

Plant and garden lovers come from around the world to visit the Quail Botanical Gardens (230 Quail Gardens Dr., Encinitas, 760/436-3036, www.qbgardens.org, 9 A.M.–5 P.M. daily, adults $10, seniors $7, children $5). The plants in this 30-plus-acre spread come from around the world too, as Quail plays home to sub-gardens highlighting rare plant species from almost every continent. Paths meander through the dozens of sub-gardens, inviting visitors to take their time and enjoy the multihued beauty surrounding them on all sides. No visit to the Quail Gardens is complete without viewing the famous Bamboo Garden and the new Undersea Garden filled with rare succulents. The Rainforest Garden has its own waterfall, and the Subtropical Fruit Garden boasts plump offerings that don't grow elsewhere even in California.

A coffee cart offers minimal refreshments, or you can bring your own picnic to enjoy in the designated picnic areas on the grounds. Restrooms hide delicately amongst the plants, and the visitors center and gift shop sit at the center of the gardens. Knowing that kids often get bored when presented with endless plants, a children's garden and a miniature railroad offer entertainment for young visitors.

# Entertainment and Events

## NIGHTLIFE
### Bars and Clubs

The Gaslamp Quarter is the hottest part of downtown San Diego for the young and energetic nighttime crowd. Consider just walking around Fourth Street and picking a club at random, or try one of the ones mentioned here. **Belo** (919 Fourth St., 619/231-9200, www.belosandiego.com, Fri.–Sat. 7 P.M.–2 A.M.) is a favorite hotspot with young club-hoppers. They're drawn by the regular appearances of big-name DJs, the size of dance floors, and the big, strong drinks that aren't *too* expensive, especially compared to those sold in competing Gaslamp clubs. Women, be aware: Lots of men at Belo are on the prowl, but security is tight and you'll still have fun, especially if you're part of a group. Dressy attire is encouraged, and cover charge run $15 and up, depending on the night.

After a fashion, you'll find truth in advertising at the **On Broadway Event Center** (615 Broadway, 619/231-0011, www.obec.tv). It is on Broadway—in the Gaslamp, not Manhattan. But it might feel like Manhattan, with the major-league weekend crowds and the overpriced drinks and the hot-stuff VIP room. (If you can get a VIP table, you'll have a blast. Otherwise, the service On Broadway is nothing to write home about.) With five dance floors with different DJs, dancers who love house, trance, '80s, and even salsa can find a place on the floor. Just beware of the lines at the door, especially if you've grabbed a spot on the VIP list, and the size of the cover charge if you're *not* on the list.

You can have it all if you get into **Aubergine** (500 Fourth St. at Island St., 619/232-8100, www.aubergineon4th.com, Fri.–Sat. 6 P.M.–2 A.M., 21 and over). This complex offers three rooms for dancing, a restaurant and sushi bar, and a comedy club all in the same (big) place. If you're coming to dance, get yourself on the guest list in advance to avoid the $20 cover. Expect a significant singles scene, good DJs spinning a mix of classics and new top hits, and crowds seeking sushi at happy hour (6–8 P.M.). The dress code tends toward the upscale, so leave the jeans behind and break out the slacks and cocktail dresses.

How can you not finish out your night at a club called **The Bitter End** (770 Fifth St., 619/338-9300, www.thebitterend.com, daily 3 P.M.–2 A.M., $10)? A step more mellow than most Gaslamp clubs, Bitter End has a distinct lounge feel with a dance club downstairs. The middle level is the main bar, which serves up pool, conversation, and the house special Black Martini. Upstairs is filled with soft couches and armchairs to recline on, plus Victorian architectural details and a historic atmosphere to please even a picky Goth. With a $10 cover, Bitter End offers one of the less expensive club experiences in the Gaslamp, but mind your dress. After happy hour, the dress code gets strictly enforced, and that means no tennis shoes.

## Gay and Lesbian

With a young, hip scene and a significant gay presence, nightlife in Hillcrest is happening most every night of the week.

**The Brass Rail** (3796 Fifth Ave., 619/298-2233, www.thebrassrailsd.com, Mon., Thurs.–Sat. hours vary) is one of San Diego's oldest gay venues. The lounge features theme nights, DJs, and live music in a historic Hillcrest location. Ladies should head to **The Flame** (3780 Park Blvd., 619/295-4163, www .flamesd.com, daily 1 P.M.–1 A.M.) on Saturdays for dancing, drinks, or just people-watching from the raised, circular couches.

## Live Music

San Diego enjoys its music, and you'll find plenty of opportunities to hear live classical, jazz, rock, and more throughout town. You'll have no trouble finding everything from tiny dive bars with mini-stages to huge multiday music festivals. Whether you prefer mellow

jazz, danceable blues, or hard-hitting rock, odds are it's playing live. Check web guides to the Gaslamp (www.gaslamp.org) and Hillcrest (http://gothere.com/sandiego/Hillcrest) for listings of who's hosting what when you're in town.

If you're in Point Loma for the evening, head to Humphrey's for live music any time of year. **Humphrey's Backstage Music** (2241 Shelter Island Blvd., www.humphreysbythebay.com/ backstagemusicclub.cfm) offers a lounge-style venue with live music or DJs spinning danceable tunes or playing charming smooth jazz to drink and converse by. Check the website for this month's schedule. If you're around in the summer season, buy tickets in advance for the local favorite concert series, **Humphreys Concerts by the Bay** (www.humphreys concerts.com). National acts come out to play against the backdrop of the marinas of Shelter Island as the sun sets over San Diego Bay. The outdoor venue takes advantage of the evening climate, so you can bask in the warm air under the stars as you listen to the tunes of your favorite rock band or folk singer.

## Comedy

Laugh it up in the Gaslamp Quarter! The **John Lovitz Comedy Club** (Fourth and Island Sts., 866/468-3399, www.jonlovitzcomedyclub .com) has comics making with the funny most every night of the week. Come out to see major stars you'll recognize from TV and film, or up-and-coming comics from the showcase specials on Comedy Central. As a part of the Aubergine complex, the John Lovitz Comedy Club offers far better dining options than the average comedy venue. (Think sushi rather than nachos.) This makes getting yourself to the two-item (food or drink) minimum an easy prospect.

# THE ARTS

Live theater lives well in San Diego. Most every area and district has at least a theater or two, and several big houses garner national acclaim for world-class productions. If you're in San Diego for more than one night, it will be worth your while to take in a show at the Old Globe,

# FESTIVALS AND EVENTS

Summer is event season in San Diego. If you're visiting between June and October, you can hardly help tripping over some fun congregation of folks. Check the web or with the tourist bureau for tickets to your favorite events, or information about what's going on in the area during your visit.

## SAN DIEGO COUNTY FAIR

The San Diego County Fair (2260 Jimmy Durant Blvd, Del Mar, 858/755-1161, www.sdfair.com, June-July) runs for several weeks every summer and boasts being one of the very best in the state. Naturally it's held at the famed Del Mar County Fairgrounds, which were purposely built for this celebration of San Diego agriculture.

## LGBT PRIDE PARADE AND FESTIVAL

There's nothing sexier than loving yourself. To celebrate being yourself, each year San Diego hosts its own LGBT Pride Parade and Festival (sandiegopride.org, June). Smaller than the mammoth festival in San Francisco each year, San Diego Pride beckons to those who want the fun of Pride without the mega-crowds. (But still, with all that bikini weather, expect plenty of people to be in attendance at all events and on both days of the festival.) The weekend is packed with events and attractions, from a 5K run to a Ferris wheel. No matter who you are or what you're into, there's something for you here. You'll find almost a dozen stages, each offering a different style of music from hip-hop to acoustic to Latino to lavender. Just about every possible lifestyle choice is represented with its own fun area; you can get hardcore in the leather space, explore your sexuality in the bisexual area, or bring your children to the family place. If you love baseball and queer life, plan ahead and purchase tickets to the Padres Pride event.

The parade and festival take place in Balboa Park, spilling out to the Hillcrest neighborhood especially in the evening, and out to Petco Park for the Padres baseball event. Check the website for information about park-and-ride services, parking, bicycle parking, public transit, and more. You can purchase tickets in advance, or at the festival. There's no smoking at the festival, but if you need wheelchair assistance, contact the festival organizers in advance.

## STREET SCENE

For a rockin' good time, check out Street Scene (Coors Amphitheater, Chula Vista, www.streetscene.com, Sept.) if you're in the San Diego area in September. This major rock-and-more festival draws name-brand pop and rock acts from around the world for a two-day show. Once you're inside the amphitheater, you'll have your choice of several stages featuring up-and-comers, experimental music, and of course the big-leaguers. Check the website for this year's lineup of musicians and a look into the stage setup and facilities for the concert. You'll find plenty of food and drink available at the indoor concessions, though it's always a good idea to eat well before venturing into a major music festival. Also, be sure to bring your sunscreen; September weekends in San Diego are often blazing hot with fiery sunshine.

## THUNDERBOAT REGATTA

For an event that's unique to San Diego and totally noisy, you can't beat the Thunderboat Regatta (www.thunderboatregatta.com, Sept.). For one weekend each September, Mission Bay revs up and gets loud, hosting a supercharged powerboat-racing event. You can see drag boat racing, Formula One, cracker box inboards, and much more. Stands are set up on beaches around the bay to allow the most people the best views of the races – be sure to buy your tickets in advance to get a good seat. The excitement at this event is contagious, and the tension is real. Be sure to bring earplugs, and extra money for parking if you want a space anywhere near the bay. (Alternately, check the website and the local resorts for deals on hotel rooms within walking distance of race-viewing areas.) Kids of all ages are welcome – check the schedule for this year's family-oriented events.

the La Jolla Playhouse, or one of the innumerable repertory theaters.

## Theater

The **Old Globe** (Copley Plaza, Balboa Park, 619/234-5623, www.oldglobe.org, box office daily noon–6 P.M. or end of show), one of the most famous theater complexes in California, sits in the middle of Balboa Park. Originally constructed to produce abbreviated Shakespeare plays for the 1935 California Pacific International Exposition, the magnificent Old Globe was remodeled to permanence in 1937. It has been producing a full season ever since, growing to add two auxiliary theaters: the Cassius Carter Centre Stage and the Lowell Davis Festival Stage. The Old Globe, restored to its original magnificence after a fire in 1978, seats almost 600 people, and has produced world premieres of plays such as *Into the Woods* and *The Full Monty* that go on to become Broadway spectaculars and worldwide hits. If you can get a ticket to something new at the Old Globe, you may find yourself seeing history being made.

The Old Globe theaters are reminiscent of the complex at the legendary Ashland Shakespeare festival. The huge outdoor Lowell Davis facility can seat almost 700 spectators and puts up shows during the summer and fall festival season. The smaller Cassius Carter Stage presents theater in the round, in an intimate black-box-style setting. See the website for a list of the shows playing at each theater, as well as for ticket sales and seating charts. At the Copley Theater complex, enjoy a snack and a drink at Lady Carolyn's Pub or browse for souvenirs at the gift shop.

For a night of high budget, fabulous Broadway theater or an adventurous off-center world premiere, check out a show at the **La Jolla Playhouse** (La Jolla Village Dr. and Gilman Dr., 858/550-1010, www.lajollaplayhouse.com, box office Sun.–Mon. noon–7 P.M., Tues.–Wed. noon–7:30 P.M., Thurs.–Sat. noon–8 P.M., shows Tues.–Sun.). This top-tier theater company produces big musicals, small experimental plays, historical dramas, and everything in between. Check the website for this year's main season schedule as well as the off-season "The Edge" plays. The Playhouse actually encompasses a building complex with three separate theater. Originally created by an ensemble of Hollywood actors, the Playhouse delights in showing off both well-known popular shows and great world premieres. Look for originality in sets and costuming, as well as top-notch acting.

For a charming night out on the North Coast, grab a seat at the **North Coast Repertory Theater** (987 Lomas Santa Fe Dr., Solano Beach, 858/481-1055, http://northcoastrep.org, shows Wed.–Sun.). The North Coast Rep produces about eight shows each year, including musicals, dramas, comedies, and family favorites. With ticket prices at around $20 per show, a laid-back evening of good repertory theater isn't hard to obtain. The theater at Lomas Santa Fe Plaza is located conveniently near I-5 and the Del Mar Racetrack, for easy access after a day's sightseeing.

## Classical Music

The **Organ Concerts in Balboa Park** (www.sosorgan.com) provide a unique, free live music experience that all visitors and locals can enjoy. Every week of the year for almost a century, the Spreckels Organ has serenaded the park with beautiful music. Concerts happen on Sundays 2–3 P.M., and on Monday nights at 7:30 P.M. in the summertime. Come out, take a seat on a park bench, and relax as the music washes over you.

If you love opera, be sure to get tickets to the **San Diego Opera** (box office 619/533-7000, www.sdopera.com, Mon.–Fri. 8:30 A.M.–4:30 P.M.) during your visit. Originally created to produce San Francisco Opera productions in the 1950s, the San Diego Opera quickly grew into an independent production company to rival even its famed neighbor to the north. In addition to the regular season filled with original productions of famous operas, you'll find the San Diego Opera hosting international stars at special concerts, and presenting a variety of musicales to the San Diego community.

All regular Opera performances take place

at the Civic Theatre (Third Ave. and B St.). You'll find several parking structures and surface lots nearby—parking usually starts at $10 and goes up on concert nights. The MTS trolley stops right behind the Theatre entrance, and is a great option if you're staying anywhere near the trolley line or are taking the train into the Santa Fe station. If you're coming from the North County for a night of culture, check the Opera's website for information about the San Diego Opera Caravan, a pay bus service to and from Carlsbad to the Civic Theatre.

## Cinema

You'll find plenty of first-run multi-screen cineplexes scattered throughout the San Diego area. But if you're looking for a fun vintage movie-going experience, try the **Ken Cinema** (4061 Adams Ave., 619/819-0236). Built in 1946, this single-screen theater now specializes in running independent and foreign films. You can also attend the Gay and Lesbian Film Festival at the Ken each year. Happily, the seats are not the same vintage as the rest of the theater—new, comfortable theater chairs were installed in 2004. There's no parking lot, so you'll have to try your luck on the street with the locals who come to the Ken regularly to see something other than the standard new Hollywood fare.

If you're in La Jolla and looking for fun and unusual film entertainment, head up to the **La Jolla Village Cinemas** (8879 Villa La Jolla Dr., 619/819-0236). This four-screener shows a variety of different styles of movie, from independent to foreign to popular. Enjoy better-than-average concessions, plus an array of good food and drink centered right around the theater. If you're looking for a midnight movie experience, call and see if they're running something while you're in town.

# Shopping

Shopping in San Diego runs primarily to malls and shopping centers that offer a good, if selective, experience. Downtown, wander the Gaslamp Quarter for San Diego—grown clothing or hit the immense Horton Plaza for stores you know. Old Town is fun for unique, Mexican souvenirs and is a short jump from Mission Valley where the mall is king. Farther north, La Jolla provides a more relaxed, upscale experience.

## DOWNTOWN
### Gaslamp Quarter

As you stroll the streets of the Gaslamp Quarter you'll find many stores are local chains, like the **San Diego Trading Company** (534 Fifth Ave., 619/237-0062, www.sandiegotrading company.com) or surfing/resort wear purveyors such as **Hilo Hattie's** (301 Fifth Ave., 619/546-7289, www.hilohattie.com) and **Quiksilver Boardriders Club** (402 Fifth Ave., 619/234-3125, www.quiksilver.com).

For the ladies, trendy clothes are sold at **Mango Clothing** (230 Fifth Ave., 619/237-1344). Men looking for serious suits go to **Boutique Voss** (946 Fifth Ave., 619/235-8999), a purveyor of fine Italian designer fashions.

In casual California, it makes sense to find several stores devoted to the sale of jeans. **G-Star** (470 Fifth Ave., 619/283-7088, www .g-star.com) offers fun, eclectic men's and women's wear made mostly from denim. You'll find familiar jeans, jackets, and accessories inside the chain **Lucky Brand Jeans** (621 Fifth Ave., 619/230-9260, www.luckybrandjeans.com).

While the district's gaslamps don't glow red anymore, you can find some risqué items here, most a couple of blocks off the main drag. The large **Hustler** (929 Sixth Ave., 619/696-9007, www.hustlerhollywood.com) chain has a presence here. This huge, two-floor emporium is astonishingly well-lit and woman friendly. The downstairs area is devoted to lingerie and novelty items—things that can be displayed in the big plate-glass windows. Upstairs, you'll find the good stuff, including young, friendly employees who will be happy to help you with any product needs you might have. A huge toy wall has something for every woman's needs, and the DVD collection makes men swoon with... er...joy. Be sure to check out the fun foam sex chairs and couches while you're up there! A small but sweet selection of home stores hang out in the Gaslamp. You can check out the latest styles at the familiar **Z Gallerie** (611 Fifth Ave., 619/696-8137, www.zgallerie.com) or the funky **Avitatt** (232 Fifth Ave., 619/338-8245, www.avitatt.com). Specialty items of obvious types are available at **Kita Ceramics + Glassware** (517 Fourth Ave. #101, 619/239-2600, www.kitaceramicsglass.com), **Urban Lighting** (301 Fourth Ave., 619/232-6064, www.urbanlighting.net), and **Fourth Avenue Rug Gallery** (827 Fourth Ave., 619/234-8700).

## Horton Plaza

Looking for a big mall to gather all your favorite shops together into one place? Visit Westfield Horton Plaza (324 Horton Plaza, San Diego, 619/239-8180, www.westfield.com/hortonplaza, Mon.–Fri. 10 A.M.–9 P.M., Sat. 10 A.M.–8 P.M., Sun. 11 A.M.–7 P.M.). With all the standard Westfield mall amenities, including day spas, salons, and plenty of food options, you'll feel right at home here.

Many of your favorite midrange to upscale chain boutiques make a home at Horton Plaza. Shop at Baby Gap, Bebe, Guess, and Victoria's Secret, among others. Horton Plaza also offers an immense array of jewelry shops, accessory stores, and leather boutiques, from Coach and Louis Vuitton for the stylish adult looking for handbags to Metal Zone and Stone Waterfall for younger shoppers looking for hot new jewelry. For shoes, you'll find everything from Crocs to Foot Locker.

## OLD TOWN
### Bazaar del Mundo

A perfect way to experience shopping in Mexico without making the trek down to Tijuana is to visit Old Town's famed Bazaar del Mundo (4133 Taylor St., 619/296-3161, Sun.–Mon. 10 A.M.–5:30 P.M., Tues.–Sat. 10 A.M.–9 P.M.). Easily accessed from I-5 and I-8, this cheerful

and colorful shopping center brings the best of Mexico across the border. From the familiar figures in the **Laurel Burch Gallerita** to the unusual and often elegant imports of **Artes,** you'll find perfect gifts for everyone on your list (and for yourself, of course). When you come down to the Bazaar, come hungry! Some of the best and most visitor-friendly Mexican food is served here (see *Food*).

## Fashion Valley

Another big urban mall, Fashion Valley (7007 Friars Rd., 619/688-9113, www.simon.com/mall, Mon.–Sat. 10 A.M.–7 P.M., Sun. 11 A.M.–7 P.M.) has plenty of the shopping experience you desire. A bit higher end than Horton Plaza, Fashion Valley focuses more on the home and offers some designer boutiques.

Appropriately, fashions for men, women, and children of all ages abound at Fashion Valley. Kids can grow up here, going from Gymboree to GapKids and on up to The Limited Too. Gentlemen have a number of options for all parts of life, from the casual times at J. Crew and Old Navy to more formal situations in Bernini, Gucci, and After Hours Formal Wear.

Not surprisingly, women have the most clothing options here at the mall. The mature crowd prefers Ann Taylor and Talbots, while the teens and twenties shoppers flock to Abercrombie & Fitch and Forever 21. For inexpensive and sporting shoes, run to Footlocker or Shiek Shoes. Fancy sunglasses peek out the windows at Occhiala da Sole and thousands of watches keep the time inside Tourneau.

## LA JOLLA

Shopping in La Jolla feels a little like a spending spree in the sophisticated areas of Los Angeles. This upscale suburb prides itself on its walking-and-shopping, much of which is centered around Prospect Street. Be sure to veer off onto the side streets, which hide some true gems!

## Prospect La Jolla

Big name and upscale chain stores rent space on Prospect, as do locally owned one-of-a-kind boutiques. You can go lingerie shopping at **Victoria's Secret** (1111 Prospect St., 858/459-0688, www.victoriassecret.com) or the unique **Neroli** (7944 Girard Ave., 858/456-9618). Look for monochromatic women's wear at **White House/Black Market** (7927 Girard Ave., 858/459-2565, www.white houseblackmarket.com), or a matching man's tuxedo at **Imperial Taylor and Formal Wear** (7744 Fay Ave., 858/459-8891). Dozens more apparel stores, from the casual to the highest of high-end cluster in La Jolla.

Naturally, only the funkiest or fanciest jewels will do to complement the lovely clothing sold in La Jolla (a town whose name translates as "The Jewel"). You can browse in dozens of jewelry stores, from reasonably priced costume jewelry all the way up to designer diamonds. For

something fun and unique, head for **The Artful Soul** (7660 Fay Ave., 858/459-2009, www.artfulsoul.com) to check out everything from earrings and bracelets to purses and belts, all sparkling and creatively designed. For local fine jewelry, visit **Jewels by the Sea** (1237 Prospect St. B, 858/459-5166) and **Jewel of La Jolla** (1250 Prospect St., Ste B20, 858/729-1849).

Elegant antique stores cluster in La Jolla, beckoning wealthy patrons to furnish and decorate their homes with the beautiful artifacts of the past. Pick up a great new piece for your collection at shops such as **AJA Antiques & Art** (955 Prospect St. E, 858/459-0333), **Renaissance Art and Antiques** (7715 Fay Ave., 858/454-3887), or the **Girard Avenue Collection** (7505 Girard Ave., 858/459-7765).

# Sports and Recreation

San Diego has more than its share of sunny days year-round, so get outside! With dozens of miles of beaches, zoos, parks, trails, and endless opportunities for recreation, even the most dedicated couch potatoes can find something great to do under the famed California sun.

## BEACHES

If you come to San Diego, you must go to the beach. It's an imperative. From Encinitas and Del Mar down almost to the Mexican border, the California coast shows off its best. The San Diego beaches all seem to be 100 yards wide, perfectly flat, 100 percent pale, soft, sugar sand, and run as far in either direction as the eye can see. A few rocks appear in spots, but they're few and far between (especially in comparison to the rugged northern coastline). Bring your towel, umbrella, sunscreen, swimsuit, and surfboard. And if it's a weekend in the summertime, come early in the morning to stake a prime spot in the sand.

For a list of beaches maintained by the City of San Diego, check out this website: www.sandiego.gov/lifeguards/beaches.

## Ocean Beach

Yes, the Ocean Beach (1950 Abbot St., Ocean Beach, 24 hours/day) sandy spot is part of the community of Ocean Beach townlet. Small for a San Diego beach, this one-mile stretch of sand beckons locals and visitors alike with its lifeguard-protected waters, multi-use areas, and famous Dog Beach. On Dog Beach, at the north end of Ocean Beach, dogs are allowed off-leash all day, every day. (Please clean up after your dog!) Farther south, you'll find designated areas for fishing, surfing, and swimming. Check with the lifeguards to figure out which is which. Be aware that rip currents can be strong at Ocean Beach, and take care when you're out in the water. At the south end of the beach, you can take a walk out on the Ocean Beach pier; some people even bring a pole to spend some quiet time fishing out on the pier.

If you need a restroom or showers, head for the main lifeguard station at Abbot Street, which has both. Lifeguards stay on duty from 9 A.M. to dusk daily. Amazingly ample parking can be found at three lots that range from the south to the north end of the beach. (The smallest lot is the one by the lifeguard station; go north or south for better parking opportunities.)

## Black's Beach

Black's Beach (south of Torrey Pines State Beach) sits north of downtown La Jolla, and this local's favorite finds fame as a surf break; head for the south end of the two-mile beachfront to find the best surfing. But pause a second before grabbing your board and clambering down the cliffs: Black's doubles as a well-known nude beach.

The main difficulty with Black's Beach is getting there. As an unofficial beach without a permanent lifeguard station, you won't find any parking lots; you'll have to do the best you can on the street. No well-built or easily climbed stairways lead down to Black's, so you can either scramble down the cliff paths, or take your chances with the tides and enter from an adjacent beach to the north or south. Finally, lifeguards are stationed here in the summer months only and the waters are unregulated, so be extremely careful of your fellow surfers and swimmers!

## Coronado Main Beach

The can't-miss Hotel del Coronado marks the Coronado Main Beach (Ocean Blvd.). Anyone can walk through the outdoor common areas of the Del to get out to this charming sandy beach. Yet another fabulous sun-drenched chunk of coastline, the Coronado Main Beach gets ultra-crowded in the summertime, so come early if you want a prime spot of your own. Do pay attention to the signs and flags—a nasty breakwater of large boulders hides under the water just in front of the Del at high tide. Also take a look at the odd-shaped dunes; from the air, they spell out "Del Coronado."

## Del Mar City Beach

Running along the length of downtown Del Mar, without tons of easy parking, Del Mar City Beach (15th St. and Coast Blvd. to the Rivermouth, Del Mar) is touted as one of the best beaches in an area famous for its welcoming sands. This huge strip of coastline has

it all. The soft sand invites sunbathers, who can spend all day soaking up rays. The ocean beckons, the cool Pacific making a perfect counterpoint to hot San Diego summer days. A decent surf break near the center of City Beach beckons to new and experienced wave riders alike. (You can even take surf lessons here.) Lifeguards protect the shores, complete with the *Baywatch*-esque pale blue towers that mark all guarded San Diego county beaches. Be sure to pay attention to the colored flags on the beach. Blue means swimming is okay, and a yellow flag with a black ball means *no surfing* in the surrounding area.

Once you find a place on the street to park (bring quarters for the meters) getting onto the beach is easy. The area is flat and simple to access, and in some places boardwalks and paths make beach access even simpler. Just off the beach, the Powerhouse community center offers restrooms, a restaurant, and a community theater.

## SURFING

With its endless sunshine, temperate water, and magnificent breaks, San Diego offers some of the best surfing in California. You can surf year-round down here, though San Diego is not the South Pacific and wet suits can be a good idea in winter.

The average water temperature of the Pacific Ocean in summer stands at 65–70°F—perfect for surfing, snorkeling, diving, kayaking, or just plain old swimming.

### Surf Breaks

San Diego boasts plenty of classic southern California surfing. For the coolest local breaks, you'll have to consult the coolest locals. But even the more popular spots offer reliable breaks. In La Jolla, **Black's Beach** is both a local's favorite and visitor's joy. Modest surfers beware: Black's also operates as a nude beach. **Del Mar City Beach** (15th St. and Coast Blvd. to the Rivermouth, Del Mar), in addition to being a great sandy spot to hang out, offers fine beginning and intermediate waves. **Mission Beach** has a good break as well as lifeguards, restroom facilities, and about a zillion tourists and sun worshippers in the summertime. If you're serious about surfing, check out **Windansea Beach** (6800 Neptune Pl.), which has a heavy shore break and a rockier coastline than most of San Diego—and therefore fewer sunbathers and swimmers hanging out here. You will find dense crowds of fellow surfers, so this isn't the best spot for beginners to try out their boards. On the other hand, the small, consistent waves at **La Jolla Shores** (8200 Camino del Oro, La Jolla) bore the hardcore masters, but are perfect for novice surfers. Just stick within the lifeguard-designated surfing areas to avoid the swimmers and scuba divers sharing the water here.

## Surf Schools

Never ridden a wave before? Always wanted to? Check out one of San Diego's many surf schools. You'll go to a small-wave beach, learn the basics of the sport on dry land, then paddle out for the first time. Most schools promise to get you up and riding (if only for a few seconds) the very first time! Or if you've come to Southern California specifically to surf, check with the schools about multi-day, all-inclusive (lodging too!) "surf camps" that get you surfing all day, every day for a few days or a whole week.

Surfari (3740 Mission Blvd., 858/337-3287, www.surfarisurf.com, $50/day group lesson, $75/day private lesson, start times 9 A.M., 11 A.M., 1 P.M., 3 P.M.) was started by competitive surfer Rick Gehris and operates close to downtown San Diego at Mission Beach. Each 2.5-hour lesson includes land instruction, interactive in-the-water instruction, and an hour afterward on your own to play. Regular group lessons happen almost every day of the year. For a more intense learning experience, book a discounted three-day lesson series.

The **San Diego Surfing Academy** (800/447-7873, www.surfingacademy.com, $60/group lesson, $55/hour private) runs year-round at the north end of South Carlsbad State Beach Campgrounds. You must make an appointment to take lessons with the SDSA, but the quality of instruction makes it worth the bother. All equipment is included in the fee—perfect for hours of fun surfing the waves of the North Coast. With two-hour group classes and by-the-hour private lessons, this safety-oriented school makes certain you'll know what you're doing out there in the surf. If you want to take your surfing to the next level, look into SDSA's surf camps, which include meals, tent cabin lodgings, and photos of you out on your board.

If you're female, and you want to learn to surf but you find the male-dominated sport intimidating, come out to **Surf Diva** (2160 Avenida de la Playa, La Jolla, 858/454-8273, www.surfdiva.com, $65/hour private lessons, $135/two-day clinic). The first all-women's surf school in the world, Surf Diva creates an estrogen-friendly, supportive atmosphere for girls ages five and up to learn the ins and outs of the waves at La Jolla Shores. (The "Guys on the Side" semi-private and group lessons include men too!) Book a private lesson, or take a two- to five-day clinic to get serious about the sport. Lessons at Surf Diva can make a fun and creative start to your best friend's bachelorette party!

### Board and Equipment Rental

Most of the surf schools, including **Surfari** and **Surf Diva,** rent and sell boards, leashes, wetsuits, and board care equipment—everything you need for your first surf set-up, and repair and replacement equipment if you're an expert.

## BOATING

In Mission Bay and San Diego Bay, the calm waters make great fun of all forms of boating, from paddle-boating to waterskiing to sailing. Kayaking is a special local favorite pastime, especially for would-be explorers of the famous La Jolla Caves. If you plan to exit the bays for the open ocean, be sure you're either competent to navigate a watercraft on the open sea, or have somebody with you who can do it. Watch the weather reports, and pay attention to local experts.

### Power Boating and Waterskiing

On the calm waters of the two bays, you can water-ski and wakeboard, dash around on a Jet-Ski, or just cruise offshore in a speedboat. **Seaforth**

**Boat Rentals** (888/834-2628, www.seaforth boatrentals.com, $35–145) has three locations: in Mission Bay, downtown San Diego, and Coronado. If you're planning to cruise, rent one of the large (up to 240 horsepower) speedboats, which has plenty of room for passengers, coolers, and snacks. If you've got an athletic crew with you, reserve a ski boat. They come with wakeboards, ski tubes, skis. For a more motorcycle-like on-the-water experience, pick up a modern, powerful Jet-Ski that rides 2–3 people.

Another multi-boat rental outfit with several locations in and around San Diego is **Action Sport Rentals** (858/581-5939, www.action sportrentals.com, $95–150). Rent yourself a three-seater Jet-Ski or a six- or seven-passenger speedboat and tool around the bays. For a bigger party, Action offers 13-passenger power pontoon boats. If you want to water-ski or wakeboard but don't have anyone to drive the boat, reserve some time with Action's professional driver. You'll get rides on whatever type of toy (wakeboard, skis, kneeboard, tube) you want behind their competitive-class ski boat.

### Sailing

Whether you want a quiet putter around the bay or an exhilarating adventure on the open ocean, you can get just the sailing experience you want in San Diego. **Seaforth Boat Rentals** (888/834-2628, www.seaforthboat rentals.com) offers rental sailboats from 14 to 36 feet. You can also book a sailing lesson, or even hire a captain to take care of the practicalities while you and your party enjoy a glass of wine and a meal or snack on the water.

### Kayaking

With so many calm, protected bays, plus an array of exciting sea caves, it's no wonder that San Diego boasts some of the best sea kayaking in the state. Whether you've got your own boat or you plan to rent or take a tour, the most popular spot to paddle are the La Jolla Caves, part of the larger **La Jolla Cove Ecological Reserve** (1100 Coast Blvd., www.sandiego .gov). **Scuba San Diego** (619/260-1880, www .scubasandiego.com) offers guided paddles of

this well-traveled area. You don't need any previous sea kayaking experience to take this easy two-hour tour; the sit-on-top kayaks are easy to get into and out of, and safe if you happen to fall off. On the tour, you'll visit soaring sea cliffs and a vast kelp forest, and paddle through the famed local sea caves.

### SNORKELING AND SCUBA

The reefs and wrecks off San Diego offer amazing sights, clear waters, and brightly colored sea life—whether you want a guided tour or go off on your own.

A great place to enjoy a calm snorkel with your family is the **La Jolla Cove.** Make a reservation with a professional outfit such as **Scuba San Diego, Inc** (619/260-1880, www .scubasandiego.com) to take a guided tour of the La Jolla Cove Ecological Reserve. They also offer an exciting night dive, and a Scuba Adventure trip for new divers who are not yet certified. Or bring your own (or rent some) equipment and kick off the shore on your own (with at least one friend, of course).

Looking for a deeper dive experience? Take a scuba trip to one of the San Diego area's many fabulous dive locations. Depending on your interests, you can view the abundance of life in the La Jolla Outer Reef, human history and mechanical failure at Wreck Alley, or the undersea forest at the Giant Kelp Beds.

### FISHING

Any number of charter companies offer half- to full-day deep sea fishing trips for everything from rock cod to yellowfin tuna and mahi-mahi, depending on the season. Most companies include both Mexican and California fishing licenses with your charter as needed, as well as rental or included tackle and fish cleaning and filleting services. The tuna season (for fishing well offshore for large tuna) runs from early summer through the fall most years.

Leaving right out of the San Diego harbor, **H&M Landing** (2803 Emerson St., 619/222-1144, www.hmlanding.com, half-day adults $40, tackle $9.50) offers half-, three-quarter-, full-day, and evening trips year-round.

Shorter trips ply the Point Loma kelp beds, while longer trips can head out to the Coronado Islands or farther into the open water. **Seaforth Sportfishing** (1717 Quivira Rd., 619/224-3383, www.seaforthlanding.com, tackle extra) offers half-day through multi-day trips to fish for most of the major species fishable in the San Diego area. You can even catch a barracuda! Seaforth's year-round half-day trips last five hours (morning or afternoon), allow the catching of more than half a dozen types of fish, and are perfect for families with children or new anglers. Three-quarter day trips really last all day (eight hours) and can range down as far as the Coronado Islands in Mexico. The Overnight Mexico and Multi-Day Tuna trips are best for more experienced fishers who don't suffer from too much seasickness, and are looking to reel in a bigger catch. On any Seaforth trip, expect a full galley with snacks, meals, and beverage service. You can get a bay skiff for $40 per half-day, plus rent tackle and buy live bait.

**Point Loma Sportfishing** (1403 Scott St., 619/223-1627, www.pointlomasportfishing.com, adults half-day from $40, multi-day from $250, tackle extra) offers more than six boats and an extensive list of fishing options. With Point Loma, hardcore anglers can book a two-week cruise that ranges more than 1,000 miles from San Diego, going after enormous deep-water tuna and other major-league sport fish. On the other hand, several of Point Loma's boats offer sedate, family- and beginner-friendly half-day (six hours) and three-quarter-day (8–10 hours) trips for rockfish, sea bass, barracuda, and yellowtail near the San Diego and northern Mexico coastlines. Private charter boats are available for parties of 5–25.

For small groups looking to fish together, **Action Sport Rentals** (2580 Ingraham St., 619/226-2929, www.danalanding.com) at Dana Landing maintains a fleet of six-passenger fishing boats that can handle half-day to two-day fishing trips. Action Sport Rentals offers bay-safe skiffs, tackle, and bait year-round. You'll also find a launch there if you've brought your own boat.

## WHALE-WATCHING

If you prefer to catch marine life with your camera rather than a hook and line, consider taking a whale-watching cruise out from the San Diego coastline. Most of the sportfishing outfits also offer whale-watching trips and charters in season (winter through mid-spring). **Hornblower Cruises** (1066 N. Harbor Dr., 619/686-8700, www.hornblower.com) offers daily nature cruises at 9:30 A.M. and 1:30 P.M. year-round. This nearly four-hour adventure is great for families, and includes a kid-friendly marine habitat video; seal, sea lion, and dolphin viewing; and guaranteed whale spotting. Hornblower offers one of the most comfortable, tourist-friendly sea experiences, with a snack bar, indoor decks with panel windows for good viewing, and a yacht highly rated for its stability.

## AIR SPORTS

With a strong military history and endlessly fabulous weather, it's no wonder that aviation-based sports are a big deal in San Diego.

### Flying and Skydiving

Yes, you really can go to "war" during your otherwise tranquil vacation in San Diego. **Biplane Air Combat & Warbird Flights** (800/759-5667, www.barnstorming.com, $200–450 per person, depending on type of flight) offers the rare opportunity to fly an air combat mission in a light plane designed for dogfighting. Or take a ride in an SNJ-4 Texan, a real World War II aircraft. For a more peaceful aviation experience, book a scenic flight for one or two people in an old-fashioned biplane.

If you prefer jumping out of planes to riding in them, head up north to **Skydive Elsinore** (20701 Cereal St., Lake Elsinore, 951/245-9939, www.skydiveelsinore.com). This full-service skydiving school and outfitter can take you on a great jump, regardless of your experience level. Beginners can take a tandem jump after a brief introductory lesson, or go more intensive with a full-fledged skydiving course culminating with a solo jump. If you're a more experienced jumper, take a look at the website for your diving options.

## Gliding

For perhaps the most unusual views of northern San Diego County you can get, go **Sky Sailing** (31930 Hwy. 79, Warner Springs, 760/782-0404, www.skysailing.com, daily, scenic trips from $70/person, lessons from $110). In a silent glider or "sail plane," you'll catch thermal updrafts, see Palomar Mountain and Warner Springs Ranch, and feel the wonder of birdlike flight. If you're interested in sightseeing, make a weekday reservation or just drop by on the weekend for a flight flown by an FAA-certified pilot. If it's actually flying a glider yourself that lights your fire, book a lesson or rent a glider of your own. (Hand-controlled gliders are available for pilots with special needs.) And if you've got a strong stomach and great faith in your ability to survive, ask about the Sensational Aerobatic Rides.

If you prefer the notion of gliding off a sea cliff into the air above the Pacific Ocean, your destination is the **Torrey Pines Glider Port** (2800 Torrey Pines Scenic Dr., 858/452-9858, La Jolla, $150–175 for a 20-minute tandem flight). Here you can book a tandem flight on either a hang glider or a paraglider with only 20 minutes of pre-flight instruction. The specialty of the house is paragliding, and you can sign up for lessons and get certified to paraglide all on your own.

## GOLF

With fabulous sunny weather year-round, San Diego and its surrounding countryside are a golfer's dream. Wherever you go, you'll find a course or two awaiting you, from easy nine-holers up to U.S. Open hosts. If you're new to the area, consider calling **Showtime Golf** (888/661-2334, www.showtimegolf.com). This golf service provider can get you advance or last-minute tee times, book you into local tournaments, and answer all your questions about the vast range of golfing options in the San Diego area.

If you know anything about golf in San Diego and La Jolla, you know that the One True Golf Course here is **Torrey Pines** (11480 N. Torrey Pines Rd., La Jolla, 858/452-3226, www.torreypinesgolfcourse.com). Home of the 2008 U.S. Open, the Torrey Pines Golf Course has two championship 18-hole courses. Plan to book well in advance for a tee time at this gorgeous course.

## HIKING

In addition to walks on the beach, the **Torrey Pines State Reserve** (North Torrey Pines Rd., 858/755-2063, www.torreypine.org, daily sunrise–sunset) offers some unusually beautiful wilderness trails. Be sure to look for *Pinus torreyana*—the rarest species of pine tree in the United States. The shortest walk is the High Point Trail, only 100 yards up to views of the whole reserve, from the ocean to the lagoon to the forest and back. For an easy, under one-hour walk, take the Guy Fleming Trail for a level two-thirds of a mile through forest, wildflower patches, and views of the ocean. For a longer walk, leave the visitors center by the road, then take the North Fork Trail west to the Broken Hill Trail, which will bring you right down to the beach stairway and a great view of Flat Rock.

## CASINO GAMBLING

If your first love is a night donating money to the local Native American tribe, a number of casinos outside the city proper can hook you up.

A few miles east of San Diego, two casinos offer a good time. **Club Sycuan** (5469 Casino Way, El Cajon, 619/445-6002, www.sycuan.com) sits in the suburb of El Cajon. This casino and resort offers fun for all comers, with a hotel, several restaurants (including a buffet), a golf course, tennis courts, and gaming floors. At Club Sycuan, you'll find thousands of slot machines, plus an array of table games including blackjack, pai gow poker, mini-baccarat, roulette, and craps. You can also enjoy the tension of the Bingo Palace and the smoke-free atmosphere of the Poker Room. Vegas-style stage acts entertain weary gamers and golfers in the evening.

Nope, that's not a Back East boarding school. That big, classically styled building east of La Jolla is actually the **Barona Valley Ranch Resort and Casino** (1932 Wildcat Canyon Rd., San Diego, 619/443-2300, www.barona.com). This upscale resort brings a touch of class to the Las Vegas–style casino. Stay in the large, posh hotel (that's the big building), eat dinner at the Steakhouse or the Buffet and grab lunch at the noodle house, pamper yourself in the day spa or out at the pool, or play around at the Barona Creek Golf Club. Finally, hit the casino for plenty of up-to-date loose slots plus 70 table games, including craps, roulette, cash baccarat, and much more. You can also hang out in the poker room, or play the ponies at the off-track betting parlor.

While no casinos grace the North County coastline, if you're vacationing in Del Mar or Encinitas, gaming possibilities lurk only a few miles east. You'll find part of the ever-popular **Harrah's** (777 Harrah's Rincon Way, Valley Center, 877/777-2457, www.harrahs rincon.com) chain off Highway 76 northeast of Oceanside. The typical Harrah's tower rises high over the tiny town of Valley Center, offering over 600 hotel rooms, nine different eateries (including an oyster bar, a buffet, and a coffee house), and a full-service spa. The gaming rooms offer hundreds of slots, a World Series of Poker room, and plenty of table games, including craps, roulette bingo, and blackjack. To cool off in the heat of summer, rent a cabana or pull up a chaise lounge at the gorgeous two-tiered pool.

Yet another large, blocky, luxurious casino, the **Pala Casino Resort and Spa** (11154 Hwy. 76, Pala, 877/946-7252, www.palacasino.com) dominates the landscape on hot, dry Highway 76 east of Oceanside. The dining options are especially fine here; you can get entertainment with your meal at Mama's Cucina Italia, a casual Asian meal at Noodles, all you can eat at the Terrace Buffet, or elegance at The Oak Room. Entertainment also comes big at the Pala, with two large theaters (one indoor, one outdoor), a lounge, and an event center. In the casino proper, you'll find the largest array of new slot machines in the area, plus more than 80 table games. A high-limit room offers fun for high rollers, and a smoke-free room provides relief for sensitive noses who still want to play.

## SPECTATOR SPORTS
### San Diego Chargers
Are you ready for some football, without snow, sleet, or freezing rain of the back east outdoor stadiums? Then grab tickets to **Qualcomm Stadium** (entrance on Friars Rd., www.san diego.gov/qualcomm) in the Mission Valley neighborhood. The San Diego Chargers (www .chargers.com) are a good team in the AFC West, and they tend to make the playoffs most years (albeit as a wildcard in 2007–2008). If you're driving in, plan to arrive at the parking lot at least two hours early since the lot often fills up and even closes an hour before kickoff. Also, try to avoid going in or out via Highway 15, which is the most congested route to the stadium. A better way to get there might be the Mission Trolley System (MTS), which has special event bus service to the stadium, as well as regular stops at Qualcomm on the Blue and Green trolley lines. The NTCD system also provides express bus service to all home games.

Once you've made it into the stadium, you'll find ample food, drink, restrooms, souvenirs, ID bracelets for your kids, and first aid and other services throughout. Alcohol sales are limited and end at the close of the third quarter. For a more posh NFL experience, check whether tickets are available at the club level, which has squishier seats and a wait staff.

### San Diego Padres
While you're in San Diego, why not take yourself and your family out to a baseball game? The San Diego Padres (http://sandiego.padres. mlb.com) play throughout the regular season (and hopefully into the World Series) at **Petco Park** (100 Park Blvd., 619/795-5000) in downtown San Diego. Few rain-outs mar the Padres' home season, and in addition to the game, you can view Balboa Park, the cityscape, and San Diego Bay from the lovely and spacious modern stadium. Sit back with a brew or a soda, enjoy the extra leg room, and bask in the perfect spring baseball weather of San Diego.

Petco Park is well situated for fans who prefer to avoid the inevitable parking nightmares and take public transit in to the game. The MTS trolleys and buses have multiple stops within a block or two of the ballpark, and the Coaster rail line offers extra trains on game nights for fans coming in from the North County towns. If you're staying in the Gaslamp Quarter, consider just walking over to the stadium from your lodgings. If you must drive, prepare to pay $8–15 for downtown lot parking and $20 for a slot right by the park.

### Del Mar Racetrack and Fairgrounds

In horseracing season, you'll find significant crowds descending on the tiny town of Del Mar and its coastside neighbors. All these folks are intent on the famous **Del Mar Fairgrounds** (2260 Jimmy Durante Blvd., Del Mar, 858/755-1141, www.sdfair.com), where some of the finest thoroughbreds ever to grace a track have raced to victory. The track was built in the late 1930s, with Bing Crosby supplying both funds and fame to create the glorious equestrian facilities that continue to delight race and horse fans to this day. The various structures at the Fairgrounds are built in the style of various California missions, and careful attention to detail has created possibly the most beautiful permanent indoor-outdoor exhibition facilities in the state.

Races usually run from July through early September. Wagering rules can be found at the track or on the Fairgrounds website, as can information about the off-season telecast racing series. Come out and join in the excitement of live thoroughbred racing in one of the most hospitable climates in the world! Show up on Friday afternoons to enjoy a concert by a big-name band in addition to the races.

If you prefer a different style of equestrian event, come to Del Mar a little bit earlier in the year for the **Del Mar National Horse Show** (www.sdfair.com/horseshow). This event lasts three weeks each spring, with a full week each devoted to Western events, dressage, and hunter/jumper activities. Be sure to book your room and buy tickets in advance, as this is one of the most popular horse shows in the western United States each year.

Any number of other events take place at the Fairgrounds every month of the year. Check the website for a calendar of upcoming events, plus ticket information. Ample pay parking surrounds the Fairgrounds, or if you're taking the train, grab a free shuttle from the Coaster straight to the racetrack.

**SAN DIEGO**

## Accommodations

### DOWNTOWN

Acres of hotels cluster throughout downtown San Diego. Whether you need a budget hostel or want a high-end luxury resort, you'll find it. Many mid-tier and upscale chains offer bed and board downtown—all you have to do is walk around to find the Sheraton, Hilton, or Holiday Inn. For a more interesting lodging experience, look to the smaller chains and the independents.

### Under $100

Looking for budget accommodations in the heart of San Diego? For a start, call the **HI-San Diego** (521 Market St., 800/909-4776, www.sandiegohostels.org, $20–30). Located perfectly right in the middle of the Gaslamp Quarter, you can get just about anywhere from this almost-elegant youth hostel. (Bring your HI card for lower rates!) Inside, you'll find private and double rooms, as well as dorm rooms that sleep 4–10 people in single beds. The amenities include all standard hostel fare: coin-op laundry, an open kitchen, common rooms with and without TVs, and a garden area. Plan to bring or buy a lock for the lockers provided in the dorm rooms. The hostel's packed events calendar includes free walking tours of Balboa Park and the downtown area, and regular free trips down to Tijuana. Between the food and nightlife of the Gaslamp and the endless stream of interesting people and activities, the HI-San Diego is the perfect resting place for young people visiting San Diego.

Looking for a Mediterranean-style student hotel? Try the **Hotel Occidental** (410 Elm St.,

619/232-1336, www.hoteloccidental-sandiego
.com, $80–150). Located only a block and a
half from the entrance to Balboa Park, you
can visit the zoo and museums, or head downtown to the Gaslamp Quarter. Don't expect
tons of in-room luxury here—smaller rooms
share baths, and even some of the larger
rooms have only a half-bath, with shower facilities down the hall. Decor feels European
(in the Ikea sense when it comes to furniture), with lots of clean lines and plain linens
and small, ingeniously used spaces. Hotel-
wide amenities include free Wi-Fi, complimentary continental breakfast, and private
kitchenettes that let you keep some of your
own food rather than depending on restaurants for every meal.

## $100-150

With enough rooms for a medium-sized motel,
but the feel of a small inn, **La Pensione Hotel**
(606 W. Date St., 800/232-4683, www.la
pensionehotel.com, $100–110) prides itself
on offering the best value in the best location
in downtown San Diego. The exterior blends
the look of a Mediterranean home with the
Spanish Colonial Revival style of Southern
California. Inside, each room has one queen-
sized bed, unusual photographic wall art, and
a clean bathroom. It's not posh or plush, but
you'll find comfort. The hotel is located in
Little Italy, within easy walking distance of
great restaurants and cafés, and only blocks
from the Gaslamp Quarter. The staff can help
you with taxis and public transit, making it
possible to avoid driving.

La Pensione does not have as many off-street
parking spots as they do rooms, so parking is
limited during the high season. And if you're
bringing your kids, be aware that trundle beds
and such are not available, and the hotel requests that only two people stay in any one
room.

## Over $250

For a fun hotel stay downtown, hit the exclusive **W Hotel San Diego** (421 W. B St.,
619/398-3100, www.starwoodhotels.com,

$250–300). This swanky, ultra-modern hotel
has the perfect location—convenient to the
airport, walking distance to the harbor, and a
short jaunt to the fabulous restaurants in the
Gaslamp Quarter. Upper-level guest rooms
offer views of city and the bay. Rooms feature cushy beds with featherbeds and down
comforters, and are done in an almost-indus-
trial, urban-chic style that echoes the grander
decor of the entrance, lobby, and bars. Despite
the hard lines and cool blue-and-silver color
scheme, touches of whimsy abound. (Be sure
to take a moment to read the labels on your
toiletries—it's worth the time.) But best of
all, the service here is exceptional, even in
this tourist-friendly region. Just call down,
and anything you want will be at your door-
step, probably in about 15 minutes. You'll find
every amenity you could dream of, from 24-
hour room service to first-aid kits to Wi-Fi
to condoms—but beware, none of these are
complimentary.

For a fun night out without the hassle of a
car or a cab, head up to The Beach, the W's
bar created with real sand and fruity umbrella
drinks to mimic an actual SoCal beach scene.

If you want to stay in *the* classic San Diego
hotel and you've got the money to do it,
book a room at the ◖ **US Grant Hotel** (326
Broadway, 619/232-3121, www.starwoodhotels
.com, $350). Built in 1910, the US Grant has
anchored the Gaslamp Quarter for almost 100
years. Inside, you'll be showered with luxury,
from the elegant lobby to the in-house spa to
the gorgeous guest rooms (which include luxurious showers). Even the standard guest rooms
have plush linens, original artwork, and the
many amenities that mark the US Grant as
worth the cost of admission.

For additional pampering, make an appointment for an in-room or in-spa massage with
Spa Velia. You've got all the restaurant options
of the Gaslamp within staggering distance, or
you can stay in the hotel and dine at the upscale California-style Grant Grill. Whether
your interests are surfing or golfing, the concierges can help you with arrangements for activities around the city.

## BALBOA PARK AND HILLCREST

Lodgings right by the park aren't plentiful. For a better selection, check out downtown and Old Town, which are within easy public transit and driving distance to the wonders of Balboa Park and the fun of Hillcrest.

### $100-150

Looking to stay at an inn that evokes the true spirit of San Diego? Try the Spanish-Colonial Revival-style **Balboa Park Inn** (3402 Park Blvd., 619/298-0823, www.balboaparkinn .com, $100–250). This funky boutique hotel offers 26 unique rooms and suites with names like Harlequin and Emma's Diary, each beautiful in its own decorative style. Smaller rooms just offer a simple bed-and-bath setup, while the more numerous suites offer multiple rooms, kitchens, decks, and often more than one bed. Balboa Park Inn is the perfect place for families looking for moderate prices and the attractions of Balboa Park. Situated just north of the park, you can walk from the inn to the San Diego Zoo. The quiet neighborhood isn't much for nightlife, but offers peace for visitors who long for a good night's sleep.

Another small, stylish charmer is the **Hillcrest Inn** (3754 5th Ave., 800/258-2280, www.hillcrestinn.net, $120–150). Situated in the up-and-coming Hillcrest neighborhood within a few minutes' drive of Balboa Park, this small hotel offers entirely acceptable rooms at reasonable prices. While amenities aren't luxe, you will get a TV, refrigerator, microwave, and clean private bathroom, as well as access to the hotel's outdoor spa. Around the Hillcrest area, you'll find the center of San Diego's gay culture, plus easy access to Downtown and the Gaslamp Quarter. If you can snag an unmetered on-street parking spot, take it, since parking at the inn costs extra. Luckily, lots of restaurants, shops, parks, bars, and clubs are within easy walking distance of the inn, so you may only need to park once.

Only a few blocks' walk from the center of the Hillcrest neighborhood, **Kasa Korbett - Hillcrest Bed and Breakfast** (4050 Front St., 800/757-5272, www.kasakorbett.com, $110–130) expresses a gentle residential charm that's hard to find in the bustling downtown. Pick from one of four charming little rooms, each done with a distinct theme and color palate. (The Gulf Coast Room is *pink*—you'll love it or you'll hate it.) Rooms here sleep one or two people; all have private baths and charming amenities. In the classic B&B tradition, no TVs or DVD players can be found in the guest rooms, and the setup is generally better for couples enjoying a romantic vacation than for families on a beach trip. Enjoy the hospitality of your host, Bob, who can provide you with the best recommendations for what to do, where to eat, and what to see in Hillcrest and beyond. Parking off-street is free, and weekly rates are available.

## OLD TOWN

You'll find a massive cluster of national chain motels in Old Town, so this is a great place to land if you need a place to stay on short notice. However, if you want something a little less generic but still reasonably priced, Old Town can hook you up with that too.

### Under $100

For thrift, exterior charm, and location, location, location, you can't beat the **Old Town Inn** (4444 Pacific Hwy., 800/643-3025, www.old town-inn.com, $60–140). Built to resemble a rancho with a low profile and narrow columns, this motel sits across the street from the Old Town Transit Center, so you can catch a bus or trolley and get virtually anywhere in San Diego County from here. The white-painted, red-tile-roofed exterior of the motel gives way to plain motel rooms inside, with muted pastels, dark carpets, and floral bedspreads. If you plan to cook your own meals, go for an efficiency room, which includes a two-burner stove, refrigerator, and microwave. This family-friendly motel allows kids 12 and under to stay free, has a heated pool, and offers a free daily continental breakfast.

### $100-150

For a cheerful modern stay in San Diego

SAN DIEGO

that feels almost like home, stay in the **Sommerset Suites Hotel** (606 Washington St., 800/962-9665, www.sommersetsuites .com, $125–225). Light, bright bedrooms offer a touch of class in this 80-unit, all-suite, non-smoking motel, and each room offers a full kitchen. Enjoy free Wi-Fi in your room or down by the pool, where you can take a refreshing dip on a hot day or a hot spa soak on a cool evening. Technically the Sommerset is in the Uptown neighborhood adjacent to Old Town, but it's easy to reach shopping and dining in Old Town, or all the major attractions in San Diego.

The **Kings Inn** (1333 Hotel Circle S., 619/297-2231, www.kingsinnsandiego.com, $140) offers spacious, nonsmoking motel rooms at affordable prices. Guest rooms are done in florals with jewel-colored carpets and light walls, with either one king or two queen beds. Outside, take a dip in the cute apostrophe-shaped pool or accompanying spa. The location is convenient to sightseeing and transportation, and attached are two family restaurants that provide room service to the motel. The Amigo Spot serves authentic Mexican cuisine, and the Waffle Spot has (surprise) waffles, as well as Mexican and American egg breakfast dishes and a kids' menu.

## $150-250

Though Craftsman architecture holds sway in much of Southern California, the Victorians had their say too. To immerse yourself in the Victorian era in San Diego, stay at **A Victorian Heritage Park Bed & Breakfast Inn** (2470 Heritage Park Row, 800/995-2470, www .heritageparkinn.com, $140–350). This B&B has a dozen amazing guest rooms, each with a unique decorative scheme that complements the classic Queen Anne lines of the mansion itself. Expect to be pampered with featherbeds, private baths (many with clawfoot or whirlpool tubs), antique canopy and poster beds, and glorious views out the windows. A traditional afternoon tea is served downstairs each day, complete with finger sandwiches. Surrounding the inn you'll find the Victorian Heritage Park

of San Diego, a small cluster of immaculately restored 19th-century homes and gardens set in almost eight acres of space, complete with cobble-stoned streets and views of downtown and the ocean to the west.

The **Padre Trail Inn** (4200 Taylor St., 619/756-7800, www.padretrailinn.com, $165–175) has upscale furniture and brandname toiletries, so you'll feel just a little bit pampered in your pleasant room here. Spend a few hours lounging by the side of the pool, or dive right into sightseeing in Old Town. The exterior matches the locale—a Spanish Revival hacienda was the inspiration for the Padre Trail Inn.

## POINT LOMA

While your kids will love the proximity to SeaWorld, you'll love the almost European stylings of the classic ocean-side resorts on Point Loma and Shelter Island. You're still within easy driving range of all major San Diego attractions, without the crowds and the downtown feel. If you own your own boat and plan to bring it to San Diego, consider one of the resorts on Shelter Island—most have private marinas that rent slips.

## Under $100

For the cheapest accommodations near the beach, book a bed or a family room in the **⟨ HI-San Diego, Point Loma Hostel** (3790 Udall St., 800/909-4776, www.sandiegohostels .org, $18–22). A short drive or a longish walk from famous Ocean Beach, this charming bright-red hostel sits in the midst of a residential area of Point Loma. The proprietors encourage bicycling exploration of San Diego by providing ample bike racks for secure storage. Or if you prefer, the bus stop is only a block away from the hostel, making it easy to get to the zoo, Old Town, the beaches, or wherever else you want to go. Inside, you'll find four- to eight-bed dorms and private or family rooms include linens, Internet access, and storage lockers. Cook in the common kitchen and eat in the living room or out in the cute courtyard. The owners love to see families, as well as budget-minded singles here at the hostel, and this is a great place to stay for a truly inexpensive family beach vacation.

For folks who want a budget bed with more privacy than a hostel can afford, the **Dolphin Motel** (2912 Garrison St., 619/758-1404, www .dolphin-motel.com, $66–100) offers comfortable rooms at reasonable rates. The white walls match the pristine white bedspreads, daring you to find fault with the cleanliness at this budget motel. Pick a queen-bed room or a slightly larger room that has a twin bed as well. While the rooms aren't huge, you'll get a comfortable bed for the duration of your stay. One building has smoking rooms. Best of all, you're only a short walk from the sea, and the fishing, kayaking, and other water sports of San Diego are easily accessible (some only across the street). Enjoy a pastry and a morning cup of coffee on the house out in the attractive little courtyard. Or get your own and sit out on the balcony, enjoying the calm air of Point Loma.

## $150-250

Consider staying across the bay from downtown San Diego, on Shelter Island at **Humphrey's Half Moon Inn & Suites** (2303 Shelter Island Dr., 800/542-7400, www.halfmooninn.com, $175–575, parking $10). This resort property looks out over the bay towards the city skyline. It has its own private marina and a lush tropical garden (heavy on the palm trees, of course). Your large, homey-styled room might look out into the greenery or over the great blue bay. If you're in the mood for luxury, add an "enhancement," such as champagne and strawberries or an in-room massage, to your room reservation. If you're feeling lazy, spend a day by the pool, enjoying fruity rum drinks from the poolside bar. On the other hand, energetic travelers can take a boat out onto the water, head into town to check out the attractions, or take a bike ride around Shelter Island. Come evening, you can dine at the on-site gourmet restaurant, then dance the night away to live music at the hotel's own club. In the summertime, get tickets to one of the famed outdoor concerts held on the resort property.

Another Shelter Island charmer, **The Bay Club Hotel and Marina** (2131 Shelter Island Dr., 619/224-8888 or 800/672-0800, www .bayclubhotel.com, $139–189) provides bay and harbor views, comfortable rooms, and charming amenities. Guest rooms have tasteful decorative touches in earth tones and soft pink florals—perfect for a restful vacation. Outside your room, you'll find a funky geometric swimming pool with matching spa, a fitness center, and a brown-and-white bar and grill with a 1950s-style tropical resort feel. Be sure to stop at the desk before heading out into town to grab discount passes to various attractions. Bringing your boat to San Diego? Call the Bay Club to make arrangements to rent a slip in the private marina, which is convenient to the bay, the open ocean, and an on-water fuel station.

The exterior of the **Kona Kai Resort** (1551 Shelter Island Dr., 619/221-8000 or 800/566-2524, www.resortkonakai.com, $189) evokes the legendary Hotel del Coronado. But on the property, you'll find a sense of peace and tranquility that feels more like a Hawaiian resort out away from the city. With a fitness center, a pool, and a full-service spa, you won't lack for pampering and amenities as you bask in the Shelter Island sunshine. Inside, your room will fulfill all your oceanside vacation ideals with soft neutral tones on the walls, and cute colorful and green accents creating a tropical paradise. If you plan to take a seagoing adventure, you can moor your personal or rental boat at the private marina (slips up to 200 feet), or you can head over to SeaWorld or downtown for land-lubbing activities. Even if you get seasick, it might be worth a stroll down to the marina to check out the mega-yacht docking area and get a glimpse at how the other 1 percent live.

## CORONADO

While the Del dominates the Coronado scenery and certainly makes for a fun place to stay, the island town also offers an array of other accommodations. You can find a good place to lay your head for a reasonable rate here, or go over the top at the Del or one of the other big beach resorts.

## Under $150

For an inexpensive stay on Coronado Island, visit the **El Rancho Motel** (370 Orange Ave., 619/435-2251, www.elranchocoronado.com). A few blocks from the Del, the beaches, and the downtown area of Coronado, the El Rancho lets you enjoy the high life without the high prices. Each unit of the El Rancho has its own air conditioning, TV, fridge, and microwave, plus a comfortable bed and a pleasant tiled bathroom. You'll feel right at home in the small lodge-like motel with its white exterior and mostly matching interior. Be sure to ask the innkeeper (who lives on-site at the motel) about the best food, shopping, and good beach spots on the island.

## $150-250

If you can't quite afford a stay at the Del this time, the next best thing might be the **Glorietta Bay Inn** (1630 Glorietta Blvd., 619/435-3101, www.gloriettabayinn.com, $185–360). Literally across the street from the Del, the stately white mansion was the dream home of John D. Spreckels, who in the latter half of the 19th century owned the Del and most of the rest of San Diego in the bargain. Today, the lovely structure oozes charm, even as the less-glamorous motel buildings behind it offer spacious budget accommodations. For a premium, you can book a room inside the mansion proper; each of these is uniquely decorated and includes upscale services and amenities. The "Inn Rooms" behind the mansion are spacious, with adequate amenities and cheerful tropical-resort decor. If you're bringing your family for several days of beach time, the Inn Suites offer a full kitchen and a living room as well as one or two bedrooms, making them an ideal base of operations. No matter which building you stay in, a free continental breakfast is served each morning in the mansion's breakfast room. Grab a pastry and your coffee and enjoy exploring the downtown common rooms boasting photos commemorating the history of the house and the Spreckels family. Then jog across the street to gape at the Del or just pass through onto Coronado Beach.

At **Villa Capri By the Sea** (1417 Orange Ave., 800/231-3954, www.villacapribythesea.com, $150) you get all the benefits of staying right at the hot center of Coronado (that is, near the Del), without the costs or the ghosts. Bring your whole family or several friends—the suites sleep up to six people, and include a full kitchen with all pots and pans necessary for cooking great meals. Yet you can still walk across the street to enjoy the restaurants and shops of the Del, and to get out onto Coronado Beach. Inside, the living rooms are dimly lit but comfortable, the kitchens are light and homey, and the bright bedrooms look perfect for a sunny beach vacation. On the hottest days, you'll appreciate your own oasis of air conditioning, cable TV, and Wi-Fi after hours out on the sand playing with on-loan beach toys. Check the website for special Internet rates.

## Over $250

**C Hotel del Coronado** (1500 Orange Ave., 800/468-3533, www.hoteldel.com, $500) dominates the landscape of Coronado Island. Even in Southern California, the Del, as it's called by its friends and neighbors, wins a prize for grandiosity. The white-painted, red-roofed mammoth sprawls for acres from the beach to the road, taking up a couple of blocks all its own. Inside, the Del is at once a historical museum, shopping mall, food court, and, oh yeah, it's a hotel too! Famously haunted, the Del offers almost 700 rooms, plus another 70-plus individual cottages at Beach Village. Your best bet to catch a ghost in action is to book a room in the Victorian Building. For a more modern hotel experience, stay in the Ocean Towers or California Cabanas. Room sizes and decor vary, from smaller Victorian-decorated guest rooms to expansive resort-themed suites. Pick what you (and your budget) like best! If you want a view, be aware that ocean-facing rooms cost extra.

The best thing about staying at the Del is that you almost never have to leave. You can fall out of the hotel onto Coronado Beach, grabbing a spot early on this oft-crowded strip of sand in the summertime. In the winter, the

© LIZ HAMILL SCOTT

**the Del from the beach side**

hotel puts up an improbable ice rink out on the "back porch." You can pick from among several restaurant (or room service) for meals, and even shop for a new bikini in the downstairs of the main building.

For a luxury-oriented longer stay on Coronado Island, rent a true condo at the **Coronado Beach Resort** (1415 Ocean Ave., 877/477-7368, www .coronadobeachresort.com, $250–475). Studio, one-bedroom, and two-bedroom units all have full kitchens (most with dishwashers) with plenty of pots and pans to help you cook your own meals as you gaze out over the beach and ocean below you. You'll eat, live, and sleep in subdued tropical-themed decor, with high-class amenities surrounding you. Head up to the roof to enjoy the spa-with-a-view, or over to Loew's to take a dip in one of their three pools or many sports facilities. If you fancy a day at the beach with your family, just call down to the desk to gather up an array of beach chairs and toys, plus the all-important boogie boards. Also nearby you can access all of downtown Coronado, with its restaurants and boutiques.

## MISSION BAY

The perfect location to find a room if you're traveling with your family to SeaWorld, or planning a wild-water vacation off the shore, Mission Bay offers plenty of inexpensive chain and independent motels. If you're looking for luxury, you can also check in to one of the up-scale resorts along the beach.

### Under $150

**Mission Bay Motel** (4221 Mission Blvd., 866/649-5828, www.missionbaymotel.com, $70–150) offers clean, comfortable accommodations at the right price near the beach and Mission Bay Aquatic Park. This cheerful, white-and-blue-painted, low-built motor hotel has small, white-painted and pastel-decorated rooms, and makes a perfect base from which to enjoy the many sights and sun-drenched beaches of San Diego. You can choose from rock-bottom priced singles (which actually sleep two people) up to multi-bed rooms with kitchenettes that can accommodate the whole family. The residential Pacific Beach neighborhood offers affordable local restaurants, a beach a block a way, and car or public transit access to the rest of the San Diego area.

## $150-250

Almost affordable rates seem a surprise at oceanside **The Dana on Mission Bay** (1710 W. Mission Bay Dr., 800/445-3339, www.thedana.com, $180–300). It's so close to SeaWorld that you can walk to the park, and it has its own private marina for serious sea-lovers. Pick from two blocks of rooms—the Marina Cove section offers less expense without views of the ocean—you might look over the garden or the pool. Inside, Marina Cove rooms are fairly small, with brightly colored, tropical-themed decor. The Waters Edge premium rooms have wonderful views out over the Pacific and a more subtle, elegant design scheme. When it's time to get out of the room and enjoy San Diego, take advantage of the many free shuttles to attractions such as the San Diego Zoo and the Gaslamp Quarter. Rent a personal watercraft or a boat directly from The Dana and take a spin on Mission Bay. Or stay on the 10-acre resort property and splash in one of the two large swimming pools.

If your reason for coming to San Diego is to loll about on the beach sipping fruity cocktails, the **Bahia Resort** (998 W. Mission Bay Dr., 800/576-4229, www.bahiahotel.com, $185–310) is the perfect place to drop your suitcase and change into your swimsuit. Set right on the beach in Mission Bay, you can stumble out of your hotel room onto a strip of sun-warmed sugar sand. If you prefer your water a bit more contained, the charming Moroccan decor surrounding the large pool and tremendous (30-person) spa is for you. For the ultimate in splendid relaxation, order from the café and waiters will deliver right to you at poolside. Inside, the understated guest rooms are done in a variety of styles. Enjoy the comfort of the plush beds, the overstuffed furniture, and the homey touches prevalent especially in the larger apartment-like suites. The hotel restaurant, Café Bahia, offers tasty traditional breakfast, lunch, and dinner with just

a touch of Middle Eastern flavor. For a treat, eat outdoors!

## Over $250

San Diego seems littered with gorgeous high-end resort hotels, and the Mission Bay area is no exception. One of the nicest of these is the **Catamaran Resort** (3999 Mission Blvd., 800/422-8386, www.catamaranresort.com, $355). Garden rooms and studios, which have one or two beds, stylish decor, and top-tier amenities (plus full kitchens in the studios), can have surprisingly reasonable rates. The premier rooms—bayfront rooms and suites—have grand views of the ocean, some with direct access right down to the Catamaran's own private beach. A great reason to stay at the Catamaran, the private beach runs to a private pier with a water-sports rental facility that can hook you up whether you prefer high-powered, wind-powered, or human-powered watercraft. (Windsurfing is a favored activity on Mission Bay.) For younger guests, the Mad Scientist Kid's Camp and Catamaran Kids Club keep children occupied and happy while their parents enjoy the sea, the spa, or the private comforts of their hotel room. Also on-site you'll find the Atoll Restaurant, which serves three meals a day and a sumptuous champagne brunch on Sunday mornings and early afternoons.

## LA JOLLA

If you want to stay in ritzy La Jolla, be prepared to bust out your credit card. This uptown burg doesn't come cheap. While a few motels offer decent rooms for under $200, you'll find the best locations and rooms well over that price point. If you simply must stay in La Jolla on a budget, a few major chain motels lurk around near downtown.

## $100-150

One of the few pleasant lower-budget La Jolla accommodations is the **Sands of La Jolla** (5417 La Jolla Blvd., 800/643-0530, www.sandsoflajolla.com). It's not located in the center of the action, which helps the price point stay a little bit lower, but you can still use a car to reach the beaches, the La Jolla Cove, and the top attractions in San Diego proper. Inside, you'll find pleasant motel rooms furnished with light woods and sunny yellow wall and window treatments. Deluxe rooms and suites offer full kitchenettes, and all rooms have refrigerators, microwaves, and toaster ovens to help you save money by buying some of your own food from the store rather than a pricey restaurant. This nice little motel also offers family-friendly, multi-bed rooms and suites for great beach vacations.

## $150-250

Perfectly located and reasonably priced (for La Jolla), the **La Jolla Inn** (1110 Prospect St., 888/855-7829, www.lajollainn.com, $159–189) sits comfortably between the main shopping drag and the sloping sidewalk down to the beach. The brick facade with dark blue awnings stands out in an area of wood and adobe-style construction. Inside, you'll think you've found a boutique hotel on the Mediterranean, with small bright rooms that feature natural wood furniture and colorful homemade quilts. Upper rooms also offer the best art ever: a view out over the Pacific. All guests get to take advantage of the free continental breakfast and the afternoon snack (served at 2 P.M.—perfect for a quick break from the beach). Be sure to take advantage of the free underground parking as this area gets crowded in high season.

## Over $250

In La Jolla, upscale accommodations abound. One of the most charming is the **[C] Estancia La Jolla Hotel and Spa** (9700 Torrey Pines Rd., 858/550-1000, www.estancialajolla.com, $350–400). Built on an historic Mexican rancho, the traditional arrangement of buildings and courtyards gleam with restoration and vitality. (When driving in, look for the resort name on a standard cross-street sign.) Palm trees and succulents grace the landscape. Inside, spacious guest rooms in neutral tones are accented with bright oranges, yellows, and

greens. Beds offer an extra-comfy night's sleep, made even better by a visit to the spa or a day spent lounging under a cabana by the vast swimming pool, sipping drinks from the poolside bar. The hotel offers many of the amenities of a full-scale resort, including a restaurant, wine bar, and casual sports bar. As you stroll the groomed paths through the endless gardens dotted with native plants, you'll also find a small store, the main lobby, and the main sitting room complete with huge stone fireplace and all the help you need from friendly concierges at the desk.

The candy-colored **La Valencia Hotel** (1132 Prospect St., 858/454-0771, www.lavalencia .com, $275) has it all: ocean views, high-end restaurants, sumptuous guest rooms, and a great downtown location. Guest rooms, suites, and villas are decorated tastefully in earth tones with splashes of bright color. Living plants provide both oxygen and a homey sense of elegance both in the rooms and throughout the resort. Downstairs, take advantage of the state-of-the-art workout room, then cool off in the large sparkling blue pool. You can walk to the cliffside boardwalk or down to the beach from the La Valencia, and enjoy the shopping and restaurants of Prospect Street.

**The Lodge at Torrey Pines** (11480 N. Torrey Pines Rd., 858/453-4420, www .lodgetorreypines.com, $450) offers luxury, service, amenities, and access to the amazing Torrey Pines Golf Course. You'll be struck by the classic Southern California Craftsman architecture—the exterior of the lodge is a work of art in itself. The Craftsman elegance continues into the rooms, with designer fabrics, tasteful appointments, gorgeous marble bathrooms, and views of the golf course and ocean. If you plan to play golf, check the golf packages and arrange your tee time through the hotel. Non-golfers have a number of great recreation options too. Book an appointment at the full-service spa, rent one of the charming cabanas down at the beach, or take a guided hike at the state reserve. If traveling with family, their are numerous kids' activities and amenities available at the resort.

## NORTH COUNTY

If your one major purpose in coming to the San Diego area is to lounge on a white-sand beach, consider booking a stay north of the city proper. Some of the best beaches cluster in the North County area. Accordingly, you'll find everything from modest motels to chi-chi resorts available in the area.

### Under $150

For a good, modest motel that's clean and reasonably close to the beach and everything else, stay at the **Moonlight Beach Motel** (233 Second St., Encinitas, 800/323-1259, www .moonlightbeachmotel.com). Cheerful budget motel rooms greet guests with floral bedspreads and light-painted walls. Most rooms have a kitchenette, complete with refrigerator and microwave, making it easy to store and chill beach drinks and snacks in your room. Rooms are clean enough to feel comfortable sleeping in, but not so fancy that you'll be horrified if a little bit of sand makes it onto the carpet. The motel sits near both U.S. 101 and I-5, making it a perfect base from which to get anywhere in the San Diego area. If you prefer to stay close by, you're only a few blocks from Moonlight Beach. Go surfing, play a game of volleyball, or just relax into the sand for a day. (From the motel on a busy summer weekend day, walk to the beach if you can to avoid the parking nightmare down closer to the sand.)

Built in the charming Spanish Colonial Revival style, **Les Artistes** (944 Camino Del Mar, Del Mar, 858/755-4646, www.les artistesinn.com, $85–200) offers something different from the standard chain motel experience. Each room is named for and decorated in the style of a particular artist or style, from the French countryside of Monet to the peace of Zen. Despite its unique and fun style, this is a budget motel; the rooms are small and you won't be able to trip over your doorsill and fall into the ocean. But the beach and downtown Del Mar with its restaurants and shops are only a few blocks away. And you can bring your family (several rooms have multiple beds), including your beloved pet, to Les Artistes and

receive a warm welcome. Don't bring your cigarettes, however, as Les Artistes is entirely non-smoking.

### $150-250

If you want a beach house of your own rather than a motel room that's part of a huge block, book a daily or weekly bungalow or suite at the **Wave Crest Resort** (1400 Ocean St., Del Mar, 858/755-0100, www.wavecrestresort.com, $200–500). Here you'll get a studio, one-bedroom, or two-bedroom private unit. These are condo-style accommodations, so you'll get nice furnishings but no daily maid service. Even if you go for a more economical garden-facing unit, you'll enjoy the view of the meticulously landscaping that makes the whole complex lovely. For a modest extra fee, your unit will face the near-enough-to-touch Pacific Ocean. Take a quick walk to Seagrove Park and down to the beach beyond. Perhaps the only downside, which can also be an upside, is its proximity to the rail line and the highways. They provide both easy transportation and noise.

### Over $250

For a classic luxury resort experience, complete with a golf course, multiple swimming pools, ocean views, and almost every service you can dream up, stay at the **Four Seasons Aviara** (7100 Four Seasons Point, Aviara, 760/603-6800, www.fourseasons.com, $395). You'll find everything in your guest room exactly as you'd expect from a Four Seasons hotel, from the L'Occitane toiletries to the specially made comfy beds to the tasteful tropical decor. Downstairs, the lobby and common areas shine with marble floors and columns. You can indulge at the various independently owned shops, including a wonderful little jewelry store that specializes in unique colored gems, many of which are mined in San Diego County. The concierge and desk staff are as friendly and helpful as possible at all times—you can get whatever you want whenever you want, pretty much.

On the Four Seasons property you can play 18 holes of golf, a set of tennis, splash with the kids in the family swimming pool, or get serious in the adults-only lap pool. Round out your day with a treatment from the hotel spa. In the evening, dine at one of the three on-site restaurants. If you've come with your family, you can get the kids involved in a number of activities tailored for the younger set, and escape and enjoy some of the more adult aspects of the resort.

For another tip-top resort experience, book a room at the newly reopened **L'Auberge Del Mar** (1540 Camino Del Mar, Del Mar, 800/245-9757, www.laubergedelmar.com, $425). Enjoy the elegant guest rooms, posh spa, upscale dining, and superior amenities, all with glorious views overlooking the ocean. For guaranteed access to the tennis courts, book a court and a time in advance.

# Food

San Diego doesn't have the celebrated culinary culture of San Francisco or the Wine Country, but you can still get a good meal in this town. Due to San Diego's proximity to the border and the ocean, you'll easily find delicious Mexican food and fresh seafood. In places like the Gaslamp Quarter, Hillcrest, and La Jolla, you can find great food just by wandering down the main drag and reading menus as you go.

## DOWNTOWN
Downtown San Diego offers an astonishing array of dining choices, from comfortable American fare to understandably fabulous Mexican food and surprisingly diverse Italian option, on to upscale California cuisine.

### California
A local legend, the **Grant Grill** (326 Broadway, 619/744-2077, www.grantgrill.com, breakfast, lunch, and dinner, $22–38) has been serving upscale cuisine since 1951. The wonderful ambiance of the posh dining room makes even the most casual of diners feel wealthy and "part of the crowd." The Grant Grill, part of the US Grant hotel, serves breakfast, lunch, and dinner every day, and offers a full-service lounge with live music and a lobby where you can enjoy top-end aperitifs and digestifs. At lunch and dinner, you'll find the fanciest of California-style cuisine on the menu. For dinner, choose from the á la carte menu, or enjoy a full five-course tasting menu that's something

of a bargain. For an extra fee, you can add wine pairings to each course of the tasting menu. The wine list is short compared to many high-end restaurants, which makes it happily manageable, and it focuses almost exclusively on California wines. On Sundays, come in late in the morning or early in the afternoon to enjoy a wonderful brunch.

If you're female, coming into the Grant Grill makes you a part of history. In the 1950s and '60s, the Grill was an exclusive and exclusionary men's club. In 1969, a group of local businesswomen staged a sit-in, and the Grant Grill was forced to move into the modern era.

### Italian
Looking for some comfortable, warm Italian food without high prices or pretenses? Go where the locals go: **Filippi's Pizza Grotto** (1747 India St., 619/232-5094, www.realcheesepizza .com, Mon.–Thurs. 11 A.M.–10:30 P.M., Fri.– Sat. 11 A.M.–11:30 P.M., Sun. 11 A.M.–10 P.M., $10–15). Walk through the tempting Italian market at the front into the dimly lit restaurant at the rear of the building. Enjoy the classic atmosphere, complete with red-and-white-check tablecloths. Order a pizza, some lasagna, or a giant meatball sandwich. Pastas come with classic and uncomplicated marinara and the pizza might be the best in all of San Diego. Best of all, Filippi's serves late into the evening—until almost midnight on weekends. You'll definitely have to jostle with the local crowd for a seat on Friday and Saturday nights.

# DINNER CRUISES

An unforgettable way to dine in this coastside community is to take a dinner cruise in the calm waters of San Diego Bay. While you shouldn't expect the food on these cruises to be the best for the price, the atmosphere and scenery make up for any culinary deficiencies. Be forewarned that the drinks tend to be a bit weak as well; if you love a strong cocktail, plan to hit one of the many downtown bars before or after your cruise.

The juggernaut of the dinner and event cruise industry in California, **Hornblower** (1066 N. Harbor Dr., 619/686-8715, boarding 6:30 P.M., $65) offers a popular three-hour dinner cruise every night. Pick up a glass of complimentary champagne as you walk down the gangplank onto the yacht. Enjoy your three-course dinner (or more, if you pay extra) as the sun drops below the horizon. Take a constitutional stroll on the deck and return for dessert, or make for the entertainment deck and dance the evening away as the yacht slowly makes its way around the bay. If you prefer a daytime cruise, book passage for a Sunday champagne brunch.

**San Diego Harbor Excursion** (1050 N. Harbor Dr., 619/234-4111, www.sdhe.com, $60 for no-host bar and dinner, $80 for hosted bar and dinner) also offers nightly dinner cruises and Sunday champagne brunches out on the bay. With an array of options, including vegetarian entrées and a children's dinner package at a reduced rate, San Diego Harbor Excursion offers a fun cruise and a tasty meal. Be sure to reserve your place at the table a few days in advance for Friday and Saturday nights and for Sunday brunches in summertime.

You can find Filippi's locations in other parts of San Diego County, but the original is this Little Italy location.

## Mexican

For some heavily hyped California-ized Mexican food in the Gaslamp, you can't beat **Fred's Mexican Café** (527 Fifth Ave., San Diego Ave., 619/232-8226, www.fredsmexicancafe.com). Blending San Diego seafood, the California fresh-ingredient craze, and tradition Mexican dishes, Fred's has earned top honors from local restaurant polls. The extensive menu offers up creative takes on burritos, tacos, enchiladas, and much more. Fred's prides itself on its margaritas as well—amazing concoctions that take the margarita concept to the next level, served in faux martini glasses or thick-stemmed bowls. The casual atmosphere features trestle tables and cluttered walls, appealing to a young crowd preparing for a night out on the town.

## Steak

Looking for a rich slab of beef after a long day playing outside? Head for the **◖ Greystone Steakhouse** (658 Fifth Ave., 619/232-0225, www.greystonesteakhouse.com, dinner only $30–48) in the heart of the Gaslamp. This upscale eatery makes a great start to a night out on the town with your sweetie. The white tablecloths light up the dim interior, where the dining area surrounds a staircase leading down into the belly of the restaurant. Or if you prefer, get a table on the small patio out front so you can people-watch as the Gaslamp heats up with the evening crowd. The menu includes all your favorite steakhouse standards—great cuts of beef, lobster and prawns, and an array of yummy sides. You'll also find some interesting California-style entrées and appetizers. Portions are big, so consider splitting an entrée with your dinner partner so you can both enjoy an appetizer and some dessert. The wine list focuses on California wines and includes a good selection of local vintages, and the full bar offers pre-dinner cosmos and martinis. The service can be a bit slow during the dinner hours, but it's friendly and helpful.

## BALBOA PARK AND HILLCREST

The fun and funky Hillcrest neighborhood offers an array of dining options, from ethnic to upscale to down-home. To pick your own favorite, wander up and down India Street and read the menus in the windows. Most every restaurant on India wins local approval.

## American

If you're looking for dinner and nightlife all in one spot, come out to the **Corvette Diner** (3946 Fifth Ave., 619/542-1476, www.cohn restaurants.com, Sun.–Thurs. 11 A.M.–10 P.M., Fri.–Sat. 11 A.M.–11 P.M., $8–14). This crazy, crowded diner is all about the atmosphere, from the outlandish 1950s decor to the rock-and-roll to the bouffant-topped waitresses. The food runs to standard American diner fare, though you'll find any number of Corvette original dishes. And don't skip the soda fountain—the fountain and dessert menu includes classics and originals galore.

If you're looking for a quiet meal, the Corvette is *not* your place. A DJ spins nightly, and on weekdays you can find child-oriented entertainers performing for an appreciative audience. Kids love the wild, loud fun of the family-friendly Corvette.

If it *is* a quiet American dinner you want, try the **Crest Café** (425 Robinson Ave., 619/295-2510, www.crestcafe.net, daily 7 A.M.–midnight, $8–16). This colorful, cheerful diner welcomes a more sedate crowd with a bright dining room and three wonderful meals per day. In amongst the traditional diner fare, you'll find a few upscale dishes, such as lemon-ricotta pancakes and orange marmalade–stuffed French toast. You'll also see a wide array of Mexican-inspired entrées, alongside diner dishes that have been made over with an eye towards modern health consciousness. Open till midnight, the Crest is the perfect place to stop and grab a late-night snack after (or during) a night out in Hillcrest.

If you're looking for a hearty breakfast or a unique American dinner, the local Hillcrest favorite hangout is **Hash House A Go Go** (3628 5th Ave., 619/298-4646, www.hashhouse agogo.com, Mon.–Fri. 7:30 A.M.–2 P.M. and 5:30–9 P.M., Sat.–Sun. 7:30 A.M.–2:30 P.M. and 5:30–10 P.M.). The Hash House puts its own spin on casual American food, including

an array of fresh local ingredients that take the dishes up a notch. You'll dine in a modern atmosphere with an industrial-urban decorative scheme, complete with brushed-metal tabletops. For breakfast, the obvious choice is of course hash, though you've got dozens of other options as well. Lunch and dinner feature especially wonderful salads, plus plenty of great entrées in a variety of styles. Look for fresh veggies and fruit, lean meats, and preparations that start to transcend American diner food and lean into the world of haute California cuisine.

If you're in Balboa Park, chances are you're visiting the museums or the zoo. At the zoo, grab a bite at **Albert's Restaurant** (Gorilla Tropics at the San Diego Zoo, 619/685-3200). This sit-down eatery serves lunch year-round and dinner during the summer nights when the zoo stays open late. Sit indoors to escape the heat, or out on the patio to enjoy the view of the gardens surrounding the animal enclosures. Relax with a drink at the bar, order a simple salad or sandwich, or enjoy a hearty steak dinner.

## Cafés

If you need a quick bite before a show at one of the Old Globe Theaters, the closest eats can be had at **Lady Carolyn's Pub** (619/231-1941, ext. 2751, Tues.–Fri. from 7 P.M., Sat.–Sun. from 1 P.M.). This walk-up snack bar offers soups in sourdough bowls, salads, wine, and Irish coffees. Open every day a show goes up (until the theater shuts its doors), Lady Carolyn's can get crowded on weekends. Dine early if you can.

## Coffee and Tea

Round out your Balboa Park experience with a cup of tea and a meal at the **Tea Pavilion** (619/231-0048, daily 10 A.M.–5 P.M., later in the summer). As advertised, the specialty of the house is tea. You'll find a great cuppa, whether you favor herbal, green, or black teas. You can also get a bowl of noodles, some sushi, or a quick snack. To take some of the Japanese experience home with you, wander into the market section to peruse the unusual imported food and drink.

If all that tromping around through the park

has tired you out, perk up with a drink from **Daniel's Coffee Cart** (House of Hospitality Courtyard, Tues.–Sun. 8 A.M.–5:30 P.M., Mon. 8 A.M.–4:30 P.M.). You'll find all your favorite espresso drinks, plain ol' coffee, tea, and pastries.

A favorite Hillcrest coffee shop is **Gelato Vero Caffe** (3753 India St., 619/295-9269, Mon.–Thurs. 6 A.M.–midnight, Fri. 6 A.M.–1 A.M., Sat. 7 A.M.–1 A.M., Sun. 7 A.M.–midnight, $10), which serves the workday-morning caffeine-jonesing crowd *and* the late-night dessert and coffee hounds. The gelato is all made in-house, and the owners and fans assert that you won't find any better this side of Italy. The small café has little seating in the main room; if you want to sit down and enjoy your coffee or gelato and there doesn't seem to be room, hit the stairway off to the side out the door of the café to find the upper deck and inside cottage seating.

## OLD TOWN

Old Town is more about the history, shopping, and sights than it is about dining. Most locals head downtown for a meal. But if you really want to eat here, Mexican food is your best bet.

In Old Town's little corner of Mexico, Bazaar del Mundo, you can find some great South-of-the-Border eats in a variety of styles and price ranges. Join the party at **Casa Guadalajara** (4105 Taylor St., 619/295-5111, http://bazaardelmundo.com/guad2006.shtml, Mon.–Thurs. 11 A.M.–10 P.M., Fri. 11 A.M.–11 P.M., Sat. 7 A.M.–11 P.M., Sun. 7 A.M.–10 P.M., happy hour Mon.–Fri. 4–7 P.M.). From the moment you see the low, whitewashed, adobe-style building with the red-tiled roof, you'll start to feel the Mexican atmosphere. Inside, enjoy the music of strolling mariachis as you sip a margarita and dine on excellent regional Mexican cuisine. The seafood-heavy menu features Mexican classics as well as the chef's unique creations. Be sure to check out the daily specials!

## POINT LOMA

Out on Point Loma, the food is all about the fish—not a surprise, considering that this spit of land sits out in the water, surrounded on three sides by bay and ocean. Whatever style you like your fish cooked (or uncooked) in, Point Loma can serve it to you.

### California

The **Embers Grill** (3924 W. Point Loma Blvd., 619/222-6877, Sun.–Tues. and Thurs. 11:30 A.M.–9 P.M., Fri.–Sat. 11:30 A.M.–10 P.M., $25–50) offers casual dining to the masses with plenty of patio room for outdoor dining. Expect sometimes-huge portions of fairly common American dishes with a California twist. If you're looking for a lighter meal, order a sandwich, salad, or personal-sized pizza. Embers is also a great place for a full-sized tasty lunch.

### Japanese

In the world of high-end seafood, the Japanese are famed for creating some of the best dishes on Earth. For some amazing sushi, go to **Umi Sushi** (2806 Shelter Island Blvd., 619/226-1135, www.umisushisandiego.com, Mon.–Sat. 11:30 A.M.–2:30 P.M., 5–10 P.M., $4–11). If you love your rolls, choose from three-dozen on the menu, plus plenty of nigiri, sashimi, specialty platters, and "sushi boats." For folks who love Japanese food but quail at the thought of raw fish, Umi offers hot entrées, noodle dishes, salads, and more. Sit up at the sushi bar to see your food put together, or pick a table out in the classically Japanese-styled dining room.

### Mediterranean

Weary of fish and looking for a respite from the endless seafood of Point Loma? Grab a bite of something completely different at the **Fairouz Cafe and Gallery** (3166 Midway Dr., 619/225-0308, www.alnashashibi.com, $14–19). The bright, cheerful dining room features the original artwork of Al Nashashibi, a painter with roots in Jerusalem. (Yes, you can purchase works you see while dining; inquire with your server.) As for the food, you'll find meat and vegetarian entrées in the Middle Eastern tradition, with lots of lamb and chicken, plus several Greek specialties, such as stuffed grape leaves. At lunchtime, look to the appetizers and salads for lighter fare.

## Steak and Seafood

For the best of the land out by the sea, visit ◖ **Island Prime** (880 Harbor Island Dr., 619/295-6801, www.cohnrestaurants.com, lunch from 11:30 A.M., dinner 5–10 P.M., $30–50). This huge house of steak and fish seats more than 600 on a top evening. Ask in advance for a window seat or a table out on the deck overlooking the harbor and the San Diego skyline. On the deck, you might find yourself by one of the fires, feeling as though you were dining at your own private beach house (well, except for the crowd, of course). The simple decor makes use of the wooden architectural features of the building. If you're boating on the San Diego waters, dock-and-dine at the neighboring Sunroad Marina. The menu boasts shellfish, finned fish, and plenty of hearty meats in a classic steakhouse-meets-California style. Start (or finish) your meal with a martini or another fabulous cocktail.

For a lighter meal, head for the C-Level cocktail lounge. In addition to the high-octane libations, the lounge serves a light dinner menu—that really isn't all that light. Whichever you choose, you'll find a pleasant trend towards local and organic ingredients in Prime's dishes.

One of the best things about dining in San Diego is the opportunity to enjoy a fabulous meal while looking out over the harbor or the ocean. That's just what you'll get at **Humphreys by the Bay** (2241 Shelter Island Blvd., 619/224-3577, www.humphreysbythebay.com, daily 7 A.M.–2 P.M., Sun.–Thurs. 5:30–9 P.M., Fri.–Sat. 5:30–11 P.M., $22–50). The white tablecloths on the candlelit tables look right out over the Humphreys Marina and off towards the San Diego city skyline. This hotel-based restaurant serves three meals a day, plus brunch on Sundays. On the dinner menu, seafood reigns, though various land-based entrées get their due as well. Or combine the two for an extravagant meal that makes for the best of everything. At lunchtime, upscale sandwiches and salads make the most of lighter midday standards. Whichever you choose, lunch or dinner, don't miss the awesome seafood soups! The breakfast menu includes all the egg-based standards, fresh fruits and pastries, and a few scrumptious surprises. Sunday brunches are buffet-style, with plenty of made and carved-to-order specialties.

If what you really want is the freshest slab of fish to be found on Point Loma, eat at the aptly named **Point Loma Seafoods** (2805 Emerson St., 619/223-1109, Mon.–Sat. 9 A.M.–6:30 P.M., Sun. 11 A.M.–6:30 P.M., $5–14). Much of the fish sold here, either as a hot meal to eat right there or chilled in paper ready to cook, comes straight off the fishing boats in the harbor. Shellfish, including local spiny lobster, is fresh, top quality, and sold only in season—making Point Loma Seafood the perfect place for a seafood lunch. Hot food and sandwiches come with slaw and fries—perfect accompaniments for fish. The cold foods include seafood salads plus a small array of sushi and sashimi. The atmosphere is the antithesis of upscale, which make it perfect for many visitors looking for reasonable prices and truly great fish.

## CORONADO

To find your own food in Coronado, stroll down Orange Avenue. While you'll definitely find your fellow tourists there, you'll also find a large number of restaurants in a bunch of different styles and ethnicities that are worth trying out.

### American

If you're a night owl and find yourself looking for nourishment after hours, you can find it at the **Night & Day Café** (847 Orange Ave., 619/522-2912, open 24 hours daily, $10). This small hole-in-the-wall diner will make you feel right at home. You'll find all your old standard American favorite foods in an atmosphere that's unique to Coronado.

### French

With the opulence of the Del overseeing the town, a night out for French cuisine seems appropriate here. You'll do well at **Chez Loma French Bistro** (1132 Loma Ave., 619/435-0661, www.chezloma.com, Tues.–Sun. 5 P.M.–close, $23–36). You can walk to this charming restaurant that's located in the historic Carez

Hizar House—a white-frame house that leads into warm, red dining rooms. The cuisine tends toward the classic French brasserie style, with the occasional hint of California color in some of the dishes. The wine list is worth a visit all on its own; it's not immense, but it shows off the best of California and France, including a large selection of flights (samples of three different wines all in one type). The food and the ambiance have caught the attention of local foodies, and Chez Loma has been highly reviewed and presented with a number of regional restaurant awards.

## Italian

Looking for a good plate of spaghetti on the island? Go to **Island Pasta** (1202 Orange Ave., 619/435-4545, www.islandpastacoronado .com, Sun.–Thurs. 11 A.M.–9 P.M., Fri.–Sat. 11 A.M.–9:30 P.M.). Island Pasta brings out the best in the Italian staples, serving up thin-crust pizzas and handmade pastas, as well as seafood and sandwiches.

## Steak and Seafood

For good food in a fanciful atmosphere, get a table at **Peohe's** (1201 First St., 619/437-4474, www.peohes.com, lunch daily 11:30 A.M.–2:30 P.M., dinner Mon.–Sat. 5:30 P.M.–close, Sun. 4:30 P.M.–close, $22–80). It offers a cute tropical atmosphere, great views of San Diego Bay, and tasty offerings from land and sea. The menu is friendly to tourists new to the fresh California fish concept, while still offering pros at the game some interesting new preparations. If you prefer to keep your fish off the grill, order from the sushi bar. To go with your meal, enjoy a festive cocktail. The Volcano is the house special, and it serves two with near-lethal potency. Finally, Peohe's prides itself on its huge and tasty homemade desserts. If you possibly can, round out your meal with a Hot Chocolate Lava cake.

## Thai

If your preference is hot and casual, eat at **Swaddee Thai Restaurant** (1001 C St., 619/435-8110, daily 11 A.M.–3 P.M., 5–10 P.M.).

Off the main tourist drag, Swaddee's tasty Thai cuisine appeals to locals, and is something of a hidden gem.

## MISSION BAY

Locals and visitors alike flock to Mission Bay for a day's entertainment. As the sun sets, the need for food kicks in. Along Mission Bay, you'll find an array of ethnic eats to please any palate.

## Italian

**Luigi's Italian** (3210 Mission Blvd., 858/488-2818, Sun.–Thurs. 11:30 A.M.–10 P.M., Fri.–Sat. 11:30 A.M.–11:30 P.M., $11–30) is the place to go for Italian food at Mission Bay. Sit outside for the best people-watching, or inside for a loud, bright, tasty meal. The house red wine accompanies the inexpensive cuisine perfectly—including the pizza. Speaking of Luigi's pizza, you'll want to order a single slice unless you're part of a large crowd. A whole Luigi's pie barely fits on a four-top. Luigi's can get loud and rowdy, especially on game day, as many locals bring their posse for pizza and the game on the big-screen.

## Mexican

For great, cheap Mexican food right on the main drag, you can't beat **Valentine's Mexican Food** (3852 Mission Blvd., 858/539-0939, daily 10 A.M.–10 P.M., $4–7). You can order tacos to go or enjoy an enchilada plate inside the restaurant, taking advantage of the free serve-yourself chips and salsa. There's nothing fancy about Valentine's food, but it's high quality and plentiful, with the proper toppings and sides, such as guacamole, sour cream, and house-made salsa. Lunching here during a day on the beach or the water will fill you up and get you back out for a long afternoon of playing in the sunshine.

## Seafood

At the boastfully named **World Famous** (711 Pacific Beach Dr., 858/272-3100, daily 7 A.M.–11 P.M., $11–30), enjoy breakfast, lunch, or dinner with a view. Fish, purchased fresh daily, is the specialty of the house here, and preparations range from classic American to a variety of ethnic stylings that might be called "fusion" if this were San Francisco. Grab a drink at the bar and take a seat either indoors in the Vegas-inspired dining room or outdoors on the seaside patio. The wine list features some of the best-known California vintners.

## Thai

Not enough heat out on the beach? Have a meal at **Jack's Thai Spices** (1768 Garnet Dr., 858/483-9830, www.jackthaispices.com, daily 11 A.M.–10 P.M., $13–20). Bright yellow walls and palm trees make this a welcoming and exotic place to dine. With Thai-style spare ribs, curries, peanut sauce dishes, noodles, rice, and a wide array of vegetarian options, Jack's has something for everyone. Jack himself might be on-site. (Look for an older Thai gentleman with a noticeably big grin.) He acts as both owner and chef, and created many of the specialty dishes himself. If you know in advance that you plan to eat at Jack's, check the website for a chance to win a free lunch in a weekly drawing. Also, check out the "Speak Thai" section to learn a few restaurant-friendly phrases.

## LA JOLLA

For a good selection of food in La Jolla, stroll or drive down Prospect Street. You'll find an array of high-class California cuisine, plus coffee shops and more casual dining options.

## California

**[** **Georges at the Cove** (1250 Prospect St., 858/454-4244, www.georgesatthecove.com) is a La Jolla institution. The complex actually includes three separate restaurants. The favorite, **Ocean Terrace** (lunch and dinner, $15–20) offers casual outdoor seating on the roof of the building year-round, with unpretentious and delicious cuisine. Enjoy seafood as you look out over La Jolla Cove, or choose a simple salad or sandwich for a lighter meal. Downstairs, you'll find the ultra-urban **Georges California Modern** (dinner, $35–40). The industrial design of the dining room precedes the chic, if sometimes a bit overwrought, dishes you'll find on the menu here. Windows

offer views of the Cove, while cushioned banquettess make diners along the wall comfortable as they settle in for a multi-course dinner. Finally, if you're really looking for a cocktail out on the balcony, **Georges Bar** (lunch and dinner, $15–20) has just what you're looking for. You can order from the Ocean Terrace menu, or just sip your drinks as you enjoy the warm evening air.

## Seafood

Looking for good seafood and a fabulous view to go with it? Have a meal at **Brockton Villa** (1235 Coast Blvd., 858/454-7393, http://brocktonvilla.com, Mon. 8 A.M.–3 P.M., Tues.–Sun. 8 A.M.–9 P.M., $30), which is open for breakfast, lunch, and dinner. Here you can enjoy classic American dishes with a California twist, plus plenty of fish, of course. The casual atmosphere of this beach bungalow blends perfectly with the sugar sand beaches of the San Diego area. Wooden tables, funky mismatched chairs, and the bright white paint inside evoke a sense of the casual resort atmosphere of historic La Jolla. For fun, read the menu for information on the quirky history of the bungalow, which dates from the late 1800s.

## NORTH COUNTY

Each town ranging up the Pacific Coast Highway to Del Mar and Carlsbad has a main drag filled with restaurants. You'll find ethnic enclaves, homey diners, and more.

## California

Looking for elegant yet casual beach town dining? Try the famed **Arterra** (11966 El Camino Real, Del Mar, 858/369-6032, www.arterra restaurant.com, Mon.–Fri. 6:30–10:30 A.M., 11:30 A.M.–2 P.M., 4–9:30 P.M., Sat. 7–11:30 A.M., 4–9:30 P.M., Sun. 7–11:30 A.M., $35). Improbably located inside the San Diego Marriott Del Mar, Arterra offers anything but standard chain hotel fare. Start with a drink and perhaps a seafood appetizer in the modern, comfortable outdoor lounge. Once you're seated for dinner inside the plush, red-splashed dining room, you'll find great service and top cuisine created from the freshest local and organic ingredients around. The tasting menus (with or without wine pairing) are a popular option, letting you sample the greatest variety of dishes. Get adventurous and try something new, since there's plenty of cutting-edge cuisine on the menu. And don't forget the wine; the list includes many boutique California charmers that pair wonderfully with the cuisine. If your preference is for uncooked fish, go for something from the surprisingly good sushi bar.

## Italian

On the almost Mediterranean-feeling north coast of San Diego County, sunny Italian food somehow seems appropriate. Some of the best just off the beach is served in Encinitas at **( Via Italia Trattoria** (569 S. Pacific Coast Hwy., Encinitas, 760/479-9757, Mon.–Thurs. and Sun. noon–9 P.M., Fri.–Sat. noon–10:30 P.M., $10–25). This Italian-owned and -operated casual restaurant feels like a real trattoria on the coast of Italy. You can get a budget-friendly yet fabulously delicious thin-crust pizza, a dish of steaming pasta with your choice of traditional sauce, or an upscale seafood entrée. The food is fresh, cooked just right, and

delectable. Whatever you order from the large menu, you'll enjoy eating it in the casual dining room with classic red-and-white-checked tablecloths. Or if you just want a quick drink and an appetizer, take a seat at the bar.

For haute cuisine with an Italian flair, make the drive out to the Four Seasons Aviara and have dinner at **Vivace** (7100 Four Seasons Pt., Carlsbad, 760/603-3773, Sun.–Thurs. 6–9:30 P.M., Fri.–Sat. 6–10 P.M., $35–50). A perfect restaurant for a romantic night out, Vivace offers California-Italian cuisine in several courses, with a menu that changes nightly and seasonally to take advantage of the freshest local ingredients. Attentive, knowledgeable servers can help you with both the menu and the wine list, which provides great menu-matching selections from California, Italy, and other wine regions of Europe. As you sip your wine, you can admire the elegant tropical-themed decor throughout the several interconnected dining spaces. (Be sure to look down; the floor is gorgeous!) Be sure to plan at least an hour and a half so that you can enjoy the whole dining experience, right through dessert and coffee.

# Information and Services

## INFORMATION
### Tourist Information

The San Diego Convention and Visitor's Bureau operates two visitors centers, each of which can help you with everything from flight information to restaurant coupons to hotel reservations. Downtown, head for the **International Visitor Information Center** (1040⅓ W. Broadway at Harbor Dr., 619/236-1212, Oct.–May daily 9 A.M.–4 P.M., June–Sept. daily 9 A.M.–5 P.M.). In La Jolla, make use of the **La Jolla Visitor Center** (7966 Herschel Ave., 619/236-1212, daily 11 A.M.–4 P.M.). To get a feel for the town before you arrive, check out the SDCVB website at www.sandiego.org. Friendly folks can answer emails and phone calls about most anything pertaining to San Diego County.

## Media and Communications

As a well-traveled tourism destination, San Diego has a wide range of publications you can pick up to help you plan the details of your visit. The daily newspaper is the **San Diego Union-Tribune** (www.signonsandiego.com).

Some stores and hotels carry **San Diego Magazine,** a glossy monthly publication focused on the culture and lifestyle of the region. While this isn't a tourist-centered magazine, you can still find good information about what's hot *right now,* especially in the dining and shopping scenes.

It's pretty easy to get online in San Diego. Most hotels have either wireless or cabled high-speed Internet access in rooms, though it isn't always free. Business-oriented accommodations also often maintain several public-access computers for guests. You can also find Wi-Fi in many coffee houses, both chain and independent, plus public libraries and some bookshops. As of this writing, San Diego does not have free municipal wireless service.

## SERVICES
### Banks and Post Offices
Banking in San Diego is easy—like most big cities, ATM machines abound not only at bank branches, but in restaurants, bars, and minimarts as well. You'll find branches of most of the major American banks here, including Wells Fargo, Bank of America, Washington Mutual, and many more.

You'll find plenty of U.S. Post Office branches scattered throughout San Diego. If you need to ship your shopping home, you'll find a **post office** at 51 Horton Plaza, convenient to the mall and much of downtown. South of Balboa Park, the post office sits at 815 E Street. In La Jolla, there's a branch only a few blocks from Prospect downtown at 720 Silver Street. Each town in the North County has its own post office, of course. In Encinitas, it's at 1130 Second Street.

### Medical Services
With UC San Diego in town, the number of major medical centers in and around San Diego is higher than the average. If you must get sick on vacation, San Diego isn't the worst place to do it. In town, the **UCSD Medical Center - Hillcrest** (200 West Arbor Dr., 619/543-6222) offers emergency and clinic services, as does **Scripps Mercy Hospital** (4077 Fifth Ave., 619/294-8111). The **Kaiser Permanente Medical Center** (4647 Zion Ave., 619/528-5000) includes a full-service, 24-hour emergency room. La Jolla also has a heavy load of hospitals, with **Scripps Green Hospital** (10666 N. Torrey Pines Rd., 858/554-9100) and **Scripps Memorial Hospital** (9888 Genesee Ave., 858/626-4123).

In the North County area, the only trauma center is within the **Palomar Medical Center** (555 East Valley Parkway, 760/739-3000) in Escondido. You can get regular hospital services at the **Scripps Memorial Hospital** (354 Santa Fe Dr., 760/633-6501) in Encinitas.

Most of the beaches in San Diego County maintain a lifeguard presence in the summertime, and many have lifeguards patrolling in the winter as well. Look for the light blue towers on the beach to find the nearest available lifeguards, or for permanent buildings bearing a large red cross.

# Getting There and Around

If you're coming to San Diego from Los Angeles, you'll be relieved by the easing of traffic. If you're coming from anyplace else, you may be horrified by the packed highways. In the grand scheme of California transit, San Diego isn't the worst place to try to get around. The highway network makes some sense, there's almost adequate in-town public transit, and the rail and air travel centers bustle with activity.

If you prefer human-powered transportation, San Diego's fabulous weather, generally safe streets, and miles of mostly along-the-coast paths make bicycling and walking eminently possible as your major mode of transportation.

## GETTING THERE
### Air
The major-league **San Diego International Airport** (3665 N. Harbor Dr., www.san.org), a.k.a. Lindbergh Field, is stuffed right along San Diego Bay, convenient to downtown, Coronado, and almost every major San Diego attraction. Short-term parking sits adjacent to the terminals and costs $1 per hour on average. Long-term lots surround the airport; check the airport website for specifics. A 60-minute

maximum, free "cell phone lot" lets drivers wait for incoming passengers without having to drive endlessly around the airport.

If you're flying a light plane in, the most convenient general aviation airports to downtown San Diego are Brown Field (8,000-foot runway) and Montgomery Field (4,600-foot runway). Eight additional general aviation airports are scattered throughout the county. For information, check www.miramarairshow .com/airports.html.

## Train

To get to San Diego by train from the north or the east, find your way aboard the **Amtrak Pacific Surfliner** (www.amtrak.com), a train that runs a dozen times a day from Paso Robles along the Pacific Coast down to San Diego. Boarding is easy from most major California destinations in the area, including San Luis Obispo, Santa Barbara, Los Angeles, and Anaheim. Check into transfers from the Coast Starlight and the Capitol Corridor routes as well. Amtrak services the Santa Fe station (1050 Kettner Blvd.) and the Old Town Transit Center (4005 Taylor St.).

For a reliable local commuter train, jump on board **The Coaster** (www.sdcommute .com). The Coaster runs from Oceanside into downtown San Diego and back a dozen times a day Monday–Friday, with five trains running Saturdays, plus special event and holiday service. Fares run $4–5.50 for adults one-way ($2–2.75 for seniors/disabled, children under 6 ride free). Purchase tickets from the vending machines in every train station. In the North County, NCTD Coaster Connecter bus routes can connect to the train station. In San Diego proper, catch the trolley or the bus from either the Old Town Transit Center or the Santa Fe station.

## Car

Most visitors drive into San Diego via the heavily traveled I-5 from the north or south. I-805 runs parallel to I-5 at La Jolla and leads south into Mission Valley. To drive between the North County and San Diego, take I-15, which runs north–south farther inland. Be sure to avoid rush hour, as the back-up on I-15 can become extensive after Poway. Both I-805 and I-15 cross I-8, which runs east–west through Mission Valley. The smaller yet surprisingly

© ROBERT HOLMES / CALTOUR

Amtrak's Santa Fe station

pretty Route 163 runs north–south from I-5 in Balboa Park north to I-15 in Miramar.

## GETTING AROUND
### Car

This is Southern California. Most people drive here whether they need to or not. Happily, this is *not* the Los Angeles Basin, so traffic sometimes relaxes into a bearable state and the people who named the freeways weren't actually insane.

Parking is the hardest at the beaches in the summertime. Everyone else in the state seems to be trying to find a parking spot close to the sand between June and September. If you possibly can, find another way to get from your accommodations to the beach, be it bicycle, public transit, or your own two feet. If you must drive, check out the parking situation ahead of time (most beaches' websites offer parking information) and plan ahead. Bring cash for pay parking, come early in the morning, and be prepared to walk up to a mile from your parking spot down to the beach itself.

In the various downtown areas, you'll find fairly average city parking issues. Happily, San Diego's major attractions and event venues tend to be accompanied by large parking structures. Just be prepared to pay a premium if you're doing something popular.

### Bus and Trolley

In downtown San Diego, Coronado, and La Jolla, the **MTS** (www.sdcommute.com) operates both an extensive bus system and trolley routes. The North County is served by the North County Transit District, or NCTD. Trolley tickets cost $1.25–6. Bus fares range $1–5, depending on where you're headed. If you plan to make serious use of the trolleys and buses, use the vending machines at trolley stations to get a day pass—a regular day pass is a bargain at $5, and two-, three-, and four-day passes can save you even more money. Day passes work on NCTD Breeze buses as well as most MTS routes.

See the website for more information about schedules, routes, and fares for both the MTS and NCTD services. If you plan to pay your fare for buses or trolleys on-board, have exact change available. The vending machines are more forgiving, as many take $1 and $5 bills and make change.

If you don't have a car with you, or just want to avoid driving for a while, hop onto the **Old Town Trolley** (www.trolleytours.com/san-diego, adults $30, children $15) for a great look at the highlights of San Diego without the headaches of parking and traffic. The trolley can take you in a loop through downtown (including the Gaslamp Quarter), Old Town, out over the bridge to the Del on Coronado, and around the San Diego Bay Harbor. You can get on and off the trolley at any time to visit a museum, go shopping, or grab a bite to eat. Another trolley will appear to take you on your way. As long as you stay onboard, the driver will narrate, pointing out the sights as you pass them and make stops at the biggest and most important. While the Old Town Trolley is way too expensive to use in place of public transportation, it's a great way to get out and see the highlights of the city in a day.

### Tours

If you've only got a limited time in the San Diego area and want to see as much as possible, consider taking a tour. Several fun, unique tours show off different sides of the city, some you may not have explored before. For instance, to see the city from the bay, consider a harbor tour. **San Diego Harbor Excursion** (619/234-4111, www.sdhe.com, adults $18, seniors $16, children $9) offers one-hour tours of the north and south ends of the bay, and a two-hour tour that covers the bay in full. You'll see some of the most famous San Diego sights from a new perspective: the Maritime Museum ships, the USS *Midway,* the Coronado Bay Bridge, and Fort Rosencrans. This excursion company also provides regular dinner and brunch cruises; reservations in advance are recommended!

For a unique look at the San Diego Bay, add a **Seal Tour** (www.trolleytours.com/san-diego, seal tour $30 or less) to your Old Town Trolley ticket. You'll get a ride on a strange-looking amphibious contraption that will take you from the road around the harbor out into the harbor to look at the city from the water.

To take your own tour of San Diego with just a little bit of help, book a cute talking **Go Car** (639 Kettner Blvd. or 2415 San Diego Ave., 619/696-9002, www.gocartours.com, daily 9 A.M.sunset). In your Go Car, you'll be directed through town by a talking GPS navigation unit that also knows stories about the sights of San Diego. With a Go Car, you can either take a standard tour, or program your own routes through the area.

Looking for something fun and a little spooky to fill the after-dark hours?

Take the **Haunted San Diego Ghost Tour** (877/642-8683, www.hauntedsandiegotours .com, $30, June–mid-Sept. nightly, mid-Sept.– May Thurs.–Sun.). This combination bus and walking tour takes about two hours, and includes stops at haunted sites in the Gaslamp District, downtown, and Old Town. Visit the haunted houses and hotels and hear the ghost stories that make each one famous. Highlights of the tour include a historic cemetery and the notorious Whaley House. For the best haunted experience, take the 8:30 P.M. tour so you'll be sure to experience the haunted places of San Diego in darkness.

# THE DESERTS

Cosmopolitan Palm Springs and its many outlying towns are havens for wealthy residents of northern climates who come down each winter to escape the cold. Great golf and wonderful day spas are hallmarks of Palm Springs proper, Rancho Mirage, Palm Desert, and Indian Wells.

But beauty can be harsh, and nowhere is this more true than in the California deserts. Only a few miles away from Palm Springs, Joshua Tree National Monument sprawls across the desert landscape, connecting two major California desert climates—the Mojave Desert and the lower Colorado Desert. Joshua Tree is easier to access from the Los Angeles area, featuring the strange shapes of the plant that is its namesake. North, the seemingly endless Mojave stretches across the state, offering hiking trails, preserve areas, ghost towns, and even camping for the hardy traveler.

Death Valley hugs the Nevada border at the east side of the state and its barrenness is legendary. In truth, Death Valley is misnamed. This vast forbidding landscape encompasses a wealth of life; a vast variety of plants, animals, birds, and even fish call the Valley home. Spring is the best time to experience this contradiction, when an astonishing bloom of wildflowers brightens the desert landscape.

The southernmost desert park of California is Anza-Borrego State Park. The biggest of all California's state parks, Anza-Borrego is part of the Colorado Desert region and home to its diverse array of wildlife. From ocotillo fields to palm oases to profuse spring wildflower blooms, the beauty of this desert's gardens

© LANCE SCOTT

# HIGHLIGHTS

**◖ Palm Springs Aerial Tramway:** For a stunning view of Palm Springs and the San Jacinto Mountains, nothing beats an exhilarating ride up the Aerial Tramway, which zips up 2.5 miles in about 10 minutes and provides a 360° view of the valley below (page 160).

**◖ Oasis of Mara:** No, it's not a mirage! The lush Oasis of Mara, accessible via a 0.5-mile nature loop, provides an up-close glimpse into the history and ecology of Joshua Tree National Park (page 177).

**◖ Keys View:** This panoramic view is one of the best in Joshua Tree. Pick a clear day to take in the vista from Palm Springs all the way out to the Salton Sea (page 180).

**◖ Scotty's Castle:** Don't miss touring the only private mansion built in Death Valley. This grand home, albeit unfinished, provides an entertaining Gold Rush–era history to the region (page 189).

**◖ Badwater Basin:** Take a walk along the esoteric landscape of this dried-out lakebed, situated at the lowest elevation in the Western Hemisphere (page 191).

**◖ Artist's Palette:** Nature is the ultimate artist here, where a combination of minerals paints the badlands in brilliant colors. Time your visit at sunset, when the fading light washes the already colorful mountains in glistening gold (page 191).

**◖ Borrego Palm Canyon:** This canyon provides the best overview of Anza Borrego flora and fauna. An easy three-mile loop takes visitors from sandy desert to shady palm groves with interpretive stops along the way (page 204).

LOOK FOR ◖ TO FIND RECOMMENDED SIGHTS, ACTIVITIES, DINING, AND LODGING.

rivals any in the world. Nearby, the former mining town of Julian offers a taste of Southern California gold rush history.

## PLANNING YOUR TIME

Palm Springs makes a great weekend getaway or a relaxing spot to kick back for a whole season—just ask the thousands of Californians who maintain vacation condos here or are regulars at the coolest hotels. In the summertime, many Los Angelenos who want to escape the summer fog at the coast come out to the desert for some serious heat and swimming pool time. In the winter, mild temperatures lure Palm Springs visitors out for easy day trips to Joshua Tree.

Death Valley makes another great weekend destination, as does Anza-Borrego. You can pick lodgings right in the center of these deserts, then spend your time on Saturday and

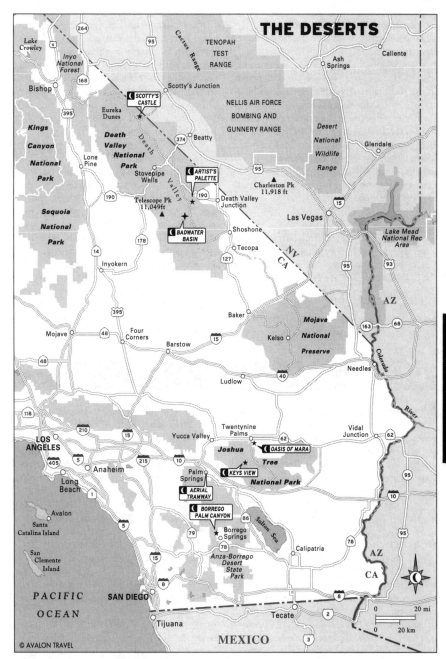

THE DESERTS

© AVALON TRAVEL

Sunday driving to the major sights and picking a few spectacular hikes before heading out on Sunday afternoon.

If you're a true desert rat and want to do a tour of all California's major deserts, plan at least a week to 10 days. The parks cover broad swaths of California's southern regions, and the distances between them can take hours to drive, especially along some of the more interesting back roads. Then you'll want to spend at least a day or two exploring within each desert. Leaving yourself enough time to enjoy the diverse ecosystems and unique sights will make the trip worthwhile.

## HISTORY

The history of the deserts of California is actually the geological history of the American continent. Two major deserts collide in California: the high-altitude Mojave to the north and the lower-lying Colorado in the southeast.

The most famous desert park in California, Death Valley, has its own story. Death Valley's formation began at least two billion years ago, and its landscape has been evolving ever since. Lakes have formed and dried up in its famous below-sea-level basin to the south, and recent volcanic activity is evident at the north end of the valley. Even as you wander around, the desert is changing all around you. Wind, gravity, and even water erode the valley's walls, shift its dunes, and create a new and different place every single day.

At heart, Palm Springs is a Hollywood town. As the movie industry heated up in the Los Angeles Basin, the industry had to find someplace to shoot desert and "Old West" locations. And the stars started seeking someplace to escape Hollywood and enjoy themselves on their own time. In the Golden Age of Hollywood (the 1930s, '40s, and '50s), film crews crowded into Palm Springs and stars built weekend homes with sparkling swimming pools. Today, many of the original 1940s and '50s inns that once housed producers and film crews now open their doors to guests of the area, and architecture buffs come to tour the original mid-century modern mansions and villas.

# Palm Springs

Palm Springs is a desert town with many faces. Some folks think of it as a wintertime snowbird retreat—that is, the spot where thousands of retired folks come to escape the harsh winter weather of their hometowns. To Hollywood star-followers, it's both a vacation haven for actors and a major on-location shooting site for many classic films of the 1940s and '50s. And for the young and vivacious gay crowd, it's a thriving and accepting town that's been known for its tolerance for more than five decades, complete with plenty of hot nightspots.

The Palm Springs area actually encompasses several medium-sized towns that have grown enough to bleed together into one sprawling urban area. Palm Springs proper maintains its status as the poshest and most happening place to be. As you drive south through Ranch Mirage, Palm Desert, Indian Wells, and down to Indio, you'll find more residential communities and country clubs with clusters of mall-style shopping but no real historic downtown areas. By the time you get to Indio, the industrial part of the area begins to take over, and the only real tourist sights are the date farms.

## SIGHTS
### ◖ Palm Springs Aerial Tramway

At first glance, Palm Springs doesn't seem like a spot where a gondola ride would be a big attraction. And yet, the Palm Springs Aerial Tramway (1 Tramway Rd., 760/325-1391, www.pstramway.com, Mon.–Fri. 10 A.M.–9:45 P.M., Sat.–Sun. 8 A.M.–9:45 P.M., adults $21.95, children 3–12 $14.95, seniors $19.95 ) draws both visitors and a surprising number of locals nearly every day of the year. The idea for the tramway was conceived by prominent and sweaty resident Francis Crocker in 1935. Crocker longed to visit the cool, snow-capped peak of Mount San Jacinto when the sun beat down mercilessly on the valley floor. It took nearly 30 years of wartime delays and political missteps to realize the dream, but in 1963 the structure was complete and the first visitors took a ride up to the peak of the 10,834-foot mountain. In 2000, the tramway was renovated, and now runs the biggest revolving cars operating in the world.

To take a ride on the tramway, you first drive up a winding road to the parking lots of the Valley Station. Purchase or pick up your tickets, then wait for your tram to depart. (Schedules vary based on season and weather conditions.)

You'll board the tram car and find a good place to stand on the circular metal platform, which can get fairly crowded. As the tram begins to climb, the platform revolves, letting passengers take in all the different views up and down the valley. The whole trip takes only 10 minutes as the tram ascends about 8,000 feet. When you get off the tram, you'll be in the Mountain Station, which includes a bar, a restaurant, a souvenir shop, and a visitors center for the surrounding Mount San Jacinto State Park (see *Sports and Recreation*).

But most folks head straight out the back door and into the park. In the wintertime, the park is usually covered by several feet of snow.

© AVALON TRAVEL

Locals bring their snowshoes, cross-country skis, sleds, and snow toys up on the tram (all of these are allowed in the car) for a fun few hours in the snow. The park creates a **Winter Adventure Center** (Thurs.–Fri. and Mon., 10 A.M.–4 P.M., Sat.–Sun. 8 A.M.–4 P.M., Nov.–Apr., ski package $21/day), a snow park with sled tracks, each winter. In the summertime when the snow is gone, those same locals take picnic supplies and walking sticks up to the mountain for a cool day's hiking and nature-loving.

## Palm Springs Art Museum

Just a couple of blocks from the main drag, the Palm Springs Art Museum (101 Museum Dr., 760/322-4800, http://psmuseum.org, Tues.–Sun. 10 A.M.–5 P.M., Thurs. until 8 P.M., adults $12.50, children $5) shows off the finest modern art in a variety of media. From your first steps up to the museum entrance, which is flanked by a pair of large sculptures, you'll be ensconced in the forms and shapes of modern art. The museum's central permanent collection is a mix of Western and Native American fine art and crafts. From local artists and craftspeople as well as those from around the Western states, these pieces evoke the sense of space and beauty found in Palm Springs and beyond. Other permanent exhibits include an ever-changing array of modern glass sculpture and an almost-new installation by Patrick Dougherty. The Palm Springs Art Museum also hosts an endless parade of traveling shows and special exhibitions, from video installations to sculpture collections to photography.

## Moorten Botanical Garden

Visitors who've come to the desert to learn and view the variety of desert wildlife will love the Moorten Botanical Garden (1701 S. Palm Canyon Dr., 760/327-6555, Mon.–Sat. 9 A.M.–4:30 P.M., Sun. 10 A.M.–4 P.M., adults $3, children $1.50). Set right near downtown, this charming garden specializes in cacti and succulents, growing over 3,000 varieties. The desert plants originate from all over the world, from South Africa and Madagascar to South America and much more locally in the Mojave

and Sonora deserts of California. You can wander the outdoor gardens, then head inside to the "Cacterium," a greenhouse in which the more delicate (and less adapted to the Palm Springs locale) specimens thrive.

The Moorten gardens were created and expanded by Patricia and "Slim" Moorten; Slim was one of the original Keystone Cops. Today, their son Clark owns and operates the gardens. Be sure to say hi if you see him out working on his pride and joy.

## The Living Desert

Do you prefer animal life to an endless parade of plants? Then head for The Living Desert (47900 Portola Ave., Palm Desert/Indian Wells, 760/346-5694, www.livingdesert.org, daily 9 A.M.–5 P.M., summer 8 A.M.–1 P.M., adults $12.50, children $7.50). The truth is you can visit a bunch more botanical gardens at The Living Desert. But you can also visit the animals—furry, scaly, feathered, and bald—that inhabit the world's great deserts. The Living Desert focuses primarily on the desert habitats of Africa and the Western United States. Some

desert bighorn sheep at The Living Desert

of the African natives, such as the gazelles and sand cats, are endangered species; others, like the meerkats, are stars of the small screen. The Discovery Center welcomes children of all ages, offering basic educational opportunities and interactive exhibits. The WaTuTu Village focuses on the lives of human natives of desert regions, and a somewhat incongruous but nonetheless impressive model train setup round out The Living Desert offerings.

Visitors can expect plenty of amenities at The Living Desert, including two café-style restaurants, two gift shops, and plenty of restrooms with baby-changing stations. The paved paths are wheelchair- and stroller-accessible. In addition, a number of shaded spots have water misters that cool off guests during the heat of summer.

## Date Farms

In the south part of the urban region, groves of dates provide most of the United States' crop of the sweet Middle Eastern staple fruit. The **Oasis Date Farm** (59–111 Hwy. 111, Thermal, 800/827-8017, http://oasisdategardens.com,

Oasis Date Farm

Mon.–Sat. 8 A.M.–5 P.M.) in the thriving metropolis of Thermal has a good-sized storefront and a demonstration "arbor" of date palms that visitors can walk around in. In the store, you can learn about the many different varieties of dates (interestingly, most dates originally come from Iraq) and taste almost all of them. You can buy whole dates, mixed boxes, and date candies. Over at the ice cream counter, the one thing you simply must try is the date shake—a super-sweet regional specialty that's perfect on both hot summer and mild winter days. Out in the orchard, you'll see how dates cluster and grow as you enjoy a few minutes in the shade of the thickly fronded palm trees.

Another famous date orchard that's open to the public is the **Shields Date Farm** (80–225 Hwy. 111, Indio, 800/414-2555, www.shields dates.com, daily 9 A.M.–5 P.M.) in Indio. If you can't make it as far as Oasis, check it out!

## Desert Memorial Park

It's not on most tourist destination lists for Palm Springs, but visiting star seekers and locals alike make pilgrimages to Desert Memorial Park (31750 Da Vall Dr., Cathedral City). Unlike the craggy old cemeteries in more historically oriented parts of California, you won't find slightly sunken marble tombstones, illegible wooden board memorials, or dried up weeds. Here all the grave markers are flat and uniform, the deep green lawn is meticulously maintained, and the shade trees are trimmed to perfection. Stop by the office to pick up a map and listing of the graves, some of which are inhabited by the remains of famous Hollywood celebrities. The best known of these are Frank Sinatra and Sonny Bono. Several members of Sinatra's family rest beside him. You might also see the markers for members of the Gabor family and actor William Powell.

## ENTERTAINMENT AND EVENTS

Unlike most of the rest of California's desert towns, Palm Springs is a thriving entertainment center. If you love to see shows, go out dancing, and stay up till 3 A.M. partying, this is the town

THE DESERTS

for you! The nightlife has a friendly vibe, the shows appeal to all ages (for real), and the festivals can fill the whole town with fun-loving visitors from around California and beyond.

## Bars and Clubs

**Red 74** (72–990 El Paseo, Palm Desert, 760/568-6774, Tues.–Sat. 6 P.M.–2 A.M., cover $5–15) in the suburb of Palm Desert offers truth in advertising; red fabric adorns the walls, and red decorative elements create a womblike monochromatic atmosphere. You'll find a younger crowd here enjoying the original signature cocktails, the dancing, and the eye candy. Beware: You might find yourself trying to grab a drink during a six-minute speed-dating session. But if you're lucky, you'll make it on a night with world music or a particularly good local DJ.

Two other suburban bar/clubs you can try out are the **Village Lounge** (73196 Hwy. 111, Palm Desert, 760/568-1200) and the **Club Rio** (68449 Perez Rd., Cathedral City, 760/321-5526).

## Gay and Lesbian

To be frank, most of the good nightlife in Palm Springs sits squarely within the gay community. The liveliest bars, the best dance clubs, the smoothest lounges—all gay.

But then again, "gay bar" doesn't mean quite the same thing in Palm Springs as it does in San Francisco or even Los Angeles. Here in the desert, there's a very casual, relaxed vibe to almost all of these spots. There's far less regimentation of straight vs. gay vs. lesbian here than elsewhere in California. It's not at all unusual to hit a gay bar at 11 P.M. on a Saturday night and find pretty shirtless boys, crew-cut lesbians, gorgeous drag queens, threesomes of indeterminate relationship, and straight married senior citizens all grooving on the same dance floor. Most "gay" bars and clubs welcome straights of all ages—just be aware that you'll see open same-sex affection, and if you freak out over it, *you'll* be the one who's asked to leave. Same goes the other way; if you're gay, you're expected to tolerate straight folks

smooching on your turf. But if you're open minded about your fun, you'll love the scene here in Palm Springs.

One of the premier gay clubs in Palm Springs offers you a respite from the desert heat at the **Oasis Nightclub & Lounge** (611 S. Palm Canyon Dr., 760/416-0950, www.cluboasis ps.com, Wed.–Thurs. 3 P.M.–midnight, Fri. until 2 A.M., Sat. until 4 A.M.). The regrettable strip-mall exterior belies the big industrial interior, which includes tons of room for dancing as well as drinking and meeting people. The unfinished ceiling and ductwork make the dance floor feel bigger, anyway. The crowd tends towards the boys, but women are welcome too. The club hosts many parties and special events each year, plus a regular calendar of nightly fun. Go to the website for more information before you come, or just show up and be surprised. Looking for a slightly mellower evening? Order your favorite fruity cocktail at the **O Lounge,** a quieter spot within the Oasis.

If your tastes run to leather, the one club in Palm Springs you must visit is **The Tool Shed** (600 E. Sunny Dunes Rd., 760/320-3299, www.toolshed-ps.com, daily 7 A.M.–2 A.M., Fri.–Sat. until 3 A.M.). Wear your leather and your Levi's when you come to shoot a game of pool or enjoy the rugged scenery. Inside, you'll find mostly men drinking and having fun in the appropriately industrial-styled bar, complete with chain-link fence. Check the website for a list of upcoming events.

For the ladies, **Delilah's** (67855 Hwy. 111, Cathedral City, 760/770-1210) offers a more estrogen-oriented atmosphere.

A newcomer on the proverbial block, **Mixie's Boy Bar** (120 S. Palm Canyon Dr., 760/203-0147) offers a big, meandering, multi-level dance floor, two bars, and a patio where you can hang out and smoke. The video system provides nonstop visual entertainment (as if the dance floor wasn't enough!) and DJ Mixtress rocks the house with a totally danceable blend of hip-hop, house, pop, and the occasional '80s classic thrown in to keep things lively. The art prints on the wall definitely have a theme, and there's actually a fair amount of seating for patrons who aren't quite up to dancing the whole night away. Is that totally shapely cocktail waitress male or female? Does it matter? This club and bar is one of the all-sexualities-welcome establishments, so feel free to climb the stairs for a fun late-night party no matter what your proclivities.

Even in gala Palm Springs, **Toucan's Tiki Lounge** (2100 N. Palm Canyon Dr., 760/416-7584, www.toucanstikilounge.com) draws notice. It's also a locals' favorite, almost a bar-around-the-corner, despite the wild tiki decor. This fun nightspot has pretty boy go-go dancers, a tiny dance floor that gets crowded on weekends, and a drag show every Sunday night. Bring a friend or four to make the most of a night out at Toucan's.

Can you picture a gay sports bar? **Score** (301 E. Arenas Rd., 760/866-1905) brings these two usually mutually exclusive concepts together to create a unique queer-jock experience on Arena Road, the longtime gay main drag. Imagine big-screen TVs, beer on tap, and dozens of beautiful men to stare at. Sounds like heaven!

## Live Shows

One of the staples of the Palm Springs entertainment scene is its exuberant Vegas-style shows. With singing, dancing, amazing costumes, and wonderful comedy, these shows delight audiences all year long.

Perhaps the most popular of the big shows is the **Palm Springs Follies** (128 S. Palm Canyon Dr., 760/327-0225, www.psfollies.com, shows Wed.–Sun. most weeks, see current schedule, $48–90). This vaudeville-meets-Vegas-style show draws national guest acts (Oct.–May). So what's the twist? Those lovely bejeweled showgirls wearing the glitter and the giant feather headdresses are old. Really, really old. The youngest performer in the Palm Springs Follies is 54 years old, and the oldest showgirl is well past her 80th birthday. You'll be surprised and delighted by a cast that's old enough to remember when this kind of live singing and dancing entertainment was more

than just a curiosity. Heck, a few of these performers remember Prohibition! Perhaps best of all, the dancers and singers come out to meet their audience after each show. Get autographs on your program and express your appreciation of the sexy seniors.

Advance reservations are highly recommended, as the Palm Springs Follies often sells out. You can purchase tickets for this three-hour show online or by phone, or at the box office. This long show can get boring quickly for small children, so it might be better to leave them at home, especially for evening shows.

Visitors who want to blend the various cultures of Palm Springs can't help but love **Copy Katz** (Casino Morongo Resort and Spa, 49500 Seminole Dr., Cabazon, 800/252-4499, www.morongocasinoresort.com or www.copykatzps.com). This celebrity impersonator and drag show features talented performers who'll make you believe you're watching Barbra Streisand or Michael Jackson. You can check online for the shows coming up in the following week, and you can buy tickets at the website. Cabazon is 20 minutes west of Palm Springs.

## Festivals and Events

With tourism and glamour as its major industries, it's no surprise that the Palm Springs area hosts an immense array of festivals each year to bring even more visitors into town.

One of the biggest festivals each year celebrates the area's signature crop: dates. The **Riverside County Fair and Date Festival** (82–503 Hwy. 111, Indio, 760/863-8247, www.datefest.org, Mon.–Fri. 10 A.M.–10 P.M., Sat.–Sun. 10 A.M.–midnight, adults $8, youth 5–12 $6) takes place in mild and lovely February of each year at the County Fairground in Indio. The Fairgrounds were created with a fun and funky Arabian Nights theme, which decorates the big space from the entrance gates inward. Be sure to get a place to view the Queen Scheherazade parade, check out the ostrich and camel races, and definitely grab a date shake from one of the many vendors. Kids and teens flock to the carnival area to ride the tilting, whirling, zipping rides (unlimited rides $23) that light up at night. You can't help but be entertained as you ramble through the rows of vendors, view the county fair contest entrants, and taste every dish that can possibly be made with dates. In the evenings, musical acts draw fairgoers to the stage to watch everything from local jazz to headlining national classic rock acts.

A perennial favorite of serious rock lovers from all over the state is the **Coachella Valley Music Festival** (www.coachella.com, single-day pass $95, three-day pass $275). Literally dozens of bands crowd onto the roster each year. In 2008, the lineup featured Roger Waters as the headliner, with such bands as The Verve, Death Cab for Cutie, and Fatboy Slim adding spice. For three days, concert-goers can immerse themselves in music from sunup to sundown and beyond. (Well, not quite from sunup…your hangover will appreciate the restraint.)

The Festival runs over a long weekend each spring, usually toward the end of April. Attendees can choose from the endless array of local motels and inns, or they can bring tents to pitch on-site so as to stick as close as possible to the action. The festival is held at the Empire Polo Field. Car access isn't too difficult, but the festival organizers encourage the use of public transit and carpooling to minimize auto traffic and crowding in the parking lots. Check the website for gate-opening hours and current prices. You can buy tickets online through the festival site, or call one of the major ticket handlers.

To no one's surprise, the Palm Springs region holds not one but many gay-themed events each year. While the annual **Greater Palm Springs Pride Parade** (www.pspride.org, Nov.) and festival are plenty of fun and well-attended, and the **Dinah Shore Weekend** (www.dinahshoreweekend.com, Apr.) is held especially for the girls, these are not *the* events of the season. Instead, break out your best croquet whites and take yourself and your friends to the annual **White Party** (277 Avenida Caballeros, www.jeffreysanker.com). Although the signature party takes place on the third Saturday night of April each year, the whole week beforehand sees pool parties, after-hours club events, and plenty of other themed social entertainments livening up the nights. The Saturday night White Party hosts up to 20,000 white-clad men intent on bumping and grinding and dancing the night away to fabulous, top-end DJs. Drag and dance shows light up the stage throughout the evening, and side lounges offer spots to sit down, kick back, and relax…or whatever…in a quieter space. The White Party typically runs 9 P.M.–5 A.M., with an after-party for seriously dedicated partiers. Other festival-sponsored parties include the fabulous and very popular Underwear Party and Pool Party. Check the website to buy tickets for your favorite events and get a look at this year's theme.

## SHOPPING

Shopping is a major pastime for the wealthy golfers and condo owners who frequent the Palm Springs area. The whole of Palm Canyon Drive from La Quinta up to Palm Springs seems to be one long strip mall, with everything from auto parts shops to Targets and on up through high-end chain clothing stores. On the other hand, for unique boutiques, your best bet is downtown Palm Springs or El Paseo.

### El Paseo

El Paseo is actually a mile-long avenue in the town of Palm Desert. Literally hundreds of shops, galleries, salons, restaurants, and more cluster on both sides of this legendary shopping street. El Paseo hosts a number of festivals each year, and weekly Art Walks during the wintertime high season. Whether you've come for the culture or for some simple retail therapy, El Paseo can hook you up.

The largest block of shops, an outdoor mall of sorts, is called **The Gardens** (El Paseo and San Pablo). The Gardens is anchored by Saks Fifth Avenue (73–555 El Paseo, 760/837-2900, www.saksfifthavenue.com, Mon.–Thurs. 10 A.M.–6 P.M., Fri.–Sat. 10 A.M.–7 P.M., Sun. 11 A.M.–6 P.M.) on one side and Tiffany & Co. (73–585 El Paseo, 760/341-3444, www.tiffany.com, Mon.–Sat. 10 A.M.–6 P.M., Sun.

11 A.M.–5 P.M.) on the other. But you can walk, or take one of the bright-yellow Courtesy Carts from end to end of the long street to make carrying your accumulation of shopping bags a bit easier.

At the south end, between Ocotillo and Sage Streets, shoppers interested in Native Americana and New Age merchandise can find an array of lovely things at shops such as **Earth Spirits** (73–130 El Paseo #N., 760/779-8766). Apparel for men and women can be purchased all up and down El Paseo—choose from chain shops or unique boutiques such as **She She** (73–061 El Paseo, Ste. 2, 760/779-0417) and **Mister Marcus** (73–540 El Paseo, Ste. B, 776-8454). Art lovers enjoy wandering in the **Edenhurst Gallery** (73–655 El Paseo, 760/346-7900) and **Gallery 1000** (73–400 El Paseo, #1, 760/346-2230), among others. The street also hosts an endless selection of interior designers and home stores for those looking to pick up just the right Southwestern item to add to their home's decor.

## Outlets

Outside of Palm Springs, you can load up on discount designer merchandise at the **Desert Hills Premium Outlets** (48400 Seminole Dr., Cabazon, 951/849-6641, http://premiumoutlets.com/deserthills, Sun.–Thurs. 10 A.M.–8 P.M., Fri. 10 A.M.–9 P.M., Sat. 9 A.M.–9 P.M.). From Palm Springs, drive west on Highway 11 to I-10 and into Cabazon. Highlights of this huge sprawl of high-end outlet stores include Dolce & Gabbana, Ralph Lauren, Gucci, Cole Haan, Waterford Wedgewood, and Bose. If all that bargain-hunting makes you hungry or you need a hit of energy, the mall has an array of coffee shops and quickie restaurants at each end to satisfy your cravings.

## SPORTS AND RECREATION

The Palm Springs and Coachella Valley area hosts a staggering 100-plus golf courses. If you're not a golf lover, beautiful desert and mountain parks beckon hikers and even cross-country skiers and showshoers. Water parks

cool children and adults alike during the long, hot desert summers.

## Parks

The closest gorgeous scenery and good hiking to downtown Palm Springs is found at the **Indian Canyons** (1097 E. Murray Canyon Rd., 760/327-6550, www.palmsprings.com/points/canyon, daily 8 A.M.–5 P.M., adults $8, children $4). These canyons were once home to the ancestors of the Agua Caliente Cahuilla Native Americans. The abundant streams and diverse plant and animal species made the series of canyons a wonderful place to live—plenty of fresh drinking water, food, and materials to build shelter sit all around. The progressive tribes even diverted water from the streams to irrigate planted crops. Today, all the canyons bear trace evidence of these long-gone communities, and it's fun for kids (and grown-ups) to search for housing foundations, dam remnants, and food-processing areas.

The most stunning (and most-visited) of the canyons is **Palm Canyon,** an aptly named 15-mile-long oasis of color, water, and beauty improbably set in the midst of a dry and barren patch of desert. You'll bask in the shade of the lush and naturally growing palm trees, admire the colorful spring wildflowers, and dip your fingers in the creek that feeds the abundant life in the canyon. The paved footpath makes it easy to explore. For an extra $3, you can take a ranger-guided one-mile walk to learn more about the history and nature of the canyon. Or if you prefer to let a strong equine do the walking, horseback riding is permitted through Palm Canyon. And in the grand tradition of popular outdoor sights in Southern California, the **Trading Post** offers souvenirs, maps, and refreshments to all comers.

Another beautiful and well-traveled spot is **Tahquitz Canyon** (500 W. Mesquite Rd., 760/416-7044, adults $12.50, children $6). The highlight of Tahquitz Canyon is a waterfall that cascades down 60 feet down and splashes into a pool. The fall is seasonal, and you'll want to come in the springtime to see the best show. Tahquitz Canyon has its own

THE DESERTS

© LIZ HAMILL SCOTT

**Snow in Palm Springs!**

visitors center, complete with an interpretive exhibit, short educational film, and observation deck.

Other canyons include **Murray Canyon** and **Andreas Canyon.** If you prefer seclusion and a wilder version of natural beauty, these canyons might be more appealing to you than the well-developed Tahquitz and Palm Canyons.

At the top of the Aerial Tramway, **Mount San Jacinto State Park** (25905 Hwy. 243, 951/659-2607, www.parks.ca.gov, daily dawn–dusk) offers fabulous hiking, camping, and winter snow play only 10 minutes from Palm Springs by gondola ride. You can also access the park from the other side by driving in from CA-243 or CA-74. The south end of the Pacific Crest Trail runs through this beautiful high-elevation park. Many day-hike trails crisscross the mountain peak, letting visitors enjoy cool, shaded forests and fabulous valley views as they walk. A number of campgrounds throughout the park, some hike-in and some car-campsites, offer outdoorsy travelers the opportunity to acclimate to the altitude and explore the area in depth. But no matter how fit you are, take care when you first arrive and begin to hike

here—you'll be well over a mile and possibly as much as two miles above sea level, and altitude sickness can be a real danger.

Nature lovers can look for lots of wildlife as they ply the trails of the park. Sniff the wildflowers and admire the butterflies drinking from them, touch the bark of a Jeffrey Pine tree, or bring your birding list and look out for winged friends. While bears aren't a problem at San Jacinto, do keep an eye out for mountain lions. If you see one, get as big as you can and don't run; face the cat down.

## Golf

*The* major form of outdoor exercise in and around Palm Springs and the Coachella Valley is golf. The region boasts more than 100 courses, about half of which are public or semi-public. The rest belong to a variety of private country clubs. Among the publicly accessible courses, players can try anything from low-fee municipal courses up to swanky PGA championship country clubs. If you're a serious golfer, pick up a guide to all the courses or look on the web to find those that will fit your game best.

**Indian Springs Golf and Country Club** (79-940 Westward Ho Dr., Indio, 760/200-8988, www.indianspringsgc.com) boasts some of the best golfing in all the region for under $100 (most of the time). Naturally, the best rates going are in the blistering summertime, but you can find bargains in the moderate months of September, October, and March as well. Whatever your skill level, this 6,770-yard, par 72 course will offer fun in the desert sunshine. You can also make good use of the driving range and pro shop, and grab breakfast, lunch, or dinner before or after your game.

Looking for hardcore championship golf the likes of which you've only seen before on TV? Book a tee time at **Trilogy La Quinta** (60–151 Trilogy Pkwy., La Quinta, 760/771-0707, www.trilogygolfclub.com/laquinta, $30–120). The likes of Tiger Woods and Annika Sorenstam have walked the greens here at the oftentimes home of the PGA Skins Game. Six tee positions provide a challenge for new, mid-level, and experienced players. As at most courses, afternoon golfers get the best price breaks, as do those willing to brave the torturous summer heat. The attached Azul Restaurant has gone modern in its decor, serving upscale California cuisine for breakfast, lunch, and dinner to golfers and non-players alike.

The **Cimarron Golf Resort** (67–603 30th Ave., Cathedral City, 760/777-6060, www.cimarrongolf.com) prides itself on offering a different experience from the plethora of country club courses. In truth it has two separate courses: Pebble and Boulder. Boulder is the par-71 championship course that draws the best golfers out on weekend morning, while Pebble's par-58 provides fun for even the newest of golfers and good practice for more advanced players who only have a couple of hours to enjoy a game. You can book your tee time up to 120 days in advance. Call for rates during your stay.

Looking for something else? A few more of seemingly infinite options include **Eagle Falls Golf Course** (84–245 Indio Springs Parkway, Indio, 760/238-5633, www.eaglefallsgolf.com,

$50), **Mesquite** (2700 E. Mesquite Ave., Palm Springs, 800/727-8331, www.palmsprings.com/golf/mesquite.html), where Bob Hope used to bring his cronies, and the ritzy **Indian Wells Golf Resort** (44-500 Indian Wells Ln., Indian Wells, 760/346-4653, www.indianwellsgolfresort.com, $75–200).

## Biking

Bicycling opportunities abound in Palm Springs. Wintertime, when the weather is mild to cool, is the best time to take a bike out on the desert roads and bike trails. In the city of Palm Springs, an interconnected maze of bike trails help folks get around with ease and relative safety. Check www.palmsprings.com/city/palmsprings/bikemap.html for a map of the in-town loops.

## Water Parks

Summer visitors and locals looking to both cool off and enjoy active outdoor fun head for **Knott's Soak City USA** (1500 S. Gene Autry Tr., 760/327-0499, www.knotts.com/soakcity/ps/index.shtml, adults $18–30, children $18). As with most major California water parks, Soak City has fast and furious slides, as well as the funky new Pacific Spin, a slow-moving river for inner tubers, a wave pool, and a children's splash area. Soak City also offers plenty of dry land, complete with some chairs and chaises. Amenities include coin-op lockers, food concessions, restrooms and changing rooms, and rentable shaded cabanas.

## Winter Sports

With the well-known scorching desert climate of the valley floor, Palm Springs doesn't seem like much of a winter sports destination. And yet, visitors and locals (especially locals) can take advantage of nearby mountains to ski, sled, snowboard, or just play in the snow for a day.

For a nearby day of snow play, cross-country skiing, or snowshoeing, grab your gear and take the Palm Springs Aerial Tramway up to **Mount San Jacinto State Park** (25905 Hwy. 243, 951/659-2607, www.parks.ca.gov, daily

THE DESERTS

dawn–dusk). If you've got sleds and kids, head out of the Mountain Station and down the main trail to the Adventure Center. Here you'll find groomed sledding tracks and even the occasional sled-racing event. For the adventurous and fit crowd, many of the summer hiking trails turn into cross-country ski and snowshoe tracks when the snow covers them. Check with the rangers at the Mountain Station for current conditions and a trail map.

SoCal downhill skiers and snowboarders think of the ski resorts at **Big Bear** (880 Summit Blvd., 800/424-4232, http://bigbear. com) as their home mountains. Choose between **Snow Summit** (909/866-5766, www.snow summit.com, adult lift tickets $20–65, children $8–53) and **Bear Mountain** (909/866-5766, www.bearmountain.com). At Snow Summit, 14 lifts service more than 30 trails. This resort caters primarily to beginning and intermediate skiers, complete with a ski school and fun beginner terrain parks. On the other hand, Bear

Mountain appeals more to the intermediate and advanced crowd. With dozens of jumps, jibs, and a Superpipe, Bear Mountain beckons to boarders and freestylers from SoCal and beyond.

Big Bear also offers cross-country ski and snowshoeing trails and tours, plus a snow park.

## Spas

With all that money running around Palm Springs, it's understandable that plenty of it gets spent on relaxing massages and rejuvenating facials. You'll find many day spas and spa resorts clustered north of Palm Springs proper in the town of Desert Hot Springs, taking advantage of the smallish locale's namesake waters. For example, **Living Waters Spa** (13340 Mountain View Rd., Desert Hot Springs, 866/329-9988, www.livingwatersspa.com, day use $45/couple or single) features multiple pools filled with the local mineral water, massage services, and comfortable European-style

# SAFETY IN THE DESERT

People who've never spent time in a desert before often underestimate the very real dangers of trekking in a harsh, dry climate, while experienced desert rats can become overconfident and complacent about their safety precautions, to their detriment.

No matter who you are, or how many times you've gone hiking or camping or backpacking or driving out into the desert, you *must* plan for problems and practice for safety. Here are a few recommendations from the various desert state and national parks:

· **Carry water.** This is possibly *the* most important desert safety tip of them all. You're not likely to find much water if you're out hiking in the desert. In Death Valley, 1-2 gallon per person per day is recommended, and they mean it. Even if you're driving around the park on mostly paved roads, carry water in your car. Water is a big concern in all the big desert parks – you won't find much, even at the major sights with big parking

lots. No matter which desert you're visiting or for how long, bring twice as much water as you think you'll need. Better to have too much than too little!

· **Wear a hat.** In the desert, wear a hat with a wide brim to shade your face and your neck. Do it even if you hate hats; if you don't have one, buy one at the gift shop. Hats are the single best way to keep the punishing desert sun off your head, a must if you get into any trouble in the desert.

· **Wear sunglasses.** Again, don shades even if they're not your usual style. The harsh sunlight bouncing off the light-colored landscape can cause real damage to unprotected eyes. Many of the visitors centers sell sunglasses.

· **Use sunscreen.** You've never experienced sun like it pounds down in the desert, so be good to your skin and go for a high-SPF sun-hotel accommodations (most with full kitchens). The other European aspect of Living Waters its clothing-optional and, in fact, somewhat clothing-discouraged facilities. Expect to see day-use and overnight guests strolling, bathing, and lounging in the nude all around the resort. The emphasis of this spa is on freedom (especially freedom from binding clothing) and relaxation for all visitors.

On the other hand, **Desert Mystique Spa** (4721 E. Palm Canyon Dr., Ste. F, Palm Springs, 760/960-4597, www.desertmystique spa.com, Mon.–Sat. 10 A.M.–7 P.M., Sun. by appt, $80–90/hour massage) in the midst of downtown Palm Springs gives more modest spa-goers a traditional day spa experience. Desert Mystique has a full menu of spa treatments, including half a dozen different massage styles and an array of facial and body treatments. The facials tend toward SoCal aesthetic and post-surgical treatments, while the massages have an almost Northern California flair.

If you're serious about pampering your face, book an appointment at **European Experience Luxury Facials** (2225 Tahquitz Canyon Rd., Ste. 6, Palm Springs, 760/902-2751, www .palmspringsfacials.com). Whether you're a man or a woman, this day spa can concoct the perfect treatment. Men also seek out the specialized back treatment, and everyone loves a relaxing Swedish massage. Ear candling and waxing services are also available.

## Casino Gambling

The **Fantasy Springs Casino** (84–245 Indian Springs Pkwy, Indio, 800/827-2946, www .fantasyspringsresort.com) has all sorts of entertainment options, from bowling to live shows. You can stay at the high-rise hotel and pass all day and half the night down on the casino floor. This isn't a full-fledged Vegas-style casino, but you'll find plenty of slot machines, table games, bingo, and even horse-race betting. Enjoy a game of easy-rules blackjack or

**THE DESERTS**

screen. (It'll also help with the unbelievably dry skin most folks get when hanging out in ultra-dry climates.)

- **Stay away from old mines and other man-made hazards.** You'll find cool old abandoned mines in Death Valley, Joshua Tree, Mojave, and possibly even Anza-Borrego. Such places have zillions of hidden dangers, from invisible vertical shafts to collapsing timbers to piles of old explosives. Don't wander into old mine shafts or touch explosives, and tell park rangers about the latter.

- **Be aware of potential flash floods.** All the desert parks in California are rife with washes – spots where water rushes across the landscape during rare but often intense desert storms. And if you're in a wash during one of those storms, you can get fatally swept away. If the weather looks stormy, take care in washes: don't park your car

in one, don't use one for a hiking trail, and don't pitch your tent in or beside a wash.

- **Tell someone where you're going.** Tell a friend or a family member back home where you're going and when you plan to be home. That way, somebody will miss you if you don't come back and can alert the park or the police to your potential location and predicament. If you're planning to go backcountry camping in a park that allows it, register with the rangers as required for the same reason.

- **If something happens, stick with your vehicle or your companions.** It's easier to find several people than one alone, and it's easier to find a bright shiny car than it is a person. So if the worst happens and you find yourself stranded, stay with your group and with your car for the best chance of being found.

mini-baccarat, or try your luck at one of the newer progressive slot machines. When you need a break, head for one of several restaurants or the nearby attached cocktail bar.

At the **Spa Resort Casino** (401 E. Amado Rd., Palm Springs, 760/883-1000, www.spa resortcasino.com) you can try your luck at one of 1,000 slot machines or 30 tables. Got lots of cash to bet? Head for the high-limit room. Poker lovers tend to stick close to the card room, while casual gamers take a break from the endless noises and flashing lights of the casino floor to get a soothing massage or facial at the resort's in-house spa.

## ACCOMMODATIONS

The range of accommodations in Palm Springs is both broad and deep. As a town with nearly 100 years' history as a tourist mecca, it's hard not to find a room here, even on the spur of the moment (as long as it's not a festival weekend). You can go for a cheap motel, a historic mid-century modern hotel with Hollywood history, or even a plush high-end casino style hotel. Sure, you can stay at one of the standard national chain motels, but why would you when so many lovely boutique hotels dot the landscape?

If you're gay, you've got even more choices. Palm Springs has an array of gay-only and gay-friendly lodgings. Most of these cater to men only, except during the woman-oriented Dinah Shore Weekend.

### Under $100

**Chase Hotel Palm Springs** (200 W. Arenas Rd., 760/320-8866, www.chasehotelpalm springs.com, $90–235) offers classic Palm Springs–style accommodations at reasonable nightly or weekly rates. The charming mid-century modern motel sits only a block from Palm Canyon Drive. Outdoors, it boasts a charming garden area complete with palm trees and a saline swimming pool. Inside, while the style of the guest room furnishings evokes the 1950s, the beds and chair are in fact comfortable and totally modern. Choose between a king or two-bed room, or a larger suite with

a kitchenette and perhaps even a mosaic-tiled fireplace. Each morning, grab a bite to eat from the tasty continental breakfast spread, and don't forget to indulge in a freshly baked chocolate chip cookie in the evening!

### $100-150

Only a few minutes from the center of town, **( A Place in the Sun** (754 E. San Lorenzo Rd., 760/325-0254, www.aplaceinthesun hotel.com, $112–340) was first built in the early 1950s to shelter the cast and crew working on the film of the same name. Then and now, a meandering set of 16 semi-individual bungalows offer spacious quarters for visitors. All guest bungalows include full kitchens, living rooms with modern TVs, and tropical-resort-style decor with old-school movie prints decorating the rather thin walls. Bedrooms have cushy mattresses and older wall heaters—you might even see a radiator unit original to the property in your vintage pink-tiled bathroom. You'll also have your own small private patio (on which you can relax with a cigarette),

A Place in the Sun

plus access to the central courtyard with its ill-kept miniature putting green and its lovely modern gentle-salt pool and spa. A continental breakfast is served in the office each day, or out in the gazebo by the pool with more variety of food and drink on the weekends in wintertime. Friendly owners will help you out with all aspects of your stay (the office is open 9 A.M.–5 P.M. six days per week). Pets are welcome.

If you want to stay in a real William F. Cody original building, check in to the **Del Marcos Hotel** (225 W. Baristo Rd., 760/325-6902, www.delmarcoshotel.com, $110–200). This small boutique hotel has won awards for its dedication to preserving its mid-century modern design. Indeed, even the guest room decor screams late 1940s and early '50s, complete with prints of Hollywood idols of the time, period artwork, and brightly colored chairs of funky design. You'll be greeted at the front entrance by the hallmark diagonally sloping roofs and faux-stonework, and muted colors of the period. The interior courtyard boasts a saline pool surrounded by chaise lounges with umbrellas and an expanse of concrete. With only 16 rooms, the Del Marcos Hotel feels more like an inn than an impersonal hotel, and it's convenient to the shops and restaurants of Palm Canyon Drive.

## $150-250

The **Movie Colony Hotel** (726 N. Indian Canyon Dr., 888/953-5700, www.movie colonyhotel.com, $180–400) takes the famed mid-century modern style and kicks it into an upper scale. While you'll still see the clean diagonal lines and blocky structural details, the amenities inside and out of the rooms and townhouses here breathe with a vintage-meets-modern luxury. You'll find high thread-count linens, light-colored designer furnishings, plenty of space, and designer accents. All rooms have California king beds and pristine bathrooms. Townhouses include large living areas with great 1950s style sofas, fireplaces, and travertine bars with refrigerators. Pay a little extra for a room with a door out to the attractive pool area. It's the focal point of the

hotel, and includes a large spa and a fire pit where complimentary wine is served in the evenings. With your room rate, you'll also receive a daily continental breakfast, concierge service, and loaner bicycles on which you can explore downtown Palm Springs.

## Over $250

If you can afford serious luxury in the desert, stay at the **Villa Royale Inn** (1620 S. Indian Trail, 760/327-2314, www.villaroyale.com, $200–350). This lovely boutique hotel seeks to evoke the feel of Europe—a Tuscan villa, perhaps. Guest rooms range from small "hideaways" to spacious two-bedroom villas that feel more like home than a hotel room. Each of the 30 rooms has its own unique antique furnishings, down duvet, fluffy bathrobes, and charming bathroom stocked with herbal toiletries. Though the rooms are fabulous, it's the amenities at Villa Royale that make you feel like royalty. Choose between two pools and one large Jacuzzi, book an in-room massage, or ask the concierge to help you get a tee time or a tennis court at one of the famed local golf courses or country clubs. Every morning you'll awaken to a full, hot, cooked-to-order breakfast, which can be served in your room. For lunch and dinner, enjoy the Continental cuisine served by the attached restaurant Europa, or have them bring the food to you in your room or out at poolside.

## Gay and Lesbian Resorts

Among the dozens of resort hotels and inns catering to gay men, **The Triangle Inn** (555 E. San Lorenzo Rd., 760/322-7993, www.pride nation.com/triangle, $135–560) stands out for a number of reasons. The Triangle was the first commercial design of one Hugh Kaptur, the architect who went on to do much important mid-century modern work in and around Palm Springs, including William Holden's home. The unique structures and interesting lines have been preserved, making the lushly landscaped buildings fun to look at for passersby outside the compound. Inside, each of the nine guest suites has a unique decorative scheme.

**THE DESERTS**

You can rent anything from a studio suite up to a fully furnished four-bedroom house. Out at the pool, in the hot tub, under the cooling misters, and in the other common areas of the Triangle, clothing is optional. Hosts Michael and Stephen live at the resort and their talent as hosts helps make the Triangle what it is today. Oh, and be sure to pet Duncan, the orange tabby cat who runs the place, when you see him prowling the grounds.

A larger oasis for gay men, the **Vista Grande Resorts** (574 S. Warm Sands Dr., 760/322-2404, www.mirage4men.com, $100–325) sits in the popular Warm Sands area. This hedonistic clothing-optional resort offers 30-some guest rooms, three pools, three spas, and a steam room. The pool-and-spa complex in the Mirage section of the three-resort complex has two waterfalls, curved naturalistic pools, and lots of foliage and rocks surrounding the swimmable waters. Rooms range from an economical studio room to a luxurious suite by the waterfall with a living room and a full kitchen. All amenities are taken care of, so kick back, relax by (or in) the pool, and concentrate on making new friends.

For the ladies, the **Queen of Hearts** (435 E. Avenida Olancha, 760/322-5793, www.queenofheartsps.com, $120–180) provides laid-back elegance for reasonable nightly rates. This recently renovated nine-room inn was the first lesbian-oriented hotel to be opened in Palm Springs nearly 40 years ago (then called the Desert Knight). Today, each room includes lovely light designer appointments, a queen bed, a full kitchen, and a comfortable bathroom. Unlike the men's resorts, guests of the Queen of Hearts wear clothes in the common areas, including while swimming in the sparkling courtyard pool or soaking in the outdoor, above-ground whirlpool tub. While you don't need to be a gay woman or couple to stay at the Queen, this inn does cater to that crowd and you should expect to see happy female couples engaging in public displays of affection here. If you're among those couples, be sure to let management know if you're celebrating a birthday or anniversary!

## FOOD

The dining in Palm Springs exemplifies the best of California. You'll find high-end California and French cuisine, fun ethnic eateries, and tasty snack foods all through the area, though the greatest concentration of serious independent restaurants collects downtown, on and around Palm Canyon Drive.

### American

A favorite local downtown breakfast spot is **Billy Reed's** (1800 N. Palm Canyon Dr., 760/325-1946, daily 7 A.M.–9 P.M., $7–22). The interior dining room and bar have low lights and air conditioning, while the out-front patio offers plenty of seating and great people-watching. The casual atmosphere welcomes everyone all day long, though shoes and shirts are required. Expect the quality of service to depend a bit on the level of crowding. The extensive menu includes everything from classic omelets and giant cinnamon rolls for breakfast to every kind of salad and sandwich for lunch and on up to prime rib and salmon for dinner. Whatever you order, you'll get hearty portions of classic American food, perhaps with a tiny Mexican twist here and there. In all honesty, the food isn't the best you'll ever taste, but it's good enough, it's hot, and it's plentiful.

### Asian

Looking for a little Eastern flair with your dinner in the desert? Try **Wang's in the Desert** (424 S. Indian Canyon Dr., 760/325-9264, www.wangsinthedesert.com, $12–20). Friday evening happy hour tends to draw a big and mostly gay crowd, and likewise a group more interested in socializing than chowing down shows up to "Chill" on Sunday afternoons with a DJ spinning to help add to the atmosphere. But if you're looking for great Chinese food, you can find it here too. Take a seat on a banquette in the attractive gold and cream dining room and order from the distinctive menu. The dishes ring familiar, but Wang's puts its own stamp on the cuisine. You'll find unique appetizers and entrées that you won't taste anyplace else. Just be sure to get reservations at least a couple of days in advance, since Wang's gets crowded with locals at dinnertime, especially on weekends.

## French

When you turn sideways to thread your way into ◖ **Pomme Frite** (256 S. Palm Canyon Dr., 760/778-3727, www.pomme-frite.com, lunch Sat.–Sun. 11:30 A.M.–2:30 P.M., dinner Wed.–Mon. 4:30–10:30 P.M., $18–28), you might believe you've somehow been transported to France or even Belgium. This hole-in-the-wall does not pretend to serve haute cuisine; instead, Pomme Frite offers casual bistro dishes cooked to perfection. The food fits in perfectly with the atmosphere—sunny yellow walls, black-and-white prints, real wooden wine boxes, and other tchotchkes. Tables are scrunched so close together in the tiny front dining room that even the wait staff has trouble getting through. Though the back dining room's setup is a tiny bit more spacious, it's still loud and has a friendly, crowded feeling. On weekends, reservations are highly recommended, though they fit in as many walk-ins as they can.

The menu provides a look at both Paris brasserie favorites such as mussels and steak and fries, plus a few fun Belgian dishes. The fresh, delicate salads are delicious too, but as you eat, try to save just a little bit of room for the delectable desserts.

## Italian

Do you just want an ultra-casual pizza meal? Walk up to the counter at **Lotza Mozza Pizza & Pasta** (119 S. Indian Canyon Dr., 760/325-5571, $10) and order a handmade pizza, a tasty pasta dish, or a big crisp salad. Grab a seat at any of the red-checker-covered tables and the cute young wait staff will bring your food out to you. Pizzas have New York–style thin crusts, tasty tomato sauce, and gooey mozzarella cheese. While the service isn't always stellar, the price is right and the food does come out piping hot and tasty.

## Mexican

Among the best of the many Mexican restaurants throughout the Palm Springs region, the **Las Casuela** (368 N. Palm Canyon Dr., 760/325-3213, www.lascasuelas .com, Sun.–Thurs. 11 A.M.–9 P.M., Fri.–Sat. 11 A.M.–9:30 P.M., $10–12) group offers some of the best and most authentic Mexican cuisine. Las Casuela Original was the first of them, opened by the Delgado family in 1958 with the recipes Maria brought up from her home. The small dining room looks bigger because of the wall-length mirror along one side, which reflects the wonderful hand-painted mural on the opposite walls that depicts pastoral life in Mexico, complete with cows. The service feels as friendly as the restaurant sounds—if you have any food allergies or special requests, they'll be happy to accommodate you. The family opened Las Casuela Nuevas and **Las Casuela Terraza** (222 S. Palm Canyon Dr.), two bigger and slightly fancier versions of the original, still using Grandma's old recipes as the basis for their menus. Terraza boasts a beautiful outdoor patio seating area and some fabulous margaritas made with top-shelf tequilas.

## Steak

The restaurateurs of Palm Springs have opened a near-countless array of steakhouses. It's hard to go more than a mile or two without running into one. The king of the local chains is undoubtedly **LG's Prime Steakhouse** (255 S. Palm Canyon Dr., Ste. B, 760/416-1779, www .lgsprimesteakhouse.com, daily 5 P.M.–close, $25–55). All three of their restaurants (one in Palm Springs, one in Palm Desert, and one in La Quinta) offer the best beef available, much of it dry aged in specially designed meat lockers on the premises. The sides are steakhouse classics that complement the huge cuts of meat, but some of the appetizers are LG's originals. While the atmosphere at LG's has a splash of upscale elegance, you'll still see plenty of exposed brick and feel a touch of casual friendliness.

## Vegetarian

Desperately looking for a meat-free meal in steak-loving Palm Springs? Head downtown

**THE DESERTS**

to **Native Foods** (1775 E. Palm Canyon Dr., Ste. F, 760/416-0070, www.nativefoods.com, Mon.–Sat. 11 A.M.–9:30 P.M., $8–15). This vegan restaurant offers a large menu of salads, sandwiches, soups, and hot food of all kinds, plus delicious desserts. You'll find some tasty seitan (a grain protein) faux meats and tempeh, as well as lots of bean dishes, veggie pizzas, and Middle Eastern–inspired cuisine. Native Foods even has a small kids' menu. This small SoCal chain also has a restaurant in Palm Desert (at 73–890 El Paseo Dr.) to satisfy the appetites of hungry vegan shoppers.

## Coffee and Tea

Okay, so it's a chain. At least it's a Southern California regional chain. Still, the **Coffee Bean and Tea Leaf** (100 N. Palm Canyon Dr., 760/325-9402, $5) at the corner of Palm Canyon Drive serves up tasty coffee in a pleasant local atmosphere. You can get your favorite espresso drink and a pastry, and sit either inside or out to enjoy a quick breakfast.

# INFORMATION AND SERVICES

Though it's the only one in the stark desert region, Palm Springs and its suburbs create a major urban center, and an affluent one at that. Expect to find all the goods and services you need and want someplace in or around Palm Springs.

## Tourist Information

For newcomers to Palm Springs, a good first stop is the **Palm Springs Visitors Center** (777 N. Palm Canyon Dr., 760/778-8415, www.palm-springs.org). Here you'll get everything you need to enjoy your visit to the area, including real opinions on local attractions and restaurants. The website can help you even before you arrive—use it to select an inn, print up maps, and get the low-down on the best events and parties while you're in town.

## Media and Communications

The local Palm Springs newspaper is *The Desert Sun* (www.mydesert.com). It's published daily and available at many local motels and restaurants, plus it's for sale at public newsstands and shops in all the various towns.

Cell phones work fine in Palm Springs, as do laptops with wireless Internet capability (though you'll often have to pay for the privilege to connect up).

All major American banks do business in Palm Springs, and you'll find a plethora of ATMs ready to help you access (and ultimately spend) your cash. Palm Springs and its satellite towns also have full-service **post offices**—at least one per town. The Palm Springs branch sits at 333 East Amado Road.

## Medical Services

In a town full of retirees, medical care is easy to come by. If you need an emergency room, you'll definitely find one. Right in downtown Palm Springs, you can head for the **Desert Regional Medical Center** (1150 N. Indian Canyon Dr., 760/323-6511, www.desertmedctr.com), which provides both emergency and trauma care services. On the other hand, if you're looking for a plastic surgeon, the phone book can hook you up. I can't.

# GETTING THERE AND AROUND

## Air

The **Palm Springs International Airport** (3400 E. Tahquitz Canyon Way, 760/318-3800, www.palmspringsairport.com) offers flights with most major carriers and a few minor airlines. It is the only commercial airport in the region—if you can't fly into or out of here, you'll be driving in from the Los Angeles Basin. While the weather in Palm Springs is usually fabulous, when it gets bad it can shut down the whole airport, so keep that in the back of your mind when you plan your wintertime flights.

## Bus

The **SunLine Transit Agency** (800/347-8628, www.sunline.org, adults $1, seniors $0.50) runs a number of bus lines throughout the Palm Springs region, running from Desert Hot Springs down through Palm Springs proper, into Indio and all the way down to Coachella and Thermal. Check out the route map online.

## Car

Palm Canyon Drive is the main drag through downtown Palm Springs. Then it takes off and connects the back sides of all the other towns, from Palm Desert down to Indio. While it might sound like it, this drive isn't all that attractive unless you're really into strip malls and chain stores. There's little scenery otherwise.

If you're driving in from Los Angeles, I-10 is the most direct route east. I-10 runs through Palm Springs and down through Indio, out east past the south entrance of Joshua Tree.

## Tours

If you love to go touring, you can find a variety of different styles and modes of transit in Palm Springs tours, self-guided or prepackaged. **Celebrity Tours** (760/770-2700, www .celebrity-tours.com, adults $35, children $14) offers two short city tours that focus on the (surprise) celebrity residents and their homes in the town of Palm Springs and in the connecting cities beyond. A luxury bus brings visitors to the homes of Bob Hope and Celine Dion, to the date farms at the edge of the urban center, then back to the Old Movie Colony of Palm Springs proper. You can also check out Celebrity's day trip tours into Los Angeles, Las Vegas, and other spots in the region.

The discerning boonie-crasher can check into **Adventure Hummer Tours** (760/285-0876, www.adventurehummer.com, adults $110–160, children $70–90). You'll board a militaristic H-1 Hummer for your open-air adventure out into the desert canyons beyond the city. Whether you want to see the remote off-road regions of Joshua Tree or check out the legendary earthquake-producing San Andreas Fault or both, Adventure Hummer can take you there.

If you prefer wait till after dark to head outside, check out **Sky Watcher Tours** (73–091 Country Club Dr., Ste. A42, Palm Desert, 760/831-0231, www.sky-watcher.com). You'll get an educational and entertaining tour of the night sky over the deserts surrounding Palm Springs that's perfect for kids and adults, plus fun takeaway sheets to help you identify constellations wherever (in the Northern Hemisphere) you are.

**THE DESERTS**

# Joshua Tree

Joshua Tree National Monument and its namesake "trees" lies just east of Palm Springs and offers easy access from the Los Angeles area. The northern half of the park sits in the high-altitude Mojave Desert. But as the park's lands stretch south, they also dip down into the lower-set Colorado Desert. It's actually not too hard to see where the landscape starts to change; Joshua trees become fewer and fewer, while ocotillos and teddy bear cacti start to pop up in their place. Even the dust-dry ground changes in color and character, with the characteristic light tan boulders of the north country giving way to a darker gray ground in the south. While many visitors stick exclusively to the north end of the park, it's worth the time to drive the main park road south to check out a really different desert region.

## SIGHTS
### ◖ Oasis of Mara

The best known and best visited oasis in Joshua Tree is undoubtedly the well-developed Oasis of Mara (Hwy. 62 and Utah Trail). A number of small springs well out of the ground along the Pinto Mountain fault here, providing the life-giving water that supports a large and lush (well, lush for the Mojave Desert) ecosystem. The earliest known residents of the Oasis were the Serrano people, who planted a new palm tree each time a boy was born, then used the products of those palm trees for tools,

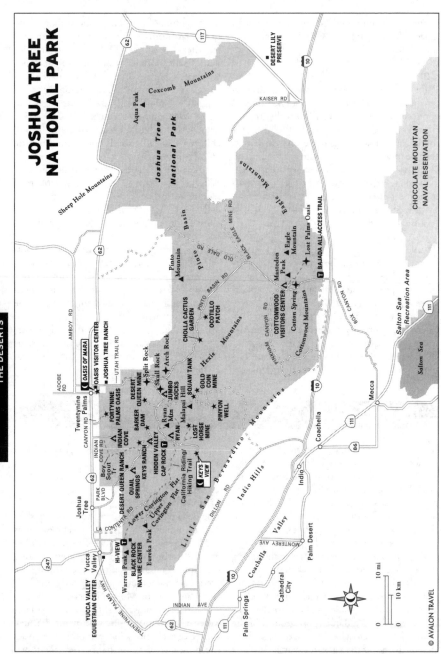

# JOSHUA TREE NATIONAL PARK

© AVALON TRAVEL

shelter, and food. With the arrival of European-American settlers, the culture around the oasis and its surrounding grasslands changed. Gold mines sprang up, and ranchers brought in cattle to graze the region. One or two homes were even constructed here.

Today, over 100,000 people come through the Oasis visitors center just outside of the town of Twentynine Palms each year. Ironically, the Oasis sits outside the park boundaries, but it's still treated as a part of the park. A lovely easy nature trail loops around the oasis for half a mile. This wheelchair- and stroller-accessible trail includes a variety of signs that teach walkers about the natural features of the oasis. You'll see the palm trees, hardy grasses, and huge light boulders that characterize the region and hint at the beauty you'll find elsewhere in Joshua Tree.

## Black Rock Canyon

West of the main entrances, just south of the tiny town of Yucca Valley, the Black Rock Canyon (Hwy. 247 at the northwest corner of the park) makes a great introduction to the park. The developed campground, nature and ranger center, and hiking trails are surrounded by the famed Joshua trees, which begin the spring bloom late each February. Lots of birds and mammals live nearby. You might see anything from a great horned owl to the threatened desert tortoise while you visit and camp here. You'll also see the famed black rocks that give the area its name. First-time visitors often walk the **Hi-View Nature Trail** (1.3 miles), a lovely interpretive stroll that points out and describes the plants and other natural features that characterize the northern Mojave Desert region of Joshua Tree National Monument. Black Rock Canyon also includes a trailhead for a 35-mile stretch of the California Riding and Hiking Trail and several other longer hiking trails. Check in at the ranger station for a wilderness permit if you plan to go on an overnight backpacking trip in the area.

## Hidden Valley

One of the centerpieces of Joshua Tree, the

© LANCE SCOTT
Joshua Tree

THE DESERTS

Hidden Valley (Park Blvd., 10 miles south of West Entrance) offers hikes, a nature trail, a campground, and a rare view of a tiny desert valley. If you're day-tripping in Joshua Tree, park in the day lot and follow the tourists off to the right to the sort-of trail onto and through the big tan boulders. You'll scramble up, getting a great up-close view of the surprising granite mineral content of the pale boulders on either side of you. Emerge from the rocky trail into a small rocky meadowlike area, which includes small signs describing the natural features. Keep walking across the clearing and on to the next miniature pass.

## Cap Rock and Skull Rock

Among the wonders of Joshua Tree are the fabulous boulder formations scattered about the landscape. As you drive or hike, especially in the northern reaches, you'll have a hard time missing at least a few of these great light orangeish-tan rocks. Sit and stare at them, thinking up different common animals and other things that the boulders and clusters resemble—kind of like cloud gazing, but without the movement.

Two rocks that are fairly close together by the road so resemble other objects that they're named and marked on park maps. If you take the east–west connecting road from Pinto Basin Road (the main north–south corridor) to the road to Keys View and Hidden Valley, you'll first pass Skull Rock (Park Blvd., seven miles east of Hidden Valley), one of the many giant stones that provide shade at the aptly named Jumbo Rocks campground. Guess what this rock is shaped like? Just past the intersection towards Hidden Valley, Cap Rock and its buddies offer interesting geology, a small picnic area, and a good spot for rock climbers to dig in and start scrambling.

## Keys Ranch

The only way to get a real look at Keys Ranch (Keys Ranch Rd., Oct.–May Sat.–Sun. 10 A.M. and 1 P.M., adults $5, children $2.50) is to take a docent-guided tour of the buildings and land. William and Frances Keys were among the

rugged settlers of the Mojave Desert. They ranched on the sparse desert grasses and raised five children on this patch that would become part of Joshua Tree. Today, visitors see the weathered pine buildings that housed the original ranch house, the schoolhouse that educated the few local children, the local general store, and a workshop. The orchard and landscaping have been replanted and revived. A collection of mining and farm equipment sits in the dry desert air, and relics like the old well dot the property here.

To get to Keys Ranch, drive half a mile north of the Hidden Valley campground, then turn off onto a bumpy one-lane dirt road (passenger cars okay) that runs for about a mile. Park near the gate and meet your tour guide just inside the property. Buying tickets in advance (you can call ahead and use a credit card) is recommended, especially on holiday weekends. If you're feeling lucky, you can just head up to the gate and ask the ranger if any spots are available on the next tour. Check the ranger schedule for weekday tours throughout the year.

## ◖ Keys View

One of the best views in all of Joshua Tree is the Keys View (end of Keys View Rd., bear right off Park Blvd. past Cap Rock). On a clear day, the view from here redefines the concept of "panoramic," letting travelers see the whole of the Palm Springs urban sprawl, the Coachella Valley farmland, the notorious San Andreas fault, and even the Salton Sea many miles to the southeast. You'll drive all the way to the end of the road out of the West Ranger Station, up to about 5,000 feet elevation and the sizeable parking lot. Get out of your car and climb a brief paved trail to the vantage point at the top of the ridge.

Sadly, crystal clear days are hard to come by. Not only is the ever-expanding Palm Springs cityscape polluting its valley, a pass to the west and prevailing winds often blow smog into the region from the Los Angeles Basin. The best time to catch a good view at Keys is the early morning, and the best way to help make the views better is to read the signs up on the path and do what you can to decrease your own emissions. Sure, you're only one person, but imagine what the mid-afternoon would look like at Keys View if even two out of three people did *only one person's* worth of responsible pollution reduction?

## Cottonwood Spring Oasis

The Cottonwood Spring Oasis (Box Canyon Rd., turn onto spur road at visitors center) gets fewer visitors than many of the northern park sights, but it's one of the most beautiful oases in Joshua Tree. The catch? No Joshua trees, because Cottonwood sits at the transitional area between the Mojave and Colorado Deserts. Instead, at the oasis you'll see a fabulous grove of desert fan palms, which are native to California. The thick growth of flora and fauna at this oasis is fed by Cottonwood Spring, a naturally occurring spring caused by the seismic activity in the region. (Caution: Do not drink the spring water! It's not potable.) The Cahuilla Native Americans used the spring water for washing, cooking, and more. They also hunted and gathered from the abundant natural resources here. You can still see

## WHAT IS A JOSHUA TREE?

You'll see them everywhere in the north end of Joshua Tree National Park, and indeed they're common throughout much of the Mojave Desert. They do look almost like deciduous trees from a distance, and up close their foliage and "bark" looks like nothing else most folks have ever seen – spiky and scaly, green and brown and odd, with funky creamy greenish flowers every once in a while. It's definitely not a "regular" tree, but it doesn't look much like a cactus species either.

So what is a Joshua tree?

Desert botanists will probably figure out on their own that Joshua trees are members of the yucca family. Specifically, Joshua trees are *Yucca brevifolia* – a type of yucca that grows almost exclusively in the high-altitude (2,000-6,000 feet) Mojave Desert ecosystem. Though the trees can be delicate – they've got a shallow root system and all those branches get heavy – Joshua trees can live up to a thousand years.

If you get to see the Joshua trees bloom, you're lucky! They don't bloom every spring; it happens only when enough rain falls at the right time, and after the tree has experienced at least one hard freeze. Once they bloom, specially adapted yucca moths fertilize the flowers by laying eggs in them. This spreads pollen, and the blossoms turn into a greenish-brown fruit filled with seeds. The fruit drops, the seeds spread out on the ground and sprout, and new Joshua trees begin to grow.

You'll see other types of yucca plants throughout California, even in unlikely spots such as the Big Sur coast. Most of the common yuccas grow wider and closer to the ground than Joshua trees, and have much longer dagger-like leaves. Once you study their shape and the way the leaves grow, then the family resemblance becomes clear.

© LANCE SCOTT

evidence of their presence in left-behind artifacts. You'll also find the remains of more recent use of the spring: primitive, hand-built gold milling equipment left over from several 19th- and early 20th-century gold mills.

In the early springtime, the Cottonwood area leads the park's beautiful wildflower bloom with colorful desert dandelions, lupine, and others. Check in February for the first flowers. Any number of hiking trails encircle the area, perfect for day trips, and a campground offers rare shady spots with the sound of trickling water to lull you to sleep at night.

## SPORTS AND RECREATION

Even more than the other California deserts, Joshua Tree invites outdoor sports enthusiast of all kinds into its wilderness to take advantage of the beauty and challenge of the diverse region. Whether you're a leave-no-trace backcountry backpacker, a hardcore climber, or a Jeep-driving boonie-crasher, you'll find your bliss here.

### Hiking

Dozens of great hikes crisscross the length and breadth of Joshua Tree. Though many of these start in or near the visitors centers and developed campgrounds, don't neglect the trails that begin off the paved and unpaved roads of the park.

Before you begin a hike here—even a short two or three mile jaunt—be sure you're properly prepared. It's not as dry as Death Valley, but Joshua Tree National Monument is still a harsh and unforgiving desert. Bring lots of water (up to a gallon per person). For longer hikes, pack more water, food, and a first-aid kit. Talk to the rangers about safety, climate, and what to bring on a long day or multi-day backcountry adventure.

A number of trails start at the Black Rock Canyon campground. In addition to the **Hi-View Nature Trail,** many longer hikes begin here. To get to the summit of **Eureka Peak** (approx. 12 miles round-trip, difficult), first take the Burnt Hill Trail south to connect to the Eureka Peak Trail. You'll ascend 1,500 feet on this all-day trek up to some of the most

beautiful views in the whole park. Another option is the **Panorama Loop** (approx. 12 miles round-trip, difficult). Be sure to bring your camera!

Down south, the Cottonwood Spring area offers everything from quarter-mile nature walks to multi-mile intense hikes. If you're more into cactus than quadriceps strain, try the **Cholla Cactus Garden** (0.25 mile, easy). It's definitely worth it to spend the $0.50 on the descriptive pamphlet that will give you a greater understanding of the "jumping" cholla catci and the rest of the surrounding ecosystem. Look for the desert wood rats and cactus wrens that feed here, but be sure not to touch the pretty but vicious teddy bear cholla—the nasty little needles seem to jump off the cactus to bury themselves in unsuspecting hands.

Farther south, only half a mile from the park gate, the **Bajada All-Access Trail** (0.25 mile, easy) offers great views of the myriad plants that populate the Colorado Desert climate. As implied by the name, this nature trail is wheelchair-accessible.

For a longer and tougher hike, climb **Mastodon Peak** (3 miles round-trip, difficult). This steep hike takes you back up above 3,000 feet, where you'll take in views of Eagle Mountain and out to the Salton Sea. Check out the Mastodon Mind and the Winona Mill on your way. One of the longest and most rewarding hikes in this region takes you out to the **Lost Palms Oasis** (8 miles round-trip, difficult). Here grows the largest grove of fan palms in Joshua Tree, fed by natural year-round pools of fresh water.

### Rock Climbing

Joshua Tree is one of the finest rock climbing parks in the United States, indeed in the world. Whether you're into bouldering or climbing, you'll find a plethora of climbing areas and routes here. The good climbing regions are almost all found in the northern reaches—the Mojave area, which is filled with granite canyons and fantastical boulder formations. Even the most dedicated of climbers can't chip the surface of Joshua Tree in just

THE DESERTS

© LIZ HAMILL SCOTT

climbing Cap Rock

one trip, which is why many come back to the park year after year.

If you need equipment and supplies, the small towns along the north border of Joshua Tree support a number of climbing outfitters. Curious newcomers can even arrange guided climbs and climbing lessons through these companies. Obviously, **Joshua Tree Rock Climbing School** (760/366-4745, www .joshuatreerockclimbing.com, $120/one-day session) is prominent among these outfits. From one-day beginning seminars that teach the fundamentals of rock climbing up through four-day intensive sessions and lead climbing classes that take newbies up to the intermediate level in only half a week, this school offers a wonderful opportunity for aspiring climbers to start building their skills.

More than a dozen climbing spots surround the Indian Cove Campground. A tangle of paved roads service the area, and a large parking lot provides easy access to the boulders and cliff faces. Test your skills against Dos Equis Wall or Apparition Rock to the west, or Upper and Lower Dodge City to the south of the central camping area.

The climbing areas associated with the Hidden Valley are more spread out, but there are more of them and several of these range out into the wilderness area of the park. Near the parking area and campground you'll find The Real Hidden Valley Area, Cyclops, Echo Cove, and a number of others. Out to the northeast, you can hike or drive a dirt road out to Willow Hole to climb the Fortress, Super Dome, or Valley of Kings.

Between the Sheep Pass and Ryan campgrounds, several parking lots make it easy to stage climbs at Cap Rock, Hall of Horrors, and Love Nest. Other good places to stage climbs include the rough roads of the Geology Tour, the Queens Valley, and Split Rock.

Do be aware that strict rules govern climbing at Joshua Tree, and climbers are responsible for knowing those rules before they start up any boulders or steep faces. Be sure to check the park website or stop in at the ranger station to pick up a copy of those rules and the Fixed

THE DESERTS

## MOJAVE DESERT NATIONAL PRESERVE

California's Mojave Desert stretches for endless miles across the state. For the best views of the unique climate, formations, and ecosystem of this famous desert, visit the Mojave National Preserve (located btwn. I-15 and I-40, www.nps.gov, free). The Mojave is vast so don't expect to see all of the desert in one trip, even if you've got a whole week to spend. Pick your drives, hikes, and attractions carefully in order to see the Joshua Trees, caverns, cinder cones, and abandoned mines that most appeal to your interests.

The **Mojave Scenic Drive** is an easy day trip from Twentynine Palms or even Palm Springs. If you've only got one day, the best (and easiest) introduction to the Preserve is at the northern edge of the park along the smooth, well-kept pavement of I-15. From the town of Baker, turn south off I-15 onto Kelbaker Road for the 35-mile drive to Kelso. You'll traverse an alien landscape composed of volcanic activity, part of the Cinder Cones

National Natural Landmark. Stop in Kelso to explore the fabulous visitors center. The Spanish Revival facade of the **Kelso Depot Visitor Center** (Kelbaker Rd., Kelso, 760/252-6108, daily 9 A.M.-5 P.M.) welcomes travelers from all over the world. The visitor center once held the all-important Kelso Depot, which served the railroad that supported the many desert mining camps. The original structure has been renovated to include exhibits on the desert landscape and natural history, historically furnished dorm rooms, and a restored lunch counter. An abundance of park rangers are on hand with advice on yearly road conditions. (Not all roads are passable in standard cars each year. Be sure to ask here or at one of the other visitors centers about passable roads before striking out on your own.)

Snap a few photos of the Kelso Dunes along the horizon before climbing back into your car to turn onto Kelso-Cima Road. The road follows the Union Pacific rail line along the edge

Anchor Checklist. The website also offers topographical maps of the major climbing areas.

## Horseback Riding

Several trails at Joshua Tree are open to equestrians as well as hikers. You can bring your own horse and ride the trails solo, or arrange with one of the local ranches to take a guided ride of the park and the area that surrounds it.

**Joshua Tree Ranch** (Park Blvd. Mile 2.9, 760/366-2788, www.joshuatreeranch.com, $65–125) offers easy rides on its own land just north of Joshua Tree, and moderately challenging rides into the park. You can also work with the ranch to create your own private ride for a higher fee. This ranch takes its horses and its riding quite seriously, so consider your real riding ability level and that of your companions and family before booking a ride with them. Reservations for all rides are required, but rides are available most days with enough advance warning.

A full-service equestrian center, the **Yucca Valley Equestrian Center** (7429 Avalon Ave.,

Yucca Valley, 760/365-4433, www.yuccavalley equestriancenter.com, $35/hour) leads easy rides across flat desert lands of Joshua Tree as well as more challenging rides through narrow canyons and up steep hills. While the standard trail tack is Western, you can request an English saddle when you reserve your ride.

If you'd rather strike out on your own, the most popular riding trail in Joshua Tree is the **California Riding and Hiking Trail.** This 35-mile section of what is actually a statewide trail has many access points throughout the north end of the park. Its park boundaries are the Black Rock Canyon campground (which includes a horse camp) in the west and the North Entrance Station to the east. You can see many of the most beautiful areas of Joshua Tree while riding this trail, many of which are not directly accessible by road. Ride through forests of Joshua trees and past amazing and rarely seen rock formations. You can do a two-day ride on this trail, stopping at the Ryan campground, which includes horse facilities, near the middle of the trail's length.

of the Providence Mountains to the town of Cima, where you'll find snacks and drinks (but no gas). Cima also serves as a convenient fork; if you're in a hurry to get back to I-15, staying left on Cima Road will get you there the quickest. The right fork, **Morning Star Mine Road,** offers a more interesting route, including a turnoff to the abandoned mine that gives the road its name. From the mine, turn left onto Ivanpah Road and continue to Nipton Road to return to the freeway.

This drive takes about 90 minutes without stops, but feel free to hike the many great desert trails, photograph the Joshua Trees or the blossoming spring wildflowers, and explore (safely) an abandoned mine.

Planning to spend a weekend or longer exploring Mojave? For a total immersion into the desert world, spend your nights in one of the park's many campgrounds. **Hole-in-the Wall** campground is accessible from the Kelso-Cima Road and has toilet facilities, potable water, and an RV dump station. If your primary goal is to explore Mitchell Caverns, Hole-in-the-Wall's 37 campsites are closest to this major attraction.

Not too far from Hole-in-the-Wall, **Mid Hills** campground also has bathrooms, water, picnic tables, and fire rings for its 26 available sites. Like Hole-in-the-Wall, no reservations are accepted – all sites are first-come, first-served, so get there early during spring wildflower season. If you've come to Mojave to ride your horse through the beautiful and varied desert, make a reservation at the **Black Canyon** equestrian and group campground ($12, reservations 760/928-2572).

Want to camp all on your own, with no other campers nearby? Mojave has a number of existing roadside campsites that have sheltered independent desert-lovers for years. Just be sure to use an already existing site; look for stone fire rings and pre-disturbed earth to avoid further disturbing the fragile desert ecosystem.

The 16-mile **Boy Scout Trail** also permits equestrian traffic. Running roughly from Indian Cove to Hidden Valley, it offers another scenic view of northern Joshua Tree for hikers and riders alike.

## Off-Roading

Unlike many of California's wilderness parks, Joshua Tree welcomes off-road vehicles and provides more than half a dozen backcountry roads for four-wheel drives to bump out to explore otherwise inaccessible parts of the park. (Mountain bikes are also allowed on these roads, so keep a lookout while driving out there.)

One of the most popular backcountry roads is **Geology Tour Road** (Geology Tour Rd. and Park Blvd.). Pick up a printed road guide at the start of the road so you'll know about each of the 16 major geological (and other landscape) features you're looking at when you stop at them. In truth, during good years regular passenger cars (but not trailers and motor homes)

can make part of this tour, from the turn off the main road to the Squaw Tank.

**Queen Valley Roads** are a network of smallish roads running for a total of about 13 miles. You'll get to see plenty of big granite boulders and Joshua trees as you bump along out here on the other side of the paved road from Hidden Valley. This makes a great mountain biking trek if you prefer to travel under your own steam.

In the south, several great roads offer a fun crash through the boonies of the Colorado Desert region of the park. The **Black Eagle Mine Road** (six miles north of Cottonwood visitors center) offers nine miles of scenic canyon vistas within the park boundaries, and BLM road and driveable side trails beyond. Outside of the park on the side roads, you'll come upon abandoned mines and old homesteads—beware of the dangerous and unstable mine shafts and equipment if you find them. Leading from the same cutoff, the **Old Dale Road** runs 23 miles through the Pinto Basin dry lakebed and up a steep mountain, then out of the park. More

THE DESERTS

unstable mines and abandoned homes greet you once you cross the park boundary.

If you're looking for a more serious adventure, the **Pinkham Canyon-Thermal Canyon Roads** is advised only for hardcore booniecrashers who know what they're doing and carry proper emergency supplies.

## Mountain Biking

As of this book's publication, the only mountain biking allowed in Joshua Tree is along the backcountry roads shared with off-road vehicles. Check with the rangers at any of the visitors centers to learn whether 29 miles of designated mountain biking trails have opened by the time of your visit.

## CAMPING

Many of the outdoors-loving visitors to Joshua Tree prefer to sleep out under the brilliantly glittering stars. If that's you, you've got your choice of mostly first-come campgrounds with tent and RV sites and at least basic facilities, and backcountry rough camping.

If you plan to backpack out into the wilderness, you must register on one of the backcountry boards or get a permit at one of the ranger stations. Most of the major drive-in campsites have backcountry boards (bulletin boards where you can sign up and indicate your general planned route and destination.

At all the developed campgrounds, you must observe quiet hours, generator use restrictions, and deal with the lack of showers. In fact, only a few campgrounds offer any water at all. If you bring a solar shower, take care! The sun in this area can quickly give you a near-boiling shower experience.

The **Black Rock** (Black Rock Canyon, reservations Sept.–May 877/444-6777, $15) campground is one of the biggest and most developed in Joshua Tree. With 100 sites, running potable water, and full bathroom facilities, Black Rock offers a semblance of comfort in the harsh desert. Some spots take RVs, and the site has a dump station. Black Rock is one of the two park facilities where equestrians can camp with their horses.

The other horse-friendly campground is **Ryan** (Park Blvd. south of Hidden Valley, first-come, first-served, $10), which has more primitive facilities and fewer sites. Expect pit toilets and no available drinking or washing water here. Each site has a grate for cooking and campfires, and a picnic table.

Two other popular campgrounds, **Hidden Valley** (Park Blvd. south of West Entrance, first-come, first-served, $10) and **Jumbo Rocks** (Park Blvd. east of Geology Tour Rd., first-come, first-served, $10), sit near the center of the most traveled areas of the park. Both are primitive, with pit toilets and no water, but Jumbo Rocks has over 100 sites in great locations. Many of these sites sit beneath the shelter of boulders, a natural and historic way to camp. Both of these campgrounds are first-come, first-served. At Hidden Valley, RVs must be 25 feet or less.

**Indian Cove** (Indian Cove Rd. south of Entrance Station, reservations Sept.–May 877/444-6777, $15) offers over 100 campsites along the north park boundary in a location convenient to the small towns just north of Joshua Tree. While there's no water on-site, it's easy to come by at Joshua Tree and Twentynine Palms—and you can even get a hot meal in the evenings with only a short drive back to your tent! The Indian Cove area offers a half-mile nature trail for tourists who want to check out the local wildlife and traces of seasonal Native American settlements.

In the south of the park, **Cottonwood** (CA-195 at the Cottonwood Visitors Center, first-come, first-served, $15) offers water and flush toilets, as well as a dump station for RVs. The nearby visitors center offers a few basic supplies, and some of the loveliest hikes and wildflower viewings start in this region.

## ACCOMMODATIONS

If you're looking for luxury in your accommodations, you'll need to stay in Palm Springs and day-trip in to Joshua Tree. A few town motels offer plain but clean and comfortable indoor beds just outside of the northern park boundary. Inside the park, your choices are campgrounds with flush toilets, campgrounds without flush toilets, and backcountry hike-to-it and do-it-yourself camping.

Most of the motel rooms adjacent to Joshua Tree lie in the town of Twentynine Palms. You'll find the usual array of national chains, plus a few independents vying for your business.

## Under $100

Any U2 fans who've come to Joshua Tree to pay homage simply must stay at the **Harmony Hotel** (71161 29 Palms Hwy., 760/367-3351, www.harmonymotel.com, $77–95). This is where the band stayed when they were hard at work on the album named for the National Monument. It's a small, casual motel with only eight rooms total. The guest rooms have been recently remodeled, and you'll find white and light-patterned linens, cute sitting and dining areas in the larger rooms, and original artwork in each room. Pick a room with a king or two double beds, request one of the rooms with a kitchenette, or make yourself a pot of coffee in the guests' kitchenette/break room. Be sure to take a break in either the piping-hot outdoor spa in the evening or the deliberately unheated pool in the heat of the summer's day. For a quick break from the natural wonders, take in the artwork that surrounds the inn.

## $100-150

**Sunnyvale Garden Suites Hotel** (73843 Sunnyvale Dr., Twentynine Palms, 760/361-3939, www.sunnyvalesuites.com, $100–190) is perfectly located downtown, but off the noisy highway, in Twentynine Palms. Don't let the rugged exterior with its Western-style weathered pine boards fool you—the interiors feature comfortable modern amenities. All rooms have vintage tubular brass-style or wooden bedsteads, simple and soothingly colored linens and curtains, and plenty of space. Rooms sleep 2–6 people, and some have full kitchens. Outside of the guest room, enjoy the fitness center and the large outdoor spa, or take a walk in the climate-appropriate desert garden that surrounds the property. Bring the kids out to the playground in the cool mornings and evenings to burn off some energy, or just take

a family stroll around the residential neighborhood of Twentynine Palms.

A favorite with repeat visitors, the **Circle C Lodge** (6340 El Ray Ave., Twentynine Palms, 760/367-7615, www.circleclodge.com, $135–150) offers lovely accommodations away from the noisy center of town and out in the desert. Choose from a guest room with a king bed or two queens; each room has its own well-equipped kitchenette (all the kitchen lacks is an oven). Light, floral decor with colorful blue and red accents and TVs with VCRs (but no DVD players just yet) make the oversized rooms pleasant and homey. Each morning head down to the courtyard for a complimentary bagel with fresh fruit, juice, and coffee. The sparkling pool and cute circular shaded spa invite visitors to relax after a dusty day of hiking at Joshua Tree.

## $150-250

**Roughley Manor** (74744 Joe Davis Dr., Twentynine Palms, 760/367-3238, www.roughleymanor.com, $150–185) seems to be poorly named; this lovely B&B is anything but rough, inside or out. Once the homestead of a young couple named Campbell who dreamed of ranching in the desert, the inn now welcomes guests all year long. With a dozen rooms, two in the lovely stone-clad main house and the rest in a handful of other buildings scattered throughout the large garden property, Roughley offers more space and better privacy than most similar inns. Each individually decorated guest room uses floral themes as they should be used—sparingly—to create the sense of a guest suite in a private elegant farmhouse. Many of the suites have kitchenettes and dining areas to create an additional sense of staying at home rather than at an impersonal motel. The prices are amazingly cheap if you're accustomed to the B&Bs of the big cities and Wine Country, and the location is perfect for sojourns out into Joshua Tree.

## FOOD

There's no food inside Joshua Tree National Park. Picnickers and campers must pack in every bite of food they intend to eat. The only

THE DESERTS

visitors centers that maintain snack bars reside just outside the park boundaries.

Multi-night campers sometimes long for a hot meal served by someone else at a clean table. If that's what you need, you can drive into Twentynine Palms or even Palm Springs for a tasty meal.

## Restaurants

The most talked-about eatery adjacent to Joshua Tree is the **Crossroads Cafe & Tavern** (61715 29 Palms Hwy., Joshua Tree, 760/366-5414, www.crossroadscafeandtavern.com, Sun.–Tues. 6:30 A.M.–8 P.M. Thurs.–Sat. 6:30 A.M.–9 P.M., $5–10). It sure doesn't look like much from the outside, with its rusted aluminum siding and bright blue painted trim. But it's what's inside that counts, and inside the Crossroads you'll find friendly owners running their own place with the assistance of a tiny tribe of well-trained employees. The food is as unpretentious and tasty as the owners. At breakfast you can get an array of egg dishes, while lunch and dinner run to salads and sandwiches. The price is right at the Crossroads, so you won't break the bank for a reasonably health conscious meal here. Plenty of vegetarian options dot the menu, though carnivores aren't left out either.

Longing for a gooey slice of pizza or a big ol' hearty sub? Try **Sam's Pizza** (61380 29 Palms Hwy., Joshua Tree, 760/366-9511, www.sams pizza.com, Mon.–Thurs. 11 A.M.–8 P.M., Fri.–Sat. 11 A.M.–7 P.M., Sun. 3–8 P.M., $5–20). The big menu features an array of reasonably priced Italian and American dishes that are perfect after a long day of hiking or climbing. Create your own pizza, or go for a classic hot meatball sub. If you're planning a late afternoon in the park, order cold subs and have them wrapped up to go. Specialties include calzones, paninis, and even a few Greek dishes beckon, while full-sized dinners appeal to seriously hungry diners.

Decent and inexpensive Mexican cuisine in the Joshua Tree desert region is served at **Santana's Mexican Food** (73680 Sun Valley Dr., Twentynine Palms, 760/361-0202, open daily, $5–10). Grab a burrito, a couple of tacos, or even a combo plate here, and top it off with an offering from the open salsa bar. Yum!

## Cafés

The **Park Rock Café** (6554 Park Blvd., Joshua Tree, 760/366-3622, Mon.–Sat. 9 A.M.–6 P.M., Sun. 9 A.M.–4 P.M., $10–20) serves casual café food and espresso drinks next door to the Joshua Tree Visitors Center near the West Entrance to the park. Park Rock is a good place to grab a quick bite before entering the park or just after leaving.

## Markets

Need to stock up on groceries before hitting the park? Two local markets can supply hungry hikers and campers in need of supplies. **Stater Bros** (58060 29 Palms Hwy., Yucca Valley, 760/365-2415) sits near the western entrances. Near the Oasis entrance, check out the **Plaza Market** (5668 Historic Plz., Twentynine Palms, 760/367-3464).

## INFORMATION AND SERVICES
## Tourist Information

It's hard to drive more than a dozen miles in Joshua Tree without tripping over a ranger station or a nature center. Most of these are tiny, but they're prolific and you'll get the information you need wherever you stop. If you're camping at any of the larger campgrounds, you'll probably find a nature center somewhere in it.

The **Oasis Visitors Center** (760/367-5500, year-round daily 8 A.M.–5 P.M.) sits at the Oasis of Mara. It's got all you need in terms of rangers, a bookshop, special exhibits including videos, and more.

West of the Oasis, you can enter the park at the **Joshua Tree Visitors Center** (760/366-1855, year-round daily 8 A.M.–5 P.M.). A fun little interpretive museum explains the origins and current fun available in Joshua Tree, and knowledgeable rangers can inundate you with maps and advice. Day-trippers often grab a quick bite and some extra water from the adjoining café before heading into the foodless desert park.

If you're entering the park from I-10 in the

south, your first stop will be the **Cottonwood Visitors Center** (no phone, year-round daily 9 A.M.–3 P.M.). This tiny center has maps and rangers, a picnic ground, and flush toilets and running water, but very little else.

## Media and Communications

The National Park publishes several pamphlets and papers for visitors. Ask for these at any of the visitors centers.

In an emergency, call **San Bernardino dispatch** (909/383-5651). Cell phone coverage is unreliable in the park, especially in the back-country. Don't depend on your cell phone in cases of emergency. You can find public phones at the Joshua Tree and Oasis visitors centers.

You won't find Internet access inside the park. You might find a Wi-Fi connection at your motel in Twentynine Palms, and there's certainly plenty of Internet in Palm Springs.

The Twentynine Palms **post office** is located at 73839 Gorgonio Drive.

## Medical Services

For non-emergency medical needs, the nearest place to find a wide variety of clinics open at all hours is Palm Springs. In an emergency, dial 911 or 909/383-5651 (San Bernardino dispatch).

## GETTING THERE AND GETTING AROUND
### Air

The nearest major airport to Joshua Tree is at **Palm Springs** (3400 E. Tahquitz Canyon Way, 760/318-3800, www.palmspringsairport. com). It only takes about an hour to drive from the airport out to the park.

### Car

You can drive from Palm Springs or even Los Angeles to the south entrance of Joshua Tree on I-10. From I-10 heading east, turn north (left) onto Box Canyon Road, which takes you right up to the Cottonwood Springs Visitors Center.

To enter at the north side of the park, find your way to Twentynine Palms Highway, also known as State Highway 62. Highway 62 originates at I-10 northwest of Palm Springs, or to avoid the freeway take Indian Avenue up through Desert Hot Springs and around to the north side of the park. From Highway 62, you can turn in to Black Rock Canyon, the Joshua Tree Visitors Center, or the Oasis of Mara.

Parking inside Joshua Tree usually isn't too difficult, as ample parking lots are provided for the major attractions. On holiday weekends, come early for the best spots and least crowded hikes.

THE DESERTS

# Death Valley

For a valley famed for its uncompromising climate, Death Valley teems with life. Desert plants, including funky pickleweed and more common creosote, wildflowers, and even desert-dwelling fish and snails live here in profusion. Even the rocks, cliffs, salt flats, and mountains seem to live and breathe here. The best way to experience the amazing world that is Death Valley is to visit for at least a weekend, driving from sight to sight and then getting out of the car to walk out into the desert.

## SIGHTS
### ◀ Scotty's Castle

If you ask the locals around Death Valley if there's one single thing not to miss, almost to a person they will tell you to see Scotty's Castle (Hwy. 267 in Grapevine Canyon, 3 miles northeast of Grapevine intersection, adults $11). The unfinished grand Spanish-styled home is the only private mansion ever built in Death Valley. Contrary to popular legend, it never was the home of infamous huckster Death Valley Scotty—he actually lived in a rough cabin on the property, only hanging out in the castle with his friend Albert Johnson. In truth, the mansion was built and furnished by Johnson and his wife, a wealthy couple from Chicago who initially invested in Scotty's oft-lauded but never seen gold mine but became

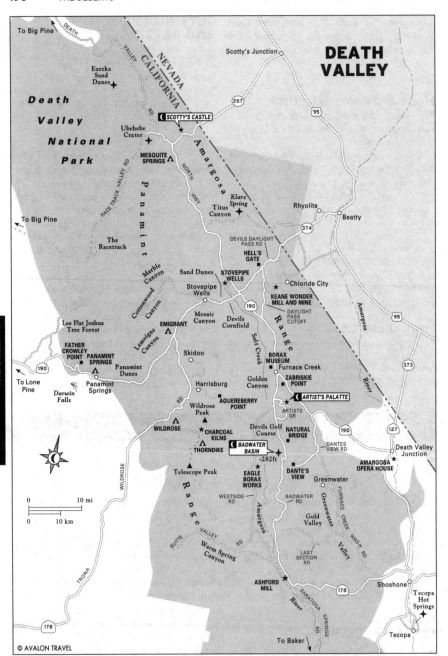

© AVALON TRAVEL

close friends to Scotty anyway. The Johnsons and Scotty often entertained at the castle, and movie stars and presidents came to stay in the guest rooms here. Once upon a time, you could have even rented one of the upstairs guest rooms by the week.

Today, several different tours give visitors different glimpses into the wonders of Scotty's Castle. For first-time visitors, docents recommend the regular main-house tour. If you've already been through the castle proper, consider the Underground Mysteries tour. Purchase tickets at the ticket booth (the first building as you enter the attraction's center). A good place to start while you wait for your tour time is the visitors center and interpretive museum, which describes the history of the castle, Death Valley Scotty, and Albert Johnson. Your tour will meet at the fountain in front of the castle entrance. All tours are conducted by Park Service employees who dress and speak as though it were still the late 1930s and you were friends of Johnson and Scotty come to dine and stay at the castle. The highlight of the tour is the magnificent player organ in the music room, which still plays for visitors every day. (Check with the visitors center for musical events at the castle.)

Once you've finished your tour, you can wander the property, climbing up a little hill to visit Scotty's grave. You'll also see the remains of the construction facilities—the building of the castle was never finished—you'll notice the empty swimming pool and some half-built exterior structures scattered about. If you'd like to buy souvenirs or a quick snack, you can do so at Scotty's Castle, which also has restroom facilities.

## ❰ Badwater Basin

Want to go down—all the way down to the lowest land on the continent? Drive out and follow the signs from Highway 190 to Badwater Basin (Hwy. 178, 18 miles south of Furnace Creek, turn off 190 onto 178 at Furnace Creek Inn). At 281 feet *below* sea level, Badwater holds the title of the lowest elevation in the Western Hemisphere. Tourists love to get their photos taken beside the elevation sign sitting out on the boardwalks that protect the tiny salt pond here. Please respect this pond; its ecosystem is frail and includes a species of snail found nowhere else in the world, and you can damage it just by walking up to its edge. Keep to the boardwalk as you gaze into the water that seems impossible in the blinding heat of the salt flats of this long-dried-out lakebed. You can walk off the boardwalk and out onto the salt flats; just follow the obviously human-created path. Ahead of you, the western mountain range might boast a coating of snow during the winter months, and the view up the valley is astonishing on a clear day. Also be sure to turn around and take a look up at the mountains just behind you. See if you can spot the Sea Level sign way up the hillside.

But be careful, since even in the wintertime the ground beneath you on the salt flats can be up to 80°F hotter than the air around you. Yes, the rubber soles of your shoes can melt right into the salt on a warm day! The National Park rangers beg you not to go to Badwater in the summertime. The danger is very real and trying to explore the salt flats in the summertime can be fatal. Even in the wintertime, bring water with you to this region, especially if you plan to go hiking here. Though there's no visitors center at Badwater, you will find potable water at the restrooms adjacent to the parking lot. Expect to find plenty of other cars in that parking lot, as Badwater is one of the most popular spots to visit in Death Valley.

## ❰ Artist's Palette

Perhaps the single most classically beautiful spot in Death Valley, the Artist's Palette (Artists Drive, turn off Hwy. 178 about 7 miles south of Furnace Creek) almost looks like some sort of manmade trick. It seems so improbably that all those brilliant colors splashed together in one spot can really be a random conglomeration of different minerals all clustered in this one spot. But if you look carefully at the mountains elsewhere in Death Valley, you'll find examples of all the colors in the Palette throughout. Even along the Artist's Palette

THE DESERTS

© LANCE SCOTT

**Artist's Palette**

cutoff, swaths of color spill down the mountains for miles through the narrow canyon. It's worth your time to slow down on the road, even to stop and photograph some of the "secret" painted spots.

The one-way road through Artist's Palette splits off from Highway 178 and runs for about five miles (entrance at the south side), and the road is paved and driveable by regular cars. The best time to hit the Palette is just before sunset, when the falling sun limns the already amazing colors with gold. You'll see bunches of people pulled off the road and walking up and down a rise to take photos of a colorful cliff, but this is *not* the Palette proper. Stop to look, but then keep driving until you see the Artist's Palette sign and turn right into the drive for the parking lot. Walk a few steps up a tiny rise and you'll see the Palette right in front of you in all its pastel glory. You'll also see a number of other tourists at all times of day. No restrooms or water are available at Artist's Palette.

## Devil's Golf Course

One of the eeriest formations in Death Valley is the ground at Devil's Golf Course (Hwy. 178 about 11 miles south of Furnace Creek). This part of the low salt flat that was the bottom of a long-vanished lake got stirred up somehow. The results are spectacular, with acre upon acre of chewed-up ground covered with delicate crystalline salt formations. It's a good idea to wear long pants and sturdy shoes and to be very careful if you plan to walk out onto the Golf Course. The ruts, holes, and crevices can be knee-deep, rocks and crystals are razor-sharp, and to call the walking "uneven" is the understatement of the year. If you're a photographer, be sure to bring your camera to capture the fragile salt crystal growths proliferating here.

Yes, every step you take out onto Devil's Golf Course destroys countless beautiful crystals. So why does the park let you walk out there? Because these crystals aren't a permanent feature of the region. Every time it rains, the crystals melt down to a salty liquid, then as the Golf Course dries out, the crystals start growing anew.

The road in to Devil's Golf Course is dirt and can get rough, but it's passable by passenger car. The slower you drive, the better condition the road will stay in. There's a parking lot in the Golf Course and a couple of plaques describing the formation and geology of the area. However, there are no restrooms or water here.

## Dante's View

One of the many glorious views of Death Valley can be accessed by car at Dante's View (end of Dante's View Rd., turn off Hwy. 190 about 10 miles southeast of Furnace Creek). From more than a mile high, you can look out over what feels like the whole valley—right down into the salt flats of Badwater, up to Furnace Creek, and beyond. Right next door you can wave at the thematically named Coffin Peak to the south of Dante's. As the main views spread out to the west, Dante's Peak is a great place to watch the sun set over Death Valley.

## Salt Creek

You may have heard of the famous Death Valley pupfish, a species of fish that lives in only one spot on the globe—here at Salt Creek (Hwy. 190, about 15 miles north of Furnace Creek, turnoff on west side of the highway). It's a strange contradiction, with a shining creek flowing through some of the most dry and desolate landscape on Earth. Toward the center of the valley off Highway 190, Salt Creek runs all year, its source a small spring, its terminus the hard ground where a miniature delta spreads out then dries up. To protect the delicate ecosystem in and around the heavily salinated creek, the Park Service has built a boardwalk that lets visitors see the plants, algae, and pupfish without treading on and in the delicate landscape here. The boardwalk runs from the parking lot up to the area where the pupfish spawn early in the wintertime. As spring comes, the pupfish swim downstream, making viewing easy even for visitors who don't want to take a hike. All around the boardwalk you'll see plants that thrive on salty water, including the funky pickleweed. That's the big bushy plant with the succulent-like tentacles divided into small greenish-orange droplets.

This plant is so salty that early pioneers in the area used it to make pickles instead of adding salt—hence its name.

The drive from the highway is about two miles on a dirt road that's passable in a passenger car. Pit toilets sit in the parking lot area. The boardwalk trail is wheelchair accessible.

## Ubehebe Crater

Just about every type of major geological feature was once a part of the Death Valley landscape. In the north end of the valley, a recent (in geologic time) volcano left behind Ubehebe Crater (8 miles west of Scotty's Castle, from Hwy. 190 take left fork at the Grapevine). A quick walk up from the parking lot takes you right to the edge of the crater, which consists of razor-sharp black volcanic rock that is on the opposite inner face of the crater fading into a bright salmon pink and even a stark white. The view over the edge of the crater back down the valley is worth coming up here, and when you turn around you see the less visited but also lovely north end of the valley. Ubehebe is a great place to go hiking if you're in good shape—among other things, you can climb up from the parking area along the crater's rim to Little Hebe crater, a smaller crater created by the same volcano about 2,000 years ago.

Get to Ubehebe Crater by taking the other fork at the intersection that takes you to Scotty's Castle. The road is easily traversable by passenger cars; there's a parking lot but no restroom or water here.

## Museums

In the town of Furnace Creek, out by the Ranch, you'll find two tiny museums that give guests a deeper understanding of both the natural and human history of Death Valley. The **Borax Museum** (admission free) at Furnace Creek Ranch focuses on the mining history of the area, with a tiny interior gallery/bookshop filled with mineral samples, books and documents, and smaller mining tools. The bulk of the museum sits outdoors, displaying an array of desiccated large mining and support equipment. Get a map indoors for $1 that

© LANCE SCOTT

Borax Museum

describes each numbered exhibit outside. You'll see hand-built mining machines, carriages and wagons, a steam locomotive, and more.

Just a few yards north of the Ranch sits the **Furnace Creek Visitors Center and Museum** (Hwy. 190 at the gas station, 760/786-3200, year-round daily 9 A.M.–5 P.M.). The interpretive museum here tells the story of Death Valley's long, slow formation and erosion. Even if you're not a rock nut, it's worth your time to stop in here to learn more about the natural wonders you'll witness when you get out on the road to explore. This is also a good spot to talk to rangers about the relative passability of the various rugged roads in the park, and to learn about the very real dangers of exploring Death Valley and how to keep yourself as safe as possible during your journey.

## ENTERTAINMENT AND EVENTS

The main entertainment in Death Valley are the sights and (lack of) sounds of the valley itself. If you're an energetic night owl, plan to

enjoy full-moon hikes rather than dance clubs, since you can count the number of saloons in the whole of the valley on one hand.

## Bars and Clubs

For a drink or two to cap off a long day out in the desert, head on down to the **Corkscrew Saloon** at Furnace Creek Ranch (Hwy. 190 at Furnace Creek, 760/786-2345, daily noon–midnight). Go ahead and wear your boots and hat into the cowboy-styled bar with its wood floor and dim lighting. Drink a mug of beer on tap, grab a glass of wine, or sip your favorite cocktail from the full bar. They've got a TV with the game on for sports fans, and a pool table for desert sharks. The crowd mixes the ubiquitous tourists and a few die-hard locals who serve as the Corkscrew's regulars.

The other local watering hole sits a little north of Furnace Creek: the **Badwater Saloon at Stovepipe Wells** (Hwy. 190 past the big bend, 760/786-2387, daily 5:30 P.M.–9 P.M.). Attached to the Toll Road Restaurant, this saloon has beer, wine, cocktails, and a small snack menu to satisfy evening munchers over 21. It's not open too late, so you'll need to get your quaffing in early in the evening.

## Live Music

Outside the park proper in the town of Amargosa Valley, Nevada, you'll find one of the most original entertainments available anywhere at the **Amargosa Opera House** (Death Valley Junction, 760/852-4441, www .amargosa-opera-house.com, adults $15, children $12). This lovely small theater is the pride and joy of Marta Beckett, a dancer from New York City who found her "home" in an abandoned theater in Death Valley Junction, where her car was getting a flat tire fixed. She and her husband repaired and renovated the theater, creating an intimate space where Marta could perform for an appreciative, if small, audience. That was in 1968. In the early 1970, Marta was inspired to paint murals on the walls and ceiling of her Opera House—a permanent audience for her ballets.

It's been 40 years, and Marta still dances at the Opera House each Saturday night from November through the middle of May. Reservations are required, as the seating is limited and Marta's shows often sell out. The show you see was created and choreographed by Marta, incorporating music, ballet, and comedy. The best way to learn about these unique entertainments is to see one for yourself.

You can also stay at the Amargosa if you like, since the old adobe hotel building has been renovated and is open to guests all year long. You can even ask for one of the rooms in which Marta has painted some of her lovely murals.

## Festivals and Events

The Death Valley mythos—a place where intrepid miners and hardy pioneers couldn't find water and sought to leave ASAP—wouldn't be complete without an annual tribute to those first white visitors. The **49er Encampment** (www.deathvalley49ers.org) takes place throughout the first week of November each year. Thousands of history buffs flock to the valley to camp, tell stories, sing songs, dance, and take tours of the park. Participants and guests alike enjoy the parade, which is one of the highlights of the many activities put on by the Encampment.

## SPORTS AND RECREATION

The outdoor recreation comprises much of Death Valley's attraction to the million visitors the park sees each year. Whether you're an extreme sandboarder, an aggro four-wheeler, or a slow walker, you'll find something worth doing out-of-doors in Death Valley.

## Off-Roading

If you've got a 4x4, or you know how to drive one and can rent one, it's well worth it to bring a hardy off-road vehicle into Death Valley. Many of the off-the-beaten-track sights and trails can only be accessed by high-clearance and four-wheel-drive vehicles.

The drive out to the **Natural Bridge** (about 1 mile off Hwy. 190, 1–2 miles south of Devil's Golf Course) isn't long or aggressive, but the road condition makes high-clearance or 4WD a good idea in most seasons. Check with the rangers for current conditions. Once you park, you've got a half-mile walk in to see the magnificent stone arch stretching across yet another beautiful desert canyon.

One of the most out-of-the-way sights in the park is **The Racetrack** (27 miles from Ubehebe Crater). You'll take a 27-mile drive on an incredibly rough road out to a patch of desert where a mysterious (but explicable) phenomenon draws hardy visitors out beyond the crowded main valley sights. You don't really need to hike anywhere—just get out of your car and stare out across the plateau at the deep grooves in the barren lakebed. The tracks are made by rocks sliding across the lakebed. See a track with no rock at the end of it? Sadly, uncaring tourists often pick up the rocks and take them home. Please leave the rocks where nature put them to allow future visitors to enjoy the unusual sight.

Also in the north end of the valley, the **Eureka Dunes** (10 miles south of Big Pine

Rd.) are some of the most unusual dunes you'll ever see, no matter how far you travel. The sand composing the dunes is the only sand nearby, and it rises 700 feet off the valley floor. You can walk up the Eureka Dunes, but no horseback riding and sandboarding aren't allowed here. This is a measure to protect the delicate ecosystem that evolved right here at the dunes and exists nowhere else on Earth. The drive runs about 40 miles or so, first on a long unpaved road running north from the Y-intersection to Scotty's Castle, then on a 4WD track about 10 miles to the dunes. Out towards the dunes, sand can get deep, so rangers recommend that *experienced 4WD drivers only* attempt this road.

The lovely **Titus Canyon** (Hwy. 190 about 20 miles north of Stovepipe Wells intersection) can be traversed on foot or by a 26-mile one-way 4WD track that connects directly to the ghost town of Rhyolite. Along the many miles of canyon, you'll see some of the most diverse and arguably most beautiful desert canyon scenery anywhere in Death Valley. It's got Native American petroglyphs, bighorn sheep, colorful mineral deposits, and skinny "narrows" where the walls soar overhead and almost black out the sun. Because the 4WD road runs only one way, you must come back into Death Valley by making a long loop into Nevada. Take Highway 374 past Rhyolite to Highway 95. Head either north to Highway 267, which will take you back to Scotty's Castle, or south to Highway 373 through Amargosa Valley, which becomes 127, then turn onto 190 which takes you back to Furnace Creek. Consider making your viewing of Titus Canyon an all-day adventure.

Out west in the Panamint Springs area, take your truck on a drive up to **Aguereberry Point** (Emigrant Canyon Rd. about 13 miles south of Emigrant intersection). This drive includes passing the ghost town of Harrisburg—an early 20th-century gold mining town that once had a population of 300 living in tents. You can actually walk right into this mine, which has been stabilized and made safe for visitors to spelunk in. Just be sure that the mine isn't closed to protect hibernating bats. All the way up the road, park and climb up to the point, which provides more beautiful valley vistas to enjoy. If you're staying in Panamint Springs, Aguereberry Point makes a good sunset or sunrise destination.

## Hiking

Though you can reach most of the major sights of Death Valley by driving and perhaps a short walk, to get off the beaten track you'll need to take a hike. In fact, that's why many visitors come here. The best time to hike in the floor of Death Valley is the wintertime, when temperatures are cool to moderate. On the other hand, if you're interested in hiking the high country, the best time to explore the ridges is in the summer when the snow has melted.

For a fun easy or moderate walk where you can control both the distance and the elevation change, park on the side of the road and wander on out to the **Sand Dunes** (2–4 miles round-trip, easy) near Stovepipe Wells. The dunes are constantly shifting, and regular visitors love them because they're never the same two years in a row. They're beautiful at sunset when the golden light hits them, and if you're visiting during a full moon you'll find few more romantic spots to share an outdoor stroll with your sweetie.

From the roadside parking area, just walk out toward the cluster of dunes. They look like they're only a few yards away, but the desert air creates false senses of distance and it's about a mile to the edge of the dunes. There's no trail. You can walk right up the sides of the dunes. The hundreds of pockmark-like footprints bear witness to other visitors' climbs. If you climb as far as you can up the tallest dune, the round-trip is four miles.

**Mosaic Canyon** (1–4 miles round-trip, moderate) offers a variable length and difficulty hike with beautiful rock formations that resemble mosaics. Check out the canyon walls on the first half-mile of the walk for the best mosaics. If you want to, you can continue a couple of miles farther into the canyon. This hike starts at the Mosaic Canyon parking lot, a couple of miles past Stovepipe Wells Village.

If you don't have a 4x4 vehicle but you want to see the charming **Titus Canyon Narrows** (3–13 miles round-trip, easy), you can leave your car at the Titus Canyon parking lot and walk down the unpaved road. The Narrows go on for about a mile and a half of level road—if you're up for a much longer walk, you can get all the way to Klare Springs and the local petroglyphs.

For a scenic summer walk, **Dante's Ridge** (1–8 miles, moderate) offers soaring vistas and cool temperatures even in July. If you want a short hike, climb 0.5 mile from the Dante's View parking lot to the first peak in the chain. If you're done, feel free to walk back down; if you're feeling energetic, keep descending and climbing the ridge to the top of Mount Perry. You'll need to be an adventurous sort, as there's no trail past the first peak, though hiking is allowed.

Bring a detailed map if you plan to take on the hike through **Fall Canyon** (6 miles round-trip, difficult). Start at the Titus Canyon parking lot and from there, head north along a trampled path, and from there you're on your own as you descend a wash into the canyon and to a "dryfall." If you're up to it, you can skirt around the dryfall and head down to the most spectacular narrows area of the canyon.

If you're into the mining history of Death Valley, the **Keane Wonder Mine Trail** (2 miles, difficult) is a must-hike. It's a rough go—steep and rocky the whole mile up from the ruins of the mill to the ruins of the mines. Ruin crawlers will love the whole area. When the Keane Wonder Mine ceased production, it was abandoned and has been slowly desiccating ever since. At the top of the trail, you'll find the abandoned and incredibly dangerous mine entrances. Do not enter these unstable structures. At time of publication, the trail was closed pending repair. Check the Visitors Center for status updates.

If you're an aggro hiker visiting Death Valley in the summertime, check out **Telescope Peak Trail** (14 miles round-trip, difficult). The trail begins at the Mahogany Flat Campground and climbs 3,000 feet to the peak of the tallest mountain in Death Valley. The sweeping views will take what's left of your breath away after your climb. The snow usually melts by the beginning of June; if you want to try this trail in the winter you'll need an ice axe, crampons, and lots of previous winter climbing experience.

## Biking

You've got to be pretty tough to bring your bike to a place called Death Valley. But plenty of folks do. The main biking road is Highway 190, which runs north–south along the east side of the valley. You can cut off the highway onto any paved road if you want to take in some sights. However, no bikes are allowed off the pavement in Death Valley.

## Horseback Riding

At Furnace Creek Ranch (Hwy. 190, 760/786-2345, www.furnacecreekresort.com), you can take a horseback ride out into the desert from October through May. Horse-and-carriage rides are also available on occasion. Call the ranch or ask at the front desk for more information and to make reservations.

## Golf

It's not a golfing destination, but if you're just burning to play a round in the hottest valley on earth, book a tee time at the **Furnace Creek Ranch Golf Course** (Hwy. 190, 760/786-2345, www.furnacecreekresort.com/golf-1203.htm, green fee $30–55, cart rental $12.50). Nope, it's not the shining green you'll find at most golf courses, for obvious reasons. Even in winter, limited water can be spared to irrigate greens and fairways. This 18-hole, par 70 course is part of the Furnace Creek Ranch complex near the center of Death Valley. You'll find restaurants and a general store at the Ranch. Check the website for golf and lodging packages.

# CAMPING

Folks who want to explore Death Valley on the cheap quickly the fill the campsites that dot the park. Whether you're in an RV or just have a tent to pitch, you'll find someplace that suits your fancy. Just be aware that during high season (winter), the popular central campgrounds fill up fast. You can make reservations for a spot at many of the popular campgrounds by calling 877/444-6777 or online at www.recreation.gov. During the summer, camping in Death Valley can be extremely unpleasant, since few campgrounds here offer shade of any kind to take the edge off the extreme heat. Camping from June to September is not recommended in the lowland areas, and many campgrounds are closed from May to September.

## RV and Tent Campgrounds

RV campers love to hang out in Death Valley. Accordingly, several full hook-up RV campgrounds offer space to settle in for a stay.

Both on the same side as the ranch and across the road, **Furnace Creek** (Hwy. 190 at Furnace Creek, 800/365-2267, www.furnacecreekresort.com, open year-round, $12–18) offers both RV spaces and tent camping. Campers gain access to the facilities at the Ranch, including the swimming pool, golf course, restaurants, and store. The RV camping sits mostly on the opposite side of Highway 190 from the Ranch, and the "campground" is in fact a stretch of barren asphalt with no shade whatsoever. This campground fills up fast during the busy winter months and you must make a reservation to get a spot here. Expect to find running water, flushies, and fireplaces at or near your site.

If you want to camp near, but not in, Furnace Creek Ranch, you can choose between **Texas Springs** (east of Furnace Creek, $12) and **Sunset** (east of Furnace Creek, north of Texas Springs, $10). Both are open from October through April, and feature running water, flush toilets, and RV dump stations. Of the two, Texas Springs has the nicest amenities, with picnic tables and fire rings. Both campgrounds are wheelchair accessible.

Another popular RV park sits at the tiny villagelet of **Stovepipe Wells** (Hwy. 190 at Stovepipe Wells, 760/786-2387, open Oct.–Apr., $12). Again, you get access to the small general store and the tavern if you park on the wide patch of asphalt here. There are also several fun sights nearby, and Stovepipe Wells is close enough to Furnace Creek to make a good spot from which to base your trip. Stovepipe Wells spots are first-come, first-served only.

**Mesquite Springs** (spur road left off Hwy. 190, south of Scotty's Castle, open year-round, $10) offers both tent and RV spots on the west side of Death Valley. It's the only campground in the high north country, near Scotty's Castle. It's a long drive to either Stovepipe Wells or Furnace Creek, the nearest spots that offer major services such as food and gasoline. But if you're specifically looking for isolation and a more rugged experience, Mesquite Springs might be just the place for you. It is first-come, first-served, with self registration, and the campground has potable water, flush toilets, and an RV dump station.

If you're willing to camp on the far west side of the park, **Panamint Springs** (Hwy. 190 past Western Entrance, west of Panamint Valley Rd., $15–30) offers a camping experience unique to all of Death Valley—that is, campsites along a river shaded by mature trees. No, really! One of the few year-round rivers in Death Valley runs and even cascades down a 20-foot fall about five miles back from the Panamint Springs Resort. With 40 RV spaces and 26 tent sites, call to make a reservation or arrive early in the morning if you want a spot in the winter months. You'll also find water and toilets throughout the campground, and 15 of the RV spots have full hookups with 50-amp electricity.

## Tent-Only Campgrounds

If you want to camp Death Valley in the summertime, head up into the Panamint mountain range to the tent-only **Thorndike** (Mar.–Nov., free) campground. Be aware that you may need a four-wheel-drive vehicle to access this campground. Thorndike is a primitive campground, so you must bring all your own water for drinking and washing (bring lots more than you think you need to be safe). You will find pit toilets, and your site will include a picnic table and a fireplace. The nearby **Wildrose** (year-round, free) campground has a lower elevation and a wintertime crowd. It offers a few more in-season amenities, including potable water from November through April and a road you can drive in a passenger car. The nearest major services, such as food and gas, are a goodly drive to either Panamint Springs or Furnace Creek.

If you're into the western side of the park, consider camping at **Emigrant** (year-round, free), which sits about halfway between Panamint Springs and Stovepipe Wells. You'll get a spot to pitch your tent, access to potable water and flush toilets, but no fire rings here.

## ACCOMMODATIONS
### Under $100

If you prefer to stay on the west side of Death Valley (a good idea for at least one night if you're driving in from the California side), book a room or a camping spot at the tiny **Panamint Springs Resort** (Hwy. 190, 775/482-7680, www.deathvalley.com/psr, $89–170). This rustic lodge-style motel is the only independently owned lodging in Death Valley, and also has a temperature that's generally 10–15°F lower than the other motels in the park. Your amenities will not include a TV or much in the way of good phone service, but the resort does offer free Wi-Fi. You will have access to the resort's restaurant, which serves three meals a day year-round. If you're visiting in the wintertime and the weather is mild, get a seat out on the patio so you can enjoy a view of the valley with your food.

### $100-250

The biggest resort complex in the park, **Furnace Creek Ranch** (Hwy. 190, 800/236-7916, www.furnacecreekresort.com, $135–225) acts as the human center of eastern Death Valley. It's in close proximity to many of the major attractions people come to see. If you stay here, you're on the same property as two restaurants, a tavern, a general store, a museum, a gas station, a golf course, an airstrip, and the main park visitors center. With a wide lawn, a playground, and a mineral spring–fed swimming pool, this is a great place to bring your kids for

© LANCE SCOTT

Furnace Creek Ranch

a desert vacation. The guest accommodations at Furnace Ranch were deliberately created to be casual and, well, ranch-like. You can choose from standard, deluxe, or cabin-style accommodations. Rooms have one or two double or queen beds, chain-motel styling, and adequate bathroom facilities. Some rooms have tiny patios or balconies overlooking the lawns and pools. No smoking is permitted in any room.

The motel at **Stovepipe Wells** (Hwy. 190 past the big bend, 760/786-2387, www.stove pipewells.com, $135) offers basic rooms and amenities at reasonable prices. Choose between king or two-bed rooms, all ground floor rooms only a few steps from the restaurant and saloon, the swimming pool, and across the street from the general store. Your room will have a TV but no phone, beds with motel-style bedspreads and wall art, and a bathroom with a shower or tub combo—everything you'd expect (well, except the phone) from an inexpensive motel. From the motel, you'll have easy access to Mosaic Canyon, the local dunes, and Salt Creek.

## Over $250

The lone high-end resort in all of Death Valley is the ( **Furnace Creek Inn** (Hwy 190. at Hwy. 178, 800/236-7916, www.furnace creekresort.com, $310–475, mid-Oct.–mid-May only). This beautiful property was constructed early in the 20th century by the Pacific Borax Company. It's a lovely place to come upon as you drive up Highway 190, with its palm oasis and multi-level adobe buildings rising up onto the hillside. As you pull up to the front of the hotel, you'll see the ingenious tunnels that perforate the complex, and the wonderful views out over the salt flats of southern Death Valley.

Inside, you might find your guest room a bit small given the price you're paying for it. The bathrooms are tiled and sparking clean, though the fixtures can be on the old side unless you're in a spa room. And not all rooms look out over the valley, so you might get a fabulous view of the Dumpsters in the back parking area. But the interior design is mellow and pleasant, with colors and patterns that

the pool at Furnace Creek Inn

THE DESERTS

© LANCE SCOTT

echo the desert outside. You've got a TV and a phone, room service, and access to all the lovely amenities the resort has to offer. Most rooms have king-sized beds and a couple of unique suites are available.

It's really those amenities you're paying so much for: the bathtub-warm mineral pool that's fed by a local hot spring and open late into the night, the poolside food service, the gazebo in the palm oasis, the fine dining room, spa services, and more. While you're visiting, be sure to take a leisurely tour of the property. The architecture and artwork are more than worth your time and attention. The staff, who take pains to provide every service a guest could ever want, will be happy to assist you in planning your park exploration as well.

## FOOD

You'll need to plan your meals each day during your trip to Death Valley, since there are no fast food joints or 24-hour supermarkets where you can grab a quick bite at 4 P.M. or 4 A.M. In fact, Death Valley has no supermarkets or fast food, period. Either bring a cooler stocked with picnic supplies to carry with you each day as you explore the valley, or plan to be near one of the three resort areas at mealtimes. If you do plan to feed yourself, stock up on staples (particularly the nonperishable stuff like soda and water) outside the park to save money.

### Casual Dining

If you're looking for a good, casual, diner-style meal, you won't do better in Death Valley than the **49er Café** (Hwy. 190 at Furnace Creek, 760/786-2345, daily until 9 P.M., $8–15) at the Furnace Creek Ranch. One of two restaurants on the property, the 49er Café is open the longest, serving a traditional American breakfast, filling lunches, and hearty dinners. While big eaters can get huge portions if they want them, it's a relief for the lighter eaters to find smaller items such as single eggs and half-grapefruits on the menu. The rustic dining room has some fun touches, including an original wood plank floor and plastic-covered maps of the valley on each table. You can plan out your day's travels

as you sit sipping your coffee and waiting for your eggs to arrive. The service staff gets the job done, and can be quite friendly especially if you choose a seat at the counter. Feel free to wear jeans and a T-shirt.

If you've burned untold hundreds of calories hiking around the valley during the day, you'll find the perfect replenishment at the **Wrangler Steakhouse** (Hwy. 190 at Furnace Creek, 760/786-2345, 6–9 A.M., 11 A.M.–2 P.M., 5–9 P.M., $23–35). The Wrangler offers a menu loaded with steaks, plus ribs and chicken smothered with tangy barbecue sauce. In the same weathered wooden structure with the 49er Café, you'll be treated to a casual atmosphere where you'll feel at home in jeans and boots. The short wine list includes a few California favorites. You can also grab a beer or a cocktail, and finish off your meal with a cappuccino or a latte. For breakfast and lunch, the Wrangler puts up a casual buffet with both hot and cold dishes.

If you're in the northern reaches of Death Valley around dinnertime, your option for a restaurant meal is the **Toll Road Restaurant** (Hwy. 190, Stovepipe Wells, 760/786-2387, www.stovepipewells.com, daily 7–10 A.M., 11:30 A.M.–2 P.M., and 5:30–9 P.M.). The Toll Road serves biscuits and gravy for breakfast, a burger for lunch, and some chicken or pasta for dinner. The small dining room manages to accommodate both the residents in the motel and the campground, plus the occasional tourist stopping in for lunch from another part of the park. But do be prepared to wait for a table on weekends in the high season.

The small size and lower traffic out west mean that the **Panamint Springs Resort Restaurant** (Hwy. 190 at west side of park, 775/482-7680, www.deathvalley.com/psr, $10–30) can serve home-cooked food to its diners all year long. Take a seat out on the large patio and enjoy a glass of beer before lunch or dinner—the restaurant offers more than 100 varieties from around the world.

### Fine Dining

The few restaurants in Death Valley tend

toward solid American food with little frill or pretense. The only high-end dining establishment in the park is the **Furnace Creek Inn Dining Room** (Hwy. 190 at Hwy. 178, 760/786-3385, www.furnacecreekresort.com, Oct.–May, $18–30). Serving three meals per day to accommodate inn guests, the Dining Room offers large portions of delectable if sometimes a little bit overwrought California cuisine. Reservations are recommended for dinner, especially on weekend evenings. The servers make sure everything you need is taken care of in a timely fashion. Bring your appetite. The appetizers can be too tempting to resist, which might make the entrée and the luscious desserts seem a bit overwhelming. The lunch menu includes lighter but no less elegant fare, and breakfast is a reasonably standard California list of egg dishes and waffle-like things. The Dining Room bleeds elegance, with its white tablecloths and designer china. If you eat here in the daytime, you'll get a lovely view towards the mountains from the picture windows. The Dining Room has a dress code, so be sure to bring at least one non-hiking outfit if you plan to dine here.

## Markets

If you need groceries, you can buy them in two spots in Death Valley. The widest selection of food, drink, and goods is sold at the **Furnace Creek Ranch General Store** (Hwy. 190 at Furnace Creek Ranch). The exterior is quaint, but the interior is stuffed with shiny modern souvenirs. You can find clothes if you need them—even swimsuits! The food clusters at the back of the store, and you can get staples, drinks, milk, produce, and other perishables. The market also has ice cream and plenty of junk food.

Much smaller, but adequate in an emergency, is the **Stovepipe Wells General Store** (Hwy. 190 past the big bend at Stovepipe Wells). This store is more like an understocked mini-mart than a real general store, and more than half of the merchandise sold is souvenirs. You can buy water, soft drinks, and a few limited food items here, but don't plan to stock up since for

that you must go to Furnace Creek or outside the park.

## INFORMATION AND SERVICES

People can be lulled into a false sense of security because Death Valley is a national park. Yes, there are rangers here, and this is a geographically large park. But you are leaving civilization for real when you go to Death Valley. You can drive for miles without seeing another living soul, a telephone, or any means of assistance. Take some time to plan your trip to this enchanted but desolate region, making sure you've got lots of water (one full gallon per person, per day), a first-aid kit, a spare tire, and a good pair of walking shoes.

That said, most of the 1.2 million visitors who come to Death Valley each year have a fabulous time and no need to worry about the lack of nearby civilization.

### Tourist Information

The main **Furnace Creek Visitors Center** (Hwy. 190, 760/786-3200, daily 9 A.M.–5 P.M.) sits just north of Furnace Creek Ranch. The rangers at this center tend to be experienced with the park and can give you good advice about the best spots to go at the best times. They'll also tell you where *not* to go. This visitors center also has a book and souvenir store, and an interpretive museum.

The other major in-park visitors center sits at **Scotty's Castle Visitor Center and Museum** (SR 267, 760/786-2392, summer daily 9 A.M.–4:30 P.M., winter daily 8:30 A.M.–5 P.M.). Here again you'll find an interpretive museum and rangers to help you with your itinerary. The bookshop is smaller, but an attached snack shop sells munchies and plenty of bottled water.

### Media and Communications

Expect your cell phone to be out of commission for the whole of your stay in Death Valley. You might get lucky if you've got the right carrier, but most folks get no bars. Even many of the motels offer no in-room telephones, and most have little or no Internet access either. To come to Death Valley is to "disconnect" from modern communication gadgets almost completely. Some adults come here specifically for that reason, but be prepared for whining from older kids and teenagers when they discover they won't be able to text their friends for days at a time.

All the major resort areas have phones that can be used in an emergency, but you won't find any call boxes along the highway. Highway 190 has plenty of traffic traversing it every day—if you need to, you'll probably see plenty of cars and ranger trucks you can flag down for assistance. If you're serious about heading into Death Valley's back country, consider bringing a long-range, two-way radio just in case.

You can pick up a wealth of literature about the park from either visitors center. The major resort motels may offer the *LA Times*.

## Medical Services

No significant medical services are available inside Death Valley. The closest hospital is **Barstow Community Hospital** (555 S. Seventh Ave., Barstow, 760/256-1761). On the Nevada side, contact the **Beatty Clinic** (775/553-2208) or the **Pahrump Urgent Care Facility** (775/727-6060).

## GETTING THERE AND AROUND

A trip to Death Valley isn't like a trip to Los Angeles. The remote, harsh valley is surrounded by treacherous mountain ranges with few paved roads

### Air

The closest major airport to Death Valley is the **Las Vegas International Airport** (5757 Wayne Newton Blvd., Las Vegas, 702/261-5211, www.mccarran.com). From Vegas, it's a two- to three-hour drive to Furnace Creek.

If you're lucky enough to have access to a light plane, you can fly right into the **Furnace Creek Ranch** (Hwy. 190, 760/786-2345, www.furnacecreekresort.com). The Ranch has an uncontrolled 3,000-foot runway with tie-down space for general aviators.

### Car

The main north–south corridor through Death Valley is CA-190. CA-190 makes a hard turn to the west just before it passes through Stovepipe Wells and on out through Panamint Springs. Numerous paved, unpaved, and four-wheel-drive-only roads branch off from CA-190 throughout the park, letting visitors access the park's main attractions and trailheads.

## THE HIGH PRICE OF GETTING STUCK

Before you visit Death Valley, check in with the rangers at the main visitors center (Furnace Creek, Hwy. 190, 760/786-3200, daily 9 A.M.–5 P.M.) to get up-to-the-minute information about the state of the four-wheel-drive roads in the park. Particularly at the north end of the park, razor-sharp volcanic rock can scatter across roads, not just cutting but actually shredding all but the heaviest all-terrain tires. The road to The Racetrack is the worst; it's not unusual for Hummers to lose more than one tire and end up stranded more than a dozen miles from the nearest paved road or source of help. Add to that the fact that most cell phones receive no signal anywhere in Death Valley, and you have a recipe for disaster.

So how do you extricate yourself from such a mess? You stay put, or walk out to the road until a park ranger comes to find you. The ranger will call the one and only tow company that makes runs out into Death Valley's backcountry. As the only game in town, this company happily charges whatever they want to help you. If they've got a spare tire or two in your size, the service might only cost you $800-1,000. But if you need a tow back to civilization, expect to shell out upwards of $2,000 for the privilege.

What's the moral of this story? Listen to the rangers if they tell you that a certain road is treacherous this season and consider carefully how much money you're willing to spend for your off-road adventure before you bump out beyond the reach of civilization.

THE DESERTS

To drive in to the park, you'll come either from NV-95 or CA-395, then turn off onto smaller roads that lead into the park. Get a map before you leave for the best navigation; GPS units also work in the park.

The nearest major California town to Death Valley is Bakersfield. (Baker is closer, but it has fewer services.) See the *Yosemite* chapter for information about this useful waypoint city.

You'll need to keep an eye on your gas gauge and plan well when exploring Death Valley by car. Gas is available *only* at the resort areas of Panamint Springs, Stovepipe Wells, and Furnace Creek. In spring of 2008, the gas station at Scotty's Castle was not functional or open for business; check with the Park Service for an update before or during your visit.

## Tours

It doesn't happen every year, but most years Death Valley receives just a very little bit of winter rainfall. When these miniscule rains bunch up, especially in January and February, the water is absorbed by the seeds of countless wildflowers. Come late February and March, these newly sprouted seeds grow up and then bloom, creating a stunning profusion of color spreading across the normally bleak and barren desert floor. The most prominent color you'll see is yellow, since the Desert Gold grows a foot or more tall and produces a brilliant golden daisy-like flower with an orange center. In amongst the gold you'll see streaks of purple, dots of pink, and puffs of white. In fact, flowers of every color in the rainbow grow in Death Valley when conditions are right.

The best way to see the flowers is to get out of your car and take a stroll out into the desert where they grow. Ironically, often the water vapor and carbon dioxide cars emit make the strips of land right beside the road the most colorful and prolific flowered areas. If you haven't studied botany recently and you'd like to know more about the beauty surrounding you, take a Wildflower Walk led by one of the park rangers during the season. Check with the Furnace Creek Visitors Center for a schedule of Walks.

# Anza-Borrego Desert State Park

Anza-Borrego has a rich human history. Native Americans hunted bighorn sheep (still found here today) and gathered from the diverse plant life here, occasionally taking the time to draw and paint on the rocks. Later, European and Colonial explorers crisscrossed the desert with trails that you can still see traces of today.

The civilized center of the region is the town of Borrego Springs, a tiny patch of land that's not part of the state park. Most folks who come to enjoy the Borrego Desert's charms spend their nights here.

Many of the 600,000 acres of Anza-Borrego Desert State Park are pristine wilderness, yet camping is allowed anywhere in the park. Two of the best times to view the park as a whole are at sunrise and sunset. When the light is low and golden, the multicolored desert spreads out from the mountains to the south.

## SIGHTS
### Visitors Center

For first-time desert park visitors, a great place to start is the Visitors Center (200 Palm Canyon Dr., 760/767-4205, www.abdsp.org, Oct.–May daily 9 A.M.–5 P.M., June–Sept. weekends only). The Visitor Centers offers information, maps, trail updates, and interactive displays. An interpretive desert garden surrounds the center and provides the names and stories of many common plants and animals in the park. The stroll is easy and mostly flat, and includes a pupfish pond.

### ◖ Borrego Palm Canyon

If there's one natural feature you must see when you visit Anza-Borrego, it should be the Borrego Palm Canyon (spur road, just north of visitors center). An easy drive or walk from the visitors center takes you to this surprising and lovely desert palm oasis. The best way to experience the canyon is to take the **Palm Canyon Nature Trail.** This three-mile loop trail takes you to the heart of the oasis, where you'll stand in a shady grove of fan palms beside the tiny creek that feeds them and the other plants whose precarious existence depend on its water. The palms you'll see are the only palm trees that are native to California. To learn more about the plants, rocks, former Native American residents, and animals that live here, pick up a trail guide from the visitors center.

Some visitors enjoy this hike and the surrounding region so much that they choose to camp at the foot of the canyon.

## Panoramic Overlook

One of the many great views you can check out in Anza-Borrego sits between the visitors center and Borrego Palm Canyon. The Panoramic Overlook offers, well, a panoramic overlook of the desert stretching out to the east and

down to the south. This is a wonderful place to take a camera or a folding chair at sunset on a clear day. The mountains turn all shades of blue, while the flat valley floor turns a light golden color with an occasional shimmering silver mirage for contrast. You can hike to the Panoramic Overlook from the Palm Canyon campground in about 1.5 miles. Expect to spend about an hour climbing up the somewhat steep hill, looking around, and walking back down. While this isn't the most strenuous trail in the park, it takes a little longer for visitors who aren't accustomed to hiking.

## Yaqui Well

It's about 1.5-mile walk out from the road to the Yaqui Well (Yaqui Pass Rd. about 1 mile west of Hwy. 78 fork), which is a natural year-round spring that's supported the life closely surrounding it for centuries. The trailhead and campground sit just off Yaqui Pass Road/S-3 (they're the same road here), which heads from the Well past the unmissable Borrego Ranch and on into Borrego Springs. A trail guide from

THE DESERTS

© LIZ HAMILL SCOTT

Anza-Borrego Desert State Park

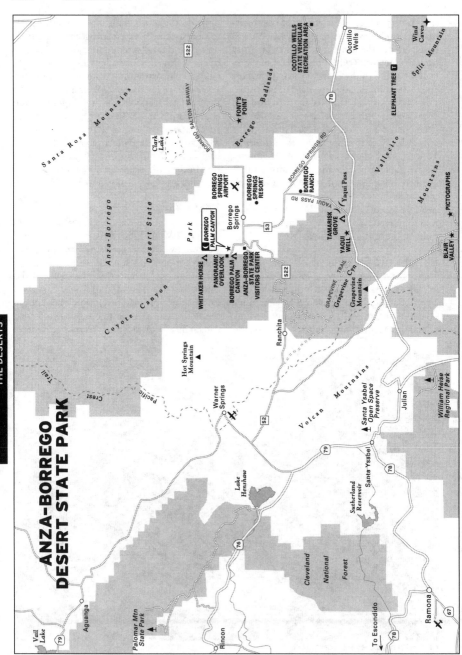

THE DESERTS

# ANZA-BORREGO
# DESERT STATE PARK

Santa Rosa Mountains

Anza-Borrego

Desert State

Park

Coyote Canyon

Clark Lake

BORREGO SALTON SEAWAY

S22

FONT'S POINT ★

Borrego Badlands

OCOTILLO WELLS STATE VEHICULAR RECREATION AREA

Ocotillo Wells

Wind Caves ★

Split Mountain

ELEPHANT TREE ▪

78

Vallecito Mountains

PICTOGRAPHS ★

BORREGO SPRINGS RD

BORREGO SPRINGS AIRPORT ✈

BORREGO SPRINGS RESORT ●

Borrego Springs

BORREGO RANCH ●

Yaqui Pass

S3

YAQUI PASS RD

TAMARISK GROVE ★

YAQUI WELL ★

BLAIR VALLEY ★

BORREGO PALM CANYON

Borrego Palm Canyon

WHITAKER HORSE ⋀

PANORAMIC OVERLOOK ⋀

BORREGO PALM CANYON ⋀

ANZA-BORREGO STATE PARK VISITORS CENTER ▪

S22

GRAPEVINE TRAIL

Grapevine Cyn

Grapevine Cyn Mountain ▲

Ranchita

Hot Springs Mountain ▲

Pacific Crest Trail

Warner Springs ✈

S2

Volcan Mountains

Santa Ysabel Open Space Preserve ⋀

Julian ○

William Heise Regional Park

79

Lake Henshaw

76

Sutherland Reservoir

Santa Ysabel

78

Cleveland National Forest

Vail Lake

79

Aguanga ○

Palomar Mtn State Park ⋀

Rincon ○

To Escondido

Ramona ○

67

78

To Escondido

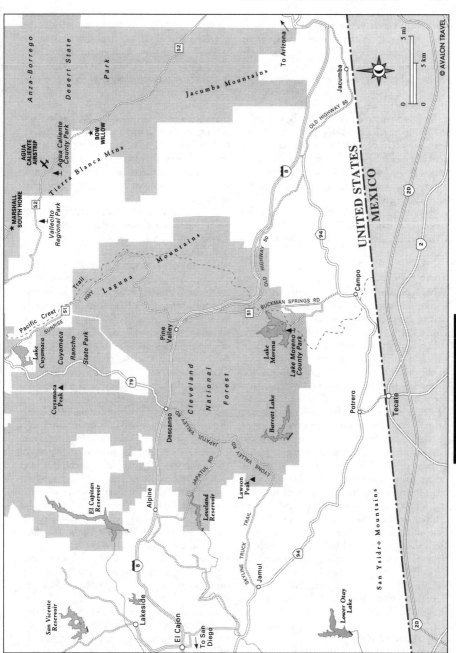

THE DESERTS

the visitors center to the north of town points out the interesting and in some cases unique features of the trail out to the spring, and of the spring itself. Because of the water, visitors get to see more abundant foliage and wildlife at Yaqui Well. Once upon a time, before conservation and state parks came along, ranchers actually grazed and watered cattle here. Before that, the Kumeyaay Native Americans camped here seasonally. Do be aware that any Kumeyaay artifacts you see lying on the ground are protected as part of the park—picking them up and taking them home is not only rude, it's actually illegal.

From the Yaqui Well trailhead you can also access the Cactus Loop Trail and the Tamarisk Campground, which has water and restroom facilities.

## Font's Point

When you stand atop the visitors center or up on the Panoramic Overlook and gaze out east to see the funky rock formation that is Font's Point (Font's Wash, off the Borrego-Salton Seaway), it looks like it's only a mile or two away. Looks can be deceiving—especially in the desert where the clear, dry air distorts distances. It's actually about 10 miles from the visitors center in the Borrego Badlands. After you negotiate the four miles of dirt road (usually passable by passenger cars) and park in the dirt lot, you'll take a short walk up to Font's Point proper. From here, you'll get arguably the best look at the formation of the desert, from its time as lakes and marshes, ancient to current fault activity, uplift and drying, all the way to current washes and canyons created by flash floods and gradual erosion. Paleontologists come here to excavate fossils from the Pliocene and Pleistocene epochs—believe it or not, woolly mammoths once lived here! Font's Point makes for another great sunrise or sunset vantage point, and there's no sight in the world quite like that of the sun hitting the badlands.

## Coyote Canyon

Coyote Canyon (entrances at the end of Horse Camp Rd. and DiGiorgio Rd.) encompasses the northernmost reaches of Anza-Borrego. Many seasonal creeks flow through this region during the flash-flood season, and the whole area is closed to human traffic from June through September to allow wildlife—especially the rare Borrego Bighorn Sheep—easy and fear-free access to the water here. Winter visitors can traverse the canyon's rough dirt roads in four-wheel-drive vehicles. Passenger cars can make it from the Borrego Springs Road cutoff up to Desert Gardens, but probably shouldn't try to go too far past due to deepening sand and rougher ruts.

**Desert Gardens** and the adjoining **Ocotillo Flats** offer some of the best cactus and ocotillo viewing in the whole of Anza-Borrego. Just park your car off to the side of the road (but not too far off—the sandy ground gets treacherously soft quickly!) and walk out into the desert to check out the variety of native plants that manage to thrive in this arid and inhospitable environment. The star of Ocotillo Flats gave the area its name and if you're there just after a rainstorm, you'll get to see the strangely beautiful ocotillos sprouting leaves and blooming. Ocotillos aren't cacti; they're a deciduous shrub that goes through a full cycle of leafing and dropping leaves each time it rains on the desert. It takes about a month for the new leaves to turn pretty colors and fall off, then the plant just sits and waits for the next rain. Out in the gardens, you'll find the misleadingly named teddy bear cactus (do not let your children hug them), the ubiquitous creosote bushes, wildflowers in the springtime, and all sorts of other desert cacti and plants.

One of the few leftovers of Anza-Borrego's years as ranchland is **Bailey's Cabin.** You can't reach the cabin from the 4WD road in Coyote Canyon. You'll have to park and hike several miles through desert sand out to the small but intact stone edifice. Originally used by the Bailey and Larner families as a line cabin on their ranch, today the state owns and maintains the cabin as part of the park. You can even camp inside it if you get there before anybody else claims it.

## Blair Valley

Off the S-2 paved road you'll find the campground and attractions in and around Blair Valley (S-2 about 7 miles south of Hwy. 78). This central western region of the park offers any number of hiking trails, plus a high density of sights worth walking out to. If you're a big fan of Native American cultural archaeology, hike on out to the **pictographs,** figures painted by early residents of the desert. One big boulder contains all the artwork—mostly Kumeyaay girls' puberty drawings that formed part of the ritual that girls went through upon becoming adult women. Though the pictographs have faded severely in the harsh sunlight over the centuries, you can still see distinctive diamond chain patterns, intricate designs, shining suns, and other symbols.

For something different and yet rather similar, take the steep three-mile hike up to the remains of the **Marshall South Home** at the top of Ghost Mountain. Marshal and Tanya South were a couple ahead of their time, heading for the middle of the desert to live an anti-commercial, totally natural, and intensely difficult existence on a lonely desert peak. They raised three children in a small hilltop cabin without electricity, running water, or access to the modern world. Today, only the skeleton of the cabin remains for visitors to poke around in.

## Split Mountain

At the eastern edge of the park, Split Mountain Road splits off from CA-78 and heads south toward the Fish Creek Mountains. It passes through the Ocotillo Wells recreation area to the north, then heads back into the park and terminates at the remains of an old **Gypsum Mine** (end of Split Mountain Rd.). From there, you can take the 4WD road out to the Split Mountain campground, or past it to the **Wind Caves** (about 5 miles south of Gypsum Mine). These are a cluster of sandstone boulders out of which the wind has carved holes, caves, and even arches over the centuries. While the formations aren't huge, they make a great place to enjoy lunch in the meager shade as the weather gets hot in the late spring and summertime. If you're visiting in the winter and looking for a walk, check out the **Elephant Tree Trail** (Split Mountain Rd., about 9 miles south of Hwy. 78) about midway down the paved road.

## Bow Willow

Down at the south end of the park, the Bow Willow (S-2, about 20 miles north of I-8) region has both water and totally dry badlands topography.

If you take a fairly stout hike, you'll find the **Mountain Palm Springs.** Several springs feed palm oases and in one case a grove of the rare elephant trees. The moderate three-mile round-trip hike seems worth it when you get the chance to rest and relax in the natural shade of the tiny groves. Sit still enough and you might get to see some of the abundant wildlife coming out to drink from the year-round water sources.

Visitors more fascinated with the harsh side of the desert head for the **Carrizo Badlands Overlook.** From here you'll get to see old washes and ridges of rock that were originally deposited by a Colorado River that ran a very different course than the modern version does.

One attraction of this region that's changed recently is the **San Diego Imperial Railway.** The tracks, some of which run across amazing trestles, cross the southern tip of the park. *But,* unlike in previous years, walking the tracks and checking the tunnels is *not* a safe activity! The railroad, which lay dormant and essentially abandoned for years, now has trains running over it on a regular basis. The tunnels and trestles are especially dangerous for explorers, because there's no safe haven. The rails and their access are now private property of the railroad, and you can be ticketed (or worse) if you're found walking the tracks.

# ENTERTAINMENT AND EVENTS

Anza-Borrego, similar to most desert parks, doesn't have too much in the way of happening nightlife. You can get a drink, though, if you're willing to do it fairly early in the evening. The **Krazy Coyote Saloon & Grille** (2220 Hoberg

THE DESERTS

Rd., Borrego Springs, 760/767-7788, www
.thepalmsatindianhead.com, daily 5 P.M.–close,
closed summer), despite its Western name, feels
more like a cocktail bar than a classic saloon.
Sure, they've got beer, but most guests at the
Krazy Coyote sip a nice California wine or
quaff a top-shelf margarita or a high-end vodka
martini. Call ahead to get the variable closing
time by season.

Another hotel bar worth looking into is
the **Hog Trough Cafe & Saloon** (221 Palm
Canyon Dr., Borrego Springs, 760/767-5341,
www.palmcanyonresort.com/saloon.htm, daily
5–10 P.M.). This saloon, with its oak bar and
eclectic decor, has more of the feel of a true
Western watering hole. The Hog Trough prides
itself on its Super Bowl party and its welcome
for two-wheeled desert travelers. So, bikers,
you've a friendly spot to show up, complete
with dedicated motorcycle parking.

## SPORTS AND RECREATION

The outdoors calls to many visitors of Anza-
Borrego. Countless acres of unspoiled desert
are just waiting to be discovered by hikers, bikers, and riders. The Borrego Springs resorts
have a few golf courses and plenty of tennis
courts and swimming pools.

As always, it's important to remember that
when you go outside, you're entering a real
desert. It's hot, dry, dangerous, and remote.
People really can, and do, die out here every
year. Before you venture on even a moderate
hike or a flat-ish 4WD road, be sure you've
got plenty of water (up to one gallon per person per day), some snacks, sunscreen, a hat, a
map, and good walking shoes (even if you're
not walking right now, you never know when
you might have to). A first-aid kit, extra gas, a
spare tire, and a vehicle emergency kit might
also be a good idea.

The best time for outdoor recreation at
Anza-Borrego is from the fall through the
spring; temperatures are moderate and in the
spring the wildflowers bloom, adding to the
beauty of a hike or off-road trek. In the summertime, the dangerously high temperatures
make serious outdoor adventuring a bad idea.

## Hiking

You can hike just about anywhere in the bounds
of Anza-Borrego State Park. If you want to, you
can just start at the visitors center and wander
straight off into the desert. On the other hand,
dozens of trails interlace the more visited and
accessible areas. Many hikes center around the
major sights in the park. Some of these trails
are more heavily maintained than others, but
don't expect pavement or boardwalks here. All
trails are primitive, and many get steep, rocky,
rough, sandy, or all of the above.

The **Bill Kenyon Overlook Trail** (Yaqui
Pass primitive camp, 1 mile round-trip, easy)
offers an easy walk in the **Tamarisk Grove
Area.** Shamble along, checking out the different kinds of cactus, before getting out to the
payoff-the view. You'll get a chance to look out
over the Pinyon Mountains, San Felipe Wash,
and other gorgeous features of the Anza-
Borrego desert.

A fascinating hike that shows off the best
of the Fish Creek Wash runs from **Mud Hills
Wash to Elephant Knees** (4.5 miles up Fish
Creek Rd. unpaved, off Split Mountain Rd.,
4 miles round-trip, moderate). Before you and
your ample supply of water set out, take a moment to read up on oyster shell reefs described
in the sign at the trail fork. The Fish Creek
Wash region was once a part of the long-gone
and dried up Gulf of California. You'll be seeing such reefs as you come upon the Mud Hills
Wash, and you'll even encounter loose shells
from more recent flooding. Once you've thor-
oughly explored the wash, it's time to climb
up the funky Elephant Knees Mesa. You'll be
tromping right up the oyster shell reef; in fact,
it's a good idea to watch your step here, because the loose shells can be hazardous. At the
top, hikers can look down and see the "knee"
formation of the bottom of the mesa. For the
best views on this hike, go at sunrise or towards sunset, when the lower sun limns the
layers of shells and ancient sediment in beautiful colors.

In the south of the park, the **Bow Willow**
region offers lots of great hiking, including
the network of trails in and around the oases

of the **Mountain Palm Springs.** The **North Fork** (2.5 miles, moderate) takes you on a good leg-stretching walk out to the Palm Bowl and Mary's Bowl Grove—a good place to see an elephant tree if you missed them to the north. The **South Fork** (3 miles, moderate) gets you to Pygmy Grove and the Totore Bowl. You can also walk the South Carrizo Creek road across S-2 and all the way out to the Carrizo Creek Wash if you're feeling energetic enough for a 20-mile round-trip trek!

For an easy and educational hike in the **Blair Valley** region, check out the **Trail to the Morteros** (unpaved Blair Valley Rd., 0.5 mile, easy). In less than an hour of easy walking, you'll get to see ancient grinding rocks used by local Native Americans to grind grains. The characteristic mortar-holes are all that remain of a once-industrious community here.

## Horseback Riding

At Anza-Borrego, all the primitive roads open to 4WD vehicles and mountain bikes are also open to equestrian traffic. That makes more than 500 miles of trails to check out within the park boundaries. In addition, part of the **California Riding and Hiking Trail** (near the visitors center) runs through the park. You can also ride on the portion of the **Pacific Crest Trail** that passes through Anza-Borrego briefly at Granite Mountain. The PCT actually runs mostly parallel to and outside the western edge of the park.

Inside Anza-Borrego, one of the best-used trails is at **Coyote Canyon** in the northern reaches. Take care, and please don't let your horse trample the delicate landscape where the road tapers off. This is where you'll find the Vern Whitaker Horse Camp, with its corrals making a desert trip with your horse both possible and comfortable. Another stand-out riding road is the **Jasper Trail** (15 miles) that runs through Grapevine Canyon in the middle western section of the park.

Didn't bring your own horse to Anza-Borrego? You can take a two-hour ride on one of the few and extremely well-tended Arabians of the **Smoketree Arabian Ranch** (302 Palm Canyon Dr., 866/408-1812, www.smoketree arabianranch.com, $95/person). This isn't your typical meat-grinding rental ranch. Yu'll find no sad, tired old nags wearing their saddles all day here. Instead, your ride will include grooming and preparing your mount as you get to know him or her before you ever climb into the saddle. You and your horse will enjoy learning about one another as you take a ride out into the beautiful desert landscape. Serious equestrians will love the way the folks at Smoketree take care of their beloved horses. But because there are few of them available for "guest" rides, be sure to call in advance to make reservations. The spring wildflower season is the busiest for Smoketree.

## Golf

Yes, there is golfing even out here in this wild desert country. The "premier" local courses sit on the land of the **Borrego Springs Resort** (1112 Tilting T Dr., 760/767-3330, www.borrego springsresort.com, greens fees $40–65, cart included). You'll find three separate nine-hole courses: The Palms, Desert Willow, and Mesquite. Pick any two to create an 18-hole day. Or take advantage of the short, cool mornings for a quick nine holes before the desert really heats up. Borrego Springs also has practice facilities, a pro shop, and regularly scheduled tournaments. Check the website for hotel-and-golf packages, as well as year-round lessons and clinics to improve your game.

Another great nine-hole course in the Borrego Springs region is **The Springs at Borrego** (2255 DiGiorgio Rd., 866/330-0003, www .springsatborrego.com/golf.htm). The Springs is adjacent to the RV park that goes by the same name. At a par-36 with a practice range, this small but technical course is perfect for golfers who want a challenging but not too-long day on a desert course. For golfers who've come to the desert specifically to play the game, there's also the **RoadRunner Golf Course** (1010 Palm Canyon Dr., 760/767-5374, www.roadrunner club.com/golf). This short 18-hole, par-3 course is great for newer golfers while helping more experienced players improve their short game.

**THE DESERTS**

## Off-Roading

Anza-Borrego State Park offers over 500 miles of dirt and sand roads accessible by highway-legal four-wheel-drive vehicles. These run around almost all areas of the park, letting you explore many places that are inaccessible otherwise. So bring your favorite tagged boonie-crasher and have a blast!

The **Jasper Trail & Grapevine Canyon** (access via Jasper Trail of S22, 13.5 miles, easy to moderate) offers a graded trail for most of the ride. You can stop and see some rare desert water welling up from Stuart Spring. Take a left here to remain on the trail and go toward the Yaqui Well primitive campground, or a right to head back out to Highway 78. If you pass Yaqui Well and head out onto the *bajada,* you'll get to see some lovely cactus varieties alongside the trail.

Want to feel like a serious boonie-crasher? Take the **Fish Creek Trail** (easy to moderate). You'll first find yourself bumping along a fault on a fairly wide track. Extremely primitive camping (no restrooms) is available at Fish Creek. From here, the trail narrows into Fish Creek Canyon, where you'll get to see the famous oyster reef cliffs. *Don't* take the Arroyo Seco del Diablo cutoff, since it's got a nasty drop that makes it dangerous to drive from this direction. Instead, keep going toward the **Sandstone Canyon Trail** (moderate to difficult). Here you'll get a great experience: tight maneuvering through narrow canyons of wind-eroded soft sandstone.

**Pinyon Mountain Road** (end of Big Rock Creek Rd., 7 miles plus 4-mile spur, easy to moderate) crosses in and out of the state park and starts close to Camp Fenner State Prison—so don't pick up any hitchhikers here! You'll get a good mix of open trail driving and creek fording, and on the spur road you can head up for a view of Devil's Punchbowl and Big Rock Creek and even on into a pine forest. Lots of out-of-the-car activities stem from this road, including access to the Pacific Crest Trail for hikers and deer hunting on the U.S. Forest Service land.

Longing for a glimpse of another country? Take the **Calcite Mine Trail** (S22 18.5 miles east of Borrego Springs, difficult). You'll bump up a difficult and slick trail (take care and use a spotter) that will take you up to a ridge that lets you look south toward Mexico. From there, the road gets even bumpier and more boulder-filled, so consider hoofing it the rest of the way to the abandoned calcite mine. When you get there, look but don't take; it's illegal to remove calcite crystals from the State Park.

While Anza-Borrego has many primitive roads worth checking out in your (mandated by the park) street-legal, possibly four-wheel-drive vehicle, the park might not make for your idea of great four-wheeling fun. Right next door, so to speak, sits the immense **Ocotillo Wells State Vehicular Recreation Area** (760/767-5391, ohv.parks.ca.gov, year-round, free). Countless (well, 80,000) acres of desert have been set aside specifically for boonie-crashers to test the mettle of their baddest trucks and best dirt bikes. Bring your rock-crawling 4WDs, open dune buggies, and other toys. Tags aren't required here. You can camp for up to 30 days, but you must bring your own water, as *no water is available inside the park.*

Be aware that Ocotillo Wells is immensely popular, and 4WD lovers come from all over California to drive here. If you're planning to visit on a holiday weekend, expect severe traffic congestion (especially when leaving) and crowding on the trails and in the camping areas.

## Biking

You're welcome to break out your mountain bike and bump along any of the primitive roads in Anza-Borrego, some of which are sandy, rough, and steep. However, no bikes are permitted on hiking trails or overland off the roads. Check out adjoining Ocotillo Wells for more extreme mountain biking opportunities.

## CAMPING

Anza-Borrego is the only state park in the California system to allow camping anywhere within its boundaries. For real. Just pull your car off the road and tromp off into the desert with your tent, find a big rock, and pitch your tent in its shadow. The catch? You'll need to take care of yourself out in the unrelenting desert. No bathrooms, no water, no nothing—just you and a shovel. If you want a more civilized desert camping experience, pick one of the RV-friendly campgrounds or even the minimally developed backcountry campgrounds.

## Developed Campgrounds

Few well-developed campgrounds grace the parched lands of Anza-Borrego. But if you really want an RV slot or a tent site with access to flush toilets and showers, you can find one. For the developed campgrounds, be sure to make a reservation in advance at 800/444-7275. Nearest to the visitors center you can stay at the **Borrego Palm Canyon Campground.** This large and somewhat desolate campground has over 100 campsites, 55 with RV hookups. (Call ahead to see if the dump station is functioning before your visit.) In addition to the showers and restrooms, working phones are available here. Some campsites have fire rings.

The **Tamarisk Grove Campground** (Road S-3 and Hwy. 78, $10–15) has 27 RV sites with access to showers, toilets, and phones. It is the southernmost fully developed campground in Anza-Borrego.

For equestrians, Anza-Borrego maintains the **Vern Whitaker Horse Camp** (Horse Camp Rd., $16). Forty corrals lie adjacent to 10 campsites, making it possible for campers to sleep near their horses. Though running water and full bathrooms grace the campground, the showers are solar heated so you may be taking a chance by using them.

## Primitive Campgrounds

Plenty of primitive campgrounds dot the land of Anza-Borrego. Also, you're permitted to camp anywhere in the park. Just be sure you've got the equipment and supplies you'll need before you pull off at your favorite cactus garden and pitch your tent. (Remember: There are no bathrooms out in the middle of the desert!) Most of the primitive campgrounds have pit or chemical toilet facilities and very little else in the way of amenities. Camping at either the primitive campgrounds or off in the rocks and sands is usually free.

The campgrounds at **Culp Valley, Yaqui Pass,** and **Arroyo** have reasonable access to paved roads. From dirt roads (most accessible via passenger cars), you can get to the sites at **Fish Creek, Yaqui Well, Blair Valley,** and **Bow Willow.** Bow Willow has more sites than most, takes reservations, and has a $7–9 per night fee. If you're interested in solitude and silence, and you're up for a hike in to your campsite, you might consider the sites at **Marshall South Home** and **Sheep Canyon.**

## ACCOMMODATIONS

Many visitors to the desert prefer not to experience its harsh beauty 24 hours a day. For them, the town of Borrego Springs, which sits right in the middle of the park, offers a wide range of motels and resorts to suit every taste and budget range.

### Under $100

The **Stanlunds Resort Inn and Suites** (2771 Borrego Springs Rd., 760/767-5501, www.stanlunds.com, $62–175) offers a convenient motel room at the right price for desert rats on a budget. Nope, it's not much to look at, but the guest rooms are reasonably clean, the beds are comfortable, and the bathroom plumbing works most of the time. You'll find the rooms rather small and decorated in standard motel florals and dark carpets, many with at least one white-painted brick wall. Larger rooms have dining areas and some have kitchens and patios as well. An outdoor pool beckons to guests who need to cool off after a long day exploring the desert, and the location downtown makes it great for dining and shopping in Borrego Springs.

### $100-150

For affordable luxury on your desert vacation, get a room at the **Borrego Springs Resort** (1121 Tilting T Dr., 760/767-5700, www.borrego springsresort.com, $115–200). Spacious rooms include comfortable modern wood-framed beds, fine cotton bedding, big bathrooms, and pretty views of mountains or the pool areas. For multiple rooms and a kitchenette, choose one of the suites. Decor tends toward the simple motel style, with quiet soothing colors. Outside of your room, take a dip in one of the two pools or lounge beside them in a covered cabana to keep the sun off. One of the biggest attractions of the resort is the attached country club golf course; check the website for packages. You can also play tennis, or ask at the desk about guided tours of Anza-Borrego State Park. Plenty of dining is available on-site, from the fancy white tablecloths at The Arches dining room to the casual Roadrunner Café. If you just want a nice before or after dinner drink, take a seat beside the column-shaped fireplace and order a classic cocktail.

## $150-250

For some travelers, it's important that their motel match with the nature and culture of its surroundings. The **Borrego Valley Inn** (405 Palm Canyon Dr., 800/333-5810, www .borregovalleyinn.com, $195–300) does just that, with low, blocky, orange adobe-style buildings with red tile roofs, and desert garden landscaping throughout. Wander the grounds,

or just sit on a wooden bench and watch the birds hop about enjoying the flowers and bugs. If you're serious about your nature loving, you can take a skinny-dip in the clothing-optional swimming pool and spa (privacy fenced for everyone's comfort, and directly accessible from rooms 1–7).

Even the smallest rooms are characteristic of its charm. All guest rooms have red-tiled floors, desert floral or Native American–inspired bedspreads and decor, matching accent decorations, cable TV, patios, and nice bathrooms. Bigger rooms might have gas fireplaces, walk-in showers, or soaking tubs, while all rooms have fridges, microwaves, and coffee makers. The largest suite offers a full homey kitchen, one bedroom, and stunning tile work.

## Over $250

For the big spenders who want the beauty of the desert without any of its discomforts, there's **( Borrego Ranch Resort & Spa** (3845 Yaqui Pass Rd., Borrego Springs, 800/824-1884, www.borregoranch.com, $400–1,700). This

Borrego Ranch Resort & Spa

© LANCE SCOTT

THE DESERTS

great sprawling resort has everything a luxury vacationer could ever need or want for a night, a week, or a month in Anza-Borrego. The recreation facilities include tennis courts, a state-of-the-art fitness center, an archery range, a tournament croquet field, and no fewer than five swimming pools. Families can enjoy pools designated just for them, complete with complimentary toys, while adults can relax or exercise in peace at the adults-only pools and spas. If you're renting one of the casitas, you may have your own private large spa or small swimming pool.

Nineteen such casitas grace the property, and they're more the size and shape of comfortable small homes than hotel rooms. You can bring your family and friends to share the comfy multiple bedrooms, beautiful desert-themed decor, and top-shelf amenities of these detached houses. Even the regular poolside rooms (yup, they're all poolside) offer tremendous space, cushy furniture, spacious bathrooms, and all the wonderful extras Borrego Ranch lavishes upon its guests to justify the lavish prices. Each room includes a full breakfast in the dining room each day.

Another reason to spend all that money on your lodgings here is the service—from the dining room to the desk staff to the fitness attendants, most everyone at Borrego Ranch will go out of their way to help you. If you need advice on activities either inside or outside the resort, they can definitely hook you up.

# FOOD
## Casual Dining

Looking for a tasty breakfast or lunch? Try locals' favorite ◖ **Red Ocotillo** (2220 Hoberg Rd., Borrego Springs, 760/767-7400, daily 7 A.M.–9 P.M., $10–20). Despite the exotic desert name, this friendly and welcoming restaurant serves up classic diner food. Just look for the Palms at Indian Head. The interior dining room is done in retro-American kitsch, while the small outdoor dining area lets diners with dogs eat in the company of their canine friends. You'll find the service good even when there's a crowd, but the real

reason to come to Red Ocotillo is the food. Diners rave about the simple but delectable fresh biscuits and gravy, served all day along with the rest of the breakfast menu. Lunch and dinner items run to classic American staple entrées, sandwiches, and so on. For a great inexpensive meal in the desert, Red Ocotillo is your best bet.

After hours out in the southwestern desert scenery of Anza-Borrego, a Mexican dinner seems like the perfect way to end the day. **Pablito's of The Desert** (590 Palm Canyon Drive, Borrego Springs, 760/767-5753, daily 11 A.M.–2:30 P.M., 5–9 P.M., $5–15) offers good solid Mexican staples with a little bit of a desert twist—such as cactus in a breakfast egg dish. Yes, they serve breakfast even though Pablito's doesn't open until later in the morning. You'll also find extremely tasty lunch and dinner options.

## Fine Dining

For an upscale meal in the low desert, you can't beat the **Cimarrón Room** at Borrego Ranch (3845 Yaqui Pass Rd., Borrego Springs, 800/824-1884, www.borregoranch.com, daily 7–11 A.M. and 11:30 A.M.–3:30 P.M., dinner nightly, $25). True, it has the advantage of being pretty much the top game in a small town, but you'll still find a low-lit, rambling dining room with a charming romantic atmosphere. Or ask for a table out on the patio on the endless warm desert evenings. The service can be variable, but the quality of the innovative dishes remains constant here. Look for high-end California stylings, including organic and sustainable produce and meat. The wine list is a star, and you'll find a long, long list of California and European wines. For a special treat, try a different glass with each course, including dessert.

The **Krazy Coyote Saloon & Grille** (2220 Hoberg Rd., Borrego Springs, 760/767-7788, www.thepalmsatindianhead.com, opens daily at 5:30 P.M., closed during summer, $20–40) is a Borrego Springs favorite. The the entrées are interesting and the homemade complimentary breads and "nibbles" make diners feel pampered. Visitors enjoy the casual-elegant atmosphere with windows overlooking the resort pool. Do expect to pay handsomely for the privilege of eating here, but most diners feel that the experience (and the martinis) are worth it.

## Markets

Need to stock up on groceries before a camping stint out in the park? Head for the **Center Market** (590 Palm Canyon Dr., # 304, Borrego Springs, 760/767-3311, Mon.–Sat 8:30 A.M.–6:30 P.M., Sun. 8:30 A.M.–5 P.M.) for the basics. For good fresh produce, join the locals at the **Borrego Springs Farmers' Market** (Christmas Circle and Palm Canyon Dr., Borrego Springs, Fri. 7 A.M.–noon) on Friday mornings. Grapefruit are the specialty of the region, so be sure to pick up some of the local Borrego breed if you can. They're sweet and pink and juicy.

## INFORMATION AND SERVICES

The only town within an easy distance of the park is Borrego Springs. It's not a one-streeter, but Borrego Springs is definitely a small town, so don't expect all the services and conveniences of a major city here.

## Tourist Infomation

The **Anza-Borrego State Park Visitors Center** (200 Palm Canyon Dr., 760/767-4205, www.abdsp.org, Oct.–May daily 9 A.M.–5 P.M., June–Sept. weekends only) sits right outside of town, beyond an odd little turnoff near the end of Palm Canyon Road. It includes a ranger station, an interpretive display area, and a demonstration desert garden outside and on its roof. Rangers here can help you plan drives and hikes, and give you advice on the best places for views, wildflowers, and wildlife.

## Media and Communications

The Internet and cell phone towers have come to Borrego Springs. Many of the resorts and motels offer Wi-Fi (sometimes free, sometimes not). Cell service is easy to come by in town, but can get spotty as you get farther out into the park. Don't expect your cell phone to save you if you get trapped in the badlands—have plenty of supplies on hand in case of emergency.

The **Borrego Sun** is the local paper, available in newspaper stands outside the Center Market.

## Medical Services

The nearest major hospital to Anza-Borrego with an emergency room is the **John F. Kennedy Memorial Hospital** (47111 Monroe St., Indio, 760/347-6191, www.jfkmemorial hosp.com), 34 miles away in Indio. The **Borrego Medical Clinic** (4343 Yaqui Pass Rd., 760/767-5051) is open 8:30 A.M.–5 P.M. on weekdays only. They do have a 24-hour answering service that can get you in touch with a doctor if you need to ask a medical question.

## GETTING THERE AND AROUND
### Air

The closest commercial airports to Anza-Borrego are the **San Diego International Airport** (3665 N. Harbor Drive, San Diego, 619/400-2400 www.san.org) and the **Palm Springs International Airport** (3400 E. Tahquitz Canyon Way, Palm Springs, 760/318-3800, www.palmspringsairport.com). There is a private airport three miles east of **Borrego Springs** (1820 Palm Canyon Dr., 760/767-7415).

### Car

Anza-Borrego State Park sits about an hour from Palm Springs to the north and from San Diego to the west. The major east–west road through the park is CA-78. County roads S-2 and S-3 run north and south through the desert, and S-22 heads east out of Borrego Springs toward CA-86.

On holiday weekends and popular spring Sundays, traffic can get very heavy on Highway 78 to the adjoining Highway 79 leaving the park to the west. Expect to creep along, possibly for hours, and plan extra time and maybe a food stop on the way out.

While you can get around the park in a passenger car, if you want to explore the dirt roads of the back country in-depth, you'll need a four-wheel-drive vehicle. Check with park rangers about current road conditions.

## Tours

Anza-Borrego has a long wildflower season, which can run from January all the way through April in moister years. Check with the state park headquarters (760/767-4684, www.parks.ca.gov) for annual wildflower predictions and status reports. You can also either call or check in at the ranger station for information on guided wildflower tours during your stay.

## JULIAN

Between San Diego and Anza-Borrego State Park sits the tiny mining town of Julian. When gold fever struck California, it quickly spread throughout the whole huge territory—even this far south. But if you've been exploring the small towns of Gold Country proper, you're in for a shock when you enter the town limits of Julian. This is a Gold Town, complete with endless crowds and parking nightmares. Residents of both San Diego and Los Angeles escape to the small-town atmosphere of Julian, with its cute shops and many public events, almost every weekend of the year.

### Sights

Most folks who come to Julian spend their time walking up and down the sidewalks of **Historic Downtown Julian.** With its many shops and restaurants, pretty old-style buildings, and attractive woodsy setting, Downtown Julian makes a nice change from the arid valleys all around it. Expect a crowd, but you'll still enjoy a stroll downtown.

Believe it or not, you can actually go wine-tasting in Julian. **Orfila Vineyards** (4470 Hwy. 78, Julian, 760/765-0102, www.orfilawines.com, Wed.–Mon. 10 A.M.–5 P.M.) has a notable reputation throughout the state. They're famous for their Rhone wines, including Viognier, Marsanne, and perhaps most of all Syrah. Their cooler weather varietals come from vineyards in coastal California. Orfila's other tasting room sits in the San Pasqual Valley north of San Diego.

The **Witch Creek Winery** (2000 Main St., Julian, 760/765-2023, www.witchcreekwinery.com, daily 11 A.M.–5 P.M.) has a fabulous long list of red wines, a few whites, and a fun cat theme running through their labels. You'll find some fascinating and unusual wines here. Ever tasted a Montepulciano before? How about an Aglianico? Witch Creek also offers a delicious array of red blends, and even a hard apple cider. Whatever your tastes, you'll find something to love at this fabulous small winery. Check out Carlsbad for the winery's other tasting room.

### Accommodations

If the heat of the desert in Anza-Borrego gets to you after a while, Julian can make a nice cool base of operations to escape back to after a day of desert explorations. Lodgings in Julian run to rustic B&Bs and vacation cabin rentals in the woods outside of town.

For a reasonably priced, rustic room in Julian, stay at the **Angels Landing Country Inn and Resort** (2323 Farmer Rd., Julian, 760/765-2578, www.angelresort.com, $90–160). Angels Landing offers quite a few family-friendly rooms and suites with multiple beds per room. Rooms fairly small with cute decor. The Lilac Building can sleep up to 10 people. The best part about this lodging is the setting—outside of town in the meadows and forested mountainside.

The **Butterfield Bed & Breakfast** (2284 Sunset Dr., Julian, 760/765-2179, www.butterfieldbandb.com, $135–185) is just as cute and country-kitsch as Julian itself. Each of the five rooms has unique decor, from elegant antique European to patchwork-quilted country Americana. All rooms have private bathrooms and cable TV, and the large private cottage can sleep up to four for an additional fee (all other rooms sleep two). Guest rooms come with a full breakfast each morning, served outdoors in the gazebo in summer and inside by the fire in winter.

A nod to luxury in Julian, **Orchard Hill Country Inn** (2502 Washington St., Julian, 760/765-1700, www.orchardhill.com, $210–500) offers 22 elegant guest rooms in a serene garden setting. Expect elegant updated decor and appointments, complete with lovely tiles, restored antique furniture, and a homelike

THE DESERTS

clutter of linens and pillows. Some cottage rooms have whirlpool tubs, and all cottages have patios or porches for summer lounging and fireplaces for winter snuggling. All guests receive a full breakfast, afternoon nibbles and wine (or beer), and upscale amenities.

For a more independent lodging experience, Julian's many vacation cabin rentals are a great choice. The **Artists' Loft, Big Cat Cabin,** and **Strawberry Hill Cabin** (4811 Pine Ridge Ave., Julian, 760/765-0765, www.artistsloft.com, $195) are all managed by the same folks. Each cabin is unique, but all share a combination of rustic construction and decoration juxtaposed with comfortable amenities. Expect to find a large sitting room with fireplace, a full kitchen with a few basic staples provided, a separate comfortable bedroom with season-appropriate bedding, and a porch or window-seat area. You're welcome to bring a full supply of groceries and cook for yourself throughout your stay at any of the cabins.

## Food

The acknowledged favorite pie shop in town is **Mom's Pie House** (2119 Main St., Julian, 760/765-2472, www.momspiesjulian .com, Mon.–Fri. 8 A.M.–5 P.M., Sat.–Sun. 8 A.M.–6 P.M., $10). Naturally, the specialty of the house is old-fashioned apple pie. You'll also find crumb-crust pies, apple-boysenberry, apple-cherry, strawberry rhubarb, and more pie flavors. If you can't take a whole pie, just stop in for a slice of your favorite flavor, maybe topped with ice cream or real whipped cream. You can also grab a sandwich and a cup of coffee while you're here. Expect crowds and lines on holiday and event weekends.

For a full meal, check out the **Julian Grille** (2224 Main St., Julian, 760/765-0173, daily 11 A.M.–3 P.M., Tues.–Sun. 5–9 P.M., $10–20), which serves higher-than-expected quality seafood and steaks in a quaint cottage. Another American diner-style eatery is the **Cowgirl Café** (2116 Main St., Julian, 760/765-2167, $10–20). The kitsch factor gets high in this tiny eatery—check out the cowgirl memorabilia on the walls. But the

main reason to brave the lines at this eight-table restaurant is the quality of the food. Expect salads to be fresh, sandwiches balanced and tasty, and desserts to be made with local apples (of course). Despite the oft-crowded dining room and small staff, service is both friendly and fast, prompting locals to give their names and wait up to 30 minutes for a table on weekends. Call for the current operating hours.

**Romano's Dodge House** (2718 B St., Julian, 760/765-1003, www.romanosjulian .com, Wed.–Mon. 11:30 A.M.–8:30 P.M., $18) is billed as the most romantic restaurant in Julian. Certainly it's cute, with its red-checked tablecloths and soft mood lighting. But what's really delightful here is the food. Sure, you can get a good bowl of pasta or a pizza but even better are the specialty entrées—unique dishes made with local ingredients (yes, apples and cider) that combine an Italian aesthetic with California creativity. The wine list features local Julian vintages as well as wines from around California and imported from Italy. Reservations are recommended for dinner, especially on weekends in fall and winter. Oh, and bring cash, as Romano's does not accept credit cards.

## Practicalities

The **Julian Chamber of Commerce** (2129 Main St., 760/765-1857, www.julianca.com, daily 10 A.M.–4 P.M.) consists of a tiny office and a big rack of brochures. You'll find almost everything you need in the brochures, including over a dozen possible places to stay overnight.

Julian lies at the junction of CA-78 and CA-79. You can drive there from Anza-Borrego in the east or San Diego to the west. Because Julian is incredibly popular as a weekend getaway destination, parking on Main Street can be challenging. You'll probably need to find parking on a side street two or three blocks from the action. During events, signs and townsfolk can help guide you to dirt lots (which you'll have to pay to use) near but not in of the center of town.

# YOSEMITE

Yosemite National Park might not be one of the seven wonders of the natural world, but its accessibility and beauty make it one of the most visited places in California. Ansel Adams' elegant black-and-white photographs turned Yosemite's stunning natural features—cascading waterfalls, striking granite cliffs, grand vistas—into international icons. Travelers come from all over the world to visit Yosemite, but other parks in the area beckon to those who prefer lighter crowds and a more unusual experience.

Mono Lake greets visitors with a serene stillness that seems almost eerie. No trees grow around this alkaline, salt-filled lake. Surrounded only by tough desert scrub, the still waters of Mono Lake have fallen and risen again amid endless state controversy. Throughout the lake and on the shore, odd calcite formations, called tufa, stand above the waterline, mute testament to the mineral content of the water. The rough High Sierra climate attracts few residents to the small towns nearby, though at one point the historic mining town of Bodie sheltered 10,000 gold-hungry residents.

The quiet, upscale town of Mammoth Lakes acts as the main access to the Mammoth Mountain ski area. Indeed, winter tourism to the mountain plays a big part in sustaining the local economy. But there's much more to do and see in and around Mammoth than just ski and snowboard. Hiking, biking, fishing, backpacking, and sightseeing are great in this part of the Eastern Sierra, and you can find bargains on lodgings in the summertime "off-season."

South of Yosemite, the Sequoia and Kings

© LIZ HAMILL SCOTT

# HIGHLIGHTS

**⟨ Yosemite Valley:** Yosemite Valley is the masterpiece of Yosemite National Park. Half Dome, El Capitan, Bridalveil Fall, Yosemite Falls, as well as miles of spectacular hiking trails can all be found here (page 222).

**⟨ Mono Lake Tufa Preserve:** Free-standing calcite towers, knobs, and spires dot the alien landscape of Mono Lake. Several interpretive trails provide history and access to these unique formations (page 243).

**⟨ Bodie State Historic Park:** A state of "arrested decay" has preserved this 1877 gold mining ghost town. Tours of the abandoned mine provide background on the settlement's sordid history (page 244).

**⟨ Devil's Postpile National Monument:** One visit to these strange natural rock formations and you'll understand how they got their name. A mix of volcanic heat and pressure created these near-perfect straight-sided hexagonal posts that have to be seen to be believed (page 249).

**⟨ Crystal Cave:** Well-lit tunnels venture into the grand chambers of this marble cavern, filled with dramatic calcite formations and polished marble (page 262).

**⟨ Mount Whitney:** With a little bit of advance planning, you can climb or even day-hike California's tallest mountain (page 263).

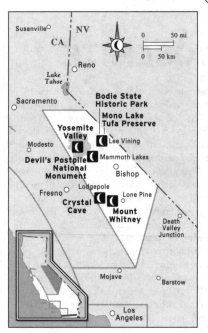

LOOK FOR ⟨ TO FIND RECOMMENDED SIGHTS, ACTIVITIES, DINING, AND LODGING.

Canyon National Parks boast gorgeous rugged mountain scenery, immense redwood trees, and far smaller crowds than their more famous neighbor. The traveled part of this area actually encompasses two distinct parks and a forest: Sequoia National Park to the south, Kings Canyon National Park to the north, and Sequoia National Forest between the two in the west.

## PLANNING YOUR TIME

This vast area deserves as much exploration time as you can give it. Both geographically huge and filled with sights and hikes and attractions, this is the perfect region to slow down and take your time.

Though summer is traditionally the high season and spring is best for the waterfalls, Yosemite is gorgeous at any time of year. During the high summer season, however, traffic jams and parking problems plague the park, just as though it were a major city. Seriously consider parking at the visitors center in Yosemite Valley and using the free shuttles to travel to different locations within the park. Tioga Pass is less congested, and parking more available, making it a viable summer option. Try to plan at least two or three days just in

YOSEMITE

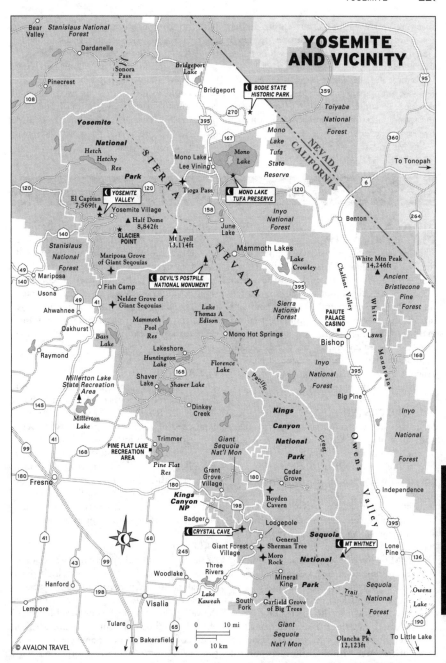

# YOSEMITE AND VICINITY

© AVALON TRAVEL

Yosemite Valley, with an excursion to Glacier Point. Adding Wawona, Tuolumne, or Hetch Hetchy? Plan a week—though it will never be long enough!

Mammoth Lakes makes a great ski weekend getaway, but prepare yourself for a long drive to get there. In winter, take a break from touring and spend your time on the slopes; in summer a week will cover you.

For Mono Lake, plan another full weekend with time to walk around the lake and explore the tufa reserves. Be sure to save a half day for the drive up to Bodie State Historic Park.

When planning a visit to Sequoia and Kings Canyon, you have a couple of options. The parks could almost be done as a day trip if all you want to do is follow the main road and maybe take a couple short hikes. To explore the parks in depth, including longer hikes, plan anywhere from 3–4 days to a week.

# Yosemite National Park

## SIGHTS
### ◖ Yosemite Valley

The first place most people go when they reach the park is the floor of Yosemite Valley (Hwy. 140, Arch Rock Entrance). From the Valley floor, you can check out the visitors center, theater, galleries, museum, hotels, and outdoor historic exhibits. Numerous pullouts from the main road invite photographers to capture the beauty of the Valley and its many easily visible natural wonders. It's the most visited place in Yosemite, and many hikes, ranging from easy to difficult, begin in the Valley.

### VISITORS CENTER

After the scenic turnouts through the park, your first stop in Yosemite Valley should be the visitors center (Yosemite Village off Northside Dr., 209/372-0200, www.nps. gov/yose, daily 9 A.M.–7 P.M., hours vary by season). Here you'll find the ranger station, as well as an intricate interpretive museum describing the geological and human history of Yosemite. Separate from the interpretive museum stands the Yosemite History Museum. Also a part of the big building complex are the theater, the Ansel Adams Gallery, and the all-important public restrooms.

A short flat walk from the visitors center takes you down to the re-created Miwok Native American village. The village includes all different types of structures, including those of the later Miwoks who incorporated European architecture into their building techniques. You can walk right into the homes and public buildings of this nearly lost culture. One of the most fascinating parts of this reconstruction is the evolution of construction techniques—as white settlers infiltrated the area, building cabins and larger structures, the Miwok took note. They examined these buildings and incorporated pieces that they saw as improvements.

### EL CAPITAN

The first natural stone monument you encounter as you enter the valley is El Capitan (Northside Rd. west of El Capitan Bridge), comprised of Cretaceous granite that's actually named for this formation. This 3,000-foot craggy rock face is accessible in two ways: You can take a long hike west from the Upper Yosemite Fall and up the back side of the formation, or you can grab your climbing gear and scale the face. El Cap boasts a reputation as one of the world's seminal big-face climbs.

### HALF DOME

At the foot of the valley perhaps the most recognizable feature in Yosemite rests high above the valley floor. Ansel Adams' famed photographs of Half Dome (visible from most of the valley floor) made it known to hikers and photo-lovers the world round. Scientists believe that Half Dome was never a whole dome—in fact, it sits now in its original formation. This

© LIZ HAMILL SCOTT

Half Dome

piece of a narrow granite ridge was polished to its smooth "dome" shape by glaciers tens of millions of years ago, giving it the fallacious appearance of half a dome. Want to climb Half Dome? See the *Hiking* section for information about this strenuous ascent.

### BRIDALVEIL FALL
Bridalveil Fall is many visitor's first introduction to Yosemite's numerous waterfalls. A pleasantly sedate water-lovers' walk, the trail to Bridalveil Fall (Southside Dr. past Tunnel View) runs a half-mile round-trip. Though the falls run year-round, their fine mist sprays strongest in spring—expect to get wet!

The trailhead comes before the main lodge, parking, and visitors center complex, making it a great first stop as you travel up the valley.

### YOSEMITE FALLS
Springtime and early summer are the best times to view the many waterfalls that cascade down the granite walls of Yosemite. You must hike to most of the falls, but Yosemite Falls are visible from the valley floor near Yosemite Lodge. Actually two separate waterfalls, Yosemite Falls together create one of the highest waterfalls in the world. But both Yosemite Falls are seasonal; if you visit Yosemite Valley during the fall or the winter, you'll see a trickle of water on the rocks or nothing at all. The best time to see a serious gush of water is the spring, when the snowmelt swells the river above and creates the beautiful cascade that makes these falls so famous.

### MIRROR LAKE
You must walk or bike a gentle mile into the park from Yosemite Valley to get to still, perfect Mirror Lake (hike past end of Southside Dr., about 4 miles round-trip). This small lake reflects the already spectacular views of Tenaya Canyon and the ubiquitous Half Dome. But come early in the season—this lake is gradually drying out, losing its water and existing as a meadow in the late summer and fall.

## Glacier Point
The best view of Yosemite Valley may not be

YOSEMITE

YOSEMITE

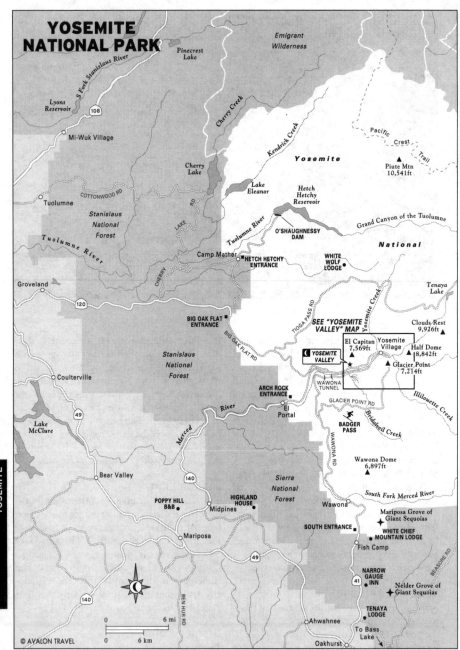

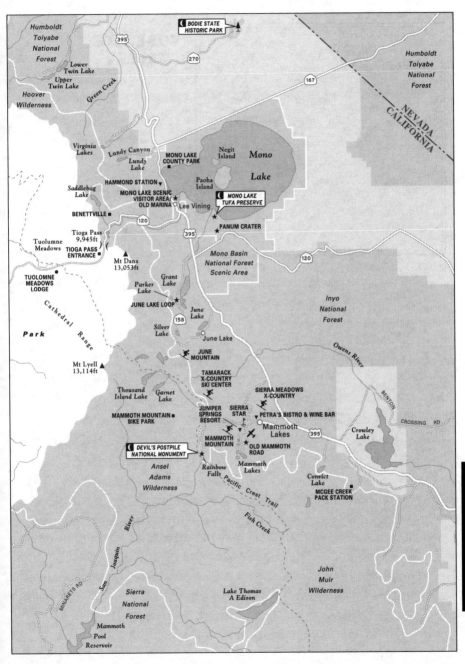

Humboldt
Toiyabe
National
Forest

Lower
Twin Lake

Upper
Twin Lake

Hoover
Wilderness

395

270

🌙 BODIE STATE HISTORIC PARK

167

Humboldt
Toiyabe
National
Forest

NEVADA
CALIFORNIA

Virginia
Lakes

Lundy Canyon
Lundy
Lake

Saddlebag
Lake

MONO LAKE
COUNTY PARK

HAMMOND STATION

Negit
Island

Mono
Lake

BENETTVILLE

MONO LAKE SCENIC
VISITOR AREA/
OLD MARINA

Paoha
Island

Lee Vining

🌙 MONO LAKE
TUFA PRESERVE

Tioga Pass
9,945ft

120

395

PANUM CRATER

Tuolumne
Meadows

TIOGA PASS
ENTRANCE

Mt Dana
13,053ft

Mono Basin
National Forest
Scenic Area

120

TUOLUMNE
MEADOWS
LODGE

Parker
Lake

Grant
Lake

Inyo
National
Forest

Cathedral Range

Park

JUNE LAKE LOOP

June
Lake

158

Silver
Lake

June Lake

Owens River

Mt Lyell
13,114ft

JUNE
MOUNTAIN

TAMARACK
X-COUNTRY
SKI CENTER

BENTON

Thousand
Island Lake

Garnet
Lake

SIERRA MEADOWS
X-COUNTRY

CROSSING RD

MAMMOTH MOUNTAIN
BIKE PARK

JUNIPER
SPRINGS
RESORT

SIERRA
STAR

PETRA'S BISTRO & WINE BAR

Mammoth
Lakes

Crowley
Lake

DEVIL'S POSTPILE
NATIONAL MONUMENT

MAMMOTH
MOUNTAIN

OLD MAMMOTH
ROAD

395

Ansel
Adams
Wilderness

Rainbow
Falls

Mammoth
Lakes

Convict
Lake

MCGEE CREEK
PACK STATION

Pacific Crest Trail

Fish Creek

San Joaquin River

MINARETS RD

Sierra
National
Forest

Mammoth
Pool
Reservoir

Lake Thomas
A Edison

John
Muir
Wilderness

YOSEMITE

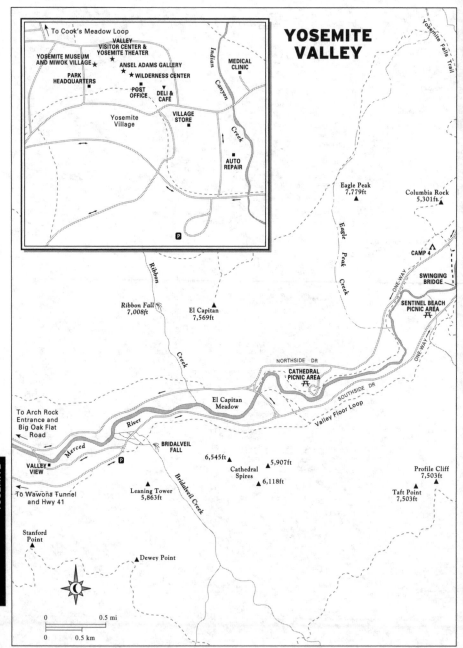

## YOSEMITE VALLEY

To Cook's Meadow Loop

VALLEY VISITOR CENTER & YOSEMITE THEATER
YOSEMITE MUSEUM AND MIWOK VILLAGE ★
ANSEL ADAMS GALLERY
PARK HEADQUARTERS
WILDERNESS CENTER
POST OFFICE
DELI & CAFÉ
MEDICAL CLINIC
VILLAGE STORE
Yosemite Village
AUTO REPAIR

Indian Canyon Creek

Yosemite Falls Trail

Eagle Peak 7,779ft
Columbia Rock 5,301ft

Eagle Peak Creek

CAMP 4
SWINGING BRIDGE
SENTINEL BEACH PICNIC AREA

Ribbon Creek

Ribbon Fall 7,008ft
El Capitan 7,569ft

ONE WAY

NORTHSIDE DR
CATHEDRAL PICNIC AREA

Creek

El Capitan Meadow

SOUTHSIDE DR

Valley Floor Loop

ONE WAY

To Arch Rock Entrance and Big Oak Flat Road

Merced River

BRIDALVEIL FALL

VALLEY VIEW

6,545ft
Cathedral Spires
5,907ft
6,118ft

Profile Cliff 7,503ft

To Wawona Tunnel and Hwy 41

Leaning Tower 5,863ft

Bridalveil Creek

Taft Point 7,503ft

Stanford Point

Dewey Point

0        0.5 mi
0      0.5 km

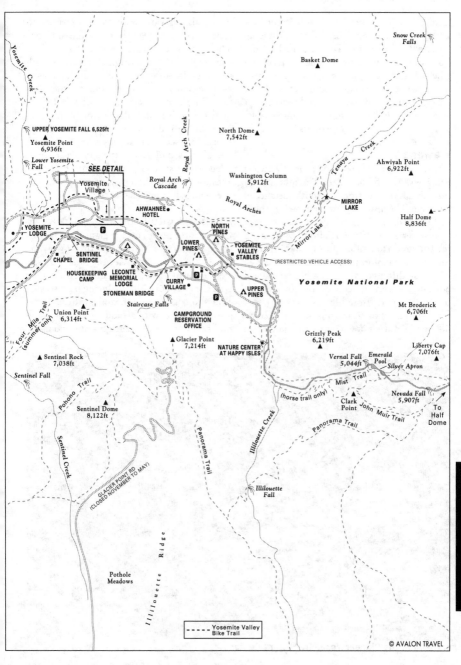

YOSEMITE

Snow Creek Falls

Yosemite Creek

Basket Dome ▲

UPPER YOSEMITE FALL 6,525ft

Yosemite Point 6,936ft

Lower Yosemite Fall

North Dome ▲ 7,542ft

Royal Arch Creek

Tenaya Creek

Ahwiyah Point 6,922ft ▲

SEE DETAIL

Yosemite Village

Royal Arch Cascade

Washington Column 5,912ft

Royal Arches

MIRROR LAKE ★

Half Dome 8,836ft ▲

AHWAHNEE HOTEL ●

Mirror Lake

YOSEMITE LODGE ●

NORTH PINES

YOSEMITE VALLEY STABLES

(RESTRICTED VEHICLE ACCESS)

CHAPEL

SENTINEL BRIDGE

LOWER PINES

HOUSEKEEPING CAMP

LECONTE MEMORIAL LODGE

STONEMAN BRIDGE

CURRY VILLAGE ●

Staircase Falls

UPPER PINES

*Yosemite National Park*

Union Point 6,314ft ▲

CAMPGROUND RESERVATION OFFICE

Mt Broderick 6,706ft ▲

Four Mile Trail (summer only)

Glacier Point 7,214ft ▲

NATURE CENTER AT HAPPY ISLES

Grizzly Peak 6,219ft ▲

Liberty Cap 7,076ft ▲

Sentinel Rock ▲ 7,038ft

Vernal Fall 5,044ft

Emerald Pool

Silver Apron

Sentinel Fall

Pohono Trail

Mist Trail

Nevada Fall 5,907ft

To Half Dome

Sentinel Dome 8,122ft ▲

(horse trail only)

Clark Point ▲

John Muir Trail

Sentinel Creek

Panorama Trail

Illilouette Creek

Panorama Trail

GLACIER POINT RD (CLOSED NOVEMBER TO MAY)

Illilouette Fall

Illilouette Ridge

Pothole Meadows

- - - Yosemite Valley Bike Trail

© AVALON TRAVEL

from the valley floor. To get a different look at the familiar formations and falls, drive up Glacier Point Road to Glacier Point. The trail from the road is any easy one—paved and wheelchair accessible—but the vista down into Yosemite Valley is anything but common. Glacier Point Road stays open all year (except when storms make it temporarily impassable) to allow access to the Badger Pass ski area.

## Wawona

The small town-like area of Wawona (Wawona Rd./Hwy. 41, 1.5 hours from Yosemite Valley) sits only a few miles from the south entrance of Yosemite. The historic Wawona Hotel was built in 1917 and also houses a popular restaurant as well as a store. Wawona also plays home to the **Pioneer Yosemite History Center** (trail from Wawona information station, open daily). The first thing you'll see is a big open barn housing an array of vehicles used over a century in Yosemite, from big cushiony carriages for rich tourists to oil wagons once used in an ill-conceived attempt to control mosquitoes on

the ponds. Onward, walk under the Vermont-style covered bridge to the main museum area. This rambling, not-overcrowded stretch of land contains many of the original structures built in the park—most over 100 years ago. Most were moved here from various remote locations. Informative placards describe the history of Yosemite National Park through its structures, from the military shacks used by soldiers who comprised the first park rangers, through homes lived in by early settlers in the area presided over by stoic pioneer women. Check your *Yosemite Guide* for living history programs and live demonstrations held at the museum.

### MARIPOSA GROVE OF GIANT SEQUOIAS

One of three groves of rare giant sequoia trees in Yosemite, the Mariposa Grove (Wawona Rd./Hwy. 41) offers a view of these majestic trees even to visitors who aren't up for long walks or strenuous hikes. During high season, a one-hour tram ride meanders through the grove, complete with an audio tour describing the botany of the trees, their history, and more.

carriage at the Pioneer Yosemite History Center

© LIZ HAMILL SCOTT

Or if you prefer, you can walk throughout the grove, taking your time admiring the ecology of the giant sequoia forest. The **Mariposa Grove Museum** (Upper Mariposa Grove, May–Sept. daily 10 A.M.–4 P.M.) brings still more information to grove visitors.

It's best to take the free shuttle to the grove from Wawona or Yosemite Valley in high season, to cut down on auto traffic and minimize use of limited grove parking areas.

## Tioga Pass

Tioga Pass, a.k.a. California State Road 120 is Yosemite's own "road less traveled." The pass (as locals call it) crosses Yosemite from west to east, leading from the populous west edge of the park out toward Mono Lake in the east. To get to Tioga Pass from Yosemite Valley, take Northside Road to Big Oak Flat Road to the Highway 120 junction, and turn east. Its elevation and location lead to annual winter closures, so don't expect to be able to get across the greater park from November through May. Along the pass, you'll find a number of developed campgrounds, plus a few natural wonders many visitors to Yosemite never see. In the spring, walk out to view the wildflowers at **White Wolf,** which sits about 10 miles east of the junction—turn north on the dirt road to get to the parking lot. Another 10 miles along, bring out your camera to take in the vista at **Olmstead Point.** Or stroll on the sandy beach at **Tenaya Lake,** two miles east of Olmstead while staring up towards **Clouds Rest.**

### TUOLUMNE MEADOWS

Once you're out of the valley and driving along Tioga Pass, you're ready to come upon Tuolumne Meadows (about 10 miles from the eastern edge of the park, accessible by road summer only). After miles of soaring rugged mountains, it's almost surprising to come upon these serene grassy High Sierra alpine meadows. Brilliant green and dotted with wildflowers in spring, gradually turning to golden orange as fall approaches, the waving grasses support a variety of wildlife. Stop the car and get out for a quiet, contemplative walk through the meadows. Or if you prefer a long trek through the backcountry, Tuolumne Meadows serves as base camp for high country backpacking.

## Hetch Hetchy and O'Shaughnessy Dam

Perhaps the most disputed valley in all California, Hetch Hetchy (Hetch Hetchy Rd. past the Hetch Hetchy park entrance) was once a valley similar to Yosemite Valley, but is now a reservoir. Hetch Hetchy supplies famously clean, clear water (plus some hydroelectric power) to the city of San Francisco and other parts of the Bay Area. But many environmental activists see the reservoir's existence as an affront, and lobby continuously to have O'Shaughnessy Dam torn down and the valley returned to its former state of natural beauty.

# HIKING

The hiking in Yosemite is second to none. From short interpretive walks on the valley floor to strenuous hikes up waterfalls and rock formations, there's something here for everyone who wants a little fresh clean air.

## Yosemite Valley

Yosemite Valley is the perfect place to take a day hike, no matter how energetic you feel. Valley hiking maps are available at the valley visitors center (Yosemite Valley at Valley Village, Northside Dr.). Read your map and talk to the rangers. Though the hikes described here provide a good sample of what's available in the valley, plenty of other trails wind through this gorgeous area. Be aware that many people love the valley trails, so you likely won't be alone in the wilderness. If you're staying at Yosemite Lodge and want a gentle walk with a great view, take the one-mile **Lower Yosemite Fall** loop. Enjoy the wondrous views of both Upper and Lower Yosemite Falls, complete with lots of cooling spray! If you can, hike this trail in the springtime or early summer, when the flow of the falls is at its peak. This easy trail works well for families with kids who love the water.

Quintessential Yosemite Valley views are visible from the **Cook's Meadow Loop,** a one-mile walk through the heart of the valley. The point of this hike is to observe Ansel Adams' famous view of Half Dome from the Sentinel Bridge, then go on to gaze up at the Royal Arches and Glacier Point.

For walkers with a little more stamina, several trails in the valley are flat, but longer. To see **Mirror Lake** (end of Southside Dr., four miles, moderate), first take the short, wheelchair-accessible paved path. For a longer walk, take the connected loop trail two miles following Tenaya Creek. Read the exhibits around the lake to learn how and why Mirror Lake is transforming from a lake into a meadow (a natural process).

If you've got several hours and a desire to extend your visit to the valley floor, take the **Valley Floor Loop** (Northside Dr. and Southside Dr., paved path alongside road). For visitors who want a mid-length hike, the half loop runs 6.5 miles and takes about three hours to traverse, going over the El Capitan Bridge and following the path of many old wagon roads and historic trails. The full loop is 13 miles long and takes all day (about six hours) to hike. But it's worth it, since you'll see all the most beautiful parts of the valley while escaping the crowds on the roads. If you want to hike the Valley Floor Loop, it's a good idea to talk to the rangers at the visitors center; the route is not entirely clear on the trail map and getting lost in the meadows or forests is a distinct possibility.

Some of the more challenging hikes in Yosemite Valley are also the most rewarding. One of these is the trek up to **Upper Yosemite Fall** (trailhead at Camp 4). You can take the shuttle (Stop #7) to the Upper Yosemite Fall trailhead rather than walking up from Lower Yosemite Fall. From the trailhead, it gets steep—you'll climb 2,700 feet in three miles (seven miles round-trip) to reach the top of America's tallest waterfall. Your reward for the work will be some of the most astonishing aerial views to be had anywhere in the world. You can look down over the fall and out over the valley, with its grassy meadows so tiny far below. Plan all day (6–8 hours) for this hike,

and bring plenty of water and snacks to replenish your energy for the tricky climb down.

Perhaps the most famous hardcore climb in Yosemite Valley takes you to the top of the monumental **Half Dome** (Mist Trail to Half Dome Trail, trail parking at the east end of Northside Dr.). This hike can be dangerous! Attempt this climb only in the summer and early fall, when the cables are up (which you hold onto for balance and use to help pull yourself up the steep granite of the last 400 feet to the top of the dome). At a round-trip distance of 17 miles and with a 4,800-foot ascent, this arduous, all-day hike (10–12 hours) is not for small children, the elderly, or the out-of-shape. Take your pack with water, food, and essentials for safety. Once you stagger to the top, you'll find a restful expanse of stone on which to sit and rest and enjoy the scenery.

Starting at the Happy Isles Nature Center, the **Mist Trail** takes you first to Vernal Fall, then on to Nevada Fall over much steep, slick granite—including over 600 stair-steps up to the top of Vernal Fall. The total distance from Happy Isles to Nevada Fall and back is seven miles, with a 2,000-foot elevation rise and fall. Plan 5–6 hours for this hike, and consider taking a lightweight parka since this aptly named trail gets intrepid visitors very wet in the spring and early summer months.

## Glacier Point Road

If you love the thrill of heights, head up Glacier Point Road and take a hike up to or along one of the spectacular (and slightly scary) granite cliffs. Hikes in this area run from quite easy to rigorous, but note that many of the cliffside trails aren't appropriate for hard-to-control children.

The two-mile round-trip hike up **Sentinel Dome** (trailhead just southwest of end of Glacier Point Rd.) makes for a surprisingly easy walk; the only steep part runs right up the dome at the end of the trail. You can do this hike in 2–3 hours, and you'll find views at the top to make the effort and high elevation (more than 8,000 feet at the top) more than worthwhile. On a clear day, you can see from

Yosemite Valley to the High Sierras and all the way out to Mount Diablo in the Bay Area to the west. Be sure to bring a camera! Be aware that there are no guardrails or walls to protect you from the long falls along the side of the trail and at the top of the dome.

Another not-too-long walk to a magnificent vista point is the hike to **Taft Point and the Fissures** (park 1–2 miles southwest of Glacier Point, Glacier Point Rd.). This two-mile round-trip hike takes you along some of Yosemite's unusual rock formations (the Fissures), through the always lovely woods, and on out to Taft Point. This precarious precipice boasts not a single stone wall—only a rickety set of guardrails to keep visitors from plummeting off the point 2,000 feet down to the nearest patch of flat ground. Thrill seekers enjoy challenging themselves to get right up to the edge of the cliff and peer down. Happily for more sedate hikers, the elevation change from the trailhead to the point is only about 200 feet.

If you're looking for a mid-level or challenging hike, plus the most spectacular view of *all* of Yosemite Falls anywhere in the park, take the **Four Mile Trail** (Glacier Point to Southside Dr., eight miles round-trip) that connects Glacier Point to Yosemite Valley. The easiest way to take this hike is to start at the top, from Glacier Point, and hike down to the valley. You can then catch a ride on the Glacier Point Tour Bus (be sure to buy tickets in advance!) back up to your car. The steep climb up the trail from the valley can be much harder on the legs and the lungs, but it affords you an ascending series of views of Yosemite Falls and Yosemite Valley that grow more spectacular with each switchback.

For a longer high-elevation hike, take the 12.5-mile walk to **Ostrander Lake** (trailhead approximately two miles past Bridalveil Creek Rd., Glacier Point Rd.) and back. (You can cross-country ski to the lake in the winter and stay overnight at the local ski hut.) This trek can take all day if you're going at a relaxed pace-especially if you're visiting during June or July and stopping to admire the wildflowers in bloom all along the trail. The lake itself is a

lovely patch of shining clear water surrounded by granite boulders and picturesque pine trees. Consider starting up the trail in the morning and packing a picnic lunch to enjoy beside the serene water. And remember to bring bug repellant since the still waters of the lake and nearby streams are mosquito heaven during hiking season.

## Wawona

It's not quite as popular (or populous) as Yosemite Valley, but the hikes near Wawona in southern Yosemite can be just as scenic and lovely. Start with the **Wawona Meadow Loop** (Pioneer Yosemite History Center), a flat and shockingly uncrowded 3.5-mile sweep around the lovely Wawona meadow and somewhat incongruous 9-hole golf course. This wide trail was once fully paved, and is still bikeable, but the pavement has eroded over the years and now you'll find much dirt and tree detritus. Best in late spring because the wildflowers bloom in profusion, this trail takes about two hours to navigate. If you'd like a longer trip, you can extend this walk to five miles (with about 500 feet of climb/descent) by taking the detour at the south end of the meadow.

If you're up for a hardcore hike and a waterfall experience few who visit Yosemite ever see, take the difficult, 8.5-mile trail to **Chilnualna Fall** (trailhead near Pioneer Yosemite History Center). Plan 4–6 hours for this 2,300-foot ascent, and bring water, snacks, and a trail map. On this amazing hike, you'll see a few fellow hikers, and many tantalizing views of the cascades. Sadly, there's no created viewing area, so you'll need to peek through the trees to get the best looks and photos. The trail runs all the way up to the top of the falls, but be careful to avoid the stream during spring and summer high flow—it's dangerous in there, what with the waterfall and everything!

## Tioga Pass and Tuolumne Meadows

For smaller crowds along the trails, take one or more of the many scenic hikes along Tioga Pass. However, be aware that they don't call it "the high country" for nothing; the altitude here *starts* at 8,500 feet and goes up on many trails. If you're not in great shape, or if you have breathing problems, take the altitude into account when deciding which trails to explore.

A great place to start your high country exploration, the loop trail to **Tenaya Lake** (Tioga Pass 20 miles west of the park's east entrance, right along the main road) offers an easy walk, sunny beaches, and possibly the most picturesque views in all of Yosemite. The trail around the lake runs about 2.5 miles, and the only difficult part is fording the outlet stream at the west end of the lake, since the water gets chilly and can be high in the spring and early summer. If the rest of your group is sick of hiking and scenery, you can leave them on the beach while you take this easy one- to two-hour stroll. Just remember the mosquito repellant!

If you're aching to see some giant trees, but you were put off by the parking problems at Mariposa Grove, try the **Tuolumne Grove of Giant Sequoias** (park and find the trailhead at the junction of Tioga Pass Rd. and Old Big Oak Flat Rd.). This 2.5-mile round-trip hike takes you down about 400 feet into the grove, which contains more than 20 mature giant sequoias. (You do have to climb back up the hill to get to your car.) While you'll likely see other visitors, the smaller crowds make this grove an attractive alternative to Mariposa, especially in the high season.

For non-athletes who just want a short walk to an amazing view, **Olmstead Point** (Tioga Pass 1–2 miles west of Tenaya Lake) may be the perfect destination. Only half a mile round-trip from the parking lot to the point, this trail exists to show off Clouds Rest in all its often-underrated grandeur. Half Dome peeks out behind Clouds Rest, and right at the trail parking lot a number of large glacial errata boulders draw almost as many tourists as the point itself.

Hikers willing to tackle somewhat longer, steeper treks will find an amazing array of small scenic lakes within reach of Tioga Pass. **Gaylor Lakes** (trailhead at the Yosemite Park border, Tioga Pass Rd.) starts high (almost 10,000 feet) and climbs a steep 600 feet up the pass to the Gaylor Lakes valley. Once you're in the valley, you can wander at will around the five lovely lakes, stopping to admire the views out to the mountains surrounding Tuolumne Meadows or visiting the abandoned 1870s mine site above Upper Gaylor Lake. The total hike spans about three miles if you don't wander around the valley. Crowd-haters will enjoy this trek, which is one of Yosemite's less crowded scenic hikes.

**May Lake** (one mile southwest of Tenaya Lake, Tioga Pass Rd.) sits peacefully at the base of the sloping granite of Mount Hoffman. While the hike to and from May Lake is only 2.5 miles, there's a steady, steep 500-foot climb from the trailhead up to the lake. One of Yosemite's High Sierra camps perches here, which makes this hike popular with the sorts of visitors who enjoy the much-less-known high-country areas. For truly hardcore hikers, a trail leads from the lake up another 2,000 feet (and six miles round-trip) to the top of Mount Hoffman.

The trail to **Elizabeth Lake** (trailhead at Tuolumne Gas Station and John Muir Trail) begins at Tuolumne Meadows and climbs almost 1,000 feet up to the lake, with most of the climb during the first mile of the 4.5-mile round-trip. Evergreens ring the lake and steep granite Unicorn Peak rises high above it. This stunning little lake makes a perfect photo op that your friends won't necessarily recognize as being Yosemite.

If altitude doesn't bother you and your legs are strong, Tioga Pass offers some stunning hikes good for a full day of hiking (or longer, if that's your thing).

For a different look at a classic Yosemite landmark, take the **North Dome** trail through the woods and out to the dome, which sits right across the valley from Half Dome. You'll hike almost nine miles round-trip, with a few hills thrown in, but getting to stare right at the face of Half Dome (and check out Cloud's Rest just beyond) at what feels like eye-level makes the effort worth it.

If you can't get enough of Yosemite's granite-framed alpine lakes, take the long walk out to one or both of the **Cathedral Lakes** (trailhead at Tuolumne Meadows visitors center, part of the John Muir Trail). Starting at ever-popular Tuolumne Meadows, you'll climb about 800 feet over 3–4 miles (depending on which lake you choose). These picture-perfect lakes show off the dramatic rocky peaks above, surrounding evergreens, and crystalline waters of Yosemite to their best advantage. Be sure to bring your camera, water, and munchies!

The **Glen Aulin Trail** (trailhead at Tuolumne Stables) to Tuolumne Fall and White Cascade is part of the John Muir trail, and several of its forks branch off to pretty little lakes and other nice spots in the area. From Tuolumne Meadows to Tuolumne Fall and back is 13 miles round trip, with some steep and rocky areas in the trail. But if you've got the lungs for it, you'll be rewarded by the fabulous views of the Tuolumne River alternately pooling and cascading right beside the trail. This hike may get a bit crowded in the high season. In the hot summertime, many hikers trade dusty jeans for swimsuits and cool off in the pools at the base of both White Cascade and Tuolumne Fall. A great way to do this hike is to enter the High Sierra Camp lottery and, if you win, arrange to stay the night at the Glen Aulin camp. If you do this, you can take your hike a few miles farther, downstream to California Fall, Le Conte Fall, and finally Waterwheel Fall.

## SPORTS AND RECREATION

The whole point of coming to Yosemite is to get outside and enjoy it. If you're craving more than just endless hiking, the park offers plenty of different outdoor activities suited to all ages and fitness levels.

### Horse and Mule Riding

Miles of trails let visitors of all ability levels take a load off their own feet and explore Yosemite from the back of a horse…or a mule! For some of Yosemite's more rugged terrain, especially in the high country, easygoing, surefooted mules are the best animals for the job of getting both people and gear around.

Three rides begin at the **Yosemite Valley Stable** (end of Southside Dr., 209/372-4386, www.yosemitepark.com/activities_mulehorse backrides.aspx, half-day $59–119). The sedate two-hour trek to Mirror Lake works well for kids and beginning riders. As part of the ride, your guide explains the geologic forces that are slowly drying out the lake. A half-day ride takes you out to Vernal Fall, where you can admire the views of Nevada Fall and the valley floor. This ride takes about four hours, but isn't terribly difficult. The all-day ride requires a great deal more stamina—going all the way out to Little Yosemite Valley and back.

You'll find more horses than mules at **Wawona Stable** (Wawona Rd. at Pioneer Yosemite History Center, $59–119), and more tourists, too—reservations for the rides out of Wawona are strongly encouraged. From Wawona you can take a sedate two-hour ride around the historic wagon trail running into the area. Or try the five-hour trip out to Chilanualna Falls—you'll get to tell your friends about a waterfall that few Yosemite visitors ever see. Be sure to bring a camera! Both of these rides are fine for less experienced riders, and the wagon trail ride welcomes children with its easy, flat terrain.

Out of **Tuolumne Meadows Stable** (Tioga Pass Rd. past Tuolumne Visitors Center, north side of the road, short dirt road to stables) you can get the perfect overview of the Yosemite high country by taking the introductory-level two-hour ride. For a longer ride deeper into the landscape, do the four-hour trip that passes Twin Bridges and Tuolumne Falls. An all-day ride with a variable route beckons the adventurous traveler, but you need to be both in good shape *and* an experienced rider for this one.

### Bicycling

Biking is a great way to get out of the car and off the crowded roads, and to explore Yosemite at a quicker-than-walking pace. Twelve miles of paved trails are mostly flat. You can bring your own bikes, or rent (www.yosemitepark .com/Activities_Biking_BikeRentals.aspx, daily 8:30 A.M.–8:30 P.M., $9.50/hour, $25/day) from

YOSEMITE

Yosemite Village. Check at Yosemite Lodge at Yosemite Falls for more information about renting and to get a bike trail map.

## Rock Climbing

The rock climbing at Yosemite is some of the best in the world. **El Capitan,** the face of **Half Dome,** and **Sentinel Dome** in the high country are challenges that draw climbers from all over. If you plan to climb one of these monuments, check with the Yosemite park rangers and the Mountaineering School well in advance of your planned climb for necessary information and permits.

But many of the spectacular ascents are *not* beginners' climbs. Go try to scale El Capitan for your first climb ever, and you'll fail (if you're lucky). The right place to start climbing in Yosemite is the **Yosemite Mountaineering School** (209/372-8344, www.yosemitepark.com/activities_mountaineeringschool.aspx). Here you'll find beginners' "Go Climb a Rock" classes perfect for older kids or adult team-building groups. You'll also find guided climbs out of Yosemite Valley and Tuolumne Meadows, and if you're looking for a one-on-one guided climb experience, you can get it through the school. Also available are guided hikes and backpacking trips, and cross-country skiing lessons and treks in wintertime.

## Skiing

Yosemite prides itself on its 350 miles of cross-country skiing tracks and trails throughout the park. In fact, many places in Yosemite are accessible in winter only by cross-country skis or snowshoes. Check out the **Cross Country Ski School** (www.yosemitepark.com/badgerpass_crosscountryskiing.aspx) for classes, rentals, and guided cross-country ski tours. If you're looking for a fun day out in the snow, the groomed tracks from Badger Pass to Glacier Point run 21 miles and are frequented by day skiers. You'll see fewer other skiers on the backcountry trails, which can also be traversed in a single day by a reasonably strong skier. For the hardcore XCer who wants a serious skiing experience, check out

the overnight and multi-day tours—hiring a guide for these trips is recommended for most skiers.

Downhill skiing at **Badger Pass** (Glacier Point Rd., five miles from Wawona, mid-Dec.–Apr., daily 9 A.M.–4 P.M., prices vary) is another favorite wintertime activity at Yosemite. Badger Pass was the first downhill ski area created in California. Today, it's the perfect resort for families and groups who want a relaxed day or three of moderate skiing. With plenty of beginner runs and classes, Yosemite has helped thousands of kids (and adults!) learn to ski and snowboard as friends and family look on from the sun decks at the lodge. There are enough intermediate runs to make it interesting for mid-level skiers, too. Double-black diamond skiers may find Badger Pass too tame for their tastes since there are just a few advanced runs. But everyone agrees that the prices are more reasonable than much of what you'll find at Tahoe's huge resorts, and the focus is on friendliness and learning rather than showing off and extreme skiing.

## Snowshoeing

Even if you're not up for hardcore skiing, you can get out and enjoy the snow-covered landscapes of wintertime Yosemite. Snowshoeing requires no experience and only minimal fitness to get started. "If you can walk, you can snowshoe," claims Yosemite's own website. You can rent snowshoes at several locations in Yosemite and acquire trail maps from the rental centers. The **Cross Country Ski School** (www.yosemitepark.com/badgerpass_snowshoeing.aspx) offers guided hikes and winter camping trips.

# ENTERTAINMENT AND EVENTS
## Photography and Art Classes

The unbelievable scenery of Yosemite inspires visitors young and old to create images to take home with them. Knowing this, Yosemite offers art and photography classes to help people catch hold of their inner Ansel Adams. In the summertime, art classes are offered for free out

# YOSEMITE AT NIGHT

Yosemite National Park does not roll up its meadows and trails at sunset. In fact, parts of the park come alive at nightfall, showing off another side of Yosemite's natural wonders. Check your *Yosemite Today* guide for more information about these and other activity programs.

If you fancy a nighttime stroll, you can take one regardless of season or weather. In summer, **Night Prowl** (90 minutes, $5) takes you along easy trails near Yosemite Lodge at Yosemite Falls, explaining the nightlife of the inhabitants of the valley floor. This fun guided tour welcomes children and adults. It takes place once or twice a week, starting at different times and places. In winter, take a **Full Moon Snowshoe Walk** ($14.75 rental, $5 without, children over 8). This two-hour trek from the Badger Pass ski lodge takes you out into the sparkling white wonderland that is Yosemite in winter. These walks are offered five days per month – the four days leading up to the full moon, and the day of the full moon itself. Also be aware that the Badger Pass shuttle *does not* run in the evenings, so you must drive yourself to and from the lodge.

If astronomy is your favorite nighttime interest, join experienced guides out in the valley meadows for the **Starry Skies** ($5, summer and fall) program. Well suited for individuals and families, this one-hour program takes groups out to look at the unpolluted lights of stars and moon over the park. You'll learn about constellations, comets, and meteors, and enjoy the myths and legends surrounding the mysteries of the night sky. Starry Skies happens several times each week in Yosemite Valley, and once a week in Wawona.

For families who find themselves tired after a long day running around the park, plenty of non-hiking evening fun can be had at various semi-sedentary evening programs. The **Campfire Program** ($5) does it old-school – groups gather around a nice big campfire (bring blankets and bug repellant!) for stories, singing, and marshmallow toasting. You might need to take a short walk to get to the fire near Camp Curry. If you're out at one of the more primitive lodges or campsites, check with your local rangers or office for campfire programs at your site, since many spring up in the summer and early fall months. **Fireside Storytelling** (fall, winter, and spring, free) focuses on, well, telling stories around the big fire inside the Ahwahnee Great Lounge. Take refuge from the bugs and the cold and listen to great tales in a comfortable indoor environment during the off-season.

of the **Yosemite Art and Education Center** (Yosemite Village, Mon.–Sat. 10 A.M.–2 P.M.). Check the *Yosemite Guide* for a list of classes during your visit. You must bring your own art supplies, chair or cushion to sit on, and walking shoes (you'll take a brief walk out to a good location to see the scenery). If you don't have supplies, you can buy them at the Village Store just before class. Also check the *Guide* for guided tours of the **Ansel Adams Gallery** in the Village.

## Theater and Music

The **Valley Visitors Center Auditorium** (Northside Dr. at Yosemite Village visitors center) in the heart of Yosemite Village acts as home to the Yosemite Theater. For an evening of indoor entertainment, check the copy of *Yosemite Today* you received at the gate for a list of what shows are playing during your visit. Most plays are one- or two-man productions; all center on the theme of the rich history and culture of Yosemite National Park. The John Muir Performances, starring resident actor Lee Stetson, have been running for 25 years.

It's worth making an evening trip out to Wawona one evening to listen to the delightful piano music and singing of legendary Tom Bopp. He plays vintage camp music (and requests, and whatever else strikes his fancy) in the **Piano Lounge at the Wawona Hotel** (209/375-1425) five nights a week. Older visitors especially love his old-style performance

YOSEMITE

and familiar songs, but everyone enjoys the music and entertainment he provides. Even if you're just waiting for a table at the restaurant, stop in to say hello and make a request.

# CAMPING

Many people come to Yosemite specifically to feel the great outdoors all around them all the time. Naturally, that experience includes camping out under the stars. Inside the park, you'll find 13 designated campgrounds and the High Sierra camps. If you prefer less expense and less need for advance reservations, try one of the campgrounds outside the park boundaries.

## Inside the Park

For any Yosemite National Park campground, make reservations early! All the major campgrounds fill up from spring through fall, and reservations can be difficult to come by. Consider making your Yosemite campground reservation *at least six months in advance* to get the campsite you want. To make a reservation, go to www.nps.gov/yose/planyourvisit/camping.htm or call 877/444-6777.

### YOSEMITE VALLEY

In Yosemite Valley, the campgrounds at **Upper, Middle,** and **Lower Pine** (reservations required, 375 campsites, $20/day) allow trailers and RVs, and you can bring your dog camping here with you. Upper Pine is open through the winter. Camp Curry offers plenty of food options within walking distance, and showers are available nearby. **Camp 4** (near Yosemite Lodge, no reservations required, 35 campsites, $5) stays open year-round. Yes, you can camp in the snow! Bring a tent—no RVs or trailers are allowed at Camp 4—but you'll find showers nearby and lots of food and groceries at Yosemite Lodge.

### WAWONA

To the south, you can camp at lovely forested **Wawona** (one mile north of Wawona, reservations required Apr.–Oct., 93 sites, $20) year-round. RVs are welcome, though there are no hookups on-site. If you want to camp with your horses, Wawona offers two horse sites. The small grocery store in town can provide a few basics, but most services (including showers) can't be found closer than Yosemite Valley. For a more picturesque southern Yosemite camping experience, check out **Bridalveil Creek** (Glacier Point Rd., no reservations required, 110 campsites, $14/night). You can reserve one of three horse sites if you're traveling with your mount. Mechanical beasts of burdens (RVs) are welcome as well.

### TIOGA PASS AND TUOLUMNE MEADOWS

Yosemite visitors who favor the high country tend to prefer to camp rather than stay in a lodge. Accordingly, most of Yosemite's campgrounds sit north of the valley, away from the largest tourist crowds (excluding the High Sierra Camps, which are also up north). ◖ **Tuolumne Meadows** (Tioga Pass Rd. at Tuolumne Meadows, reservations suggested, $20/night) hosts the largest campsite in the park, with over 300 individual campsites, plus four horse sites. Expect Tuolumne to be crowded for the whole of its season (July–Sept.). Tuolumne is RV-friendly and has most necessary services, including food and showers available at the Tuolumne Meadows Lodge. Other good-sized campgrounds off Tioga Pass include **Crane Flat** (reservations required, 166 campsites, $20/night, RVs ok, open mid-June–mid-Oct.), **White Wolf** (no reservations, 74 campsites, $14/night, open July–mid-Sept.), and **Hodgdon Meadow** (reservations required high season, 105 campsites, $20/night, open year-round) at the west edge of the park.

If you're looking to ditch the RV traffic and crowded central visitor areas, head for **Yosemite Creek** (no reservations, $10/night). This tents-only campground boasts only 40 campsites on a first-come, first-served basis from July through September. The creek flows right through the campground, perfect for cooling off on a hot day, and you can even drink the water if you first treat it properly. Yosemite Creek offers few amenities—no groceries, showers, or on-site potable water. It's just what many outdoorsy visitors want! Another option is **Tamarack Flat** (Tioga Pass Rd., no reservations, 52 campsites, $10/night). Here you'll be closer to Yosemite Valley but still in a more primitive environment.

The **High Sierra Camps** (www.yosemite park.com/accommodations_highsierra_how toapply.aspx) at Yosemite offer far more than your average backcountry campground. Rather than carrying heavy packs filled with food, tents, and bedding, multi-day hikers can plan to hit the High Sierra Camps, which provide tent cabins with amenities, breakfast and dinner in camp, and a box lunch to take along during the day. Choose from among the Merced Lake, Vogelsang, Glen Aulin, May Lake, and Sunrise Camp—or hike from one to the next if you get lucky. Why do you need luck? Because you can't just walk up to a High Sierra Camp one weekend at random and expect to find a bed. In the fall, a lottery takes place for spots at High Sierra Camps through the following summer. You'll need to submit an application if you want to join the lottery, and even if you get a spot there's no guarantee you'll get your preferred dates. You can check in at the website during the camping season (June–Sept.) to see if any dates are available.

The bottom line? If you want to take advantage of the Yosemite backcountry, plan for a summer when you can be flexible in your dates, and start making your arrangements a year in advance.

## Outside the Park

Some campers prefer a bit more seclusion, lower campsite prices, or just a different atmosphere. They tend to go for the campgrounds outside Yosemite's boundaries, which abound in the woodsy wilderness surrounding the park.

### GROVELAND

To camp in Big Oak Flat along Hwy. 120 near Groveland, try the Thousand Trails RV campground at **Yosemite Lakes** (31191 Harden Flat Rd., 800/533-1001, ranger station 209/962-0103, www.1000trails.com). This sprawling wooded campground beside the water has more than 250 RV sites with full hookups, 130 tent sites, a few dozen cabins, tent cabins, and yurts, and a 12-bed hostel. It's only five miles from the park entrance, and it's got a full slate of recreational amenities, laundry facilities, and Wi-Fi. You're right on the Tuolumne River, you've got great access to the boating opportunities on Lake Don Pedro, and the Moaning Cavern (see the *Sacramento and Gold Country* chapter) is only a few miles away.

### MARIPOSA

Several campgrounds surround the Arch Rock Entrance to Yosemite on Hwy. 140, near the border town of Mariposa. The **Yosemite Bug Rustic Mountain Resort** (6979 Hwy. 140, 866/826.7108, www.yosemitebug.com, $23/dorm bed, $35–55/tent cabin, $65–135/private cabin rooms) is part hostel, part rustic cabin lodge. This facility includes five hostel dormitories, a number of attractively appointed tent cabins with real beds, and a few cabins with private rooms, some with private baths. Solo travelers and families on tight budget favor Yosemite Bug for its comfortable and cheap accommodations. It's not the Ritz, but the bathrooms are clean and the linens are fresh when you arrive, and the location is great for Yosemite visitors who want to exit the park each night.

RVers aiming for the Arch Rock Entrance flock to the **Indian Flat RV Park** (9988 Hwy. 140, 209/379-2339, www.indianflatrvpark .com, tent sites $20–30, RV sites $35–40, tent cabins $60, cottages $110, pet fee $5). This park is a full-service low-end resort, with everything from minimal-hookup RV sites up through tent cabins and full-fledged cottages. Showers are available here, even for passers-through who aren't staying at Indian Flat. The lodge next door has extended an invitation to all Indian Flat campers to make use of their outdoor pool. Because Indian Flat is relatively small (25 RV sites, 25 tent sites), reservations are strongly recommended. You can make your booking up to a year in advance, and this kind of planning is a really good idea for summertime Yosemite visitors.

YOSEMITE

## SOUTH ENTRANCE

At the South Entrance down by the spread-out forest town of Fish Camp, book a site at the small, attractive **Summerdale Campground** (northeast of Fish Camp on Hwy. 41, 877/444-6777, www.reserveusa.com, two-night minimum weekends, three-night minimum holiday weekends, $19, June–Nov.). This lovely spot has only 29 campsites and a strict limit on RV size (24 feet), making it a bit quieter and less city-like than the mega-campgrounds. You'll have a fire ring and a grill at your site, plenty of room under mature shade trees for yourself and your friends, and maybe even a running water spigot (on some sites, boiling before drinking recommended).

## INYO NATIONAL FOREST

Out east, near Highway 395 and Tioga Pass, campgrounds tend to cluster in the Inyo National Forest. You can stay at **Ellery Lake** (Hwy. 120 in Upper Lee Vining Canyon, 877/444-6777, www.fs.fed.us/r5/inyo/recreation/campgrounds.shtml, $17, no reservations, pit toilets, garbage cans), which boasts 21 campsites perched at 9,500-feet elevation with available running water. Get there at dawn if you want a site on a weekend!

Another option is **Sawmill Walk-In** (Saddlebag Rd., 1.6 miles from Hwy. 120, 877/444-6777, www.fs.fed.us/r5/inyo/recreation/campgrounds.shtml, $12, June–Oct.). This primitive, no-reservations, hike-in campground (no water) has an astonishing 9,800-foot altitude that will, after a day or two, prepare you for any high-altitude activity you want to engage in.

# ACCOMMODATIONS
## Inside the Park

All the lodges, hotels, and cabin-tent clusters in Yosemite are run by the same booking agency. Contact the Yosemite Park concessionaire (801/559-4884, www.yosemitepark.com) to make reservations. Coming to Yosemite in the summer high season? Make reservations early-6–9 months early, if you have a preference as to where you want to stay. If you wait until the week before your trip, you'll either find the park sold out or end up in a tent cabin at Curry when you wanted a suite at the Ahwahnee.

## YOSEMITE VALLEY

**Curry Village** offers some of the oldest lodgings in the park. Locally called Camp Curry, this sprawling array of wood-sided and tent cabins was originally created in 1899 to provide affordable lodgings so that people of modest means could afford to visit and enjoy the wonders of Yosemite. At Curry Village, you can rent a hard-walled cabin or a tent cabin, with or without heat and with or without a private bath depending on your budget and your needs. The tent cabins ($95), the most affordable option, are small, fitting cot beds and a small dresser on the wood floor. Bear-proof lockers sit outside each tent cabin. Wood cabins ($179) have double beds (one or two) and electricity, but little else. The cabins with private baths are heated and boast daily maid services, but no TVs or phones. A few motel rooms and unique cabins have TVs and more amenities, but still no phones or significant distractions of the modern world. With its perfect location on the valley floor, a swimming pool in the summer and an ice skating rink in the winter, Camp Curry makes an inexpensive vacation at Yosemite a joyful reality.

Want to camp, but don't want to schlep all the gear into the park? Book a tent cabin at **Housekeeping Camp** ($76). Located on the banks of the Merced River, Housekeeping Camp has its own sandy river beach for playing and sunbathing. Cabins have cement walls, white canvas roofs, and a white canvas curtain that separates the bedroom from the covered patio that doubles as a dining room. Every cabin has a double bed plus two bunks (with room for two additional cots), a bear-proof food container, and an outdoor fire ring. You can bring your own linens, or rent a "bed pack" (no towels) for $2.50 per night. No maid service is provided, but you won't miss it as you sit outside watching the sun set over Yosemite Valley.

◀ **Yosemite Lodge at the Falls** ($150–250), situated near Yosemite Village on the Valley floor, has a location perfect for touring all over the park. The motel-style rooms are light and pretty, with polished wood furniture, bright-colored bed linens, and Native American design details. Lodge rooms with king beds offer romantic escapes for couples, complete with balconies overlooking the valley, while the standard rooms can accommodate singles, couples, or families. Enjoy the heated pool in the summertime and the free shuttle transportation up to the Badger Pass ski area in winter. The amphitheater at the middle of the lodge runs nature programs and movies all year. The lodge has a post office, ATM, and plenty of food options, and is central to the Yosemite shuttle system.

If you're looking for luxury amongst the trees and rocks, check in to the **( Ahwahnee Hotel** ($379–1,189). Built as a luxury hotel in the early 20th century, the Ahwahnee lives up to its reputation with soaring ceilings in the common rooms, a gorgeous stone facade, and striking stone fireplaces. Guest rooms, whether in the hotel or in the individual cottages, drip sumptuous appointments. The theme is Native American and you'll find intricate, multicolored geometric and zoomorphic designs on linens, furniture, and pillows. Rooms with king beds invite romance for couples, while those with two doubles are perfect for families.

### WAWONA
Consider staying at the charming **Wawona Hotel** ($120–190) near the south entrance of the park. The black-and-white exterior of the hotel complex reminds onlookers of a 19th-century Mississippi riverboat. Indeed the hotel opened in 1879, and has been a Yosemite institution ever since. The interior matches the outside well, complete with Victorian wallpaper, antique furniture, and a noticeable lack of in-room TVs and telephones. The Wawona feels more like a huge European pension than an American motel, complete with shared bathrooms for the more economically minded traveler. (Rooms with private baths are also available.)

### TIOGA PASS AND TUOLUMNE MEADOWS
In the high country, **Tuolumne Meadows Lodge** ($78, June 1–Sept. 16) offers rustic lodgings and good food in a gorgeous sub-alpine meadow setting. Expect no electricity, no private baths, and no other plush amenities. What you will find are small, charming wood-framed tent cabins that sleep up to four, central bath and hot shower facilities, and a dining room. The location is perfect for starting or finishing a backcountry trip through the high-elevation areas of the park.

Another rustic high-country accommodation, the **White Wolf Lodge** ($75–110, July–Sept.) sits back in the trees off Tioga Pass. Here you can rent either the standard wood-platform tent cabin with use of central bath and shower facilities, or a solid-wall cabin with a private bathroom, limited electricity, and daily maid service. All cabins and tent cabins at White Wolf include linens and towels, plus breakfast and dinner served family style in the dining room. You can order box lunches to take with you each day. Amenities are few, but breathtaking scenery is everywhere at White Wolf. Take a day hike to Hardens Lake, or a horseback ride through the backcountry. White Wolf works well for visitors who prefer a smaller crowd, since the lodge boasts only 28 cabins.

## Outside the Park
If you seek a small inn or inexpensive motel for your visit to Yosemite, consider staying outside the park proper and driving in each day. A wealth of inns, lodges, and B&Bs cluster near both the west and south entrances to the park. If you prefer a standard chain motel, Oakhurst (south of Fish Camp on Highway 41) and Mariposa (to the west on Highway 140) have most of the usual suspects.

If you're planning an extended stay at Yosemite with friends or family, it might be more convenient and economical to rent a condo or house with a full kitchen, privacy, and the comforts of home. You can find these at the **Yosemite West Condominiums** (800/669-9300), rented through the Yosemite Four Seasons Vacation Rentals. Modular buildings can be divided into a number of separate units—or not, if you want to rent a large space for a big crowd. The studio and loft condos sleep 2–6 people and have full kitchen and access to all complex amenities. Luxury suites are actually one-bedroom apartments with full kitchens, pool tables, hot tubs, four-poster beds, and all sorts of other amenities. Two- and three-bedroom apartments sleep 6–12 people. And the full houses can fit up to 22 guests, so you can fit an entire family reunion or college ski party into one huge house!

## MARIPOSA

You can't miss the **River Rock Inn and Deli Garden Café** (4993 7th St., Mariposa, 800/627-8493, www.riverrockncafe.com, $100–132) with its vivid orange-and-purple exterior in the heart of Mariposa. What was once a run-down 1940s motor lodge is now a quirky, fun motel with uniquely decorated rooms that make the most of modern Pottery Barn-esque wrought-iron and wood styling and the spaces the decorators had to work with. Never fear: The colors become softer as you step through the door of your reasonably priced guest room. Two suites provide enough space for families, while the other five rooms sleep couples in comfort. The River Rock is a 45-minute drive from the west entrance to Yosemite, and at the southern end of the long chain of Gold Country towns, making it a great base of operations for an outdoorsy, Western-style California vacation.

If you prefer cozy seclusion to large lodge-style hotels, stay at the **Highland House** (3125 Wild Dove Ln., 209/966-3737, www.highland housebandb.com, $127–165) outside Mariposa to the west of Yosemite. The house is set deep in the forest far from town, providing endless peace and quiet away from civilization. This tiny B&B has only three guest rooms, each uniquely decorated in soft colors and warm, inviting styles. All rooms have down comforters, sparkling clean bathtubs and showers, and TVs with DVD players.

Another lovely small B&B, **Poppy Hill Bed and Breakfast** (5218 Crystal Aire Dr., Mariposa, 800/587-6779, www.poppyhill .com, $137–165) sits 27 miles from the west

entrance to the park. The four airy guest rooms are done in bright white linens, white walls, lacy curtains, and antique furniture. No TVs mar the sounds of the expansive gardens surrounding the old-style farmhouse. But you can take a dip in the totally modern hot tub any time. A full gourmet breakfast served on your schedule puts the right start on a day spent exploring Yosemite or the Mariposa County area. This inn can be hard to find, especially at night. Double-check the directions on the website and consider using a GPS device if you have one.

## SOUTH ENTRANCE

Near the south entrance to Yosemite on Highway 41, the **Narrow Gauge Inn** (48571 Hwy. 41, Fish Camp, 888/644-9050, www .narrowgaugeinn.com, $132–215) recalls the large lodges inside the park, in miniature. This charming 26-room mountain inn offers one- and two-bed guest rooms done in wood paneling, light colors, white linens, or vintage-style quilts. Each room has its own outdoor table and chairs to encourage relaxing outside with a drink on gorgeous summer days and evenings. The restaurant and common rooms feature antique oil lamps, stonework, and crackling fireplaces. Step outside your door and you're in the magnificent High Sierra pine forest. A few more steps takes you to the Yosemite Mountain Sugar Pine Railroad—the narrow-gauge steam train from which the inn takes its name.

For inexpensive lodge-style accommodations in Fish Camp, check in to the **White Chief Mountain Lodge** (east of Fish Camp, 559/683-5444, www.sierratel.com/whitechief mtnlodge, $112–118). The basic rooms feature light wood paneling, tribal-design textiles, and inoffensive accents and lighting. Small TVs offer in-room entertainment, but the woods outside your door invite you outside to enjoy all that the rich Sierras have to offer. The lodge has its own restaurant and offers packages that show off the best of the Wild West heritage of the area.

The ◖**C**◗ **Tenaya Lodge** (1122 Hwy. 41, 888/514-2167, www.tenayalodge.com, $345–400) sits just outside the south entrance of Yosemite, offering plush lodge-style accommodations at a more reasonable price than comparable rooms inside the park. Guest rooms are styled with rich fabrics in bright oranges and other bold, eye-catching colors. The modern wall art evokes the woods and vistas of Yosemite. The beds are comfortable, the baths attractive, and the views forest-filled. Tenaya Lodge focuses on guest care, offering a three-meal-per-day dining room, a full-service spa that specializes in facials, and daily (and nightly) nature walks complete with costumed guides. Check at the desk for events occurring during your stay.

If you plan to do some fishing during your trip to the Yosemite area, the **Pines Resort** (54432 Road 432, Bass Lake, 800/350-7463, www.basslake.com, $245–375) is perfectly located for your angling convenience right on the shores of Bass Lake; bring your boat! You can choose a suite (a split-level king room with dark floors, light walls, fireplaces, and mountain-y touches, some with spa tub) or rent a chalet (a two-story cabin in a rustic mountain style that sleeps up to six, with a full kitchen and outdoor mini-barbecue). The Pines is a full-service resort, with a restaurant (Ducey's), bar and grill, market, all-weather tennis courts, summer swimming pool, year-round hot tubs, spa services, shaded lakefront chaise lounges, and wedding and meeting facilities.

# FOOD
## Yosemite Valley
There's plenty to eat inside Yosemite National Park, but if you leave the valley floor you'll need to plan for meals. In Yosemite Valley, you have a number of dining options. The **( Ahwahnee Dining Room** (Ahwanee Hotel, 209/372-1489, daily 7–10:30 A.M., 11:30 A.M.–3 P.M., 5:30–9 P.M., $20–35) enjoys a reputation for fine cuisine that stretches back to the 1920s. The grand dining room features expansive ceilings, wrought-iron chandeliers, and a stellar valley view. The restaurant serves three meals daily, with dinner the highlight. The California cuisine of an Ahwahnee dinner mirrors that of top-tier

San Francisco restaurants (with a price tag to match). Reservations are recommended for all meals, though it's possible to walk in for breakfast and lunch. Dinner requires more formal attire.

At the other side of the valley, you can enjoy a spectacular view of Yosemite Falls at the **Mountain Room Restaurant** (Yosemite Lodge, 209/372-1274, 5:30–9 P.M., year-round, $15–20), part of Yosemite Lodge at the Falls. The glass atrium lets every guest at every table take in the view. The menu runs to American food, and drinks are available from the full bar. A casual bar menu is available at the **Mountain Room Lounge** (noon–11 P.M., inexpensive) immediately across from the restaurant.

For more casual food options, head to Yosemite Village for **Degnan's Loft** (spring–fall) for hot pizza, soups, and appetizers, and **Degnan's Delicatessen** (daily 7 A.M.–5 P.M.) for an array of sandwiches, salads, and other take-away munchies.

Curry Village is where to go for (relatively) cheap, fast food. Hiking clothes are expected! The **Curry Pavilion** (daily Mar.–Nov., $10–15) hosts an all-you-can-eat buffet for breakfast and dinner. There is also a deck, with a full-service bar, a taqueria, pizza, ice cream, and coffee.

## Wawona
If you can, plan a meal at the south end of the park in the **( Wawona Dining Room** (Wawona Hotel, 209/375-1425, moderate–expensive). This lesser-known gem of a restaurant serves upscale homey California cuisine for reasonable prices to all comers. No reservations are accepted-all seating is first come, first served. The large, white painted dining room is family friendly, and the menu offers options for vegetarians as well as devout carnivores. Because you'll probably have to wait for a table on high-season weekends, a large common area invites seating, drinks, and live piano music by local legend Tom Bopp. The Wawona Dining room serves breakfast, lunch, dinner, Sunday brunch, and a weekly outdoor barbecue on Saturday evenings during the summer.

## INFORMATION AND SERVICES

With the high density of visitors to Yosemite Valley, the Park Service has thoughtfully put in place any number of guest services, going above and beyond most other venues in the national park system.

### Media and Communications

The print guide you absolutely need as you tour Yosemite is the monthly or biweekly published *Yosemite Guide*. This paper provides general information about the park's places and services. More importantly, it's got a detailed schedule of all classes, events, programs, and so on for the coming two weeks (in summer) or month (spring, fall, winter). You'll receive your copy when you enter the park at one of the entrance stations.

Limited Internet access is available in a few spots in Yosemite Valley. The only Wi-Fi to which you can connect your own laptop sits inside Yosemite Lodge. Kiosks are available in Degnan's Café and the Mariposa County Library—the library is free, while the café kiosks are available for a fee.

### Banks and Post Office

A number of ATMs are available throughout Yosemite, making it easy to extract cash with which to pay for souvenirs, food, and more souvenirs. You'll find at least one ATM in Yosemite Village at the Art and Education Center, one in Yosemite Lodge, one at Curry Village, and one at Wawona.

Several post offices provide mailing services in Yosemite. Look for a post office in Yosemite Village (Mon.–Fri. 8:30 A.M.–5 P.M., Sat. 10 A.M.–noon), inside Yosemite Lodge (12:30 P.M.–2:45 P.M.), and in El Portal (Mon.–Fri. 8:30 A.M.–5 P.M., closed 12:30–1:30 P.M.).

### Gas and Automotive Services

No gas is available anywhere inside Yosemite Valley. The nearest gas station sits at **El Portal** (24 hours, pay-at-pump). Limited seasonal gas is also available up at **Tuolumne Meadows** just past the visitors center on Tioga Pass. There's also gas in Mariposa at a **Pioneer Gas/Texaco** (5177 Hwy. 140, Mariposa) that also has a mini-mart.

If your car breaks down, you can take it to the **Village Garage** (Yosemite Village off Northside Dr., 209/372-8320, daily 8 A.M.–5 P.M., towing 24 hours). Because it's the only game in town, expect to pay a high premium for towing and repairs here.

### Laundry and Groceries

There are laundry facilities available to all comers at the Housekeeping Camp inside the Curry Village complex (Apr.–Oct. daily 8 A.M.–10 P.M.). Limited-stock, expensive grocery stores sit in Curry Village at the **Gift and Grocery** (daily 8 A.M.–10 P.M.) and in the **Housekeeping Camp Grocery** (Apr.–Oct. daily 8 A.M.–6 P.M.). For a better selection of goods and much lower prices, you're better off shopping outside the park. You can check out **Bear Valley Grocery** (7313 Hwy. 49 at Road J-16, North Mariposa, 209/377-8424) or the **Pioneer Market** (5034 Coakley Cir. 104, Mariposa, 209/742-5097).

### Medical Services

Yosemite maintains its own **medical center** (209/372-4637) in Yosemite Village at the floor of the valley. It's got a 24-hour emergency room, 8 A.M.–7 P.M. walk-in urgent care center, and a domestic violence crisis center. **Dental services** (209/372-4200) are also available adjacent to the medical center.

## GETTING THERE AND AROUND

### Car

Almost all the most popular sights, attractions, and trailheads are accessible by road. The Arch Rock entrance to the west of the park is accessed via Highway 140. The Big Oak Flat entrance is accessed via Highway 120 from the north; it's about another 45 minutes to Yosemite Valley from there. Both entrances provide access to Tioga Pass Road via Big Oak Flat Road. Tioga Pass reconnects to Highway 120 at the Tioga Pass Entrance on the east side of the park. Tioga Pass closes in November or December each year and reopens in the spring, usually in May. Yosemite's south entrance is accessed via Highway 41 from Oakhurst. Wawona Road leads from the south entrance, through Wawona, and into Yosemite Valley. Glacier Point Road is reached from Wawona Road and allows access to the Badger Pass Ski Area. In winter, chains can be required on any road at any time, so check the website (www .nps.gov/yose) for current road conditions.

### Train and Bus
**Amtrak** (www.amtrak.com) services Merced, an hour away from the park. From Merced,

bus service is available on **VIA Bus Lines** (209/384-1314, www.via-adventures.com); call for reservations. The **YARTS** (877/989-2787, www.yarts.com) bus system services Mariposa and Merced.

### Shuttle Services
Yosemite runs an extensive network of shuttles in different areas of the park. One of the most-used travels through **Yosemite Valley** (daily 7 A.M.–10 P.M., year-round, free). The **El Capitan Shuttle** (mid-June to early Sept, daily 9 A.M.–6 P.M., free) also runs around certain parts of Yosemite Valley during the summer season.

# Mono Lake

Mono Lake itself, eerie in its stillness, is the main attraction to this remote area of the Eastern Sierra. It might be enough just to sit on the edge of the lake and enjoy its beauty. Or in the summertime, enjoy an oddly buoyant swim in the heavily salted waters or even a boat trip out to some of the silent uninhabited islands. But if you'd prefer more adventure or exploration, a number of options await.

## SIGHTS
### Mono Lake Scenic Visitor Area
The large building that houses the visitors center for Mono Lake is easy to see from Highway 395, and only a short drive from the highway. The Mono Lake Scenic Visitor Area (Hwy. 395 just north of Lee Vining on the lake side, 760/647-3044, www.monolake.org) is the perfect place to start learning about Mono Lake, to start walking around the lake, and to start taking photos of the unique landscape. The interpretive museum inside the distinctive building describes in detail the natural and human history of the lake, from the way tufa towers form to the endless litigations surrounding the lake like papery ghosts. Walk out the back of the building to take your first closer look at the grassy meadows leading down to the shores of

the lake. Talk to the staff to learn about the best hikes and spots to visit, swim, launch a boat, or cross-country ski.

At the visitors center, you can also learn about various guided walks and hikes at Mono Lake, which can give you and your family a more in-depth look at the wonders of the area.

### ◖ Mono Lake Tufa Preserve
The tufa formations—freestanding calcite towers, knobs, and spires—make Mono Lake unique. The Mono Lake Tufa Preserve (Hwy. 395 just north of Lee Vining, 760/647-6331, www.parks.ca.gov, park hours and fees vary) educates and amazes visitors. A one-mile interpretive trail winds through the South Tufa area (southeast of the visitors center, adjacent to Navy Beach, fee for parking) describing the natural history of the area and formations. With some of the most spectacular tufa towers at the lake, this is a good place for newcomers to the lake to start exploring. A boardwalk trail (adjacent to the County Park) provides access to the North Tufa area. Enjoy wandering through the different chunks of this preserve, which appear along the shore all the way around the lake. Be aware that much of the land adjacent to the State Reserve areas is

Mono Lake

restricted—please care for this delicate terrain and do not venture out of the designated visiting areas. Also, to access some of the reserve at the east side of the lake, you'll need either a boat or a four-wheel-drive vehicle since no paved roads circle Mono Lake.

## Old Marina

Years ago, the stillness of Mono Lake was broken by quite a bit of boat traffic. (Private boats and small tour operators still ply the salt-alkaline lake in the summer, but no major commercial water traffic remains.) The hub of this activity was the Marina a few miles north of Lee Vining. Today, the Old Marina is merely spot off Highway 395 north of town at which you can take a short stroll down to the edge of the lake. From here you can see the two large islands in the middle of the lake, several nearby tufa towers, and much of the lakescape itself. The boardwalk trail here is wheelchair accessible.

## ◖ Bodie State Historic Park

Bodie State Historic Park (end of Dirt Road 270, 760/647-6445, www.parks.ca.gov, daily 9 A.M.–4 P.M., weekends Memorial Day–Labor Day 8 A.M.–7 P.M., fees) is the largest ghost town in California. Preservation in a state of "arrested decay" means you get to see each home and public building just as it was when it was abandoned. What you see is not a bright shiny museum display. You get the real thing: dust and broken furniture and trash and all. It would take all day to explore the town on foot, and even then you might not see it all. Tours let you into the abandoned mine and gain a deeper understanding of the history of the buildings and the town.

The town of Bodie sprang up around a gold mine in 1877. It was never a nice place to live— at all. The weather, the work, the scenery, the people...all tended toward the bleak or the foul. By the 1940s, mining had dried up and the remote location and lack of other viable industry in the area led to Bodie's desertion.

A visit to Bodie takes you back in time, to a harsh lifestyle in an extreme climate at least 10 miles from the middle of nowhere. As you stroll down the dusty streets, imagine the whole

© LIZ HAMILL SCOTT

Bodie's historic ghost town

town blanketed in 20 feet of snow in winter, then scorched by 100° temperatures in summer with precious few trees anywhere around to provide shade or a hint of green in the unending brown landscape. In a town filled with rough men working the mines hundreds of miles from civilization, you'd hear the funeral bells tolling at the church every single day—the only real honor bestowed upon the many murder victims Bodie saw in its lifetime. Few families came to Bodie (though a few hardy souls did raise children in the hellish town), and most of Bodie's women earned their keep the old-fashioned way. The prostitution business boomed just as mining did.

Today, most of the brothels, stores, and homes of Bodie aren't habitable or even tourable. Structures have been loosely propped up, but it's dangerous to go inside so doors remain locked. However, you can peer in the windows at the remains of the lives lived in Bodie, and get a sense of hard-core California history.

### Panum Crater

Even if you aren't a professional geologist, the volcanic Panum Crater (Hwy. 120 three miles east of Hwy. 395, short dirt road to parking) is worth visiting. This rhyolite crater is only 600 years old—a mere baby in geologic time! Take a hike around the rim of the crater, and if you're feeling up to it climb up the trail to the top of the plug dome. Be sure to slather on the sunscreen since no trees shade these trails and it gets quite warm in the summertime. Check the Mono Lake website for occasional guided tours of Panum Crater.

## SPORTS AND RECREATION
### Hiking

Mono Lake is not like Yosemite, with clusters of trailheads everywhere. But the hiking near Mono Lake affords things the big park can't: unusual scenery and plenty of solitude.

For an easy walk along the lake, go to the **Mono Lake County Park** (Cemetery Road, trailhead 0.5 mile east of the road) and take the boardwalk trail 0.25 mile down to the tufa formations. Wandering through the tufa will add distance to your walk, but the ground is flat and the scenery is diverting.

A lovely interpretive trail, the **Tioga Tarns Nature Walk** (Hwy. 120, east of Tioga Lake) spans about half a mile and includes numerous signs describing the flora, fauna, and geology of the area. Another nature walk is the **Lee Vining Creek Nature Trail** (Best Western Motel, Hwy. 395, moderate). This trail follows the Lee Vining Creek, currently under restoration, returning to its natural state after decades of diversion. The total walk is about three miles and takes an hour or two, depending on how much time you spend admiring the revitalized ecosystem.

You can find any number of moderate hikes in the Mono Lake vicinity. The **Lundy Canyon** (Lundy Lake Rd., dirt lot at trailhead) trail can be anywhere from 0.5 mile of fairly easy walking through Lundy Canyon to a strenuous seven-mile hike all the way out to Saddlebag Lake. Another variable hike takes you out to **Parker Lake** or **Parker Bench** (Parker Lake dirt road off Hwy. 158). This hike is a minimum of four miles round-trip, and can be 10 miles if you take the left trail fork out to Silver Lake and Parker Bench. Steep sections make this trek a bit more demanding, but you'll love the scenic, shady trail that follows Parker Creek out the shorter right fork to Parker Lake. If one or two lakes just aren't enough, take the longish but only moderately tough **20-Lakes Basin Trail** (Saddlebag Lake Rd., parking across from the dam). This six-mile loop trail will take you out past many of the lakes for which the basin is named. Or if you're tired of all that water, take a moderate two-mile round-trip pilgrimage out to the remains of the mining town at **Bennettville** (Junction Campground Rd.). You can prowl around the abandoned mine, but be careful! Old mine shafts and abandoned buildings can be extremely hazardous.

## Boating and Swimming

Go ahead and bring your powered boat, canoe, kayak, or even sailboat out to Mono Lake. A parking lot near the water at Navy Beach makes launching lightweight kayaks and canoes reasonable. If you're putting a heavier boat into the lake, check with the staff at the Mono Lake Scenic Visitor Area for directions to the launch ramp near Lee Vining Creek. Also note that no matter what kind of craft you're piloting, you cannot beach on the islands April 1–August 1.

During the summer, the **Mono Lake Boat Tours** (meet at Tioga Lodge, 760/647-6446, www.monolakeboattours.com, adults $70, children/seniors $65) offers water tours of the lake. You'll get an utterly experienced guide who's been traveling on the lake for ages.

Swimming is allowed (and even encouraged!) in Mono Lake in the summertime. You can swim from your boat, or from any of the unrestricted shore access points. You'll find yourself floating easily since the salt content of Mono Lake is several times that of the ocean. But take care and watch your kids closely, because no lifeguards patrol the area and you're swimming at your own risk.

## ACCOMMODATIONS

You won't see any five-star resorts in the Mono Lake area. The outdoorsy and naturalist types who favor this region find the no-frills motels, lodges, and campgrounds perfectly suitable for their activities.

No camping is allowed on the shores of Mono Lake. Visitors can rent affordable rooms at several motels and lodgings in the lakeside town of Lee Vining.

### Under $100

Rent clean, comfortable, affordable lodgings at **Murphey's Motel** (51493 Hwy. 395, 800/334-6316, www.murpheysyosemite.com, $58–118). Open all year, this motel provides double-queen and king beds with cozy comforters, TVs, tables and chairs, and everything you need for a pleasant stay in the Mono Lake area. Its central location in downtown Lee Vining makes dining, shopping, and trips to the visitors center and Chamber of Commerce convenient. If you plan to make a winter trip to Mono Lake, call to find out about Murphey's discounts for ice climbers.

The **El Mono Motel** (Hwy. 395 at Third St., 707/647-6310, www.elmonomotel.com) offers comfy beds and clean rooms at very reasonable prices. Enjoy the location in downtown Lee Vining, and start each morning with a fresh cup of organic coffee from the attached Latte Da Coffee Café.

## $100-150

Just across the freeway from Mono Lake, the **Tioga Lodge** (54411 Hwy. 395, 760/647-6423, www.tiogalodgeatmonolake.com, $133–165) boasts an astonishing view of the lake from every room. This older lodge at the center of the town of Lee Vining offers the perfect location for sightseeing and outdoor adventures, plus heated rooms and comfortable beds. Guest rooms are simple and uniquely decorated, each with tile floors and a full private bath. Some rooms sleep two, others up to four in two-bedroom suites are perfect for families. Don't expect to find TVs or other digital entertainment here—in keeping with the area, you're encouraged to get outside to find your entertainment. Friendly, helpful staff can assist with everything from room amenities to local restaurants to great places to visit in the area.

At the intersection of Highways 120 and 395, stay at the comfortable and affordable **Lake View Lodge** (51285 Hwy. 395, Lee Vining, 800/990-6614, www.lakeviewlodgeyosemite .com, $138–220). This aptly named lodge offers both motel rooms and cottages. The cottages can be rented in the summer only, but the motel rooms are available all year. Whether you choose a basic room for only a night or two, or a larger accommodation with a kitchen for more than three days, you'll enjoy the simple country-style decor, the outdoor porches, and the views of Mono Lake. All rooms have TVs with cable and Internet access is available. Pick up supplies at the local market for a picnic on the lawns of the lodge, get yourself a latte at the on-site coffee shop, or enjoy one of the nearby restaurants in Lee Vining.

Named for its location only 14 miles from Yosemite's east gate, the **Yosemite Gateway Motel** (51340 Hwy. 395, 760/647-6467, www .yosemitegatewaymotel.com, $143–154) offers a charming rustic experience for travelers to the Eastern Sierra. The red and white exterior echoes in the decoration of the guest rooms, supplemented with gleaming wood, new furnishings, and clean bathrooms. A TV and the Internet provide entertainment on chilly evenings, and of course the wonderful outdoor recreation opportunities of the Eastern Sierra are just outside the door. Enjoy your crystal-line views of Mono Lake, or take a day trip to Bodie or indulge in some skiing at Mammoth Lakes or June Lake. Room rates are deeply discounted in the wintertime, making the trek worth the effort.

## FOOD

Your food choices around the Mono Lake area might feel limited if you're coming right from Los Angeles or San Francisco. Nor will you see many of the standard fast-food chains. However, the town of Lee Vining offers a number of respectable eateries, plus adequate groceries for campers and picnickers.

### Restaurants

The **Hammond Station Restaurant** (54411 Hwy. 395, 760/647-6423, www.tioga lodgeatmonolake.com, $8–20) at the Tioga Lodge serves breakfast, lunch, and dinner. Choose from the health-conscious vegetarian/spa menu (which includes a number of vegan items), the American menu, or the Mexican menu. If you're planning a day out hiking or sightseeing, get a sandwich or a wrap from the "Picnic to Go" menu before you leave for the day. If you're dining in, expect a small dining room with attractive wrought-iron furniture, plus an ample outdoor seating area perfect for warm summer evenings. The food is tasty, and the service makes you feel like a local even if you're from far out of town.

A classic American diner, **Nicely's** (Hwy. 395 and Fourth St., 760/647-6477, summer daily, winter Thurs.–Mon.) offers friendly service and familiar food to locals and visitors alike. Inside, you'll find a large dining room with half-circle booths upholstered in vinyl and many other diner-style touches. The cuisine runs to sandwiches, burgers, and egg

YOSEMITE

breakfasts. Portions are generous, though the service can be slow when the restaurant is busy. Nicely's opens early and stays open through dinnertime, making it a viable dining option year-round—something of a rarity in the area. This is a good place to take the kids for burgers and fries.

If you're looking for a Wild West atmosphere and a good spicy sauce, have dinner at **Bodie Mike's Barbecue** (51357 Hwy. 395, 760/647-6432, summer only). Use your fingers to dig into barbecued ribs, chicken, beef, brisket, and more. A rustic atmosphere with rough-looking wood, red-check tablecloths, and local patrons in cowboy boots completes your dining experience. Just don't expect the fastest service in the world. At the back of the dining room you'll find the entrance to a small, dark bar populated by local characters. The good news is that the bar serves drinks to the dining room.

## Bakeries and Delis

For a unique deli dining experience, stop in for a tank of gas and a meal at the **Whoa Nelly Deli** (Hwys. 120 and 395, 760/647-1088, Apr.–Nov. daily 7 A.M.–9 P.M.) at the Tioga Gas Mart. You'll get a full, hearty meal from the daily offering, be it ribs or meatloaf or something else. Sandwiches and drinks are also available for lighter noshing. Expect to wait in line for a while at the counter to order, then to wait to pick up your own food. Seating, both indoor and out, tends to be limited during high-traffic mealtimes, and heaven help you if you get there in conjunction with a tour bus. But still, compared to the so-called food offered in most gas station mini-marts, you'll find some great stuff at Whoa Nelly, and the rowdy cooks provide something of a show for the dinner crowd.

A great place to get a to-go breakfast or lunch is the **Mono Market** (51303 Hwy. 395, 760/647-1010, daily summer 7 A.M.–10 P.M., winter 7:30 A.M.–8 P.M.). An array of breakfast sandwiches and pastries are made fresh daily, as are the sandwiches, wraps, and messier napkin-requisite entrées you can carry out for lunch or dinner.

## Coffee

Even dedicated outdoor lovers often need their morning coffee to get going on a long day of hiking, climbing, or kayaking. To that end, you'll find some charming independent coffee shops in Lee Vining. The **Latte Da Coffee Café** (1 Third St. at Hwy. 395, 760/647-6310) uses organic coffee and local fresh water to create delicious coffee drinks at the El Mono Motel. Over at the Lakeview Lodge, grab a cup of joe at the **Garden House Coffee Shop** (5185 Hwy. 395, Lee Vining, 760/647-6543, www.lakeviewlodgeyosemite .com, daily 7–11 A.M.). In addition to your favorite espresso drinks, you can pick up a smoothie or a fresh pastry to get a great start to your day.

## Markets

In addition to prepared food, the **Mono Market** (51303 Hwy. 395, 760/647-1010, daily summer 7 A.M.–10 P.M., winter 7:30 A.M.–8 P.M.) offers standard grocery staples and a liquor section.

# INFORMATION AND SERVICES

The **Mono Basic Scenic Area Visitors Center** (Hwy. 395 just north of Lee Vining on the lake side, 760/647-3044, www.mono lake.org) includes an interpretive museum that describes the creation of Mono Lake and the strange tufa formations that define it. This visitors center also has a ranger station with knowledgeable staff who can help you with the best seasonal trail and lake advice.

You can use mail services at the **Lee Vining Post Office** (121 Lee Vining Ave., 760/647-6371). Lee Vining boasts few ATMs, but you can find one or two places to grab cash (which you'll need, because many places out here don't take plastic). Try the gas stations, the visitors center, and the local grocery/mini mart.

The nearest medical facilities to Mono Lake lie to the south in Mammoth Lakes at **Mammoth Hospital** (85 Sierra Park Rd., 760/934-3311, mammothhospital.com), which has a 24-hour emergency room.

## GETTING THERE AND AROUND

Getting to Mono Lake from San Francisco or Los Angeles or anyplace else in California with a major airport is, frankly, a royal pain in the you-know-what. Mono Lake sits almost on top of the junction between Tioga Pass Road and Highway 395.

Tioga Pass is closed between November and May each year—check with the Yosemite website to get the exact closing and opening dates for this road. Highway 395 remains open all year (though storms can close it briefly until it is plowed). But accessing Highway 395 from the north or south involves long drives. You might want to consider flying in to Las Vegas or even Reno to get to Mono Lake as directly as possible.

Very little public transit of any kind gets as far as Lee Vining and Mono Lake. To adequately explore this region, you need a vehicle of your own. On the bright side, parking in Lee Vining and around the lake tends to be both easy and free. Few enough others are vying for spots that you won't spend much time looking for your own space.

# Mammoth Lakes

## SIGHTS
### 【 Devil's Postpile National Monument

Compared to the area's other national parks, Devil's Postpile National Monument (Minaret Vista Rd., 760/924-5500, www.nps.gov/depo, summer only, daily 9 A.M.–5 P.M., adults $7, children $4) seems small. But what you'll see is unique to the region. The gem and namesake of the park is the strange, unbelievably natural rock formation called the Devil's Postpile. It's hard to imagine that the near perfect straight-sided hexagonal posts are a natural phenomenon, created by volcanic heat and pressure. You

PHOTO COURTESY OF THE MAMMOTH LAKES VISITORS BUREAU

Devil's Postpile National Monument

YOSEMITE

PHOTO COURTESY OF THE MAMMOTH LAKES VISITORS BUREAU

June Lake

have to see it to believe it. Less heavily traveled than many other parks, you'll also find hikes to serene meadows, unspoiled streams, and perhaps even see the occasional deer grazing in the woods. If you're lucky, you might get a trail all to yourself for a while.

Also part of the Monument is the crystalline, beautiful **Rainbow Falls.** The thick sheet of water cascades 101 feet down to a pool, throwing up stunning rainbows of mist. For the best rainbows at the falls, hike the three miles (roundtrip) from Red Meadow toward the middle of the day when the sun is high in the sky.

In an effort to limit traffic on the narrow road down into the Monument, a shuttle runs from a spot near the gate down to the trailheads. Ample parking is available, and the shuttles run every half-hour, letting you jump on and off as you wish to hike, have a picnic, or just enjoy the fresh smell of the clean woods.

## June Lake Loop

This 15-mile scenic drive takes you out away

from the high-traffic tourist areas of the Eastern Sierra. Along the June Lake Loop (Hwy. 158, accessible from Hwy. 395 south of Lee Vining), you get the full-fledged alpine experience. Naturally, the loop's namesake June Lake has the most recreation along its shores. You can take a hike, go fish, or even plan to stay overnight at one of the campgrounds. Next you'll come to Gull Lake, then Silver Lake—two other popular boating and angling waterways. As you drive north on the loop, stop at least once to admire Reversed Peak, a 9,500-foot Sierra peak. Finally, you'll come to Grant Lake. No resorts cluster here, nor will you find any major trailheads. What you will find are a boat launch and some spectacular alpine trout fishing. Finally, take a break at the Mono Craters Monument before heading back out to Highway 395 toward Lee Vining or Mammoth Mountain.

## Mammoth Ski Museum

One of the jewels of Mammoth Lakes, the

Mammoth Ski Museum (100 College Pkwy., 760/934-6592, www.mammothskimuseum .org, Thurs.–Mon. 11 A.M.–6 P.M., $5 adults, $3 children) houses the largest collection of skiing-related art in the world. Here you'll find artistic homage in every medium the human fascination with sliding down snowy mountains on boards. The museum features the permanent Beekley Collection of sculptures, original paintings, vintage posters, and much more. Short films run daily, and each Friday night at 6 P.M. a full-length ski-themed feature film runs in the Pioneer Theater. Visit the gift shop to purchase your own reproduction vintage ski posters, books, and DVDs.

### Old Mammoth Road

Like most of the Eastern Sierra region, Mammoth Lakes became of interest to miners in the 19th century after the Gold Rush began—miners got out this far in 1877. Along Old Mammoth Road (Hwy. 203 to Main St., turn left on Old Mammoth Rd.) you'll find a number of old mining sites. At the height of the short-lived boom in Mammoth, about 20 different small mines operated in the area.

You'll see the grave of a miner's wife, a stamp mill's flywheel, and then the meager remains of Mammoth City and the nearby Mammoth Mine. The highlight of this summertime half-day trip is the ruins of the Mammoth Consolidated Mine. You can still see some bits of the camp, housing buildings, the assay office, mill, and mining equipment. The mine shaft also appears, but *do not attempt to get around the security features to head down there!* Old mine shafts are unbelievably dangerous, and should not be explored by anyone for any reason.

## SKIING AND SNOWBOARDING

Mammoth Lakes exists primarily to support the winter sports industry. The downhill skiing, snowboarding, and cross-country skiing here attract sports enthusiasts of all ages and ability levels. If you don't own your own equipment, you can rent skis, snowboards, and all the necessary accessories at a dozen different shops in town.

### Mammoth Mountain

The premier downhill ski and snowboard mountain is, aptly, Mammoth Mountain (800 Mammoth, ski school 760/934-0685,

PHOTO COURTESY OF THE MAMMOTH LAKES VISITORS BUREAU

YOSEMITE

A bronze mammoth by sculptor Douglas Van Howd stands at the main lodge of Mammoth Mountain.

snow report 760/934-6166, http://mammoth mountain.com, lift hours daily 8:30 A.M.–4 P.M.). Whether you're completely new to downhill thrills or a seasoned expert looking for different terrain, you'll find something great on Mammoth Mountain. More than two-dozen lifts (including three gondolas and nine express quads) take you up the 3,100-foot vertical rise to the 3,500 acres of skiable and boardable terrain (plus three pipes). If you're staying at Eagle Lodge, Canyone Lodge, Mammoth Mountain Inn, or the Village, enjoy the convenience of a lift or gondola right outside your lodging door. All these, plus the Mill Café and McCoy Station halfway up the mountain offer hot drinks, tasty snacks, and a welcome spot to rest during a long day of skiing.

The easiest runs on the mountain cluster mostly around the ski school and the lower area around the Mammoth Mountain Inn, and are recognizable for their cute nursery-school names. If you're an intermediate skier, runs swing down all over the mountain just for you. Build your confidence by taking the Panorama Gondola up to Panorama Lookout at the top of the mountain, then skiing all the way down the east side of the mountain along the intermediate-to-a-bit-harder ridge runs. Advanced skiers favor the bowls and chutes at the front of the mountain, and hardcore experts go west from Panorama Lookout to chase the dragon.

## June Mountain

South of Mammoth Lakes, the June Mountain ski area (3819 Hwy. 158, 760/648-7733, www .junemountain.com, lifts 7:30 A.M.–4 P.M., adults $60, youth $54, teens $45, children/ seniors $30) offers more than 2,500 feet of vertical rise on more than 500 skiable acres. This resort caters to beginners and intermediate skiers, and 80 percent of its trails are green or blue. Beginners can even take a lift up to the top of Rainbow Summit and enjoy a long run down the Silverado Trail. However, a number of black and double-black diamond slopes make a trip to June Mountain fun for more advanced skiers and boarders as well. Thrill-

seeking experts and adventurous intermediates head up to the top of June Mountain Summit then plummet down the bowl (hardcore double-blacks) or slide along the ridgeline (blue). Be sure to check your trail map before going up this way unless you're very sure of your abilities. For a cup of hot coffee or chocolate, stop at the June Meadows Chalet at the center of the ski area.

## Sierra Meadows

Go just south of Mammoth Lakes to get to the Sierra Meadows (1 Sherwin Creek Rd., 760/934-6161), a cross-country ski area with 20 miles of groomed trails. Sierra Meadows is perfect for beginner cross-country skiers, offering ski rentals, lessons, and beginner terrain that's easy on the legs—and the mind!

## Tamarack Cross Country Ski Center

Here's your chance to explore the snow-covered Mammoth Lakes Basin in wintertime. Tamarack (Lake Mary Rd. at Twin Lakes, 760/934-2442, www.tamaracklodge.com/ xcountry, Nov.–Apr. daily 8:30 A.M.–5 P.M.) offers almost 25 miles of groomed cross-country ski tracks geared for all ability levels. For non-skiers, you'll also fined groomed skating lanes, plus a restaurant in which to enjoy a nice cup of hot chocolate and good book while your more outdoorsy friends and family ply the terrain.

## Blue Diamond Trails

This trail system starts just behind the Mammoth Lakes visitors center and winds through 25 miles of Mammoth forest land, predictably marked by signs bearing a blue diamond on the trees. Blue Diamond Trails (www.mammothdirect.com) are not groomed, so be prepared to deal with varying snow conditions and unbroken trails. However, there's plenty of relatively flat land here for beginners. The Shady Rest Trails (off Hwy. 203 just before visitors center) might sound like a cemetery, but in fact they are beginners' loops with plenty of shade trees that keep skiers cool through their exertions. The Knolls Trail (Mammoth Scenic

Loop 1.5 miles north of Hwy. 203) makes a good intermediate day out, passing through lovely stands of Jeffery and Lodgepole pines. If you're up for a serious expert trek, try the Earthquake Fault Trail (Minaret Rd., unlabeled parking lot before Mammoth Mountain Main Lodge). Expect steep descents, unused areas, and narrow paths along this approximately 12-hour trail. Beginners beware of the deceptively named Scenic Loop Trail (Mammoth Scenic Loop across from Knolls Trail); this reasonably short trail (about four miles) includes steep descents and some more difficult terrain.

## SPORTS AND RECREATION

Even beyond skiing and snowboarding, outdoor activities are a central focus of life in and around Mammoth. People come here from all over to hike, bike, fish, and more.

### Hiking

Not surprisingly, hikers find plenty of worthwhile terrain around Mammoth Lakes for both short day walks and longer backpacking adventures. The **Mammoth Mountain Bike Park** (1 Minaret Rd., 800/626-6684, www.mammoth mountain.com/bike_ride, daily 8 A.M.–6 P.M.) includes a number of great hiking trails. For an all-downhill walk, take the Scenic Gondola up to the Panorama Overlook and hike back down to town. Just be sure to get a trail map at the **Mammoth Adventure Center** (1 Minaret Rd., 800/626-6684, www.mammothmountain .com/bike_ride/index.cfm, June.–Sept. daily 8 A.M.–6 P.M.) so you can keep to the hiking areas and avoid being flattened by fast-moving mountain bikers.

Mammoth Lakes also acts as a jumping-off point for adventurers who want to take on the **John Muir Wilderness** (south of Mammoth Lakes to Mount Whitney, http://sierrane-vadawild.gov/wild/john-muir). John Muir pioneered sustainability and preservation in the Sierra Nevadas, and more than half a million acres in the area have been designated national wilderness areas in his honor. Day hikers are welcome and there's plenty to see. Check with the Inyo National Forest service

and the Sierra National Forest for trail maps of the area. But the main attractions to the John Muir (as it's called locally) are the John Muir and Pacific Crest Trails—both hundreds of miles long and sought by backpacking enthusiasts around the world. If you're planning an overnight camping trip in the area—on your own or with a tour or guide company—you must obtain a permit. It's also a good idea to plan backcountry trips well in advance, to make sure you've got everything you need and all the proper permits and information ready at hand.

### Biking

Come summertime and melting snow, Mammoth Mountain transforms from a ski resort to a mountain bike mecca. The **Mammoth Mountain Bike Park** (1 Minaret Rd., 800/626-6684, www.mammoth mountain.com/bike_ride, daily 8 A.M.–6 P.M., $10–39) spans much of the same terrain as the ski areas, with almost 90 miles of trails that suit all biking ability levels. The park headquarters sits at the **Mammoth Adventure Center** (1 Minaret Rd., 800/626-6684, www .mammothmountain.com/bike_ride/index. cfm, June.–Sept. daily 8 A.M.–6 P.M.). You can take your bike onto the Scenic Gondola and ride all the way to the top of Mammoth Mountain, then ride all the way down (3,000-plus feet) on the single tracks. Be sure to pick the trails that best suit your fitness and experience level! Several other major lodges offer rider services, including the Village at Mammoth, Juniper Springs, the Panorama Lookout, and Outpost 14. If you value scenery as much as extreme adventure, pack your camera and plan to rest at the various scenic overlooks throughout the trail system.

If you need to rent a bike (and to buy park tickets), go to the Adventure Center or to the **Mammoth Mart at the Village** (6201 Minaret Rd., inside The Village, 760/934-2571, ext. 2078). Both locations offer new high-end bikes for adults and kids. These shops can also help with parts and repairs for bikes you've brought up with you, and sell accessories.

## Horseback Riding

Perhaps the most traditional way to explore the Eastern Sierra is on the back of a horse or mule. Early pioneers to the area came on horseback, and you can follow their example from several locations near Mammoth. From the **McGee Creek Pack Station** (760/935-4324, www.mcgeecreekpack station.com, one hour $30) 10 miles south of Mammoth Lakes on Highway 395, you can ride into McGee Canyon, a wilderness area little visited by tourists. Other one-day destinations include Baldwin Canyon and Hilton Lakes. Standard rides range from one hour to all day. But McGee's specialty is multi-day and pack trips that let you really get out beyond the reach of paved roads to camp for a number of days out by one of the many pristine lakes dotting the mountains. If you love the outdoors and really want a vacation as far "away from it all" as you can get, consider a few days' camping in Convict Basin or near Upper Fish Creek in the John Muir Wilderness. The McGee Creek guides will help you pack your gear and guide you through the incredible backcountry of the Eastern Sierra.

Operating out of Bishop, **Rainbow Pack Outfitters** (760/873-8877, www.rainbow packoutfit.com) offers day trips to a number of lovely local destinations, plus a full-day fishing trip with all gear carried by mule. Small children will enjoy an at-the-stables led ride on a pony or horse, while the bigger kids and adults can get out for rides to local meadows and lakes. If you're looking for a longer horseback vacation, check into Rainbow's options for full-service guided trips, hunting and fishing trips, photography and birding treks, and more. Rainbow operates from the John Muir Wilderness near Mammoth and Bishop all the way down to Sequoia and Kings Canyon parks. Pick your ideal destination and pack in!

## Snowshoeing

If you prefer walking to all that sliding around on planks, rent or bring your own snowshoes to Mammoth and enjoy a snowy hike through the mountains and meadows. Check the cross-country ski areas first—many have specifically designated snowshoe trails. Or head out to the backcountry and explore Mammoth Lakes Basin or the Sherwin Range. Groomed trails head off from right behind the Mammoth Lakes Welcome Center.

## ATVs and Snowmobiles

ATVs, dirt bikes, and snowmobiles are a big no-no at most national parks. Not so at Mammoth! Here you'll find miles of trails set aside for motorized fun. Eighty miles of groomed trails and 75,000 acres of snow-covered meadows and mountainsides await snowmobilers each winter. Much of the same territory is open to ATV and dirt bike traffic in the summer. Get a copy of the *Mammoth Lakes Winter Recreation Guide* for a complete trail and area map to find the best (and legal) places to play.

If you want to rent a vehicle, you can get single- and double-seat snowmobiles and ATVs at **Arctic Cat/Yamaha of Mammoth** (58 Commerce Dr., Mammoth Lakes, 760/934-0347, www.sierraengine.com). Reservations are recommended! Your rental includes instructions on how to operate your vehicle, local trail maps, and helmets for everyone who's going to ride. At **Bishop Motorsports** (156 E. Pine St., Bishop, 888/872-4717, www.harleyrentalsbishop mammoth.com), in addition to snowmobiles and side-by-side ATVs, you can rent Harleys and dirt bikes to take out on the Eastern Sierra roads and trails. If you're on an extended vacation, check out the weekly rental rates.

## Golf

If you're in the Mammoth area in summertime, you can enjoy a round of golf at a beautiful course with stunning mountain views. The 18-hole, par 70 **Sierra Star Golf Course** (2001 Sierra Star Pkwy., 760/924-4653, http://mammothmountain.com, $125 weekends, $100 weekdays) is open to the public. Walk this wonderful course for the best views of the surrounding Sierras, or concentrate all your efforts on the game. Amenities include a full-service pro shop, PGA golf pro on-site, and a café with full bar.

## Spas

If you want to enjoy some pampering after a hard day of skiing, book a treatment at one of Mammoth Lakes' day spas. The **Bodyworks Mountain Spa** (3399 Main St., 760/924-3161, www.bodyworksmountainspa.com) located upstairs at the Luxury Outlet Mall, offers massage therapy, spa treatments, and facials, plus a wide range of combination packages to maximize your time and money at the spa.

The **InTouch MicroSpa** (3325 Main St., 800/786-4414, www.intouchmicrospa.com) offers a full menu of treatments with a focus on the four elements of earth, air, fire, and water. Using Aveda products exclusively, InTouch caters to spa-goers who care about what's put onto their skin. A number of different styles of facials and aesthetic treatments are available. If you're in town with a group, InTouch offers several spa-party options that get everyone great treatments at discounted rates.

Somewhat incongruously located inside the local Holiday Inn, the **BellaDonna** (3236 Main St., 760/934-3344, www.belladonna mammoth.com) day spa offers a crackling fireplace, serene setting, and massage and aesthetic services. Come for a hot stone massage, a mani-pedi, or a complete makeover with natural mineral-based makeup products. If you're looking for romance, check out the couples side-by-side fireside massage. Yum!

## Casino Gambling

If an hour or three at the slots or the blackjack tables sounds like a good way to unwind, go to the **Paiute Palace Casino** (2742 N. Sierra Hwy., Bishop, 888/372-4883, www.paiute palace.com). You can play over 300 slots, plus table blackjack and poker. Look for Texas Hold 'Em tournaments every Wednesday and Sunday. The in-house restaurant is open for breakfast, lunch, and dinner.

# ENTERTAINMENT AND EVENTS
## Bars and Clubs

What would a ski resort town be without a selection of aprés-ski activities? Mammoth Lakes has a number of bars that open their doors to chilled and thirsty skiers.

For possibly the best (night) time in Mammoth, try the **Clocktower Cellar Pub** (6080 Minaret Rd. at Alpenhof Lodge, 760/934-2725, www.alpenhof-lodge.com, daily until 2 A.M.). This happening nightspot offers 30 luscious brews on tap and served properly, glasses of fine wine cadged from Petra next door, and a casual atmosphere complete with sports on TV, vintage video games, and a pool table. Instead of an obnoxious yuppie tourist pick-up joint, the Clocktower acts as a refuge for locals looking for some after-work relaxation and a pint or two. Expect informal dress and friendly conversation up at the bar, along with the delicious and unusual variety of beers. The location is perfect—in the basement of the Alpenhof just across the street from the Village.

If you prefer a French-style wine bar experience to a noisy British-ish pub, try the vintages at the **Side Door** (100 Canyon Blvd., #229, 760/934-5200, www.sidedoormammoth.com, daily 6 A.M.–midnight). The bad news: Side Door is only open until midnight. The good news: Not only can you enjoy several glasses of California's top wines, you can order up a delicious dinner or dessert crepe to go with your favorite varietal. Expect to pay ski resort prices here, and to be somewhat disappointed in plain sandwiches. But the crepes rate as excellent and the wine list is sometimes called the best in the Village.

Didn't get enough sports during your day at Mammoth? Spend the evening at **Grumpy's** (361 Old Mammoth Rd., 760/934-8587, http://grumpysmammoth.com, daily 11 A.M.–2 A.M., kitchen closes 10 P.M.). This sports bar has the usual array of TVs showing major sporting events, plus pool tables and an arcade. Grumpy's has a full bar and serves up a full lunch and dinner menu of both Mexican and American specialties. Come for the big-screens, stay for the surprisingly tasty food and drink.

The **Lakanuki Tiki Bar** (6201 Minaret Rd., 760/934-7447, www.lakanuki.com, Mon–Thurs 2 P.M.–2 A.M., Fri–Sun 10 A.M.–2 A.M., kitchen closes 10 P.M.) does serve food, but it's the nightlife in the tacky tiki bar that packs the place, especially on weekends. Just expect the name to hold true—the vast majority of the clientele at the Lakanuki run to the young, male, snowboarding variety. That makes it tough to pick up any cute chicks—they're drinking elsewhere.

## Live Music

For a high-class evening of classical music in the mountains, check out a performance of **Chamber Music Unbound** (760/934-7015, www.chambermusicunbound.org). This nonprofit orchestra performs at several locations in Bishop and Mammoth Lakes, creating unique (often humorous and fun) concerts from familiar and out-of-the-way classical pieces. With titles like Bass-Ic Instinct and Sense and Sensuality, CMU concerts may sound like adult fare, but in fact they are family-oriented shows geared for all ages and genteel musical tastes. At Christmas you might catch a performance of the classic Nutcracker, and in the spring an uplifting vocalist show.

## SHOPPING

While it's not a heavy shopping town, the upscale boutiques and galleries, plus a small outlet mall, allow weary outdoors-lovers to take a day off the slopes and engage in some retail therapy.

If you'd like to take in some art while you're in the Mammoth area, several galleries offer an array of photographic art, some for reasonable prices. The **Mountain Light Gallery** (106 S. Main St., Bishop, 760/873-7700, www.mountainlight.com) showcases the wild scenic photography of Galen and Barbara Rowell, world adventurers who died in an accident in 2002. At the gallery, you can view and purchase prints of their scenic photos as well as calendars, note cards, posters, and books. The guest gallery features the work of other landscape photographers. You can even take classes in nature photography and attend other special events.

Another photo gallery in Bishop, the

**Vern Clevenger Gallery** (905 N. Main St., 888/224-8376, www.verclevenger.com) features only the nature photography of Mr. Clevenger himself. Each of Clevenger's photos is shot on film, then a mixed digital and traditional wet process creates the large-format prints you see in the gallery. What you see is all natural, without digital enhancement to the images or colors. Inexpensive note cards and posters are available for purchase in addition to the lovely framed fine-art prints. Or take a workshop to learn how to create these gorgeous images for yourself.

In downtown Mammoth Lakes, visit the **Mammoth Gallery** (425 Old Mammoth Rd. and Minaret Rd., 888/848-7733, http://mammothgallery.com, daily 10 A.M.–5 P.M.). Here you'll see the work of a number of local photographers and watercolor artists, plus a large collection of vintage ski poster reproductions.

## ACCOMMODATIONS

Accommodations at Mammoth run to luxurious ski condos with full kitchens, perfect for spending a week plying the slopes of the local mountains with family or friends. Motels and inns offer comfort as well, often for a little less money and shorter minimum stays.

### Under $100

Want to ski the slopes of exclusive Mammoth, but can't afford the hoity-toity condo resorts? Stay at the **Innsbruck Lodge** (Forest Trail btwn. Hwy. 203 and Sierra Blvd., 760/934-3035, www.innsbrucklodge.com, $93–240). Economy rooms offer twin beds, table and chairs, and access to the motel whirlpool tub and lobby with stone fireplace at super-reasonable nightly rates. Other rooms can sleep 2–6, and some include kitchenettes. The quiet North Village location sits on the ski area shuttle route for easy access to the local slopes.

If you're planning to ski June Mountain, stay at the **Boulder Lodge** (2282 Hwy. 158, 800/455-6355, $77). This inexpensive lodge provides an array of options, from simple motel rooms for short stays to multi-bedroom

PHOTO COURTESY OF THE MAMMOTH LAKES VISITORS BUREAU

Austria Hof

apartments and even a five-bedroom lake house for longer trips and larger groups. The Boulder Lodge takes guests back a few decades with its decorating style—the browns, wood paneling, and faux leather furniture recall the 1950s. But the views of June Lake, the indoor pool and spa, and the wonderful outdoor recreation area surrounding the lodge are timeless.

## $100-150

The **Sierra Lodge** (3540 Main St., 800/356-5711, www.sierralodge.com, $125–135) boasts reasonably priced all-non-smoking rooms located right on the ski shuttle line, and only a mile and a half from the Juniper Ridge chair lift. This small motel's rates are rock-bottom in the off-season and on weekdays in wintertime. Rooms have either a king or two double beds, a kitchenette with microwave and dishes, and plenty of space for your snow and ski gear. The decor shows simple motel styling in cool, relaxing blues. Breakfast, cable TV, and Wi-Fi access are included with your room.

## $150-250

From the outside, the ornate, carved-wood, fringed **Austria Hof** (924 Canyon Blvd., 866/662-6668, www.austriahof.com, $170–195) might be a ski hotel tucked into a crevice of the Alps. But on the inside, you'll find the most stylish American appointments. Peaceful sea-green motel rooms—even those with a king bed and a spa bathtub—can be rented for under $200 per night. If you've got a larger party or a desire to cook your own meals, check out the one- and two-bedroom condo options. Austria Hof's location adjacent to the Canyon Lodge and the Village gondola make it a great winter ski or summer mountain bike base camp. In the evenings, head down to the restaurant and bar for some hearty German food and drink. Or if you prefer, slip into a swimsuit and enjoy the views from the large outdoor spa.

## Over $250

It's not cheap, but the **( Juniper Springs Resort** (4000 Meridian Blvd., 800/626-6684, www.mammothmountain.com, $290) has

YOSEMITE

absolutely every luxury amenity you could want to make your ski vacation complete. Condos come in studio, one-bedroom, two-bedroom, three-bedroom, and townhouse sizes, sleeping up to eight people. The interiors boast stunning appointments, from snow-white down comforters to granite-topped kitchen counters to 60-inch flat-screen TVs. Bathrooms include deep soaking tubs, perfect to privately relax aching muscles after a long day on the slopes. The resort also features heated pools year-round and three outdoor heated spas—there's nothing like jumping into a steaming hot tub on a snowy evening, then jumping back out to find the cold perfect and refreshing. The Talon restaurant serves breakfast and lunch, and the Daily Grind offers coffee and take-out snacks. Juniper Springs is located next door to the Eagle Lodge, which serves as one of the Mammoth Mountain base lodges complete with a six-person express chair up to the main ski area. You can rent skis right inside the hotel, and ski back down to Juniper after a day on the slopes. In the summertime, Juniper Springs' proximity to local golfing and the Mammoth Mountain bike park make it a perfect retreat.

The company that owns Juniper Springs also owns the luxury condo complex at **The Village at Mammoth** (1111 Forest Trail, 800/626-6684, www.mammothmountain .com, $360). Check them out if you can't get the condo of your dreams at Juniper.

For a unique condo rental, check out **Mountainback** (Lakeview Blvd,. 800/468-6225, www.mountainbackrentals.com, $290–460, two-night minimum). This complex boasts an array of all two-bedroom units, some of which sleep up to six people. Every individual building has its own outdoor spa, and the complex has a heated pool and a sauna. Every condo is decorated differently (and you might be able to buy and redecorate one if you want to and have enough cash). Check the website for photos to find what you like—big stone everywhere, wood paneling, gentle cream walls, or even red-and-green holiday-themed furniture. Walk to the ski lifts, or enjoy a round of golf or day of fishing in the summertime.

## FOOD

Plenty of dining options cluster in Mammoth Lakes. You can get your fast-food cheeseburger and your chain double-latte here, but why would you with so many more interesting independent options just lying around? Fare runs to American food and pizza, with a few ethnic options thrown in for variety.

### American

A favorite with locals and repeat visitors, the **Whiskey Creek** (24 Lake Mary Rd., 760/934-2555, daily 5:30 P.M.–2 A.M., $15–30) combines casually elegant California fare in the downstairs dining room with a homey nighttime bar up above. Only half a block from the Village, you can walk in and enjoy an unusual array of entrées, a surprisingly wide selection of wines, and tasty beers. Whisky Creek maintains its own tiny on-site brewery, so some of the beers they serve really are as local as it gets. The crowd, both for dining and for drinking, feels warm and friendly, as do the hearty dishes served to hungry après-skiers. Be sure to make reservations on weekends as it can get crowded here. If you've just come for a drink and a good time, expect live music to heat up the upstairs starting at about 9 P.M., and to keep on playing long past midnight.

### California

◖ **Petra's Bistro and Wine Bar** (6080 Minaret Rd., 760/934-3500, dinner Tues.–Sun.) brings a bit of the California wine country all the way out to Mammoth Lakes. This eatery offers a seasonally changing menu that's designed to please the palate and complement the wine list. That wine list is worth a visit itself—an eclectic mix of vintages highlights the best of California, while giving a nod to European and South American wines. Wine-lovers will recognize many names, but still might find something new on the unusual list. The by-the-glass offerings change each night, and your server will happily cork your half-finished bottle to take home for tomorrow. Two dining rooms and a wine bar divide up the seating nicely, and the atmosphere succeeds in feeling romantic without being cave-dark. Petra's stays open all year, so if you're visiting in the off-season you'll get a pleasantly uncrowded treat. Reservations are a good idea during high season.

A popular gourmet establishment, **Skadi** (587 Old Mammoth Rd., Ste. B, 760/934-3902, http://restaurantskadi.com) describes their menu as containing "alpine cuisine." In truth, this chef-owned restaurant boasts a menu filled with California-style innovation using mountain-inspired ingredients to their best advantage. (You'll see a lot of venison!) Everything on the list looks tasty, but if you're not ready for a heavy entrée, consider ordering a couple of items from the long list of appetizers for a "small plates" experience. Oh, and don't skip dessert! Whatever you choose, the European-heavy wine list will have something perfect to pair with it. If you're in town in the ski season, make reservations in advance, especially on weekends.

### Mexican

Even Californians who eat Mexican food on a regular basis tend to agree on the quality of the fare at **Roberto's Mexican Café** (271 Old Mammoth Rd., 760/934-3667). This casual spot serves classic California-Mexican food (*chiles rellenos,* enchiladas, burritos, and so on) in great quantities (check out the huge three-combo platter) perfect for skiers and boarders famished after a long day on the slopes. For a quiet meal, stay downstairs in the main dining room. To join in with a lively younger crowd, head upstairs to the bar, which has tables and serves the full restaurant menu. Wherever you sit, even the stoutest of drinkers should beware Roberto's lethal margaritas.

## INFORMATION AND SERVICES
### Tourist Information

The town of Mammoth Lakes has an awesome **Visitors Bureau** (2520 Main St., 760/934-2712, www.visitmammoth.com) that can help you with everything from condo rentals and restaurant reservations before you

arrive, to the latest bar openings and advice about best seasonal recreation options. These folks are well worth a stop early in your visit.

### Media and Communications

Mammoth Lakes does indeed publish its own newspaper, the **Mammoth Times** (www .mammothtimes.com). This weekly paper serves the whole of the Eastern Sierra region. Check for local events and good nightspots, and visit the website for up-to-date weather and road conditions.

Despite its tiny size, the town of Mammoth Lakes boasts a cosmopolitan atmosphere that includes plenty of Internet access. Many of the condos and hotel rooms have some species of Internet access, and you're likely to find a Starbucks with Wi-Fi somewhere downtown.

### Banks and Post Offices

Plenty of ATMs crowd into Mammoth Lakes at gas stations, mini-marts, and even bank branches. Check the Village, Main Street, and Minaret Road for the most likely places to find banks and cash machines in town.

The **Mammoth Lakes post office** (760/934-2205) sits at 3330 Main Street, a.k.a. CA-203.

### Gas and Automotive Services

Mammoth Lakes is a great place to gas up before hitting the more wild parts of the Eastern Sierra. Gas stations cluster right at the eastern edge of town, where CA-203 becomes Main Street, and more gas can be found throughout the downtown area. Just be prepared to pay a premium. This is a resort town, and they know how far away the next gas station is!

Many gas stations, plus big-box stores and even pharmacies and supermarkets sell tire chains in the wintertime.

### Medical Services

Need medical service beyond that offered at the ski resorts? You can get it at **Mammoth Hospital** (85 Sierra Park Rd., 760/934-3311, mammothhospital.com), which has a 24-hour emergency room.

## GETTING THERE AND AROUND
### Air
The nearest airport to Mammoth is the **Mammoth Yosemite Airport** (MMH, 437 Old Mammoth Rd., 760/934-8989, www.ci.mammoth-lakes.ca.us/airport/awos.htm). Extensively remodeled in 2008, this airport offers limited, expensive commercial service in and out of the Eastern Sierras, plus a single rental-car outlet. For a less expensive spot to fly into, try the Reno airport and drive in from there.

### Car
California's Highway 395 acts as the main access road to the Mammoth Lakes area. To get to Mammoth Lakes proper, from Highway 395 north or south, turn onto State Highway 203, which will take you right into town.

Mammoth Lakes (and most of the rest of the Eastern Sierra) isn't near any of California's major hot spots. Expect a six-hour drive from Los Angeles and (at best!) a seven-hour drive from San Francisco if the traffic and weather cooperate. If you fly into Reno, the drive out to Mammoth takes about three hours.

In the wintertime, be aware that it snows in Mammoth more than it does in almost any other place in California. Carry chains! Even if the weather is predicted to be clear for your visit, having chains can prevent a world of hurt and turning back in sudden storms. The longer you plan to stay, the better you should stock your car with items such as ice scrapers, blankets, water, food, and a full tank of gas whenever possible. For the latest traffic information, including chain control areas and weather conditions, call CalTrans at 800/427-7623.

Parking in Mammoth Lakes in the off-season is a breeze. In the winter, it can get a bit more complicated, as constant snow removal means that parking on the street is illegal throughout town. Most of the major resorts and hotels offer heated parking structures, and many of the restaurants, bars, and ski resorts have plenty of parking in their outdoor lots. If you're concerned about parking, call ahead to your resort and restaurants to get the lowdown on how best to get there and where to leave your car.

### Shuttles and Buses
Devil's Postpile National Monument (760/924-5500, www.nps.gov/depo, $7) runs a shuttle into the park that's mandatory for all visitors during high season (vehicles with handicap placards excepted). The shuttle runs every 20–30 minutes between Mammoth Mountain Ski Area and Reds Meadow Valley 7 A.M.–7 P.M. mid-June–mid-September.

A daily **Mountain Express Shuttle** (760/924-3184, adults $5.50, reservations recommended) runs from the Mammoth Lakes McDonald's to the June Lake ski area, arriving at 9 A.M. The return shuttle leaves June Lake at 3:30 P.M.

# Sequoia and Kings Canyon National Parks

The trees are the stars of the show at Sequoia and Kings Canyon National Parks (www.nps.gov/seki). Groves of giant sequoias, including the largest known tree on earth, soar out of the fertile Sierra soil. But in these parks you'll also find rugged granite formations (including Kings Canyon—a deeper gulch than the Grand Canyon), marble caverns, rushing rivers, and an astounding variety of ecosystems, from chaparral to alpine meadow.

## SIGHTS
### General Grant Grove
One of the largest of these parks' giant sequoia groves, the General Grant Grove (one mile northwest of the Kings Canyon Visitor Center) is home to dozens of monumental trees. The largest of these is the General Grant Tree, the third-largest tree on earth, an American National Shrine, and "America's Christmas Tree." Another feature of this area, the Fallen Monarch was once

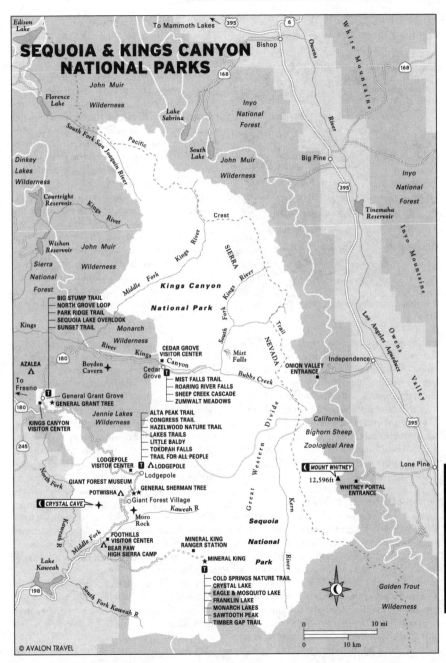

# SEQUOIA & KINGS CANYON NATIONAL PARKS

Edison Lake

To Mammoth Lakes 395

6

Bishop

168

John Muir

Wilderness

Florence Lake

Lake Sabrina

Inyo National Forest

South Fork San Joaquin River

Pacific

South Lake

John Muir

Big Pine

Inyo

Dinkey Lakes Wilderness

Wilderness

395

National

Courtright Reservoir

Kings River

Crest

Forest

Tinemaha Reservoir

Wishon Reservoir

John Muir

Middle Fork Kings River

SIERRA

Inyo Mountains

Sierra National Forest

Wilderness

Kings Canyon

South Fork Kings River

NEVADA

Owens Valley

Los Angeles Aqueduct

Kings

**National Park**

— BIG STUMP TRAIL
— NORTH GROVE LOOP
— PARK RIDGE TRAIL
— SEQUOIA LAKE OVERLOOK
— SUNSET TRAIL

River

Monarch

Trail

Independence

AZALEA △

Kings

Canyon

Mist Falls

ONION VALLEY ENTRANCE

180

Wilderness

CEDAR GROVE VISITOR CENTER

Bubbs Creek

395

To Fresno

Boyden Cavern ✛

Cedar Grove

— MIST FALLS TRAIL
— ROARING RIVER FALLS
— SHEEP CREEK CASCADE
— ZUMWALT MEADOWS

180

General Grant Grove
★ GENERAL GRANT TREE

Jennie Lakes

— ALTA PEAK TRAIL
— CONGRESS TRAIL
— HAZELWOOD NATURE TRAIL
— LAKES TRAILS
— LITTLE BALDY
— TOKOPAH FALLS
— TRAIL FOR ALL PEOPLE

California Bighorn Sheep Zoological Area

KINGS CANYON VISITOR CENTER

245

Wilderness

LODGEPOLE VISITOR CENTER △ LODGEPOLE

Western

◖ MOUNT WHITNEY

12,596ft ▲

Lone Pine

Lodgepole

GIANT FOREST MUSEUM

POTWISHA △

GENERAL SHERMAN TREE

Divide

WHITNEY PORTAL ENTRANCE

North Fork

◖ CRYSTAL CAVE →✛

★★ Giant Forest Village

Kaweah R

Great

Kaweah R

Moro Rock

Sequoia

Kern

FOOTHILLS VISITOR CENTER

BEAR PAW HIGH SIERRA CAMP

MINERAL KING RANGER STATION

National

Middle Fork

Lake Kaweah

MINERAL KING

Park

River

Golden Trout

198

— COLD SPRINGS NATURE TRAIL
— CRYSTAL LAKE
— EAGLE & MOSQUITO LAKE
— FRANKLIN LAKE
— MONARCH LAKES
— SAWTOOTH PEAK
— TIMBER GAP TRAIL

Wilderness

South Fork Kaweah R

0          10 mi

0          10 km

© AVALON TRAVEL

YOSEMITE

© LIZ HAMILL SCOTT

**General Grant Tree, "America's Christmas Tree"**

an immense tree but now acts as a tunnel along the trail, with enough head room for almost the tallest of visitors to get through without ducking. The walk among the sequoias at all stages of development is easy, with a well-built flat half-mile trail (much of this area is wheelchair accessible). But consider purchasing a trail guide at the nearby visitors center, because the circuitous trail can be difficult to follow and you may find yourself lost in the beautiful forest trying to find its star attraction.

## General Sherman Tree

There can be only one. The General Sherman Tree (Wolverton Rd. off Generals Hwy.) is the largest tree known on the planet. At just under 275 feet, it is not the tallest tree, nor at 2,200 years old is it the oldest, but by sheer volume of wood it is the biggest. If you love statistics, pick up a sheet at any of the visitors centers that lists the worlds' 30 largest giant sequoias. Take the trail down the hill to visit the tree, then past it to the shuttle stop where you can catch a shuttle back up the hill to your car.

## Giant Forest Museum

The Giant Forest Museum (559/565-4480, 16 miles from the Hwy. 198 entrance) perches on the side of the Generals Highway. Inside this fun interactive museum, you'll learn everything you ever wanted or needed to know about giant sequoia trees, which grow only here in the Sierra Nevada range. Kids and adults alike love the touchable, spinnable exhibits that provide context to the stated sizes of the trees. This newer museum goes into great detail about the importance of fire in the life of a giant sequoia (and other plants and trees that grow in the same areas). Ironically, a commitment to stamping out *all* forest fires, even those caused naturally by lightning strikes, severely endangered the giant sequoias, which rely on fire to create the right habitat for their growth and reproduction. You'll also learn about how the park used to look, and why many of the buildings have been removed to make way for more trees. This is a great stop for families whose kids need a rest from hiking and long intervals in the car.

## 📢 Crystal Cave

You'll find no trees in the Crystal Cave (Generals Hwy., three miles south of the General Sherman Tree). Instead, you'll find immense underground rooms filled with incredible natural calcite formations and shining polished marble. This is the underside of the parks—perhaps the most impressive (and one of only two publicly accessible) of the over 250 marble caverns within the park and national forest boundaries. The regular tour lasts 45 minutes and takes visitors through walkable, well-lit tunnels and into grand chambers filled with curtains, stalactites, and other weird and beautiful calcite creations. A longer two-hour tour takes you deeper into the caverns, and gives you a much more detailed lesson on the cave's history and geology. Best of all, serious spelunkers can sign up for the Wild Cave Tour, a four- to six-hour crawl off the lit tourist trails in Crystal Cave. With a limit of six people per party, you'll get the most serious caving experience available anywhere in Sequoia and Kings Canyon National Parks.

You can't buy a ticket for a tour at the

© LIZ HAMILL SCOTT

**Sequoia and Kings Canyon**

entrance to Crystal Cave. You'll need to stop at either the Foothills or the Lodgepole visitors center to purchase your tickets. Then proceed on to the cave parking lot, which can take over an hour from either visitor center. No trailers or RVs over 22 feet are allowed on the road. Be aware that even in the fall, tours fill up quickly so if possible get tickets early in the morning or even a day in advance.

### Mineral King

Ironically, the onetime boom town of Mineral King (25 miles off Hwy. 198) never had a successful mining industry nearby. Silver was discovered here and mining began in 1873, but not many minerals moved out of the mountain. Instead, the road built in 1879 attracted loggers and the hydroelectric industry, and the town managed to flourish for a while. Today, visitors drive up the long, winding road to enjoy the resurgence of nature in the area at the expense of human construction. Mineral King Valley draws both geology and botany buffs with its unique glacier-carved array of rocks and minerals, some overgrown with a variety of native plants. The Atwell Mill that once cut first-growth sequoia timber has been reduced to a few relics—a steam engine, a wheel, miscellaneous junk—while all around young giant sequoias reclaim their territory. High above the former town, Sawtooth Peak, at more than 12,000 feet, looms large and reminds many visitors and scientists of similar mountains in the Rockies. The peak is perfect for intrepid day hikers, and also allows multi-day treks with a backcountry permit.

Trying to drive your RV or trailer up Mineral King Road is hazardous to you, your vehicle, and other motorists. Also, marmots frequent the Mineral King area, and these furry critters won't seem quite so cute after you discover they've chewed through your radiator hoses! Check with the ranger station for current activity, and notify the rangers if your car has been disabled.

### ◖ Mount Whitney

It's not just the tallest mountain in California. At 14,505 feet, Mount Whitney (www.nps .gov/seki/planyourvisit/whitney.htm) boasts

YOSEMITE

the highest altitude of any peak in the 48 contiguous United States. Yes, it beats out all the mighty Rocky Mountains! You can see and photograph the impressive peak from several points along the Generals Highway in Sequoia and Kings Canyon. However, it's well away from the main part of the parks, sitting near the town of Lone Pine to the southeast. Plan a long drive to get there from either park entrance.

Amazingly, you can climb all the way to the top of Mount Whitney and back in one day, if you're in good shape and prepared properly for the journey. However, you can't just park at the trailhead and head out during high season (May–Nov.). To preserve the natural beauty of the fragile mountain ecosystem, only 100 day-hikers and 60 backpackers are permitted to hit the main trail each day, and you'll find some severe restrictions on how you must behave. Whitney Portal (13 miles west of Lone Pine) provides the most direct access along a 10.7-mile trail.

If you want to make the climb (or even day-hike), apply for a permit in advance and check reservations (Wilderness Permit Office, 760/873-2483, www.fs.fed.us/r5/inyo/recreation/wild/whitneyavail.shtml, daily 8 A.M.–4:30 P.M.). Also check the website for information about how to prepare for a Mount Whitney hike. Mount Whitney also marks the southern end of the John Muir Trail. Whether you begin here or end here, you'll find the mountain a worthwhile marker on this epic foot journey through California.

## Boyden Cavern

Tucked back in the wilds of the Sequoia National Forest, between Sequoia and Kings Canyon Parks, Boyden Cavern (74101 E. Kings Canyon Rd., 559/338-0959, www.caverntours.com/boydenr.htm, tours daily mid-Apr.–mid-Nov., $20 park fee plus tour cost) gives visitors an up-close and personal cave experience. Inside Boyden, "please try not to touch the formations" takes on a new meaning—that is, turn sideways to avoid the walls and duck to keep from hitting your head on stalactites

that are many thousands of yeards old. This modest-sized cavern network contains plenty of draperies, pancakes, stalactites, and other calcite structures. You can stare right at them, up into them, and in some cases walk all the way around them.

## SPORTS AND RECREATION
### Hiking

Sequoia and Kings Canyon attract hikers all year long-especially those looking for a wild Sierra experience without the overcrowding that's so often prevalent at Yosemite. Many areas of the parks offer lovely day hikes, or you can get a backcountry permit for a backpacking trek through this large, gorgeous area, much of which is only accessible on foot.

### GENERAL GRANT GROVE

This popular stop just north of the northern Kings Canyon park entrance offers a variety of short, flat trails that are perfect for day visitors. After visiting the General Grant Tree, take the **North Grove Loop** half a mile along an old park road through the grove. You might find yourself on the North Grove Loop even if you didn't intend to; it's not particularly well differentiated from the General Grant Tree Trail and it takes in much of the same area.

Outside the grove, take the **Big Stump Trail** (near the Big Stump park entrance) one mile round-trip through a grove that was heavily logged in the late 19th century, but is now reclaiming its true nature as a sequoia grove. Or enjoy the vistas from the **Park Ridge Trail** (Panoramic Point Rd. parking area, closed in winter). If you pick a clear day, you can see all the way out to the Coast Range of mountains in the San Francisco Bay Area from this trail! While there's little elevation change on this almost five-mile walk, consider the altitude of the area before deciding that this trail and the fire-road route back will be an easy trip. For a different view on the life and death of the giant sequoias, and humanity's intervention in this area, hike the **Sequoia Lake Overlook/ Dead Giant Loop** (lower end of General Grant Tree parking area). The two-mile trail takes you to the Dead Giant, a first-growth giant sequoia that was mostly likely killed by loggers trying (and failing) to cut it for lumber. Sequoia Lake is actually an old mill pond from the logging days.

For a longer, more demanding day hike, check out the **Sunset Trail** (Grant Grove Visitor Center). You'll climb about 1,400 feet over this six-mile (round-trip) trail, which takes you past Viola Falls and through the magnificent mixed forests.

## MINERAL KING

A good place to start walking in Mineral King is the **Cold Springs Nature Trail.** This easy, one-mile interpretive walk describes and displays the natural wonders and the formation of the valley.

A bit more strenuous, the **Timber Gap Trail** follows an old mining road through a forest of red fir trees. You'll see pretty views out to Alta Peak and the middle fork of the Kaweah River. The short version of this trail runs four miles round-trip. Note the altitude: You'll start at over 7,500 feet. For a longer hike, take the fork to **Monarch Lakes.** This trek runs about 8.5 miles round-trip, but it's mostly flat and easy walking. Consider bringing a picnic to enjoy beside the lakes. For hikers in great shape looking for the most tremendous views of the southern Sierra Nevada range, keep on going past the lakes up to the top of **Sawtooth Peak.** This trail isn't for the faint of breath or shaky of leg. It climbs 1,200 feet in just over a mile of loose, difficult ground. But once you're at the top, you'll get a fine chance to rest as you photograph the majestic peaks all around you.

Many other hikes begin in Mineral King Valley. You can visit a number of charming alpine lakes if you're up for a hike of 7–11 miles. Plan to take food and water and spend all day on hikes out to **Eagle and Mosquito Lakes** or **Crystal Lake.** You can also get to **Franklin Lake** and back in a day, though the pristine beauty of the water and fascinating geology of the area often draw backpackers on their way to Mount Whitney over several days.

## LODGEPOLE

For a charming interpretive walk at the Lodgepole Village area, head down the **Hazelwood Nature Trail** (Giant Forest Lodge). Signs along this flat one-mile stroll tell the history of humans' relationship with the giant sequoia trees—good and bad, beneficial and destructive. This walk works well for families with school-aged kids. In the same vicinity, you can putter along the quarter-mile **Trail For All People.** This interpretive nature walk's pride comes in spring, when the wildflowers bloom. A bit longer but perhaps the most representative of life in Sequoia National Park, the **Congress Trail** starts at the General Sherman Tree. Grab a pamphlet with map at the Sherman Tree to get the best experience on this trail, which includes many of the park's most famous named giant sequoias. This two-mile round-trip trail is paved, making it wheelchair accessible and a non-strenuous walk even for folks who usually aren't big hikers.

How can you resist a hike to a granite formation called **Little Baldy** (11 miles north of General Grant Grove)? This moderate climb takes you up about 700 feet to the top of the cutely named granite dome. Look down from the peak, which tops out at over 8,000 feet, into the Giant Forest and snap a few photos. Or if you prefer water to stone, head for **Tokopah Falls** (Lodgepole Campground). Early summer, when the flow is at its peak, is the best time to trek out the almost two miles along the Marble Fork of the Kaweah River to this fantastic 1,200-foot waterfall.

Hardcore hikers willing to brave steep climbs at high altitudes can either take day hikes or obtain overnight backcountry passes for the region's major trails. The **Lakes Trails** (Wolverton picnic area) vary in length, but you're definitely going to have to climb a ways up to the glacial lake areas. From the trail, you'll be able to visit Heather Lake, Emerald Lake, and Pear Lake. The minimum distance round-trip for a day hike to Heather Lake is eight miles. Heights-lovers choose the **Alta Peak Trail,** which ascends all the way up to the 11,204-foot summit of Alta Peak. Pick a

Sequoia's namesake stars

clear day for this grueling 14-mile hike and you'll get a view of Mount Whitney across the Great Western Divide.

### CEDAR GROVE

Even if you hate hiking, you'll want to get out of the car and stroll the negligible distance (less than 0.25 mile) from the parking area three miles east of Cedar Grove Village to the **Roaring River Falls.** The whole tiny trail sits under a canopy of trees, making it cool even in the hottest parts of summer, and just looking at the falls feels refreshing after driving the Generals Highway. Another easy meander comes only a mile from Road's End (the northeast terminus of Generals Highway). **Zumwalt Meadows** offers a flat one-mile loop around the meadow of the same name, then a shady walk through a grove of heavenly smelling incense cedar and pine trees along the Kings River.

Moderate hikes abound in this area. A good place to bring a picnic is **Sheep Creek Cascade.** This hike takes about an hour and a half, ascends 600 feet, and runs about two

miles total. You end up in a picturesque shaded glen that's perfect for taking a load off your feet and enjoying the serene surroundings. The **Mists Falls Trail** (Road's End) is a popular jumping-off point for backpackers destined for the Kings Canyon backcountry. However, you can go eight miles out and back to Mists Falls in about five hours. Plan for dust and heat on the first couple of miles of the trail, then steep switchbacks that take you up 1,500 feet to the falls. If you're passing through on your way to the John Muir Trail for a longer trek, keep going past the falls, up to Paradise Valley, then to the trail crossing at Upper Woods Creek.

### Climbing

It shouldn't surprise anyone to learn that **Mount Whitney** is a wonderful place to rock climb. You can climb up the steep East Face of the mountain or head up the Needles. These climbs are not beginners' journeys, but the East Face isn't the hardest climb ever either. First climbed by John Muir himself in 1931, most of the East Face rates at a Class 3, with the worst bits rated 5.4. The Needles are famed among big-wall climbers who attack the Sierras each year. See the *Mount Whitney* section for permit information and regulations.

### Horseback Riding

A number of horse-accessible trails meander through Sequoia and Kings Canyon. Rent a horse for a day ride from the pack stations at **Cedar Grove** (559/565-3463 summer, 559/337-2314 off-season) and **Grant Grove** (559/335-9292 summer, 559/337-2314 off-season). If you're new to horses, pick a gentle one-hour ride. For more hardy or experienced riders, both pack stations offer half-day and full-day rides.

If you're looking for a multi-day horseback adventure, you can find that too at Sequoia and Kings Canyon. Call either of the pack stations to arrange a guided backcountry pack trip.

### Fishing

Fishing is allowed in any of the lakes inside Sequoia and Kings Canyon. You can purchase a fishing license and tackle at the markets at the Grant Grove, Cedar Grove, and Lodgepole visitors centers. The visitor centers can also advise about season opening and closing dates. Anglers are permitted up to five trout per day. The lakes and the Kaweah drainage hold rainbows, eastern brook, German brown, and golden trout.

## ACCOMMODATIONS
### Camping
The park offers 13 campgrounds, three of which are open year-round (Lodgepole, Azalea, and Potwisha). Campgrounds are first-come, first-served, except for Lodgepole (summer visits only). A list and map of all campgrounds is available at www.nps.gov/seki/planyourvisit/campgrounds.htm.

**Lodgepole** (summer reservations 877/444-6777, www.recreation.gov, $18–20) is located along the Kaweah River and is 21 miles from the Sequoia entrance. In summer, there are 214 sites for tents and RVs, flush toilets, showers, laundry, and bear-proof containers. Off-season, there are 25 walk-in tent sites (first-come, first-served).

**Azalea** (Grant Grove, 110 sites, $18) is located 3.5 miles from the Kings Canyon park entrance and within a half-mile of the visitor center. **Potwisha** (42 sites, $18) is also on the Kaweah River, about four miles from the Sequoia entrance. Amenities include flush toilets, RV disposal, and bear-proof containers.

More adventurous campers should check out the High Sierra Camps. Start at Crescent Meadow, about 10 miles south of Wuksachi on Generals Highway, to get to the **Bearpaw High Sierra Camp** (866/807-3598, www.visitsequoia.com, June–Sept.), an 11.5-mile hike into the gorgeous Sequoia back country. This camp takes a leaf from Yosemite's book with its accommodations and amenities. This camp offers six tent cabins that sleep two people apiece, and come complete with bedding, towels, and sleeping pads. You can even fit a third person on the floor of your cabin, if that person brings bedding and a towel for herself. A bath house offers flush toilets and hot showers

(heaven!), and each stay comes with a full dinner and full breakfast, served family-style. You can even buy a box lunch to take with you on your next day's journey.

### Under $100
Centrally located in the Grant Grove Village, the **Grant Grove Cabins** (866/522-6966, www.sequoia-kingscanyon.com, $65–75/tent cabins) offer a wide array of lodging styles for a variety of prices. Many of these cabins have been around awhile—some since the early days of what was then the General Grant National Park. The economy option here are the tent cabins, which are short on amenities, with no electricity or heat and with shared, central bathrooms. From May through October, a number of Camp, Rustic, and Oversized cabins offer solid walls ($77–140), a small propane heater plus an outdoor wood-burning stove, electricity, and daily maid service. When you make reservations, ask about larger cabins if you've got a bigger group or family. It can start snowing in Sequoia and Kings Canyon as early as mid-September. If you're visiting in the spring or the fall, consider whether you're willing to chance an unheated or minimally heated cabin should a storm come up in the park. Open all year are the historic cabins with private baths. Most are duplexes, one log cabin is a single that sleeps two. These cabins have heating, historic Mission-style decor, and amenities such as coffee makers.

### $150-250
Built in 1999, the **Wuksachi Lodge** (Hwy. 198 just west of Lodgepole, 866/786-3197, www.visitsequoia.com, $215–285, year-round) offers the most luxurious accommodations available inside the parks. With 102 rooms of various sizes, the Wuksachi Lodge offers ample luxury housing for tree-lovers who just can't give up their creature comforts. Guest rooms boast "woodsy-motel" decor, with colorful Native American print bedspreads and slightly more interesting Mission-style wooden furniture. Each room has a private bath, a TV, a phone, a coffee maker, ski racks, and daily maid service.

© LIZ HAMILL SCOTT

**Clear water runs through Sequoia National Park.**

The Wuksachi's superior rooms offer space and comfort, particularly for families who cannot imagine a vacation without digital entertainment readily available. An on-site restaurant (the best in the parks), a Native American thematic gift shop, and close access to the Lodgepole visitors complex round out the attractions of this popular lodge.

The shining new **John Muir Lodge** (Grant Grove Village, 866/522-6966, www.sequoia-kingscanyon.com, $150–200, year-round) brings together the concepts of a comfortable motel and a classic woodsy lodge. Expect big timber poles combining form and function in the huge common room. This space acts as a living room or lounge, with a fireplace, wireless Internet access, tables, sofas, and a number of board games. Guest rooms are simply decorated in an alpine theme, complete with comfortable beds, clean bathrooms, and charming views out into the forest. Since you're up at the edge of General Grant Village, you'll find plenty of nearby food and services, including the Village restaurant, mini-mart, souvenir shop, and the Grant Grove visitors center.

The lodge is convenient to hiking, and to the Generals Highway through the park.

## FOOD
### Restaurants

The national parks have their visitors good and trapped when it comes to dining options. Guests who want a wide range of options should bring in their own food. One option is to bring a cooler and stop at a supermarket before you enter the park.

One of the Sequoia restaurants sits at the Grant Grove complex, servicing both the John Muir Lodge and the surrounding tent cabins. **Grant Grove Restaurant** (Hwy. 180 at Generals Hwy., 559/335-5500, Sun.–Thurs. 8 A.M.–2 P.M., 5–7 P.M., Fri.–Sat. 8 A.M.–2 P.M., 5–8 P.M.) serves three meals each day, and is closed in between. This basic dining room offers standard American fare at pretty high resort prices. Though the food is nothing special at lunch or dinner, you can get a palatable meal and a glass of wine. Breakfast, on the other hand, is a monument to the value of cereal bars, apples, and OJ. Morning service at the Grant Grove

Restaurant is weak to disastrous (expect to wait 20–30 minutes for a table in a half-empty dining room), the coffee has both mediocre taste and strength, and the food is simply appalling. If you have *any* other breakfast option, go with it.

The closest thing to an upscale restaurant in Sequoia and Kings Canyon is the **Wuksachi Lodge Restaurant** (off Generals Hwy. west of Lodgepole, open daily year-round for breakfast, lunch, and dinner, $9–24). The elegant dining room has white cloths on the tables and sweeping forest views outside the picture windows. The Wuksachi Restaurant offers three meals per day to service the lodge's overnight guests. But dinner stars as *the* meal of the day, boasting fancier preparations and California-style ingredients. Make a reservation if you plan to dine at the Wuksachi on a summer weekend.

On the other end of the dining spectrum, but no less fun, you'll find the **Kings Canyon Lodge Restaurant** (Hwy. 180 approx 20 miles east of Grant Grove Village). Warning: If taxidermy puts you off your food, do not eat here! Stuffed heads of deer, elk, and other animals decorate the walls, and every other inch of space in the long narrow dining room/lobby is covered with Western-themed knickknacks, geegaws, and tchotchkes. Some of these might even be antiques. Ancient refrigerators and freezers hold cold soft drinks, beer, and ice cream, and the classic diner food is made to order in the least pretentious open kitchen anywhere in the state of California. The restaurant remains open through the long, hot afternoon, making the Kings Canyon Lodge a welcome rest stop for kids needing ice cream and to run around, and adults who prefer to eat late (or have no other choice).

## Markets

You'll find minimally stocked mini-marts at both the **Grant Grove Village** (Hwy. 180 at Generals Hwy., Sun.–Thurs. 9 A.M.–7 P.M., Fri.–Sat. 9 A.M.–8 P.M.) and the **Lodgepole Market** (Generals Hwy. at Lodgepole, daily late May–fall 8 A.M.–8 P.M., fall–spring 9 A.M.–6 P.M.). These sell a few staples, soda, beer, s'mores makings, and some packaged food suitable for reheating over a campfire.

# INFORMATION AND SERVICES
## Tourist Information

Sequoia and Kings Canyon National Parks boast several visitors centers and rangers stations. When you enter the park, you'll be given both the glossy pamphlet and the up-to-date National Park Guide for Sequoia and Kings Canyon. These will provide you with all the in-park information you need to have a great time and keep up on any activities and events.

In Sequoia, the **Foothills Visitor Center** (559/565-3135, daily) is located on Generals Highway, one mile from the park entrance. Crystal Cave tour tickets are sold here until 3:45 P.M. and wilderness permits are issued here as well. **Lodgepole Visitor Center** (Lodgepole Rd., 559/565-4436, spring–fall), off Generals Highway, is 21 miles from the Sequoia entrance. Crystal Cave tour tickets are sold until 3:30 P.M. and wilderness permits are issued here. The **Mineral King Ranger Station** (Mineral King Rd., 559/565-3768, May–Sept.) is located up a narrow road and offers basic seasonal services.

In Kings Canyon, there is the **Kings Canyon Visitor Center** (Grant Grove, 559/565-4307, Apr.–Oct. daily 8 A.M.–5 P.M., Nov.–Mar. daily 9 A.M.–4:30 P.M.) three miles east of the Highway 180 entrance and **Cedar Grove Visitor Center** (559/565-3793, mid Apr–mid–Nov.) in Cedar Grove Village.

## Media and Communications

You're a long way from civilization when you visit Sequoia and Kings Canyon National Parks. Don't expect flawless coverage from your cell phone. If you're lucky you might find some signal; if you're unlucky, you're stuck with land lines at the visitors centers and lodgings for the duration of your stay. Likewise with Internet service. The more cosmopolitan lodges inside the park offer some Wi-Fi in common areas, but that's about the extent of Internet service here. So consider forgetting the laptop and the PDA and unplugging for a few days so you can get to understand the sights and sounds of the woods all around you.

## Banks and Post Offices

No banks lie inside the park, but you can find ATMs at the major visitors complexes at Grant Grove, Lodgepole, and Cedar Grove (summer only).

Though you can no longer post a letter from the old log cabin post office, you can make use of the **Park Post Office at Lodgepole** (Lodgepole Visitor Center, Mon.–Fri. 8 A.M.–1 P.M., 2–4 P.M.). Address any mail to General Delivery, Sequoia National Park, 93262.

## Medical Services

No medical services beyond the first aid provided by rangers are available in Sequoia and Kings Canyon. In a medical emergency, dial 911 from your cell phone, your lodgings, or a call box if possible. The nearest hospitals sit out in Fresno and Visalia.

## GETTING THERE AND AROUND
### Car

Visitors can enter Sequoia at the Ash Mountain entrance on Highway 198 or at Big Stump in Kings Canyon on Highway 180. There are no road entrances on the east side of either park.

The closest major highway to the park is Highway 99. Turn east onto CA-180 from Fresno to get to the north entrance and onto CA-198 from Visalia in the south. The main road running through the two parks is called **The Generals Highway.** It connects CA-180 (Kings Canyon Highway) in the north to CA-198 in the southwest.

Drive carefully in Sequoia and Kings Canyon. They might call it a "highway," but in truth the Generals Highway is a steep, narrow, twisting mountain road that can be treacherous in bad weather and when driven too fast by unfamiliar and inexperienced motorists. Maximum RV length is 22 feet on Generals Highway and Crystal Cave Road (no trailers permitted on the latter). RVs and trailers are not permitted on Mineral King Road or Moro Rock/Crescent Meadow Road.

Parking lots grace most major attractions, but these can fill up quickly in the summer. Some parking is permitted along the roadsides, but *please* don't park your hot car on dry grass—you can set the park (and your car) on fire this way.

Several of the park's roads close in the winter, though the Generals Highway remains open. The Mineral King Road, Crystal Cave Road, and Panoramic Point Roads close from about the beginning of November to the end of May each year. Check the website or call 559/565-3341 for current road information.

Drive times from either San Francisco or Los Angeles can easily run 5–7 hours, depending on traffic and weather conditions.

When you approach the parks, you'll be told by everybody and their little dog Spot that there's no gas anywhere in Sequoia or Kings Canyon National Parks. And technically, that's true. The Kings Canyon Lodge gas station sits on national forest land rather than inside the park borders proper. And many visitors are dubious when they see the genuine antique gravity gas pumps sitting outside the funky old lodge. But those pumps work, and while you can't fill up your SUV, you can get enough gas here to at least get you out of the park and to one of the border towns.

Two other stations sit in the national forest at Hume Lake (Hwy. 180, 11 miles north of Grant Grove) and Stony Creek (Generals Hwy., btwn. Lodgepole and Grant Grove).

## Shuttles

Sequoia National Park provides free shuttle service (559/565-3341, www.nps.gov/seki/plan yourvisit/publictransportation.htm) within the park May 21–September 1. The "green" route connects Giant Forest with the Lodgepole Visitor Center, the General Sherman Tree, and the Giant Forest Museum. The "gray" route connects the Giant Forest Museum to Moro Rock and Crescent Meadow.

The **Sequoia Shuttle** (877/287-4453, www. sequoiashuttle.com, $15) connects Visalia to the Giant Forest Museum.

# CENTRAL COAST

Here begins the California coast that movies and literature have made legendary. Soaring cliffs drop straight down into the sea in some areas, making the white sand beaches that occasionally appear beneath and beyond them all the more inviting. From north to south, the Pacific Ocean changes from slate gray to a gentler blue. Scents of salt and kelp waft up the beaches, and the endless crash of the breakers against the shore is a constant lullaby in the coastal towns.

The seacoast city of Santa Cruz, with its ultra-liberal culture, redwood-clad university, and general sense of funky fun, prides itself on keeping things weird. The beach and Boardwalk are prime attractions for surfing and enjoying the sun.

Gorgeous Monterey Bay is famous for its sealife. Sea otters dive and play at the world-renowned aquarium while sea lions beach themselves for sunning pleasure on offshore rocks. The historic Cannery Row was immortalized by Steinbeck in his novel of the same name, but the now touristy wharf area bears only a superficial resemblance to its fishing past.

One of the most exclusive enclaves of the wealthy in all of California, nearby Carmel rivals Malibu for its charming ocean views, well-traveled beaches and parks, and, most of all, for its unbelievably expensive real estate. (Clint Eastwood was once mayor here.) The legendary Pebble Beach golf course and resort sits just north of downtown.

South of Carmel, Highway 1 begins its scenic tour down Big Sur. The Big Sur coast might be the single most beautiful part of

© MONTEREY COUNTY CONVENTION AND VISITORS BUREAU

# HIGHLIGHTS

◖ **Santa Cruz Beach Boardwalk:** This is the best traditional beach boardwalk in the state (page 273).

◖ **Monterey Bay Aquarium:** This mammoth aquarium was the first of its kind in the United States and still astonishes with a vast array of sea life and exhibits (page 287).

◖ **17-Mile Drive:** This gorgeous scenic drive is worth the toll for an introduction to the region's coastal beauty (page 295).

◖ **Carmel Mission:** Father Junipero Serra's favorite California mission is still a working parish, with an informative museum and stunning gilded altar (page 297).

◖ **Big Sur Coast Highway:** This twisty, coastal drive is iconic Big Sur, with jutting cliffs, crashing surf, and epics views all the way (page 304).

◖ **Pfeiffer Big Sur State Park:** Whether you're camping at the park or not, it's worth your time to hike through the stunning redwoods of Pfeiffer Big Sur (page 307).

◖ **Hearst Castle:** No visit to the Central Coast is complete without a tour of Hearst Castle, the grand mansion on a hill conceived and built by publishing magnate William Randolph Hearst (page 318).

◖ **Santa Barbara Museum of Natural History:** The museum's large galleries house exhibits highlighting the natural history and inhabitants of the area. Take a stroll along the nature trail or peruse the accompanying planetarium (page 327).

LOOK FOR ◖ TO FIND RECOMMENDED SIGHTS, ACTIVITIES, DINING, AND LODGING.

California. The rugged cliffs and protected forests have little development to mar their natural charms. Travelers called to the wilderness will feel right at home in Big Sur. It's a sin to remain in your car, however, when an such an embarrassment of natural riches await. Waterfalls and redwoods beckon hikers and campers while cliffside resorts pamper guests.

Seaside Cambria makes a good base from which to visit much of the Central Coast, including Paso Robles and San Simeon, home to the grand Hearst Castle, an homage to excess.

The coast becomes less rugged here, though no less beautiful.

Beach lovers will flock to temperate Santa Barbara farther south, where the relaxed yet cultured pace reflects its mission and university influences, as well as its affluence. Wine is a growth industry here as well—look for the Central Coast to become the next great California wine region.

## PLANNING YOUR TIME

The Central Coast is a favorite of many California residents for romantic weekend getaways. If you're coming to this part of the state for a weekend, pick an area and explore it in depth. Don't try to get everywhere in only two days—this is a big region and driving from one spot to another can take hours.

For a relaxed weekend without much travel, focus your trip on Santa Cruz, Carmel, Big Sur, Cambria, or Santa Barbara. If you're up for more adventure, add a day of wine tasting in Paso Robles to your Cambria trip, or head over to the Monterey Bay Aquarium from Carmel one morning.

If you've got a whole week, start in either Santa Cruz or Santa Barbara and work your way down or up the coast on Highway 1, with side trips into the Carmel Valley and Paso Robles. Alternately, it's easy to spend a whole week chilling out and becoming one with nature in Big Sur.

# Santa Cruz

There's no place like Santa Cruz. Not even elsewhere in the wacky Bay Area can you find another town that has embraced the radical fringe of the nation and made it into a municipal-cultural statement quite like this. In Santa Cruz, you'll find surfers on the waves, nudists on the beaches, tree-huggers in the redwood forests, tattooed and pierced punks on the main drag, and families walking the dog along West Cliff Drive. Oh, and by the way, that purple-haired woman with the tongue stud might well be a dedicated volunteer at her local PTA. With the kind of irony only Santa Cruz (a town that has openly decriminalized marijuana) can produce, a massive illegal fireworks storm erupts over the beaches in patriotic celebration each Fourth of July.

Most visitors come to Santa Cruz to hit the Boardwalk and the beaches. Locals and UCSC students tend to hang at the Pacific Garden Mall and stroll on West Cliff. The east side of town can get dicey, especially a few blocks from the Boardwalk, while the Westside tends more towards families with children. The food of Santa Cruz qualifies as a hidden treasure, with myriad ethnicities represented.

The Santa Cruz area includes several tiny towns that aren't inside Santa Cruz proper, but blend into each other with the feeling of beach-town suburbs. Aptos, Capitola, and Soquel all lie to the south of Santa Cruz along the coast. Each has its own small shopping districts, restaurants, and lodgings. They've also got charming beaches all their own, which can be as foggy, as crowded, or as nice to visit as their northern neighbors.

## SIGHTS
### ◖ Santa Cruz Beach Boardwalk
The Santa Cruz Beach Boardwalk (400 Beach St., 831/423-5590, www.beachboardwalk.com, daily 11 A.M.–close, parking $10), or just "the Boardwalk" as it's called by the locals, has a rare appeal that beckons to young children, too-cool teenagers, and adults of all ages.

The amusement park rambles along each side of the south end of the Boardwalk; entry is free, but you must buy either per-ride tickets or an unlimited ride wristband. The Great Dipper boasts a history as the oldest wooden roller coaster in the state, still giving riders a thrill after all this time. The spinner and the Zipper tend to be more fun for kids (or at least folks with hardy inner ears). In summertime, a log ride cools down guests hot from hours of tromping around. The Boardwalk also offers several toddler and little-kid rides.

At the other end of the Boardwalk, avid gamesters choose between the lure of prizes from the traditional midway games and the large arcade. Throw baseballs at things, try your arm at skee-ball, or take a pass at classic or newer video game. The traditional carousel actually has a brass ring you (or your children) can try to grab.

After you've worn yourself out playing games and riding rides, you can take the stairs down to the broad, sandy beach below the

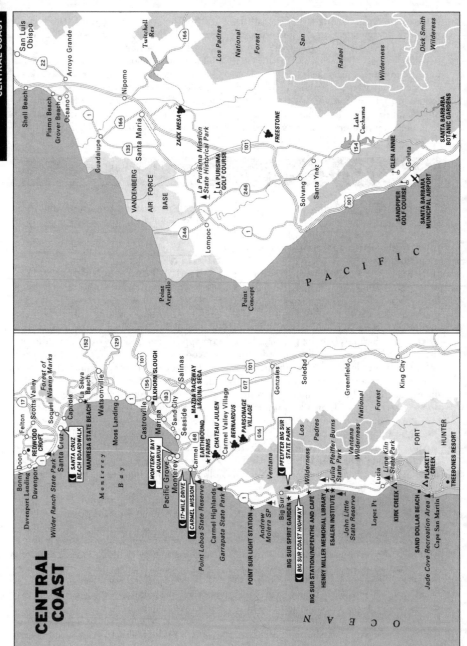

CENTRAL COAST

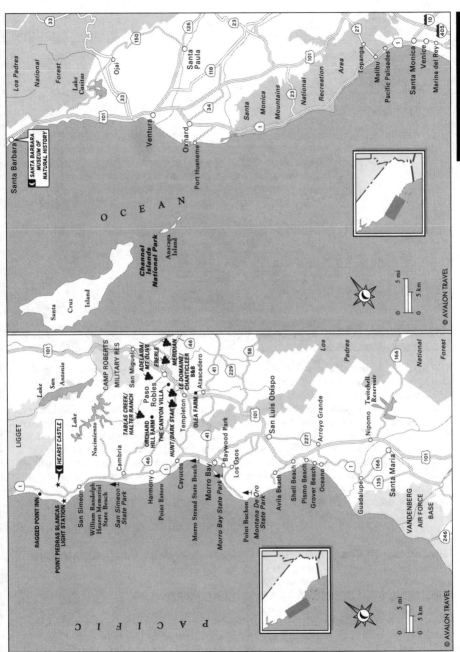

**PACIFIC OCEAN**

© AVALON TRAVEL

0 5 mi
0 5 km

LIGGET

101

Lake San Antonio

CAMP ROBERTS MILITARY RES

Lake Nacimiento

TABLAS CREEK/ HALTER RANCH

San Miguel

ADELAIDA/ MT. OLIVE

EBERLE

MERIDIAN

46

HEARST CASTLE

Cambria

ORCHARD HILL FARM

Paso Robles

LE DOMAINE/ CHANTICLEER

58

★ RAGGED POINT INN

★ POINT PIEDRAS BLANCAS LIGHT STATION

San Simeon

William Randolph Hearst Memorial State Beach

San Simeon State Park

THE CANYON VILLA

OLEA FARM

Atascadero

229

41

Los Padres

National Forest

166

Harmony

HUNT/PARK STAR

Templeton

46

1

Point Estero

Cayucos

41

Baywood Park

San Luis Obispo

101

Morro Strand State Beach

Morro Bay

Los Osos

227

Arroyo Grande

Twitchell Reservoir

Morro Bay State Park

Point Buchon

Montana De Oro State Park

Avila Beach

Shell Beach

Pismo Beach

Grover Beach

Oceano

Nipomo

135

1

Guadalupe

166

Santa Maria

101

VANDENBERG AIR FORCE BASE

246

© AVALON TRAVEL

0 5 mi
0 5 km

33

150

126

23

10

405

Los Padres

National Forest

Lake Casitas

Ojai

33

Santa Paula

118

27

Topanga

Santa Monica

Venice

101

Ventura

34

Santa Monica Mountains

23

National

Recreation

Area

Malibu

Pacific Palisades

Marina del Rey

Oxnard

1

Port Hueneme

Santa Barbara

⚓ SANTA BARBARA MUSEUM OF NATURAL HISTORY

OCEAN

Channel Islands National Park

Anacapa Island

Santa Cruz Island

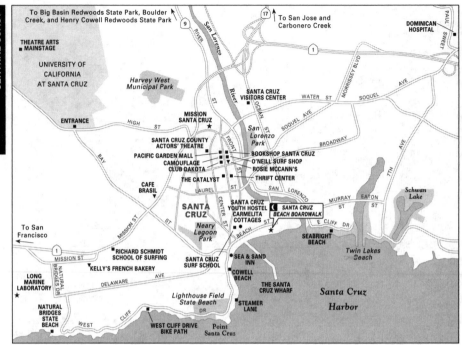

To Big Basin Redwoods State Park, Boulder Creek, and Henry Cowell Redwoods State Park

To San Jose and Carbonero Creek

DOMINICAN HOSPITAL

THEATRE ARTS MAINSTAGE

UNIVERSITY OF CALIFORNIA AT SANTA CRUZ

Harvey West Municipal Park

SANTA CRUZ VISITORS CENTER

ENTRANCE

MISSION SANTA CRUZ

San Lorenzo Park

SANTA CRUZ COUNTY ACTORS' THEATRE

PACIFIC GARDEN MALL
CAMOUFLAGE
CLUB DAKOTA

BOOKSHOP SANTA CRUZ
O'NEILL SURF SHOP
ROSIE MCCANN'S

CAFE BRASIL

THE CATALYST

THRIFT CENTER

SANTA CRUZ

Schwan Lake

To San Francisco

Neary Lagoon Park

SANTA CRUZ YOUTH HOSTEL
CARMELITA COTTAGES

SANTA CRUZ BEACH BOARDWALK

SEABRIGHT BEACH

Twin Lakes Beach

RICHARD SCHMIDT SCHOOL OF SURFING

KELLY'S FRENCH BAKERY

SANTA CRUZ SURF SCHOOL

SEA & SAND INN

COWELL BEACH

THE SANTA CRUZ WHARF

Santa Cruz Harbor

LONG MARINE LABORATORY

NATURAL BRIDGES STATE BEACH

Lighthouse Field State Beach

STEAMER LANE

WEST CLIFF DRIVE BIKE PATH

Point Santa Cruz

Boardwalk. It's a great place to flop down and sun yourself, or brave a dip in the cool Pacific surf. Granted, it gets a bit crowded in the summertime. But you've got all the services you could ever want right there at the Boardwalk, plus the sand and the water (and the occasional strand of kelp). What could be more perfect?

Looking for something tasty to munch on or a drink to cool you off? You can definitely find it at the Boardwalk. An old-fashioned candy shop sells sweets to the sweet, while the snack stands offer corn dogs, burgers, fries, lemonade, and other generally unhealthy traditional carnival food.

## Mission Santa Cruz

Believe it or not, weird and funky Santa Cruz started out as a Mission town. Mission Santa Cruz (126 High St., 831/426-5686, Tues.–Sat. 10 A.M.–4 P.M., Sun. 10 A.M.–2 P.M.) was one of the later California missions, dedicated in 1791. Today, the attractive white of the building with its classic red-tiled roof welcomes parishioners to

the active Holy Cross church and fourth-grade students from around the Bay Area to the historic museum areas of the old mission. In fact, the buildings you can visit today, like many others in the mission chain, is not the original complex built by the Spanish fathers in the 18th century. Indeed, none of the first mission and only one wall from the second mission remains on the site today—the rest was destroyed in an earthquake. The church you'll tour today is the fourth one, built in 1889. After you finish your tour of the complex and grounds, be sure to stop in at the Galeria, which houses the mission gift shop and a stunning collection of religious vestments—something you won't see in many other California missions.

## Long Marine Lab

If you love the sea and all the critters that live in it, be sure to come take a tour of the Long Marine Laboratory (Delaware Ave., 831/459-3800, www2.ucsc.edu/seymourcenter, Tues.–Sat.

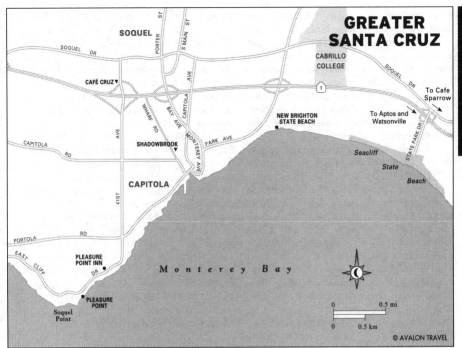

**GREATER
SANTA CRUZ**

SOQUEL

CABRILLO
COLLEGE

CAFÉ CRUZ

To Cafe
Sparrow

NEW BRIGHTON
STATE BEACH

To Aptos and
Watsonville

SHADOWBROOK

Seacliff

State

CAPITOLA

Beach

PLEASURE
POINT INN

*M o n t e r e y   B a y*

PLEASURE
POINT

Soquel
Point

0        0.5 mi

0        0.5 km

© AVALON TRAVEL

10 A.M.–5 P.M., Sun. noon–5 P.M., adults $6, children $4). The large, attractive gray building complex at the end of Delaware Avenue sits right on the edge of the cliff overlooking the ocean— convenient for the research done primarily by students and faculty of UCSC. Your visit will be to the **Seymour Marine Discovery Center**— the part of the lab that's open to the public. You'll be greeted outside the door by a full blue whale skeleton that's lit up at night. Inside, instead of a standard aquarium setup, you'll find a marine laboratory similar to those used by the scientists elsewhere in the complex. Expect to see pipes and machinery around the tanks, which are de- signed to display their residents rather than to mimic habitats. Kids particularly love the touch tanks, while curious adults enjoy checking out the seasonal tank that contains the wildlife that's swimming around outside in the bay *right now.*

If you've never been to Long/Seymour be- fore, the best way to introduce yourself to the lab is to take a tour. Tours run at 1 P.M., 2 P.M.,

and 3 P.M. each day; sign up an hour in ad- vance to be sure of getting a slot.

## UC Santa Cruz

The University of California at Santa Cruz (Bay St., 831/459-0111, www.ucsc.edu) might be the single most beautiful college campus in the country. Set up in the hills above down- town Santa Cruz, the classrooms and dorms sit underneath groves of coast redwood trees, amongst tangles of ferns and vines and cute woodland creatures. Call 831/459-4118 for a tour of the campus (groups of six or more, res- ervations required). Or just find a parking lot and wander out into the woods like the stu- dents do, looking for a perfect circle of trees to sit and meditate within.

## ENTERTAINMENT AND EVENTS
### Bars and Clubs

Down on the Mall, you can stroll upstairs to

**Rosie McCann's** (1220 Pacific Ave., 831/426-9930, www.rosiemccanns.com) for a pint and a bite. This dark-paneled, Irish-style saloon serves Guinness, Black and Tans, Snake Bites, and several tasty draft beers. You can also get a hefty meal at Rosie's, whose menu runs to sausage, mashed potatoes, and other weighty pub foods. A largely local crowd hangs out here, and you'll find the bar crowded and noisy, but the vibe friendly and entertaining.

For club-goers of the gayer persuasion, there's **Club Dakota** (1209 Pacific Ave., 831/454-9030). This local favorite tends toward the less crowded and more friendly end of the spectrum; the dance club might not be packed, but the bartenders are more likely to be happy when they get you your drinks. The only times the Dakota really gets crowded are on Saturday nights after 11 P.M., and on Pride and Party nights. If you come in before 10 P.M., you won't be charged a cover and you're likely to find plenty of space out on the dance floor. This being Santa Cruz, you might find more straight women than gay men dancing in the Dakota—it's known as a safe haven where few slimy guys hit on women. If you're a guy…well, the bouncers do a good job of keeping things fun rather than creepy here. Thursday nights equal cheap drinks, so come early to imbibe your fill.

## Live Music

**The Catalyst** (1011 Pacific Ave., advance tickets 866/384-3060, door tickets 831/423-1338, www.catalystclub.com, $12–35), right downtown on the Mall, is *the* Santa Cruz nightclub. This live rock venue hosts all sorts of big-name national acts, most of whom now play clubs rather than stadiums. The Catalyst is completely democratic in its booking—you might see Ted Nugent one week, the Indigo Girls the next, and a ska band the week after that. In between, the Catalyst hosts DJ dance nights, teen nights, and other fun events. Be sure to check the calendar when you buy tickets—some shows are 21 and over only. (Mmm… music, dancing, and a full bar!) The main concert hall is a standing-room-only space, while

the balconies offer seating. The bar sits downstairs adjacent to the concert space. The vibe at the Catalyst tends to be low-key, but it depends on the night and the event. Some of the more retro acts definitely draw an older crowd, while the techno-DJ dance parties cater to the UCSC set. You can buy tickets online or by phone; purchasing in advance is recommended, especially for national acts.

The **Crow's Nest** (2218 East Cliff Dr., 831/476-4560, www.crowsnest-santacruz.com) functions as a venue for all kinds of live musical acts. You might see a contemporary reggae-rock group one night and a Latin dance band the next. Lots of funk bands play the Nest—it's just appropriate for the Santa Cruz ethos. A few tribute bands, usually to hippie 1960s and '70s legends like Jimi Hendrix and Santana, perform on occasion as well. Most shows are free, but if there's a really popular act you might be charged $5 at the door. Check the website for a performance calendar, but it's a good bet that you'll get live musical entertainment here every night from Wednesday through Saturday.

## Comedy

For a good laugh in Santa Cruz, the **Crow's Nest** (2218 East Cliff Dr., 831/476-4560, www.crowsnest-santacruz.com, comedy Sun. 9 P.M., $7) also hosts a weekly stand-up comedy show. Because the show runs on Sunday nights, the Crow's Nest takes advantage of the opportunity to hire big-name comics who have been in San Francisco or San Jose for weekend engagements. This lets folks see headliners in a more casual setting for a fraction of the cost of the big-city clubs. The Crow's Nest, with its great views out over the Pacific, also has a full bar and restaurant. You can enjoy drinks and dinner while you get your giggle on.

## Theater

Santa Cruz is home to several community theaters and an outdoor summer Shakespeare festival that draws theatergoers from around the Bay Area.

The **Santa Cruz County Actors' Theatre** (1001 Center St., 831/425-7529, www.actorssc

.org) acts as Santa Cruz's permanent local theater company. The Actors' Theatre does it all: performs a subscription season, holds theater arts workshops, sponsors playwriting contests for kids and adults, and stages improv shows. All shows at this low-cost theater are contemporary works, including the full production series plays. But the most exciting (though not necessarily the highest quality) shows you can see here are the new works festivals featuring completely new plays, mostly by local authors, which have won Actors' Theatre contests. If one of these, especially the "Eight Tens at Eight," appears during your stay, consider getting tickets so you can see something completely different.

If you prefer historic theater to modern, UCSC puts on an annual summer Shakespeare festival: **Shakespeare Santa Cruz** (831/459-2121, http://shakespearesantacruz.org, adults $32–44, seniors/students $29, children $18). This six-week festival usually runs in the second half of July and through August. Venues both sit on the UCSC campus, one indoor at the Theatre Arts Mainstage (1156 High St.) and the other out in the redwood forests in the Festival Glen (Meyer Dr.). Each year the festival puts up at least two Shakespeare plays— 2008 selections included *Romeo and Juliet* and *All's Well That Ends Well*—plus at least one other production (often a more contemporary play). At the outdoor glen, audience members are encouraged to bring their own picnics. This can make for the perfect romantic date, or a fun outing for the whole family.

## SHOPPING

There's no shopping area in California quite like the **Pacific Garden Mall** (Pacific Ave., 831/429-8433). Hanging out "on the Mall," as the locals call it, is a pastime for many teens and adults from Santa Cruz and beyond. The Mall runs on Pacific Avenue and its offshoots, and is usually open to (very slow) auto traffic. Park in one of the structures a block or two off the Mall proper and walk from there. At the north end, shoppers peruse antiques, boutique clothing, and kitchenware. Down at the seedier south end of the mall, visitors can get shining

new body jewelry, a great new tattoo, or a silicone sex toy. In the middle (and to a lesser degree throughout the Mall), you can grab a bite to eat, a cappuccino, or a cocktail in one of the many independent eateries. You'll find only a select few chain stores on the Mall, and those are uniformly reviled by the fiercely anti-mega-corporation residents of Santa Cruz. The Borders across the street from the **Book Shop Santa Cruz** (1520 Pacific Ave., 831/423-0900, www.bookshopsantacruz.com, Sun.–Thurs. 9 A.M.–10 P.M., Fri.–Sat. until 11 P.M.) takes shockingly little business away from its local independent rival.

Sure, you will find an **O'Neill Surf Shop** (110 Cooper St., 831/469-4377) on the Mall, but surf shops are a staple of Santa Cruz. This one specializes in surfboards, wetsuits, and brand-name clothing. If your trip to California has gotten you hooked on riding the waves, and you just have to invest in your own equipment, O'Neill can be a good place to start. (If you're an expert who prefers custom work, you already know that pre-fab chain stuff isn't for you.) You can also buy a T-shirt or some sweats here—handy if you didn't pack quite right for Central Coast summer fog.

If you're wanting to buy clothes in Santa Cruz, chances are you're looking for a secondhand store. This town has plenty of 'em. One of the largest of these sits only a block off Pacific Avenue—the aptly if redundantly named **Thrift Center Thrift Store** (504 Front St., 831/429-6975). This big, somewhat dirty retail space offers a wide array of cheap secondhand clothes. You'll need to hunt a bit to find that one perfect vintage item that's just too perfect, but isn't that the fun of thrift shopping?

Down toward the great divide between the "good side" and the "less good side" of the Mall you can price some more adult merchandise. **Camouflage** (1329 Pacific Ave., 888/309-2266, http://experiencethefantasy. com, Mon.–Thurs. 10 A.M.–8 P.M., Fri.–Sat. 10 A.M.–10 P.M., Sun. 11 A.M.–7 P.M.) is an independent, women-operated and women-friendly adult store. The first room contains mostly lingerie and less-shocking items. Dare

CENTRAL COAST

to walk through the narrow black-curtained passage, and you'll find the *other* room, which is filled with grown-up toys designed to please women of every taste and proclivity. (A few cool gizmos and gadgets can make things fun for the men as well.) As many ladies as men shop here, and can feel comfortable doing so.

## SPORTS AND RECREATION
### Beaches

At the tip of the West Side, **Natural Bridges State Park** (West Cliff Dr., 831/423-4609, www.parks.ca.gov, daily 8 A.M.–sunset) offers nearly every kind of beach recreation possible. The sand strip doesn't stretch wide, but falls back deep, crossed by a creek that feeds out into the sea. An inconsistent break makes surfing at Natural Bridges fun on occasion, while the near-constant winds that sweep the sands bring out windsurfers nearly every weekend. Hardy sun-worshippers brave the breezes, bringing out their beach blankets, umbrellas, and sunscreen on rare sunny days (usually in late spring and fall). Back from the beach, a wooded picnic area has tables and grills for small and larger parties. Even farther back, the visitors center can provide great stories about the various national wonders of this surprisingly diverse state park. Rangers offer guided tours of the tidepools that range out to the west side of the beach. You can access these by a somewhat scrambling short hike (0.25–0.5 mile) on the rocks cliffs. These odd little holes filled with sea life aren't like most tidepools—many are nearly perfect round depressions in the sandstone cliffs worn away by harder stones as the tides move tirelessly back and forth. Just don't touch the residents of these pools, since human hands can hurt delicate tidepool creatures.

At **Cowell Beach** (350 West Cliff Dr.), it's all about the surfing. This West Side beach sits right at a crook in the coastline, which joins with underwater features to create a reliable small break that lures new surfers by the dozens. (See *Surfing* section for more information about surfing Cowell.)

At the south end of Santa Cruz, down by the harbor, beachgoers flock to **Seabright Beach** (East Cliff Dr. at Seabright Ave., 831/685-6500, www.santacruzstateparks.org, daily 6 A.M.–10 P.M., free) all summer long. This miles-long stretch of sand, protected by the cliffs from the worst of the winds, is a favorite retreat for sunbathers and loungers. While there's little in the way of snack bars, permanent volleyball courts, or facilities, you can still have a great time at Seabright. There's lots of soft sand to lie in, plenty of room to play football or set up your own volleyball net, and, of course, easy access to the chilly Pacific Ocean. There's no surfing here—Seabright has a shore break that delights skim-boarders, but makes wave riding impossible.

Each Fourth of July, the Santa Cruz police force cordons off the area surrounding Seabright Beach. No one can park nearby or even walk in after a certain point in the afternoon (which seems to change annually). But if you show up early to cart in yourself and all your stuff down onto the sand, you can participate in the unbelievable fireworks extravaganza that starts almost as soon as the sun goes down. Though it's technically illegal, people still create professional-grade pyrotechnical productions and launch them from Seabright. The effect quickly becomes overwhelming, but for those who can handle, the night is truly magical.

Down in Capitola, one of the favorite sandy spots is **New Brighton State Beach** (1500 Park Ave., Capitola, 831/464-6330, www.parks.ca.gov). This forest-backed beach has everything: a strip of sand that's perfect for lounging and cold-water swimming, a forest-shaded campground for both tent and RV campers, hiking trails, and ranger-led nature programs. If you plan to camp, call in advance to make reservations at this popular state park, or just come for the day and set up your spot out on the sand. New Brighton can get crowded on rare sunny summer days, but it's nothing like the wall-to-wall people of the popular Southern California beaches.

### Surfing

The coastline of Santa Cruz has more than its share of great surf breaks. The water is cold, demanding full wetsuits year-round, and the shoreline is rough and rocky—nothing at all like the flat sandy beaches of SoCal. But that doesn't deter the hordes of locals who ply the waves every day they can. The surfing culture pervades the town—if you walk the cliff, you'll likely pass the *To Honor Surfing* sculpture. Santa Cruz loves this statue, and it's often dressed up and always gets a costume for Halloween.

If you're a beginner, the best place to start surfing Santa Cruz is **Cowell's** (stairs at West Cliff and Cowell Beach). The waves are low and long, making for fun longboard rides perfect for surfers just getting their balance. Because the Cowell's break is acknowledged as the newbie spot, the often sizeable crowd tends to be polite to newcomers and tourists.

For more advanced surfers looking for smaller crowds in the water, **Manresa State Beach** (San Andreas Rd., Aptos, www.parks .ca.gov) offers fun rides under the right conditions. Manresa is several minutes' drive south toward Aptos. You'll usually find a good beach break, and the waves can get big when there's a north swell.

Visitors who know their surfing lore will want to surf the more famous spots along the Santa Cruz shore. **Pleasure Point** (btwn. 32nd Ave. and 41st Ave., Soquel) encompasses a number of different breaks. You may have heard of The Hook (steps at 41st Ave.), a well-known experienced longboarder's paradise. But don't mistake The Hook for a beginner's break; the locals feel protective of the waves here and aren't always friendly towards inexperienced tourists. The break at 36th and East Cliff (steps at 36th Ave.) can be a better place to go on weekdays—on the weekends, the intense crowding makes catching your own wave a challenge. Up at 30th and East Cliff (steps at 36th Ave), you'll find challenging sets and hot-dogging shortboarders.

The most famous break in all of Santa Cruz can also be the most hostile to newcomers. **Steamer Lane** (West Cliff btwn. Cowell's and the Lighthouse) has both a fiercely protective crew of locals and a dangerous break

that actually kills someone about every other year. But if you're into adrenaline and there's a swell coming in, you'll be hard pressed to find a more exciting ride on the Central Coast, or indeed in most of California.

Yes, you can learn to surf in Santa Cruz despite the distinct local flavor at some of the breaks. Check out either the **Santa Cruz Surf School** (322 Pacific Ave., 831/426-7072, www.santacruzsurfschool.com) or the **Richard Schmidt School of Surfing** (849 Almar Ave., 831/423-0928, www.richardschmidt.com) to sign up for lessons. Who knows, maybe one day the locals will mistake you for one of their own!

## Windsurfing and Parasurfing

If you prefer to let the wind help you catch the waves, you probably already know that Santa Cruz has some prize windsurfing and parasurfing locales. Beginning windsurfers vie with longboarders for space at **Cowell's,** which sits right next to the City Wharf (stairs at West Cliff and Cowell Beach). For a bigger breeze, head up West Cliff to **Natural Bridges State Park** (West Cliff Dr., www.parks.ca.gov, $6 parking). Natural Bridges offers the best spot to set up, plus restroom facilities and ample parking. Serious sailors head farther north to **Davenport Landing** (Hwy. 1, 20 miles north of Santa Cruz). You'll be able to discern that you've found the right rugged and windswept stretch of coast by the endless crowd of sailors and parasurfers out on the waves. Parking can be a bit haphazard here, but even if you're just stopping by to watch, it can be worth your time since the sight of these athletes using both wind and waves to create ultra-fast rides is nothing short of amazing.

If you want to try your luck at windsurfing for the first time, contact **Club Ed** (831/464-0177, www.club-ed.com) to set up a lesson. They operate in the gentle breezes and small swells at Cowell's, and make it easy for first-timers to gain confidence and have a great time.

## Hiking and Biking

To walk or bike where the locals do, just head

out to **West Cliff Drive.** This winding street with a full-fledged sidewalk-trail running its length on the ocean side is the town's favorite walking, dog-walking, jogging, skating, scootering, and biking route. You can start at Natural Bridges (the west end of West Cliff) and go for miles. The *To Honor Surfing* statue lies several miles down the road, as do plenty of fabulous views. Bring your camera if you're strolling West Cliff on a clear day—you won't be able to resist taking photos of the sea, cliffs, and sunset. Just be sure to watch for your fellow path-users. What with the bicyclists and skaters and such, it can get a bit treacherous if you don't watch where you're going.

## ACCOMMODATIONS
### Under $100
Staying at a hostel in Santa Cruz just feels right. And the **Santa Cruz Youth Hostel Carmelita Cottages** (321 Main St., 831/423-8304, www.hi-santacruz.org, $25 dorm, $55 private room, $150 cottage) offers a great local atmosphere. Like most historic Santa Cruz edifices, it doesn't look like much from the outside. And certainly the interior doesn't have the newest furniture and paint. But it's clean, cheap, friendly, and close to the beach. You'll find a spot to store your surfboard or bike for free, and car parking is $1 per day. The big homelike kitchen is open for guest use, and might even be hiding some extra free food in its cupboards. Expect all the usual hostel-style amenities, a nice garden out back, free linens, laundry facilities, and a free Internet kiosk.

### $100-150
The four-room **Adobe on Green Street** (103 Green St., 831/469-9866, www.adobeongreen .com, $132–242) offers lovely bed-and-breakfast accommodations close to the heart of downtown Santa Cruz. The location, within walking distance of the Pacific Garden Mall, lets you soak in the unique local atmosphere to your heart's content. A unifying decorative scheme runs through all four guest rooms—a dark and minimalist Spanish

Mission style befitting Santa Cruz's history as a mission town. Each room has a queen bed, a private bathroom (most with tubs), a small TV with DVD player, and lots of other amenities that can make you comfortable even over a long stay. An expanded continental spread is set out in the dining room each morning 8–11 A.M. Expect yummy local pastries, organic and soy yogurts, and multicolored eggs laid by a neighbor's flock of chickens. In keeping with the Santa Cruz ethos, the Adobe runs on solar power.

### $150-250
For a room overlooking the ocean, stay at the **Sea & Sand Inn** (201 West Cliff Dr., 831/427-3400, www.santacruzmotels.com/ sea_and_sand.html, $189–229). In an unbeatable location on the ocean side of West Cliff at Bay Street, you'll be close enough to downtown and the Boardwalk to enjoy the action of Santa Cruz. But you'll also have a touch more quiet in a neighborhood that's starting to tend toward the residential. Every room in the house comes with an ocean view (hence the high price for what's really a pretty basic motel room), and suites with hot tubs and private patios make for a wonderful seaside vacation. Rooms and suites do have nicer than average decor with pretty furniture, private baths, and free Internet access.

Some travelers prefer to stay in the woods rather than downtown or out by the busy Boardwalk. **Redwood Croft Bed & Breakfast** (275 Northwest Dr., Bonny Doon, 831/458-1939, www.redwoodcroft.com, $145–230) is a funky two-room B&B, set back in the recently charred ruins of the forest to the northwest of Santa Cruz, formerly a beautiful redwood forest. The inn itself takes the woodsy theme indoors, using natural wood in the walls and furniture to create a serene retreat-house feeling. Each of the two guest rooms bursts with beautiful appointments, lovely stone bathrooms, and views out into the recovering woods.

### Over $250
Despite its bohemian reputation, there's plenty of

money flowing through Santa Cruz. For plush accommodations, consider staying at the **Pleasure Point Inn** (23665 E. Cliff Dr., 831/475-4657, www.pleasurepointinn.com, $275–325). This small, exclusive inn boasts a rooftop deck with a hot tub, an expansive common living room with views out over the ocean, and four luxurious guest rooms. Each room has wood floors, a gas fireplace, a private deck or patio, a private bathroom, and all sorts of posh amenities. Expect to find a TV, phone, and Internet access in your room. A continental breakfast is laid out each morning, giving you just the right start to the day. All rooms also boast views out over the ocean—the inn does indeed sit on *that* Pleasure Point, so you can sit and watch the surfers as you drink your morning coffee. Or if you prefer to be a part of the action, ask about setting up surfing lessons through the inn and Club Ed when you reserve your room.

## FOOD
## American
At **Cafe Cruz** (2621 41st Ave., Soquel, 831/476-3801, www.cafecruz.com, Mon.–Sat. 11:30 A.M.–2:30 P.M., daily 5:30 P.M.–close, $16–30), the menu runs toward homey American favorites done up with a California twist (ribs, rotisserie chicken, bowls of pasta, and crunchy fresh salads). Cafe Cruz purchases the freshest local produce, meats, seafood, and even drinks they can find. You can munch locally caught fish with goat cheese from Half Moon Bay and an organic soda from Monterey. The attractive white-tablecloth dining room welcomes casual and elegant diners alike, and if you choose wisely you can get an upscale meal for medium-scale prices.

## Asian
When locals who love their sushi get that craving for raw fish, they head for **Shogun Sushi** (1123 Pacific Ave., 831/469-4477, Mon.–Wed. 5–9 P.M., Thurs.–Fri. 5–10 P.M., Sat. 3–10 P.M.). Right on the Pacific Garden Mall, Shogun serves big fresh slabs of nigiri and an interesting collection of maki (rolls). The fish served here is some of the freshest you'll find in this seacoast city. Their meats and other dishes also please diners with fresh ingredients and tasty preparations. While service can be spotty, usually it's efficient—you'll get your order quickly and it will be right on. If you're not used to sushi prices, you may find Shogun expensive, but if you're a connoisseur you'll feel that they're quite reasonable. Do be aware that there's often a wait for a table in the evenings, especially on weekends.

## California
The Santa Cruz region boasts one serious upscale eatery. The **( Shadowbrook** (1750 Wharf Rd., Capitola, 800/975-1511, www.shadowbrook-capitola.com, Mon.–Fri. 5–8:45 P.M., Sat. 4:30–9:30 P.M., Sun. 4:30–8:45 P.M., $25) has long been worth driving over the hill for. The cliffside location, complete with the namesake brook flowing through the dining room, has perhaps the most impressive views and atmosphere of any restaurant in the area. The Shadowbrook makes for a perfect spot to stage the ultimate romantic date, complete with roses, candlelight, and fine chocolate desserts.

## French
In Aptos, **Cafe Sparrow** (8042 Soquel Dr., Aptos, 831/688-6238, www.cafesparrow .com, Mon.–Sat. 11:30 A.M.–2 P.M., Sun. 9:30 A.M.–2 P.M., daily 5:30 P.M.–close, $20) serves country French cuisine that's consistently tasty. Whatever you order, it will be fantastic. The seafood is noteworthy (especially the Friday night bouillabaisse), as are the steaks. Cafe Sparrow's kitchen prepares all the dishes with fresh ingredients, and the chef (who can sometimes be seen out in the dining room checking on customer satisfaction with the food) thinks up innovative preparations and creates tasty sauces. He's also willing to accommodate special requests and dietary restrictions with good cheer. The best deal for your money is the daily-changing prix-fixe menu. For dessert, treat yourself to the profiteroles, which can be created with either ice cream or pastry cream.

## South American

**Cafe Brasil** (1410 Mission St., 831/429-1855, www.cafebrasil.us, daily 8:00 A.M.–3:00 P.M., $10–20) serves up the Brazilian fare its name promises. Painted jungle green with bright yellow and blue trim, you can't miss this totally Santa Cruz breakfast and lunch joint. In the morning, the fare runs to omelets and ethnic specialties, while lunch includes pressed sandwiches, meat and tofu dishes, and Brazilian house specials. A juice bar provides rich but healthy meal accompaniments that can also act as light meals on their own. To try something different, get an acia bowl—acia is a South American fruit—or an Amazon cherry juice and OJ blend.

## Coffee and Bakeries

For a casual sandwich or pastry, head for **Kelly's French Bakery** (402 Ingalls St., 831/423-9059, www.kellysfrenchbakery.com, Mon.–Thurs. 7–11 A.M. and 11:30 A.M.–7 P.M., Fri. 7–11 A.M. and 11:30 A.M.–8 P.M., Sat.–Sun. 7 A.M.–11:30 A.M. and noon–7 P.M., $10). This popular bakery makes its home in an old industrial warehouse-style space, and its domed shape constructed out of corrugated metal looks like anything but a restaurant. It's got both indoor and outdoor seating, and serves full breakfasts and luncheon sandwiches. You can order to stay in or to go, and pick up a breakfast or sweet pastry, some bread, or a cake while you're there.

## INFORMATION AND SERVICES
### Tourist Information

While it can be fun to explore Santa Cruz just by using your innate sense of direction and the bizarre, those who want a bit more structure on their travels can hit the **Santa Cruz Visitors Center** (1211 Ocean Ave., 800/833-3494, www.santacruzca.org) for maps, advice, and information.

## Media and Communications

Santa Cruz publishes its own daily newspaper, the *Santa Cruz Sentinel* (www.santacruz sentinel.com). You'll get your daily dose of national wire service news and current events, local news, plus some good stuff for visitors. The *Sentinel* has a Food section, a Sunday Travel section, and plenty of up-to-date entertainment information.

You can get your mail on at the **post office** near the Mall on 850 Front Street (831/426-0144).

Santa Cruz is like totally wired, man. You'll definitely be able to access the Internet in a variety of cafés and hotels. There are Starbucks locations here, and the many indie cafés often compete with their own (sometimes free) Wi-Fi.

Santa Cruz has plenty of banks and ATMs (including some ATMs on the arcade at the Boardwalk). Bank branches congregate downtown near the Pacific Garden Mall. The West Side is mostly residential, so you'll find a few ATMs in supermarkets and gas stations, but little else.

## Medical Services

Despite its rep as a funky bohemian beach town, Santa Cruz's dense population dictates that it have at least one full-fledged hospital of its own. You can get medical treatment and care at **Dominican Hospital** (1555 Soquel Ave., 831/426-7700, www.dominicanhospital.org).

## GETTING THERE AND AROUND
### Car

If you're driving to Santa Cruz from Silicon Valley, you've got two choices of roads. Most drivers take fast, dangerous Highway 17. This narrow road doesn't have any switchbacks and is the main truck route "over the hill." Most locals take this 50-mile-per hour corridor fast—probably faster than they should. Each year, several people die in accidents on Highway 17, and I once crashed my vehicle into an overturned pickup truck on Big Moody curve. So if you're new to the road, keep to the right and take it slow, no matter what the traffic to the left of you is doing. Check traffic reports before you head out; Highway 17 is known to be one of the worst commuting roads in all of the

Bay Area, and the weekend beach traffic in the summer jams up fastin both directions too.

For a more leisurely drive, you can opt for two-lane Highway 9. The tight curves and endless switchbacks will keep you at a reasonable speed; use the turnouts to let the locals past, please. On Highway 9, your biggest obstacles tend to be groups of bicyclists and motorcyclists, both of whom adore the slopes and curves of this technical driving road. The good news is that you'll get an up-close-and-personal view of the gorgeously forested Santa Cruz Mountains, complete with views of the valley to the north and ocean vistas to the south.

## Parking

Visitors planning to drive or bike around Santa Cruz should get themselves a good map, either before they arrive or at the visitors center in town. Navigating the winding, occasionally broken-up streets of this oddly shaped town isn't for the faint of heart. Highway 1, which becomes Mission Street on the West Side, acts as the main artery through Santa Cruz and down to Capitola, Soquel, Aptos, and coastal points farther south. You'll find that Highway 1 at the interchange to Highway 17,

and sometimes several miles to the south, is a parking lot most of the time. No, you probably haven't come upon a major accident or a special event. It's just like that all the time, and will be until the construction widening the highway to deal with the heavy traffic is complete.

Parking in Santa Cruz can be its own special sort of horror. Downtown, head straight for the parking structures one block away from Pacific Avenue on either side. They're much easier to deal with than trying to find street parking. The same goes for the beach and Boardwalk areas. At the Boardwalk, just pay the fee to park in the big parking lot adjacent to the attractions. You'll save an hour and a possible car break-in or theft trying to find street parking in the sketchy neighborhoods that surround the Boardwalk.

## Bus

In town, the buses are run by the **Santa Cruz METRO** (831/425-8600 www.scmtd.com, adults $1.50/single ride, passes available). With 42 routes running in Santa Cruz County, you can probably find a way to get nearly anywhere you'd want to go on the METRO.

# Monterey

Monterey is the "big city" on the well-populated southern tip of the wide-mouthed Monterey Bay. The outlying agricultural towns of Sand City and Marina lie to the northeast (closer to the Bay Area), while sleepy residential Pacific Grove lies to the northeast closer to the big golf courses of Pebble Beach.

Neighboring Carmel-by-the-Sea caters to the wealthy, the artsy, and golf afficianados, while Monterey has a long history as a working class town. Originally inhabited by Native Americans, who fished the bay, Monterey became a fishing hub for the European settlers in the 19th century as well. (Author John Steinbeck immortalized the unglamorous fish-canning industry here in his novel *Cannery*

*Row.*) It wasn't until the 20th century that the city began to lean toward gentrification—the bay just off the shore became a wildlife preserve, the Monterey Bay Aquarium opened, and the tourist trade became a mainstay of the local economy. Today, Cannery Row resembles a giant shopping mall and the Aquarium is constantly packed with visitors.

## SIGHTS
### Cannery Row

Welcome to Monterey's own version of Tourist Hell. Cannery Row (Cannery Row, www.cannery row.com), sitting right on the water, did once look and feel as John Steinbeck described it in his famed novel of the same name. In days

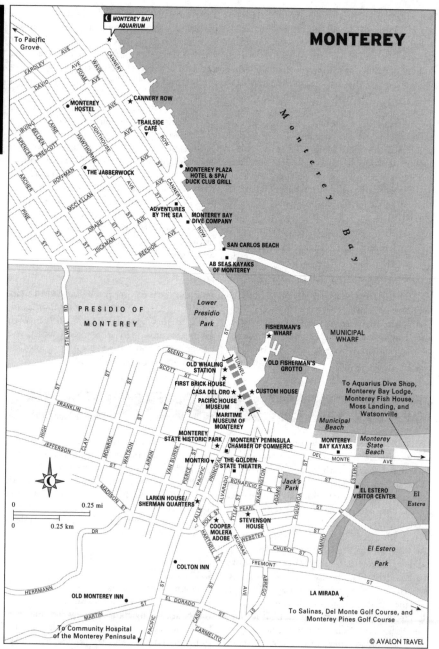

MONTEREY

Monterey Bay

To Pacific Grove

PRESIDIO OF MONTEREY

Lower Presidio Park

MUNICIPAL WHARF

To Aquarius Dive Shop, Monterey Bay Lodge, Monterey Fish House, Moss Landing, and Watsonville

Municipal Beach

Monterey State Beach

El Estero Park

To Salinas, Del Monte Golf Course, and Monterey Pines Golf Course

To Community Hospital of the Monterey Peninsula

© AVALON TRAVEL

gone by, it was easy for fishing boats to dock and offload their catches straight into the huge warehouse-like cannery buildings. Low-wage workers processed the fish and put it into cans, ready to ship across the country and around the world.

Today, what was once a workingman's wharf is now a conclave of high-end apartments, boutique hotels, big seafood restaurants, and cheesy souvenir stores. It's anchored at one end by the aquarium and runs for several blocks, which include a beach, then leads into the wharf area. All that's left of the historic Cannery Row are some of the exteriors of the buildings. Inside, history has given way to a wax museum, a Thomas Kincaide gallery, and kitsch by the yard. Kids have fun running from shop to shop, but adults may grow tired of the chain stores and tacky souvenir stalls after a while.

## ◖ Monterey Bay Aquarium

The first aquarium of its kind in the country, the Monterey Bay Aquarium (886 Cannery Row, 831/648-4800, www.mbayaq.org, daily 10 A.M.–6 P.M., adults $24.95, children $15.95) is still unique in many ways. From the very beginning, the aquarium's mission has been conservation, and they're not shy about it. They have taken custodianship of the Pacific coastline and waters in Monterey County down to Big Sur, and take an active role in the saving and conservation of at-risk wildlife in the area. Many of the animals in the aquarium's tanks were rescued, and those that survive may eventually be returned to the wild. All the exhibits you'll see in this mammoth complex contain only local sea life. If you fear that the tight focus might make the tanks dull, you needn't worry. The exhibits and shows put on by the residents of Monterey Bay delight children and adults alike.

The aquarium displays a dazzling array of species. When you come to visit, a good first step is to look up the feeding schedules for the tanks you're most interested in. The critters always put on the best show at feeding time, and it's smart to show up several minutes in advance of feeding to get a good spot near the glass.

The living, breathing **Kelp Forest** is just like the kelp beds outside the Bay proper—except this one is 28 feet tall. Try to time your visit for either the 11:30 A.M. or 4 P.M. feeding time, when the fish in the tank put on quite a show.

The deep-water tank in the **Outer Bay**

Kelp Forest at the Monterey Bay Aquarium

# STEINBECK

John Ernst Steinbeck was born in Salinas, California in 1902 and grew up in its tiny, isolated agricultural community. He somehow managed to escape life as a farmer, a sardine fisherman, or a fish canner, and ended up living the glamorous life of a writer for his too-short 66 years.

Steinbeck's experiences in the Salinas Valley farming community and in the fishing town of Monterey informed many of his novels. The best known of these is *Cannery Row*, but *Tortilla Flat* is also set in working-class Monterey (though no one knows exactly where the fictional "Tortilla Flat" neighborhood was supposed to be). The Pulitzer Prize-winning novel *The Grapes of Wrath* takes more of its inspiration from the Salinas Valley. Steinbeck used the Valley as a model for farming in the Dust Bowl – the wretched, impoverished era that was the Great Depression.

In fact, Steinbeck was fascinated by the plight of working men and women; his novels and stories generally depict ordinary folks going through tough and terrible times. Steinbeck lived and worked through the Great Depression – thus it's not surprising that many of his stories do *not* feature happy Hollywood endings. Steinbeck was a realist in almost all of his novels, portraying the good, the bad, and the ugly of human life and society. His work gained almost immediate respect – in addition to his Pulitzer, Steinbeck also won the Nobel Prize for Literature in 1962. Almost every American high school student from the 1950s onward has read at least one of Steinbeck's novels or short stories; his body of work forms part of the enduring American literary canon.

As California's most illustrious literary son in the 20th century, Salinas became equally famous for spawning the author and inspiring his work. You'll find a variety of Steinbeck maps online (www.mtycounty.com/pgs-mty-stnbeck/mty-steinbeck.html) that offer self-guided tours of the regions made famous by his various novels. Poor Steinbeck's name is taken in vain all over now-commercial Cannery Row – even the cheesy Wax Museum tries to draw customers in by claiming kinship with the legendary author. More serious scholars of Steinbeck prefer the **National Steinbeck Center** (1 Main St., 831/796-3833, www.steinbeck.org, Salinas, daily 10 A.M.-5 P.M., $10.95) and the **Steinbeck House** (132 Central Ave., Salinas, 831/424-2735, www.steinbeckhouse.com, summer tours 1-3 P.M.), both in the still-agricultural town of Salinas. And if the museums aren't enough, plan to be in Monterey County in early August for the annual **Steinbeck Festival** (www.steinbeck.org), a big shindig put on by the Steinbeck Center in order to celebrate the great man's life and works in fine style.

---

exhibit area always draws a crowd. Inside its depths, a monster bluefin tuna that's been an aquarium resident for many years rules the roost. Even the fierce hammerhead sharks and odd-looking enormous sunfish steer clear of the tuna and its brethren.

The **Wild About Otters** exhibit gives visitors an up-close and personal view of rescued otters. The adorable, furry marine mammals come right up to the glass to interact with curious children and enchanted adults. You can watch aquarists feed and train the otters daily at 10:30 A.M., 1:30 P.M., and 3:30 P.M.

In addition to the many exhibits, be sure to check out the life and times of local tidepools, surflines, and even the ecosystems that surround the pillars, cement blocks, chains, and trash of the Monterey piers.

It's easy to spend all day at the aquarium. If you get hungry, try for a table at the full-service restaurant and bar, complete with white tablecloths and a view of the bay. A self-service café offers sandwiches, salads, and ethnic dishes. You'll hardly be able to escape the souvenirs as a different gift shop sits in a corner of almost every exhibit hall.

If you possibly can, plan your visit to the Monterey Bay Aquarium on a weekday rather than a weekend. The aquarium is a wildly popular weekend destination. Especially in the summer, the crowds can be forbidding. Weekdays can be less crushing (though you'll run into school groups during much of the year), and the off-season is almost always a better time to visit. The aquarium has facilities for wheelchair access to almost all exhibits.

## Monterey State Historic Park

Monterey State Historic Park (20 Custom House Plaza, 831/649-7118, www.parks.ca.gov, daily 10 A.M.–5 P.M., free), usually called Old Monterey by locals, pays homage to the long and colorful history of the city of Monterey. This busy port town acted as the capital of California when it was under Spanish rule, and then later when the area became part of United States territory. Today, this park provides a peek into Monterey as it was in the middle of the 19th century—a busy place filled with dock workers, fishermen, bureaucrats, and soldiers. And yet it blends into the modern town of Monterey as well, and modern stores, galleries, and restaurants sit next to 150-year-old adobe structures. Free guided tours of several of the museums and adobes are offered most days; a walking tour of Old Monterey takes place at 10:30 A.M. on Monday–Wednesday and on Friday.

It's tough to see everything in just one visit to Old Monterey. If you only get to one spot on your first trip, make it the **Custom House** (Sat.–Thurs. 10 A.M.–4 P.M., Fri. 10:30 A.M.–4 P.M.). It's California State Historic Landmark Number 1, and the oldest bureaucratic building known to still stand in the state. You can spend some time wandering the adobe building, checking out the artifacts on display, or even just looking out the upstairs window towards the sea. Also on the plaza is the **Pacific House Museum** (Fri.–Wed. 10 A.M.–4 P.M., Thurs. 10:30 A.M.–4 P.M.) with exhibits of Native American artifacts.

There are 10 other buildings that comprise the park; most were built with adobe and/or brick between 1834 and 1847. These include: the **Casa del Oro;** the **Cooper-Molera**

**Adobe** (525 Polk St., guided tours Fri.–Wed. 3 P.M.); the **First Brick House;** the **Larkin House** (510 Calle Principal, guided tours Tues.–Wed. 11:30 A.M. and Sat.–Sun. noon); the **Old Whaling Station;** the **Pacific House;** the **Sherman Quarters;** and the **Stevenson House** (530 Houston St., guided tours Mon. and Fri. 2 P.M. and Sat.–Sun. 10:30 A.M.), the former residence of Robert Louis Stevenson.

Famous artists, writers, and military men have stayed in some of these spots, most of which have long histories playing several different roles. Look down as you walk to see if you're stepping on antique whalebone sidewalks. And be sure to take a few minutes to admire the many beautiful gardens surrounding the adobes, which are lovingly maintained by local groups.

## Maritime Museum of Monterey

Part of Old Monterey, the Stanton Center includes the Maritime Museum of Monterey (5 Custom House Plaza, 831/372-2608, www.montereyhistory.org, Tues.–Sun. 10 A.M.–5 P.M.). The large modern facilities provide plenty of space for the art and historical artifacts collected over the decades, most of which pertain directly to the area's history, maritime or otherwise. In the Maritime Museum, explore the history of the native Rumisen and Ohlone people, going through the Spanish exploration and conquistador era, and on in to the American military and fishing presence on the Central Coast. The original Fresnel lens from the Point Sur light station sits in here, as does an array of sardine fishing equipment.

## ENTERTAINMENT AND EVENTS
### Live Music

Classical music aficionados will appreciate the dulcet tones of the musicians who perform for **Chamber Music Monterey Bay** (831/625-2212, www.chambermusicmonterey bay.org). This society brings talented ensembles and soloists in from around the world to perform on the lovely Central Coast. One night you might find a local string quartet, and on another night you'll get to see and hear a chamber ensemble. (String quartets definitely rule the small stage and intimate theater.) Far from banning young music fans from the **Sunset Cultural Center** (San Carlos St. btwn. 8th and 10th Sts., Carmel), Chamber Music Monterey Bay reserves up-front seats at all its shows for children and their adult companions.

One of the coolest small-rock venues in California is the **The Golden State Theater** (417 Alvarado St., 831/372-3800, www.golden statetheatre.com) in Monterey. This beautiful theater is done up in 1920s era Arabian Nights–style Middle Eastern revival. It's easy to get to, sitting right downtown near the big Hyatt hotel. Get there early so you can spend some time admiring the decor before the lights lower and the show starts. The Golden State hosts acts that often play larger venues, which means that show goers get a reasonably intimate experience in which they can actually *see* their favorite performers. A few performances in 2008 included Los Lonely Boys, the Doobie Brothers, comedienne Paula Poundstone, and a special engagement of the Sally Struthers musical *Nunsense.*

## Festivals and Events

The Monterey region hosts numerous festivals and special events each year. Whether your pleasure is fine food or funky music, you'll probably be able to plan a trip around some sort of multi-day festival with dozens of events and performances scheduled during Monterey's busy year.

In keeping with the Central Coast's obsession with food and wine, the annual **Monterey Wine Festival** (800/422-0251, www.montereywine .com, mid-Oct.) celebrates wine with a generous helping of food on the side. A number of tasting events mark this weekish-long festival, including a major day event at the fairgrounds and possibly a swanky nighttime soiree at the Monterey Bay Aquarium. You can also expect a few private events and parties at participating wineries and restaurants. Check the website for this year's venues, ticket prices, and event dates and times. This festival offers the perfect opportunity to introduce yourself to Monterey

and Carmel wineries, many of which have not yet hit the "big time" in major wine magazines. The Wine Festival is just one of many similar events held each year in the region, so if you can't make it you'll have plenty of other opportunities to enjoy all the best edibles and drinkables the Central Coast has to offer.

One of the biggest music festivals in California is the **Monterey Jazz Festival** (2000 Fairground Rd., Monterey, 831/373-3366, www.montereyjazzfestival.org). As the site of the longest-running jazz festival on earth, Monterey attracts the top performers from around the world. Held each September—a month that offers the best chance for beautiful weather on the Monterey Bay—this long weekend of amazing music can leave you happy for the whole year. The event is held at the Monterey County Fairgrounds, which lets visitors enjoy all the different concerts without having to drive from venue to venue. Nine stages put up acts day and night, making it easy to either find your favorite stage and settle in for a long stay and multiple musicians, or wander the length and breadth of the fairgrounds to sample the acts at each unique venue. Camping is not permitted at the fairgrounds, but you can camp nearby, or get a room in one of the Monterey lodgings that partner with the festival to provide reasonably priced lodgings for attendees.

## SPORTS AND RECREATION

The Monterey Bay is the premier Northern California locale for a number of water sports, especially scuba diving.

### Scuba

Any native Northern Californian knows that there's only one really great place in the region to get certified in scuba diving—the Monterey Bay. Even if you go to a dive school up in the Bay Area, they'll take you down to Monterey for your open-water dive. Accordingly, dozens of dive schools cluster in and around the town of Monterey (check Carmel and Santa Cruz as well, if you prefer).

The **Monterey Bay Dive Company** (225 Cannery Row, 831/656-0454, www.mbdcscuba

.com) sits right in the midst of Cannery Row, where all visitors to Monterey eventually end up. You can take dive classes year-round, get certified, rent equipment, fill your own tanks, and even take a quick dive right off San Carlos Beach just behind the dive shop. Monterey Bay Dive Company also maintains its own dive boat, offering both boat and shore guided dive tours of the famous Monterey Bay undersea world.

Another of your many dive shop options is the **Aquarius Dive Shop** (2040 Del Monte Ave., 831/375-1933, www.aquariusdivers .com). Aquarius offers everything you need to go diving out in Monterey Bay, including air and nitrox fills, equipment rental, certification courses, and help booking a trip on a local dive boat. Aquarius works with four boats to create great trips for divers of all interests and ability levels. Call or check the website for current local dive conditions as well.

## Kayaking

With all the focus on sustainable tourism in Monterey, coupled with the lovely recreation area formed by Monterey Bay, it's no wonder that sea kayaking is popular here. Whether you want to try paddling your first kayak, or you're an expert who hasn't brought your own gear out to California, you'll find a local outfit ready and willing to hook you up.

**Adventures by the Sea** (299 Cannery Row, 831/372-1807, www.adventuresbythesea .com, 9 A.M.–sunset, tours $50/person, rentals $30/day) rents kayaks for whole days to let you choose your own route in and around the magnificent Monterey Bay kelp forest. If you're not confident enough to go off on your own, Adventures offers tours from Cannery Row. Your guide can tell you all about the wildlife you're seeing: harbor seals, sea otters, pelicans, seagulls, and maybe even a whale in the wintertime! The tour lasts about 2.5 hours, cost $50 per person, and the available tandem sit-on-top kayaks make it a great experience for school-age children. Adventures by the Sea also runs a tour of Stillwater Cove at Pebble Beach. Reservations are recommended for all tours, but during the summer the Cannery Row tour leaves regularly

at 10 A.M. and 2 P.M., so you can stop by on a whim and see if there's a spot available.

**Monterey Bay Kayaks** (693 Del Monte Ave., 831/373-5357, www.montereybay kayaks.com, tours $50–60/person) specializes in tours of both central Monterey and up north in Elkhorn Slough. You can choose between open-deck and closed-deck tour groups, beginning tours perfect for kids, romantic sunset or full moon paddles, or even long paddles designed for more experienced sea kayakers. Most tours cost $50–60 per person; check the website for specific tour prices, times, and reservation information. If you prefer to rent a kayak and explore the bay or slough on your own, Monterey Bay Kayaks can help you out there too. If you really get into it, you can also sign up for closed-deck sea kayaking classes to learn about safety, rescue techniques, tides, currents, and paddling techniques.

A third company, **AB Seas Kayaks of Monterey** (32 Cannery Row, #5, 831/647-0147, www.montereykayak.com, tours $60/person, rentals $30/day), also has plenty of sit-on-top sea kayaks for rent—choose a single or double kayak as you need. Or take a tour of Monterey Bay with an experienced guide.

## Fishing and Whale-Watching

Whales pass quite near the shores of Monterey year-round. While you can sometimes even see them from the beaches, any number of boats can take you out for a closer look at the great beasts as they travel along their own special routes north and south. The area hosts many humpbacks, blue whales, and gray whales, plus the occasional killer whale, Minke whale, fin whale, and pod of dolphins. Bring your own binoculars for a better view, but the experienced boat captains will do all they can to get you as close as possible to the whales and dolphins. Most tours last 2–3 hours and leave from Fisherman's Wharf, which is easy to get to and has ample parking. If you prefer not to rise with the sun, pick a tour that leaves in the afternoon.

**Monterey Bay Whale Watch** (84 Fisherman's Wharf, 831/375-4658, www.montereybay whalewatch.com) leaves right from an easy-to-find red building on Fisherman's Wharf and runs tours in every season. (Call or check the website for schedules.) You must make a reservation in advance, even for regularly scheduled tours. Afternoon tours are available. **Monterey Whale Watching** (96 Fisherman's Wharf, 800/979-3370, www.baywatchcruises .com) prides itself on its knowledgeable guides/ marine biologists and its comfortable, spacious cruising vessels. The *Princess Monterey* offers morning and afternoon tours, and you can buy tickets online or by phone.

If you'd rather catch fish than watch mammals, **Randy's Fishing Trips** (800/979-3370, www.randysfishingtrips.com) can take you out for salmon, halibut, albacore, mackerel, rock cod, flatfish, and even squid and Dungeness crab in season. They can also take you out for a whale-watching trip if that's your preference. Trips begin early in the morning and can last for several hours. You can bring your own food—catering is not provided—including a small cooler for your drinks. If you don't have a California fishing license, you can purchase a one-day license at the shop before your trip. While you can try to walk up to the bright teal-painted shop at Fisherman's Wharf, it's best to get tickets for your trip in advance; either call or buy online from Randy's website.

**Chris's Fishing Trips** (48 Fisherman's Wharf, 831/372-0577, www.chrissfishing.com, $55–90/per person) offers both scheduled trips and boats for charter. If you want to go solo, get on one of the daily salmon or cod trips, which include bait and ice; tackle, a one-day license, and fish cleaning are extras.

### Bird-Watching

Some of the best birding in the state can be had at **Elkhorn Slough** (1700 Elkhorn Rd., Watsonville, 831/728-2822, www.elkhorn slough.org, Wed.–Sun. 9 A.M.–5 P.M., free), a few miles north of Monterey proper in Moss Landing. This large waterway/wetland area is incongruously marked by the mammoth smokestacks of the Moss Landing power plant. While you can access the wetlands and bird habitats from Highway 1 in Moss Landing, to

get to the visitors center you must drive several miles into the agricultural backcountry. But once you're there, knowledgeable and dedicated rangers can provide you with all the information you need to spot your favorite birds, plus find a few you've never seen before.

### Golf

Yes, you can play golf in middle-class Monterey! And it's often much cheaper to play here than to head for the hallowed courses of Carmel.

The public **Monterey Pines Golf Course** (1250 Garden Rd., 831/656-2167, $25–38, cart $20) offers 18 holes for a comparatively tiny green fee. It's a short par-69 course that's got four levels of tee to make the game fun for players of all levels. Monterey Pines was originally built as a private Navy course for the pleasure of the officers at the major naval installation north of town. Today, it is open to all who want to play. Call ahead for tee times.

A bit more pricy but still not Poppy Hills or Pebble Beach, **Del Monte Golf Course** (1300 Sylvan Rd., 831/373-2700, www.pebblebeach .com, $34–95, cart $20) is part of that legendary set of courses. This historic 18-hole, par-72 course, along with two other courses, still plays host to the Pebble Beach Invitational each year. You won't get the ocean views of Pebble Beach, but you will be treated to lovely green mountains surrounding the course as you play through. The property includes a full-service pro shop and the Del Monte Bar & Grill. You can check available tee times online, then call 800/877-0597 to book your preferred time.

### Motor Sports

If you're feeling the need for speed, you can get lots of it at the **Mazda Raceway Laguna Seca** (1021 Monterey-Salinas Hwy., 831/242-8201, www.laguna-seca.com), one of the country's premier road-racing venues. Here you can see historic auto races, superbikes, speed festivals, and an array of Grand Prix events. The major racing season runs May–October of most years. In addition to the big events, Laguna Seca hosts innumerable auto clubs and small sports car and stock car races. If you've always wanted to learn to drive or ride racecar-style, check the schedule to see if one of the track classes is happening during your visit. These often happen in the middle of the week, and are a near daily event in the off-season.

Be sure to check the website for parking directions specific to the event you plan to attend—this is a big facility. You can camp here, and certainly you'll find plenty of concessions during big races.

## ACCOMMODATIONS
### Under $100
The **Monterey Hostel** (778 Hawthorne St., 831/649-0375, http://montereyhostel.com, $28/bunk, $62/private room) offers inexpensive accommodations within walking distance of the major attractions of Monterey. Frankly, when it comes to rooms and amenities, this isn't the best hostel in California. You must pay extra to rent a locker, there's no laundry facility on-site, and the dorm rooms can be pretty crowded. On the other hand, the hostel puts on a free pancake breakfast every morning, linens are included with your bed, and there are comfy, casual common spaces with couches and musical instruments. And then there's that location…. You can walk to the aquarium and Cannery Row, stroll the Monterey Bay Coastal Trail, or drive over to Carmel to see a different set of sights.

### $100-150
A cute, small, budget motel, the **Monterey Bay Lodge** (55 Camino Aguajito, 831/372-8057, www.montereybaylodge.com, $134) brings a bit of the Côte d'Azur to the equally beautiful coastal town of Monterey. With small rooms decorated in classic yellows and blues, a sparkling pool with a fountain in the shallow end, and an on-site restaurant serving breakfast and lunch, the Lodge makes a perfect base for budget-minded families traveling in the Monterey region.

### $150-250
The **Colton Inn** (707 Pacific St, 831/649-6500, www.coltoninn.com, $165) offers a touch of class above that of a standard beach-town motel. Located in the midst of downtown Monterey, the queen and king bedrooms boast attractive fabrics, designer bathrooms, and pretty appointments. While you'll find restaurants and historic adobe buildings adjacent to the Colton, expect to drive or take public transit to Cannery Row and the Aquarium.

Be sure to call in advance to get a room at ◖ **The Jabberwock** (598 Laine St, 831/372-4777, www.jabberwockinn.com, $215), a favorite with frequent visitors to Monterey. This Alice in Wonderland—themed B&B is both whimsical and elegant; expect to find a copy of the namesake novel in your tastefully appointed guest room. Be sure to take the owners up on their daily wine and cheese reception in the afternoon-they are gold mines of information about the area, and will be happy to recommend restaurants and activities for all tastes. Though located up a steep hill, the Jabberwock is within walking distance of Cannery Row and all its adjacent attractions (it's worth the extra exercise to avoid the cost or hassle of parking in the tourist lots).

### Over $250
Monterey visitors looking for elegant accommodations love the **Old Monterey Inn** (500 Martin St., 831/375-8284, www.oldmonterey inn.com, $275–400). The lovely old edifice stands in the midst of mature gardens that blossom all spring and summer, showing their sedate green side in autumn and winter. Inside the inn, the garden motif echoes in the upscale bed linens and window treatments, which compliment the pretty furnishings and cozy fireplaces. Spa bathtubs pamper guests. Additional amenities include a full breakfast (often served in the garden) and a menu of spa treatments that can be enjoyed downstairs in the serene treatment room.

Want to stay right on Cannery Row in a room overlooking the bay? You'll pay handsomely—but it's worth it—at the **Monterey Plaza Hotel & Spa** (400 Cannery Row, 831/646-1700, www.montereyplazahotel.com, $388). This on-the-water luxury hotel has it all: two restaurants, a spa, a private beach, room service, and upscale guest room goodies. Rooms range from "budget" garden and Row-facing accommodations to ocean-view rooms with private balconies and huge suites that mimic a posh private apartment. Bring your credit card and enjoy!

## FOOD

The organic and sustainable food movements have caught hold on the Central Coast. The Monterey Bay Seafood Watch program (www .montereybayaquarium.org) is the definitive resource for sustainable seafood, while the Salinas Valley inland hosts a number of organic farms.

### American

For coffee, espresso, and homebaked beignets, head to the **Trailside Café** (550 Wave St, 831/649-8600, www.trailsidecafe.com, daily 8 A.M.–4 P.M., $10–15). This Cannery Row restaurant offers breakfast, lunch, and dinner on a heated patio overlooking the bay.

For more views and exemplary American cuisine, stop by the **Duck Club Grill** (400 Cannery Row, 831/646-1706, www.montereyplazahotel .com, daily 6:30–11 A.M. and 5:30–9:30 P.M., $30) in the Monterey Plaza Hotel. Steaks, lamb chops, and the namesake duck are what's on order here and the extensive wine list offers many complements. **Montrio** (414 Calle Principal, 831/648-8880, www.montrio.com, $15–20) is another entry in elegantly casual Monterey dining. The crab cakes are legendary.

### Seafood

The **Old Fisherman's Grotto** (39 Fisherman's Wharf, 831/375-4604, daily 11 A.M.–10 P.M., $) is a relaible wharf staple for both seafood and views over Monterey Bay. The menu focuses on fresh seafood and Italian standards and the restaurant includes a full bar. If you're craving fresh seafood but want to esacpe the touristy wharf, head to the **Monterey Fish House** (2114 Del Monte Ave., 831/373-4647, daily 11:30 A.M.–2:30 P.M. and 5–9:30 P.M., $15–25) where the local go for cioppino and

grilled oysters. The tiny dining room ensures its social atmosphere.

### Markets

The **Monterey Bay Farmers Market** (980 Fremont St., www.montereybayfarmers.org, Thurs. 2:30–6:30 P.M.) showcases almost 50 farmers and vendors selling fresh produce, flowers, plants every Thursday afternoon.

## INFORMATION AND SERVICES

In Monterey, the **El Estero Visitors Center** (401 Camino El Estero, www.montereyinfo .org) is the local outlet of the Monterey Country Convention & Visitors Bureau. The **Monterey Peninsula Chamber of Commerce** (380 Alvarado St., 831/648-5360) can also provide helpful information.

The local newspaper is the **Monterey County Herald** (www.montereyherald.com). Monterey has two convenient **post offices:** one at 565 Hartnell St. and another at 686 Lighthouse Ave.

For medical needs, the **Community Hospital of the Monterey Peninsula** (CHOMP, 23625 Holman Hwy., 831/624-5311) provides emergency services to the area.

## GETTING THERE AND AROUND

Most visitors drive into Monterey via the scenic Highway 1. Inland, U.S. 101 allows access into Salinas from the north and south. From Salinas, Highway 68 travels west into Monterey.

For a more leisurely ride, **Amtrak's** Coast Starlight train (Station Pl. and Railroad Ave., Salinas, daily 8 A.M.–10 P.M.) travels through Salinas daily. For Amtrak travelers, there is free bus service to downtown Monterey (30 min.); for everyone else, the **Greyhound** bus station (19 W. Gabilan, Salinas, 831/424-4418, www .greyhound.com, daily 5 A.M.–11:30 P.M.) offers service into Monterey.

Once in Monterey, take advantage of the free **WAVE** bus (9 A.M.–7:30 P.M.) which loops between downtown Monterey and the Aquarium.

# Carmel

Carmel's landscape is divided into two distinct parts. The adorable village of Carmel-by-the-Sea perches on the cliffs above the Pacific, surrounded to the north and the south by golf courses and beach parks. Carmel-by-the-Sea boasts the highest number of art galleries per capita in the United States. When most Californians talk about Carmel, they mean Carmel-by-the-Sea. The streets are perfect for strolling, and if ever there was a town that feels comfortable and safe for a woman traveling alone, it's Carmel.

Inland, the far less-traveled Carmel Valley has its share of huge estates owned by some of the wealthiest folks in the state. The narrow valley, surrounded by verdant hillsides, has recently discovered its footing as a niche wine region. Visitors can also play a few holes at the inevitable golf courses and check out the tiny hamlets that line the lone main road through the valley.

Both Carmel by-the-Sea and Carmel Valley residents love dogs. Your pooch is welcome at many establishments, and a number of stores and restaurants offer doggie treats and keep fresh water outside for the canine set.

## SIGHTS
### ◖ 17-Mile Drive

If you're a first-time visitor to the Carmel and Monterey area, 17-Mile Drive ($9/vehicle) can introduce you to some of the most beautiful and representative land and seascapes on the Central Coast. But don't get too excited yet—long ago, the locally all-powerful Pebble Beach Corporation realized what a precious commodity they held in this road, and began charging a toll. The good news is that when you pay your fee at the gatehouse, you'll get a map of the drive that describes the parks and sights that you will pass as you make your way along the winding coastal road. These include the much-photographed Lone Cypress, the beaches of Spanish Bay, and Pebble Beach's golf course,

© LIZ HAMILL SCOTT

the view along 17-Mile Drive

CENTRAL COAST

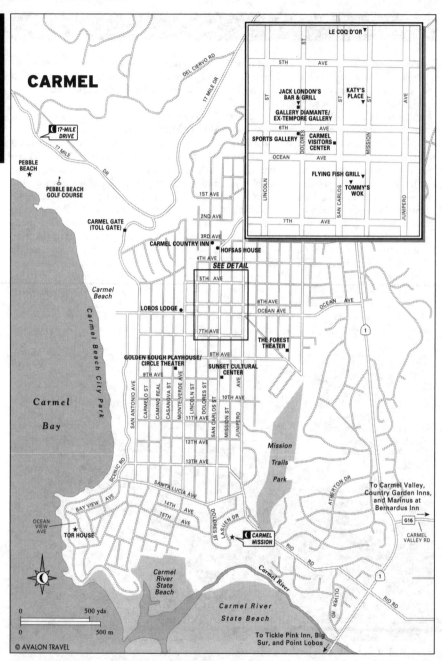

**CARMEL**

LE COQ D'OR
JACK LONDON'S BAR & GRILL
GALLERY DIAMANTE/ EX-TEMPORE GALLERY
KATY'S PLACE
SPORTS GALLERY
CARMEL VISITORS CENTER
FLYING FISH GRILL
TOMMY'S WOK

5TH AVE
6TH AVE
OCEAN AVE
7TH AVE

ST
DOLORES
LINCOLN
SAN CARLOS
MISSION
JUNIPERO

17-MILE DRIVE

DEL CIERVO RD
17-MILE DR

17 MILE DR

PEBBLE BEACH
PEBBLE BEACH GOLF COURSE

1ST AVE

CARMEL GATE (TOLL GATE)

2ND AVE
3RD AVE

CARMEL COUNTRY INN
HOFSAS HOUSE

4TH AVE

**SEE DETAIL**

5TH AVE

*Carmel Beach*

6TH AVE
OCEAN AVE

LOBOS LODGE

7TH AVE

OCEAN AVE

8TH AVE

THE FOREST THEATER

GOLDEN BOUGH PLAYHOUSE/ CIRCLE THEATER

SUNSET CULTURAL CENTER

9TH AVE

SAN ANTONIO AVE
CARMELO ST
CAMINO REAL
CASANOVA ST
MONTE VERDE ST
LINCOLN ST
DOLORES ST
SAN CARLOS ST
MISSION ST
JUNIPERO

10TH AVE
11TH AVE
12TH AVE
13TH AVE

*Carmel Bay*

*Carmel Beach City Park*

SCENIC RD

*Mission Trails Park*

SANTA LUCIA AVE

BAY VIEW AVE

14TH AVE
15TH AVE

ATHERTON DR

To Carmel Valley, Country Garden Inns, and Marinus at Bernardus Inn

G16
CARMEL VALLEY RD

OCEAN VIEW AVE

TOR HOUSE

DOLORES ST
LAS SS DR

CARMEL MISSION

RIO RD

*Carmel River State Beach*

*Carmel River*

RIO RD
OLIVER RD

*Carmel River State Beach*

To Tickle Pink Inn, Big Sur, and Point Lobos

0        500 yds
0        500 m

© AVALON TRAVEL

resort, and housing complex. There are plenty of turnouts where you can stop to take photos of the stunning ocean and the iconic cypress trees. You can picnic at many of the formal beaches, most of which have basic restroom facilities and ample parking lots. The only food and gas to be had are at the Inn at Spanish Bay and the Lodge at Pebble Beach. If you're in a great hurry, you can get from one end of the 17-Mile Drive to the other in 20 minutes—but that would defeat the main purpose of taking 17-Mile Drive, which is to go slowly and stop often to enjoy the beauty of the area.

## ◖ Carmel Mission

The Carmel Mission (3080 Rio Rd., 831/624-1271, www.carmelmission.org, Mon.–Sat. 9:30 A.M.–5 P.M., Sun. 10:30 A.M.–5 P.M., adults $5, children $1), formally called the San Carlos Borromeo de Carmelo Mission, was Father Junipero Serra's personal favorite among his California mission churches. He lived, worked, and eventually died here, and visitors today can see a replica of his cell. A working Catholic parish remains part of the complex, so please be respectful when taking the self-guided tour. The rambling buildings and courtyard gardens show some wear, but enough restoration work has gone into the church and living quarters to make them attractive and eminently visitable. The Carmel Mission has a small memorial museum in a building off the second courtyard, but don't make the mistake of thinking that this small and outdated space is the only historical display. In fact, the "museum" runs through many of the buildings, showing a small slice of the lives of the 18th- and 19th-century friars. The highlight of the complex is the church with its gilded altar front, its shrine to the Virgin Mary, the grave of Father Serra, and ancillary chapel dedicated to the memory of Father Serra. Round out your visit by walking out into the gardens to admire the flowers and fountains and to read the grave markers in the small cemetery.

## Tor House

Local poet Robinson Jeffers built this rugged-looking castle on the Carmel coast in 1919. He named it Tor House (26304 Ocean View

© LIZ HAMILL SCOTT

**Carmel Mission**

Ave., 831/624-1813, www.torhouse.org, tours Fri.–Sat. 10 A.M.–3 P.M., $7), after its rocky setting, and added the majestic Hawk Tower a year later. The granite stone structure exists today as an example of the Carmel ethos that Jeffers embodied and as a monument to his work and poetry.

## Earthbound Farms

One of the largest purveyors of organic produce in the United States, Earthbound Farms (7250 Carmel Valley Rd., 831/625-6219, www.ebfarm.com, Mon.–Sat. 8 A.M.–6 P.M., Sun. 10 A.M.–5 P.M.) offers visitors easy access to its smallish facility in the Carmel Valley. Drive up to the farm stand and browse a variety of organic fruits, veggies, and flowers. Outdoors, you can ramble into the fields, checking out the chamomile labyrinth and the kids' garden (yes, your kids can look *and* touch). Select and harvest your own fresh herbs from the cut-your-own garden, or leave the cooking to the experts and purchase delicious prepared organic dishes at the farm stand. If you're interested in a more in-depth guided tour of the farm, check the website for a schedule of walks, which will take you, a group, and an expert guide—perhaps a chef or local famous foodie—out into the fields for a look at what's growing and how to use it.

## Pebble Beach

While the legends of Pebble Beach (Palmero Way, www.pebblebeach.com) surround its championship golf course, there's a lot more to it than just greens and sand traps. A gated community surrounding the course and spreading back towards the trees encompasses some of the most expensive homes in California. From 17-Mile Drive, turn off onto the lengthy driveway to visit the ultra high-end resort. Any visitor can park and walk into the main lobby of the hotel area. Most tourists walk right through and out onto the immense multi-level patio area to take in the priceless and oft-photographed views. Whether you stay on the flagstones and enjoy a drink from the lobby bar or take a walk out onto the wide lawns, your eyes will be caught by the dramatic cliffs plummeting down to the small blue-gray bay. The golf

Pebble Beach

© LIZ HAMILL SCOTT

course draws right up to the lawns, allowing even the poorly heeled to check out a couple of the hallowed greens and fairways dotted with cypress trees. The lodge itself is worth touring, too; you can take footpaths to see the outsides of the posh accommodations, walk in to the lobby of the exclusive spa, and peer at the tables of the gourmet dining room.

## WINERIES

Its tiny size necessarily limits the number of vineyards and wineries that can set up shop in the Carmel Valley. But this small, charming wine region makes for a perfect wine-tasting day trip from Carmel, Monterey, or even Big Sur. Small crowds, light traffic, and meaningful tasting experiences categorize this area, which still has many family-owned wineries. You'll get personal attention and delicious wines, all in a gorgeous green setting.

The **Bernardus Winery** (5 W. Carmel Valley Rd., 800/223-2533, www.bernardus.com/winery, daily 11 A.M.–5 P.M., $5–10) sits on a vineyard estate that also hosts a connected luxurious lodge and gourmet restaurant. Bernardus creates a small list of wines. The grapes growing all around you go into the pride of the winery: the Bordeaux-style blended red Marinus Vineyard wine. Other varietals (Chardonnay, Pinot Noir, and Sauvignon Blanc) come from cool coastal vineyards. If you're interested and lucky, you might also get to sip some small-batch vintages of single-vineyard wines that are available only in the tasting room.

The biggest name in the Carmel Valley is **Chateau Julien** (8940 Carmel Valley Rd., 831/624-2600, www.chateaujulien.com, Mon.–Fri. 8 A.M.–5 P.M., Sat.–Sun. 11 A.M.–5 P.M.). The European-styled white estate building with the round turret is visible from the road. The light, airy tasting room is crowded with barrels, wine cases, souvenirs, and tasting glasses. When you enter, you'll be offered sips from the wide selection of Chardonnays, Cabernets, Syrahs, Merlots, and more. If you're lucky, you might find yourself tasting a rare Reserve blended red or a 10-year-old port. For a treat, call ahead and reserve a spot on the

twice-daily complimentary vineyard and winery tours. These tours conclude with a special tasting outside on the flagstone patio when weather permits.

On the other end of the spectrum, tiny **Parsonage Village Vineyard** (19 E. Carmel Valley Rd., 831/659-7322, www.parsonage wine.com, Fri.–Mon. 11 A.M.–5 P.M., $5) often doesn't make it onto Carmel Valley wine maps—which is a shame, because some of the best Syrah coming out of California (arguably) comes from this unpretentious little winery with only a nine-acre estate vineyard to work with. The tasting room sits in a tiny strip of shops, the space glowing with light that bounces off the copper of the bar. On the walls, you'll find an array of quilts made by Mary Ellen Parsons herself. At the bar, you'll taste wonderful Syrahs, hearty Cabernet Sauvignons, and surprisingly deep and complex blends—the Snosrap (that's Parsons spelled backwards) table wine is inexpensive for the region and incredibly tasty. If you find a vintage you love at Parsonage, buy it then and there since they sell out of many of their wines every year.

## ENTERTAINMENT AND EVENTS

The events and entertainment in Carmel tend to center around either art or food. This town loves its haute culture, so you won't find too many sports bars or generic movie theaters here. Instead, enjoy classical music, a wealth of live theater, and a glass of wine in the mild evenings.

### Bars and Clubs

The population of Carmel tends toward wealthy seniors. Hence, the nightlife isn't too hopping here, and live music in bars in Carmel was illegal until 2006—seriously. Most of the drinking tends toward restaurants and the occasional hotel lounge. If you're looking for an evening out within Carmel city limits, try a night at the theater.

If you simply must go out for a drink, try **Jack London's Bar & Grill** (Dolores St. and Fifth Ave., 831/624-2336, www.jacklondons

.com). All dark wood, fancy ceiling, and quiet elegance, it's no surprise that Jack London's has a full menu of fancier-than- average bar food and a wine list that would do a high-end restaurant proud. But it's also got big-screen TVs tuned to the games of the day and live blues each Friday. If you've brought your favorite canine companion, you'll find a welcoming seat outside on the patio, where the full menu is served.

## Theater

Despite its small size, Carmel has nearly a dozen live theater groups. In a town that defines itself by its love of art, theater arts don't get left out. Don't hesitate to ask the locals what's playing where when you're in town. The **Pacific Repertory Theater** (831/622-0100, www.pacrep.org, adults $16–38, students $10–20, children $7) is the only professional theater company on the Monterey-Carmel Peninsula. Its shows go up all over the region, most often in the **Golden Bough Playhouse** (Monte Verde St. and Eighth Ave.) the company's home theater. Other regular venues include the **The Forest Theater** (Mountain View St. and Santa Rita St.), and the **Circle Theater** (Casanova St. btwn. Eighth and Ninth Aves.) within the Golden Bough complex. Also look for their plays in the Monterey State Historic Park and in Pebble Beach. The company puts up dramas, comedies, and musicals both new and classic. You might see a work of Shakespeare or John Patrick Shanley's *Doubt,* enjoy your favorite songs from *The Fantasticks,* or sing along to the newer tunes of *High School Musical.* Check the website for upcoming shows, and buy tickets online or over the phone to guarantee you'll get seats while you're in town.

Each fall, PacRep puts up the **Carmel Shakespeare Festival** (www.pacrep.org), a short showing of Shakespeare that's good enough to draw the notice of Bay Area theater snobs. Check the website for information on this year's shows and the venues.

## Festivals and Events

In a town famed for art galleries, one of the biggest events of the year is the **Carmel Art Festival** (Mission St., Carmel-by-the-Sea, www.carmelartfestival.org, May). This four-day event celebrates visual arts in all media with shows by internationally acclaimed artists at galleries, parks, and other venues all across town. This wonderful festival also sponsors here-and-now contests, including the prestigious Plein Air (outdoor painting). Visitors get a rare opportunity to witness the artists outdoors, engaging in their creative process as they use the Carmel scenery for inspiration. Round out your festival experience by bidding on paintings at the end-of-event auction. You can get a genuine bargain on original artwork while supporting both the artists and the Festival. Perhaps best of all, the Carmel Art Festival is a great place to bring your family—a wealth of children's activities help even the youngest festival goers become budding artists.

For a more classical experience, one of the most prestigious festivals in Northern California is the **Carmel Bach Festival** (www.bachfestival.org). For three weeks each July and August, Carmel-by-the-Sea and its surrounding towns host dozens of classical concerts. Naturally the works of J. S. Bach are featured, but you can also hear renditions of Mozart, Vivaldi, Handel, and other heavyweights of Bach's era. Choose between big concerts in major venues or intimate performances in smaller spaces with only a small audience between you and the beautiful music. Concerts and recitals take place literally every day of the week—budget-conscious music lovers can just as easily enjoy the Festival in the middle of the week as on the weekends.

## SHOPPING

Downtown Carmel-by-the-Sea is a great place to get out of your car and stroll the streets, peering in the windows of the boutiques and countless galleries.

Carmel boasts more art galleries per capita than any other town in the United States. Accordingly, shopping in the downtown pedestrian area means "checking out the galleries." **Gallery Diamante** (Dolores St. betw. 5th and 6th, 831/624-0852, www.gallerydiamante .com) represents a typical Carmel Gallery, with a large collection of landscape paintings by different artists and interesting sculptures scattered about. The most popular modern styles in painting, sculpture, and even art glass and jewelry are on display. Jewelry here can be reasonably priced, but expect to spend a more for an original painting.

Bucking the current trends in Carmel art is Boban Bursac, sole owner of the tiny **EXtempore Gallery** (Dolores St. betw. 5th and 6th, 831/626-1298, bobanart@yahoo.com). Burasac's amazing large-format paintings evoke feelings in even the most casual passerby; lucky visitors might even get to chat with the artist. Sadly, these works of art do not come cheap, understandable given their size and the skill and devotion with which they are painted.

For something altogether different and perhaps less intimidating, there's the **Sports Gallery** (Dolores St. betw. Ocean and 6th, 831/624-6026, www.sportsgalleryweb.com). In this more casual and down-to-earth space is memorabilia, signed photos, and even paintings of your favorite sports heroes and legends, many at reasonable prices. This is a great spot to look for gifts for that sports fanatic back home.

## SPORTS AND RECREATION
### Beach
At the west end of Ocean Avenue, you'll find the (occasionally) sparkling white sands of **Carmel Beach** (Ocean Ave., 831/624-4909, daily 6 A.M.–10 P.M.). This lovely stretch of south-facing sand offers free running for canine guests, bonfires south of 10th Avenue, and all the surfing, wading, and sunbathing (when there's sun) you can handle. Enjoy the beautiful local cypress trees and consider bringing a kite to fly on this often windy beach.

### Biking
**17-Mile Drive** also makes a great bike route. Cyclists can follow this road and enjoy the smells and sounds of the spectacular scenery in a way that car drivers just can't. Expect fairly flat terrain with lots of twists and turns, and a ride that runs…about 17 miles. Foggy conditions can make this ride a bit slick in the summer, but spring and fall weather are perfect for pedaling here.

### Golf
There's no place for golfing in all of California like Carmel-by-the-Sea. You can play courses trodden by the likes of Tiger Woods and Jack Nicholson, pause a moment before you putt to take in the sight of the stunning Pacific Ocean, and pay $300 or more for a single round of golf. Golf has been a major pastime here since the late 19th century, and today avid golfers come from around the world to tee off in Carmel.

One of the Pebble Beach Resort courses, **Spyglass Hill** (1700 17-Mile Dr., Pebble Beach, 800/654-9300, www.pebblebeach .com, 18-hole Par 72) gets its moniker from the Robert Louis Stevenson Novel *Treasure Island*. But don't be fooled—the holes on this beautiful course may be named for children's characters, but that doesn't mean they're easy. Spyglass Hill boasts some of the most challenging play even in the golf course-laden Carmel region. Expect a few bogeys if you choose to play here, and tee off from the Championship level at your own (ego's) risk.

Another favorite with the Pebble Beach golf crowd is the famed **Poppy Hills Golf Course** (3200 Lopez Rd, Pebble Beach, 831/622-8239, www.poppyhillsgolf.com, 18-hole Par 72). Though it's not managed by the same company, Poppy Hills shares amenities with Pebble Beach golf courses; you can expect the same level of care and devotion to the maintenance of the course and your experience as a player there. If you're looking to improve your game, check out their program that runs two days and gets you out onto both Poppy and Spyglass Hill for a great chance to really pick up some new skills (and a few incidentally gorgeous views).

### Hiking
South of Carmel-by-the-Sea, is **Point Lobos State Reserve** (62 Hwy. 1, 831/624-4909, http://pt-lobos.parks.state.ca.us, daily 8 A.M.– sunset, $10). Known as one of the most

beautiful parks in the state park system, Point Lobos offers hiking through forestland and along the beach, scuba diving (831/624-8413) off the shore, picnicking, and nature study. Take a walk through unique ecosystems and observe the indigenous wildlife while strolling through the rugged landscape. Be aware that from July through September fog often dims the summer sun at Point Lobos, even mid-day. Spring and fall are the best times to visit, weather-wise.

## ACCOMMODATIONS
### $100-150

**Lobos Lodge** (Monte Verde and Ocean Aves., 831/624-3874, www.loboslodge.com, $147) sits right in the midst of downtown Carmel-by-the-Sea, making it a perfect spot from which to dine, shop, and admire the endless array of art in the upscale town. Each of the 30 rooms and suites offers a gas fireplace, a sofa and table, a bed in an alcove, and enough space to stroll about and enjoy the quiet romantic setting. Do be aware that Lobos Lodge bills itself as an adult retreat. While families with children can stay here, expect to pay extra for more than two guests in your room, and there is little in the way of child-friendly amenities.

### $150-250

The name and exterior of the **Hofsas House** (San Carlos St. and 3rd Ave., 831/624-2745, www.hofsashouse.com, $150) evokes a quaint inn set in the Netherlands countryside. Yet the Hofsas House actually sits in a quiet semi-residential neighborhood within easy walking distance of downtown Carmel-by-the-Sea. Rooms in the rambling multi-story structure are surprisingly spacious, with nice furniture and linens that show just a touch of wear, and adequate bathrooms. If you can, get an ocean-view room with a patio or balcony, buy a bottle of wine, and spend some time sitting outside looking over the town of Carmel out toward the serene (from a distance) Pacific waters.

For folks who come to Carmel to taste wine, hike in the woods, and enjoy the less expensive golf courses, **Country Garden Inns** (102 W. Carmel Valley Rd., Carmel Valley, 831/659-5361, www.countrygardeninns.com, $170) offers a perfect spot to rest and relax. Actually composed of two inns, the Acacia and the Hidden Valley, Country Garden's small B&Bs offer violet and taupe French Country—style charm in the guest rooms, as well as a pool, a self-serve breakfast bar, and strolling gardens outdoors. Rooms run from romantic king-bed studios up to big family suites and most sleep at least four people (with daybeds in the window nooks).

### Over $250

Travelers with dogs and cats are welcome at the pet-friendly **Carmel Country Inn** (Dolores and 3rd Aves., 831/625-3263, www.carmelcountry inn.com, $245). The Inn does not, however, welcome children under six years old-it's a romantic hideaway, not a family motel. Rooms and suites boast comfortable furnishings that feel more like a friend's home than a generic hotel—you may find a fireplace, a reading nook, or even a Jacuzzi tub inside.

Despite its ghastly name, the cliff top **Tickle Pink Inn** (155 Highland Dr., 831/624-1244, www.ticklepinkinn.com, $314) offers tasteful luxury. Each room has a view of the ocean, an array of high-end furniture and linens, and all the top-end amenities you'd expect from a distinctive Carmel hostelry. For a special treat, shell out for the spa bath suite and watch the ocean while you soak in the tub with your sweetie.

## FOOD
### Breakfast

Need breakfast? Get it at **Katy's Place** (Mission and 6th Aves., 831/624-0199, www.katysplace carmel.com, daily 7 A.M.–2 P.M., $10–20), a self-described "Carmel Tradition" that can get quite crowded on weekend mornings. You can get your favorite breakfast all day, whether you love heavy eggs Benedict or light Belgian waffles…well, as long as they're open.

### Asian

For a more authentic hole-in-the-wall locals' dining experience, seek out **Tommy's Wok**

(Mission St. and Ocean Ave., 831/624-8518, Tues.–Sun. 11:30 A.M.–2:30 P.M. and 4:30–9:30 P.M., $10–20). All the veggies are fresh and organic, and the dishes taste reliably good whether you dine in or order takeout to enjoy elsewhere.

## California
For a taste of wine country cuisine in the Carmel Valley, reserve a table at **Marinus at Bernardus Lodge** (415 W. Carmel Valley Rd., Carmel Valley, 831/658-3550, www .bernardus.com, daily 6–10 P.M., $40–70). The exquisite California cuisine features the produce, fish, and meat of local producers, and has been served to the likes of Julia Child and Leonardo diCaprio. Choose a three-, four-, or five-course meal, or go for broke and get the chef's tasting menu.

## French
Let go of any prejudices against "fancy French restaurants" and try a country-style meal in the unprepossessing dining room of **Le Coq D'Or** (Mission and 4th Sts., 831/626-9319, www .lecoqdor.com, daily 5–10 P.M., $35). Order a classic French beef stew or a German schnitzel, and perhaps share a juicy morsel with your canine companion, who is always welcome to dine with you out on the heated porch.

## Mediterranean
For cute ambiance, you can't beat the flower gardens and traditional cottage of **PortaBella** (Ocean Ave. and Monte Verde, 831/624-4395, www.carmelsbest.com, daily 11:30 A.M.– 11 P.M., $20–40). This upscale-meets-kitsch restaurant serves Mediterranean inspired cuisine with a distinct local flair.

## Seafood
The **Flying Fish Grill** (Mission St. betw. Ocean and 7th Aves., 831/625-1962, Sun.– Thurs. 5–9 P.M., Fri.–Sat. 5–9:30 P.M., $30–40) serves Japanese-style seafood with a California twist in the Carmel Plaza open-air shopping mall. While the food isn't universally revered, the service at the Flying Fish and the

presentation of the plates makes a visit worth the time and expense.

## INFORMATION AND SERVICES
You'll find the **Carmel Visitors Center** (San Carlos betw. 5th and 6th, 831/624-2522, www. carmelcalifornia.org, daily 10 A.M.–5 P.M.) right in the midst of downtown Carmel-by-the-Sea.

For more information about the town and current events, pick up a copy of the weekly *Carmel Pine Cone* (www.pineconearchive. com), the local newspaper.

The nearest major medical center to Carmel-by-the-Sea and the Carmel Valley is in nearby Monterey. For minor issues, head for the **Community Hospital of Monterey** (23625 Holman Hwy, Monterey, 831/622-2746, www .chomp.org).

## GETTING THERE AND AROUND
If you've made it to Monterey by car, getting to Carmel is a piece of cake. The quick and free way to get to Carmel from the north or the south is via Highway 1. From Highway 1, take Ocean Avenue into the middle of downtown Carmel. A more expensive but more beautiful route is the 17-Mile Drive (see *Sights*).

To get to the Carmel Valley, take Highway 1 to Carmel Valley Road, which is a major intersection with a stop light. Signs point the way to Carmel Valley.

As you read the addresses in Carmel-by-the-Sea and begin to explore the neighborhoods, you'll realize something interesting. There are no street addresses. (Some years ago Carmel residents voted not to enact door-to-door mail delivery, thus there is no need for numeric addresses on buildings.) So you'll need to pay close attention to the street names and the block you're on. Just to make things even more fun, street signs can be difficult to see in the mature foliage and a dearth of streetlights can make them nearly impossible to find at night. If you can, show up during the day to get the lay of the land before trying to navigate after dark.

# Big Sur

Big Sur beckons to many types of visitors. Nature-lovers come to camp and hike the pristine wilderness areas, to don thick wetsuits and surf the oft-deserted beaches, and even to hunt for jade in rocky coves. Some of these folks come to stay and find themselves at the amazing retreats hosted by the Esalen Institute.

On the other hand, some of the wealthiest people from California and beyond visit Big Sur to luxuriate at unbelievably posh hotels and spas with dazzling views of the ocean, flower-strewn meadows, art galleries, and fabulous cuisine.

Whether you prefer a low-cost camping trip or a pampered look into how the other 0.01 percent live, Big Sur offers its beauty and charm to all comers. Part of that charm is Big Sur's determination to remain peacefully apart from the Information Age—yes, this means that your cell phone won't work in many parts of Big Sur. Horrors!

Note: The term "Big Sur" can be confusing to non-locals. It's both a town and the semi-official name of the coastal region that runs south of Carmel and north of San Simeon delineated by Highway 1.

## SIGHTS
### ◖ Big Sur Coast Highway

Even if you're not up to tackling the endless hiking trails and deep wilderness backcountry of Big Sur, you can still get a good sense of the glory of this region just by driving through it. The Big Sur Coast Highway, a 90-mile stretch of Highway 1, runs along jagged cliffs and rocky beaches, through dense redwood forest, over historic bridges, and past innumerable parks. Construction on this stretch of road was completed in the 1930s, connecting Cambria to Carmel. You can start out at either of these towns and spend a whole day making your way to the other end of the road. The road has plenty of wide turnouts set into picturesque cliffs to make it easy to stop to admire the glittering ocean and stunning wooded

Big Sur's famous coastline

cliffs running right out to the water. Be sure to bring a camera on your trip along Highway 1-you'll find yourself wanting to take photos every mile for hours on end.

## Bixby Bridge

You'll probably recognize the Bixby Bridge when you come upon it on Highway 1 in Big Sur. The picturesque cement open-spandrel arched bridge is one of the most photographed bridges in the nation, and it's been used in countless car commercials over the years. The bridge was built in the early 1930s as part of the massive Government Works project that completed Highway 1 through the Big Sur area to connect the road from the north end of California to the south. Today, you can pull out either to the north or to the south of the bridge to take photos or just look out at the attractive span and Bixby Creek flowing into the Pacific far below.

Are there two Bixby Bridges? Nope, but the Rocky Creek Bridge (north of Bixby Bridge on Hwy. 1) is similar in design, if not quite as grand and picturesque.

## Big Sur Station

If you haven't yet stopped at one of the larger state parks in the area and hit the visitors center, pull in at Big Sur Station (Hwy. 1 south of Pfeiffer Big Sur, 831/667-2315, daily 8 A.M.– 4:30 P.M.). The ranger station offers maps and brochures for all the major parks and trails of Big Sur, plus a minimal bookshop. Frankly, the visitor center and attendant services at Pfeiffer Big Sur State Park have the same or superior information to that available at Big Sur Station, so if you're planning to hit that park, skip this stop. However, several of the lesser parks and beaches (Limekiln, Garrapata, Sand Dollar) have no visitors services, so Big Sur Station serves a good purpose for visitors who plan to go only to those less-traveled spots. You can also get a free backcountry permit for the Ventana Wilderness here.

## Henry Miller Memorial Library

A number of authors have done time in Big Sur, soaking in the remote wilderness and sea air to gather inspiration for their work. Henry Miller lived and wrote in Big Sur for 18 years, and one of his works is titled for the area. Today the Henry Miller Memorial Library (Hwy. 1, 0.25 mile north of Deetjens, 831/667-2574, www .henrymiller.org, Wed.–Mon. 11 A.M.–6 P.M.) celebrates the life and work of Miller and his brethren in this quirky community center/ museum/coffee shop/gathering place. The library is easy to find as you drive either north or south on Highway 1—look for the hand-painted sign and funky fence decorations. What you won't find is a typical lending library, bookshop, or slicked-up museum. Instead, you'll wander the lovely sun-dappled meadow soaking in the essence of Miller's life here, come inside and talk to the docents about the racy novels Miller wrote, and maybe sit back with a cup of coffee to meditate on life and art and isolated gorgeous scenery. The library offers a glimpse into the "real" world of Big Sur as a spread-out artists' colony that has inspired countless works by hundreds of people.

## Point Sur Light Station

Sitting lonely and isolated out on its cliff, the Point Sur Light Station (Hwy. 1, 0.25 mile north of Point Sur Naval Facility, 831/625-4419, tours year-round Sat.–Sun. 10 A.M. and 2 P.M., plus Apr.–Oct. Wed. 10 A.M. and 2 P.M., July–Aug. Thurs. 10 A.M., adults $8, children $4) keeps watch over ships navigating near the rocky waters of Big Sur. It's the only complete 19th-century light station in California that you can visit, and even here access is severely limited. First lit in 1889, this now fully automated light station still provides navigational aid to ships off the coast; families stopped living and working in the tiny stone-built compound in 1974. But is the lighthouse truly uninhabited? Take one of the moonlight tours (call for information) to learn about the haunted history of the light station buildings.

You can't make a reservation for a Point Sur tour, so you should just show up and park your car off Highway 1 on the west side by the farm gate. Your guide will meet you there and lead you up the paved road 0.5 mile to the light station. Once there, you'll climb the stairs up to the light, explore the restored keepers' homes and service buildings, and walk out to the cliff edge. Expect to see a great variety of wildlife, from brilliant wildflowers in the spring to gray whales in the winter to flocks of pelicans flying in formation at any time of year. Be sure to dress in layers; it can be sunny and hot or foggy and cold, winter or summertime, and sometimes both on the same tour! Tours last three hours and require more than a mile of walking, with a bit of slope and more than 100 stairs.

The farm gate is locked and there's no access to the light station without a tour group. Tour schedules can vary from year to year and season to season; it's a good idea to call ahead before showing up. If you need special assistance for your tour or have questions about accessibility, call 831/667-0528 as far in advance as possible of your visit to make arrangements. No strollers, food, pets, or smoking are allowed on light station property.

### Big Sur Spirit Garden

A favorite among local art-lovers, the Big Sur Spirit Garden (Hwy. 1, Loma Vista, 831/667-1300, www.bigsurspiritgarden.com, daily 9 A.M.–6 P.M.) changes a little almost every day. The "garden" part includes a variety of exotic plants, while the "spirit" part devotes itself to modern and postmodern Fair Trade art from as nearby as a few miles and as far away as India. The artwork tends toward brightly colored small sculptures done in a childlike, exuberant style. The Spirit Garden offers educational programs, community celebrations, musical events, and more. Call ahead for information on upcoming events.

## HIKING

The main reason to come to Big Sur is to hike its beaches and forests. As you cruise Highway 1, the parks line up for you.

### Garrapata State Park

A narrow two-mile long band of pretty light sand creates the beach at Garrapata State Park

(Hwy. 1, gate 18 or 19, 831/624-4909, www .parks.ca.gov), north of the Point Sur Light Station. Stroll along the beach, scramble up the cliffs for a better view of the ocean, or check out the seals, sea otters, and sea lions near Soberanes Point. In the wintertime, grab a pair of binoculars to look for migrating gray whales passing quite close to shore here. The **Soberanes Canyon Trail** to the east of the highway is one of the more challenging and fun hikes to tackle at Garrapata.

Expect little in the way of facilities here—you'll park in a wide spot on Highway 1, and if you're lucky you might find a pit toilet open for use.

### Andrew Molera State Park

The first "Big Sur" park you'll encounter is Andrew Molera State Park (Hwy. 1, 22 miles south of Carmel, 831/667-2315, www.parks .ca.gov, day use $8). Once home to small camps of Esselen Native Americans, then a Spanish land grant, this chunk of Big Sur eventually became the Molera ranch. The land was used to grow crops and ranch animals, and as a hunting and fishing retreat for family and friends. In 1965, Frances sold the land to the Nature Conservancy, and when she died three years later the ranch was sold to the California State Park system as per her will. Today, the **Molera Ranch House Museum** (831/620-0541, bshs@ mbay.net, Sat.–Sun. 11 A.M.–3 P.M.) displays stories of the life and times of Big Sur's human pioneers and artists as well as the wildlife and plants of the region. Take the road toward the horse tours to get to the ranch house.

The park has numerous hiking trails that run down to the beach and up into the forest along the river—many are open to biking and horseback riding as well. Most of the park trails lie to the west of the highway. The beach is a one-mile walk down the easy, multi-use **Trail Camp Beach Trail.** From there, climb on out on the **Headlands Trail,** a 0.25-mile loop, for a beautiful view from the headlands. If you prefer to get a better look at the Big Sur River, take the flat, moderate **Bobcat Trail** (5.5 miles round-trip) and perhaps a few of its ancillary loops. You'll walk right along the riverbanks, enjoying the local microhabitats. Just be sure to look out for bicycles and the occasional horse and rider. For an even longer and more difficult trek up the mountains and down to the beach, take the eight-mile **Ridge Bluff Loop.** You'll start at the parking lot on the Creamery Meadow Beach Trail, then make a left onto the long and fairly steep Ridge Trail to get a sense of the local ecosystem. Then turn left again onto the Panorama Trail, which runs down to the coastal scrublands, and finally out to the Bluffs Trail, which takes you back to Creamery Meadow.

At the park entrance, you'll find bathrooms but no drinkable water and no food concessions. If you're camping here, be sure to bring plenty of your own water for washing dishes as well as drinking. If you're hiking for the day, pack in bottled water and snacks.

### ( Pfeiffer Big Sur State Park

The biggest, most developed park in Big Sur is Pfeiffer Big Sur State Park (47225 Hwy. 1, 831/667-2315, www.parks.ca.gov, day use $8). It's got the Big Sur Lodge, a restaurant and café, a shop, an amphitheater, a somewhat incongruous softball field, plenty of hiking-only trails, and lovely redwood-shaded campsites. This park isn't situated by the beach; it's up in the coastal redwoods forest, with a network of roads that can be driven or biked up into the trees and along the Big Sur River.

Pfeiffer Big Sur has the tiny **Ernest Ewoldsen Memorial Nature Center,** which features stuffed examples of local wildlife. It's open seasonally; call the park for days and hours. Another historic exhibit is the **Homestead Cabin,** once the home of part of the Pfeiffer family—the first European immigrants to settle in Big Sur. Day-trippers and overnight visitors can take a stroll through the cabins of the Big Sur Lodge, built by the Civilian Conservation Corps during the Great Depression.

No bikes or horses are allowed on trails in this park, which makes it quite peaceful for hikers. For a starter walk, take the easy, 0.7-mile **Nature Trail** in a loop from Day Use Parking Lot 2. Grab a brochure at the lodge to learn about the park's plant life as you walk the trail. For a longer

McWay Falls

© LIZ HAMILL SCOTT

stroll, head out on the popular **Pfeiffer Falls Trail,** 1.5 miles round-trip. You'll find stairs on the steep sections and footbridges across the creek, then a lovely platform at the base of the 60-foot waterfall where you can rest and relax midway through your hike. For a longer, more difficult, and interesting hike deeper into the Big Sur wilderness, start at the Homestead Cabin and head to the **Mount Manuel Trail** (10 miles round trip, difficult). From the Y-intersection with the Oak Grove Trail, it's four miles of sturdy hiking to Mount Manuel, one of the most spectacular peaks in the area.

Need to cool off after hiking? Scramble out to the entirely undeveloped Big Sur River Gorge, where the river slows and creates pools that are great for swimming. Relax and enjoy the water, but don't try to dive here.

This is one of the few Big Sur parks to offer a full array of services. Before you head out into the woods, stop at the Big Sur Lodge restaurant and store complex to get a meal and some water, and to load up on snacks and sweatshirts. Between the towering trees and the summer fogs, it can get quite chilly and somewhat damp on the trails.

CENTRAL COAST

## Julia Pfeiffer Burns State Park

One of the best-known and easiest hikes in all of the Big Sur region sits in Julia Pfeiffer Burns State Park (Hwy. 1, 12 miles south of Pfeiffer Big Sur State Park, 831/667-2315, www .parks.ca.gov). The **Overlook Trail** runs only two-thirds of a mile round-trip, along a level wheelchair-friendly boardwalk. Stroll under Highway 1, past the Pelton wheel house, and out to the observation deck and the stunning view of McWay Falls. The medium-sized waterfall cascades year-round off a cliff and onto the beach of a remote cove, where the water wets the sand and trickles out into the sea. The water of the cove gleams bright cerulean blue against the just-off-white sand of the beach— it looks more like the South Pacific than Northern California. Anyone with an ounce of love for the ocean will want to build a hut right there beside the waterfall. But you can't—in fact, the reason you'll look down on a pristine and empty stretch of sand is that there's no way down to the cove that's even remotely safe.

The tiny Pelton wheel exhibit off the Overlook Trail isn't much unless you're a huge fan of hydraulic engineering history. It does have an interpretive exhibit (including the old Pelton wheel itself) describing what a Pelton wheel is and what it does. No other museums make their homes here, though there's a small visitors center adjacent to the parking lot.

If you're up for a longer hike after taking in the falls, go back the other way to pick up the **Ewoldsen Trail** (4.5 miles round-trip, moderate–difficult). This trek takes you through McWay Canyon, and you'll see the creek and surrounding lush greenery as you walk. Then you'll loop away from the water and climb up into the hills. Be sure to bring water, as this hike can take several hours.

If you want to spend all day at Julia Pfeiffer Burns State Park, drive north from the park entrance to the Partington Cove pullout and park along the side of the highway. On the east side of the highway, start out along the **Tanbark Trail** (6.4 miles round-trip, difficult). You'll head through redwood groves and up steep switchbacks to the top of the coastal ridge. Be sure to bring your camera to record the stunning views before you head back down the fire road to your car.

## Jade Cove Recreation Area

Jade Cove Recreation Area (Hwy. 1, two miles south of Sand Dollar Beach) is easy to pass as you barrel down Highway 1 towards San Simeon. A road sign marks the area, but there's not much in the way of a formal parking lot or anything else to denote the treasures of this jagged, rough part of the Big Sur coastline. Park in the dirt/gravel strip off the road and head past the fence and into the park. It's fun to read the unusual signs along the narrow, beaten path that seems to lead to the edge of a cliff. The signs explain that you cannot bring in mining equipment, or take away rocks or minerals obtained from behind the high-tide line. If you're into aerial sports, you can hang-glide off the cliffs here.

Once you get to the edge of the cliff, the short trail gets rough. It's only 0.25 mile, but it's almost straight down a rocky, slippery cliff. Don't try to climb down if you're not in reasonable physical condition, and even if you are, don't be afraid to use your hands to steady yourself. At the bottom, you'll find huge boulders and smaller rocks and very little sand. You may also see a small herd of locals dressed in wetsuits and scuba gear. But most of all, you'll find the most amazing minerals in the boulders and rocks. Reach out and touch a multiton boulder shot through with jade. Search the smaller rocks beneath your feet for chunks of sea-polished jade. If you're a hard-core rock nut, you can join the locals in scuba diving for jewelry-quality jade. As long as you find it in the water or below the high-tide line, it's legal for you to take whatever you find here.

Jade Cove has no water, no restrooms, no visitors center, and no services of any kind.

# SPORTS AND RECREATION
## Horseback Riding

You can take a guided horseback ride into the forests or out onto the beaches of Andrew Molera State Park with **Molera Horseback Tours** (831/625-5486, http://molerahorsebacktours.

com, $25–60). Tours of 1–2.5 hours depart each day starting at 9 A.M.—call ahead to guarantee your spot, or take a chance and just show up at the stables 15 minutes ahead of the ride you want to take. If you prefer, call to book a private guided ride for yourself and your party. Each ride takes you from the modest corral area along multi-use trails through forests or meadows, or along the Big Sur River, and down to Molera Beach. You'll guide your horse along the solid sands as you admire the beauty of the wild Pacific Ocean.

Molera Horseback Tours are suitable for children over six and riders of all ability levels; you'll be matched to the right horse for you. All rides go down to the beach. Tours can be seasonal, so call ahead if you want to ride in the fall or winter. Guides share their knowledge of the Big Sur region and wildlife, and welcome questions about the plants you're seeing as you walk your horse down the trail. Early-morning and sunset rides tend to be the prettiest and most popular.

## Backpacking

If you long for the lonely peace of backcountry camping, the **Ventana Wilderness** (www .ventanawild.org) area is ideal for you. This area comprises the peaks of the Santa Lucia Mountains and the dense growth of the northern reaches of the Los Padres National Forest. You'll find many trails beyond the popular day hikes of the state parks, especially as Big Sur stretches down to the south. Check the website to find reports on the conditions of the trails you've decided to tackle in advance, and stop in at Big Sur Station or the ranger station at Pfeiffer Big Sur State Park to get the latest news on the backcountry areas.

## Fishing

No harbors offer deep-sea charters around Big Sur, but if your idea of the perfect outdoor vacation must include a rod and reel, you can choose between shore and river fishing. Steelhead run up the Big Sur River to spawn each year, and a limited fishing season follows them up the river into **Pfeiffer Big Sur State Park** and other accessible areas. Check with

Fernwood Resort (831/667-2422, www.fern woodbigsur.com) and the other lodges around Highway 1 for the best spots this season.

The numerous creeks that feed into and out of the Big Sur River also play home to their fair share of fish. Cast for trout in the creeks of Pfeiffer Big Sur and other clear-water streams in the area. The California Department of Fish and Game (www.dfg.ca.gov) can give you specific locations for legal fishing, season information, and rules and regulations.

If you prefer the fish from the ocean, you can cast off several of the beaches for the rock fish that scurry about in the near-shore reefs. **Garrapata State Beach** has a good fishing area, as do the beaches at **Sand Dollar.**

## Scuba Diving

There's not much for beginner divers in Big Sur, but if you've got some underwater experience, you'll want to bring your gear when you visit this region. Expect cold water. Temperatures range in the mid 50s in the shallows, dipping into the 40s as you dive deeper down. Visibility is 20–30 feet, though rough conditions can diminish this significantly; the best season for clear water is September through November.

The biggest and most interesting dive locale here is the **Julia Pfeiffer Burns State Park** (Hwy. 1, 12 miles south of Pfeiffer Big Sur, 831/667-2315, www.parks.ca.gov, daily sunrise–sunset). You'll need to acquire a special permit at Big Sur Station and prove your experience to dive at this protected underwater park. The park, along with the rest of the coast of Big Sur, is part of the Monterey Bay National Marine Sanctuary. You enter the water from the shore, which gives you the chance to check out all the ecosystems, beginning with the busy life of the beach sands and heading out to the rocky reefs, then into the lush green kelp forests.

Divers at access-hostile **Jade Cove** (Hwy. 1, two miles south of Sand Dollar Beach) aren't usually interested in cute, colorful nudibranchs or even majestic gray whales. Jade Cove divers come to stalk the wily jade pebbles and rocks that cluster in this special spot.

The semi-precious stone striates the coastline right here, and storms tear clumps of jade out of the cliffs and into the sea. Much of it settles just off the shore of the tiny cove, and divers hope to find jewelry-quality stones to sell for a huge profit.

If you're looking for a guided scuba dive of the Big Sur region, contact **Adventure Sports Unlimited** (303 Potrero St., #15, Santa Cruz, 831/458-3648, www.asudoit.com).

## Bird-Watching

Many visitors come to Big Sur just to see the birdies. The Big Sur coast is home to innumerable species, from the tiniest bush tits up to grand pelicans and beyond. The most famous avian residents of this area are no doubt the rare and endangered California condors. Once upon a time, condors were all but extinct, with only a few left alive in captivity and conservationists struggling to help them breed. Today, more than 30 birds soar above the trails and beaches of Big Sur. You might even see one swooping down low over your car as you drive down Highway 1! (You'll know it if one does this—a condor's wingspan can exceed nine feet.) Check with the park rangers for the best times and places to see condors during your visit.

The **Ventana Wilderness Society** (www .ventanaws.org) watches over many of the endangered and protected avian species in Big Sur. As part of their mission to raise awareness of the condors and many other birds, the VWS offers bird-watching expeditions; these can be simple two-hour tours or overnight wilderness camping trips, depending on your level of interest. Check their website for schedules and prices.

One of the hot spots of VWS conservation efforts and tours is Andrew Molera State Park. You can head out on your own to take a look around for some of the most interesting species in the Big Sur area. But wherever you choose to hike, be it beach or forest, you're likely to see a variety of feathered friends fluttering about.

## Spas

The **Allegria Spa at Ventana** (831/667-4222, www.ventanainn.com/spa.asp, daily 9 A.M.–7 P.M.,

Japanese baths at the Allegria Spa, Ventana

© LIZ HAMILL SCOTT

until 8 P.M. in summer, $120/50-minute massage) offers a large menu of spa treatments to both hotel guests and visitors. You'll love the serene atmosphere of the treatment and waiting areas. Greenery and weathered wood create a unique space that help to put you in a tranquil state of mind, ready for your body to follow your mind into a state of relaxation. Indulge in a soothing massage, purifying body treatment, or rejuvenating or beautifying facial. Take your spa experience a step further in true Big Sur fashion with a reiki or craniosacral treatment. Or go for a private New Age reading, a personal yoga or meditation session, or a private guided hike. If you're a hotel guest, you can choose to have your spa treatment in the comfort of your own room or out on your private deck.

Just across the highway from the Ventana, the **Post Ranch Inn and Spa** (Hwy. 1, 831/667-2200,, $135/hour massage) is another ultra-high-end resort spa. Massage, body, and facial work focuses on organics and gem and crystal therapies. You can also indulge in private sessions, including Shamanic meetings

## ESALEN: AN ADVANCED CALIFORNIA EXPERIENCE

The Esalen Institute is known throughout California as the home of California massage technique, a forerunner and cutting-edge player in ecological living, and a space to retreat from the world and build a new and better sense of self. Visitors journey from all over the state and beyond to sink into the haven that's sometimes called "The New Age Harvard."

One of the biggest draws of the Institute sits down a rocky path right on the edge of the cliffs overlooking the ocean. The bath house includes a motley collection of mineral-fed hot tubs looking out over the ocean – you can choose the Quiet Side or the Silent Side to sink into the water and contemplate the Pacific Ocean's limitless expanse, meditate on a perfect sunset or arrangement of stars, or (on the Quiet Side) get to know your fellow bathers. Who will be naked. Regardless of gender, marital status, or the presence of others.

Esalen's bath house area is "clothing optional," its philosophy puts the essence of nature above the sovereignty of humanity, and it encourages openness and sharing among its guests – to the point of chatting nude with total strangers in a smallish hot tub. You'll also find a distinct lack of attendants to help you find your way around. Once you've parked and been given directions, it's up to you to find your way down to the cliffs. You'll have to find your own towel, ferret out a cubby for your clothes in the changing rooms, grab a shower, then wander out to find your favorite of the hot tubs. Be sure you go all the way outside past the individual clawfoot tubs to the glorious shallow cement tubs that sit right out on the edge of the cliff with the surf crashing just below.

In addition to the nudity and new-age culture of Esalen, you'll learn that this isn't a day spa. You'll need to make an appointment for a massage (at $150 a pop), which grants you access to the hot tubs for an hour before and an hour after your 75-minute treatment session. If you just want to sit in the mineral water, you'll need to stay up late. Very late. Inexpensive ($20) open access to the Esalen tubs begins on a first-come, first-serve basis at 1 A.M. and ends at 3 A.M. Many locals consider the sleep deprivation well worth it to get the chance to enjoy the healing mineral waters and the stunning astronomical shows.

If you're not comfortable with your own nudity or that of others, you don't approve of meditation or non-Christian spiritual philosophy, or you find it impossible to lower your voice or stop talking for more than 10 minutes, Esalen is not for you. If you've never done anything like this before, think hard about how you'll really feel once you're in the changing area with its open cubbies and naked hippies wandering about.

But if this description of a California experience sounds just fabulous to you, make your reservations now! The Esalen Institute (55000 Hwy. 1, 831/667-3000, fax 831/667-2724, www.esalen.org) accepts reservations by fax, mail, and phone if necessary. Go to the website for more information.

---

that focus on indigenous techniques that are said to enhance your life.

## ENTERTAIMENT AND EVENTS

The primary entertainment in Big Sur takes place out of doors. Listen to the symphony of the surf against the cliffs, admire the sculpture of 1,000-year-old coast redwoods, and pick up jewelry in the raw right off the beaches. But if you need a bit more, a few events and entertainment options appear in quiet, nature-loving Big Sur.

### Live Music

It probably won't surprise you to learn that Big Sur is not a hotbed of cutting-edge clubs and bars. Most folks who come here spend their days outside, hiking or doing some other vigorous activity. They drop into bed early, exhausted and needing the rest to get back out into the wilderness again the next day. But if you just can't bear to hit the sack before 10 P.M., you can find some fun at the **Fernwood Tavern** (Hwy. 1, 831/667-2422, Sun.–Thurs. noon–midnight, Fri.–Sat. noon–1 A.M.). Live music acts entertain locals and visitors alike, and you might hear country, folk, or even indie rock from the small stage. Most live music happens on weekends, especially Saturday nights, starting at 9 P.M. Even without the music, the tavern can get lively in the evenings (it's good to be the only game in town), with locals drinking from the full bar, eating, and holding parties in the meandering dim rooms.

## Festivals and Events
Each year, the Pacific Valley School hosts the fundraising **Big Sur Jade Festival** (www.big surjadeco.com/festival.html, Oct.). Come out to see the artists, craftspeople, jewelry makers, and rock hunters displaying their wares in the early fall. The school is located across Highway 1 from Sand Dollar Beach. Munch snacks as your feet tap to the live music playing as part of the festival. Check the website for the exact dates and information about this year's festival.

## CAMPING
Many visitors to Big Sur want to experience the unspoiled beauty of the landscape daily. To accommodate true outdoors lovers, many of the parks and lodges in the area have overnight campgrounds. You'll find all types of camping here, from full-service, RV-accessible areas to environmental tent campsites to wilderness backpacking. You can camp in a state park, or out behind one of the small resort motels near a restaurant and a store and possibly the cool refreshing Big Sur River. Pick the option that best suits you and your family's needs.

### Andrew Molera State Park
Andrew Molera State Park (Hwy. 1, 22 miles south of Carmel, 831/667-2315, www.parks .ca.gov, $10/night) offers 24 walk-in, tent-only campsites located 0.25–0.5 mile from the parking lot via a level, well-maintained trail. You'll pitch your tent in a pretty meadow near the Big Sur River, in a site that includes a picnic table and a fire ring. No reservations are taken, so come early in summertime to get one of the prime spots under a tree. While you're camping, look out for bobcats, foxes, deer, raccoons (stow your food securely!), and any number of birds.

As of 2007, no potable water was available at Andrew Molera. Toilets sit a short walk from the camping area, but you cannot shower here.

### Fernwood Resort
The Fernwood Resort (Hwy. 1, 831/667-2422, www.fernwoodbigsur.com) maintains a large campground area on both sides of the Big Sur River. You can choose between pitching your own tent, pulling in in an RV, or renting a tent cabin. The resort has easy access to the river, where you can swim, inner tube, and hike. You'll also have access to the restaurant, store, and tavern.

Tent cabins offer small canvas-constructed spaces with room for four in a double and two twins. You can pull your car right up to the back of your cabin. Bring your own linens or sleeping bags, pillows, and towels to make up the inside of your tent cabin. Hot showers and bathrooms are a short walk away. Tent campsites are scattered in great places—tucked in down by the river under vast shady redwood trees. You can even park your RV under a tree, then hook it up to water and electricity.

### Pfeiffer Big Sur State Park
The biggest and most developed campground in Big Sur sits at Pfeiffer Big Sur State Park (Hwy. 1, 800/444-7275, www.parks.ca.gov, $20). With 212 individual sites, each of which can take two vehicles and eight people or an RV (32 feet or shorter, trailers 27 feet max, dump station on-site), there's enough room for almost everybody here. During the summer, a grocery store and laundry facilities operate within the campground for those who don't want to hike down to the lodge, and plenty of flush toilets and hot showers are scattered

throughout the campground. In the evenings, walk down to the Campfire Center for entertaining and educational programs. If you prefer a quieter and less asphalt-oriented camping experience, check out the hike-in and bike-in campgrounds that make up part of the Pfeiffer Big Sur complex.

Pfeiffer Big Sur fills up fast in the summertime, especially on weekends. Advance reservations (800/444-7275, www.reserveamerica .com) are highly recommended. Note that some campground sites were scheduled to be under construction until December 2009.

### Limekiln State Park

The small but pretty campground at Limekiln State Park (Hwy. 1 two miles south of Lucia, 831/667-2403, www.parks.ca.gov, summer only, $18) offers 33 campsites with hot showers and flush toilets out along an attractive creek that runs toward the nearby ocean. RVs and trailers can stay here (call for maximum length restrictions), though hookups and dump stations aren't available. In the summertime, the park recommends making reservations early. In the winter, no reservations are available and many sites are closed. Call for more information if you want to camp here in the off-season.

### Treebones Resort

For the ultimate high-end California green lodging-cum-camping experience, book a yurt (a circular structure made with a wood frame covered by cloth) at the Treebones Resort (71895 Hwy. 1, 877/424-4787, www .treebonesresort.com). The resort got its name from the locals' description of this scrap of land, which was once a wood recycling plant with sun-bleached logs lying about—"tree bones." Yurts ($155–280) at Treebones tend to be spacious and charming, with polished wood floors, queen beds, seating areas, and outdoor decks for lounging. There are also five walk-in campsites ($65 for two people). In the central lodge, you'll find nice hot showers and usually clean restroom facilities. Treebones offers a somewhat pricey casual dinner each night, and

basic linens. If you like extra pillows and towels, you'll have to bring your own. Check the website for a list of items to bring and the FAQ about the resort facilities to make your stay more fun. While children are allowed in four of the yurts, Treebones recommends leaving behind kids under 12 years old—without any TVs, phones, or digital entertainment, little ones often get bored and unpleasantly loud.

## ACCOMMODATIONS
### Under $100

When locals speak of Deetjens, they could be referring to the inn, the restaurant, or the family that created both. But they all do speak of Deetjens, which operates as a non-profit organization dedicated to offering visitors to the Big Sur region great hospitality for reasonable rates. To stay at **Deetjens Big Sur Inn** (48865 Hwy. 1, 831/667-2377, www.deetjens .com, $80–200) is to become a small part of Big Sur's history and culture. It doesn't look like a spot where legions of famous writers, artists, and Hollywood stars have laid their precious heads, but Deetjens can indeed boast a guest register that many hostelries in Beverly Hills would kill for. And yet, the motley collection of buildings also welcomed transient artists, San Francisco bohemians, and the occasional criminal looking for a spot to sleep as they traversed the coast on bicycles or even on foot.

Your guest room will be unique, still decorated with the art and collectibles chosen and arranged by Grandpa Deetjen many moons ago. The inn prides itself on its rustic historic construction—expect thin weathered walls, funky cabin construction, no outdoor locks on the doors, and an altogether unique experience. Many rooms have shared baths, but you can request a room with private bath when you make reservations. Deetjens prefers to offer a serene environment, and to that end does not permit children under 12 unless you rent both rooms of a two-room building. Deetjens has no TVs or stereos, no phones in guest rooms, and no cell phone service. Two pay phones are available for emergencies, but other than that you're truly cut off from the outside world.

Decide for yourself whether this sounds terrifying or wonderful.

## $100-150

Along Highway 1 in the town of Big Sur, you'll find a couple of small motels. One of the more popular of these is the **Fernwood Resort** (Hwy. 1, 831/667-2422, www.fernwoodbigsur .com, $110). The low sprawl of buildings includes a 12-room motel, a small grocery-cum-convenience store, a restaurant, and a tavern that passes for the local nighttime hot-spot. Farther down the small road, you'll find the campgrounds, which include a number of tent cabins as well as tent and RV sites. If all this a "resort" makes, so be it. Your motel room will be a modest space in a blocky, one-level building off to the side of the main store and restaurant buildings. Not too much sunlight gets into the guest rooms, but the decor is light-colored and reasonably attractive. Rooms have queen beds and attached private bathrooms, but no TVs. If you tend to get chilly in the winter (or the summer fog), ask for a room with a gas stove. One room has a two-person hot tub sitting just outside on the back deck. In the summertime, book in advance to be sure of getting a room, especially on weekends.

Another lodge-style motel set in the redwood forest, the **Big Sur River Inn** (Hwy. 1 at Pheneger Creek, 800/548-3610, www .bigsurriverinn.com, $125–150) sits in one of the "populated" parts of Big Sur. First opened in the 1930s by a member of the legendary Pfeiffer family, the inn has been in continuous operation ever since. Today, it boasts 20 motel rooms, a restaurant, and a gift shop. Guest rooms are small but comfortable, with a juxtaposition of chain-motel comforters and curtains with rustic lodge-style wooden interior paneling. Budget-conscious rooms have one queen bed. Families and small groups can choose between standard rooms with two queen beds and two-room suites with multiple beds and attractive back decks that look out over the Big Sur River. All guests can enjoy the attractively landscaped outdoor pool with its surrounding lawn leading down to the river.

The attached restaurant offers three meals a day. Be sure to make reservations in advance for summertime weekends!

## $150-250

If you want to stay inside one of the parks but tents just aren't your style, book a cabin at the **Big Sur Lodge** (47225 Hwy. 1, 800/424-4787, www.bigsurlodge.com, $199–289) in Pfeiffer Big Sur State Park. The lodge was built in the 1930s as a Government Works project to create jobs for people suffering in the Great Depression—by then Big Sur's astounding beauty and peace had been recognized by both federal and state governments, and much of the land was protected as parks for the enjoyment of the populace. Though the amenities have been updated, the cabins of Big Sur Lodge still evoke the classic woodsy vacation cabin. Set in the redwood forest along an array of paths and small roads, the cabins feature patchwork quilts, rustic furniture, understated decor, and simple but clean bathrooms. Many cabins have lots of beds—perfect for larger families or groups of adults traveling together. The largest cabins have fireplaces and kitchens. You can stock your kitchen at the on-site grocery store, or just get a meal at the lodge's restaurant or café.

The lodge has a swimming pool for those rare sunny summer days in the Big Sur forest. But the real attraction is its right-outside-your-door access to the Pfeiffer Big Sur trails. You can just leave your car outside your room and hike the day away inside the park. Or take a short drive to one of the other state parks and enjoy their charms for free with proof of occupancy at Big Sur Lodge.

Despite the forbidding name, **Ragged Point Inn** (19019 Hwy. 1, 805/927-4502, http:// raggedpointinn.net, $200–300) takes advantage of its location to create an anything-but-ragged hotel experience for its guests. If you've come to Big Sur to bask in the grandeur of the Pacific Ocean, this is your hotel. The Ragged Point Inn perches on one of Big Sur's famous cliffs, offering stellar views from the purpose-built glass walls and private balconies or patios of almost every room in the house. Budget-friendly rooms still have plenty of space, a comfy king or two double beds, and those unreal ocean views. If you've got a bit more cash to burn, go for a luxury room, with optimal views, soaring interior spaces, plush amenities, and romantic two-person spa bathtubs. Outside your room, enjoy a meal in the full-service restaurant or get picnic supplies from the snack bar or the mini-mart, fill up for a day trip at the on-site gas station, or peruse the works of local artists in the gift shop or jewelry gallery. A special treat is the hotel's own hiking trail, which makes a 400-foot drop past a waterfall to Ragged Point's private beach.

## Over $250

If money is no object, you cannot possibly beat the lodgings at 【 **Ventana** (48123 Hwy. 1, 800/628-6500, www.ventanainn.com, $385), a place where the panoramic ocean views begin in the parking lot. This might well be the best hotel in all of California. Picture home-baked pastries, fresh yogurt, in-season fruit, and organic coffee delivered to your room in the morning, then enjoying that sumptuous breakfast outdoors on your own private patio overlooking a wildflower-strewn meadow that sweeps out toward the blue-gray waters of the ocean. And that's just the beginning of an unbelievable day at the Ventana. Next, don your plush spa robe and rubber slippers (all you are required to wear on the grounds of the hotel and spa) and head for the Japanese bathhouse. Choose from two bath houses, one at each end of the property. Both are clothing-optional and gender segregated, and the upper house has glass and open-air windows that let you look out to the ocean. Two swimming pools offer a cooler hydro-respite from your busy life; the lower pool is clothing-optional, and the upper pool perches on a high spot for enthralling views. Almost every other amenity imaginable, including daily complimentary yoga classes, can be yours for the asking.

The guest rooms range from the "modest" standard rooms with king beds, tasteful exposed cedar walls and ceilings, and attractive green and earth tone appointments, all the way up through generous and gorgeous suites to full-sized multi-bedroom houses. If you have a stupid amount of money available, the Vista Suites boast the most beauteous hotel accommodations imaginable. You'll reach your room by walking along the paved paths crowded by lush landscaping, primarily California native plants that complement the wild lands of the trails behind the main hotel buildings. You can also take an evening stroll down to the Cielo dining room—the only spot on the property where you need to wear more than your robe and flip-flops. If you're headed to the Allegria Spa for a treatment, you can go comfy and casual.

**Post Ranch** (47900 Hwy. 1, 800/527-2200, www.postranchinn.com, $550–2,185) is another exclusive luxury resort perched on the cliffs of Big Sur. Spa, yoga, and a unique yet rustic atmosphere are just a few of its perks.

## FOOD

As you traverse the famed Highway 1 through Big Sur, you'll quickly realize that a ready meal isn't something to take for granted here. You'll see no McDonald's, Starbucks, 7-11s, or Safeways lining the road here. While you can find groceries, they tend to appear in small markets attached to motels. The motels and resorts usually have restaurants attached as well, but they're all-meals all-day or 24-hour kinds of places. Plan in advance to make it to meals during standard hours, and expect to have dinner fairly early. Pick up staple supplies before you enter the area if you don't plan to leave again for a few days to avoid paying premiums at the mini-marts.

### Casual Dining

Serving three meals each day to lodge guests and passersby, the **Big Sur Lodge Café and Restaurant** (47225 Hwy. 1, 800/242-4787, www.bigsurlodge.com, daily 7 A.M.–9 P.M., $23) has a dining room as well as a cute espresso and ice cream bar out front. The dining room dishes up a full menu of American classic for every meal, while you can grab a quick sandwich to go from the espresso bar.

The **Redwood Grill** (Hwy. 1, 831/667-2129,

www.fernwoodbigsur.com, daily 11:30 A.M.–9 P.M., $20) at Fernwood Resort looks and feels like a grill in the woods ought to. Even in the middle of the afternoon, the aging, wood-paneled interior is dimly lit and strewn with slightly saggy couches and casual tables and chairs. Walk up to the counter to order somewhat overpriced burgers and sandwiches, then on to the bar to grab a soda or a beer.

The northernmost restaurant on the Big Sur coast, **Rocky Point Restaurant** (36700 Hwy. 1, 831/624-2933, www.rocky-point.com, daily 9 A.M.–3 P.M. and 5 P.M.–close, $35) offers decent food and great views to Highway 1 travelers. Enjoy the smell of mesquite from the grill as you wait for your steak or fish to bring that scent right to your nose. Though meat-eaters will find all the good solid dishes they want for breakfast, lunch, and dinner, vegetarian options are limited.

The **Big Sur Bakery** (47540 Hwy. 1, 831/667-0520, www.bigsurbakery.com, Tues.–Sat. 5:30 P.M.–close, Sat.–Sun. 10:30 A.M.–2:45 P.M.) might sound like a casual, walk-up eating establishment, and the bakery part of it is. You can stop in from 8 A.M. every day to grab a fresh-baked scone, a homemade jelly donut, or a flaky croissant sandwich for lunch later on. But on the dining room side, an elegant surprise awaits diners who've spent the day hiking the redwoods and strolling the beaches. Be sure to make reservations or you're unlikely to get a table, and you'd miss out on the amazing clam chowder (with whole clams in their shells) and other unique California takes on classic American cuisine.

According to Big Sur locals, the best breakfast in the area can be had at **Deetjens** (48865 Hwy. 1, 831/667-2377, www.deetjens.com, breakfast and dinner daily, $10–28). The funky dining room with its mismatched tables, dark wooden chairs, and cluttered wall decor belies the high quality of the cuisine served here. Enjoy delectable dishes created from the freshest local ingredients for breakfast and then again at dinnertime.

## Fine Dining

You don't need to be a guest at the gorgeous Ventana to enjoy a fine gourmet dinner at **The Restaurant at Ventana** (Hwy. 1, 831/667-4242, www.ventanainn.com, daily noon–3:30 P.M., 6–9 P.M., $28–38). The spacious dining room boasts a warm wood fire, an open kitchen, and comfortable banquettes with plenty of throw pillows to lounge against as you peruse the menu. If you're visiting for lunch or an early supper on a sunny day, be sure to request a table outside so you can enjoy the stunning views with your meal. The inside dining room has great views from the bay windows too, along with pristine white tablecloths and pretty light wooden furniture. Even with such a setting as Cielo has, the real star at this restaurant is the cuisine. The chef offers a daily-changing spread of haute California cuisine dishes, many of which feature organic or homegrown produce and local meats. To go with the seascape theme, Cielo's menu is heavy on sustainable seafood offerings. Be sure to tell your server if you're a vegetarian or have other dietary limitations—the chefs can whip up something special just for you. The best value at Cielo is the prix fixe menu, from which you can choose several courses. If you can possibly afford it, get the wine pairing with each course, and be sure to save room for dessert.

When you dine at **Nepenthe** (48510 Hwy. 1, 831/667-2345, www.nepenthebigsur.com, daily 11:30 A.M.–10 P.M., $30), be sure to ask for a table outdoors on even the partly sunny days. That way you get to enjoy both your Ambrosiaburger and the phenomenal cliff-top views. Open for lunch and dinner, the restaurant offers a short but tasty menu of meats, fish, and plenty of vegetarian dishes.

Outside, the seasonal **Café Kevah** at Nepenthe (breakfast and lunch Mar.–Jan., $10–12) patio offers a similar sampling at slightly lower prices. Just remember to keep munching on your Benedict or sandwich as you drape your arms over the wrought-iron railing and stare out into the mesmerizing blue-gray of the Pacific below and beyond you.

The **Sierra Mar** (47900 Hwy. 1, 831/667-2800, www.postranchinn.com, daily 8–10:30 A.M., noon–3 P.M., and 3–9 P.M., $100) restaurant at the Post Ranch Inn offers a decadent four-course prix fixe dinner menu in a stunning ocean-view setting. Lunch and snacks are served all through the afternoon to casual travelers, but expect to put on the ritz for a formal, white-tablecloth dining experience at this over-the-top-of-upscale restaurant.

## Markets
With no supermarkets or chain mini-marts in all of the Big Sur region, the local markets do a booming business. You can stock up on staples such as bread, lunch meat, eggs, milk, marshmallows, and graham crackers at various local stores. In town, the all-encompassing **Fernwood Resort** (Hwy. 1, 831/667-2422, www.fernwoodbigsur.com) has a market. You'll also find a seasonal market in the campground at Pfeiffer Big Sur State Park.

## INFORMATION AND SERVICES
The two most comprehensive visitors centers in Big Sur lie within **Pfeiffer Big Sur State Park** (47225 Hwy. 1, 831/667-2315, www .parks.ca.gov) and **Julia Pfeiffer Burns State Park** (Hwy. 1, 12 miles south of Pfeiffer Big Sur, 831/667-2315, www.parks.ca.gov). At Pfeiffer Big Sur, you'll find the visitors center grouped in with the Big Sur Lodge Restaurant, the hotel check-in, and a small store. A tiny nature museum lies a quarter mile or so up the park's main road. This visitors center is a good spot to get maps and information for hiking here and at other Big Sur parks that don't have manned visitors centers. This large park also offers laundry facilities, some basic staples at the store, and food all day long at the restaurant and attached espresso bar.

Farther south at Julia Pfeiffer Burns, the visitors center is easily accessible from the main parking lot. Again, rangers can advise you about hiking and activities both in their park and at other parks in the region. You'll find fewer services here than at Pfeiffer Big Sur—if you need to shop, do laundry, or gas up, head north.

Be aware that your cell phone may not work in all of Big Sur, especially out in the undeveloped reaches of forest and on Highway 1 away from the town of Big Sur and the Post Ranch. Call boxes are set at regular intervals along the highway.

For health matters, the **Big Sur Health Center** (46896 Hwy. 1, Big Sur, 831/667-2580, Mon.–Fri. 10 A.M.–5 P.M.) can take care of minor medical needs, and provides an ambulance service and limited emergency care. The nearest full-service hospital is the **Community Hospital of the Monterey Peninsula** (23625 Holman Hwy., Monterey, 831/624-5311).

## GETTING THERE AND AROUND
"Highway 1" sounds like a major freeway to many visitors, and down south it does get big and flat and straight. But along Big Sur, Highway 1 is a narrow, twisting, cliff-carved track that's breathtaking both because of its beauty and because of its dangers. Once you get five miles or so south of Carmel, expect to slow down—in some spots north of the town of Big Sur you'll be driving no more than 20 miles per hour around hairpin turns carved into vertical cliffs. If you're coming up from the south, Highway 1 is fairly wide and friendly up from Cambria, only narrowing into its more hazardous form as the cliffs get higher and the woods thicker. Be aware that fog often comes in on the Big Sur coast at sunset, making the drive even more hazardous (and much less attractive). If you must drive at night, take it slow!

Plan to spend several hours driving from Carmel to Cambria, partly to negotiate the difficult road and partly to make use of the many convenient turnouts to take photos of the unending spectacular scenery. Most of the major parks in the Big Sur region spring right off Highway 1, making it easy to spend a couple of days meandering along the road, stopping at Julia Pfeiffer or Andrew Molera to hike for a few hours or have a picnic on the beach.

# Cambria and San Simeon

The small beach town of Cambria becomes surprisingly spacious when you start exploring it. Plenty of visitors come here to ply Moonstone Beach, peruse the charming downtown area, and just drink in the laid-back, art-town feel. But Cambria owes much of its prosperity to the immense tourist trap on the hill that is Hearst Castle. Located about seven miles north in San Simeon, Hearst Castle, quite frankly, *is* San Simeon; the town grew up around it to support the overwhelming needs of its megalomaniacal owner and never-ending construction.

## SIGHTS

When it comes to this area, there is only one true sight. But once you're through with the castle tours, a few attractions in the lower elevations beckon as well. Nearby Cambria began and to a certain extent still is an artists colony; the windswept hills and sparkling ocean provide plenty of inspiration for painters, writers, sculptors, glassblowers, and more.

### ◖ Hearst Castle

There's nothing else in California quite like Hearst Castle (Hwy. 1 and Hearst Castle Rd., 800/444-4445, www.hearstcastle.com, tours daily 8:20 A.M.–3:20 P.M., $24). Newspaper magnate William Randolph Hearst conceived of the idea of a grand mansion in the Mediterranean style, on the land his parents bought along the central California coast. His memories of camping on the hills above the Pacific led him to choose the spot on which the castle now stands. He hired Julia Morgan, the first female civil engineering graduate from UC Berkeley, to design and build the house for him. She did a brilliant job with every detail, despite the ever-changing wishes of her employer. By way of decoration, Hearst assisted in the relocation of hundreds of European medieval and Renaissance antiquities, from tiny tchotchkes to whole gilded ceilings. William Randolph also adored exotic animals, and created one of the largest private zoos in the nation on his

thousands of Central Coast acres. Though most of the zoo is gone now, you can still see the occasional zebra grazing peacefully along Highway 1 to the south of the castle, acting as heralds to the exotic nature of Hearst Castle ahead.

The visitors center is a lavish affair with a gift shop, restaurant, café, ticket booth, and movie theater. Here you can see the much-touted film *Hearst Castle—Building the Dream,* which will give you an overview of the construction and history of the marvelous edifice, and of William Randolph Hearst's empire. After buying your ticket, board the shuttle that takes you up the hill to your tour. (No private cars are allowed on the roads up to the castle proper.) There are five tours to choose from, each focusing on different spaces and aspects of the castle. Tour 1 is recommended for first-time visitors, and you're welcome to sign up for several tours over the course of one day. Tour 5 is a seasonal evening tour with volunteers

**Hearst Castle**

© ROBERT HOLMES / CALTOUR

dressed in 1930s fashion welcoming guests as if to one of Hearst's legendary parties.

Expect to walk for at least an hour on whichever tour you choose, and to climb up and down many stairs. Even the most jaded traveler can't help but be amazed by the beauty and opulence that drips from every room in the house. Lovers of European art and antiques will want to stay forever. The two swimming pools—one indoor and one outdoor—shine with grandeur, all marble, glass tile, and mixed antique and custom-created statuary and fixtures.

The park recommends that visitors buy tour tickets at least a few days in advance, and even further ahead for Tour 5 and on summer weekends. For visitors with limited mobility, a special wheelchair-accessible tour is available. Strollers are not permitted. The restrooms and food concessions all cluster in the visitors center—but no food, drink, or chewing gum is allowed on any tour.

### Historic San Simeon

The tiny town of San Simeon existed primarily to support the construction efforts up the hill at Hearst Castle. The town dock provided a place for ships to unload tons of marble, piles of antiques, and dozens of workers. The general store and post office acted as a central gathering place for the community, and you can still walk up the weathered wooden steps and make a purchase here. Around the corner at the building's other door, you can buy a book of stamps or mail a letter at the tiny but operational post office.

The **William Randolph Hearst Memorial State Beach** (750 Hearst Castle Rd., San Simeon, 805/927-2020, www.parks.ca.gov, daily dawn–dusk) sits in San Simeon's cute little cove and encompasses the remaining structure of the old pier. You can lie on the beach or have a picnic up on the lawn above the sand.

### Nitt Witt Ridge

While William Randolph Hearst built one of the most expensive homes ever seen in California, local eccentric Arthur Harold Beal (a.k.a. Captain Nit Wit or Der Tinkerpaw) got busy building the cheapest "castle" he could.

Nitt Witt Ridge (881 Hillcrest Dr., 805/927-2690, tours free by appointment only) is the result of five decades of scavenging trash and using it as building supplies to create a multistory home like no other on the coast. Today, you can make an appointment with owners Michael and Stacey O'Malley to take a tour of the property. (Please don't just drop in.) It's weird, it's funky, and it's fun—an oddly iconic experience of the Central Coast.

### Cambria Cemetery

"Artsy" isn't a word that's usually associated with graveyards, but in Cambria it fits. The Cambria Cemetery (6005 Bridge St., 805/927-5158, www.cambriacemetery.com) reflects the artistic bent of the town's residents in its tombstone decor. Unlike many cemeteries, at Cambria the family and friends of the deceased are allowed to place all manner of personal objects at their loved ones' graves. You'll see painted tombstones, beautiful panes of stained glass, unusual wind chimes, and many other unique expressions of love, devotion, and art as you wander the 12 wooded acres.

## ACCOMMODATIONS
## $100-150

A favorite even among the many inns of Cambria, the **Olallieberry Inn** (2476 Main St., Cambria, 888/927-3222, www.olallie berry.com, $145) sits in a charming 19th-century Greek Revival home and adjacent cottage. Each of the nine rooms features its own quaint Victorian-inspired decor with comfortable beds and attractive appointments. A full daily breakfast (complete with olallieberry jam) rounds out the comfortable personal experience.

Her **Castle Homestay Bed and Breakfast Inn** (1978 Londonderry Ln., Cambria, 805/924-1719, www.HerCastle.cc, $127–170) is a bit different from your average B&B, with only two rooms available and lots of personal attention from the owners. When you make your reservations, you can ask about a half-day wine tour, dinner reservations, or even lunch and dinner provided by the inn. The Her Castle can be the perfect hideaway for two couples traveling together who desire the privacy of "their own house."

## $150-250

Many of the accommodations of Cambria sit along the small town's very own Hotel Row, a.k.a. Moonstone Beach Drive. One of these is the **Moonstone Landing** (6240 Moonstone Beach Dr., Cambria, 805/927-0012, www .moonstonelanding.com, $155), which provides inexpensive partial-view rooms with the decor and amenities of a mid-tier chain motel, as well as oceanfront luxury rooms featuring travertine marble bathrooms.

A charming log cabin structure shelters the eight rooms of the **J. Patrick House Bed and Breakfast** (2990 Burton Dr., Cambria, 805/927-3812, www.jpatrickhouse.com, $175). Each room has modern-country kitschy decor, a private bath, and plenty of amenities. They're dedicated to feeding you at the J. Patrick, with a big breakfast in the morning, hor d'oevres in the afternoon, and chocolate chip cookies at bedtime.

The **Burton Inn** (4022 Burton Dr., Cambria, 805/927-5125, www.burtoninn.com, $225) offers modernity in an attractive setting. Even the standard guest rooms offer tons of space, and the family suites have multiple bedrooms that promote both togetherness and privacy.

One of the cuter and more interesting lodgings on Moonstone Beach Drive, **Moonstone Cottages** (6580 Moonstone Beach Dr., Cambria, 805/927-1366, http://moonstonecottages.com, $234) offers peace and luxury along with proximity to the sea. Expect your cottage to include a fireplace, a marble bathroom with a whirlpol tub, a flat-screen TV with a DVD player, Internet access, and a view of the ocean.

For a great selection of anything from economical standard rooms up to sizeable cabins, pick the **Cambria Pines Lodge** (2905 Burton Dr., 800/445-6868, www.cambria pineslodge.com, $150-400). All rooms have plenty of creature comforts, including TVs, private bathrooms, kitchenettes, and, in some cases, fireplaces.

## FOOD

The **Sow's Ear** (2248 Main St., Cambria, 805/927-4865, www.thesowsear.com, daily 5–9 P.M., $10–30) does its best to create the proverbial "silk purse" dining experience with its upscale comfort foods and romantically dim atmosphere. Some diners feel that the prices for items such as lobster pot-pie and chicken and dumplings can run a bit high, but if you're longing for a taste of old-fashioned Americana, you can get it here.

If the smell of the salt air on Moonstone Beach leaves you longing for a seafood dinner, head for the **Sea Chest Oyster Bar** (6216 Moonstone Beach Dr., Cambria, 805/927-4514, daily 5:30–9 P.M., $20–30, cash only). No reservations are accepted, so expect a long line out the door at opening time, and prepare to get there early (or wait a long while) for one of the window-side tables. The seafood here tends to be fresh, with a good selection of raw oysters, and touristfriendly.

Perhaps the most famous, if slightly overrated, restaurant in Cambria is the **Black Cat Bistro** (1602 Main St., Cambria, 805/927-1600, www .blackcatbistro.com, Thurs.–Mon. 5 P.M.–close, $20–40). An interesting California-French menu contains both small and large plates, each with a suggested wine pairing. Despite its fancy food, the Black Cat prides itself on its casual resort-town atmosphere.

Part of an expansive but still totally local family business, **Linn's Restaurant** (2277 Main St., Cambria, 805/927-0371, www.linnsfruitbin.com/restaurant, daily 8 A.M.–9 P.M., $10) serves tasty, unpretentious American favorites in a casual, family-friendly atmosphere. If you love the olallieberry pie with your meal, you can purchase a ready-to-bake pie, jam, or even vinegar at the Linn's café, gourmet shop, or their original farm stand while you're in Cambria.

In ubiquitously high-priced Cambria, one of the best food bargains in town is ◖ **Wild Ginger** (2380 Main St., Cambria, 805/927-1001, www.wildgingercambria.com, Fri.–Wed. 11 A.M.–2:30 P.M., 5–9 P.M., $15). This tiny pan-Asian café serves delicious, fresh food at its few tables, and carries an array of take-out fare displayed in a glass case crammed into the back of the dining room. Come early for the best selection of dishes.

## INFORMATION AND SERVICES

The town of Cambria does not boast a bricks-and-mortar visitors center, but you can do research in advance of your stay at http://cambriavisitorsbureau.com. If your primary interest is Hearst Castle, you'll find a huge visitors center at the parking lot below the castle where all tours start. Inside, you can buy and pick up tour tickets, grab a cup of coffee and a meal, and peruse the extensive bookshop, which includes many books about the Hearst family, the castle, and the town of Cambria.

The nearest hospital to Cambria is the **Twin Cities Hospital** (1100 Las Tablas Rd., Templeton, 805/434-3500), well east of the coast town. It sits near U.S. 101, just south of the junction of state Highway 46 and U.S. 101.

## GETTING THERE AND AROUND

Most Californians making a weekend getaway to Cambria from either Northern California or Southern California drive there. You can drive the Pacific Coast Highway (Highway 1) right into Cambria—this is the prettiest but not the fastest way to get there. For a quicker route, take U.S. 101 to the Paso Robles area and then turn west onto CA-46, which brings you right to the town of Cambria.

If you prefer to travel by rail, you can take **Amtrak's** Coast Starlight (www.amtrak.com) to either the Paso Robles or the San Luis Obispo (SLO) stations, and make arrangements to rent a car (easiest from SLO) or get alternative transportation out to the coast.

# Paso Robles

As an up-and-coming wine-growing region, Paso Robles has become a familiar destination and appellation for state residents and as well as a popular side trip from nearby Cambria. Huge crowds do not descend on Paso every weekend as they do in the more popular wine regions and you can still find room at the tasting bars, engage with knowledgeable tasting room staff, meet the occasional winemaker tending bar, and enjoy a friendly country atmosphere both in town and on the wine roads. For the best tasting experience, visit the Paso region over the weekend—many of the smaller winery tasting rooms are open only Thursday–Monday or even only Friday–Sunday.

## WINERIES

The wine industry is growing by leaps and bounds in and all around Paso. The Paso Robles region now boasts more than 200 wineries, over 100 of which have tasting rooms open to the public. For the purposes of this book, the sprawled landscape is divided into four easily navigable parts: Highway 46 West, Highway 46 East (which does not directly connect to Hwy. 46 West), Downtown Paso Robles, and Remote—the area to the north of town on several roads branching away from U.S.101.

### Highway 46 West

The densest concentration of wineries cluster along Highway 46 West and the little roads that spring off that main thoroughfare. Many intrepid wine tasters never make it past this short and easy-to-travel stretch, which locals refer to as the Westside.

One of the best of wineries in these parts is **Hunt Cellars** (2875 Oakdale Rd., 805/237-1600, www.huntcellars.com, daily 10:30 A.M.–5:30 P.M., tasting fee $5–10). Friendly and intensely knowledgeable staff members pour some of the best wines in Paso at this mid-sized, informal tasting room. You'll enter a building that looks more like a house than a winery, then choose the regular or reserve tasting. Also be sure to check the chalkboard behind the bar for the day's specialty offerings. All the wines at Hunt are grown in the family-owned Destiny Vineyard. The specialty of the house is Cabernet Sauvignon, and Hunt makes some of the best in California. You'll also get to taste a few Chardonnays, other red varietals, some red blends, and the famed (and expensive) port and dessert wines.

If you favor small wineries that only produce tiny runs of wine, **Dark Star Cellars** (2985 Anderson Rd., 805/237-2389, www.darkstar cellars.com, Fri.–Sun. 10:30 A.M.–5 P.M.) is perfect for you. Be sure to ask at the bar about the "synthetic gravity" that's so important to the slow fermentation process used at Dark Star. You'll taste about five vintages here—all red wines of the Bordeaux tribe. Most visitors think that the best of the lot is the much-lauded Ricordati, a Bordeaux blend that wins international awards year after year. Perhaps the nicest surprise of all comes when you've picked your favorites; prices at Dark Star range up to about $35 a bottle, and many are under $30.

## Highway 46 East

It's not as crowded as 46 West, but Highway 46 East has plenty of great wineries. You might even recognize one or two names out in the Eastside.

One of the biggest winemakers to maintain a tasting room in the Paso region is **Meridian** (7000 Hwy. 46 E., 805/226-7133, www .meridianvineyards.com, daily 10 A.M.–5 P.M., tasting fee $5). You've no doubt seen Meridian on many menus and countless supermarket shelves. Meridian makes all the classic California varietal vintages, with bestsellers in Chardonnay and Cabernet Sauvignon. Check out the Limited Release list for, well, a bunch more of the same plus a few slightly less common wines like a Gewurztraminer and a Sangiovese. Meridian's deli and store provide a perfect place to gather up everything you need for the perfect wine picnic.

It might not be the biggest, but **Eberle Winery** (3810 Hwy. 46 E., 3.5 miles east of U.S. 101, 805/238-9607, www.eberlewinery.

com, daily 10 A.M.–5 P.M., until 6 P.M. in summer, free) is one of the pioneers of the Paso wine region. Gary Eberle has been making wine here for more than 25 years, and winning a passel of gold medals over that time. Be sure to get a spot on a cave tour while you're visiting, then head to the light-wood tasting room. Despite the fun statuary and the great caves at Eberle, the star attraction here is the wine. The medium-sized list features mostly hearty, bold red wines such as Cabernet Sauvignon, Barbera, Zinfandel, and a few fabulous blends. A few whites find their way to the bar, such as the Paso favorite Viognier and the lesser-known Roussanne. Taste as many as you possibly can—and you'll be surprised at how many bottles you'll want to walk away with. With most vintages selling for $15–25, you might be able to afford a few extras.

## Downtown Paso Robles

Many wineries have set up tasting rooms right in the middle of downtown Paso. It's hard to resist walking into a tasting room that bears the name **Midlife Crisis Winery** (1244 Pine St., Ste. A, 805/237-8730, www.midlifecrisis winery.com, Thurs.–Mon. 10:30 A.M.–6 P.M.). Midlife Crisis is just that according to its owners, two veterans of the Los Angeles media circus who come up to Paso on the weekends to tend to their new pet winery. They got started in 2004, so you'll find mostly young vintages in the large, eclectic tasting room that's built into an historic Paso building. Heck, you might find one of the owner/winemakers in there, pouring, stocking, or just talking with employees and guests. Though the wines here leave plenty of room for improvement, the chatter and gossip are the best in the area. If you just ask a question or two, you'll learn everything you ever wanted to know about the wines and vineyards of the Paso Robles region.

If you're in town to find the best vintages possible, stop in at **Edward Sellers Vineyards & Wines** (1220 Park St., 805/239-8915, www.edward sellers.com, Thurs.–Mon. 11 A.M.–6 P.M.). This one's a favorite of California cork dorks, creating a number of Rhone varietals and some fabulous blends that transcend their French roots and California styles to create something new. If you're a varietal lover, try Edward's Grenaches and Viogniers—less common wines that are picking up popularity with serious wine aficionados in California. The small tasting room with distressed white woodwork and a shining black counter makes room for several tasters at once, so belly on up and ask for a glass! And if you don't know your Cinsault from your Counoise, be sure to ask. The pourers are happy to answer any and all questions pertaining to Edward Sellers wines and vineyards.

What matches more perfectly with a glass of small-lot wine than a chunk of artisanal cheese? At **Orchid Hill Vineyard** (1140 Pine St., 805/237-7525, www.orchidhillwine.com, daily 11:30 A.M.–6 P.M.), you can get both. From Friday through Sunday, a tasting at Orchid Hill includes pairings with fine, flavorful cheeses that catch the attention of many a taster. Visitors also spend some time gaping at the walls, which bear original modern artwork by Jean Pierre de Rothschild. The small list of varietals, which includes Viogniers, Syrah, Sangiovese, and Zinfandel, includes some tasty wines (but they aren't the best in the area).

## Remote Wineries

Even if you don't love wine, it's worth the trip up to **Adelaida Cellars** (5805 Adelaida Rd., 800/676-1232, www.adelaida.com, daily 10 A.M.–5 P.M.). You'll get stunning views of Adelaida's mountain vineyards and down to the valley below. Adelaida wines are made with grapes grown on the estate vineyards, and the results can be fabulous. Adelaida takes advantage of its high elevation and difficult soil to raise grapes that produce small lots of top-tier boutique wines. Smoky, rich, angry-tasting Syrahs make up the backbone of Adelaida's list, which also includes Chardonnays, Rousannes, Vin Gris, Zinfandel, Pinot Noir, Cabernet Sauvignon, and a number of different and delicious blends. The winery produces vintages under four labels; the Reserve and Adelaida labels run toward the higher end, while the

SLO and Schoolhouse labels provide tasty and affordable table wines suitable for everyday drinking.

A local producer with prestigious founders and backers, **Tablas Creek Vineyard** (9339 Adelaida Rd., 805/237-1231, www.tablascreek .com, daily 10 A.M.–5 P.M.) specializes in Rhone and Chateauneuf-du-Pape varietals and blends. Taste from the longish list of current commercial and winery-only vintages. Tablas Creek takes its winemaking seriously, maintaining its own grapevine nursery, keeping its vineyards organic, and using only its own yeasts created on-site. If such practices interest you, call in advance to get a spot on the daily vineyard and winery tours. End your survey of this showplace with a visit to the dark bar and bright artwork of the tasting room. You'll find many uncommon-for-California blends and varietals here, and the Tablas Creek bar staff can help you expand your palate and your knowledge of wine.

**Halter Ranch Vineyard** (8910 Adelaida Rd., 805/226-9455, www.halterranch.com, daily 11 A.M.–5 P.M.) sits on a 900-acre ranch property once owned by a pioneer of the Paso Robles area. In 2000, the ranch was bought by a Swiss emigrant who planted almost 250 acres to grapes from the Bordeaux and Rhone varietal families. All the vineyards are farmed using organic and sustainable methods, which combine with the limestone-rich soil and unique climate to help create intensely flavorful wines. The ranch is fronted by a charming white Victorian farmhouse, and tours (call in advance) take you around both this house and the other historic buildings on the property, as well as the two winemaking facility structures. This newish winery has a small list from which to taste and purchase; its flagship vintages are Syrah and Cabernet Sauvignon, but the less expensive Ranch Red and Ranch White blends are also good buys.

## Wine Festivals and Events

Consider coming to town during one of the several wine-oriented festivals held in and around Paso Robles each year. The biggest is the **Paso Robles Wine Festival** (www.paso wine.com/events/winefestival.php, $55–125), which happens over the third weekend of May each year. The central event of the festival, the Outdoor Wine Tasting, happens on Saturday in the Paso's downtown city park. More than 80 wineries bring out their wares, making it fabulously easy to find your favorites and learn about some new vintners in the region. In addition to the central tasting, most Paso wineries keep their tasting room doors open, offering tours, special tastings, food pairings, winemakers, and more. A recent addition to the festival, a golf tournament held on the festival weekend brings golfers from all over out for a round in the perfect Central Coast spring weather. Buy your tickets for the wine festival and the golf

tournament well in advance; both events always sell out.

At the other side of the year, the **Harvest Wine Tour Weekend** (www.pasowine.com/events/harvest.php) celebrates the changing foliage of the grapevines and the frantic rush to bring in the grapes and start the juices fermenting. Nearly 100 wineries throughout Paso put on events during the third weekend of October. Check with your favorites to learn what's coming this year. You might want to sign up early for a cooking class, or just show up to join in on some messy but fun grape stomping. If you're lucky, you might even get to take a tour of a winemaking facility in full furor, and learn a bit about how your favorite vintages are made. As with the

## MORE THAN WINE

The warm Mediterranean valley climate makes a good landscape for growing olives as well as the grape. Several groves of the silvery-green trees produce high-quality fruit that orchard owners press into small batches of artisan olive oil. A number of orchards cluster here, offering fresh local olive oil and an array of cured olives. If you just can't stomach another ounce of wine, clear your palate at one of the open olive tasting rooms.

One of these growers is **Olea Farm** (2985 Templeton Rd., Templeton, 805/610-2258, www.oleafarm.com, Sat.-Sun. 10 A.M.-4:30 P.M.). This orchard and its tasting room are located to the east of downtown Paso Robles. On a visit, you can take a tour of the orchards, then head inside to taste the different types of olive oil made from the Arbequina olive trees grown here. With five or more distinct flavors of oil to choose from, you'll certainly find a favorite to bring home with you. Be sure to say hi to Oak, the orchard dog, when you visit.

**Mt. Olive Organic Farm** (3445 Adelaida Rd, Paso Robles, 805/237-0147, www.mtoliveco. com, Thurs.-Sun. 10 A.M.-5 P.M., Apr.-Oct. until 7 P.M.) grows far more than just olives. The diverse crops at Mt. Olive range from cherries and apricots to sprouts to vegetables, as well as grass-fed beef and free-range chick-

ens. The storefront sells meat, eggs, and the wide variety of produce grown here, plus an array of products made from the produce – such as jams, fruit leathers, dried fruits, and nuts. If you've been trekking through the Far Out wineries and need a meal, you can also get fresh, hot, organic cuisine here. The small menu might include steak and chicken dishes, spaghetti, pizza, and soup. To drink, try the fresh-squeezed seasonal juices and slushies.

Down in Atascadero, call ahead to schedule a visit to the **Green Acres Lavender Farm** (8865 San Gabriel Rd., Atascadero, 805/466-0837, www.greenacreslavenderfarm.com, daily 10 A.M.-6 P.M., by appointment). One thing is certain: You will leave smelling good. This four-plus-acre farm grows 12,000 lavender plants – mostly Grosso and Provencal for their high oil production. At the farm stand or on the website you can purchase an array of natural products made from and with lavender oil. Choose a bottle of pure essential oil to create your own means for scenting your home, soy candles, lavender soaps, lavender sachets, or even a jar of culinary lavender you can use in cooking. The owners and staff will be happy to give you suggestions for using their products, and to expound on the benefits of lavender in your home.

spring Wine Festival, it's a good idea to book your room and make your plans early for the Harvest Tour—the event has become quite popular with wine aficionados across the state and beyond.

## Wine Tours

If you prefer not to do your own driving on your wine-tasting excursions (something to consider if everyone in your party enjoys wine), take one of the many available wine tours. **The Wine Wranglers** (866/238-6400, http:// thewinewrangler.com, $90–120 depending on pick-up location) offers daily group tours, plus customized individual tours for a higher fee. Experienced guides will take you to some of the biggest and best wineries in the region. Group tour guests ride in the comfort of a small luxury bus; buses pick up tasters from Cambria, San Luis Obispo, Morro Bay, Pismo Beach, Paso Robles itself, and a number of other towns in the county. A picnic lunch in one of the vineyards is included, as are all tasting fees at the wineries you visit. If you know the region, feel free to request a stop at your favorite winery!

If you prefer to tour the vineyards in the privacy of your own rented limo, book a car with **At Your Service Limousine** (805/239-8785, www.tcsn.net/ays, $200–325). This company offers Paso wine tours up to five hours long, with room for up to eight riders for no additional fee. Tasting fees are included with your car.

## SIGHTS

It's not the biggest or most diverse, but you'll have fun exploring the **Charles Paddock Zoo** (Lago Ave. at Hwy. 41, Atascadero, 805/461-5080, www.charlespaddockzoo.org, daily 10 A.M.–4 P.M., adults $5, children $4). Plan an hour or two to make a leisurely tour of the fierce tigers, funky prehensile-tailed raccoons, and famous slender-tailed meerkats. You can also visit the aviary to enjoy the twitters and squawks of more than a dozen varieties of common and exotic birds. The Zoo makes a fun destination if you've brought your kids to the largely adult playground that is Paso Robles.

A good spot for younger kids is the **Paso Robles Children's Museum at the Volunteer Firehouse** (623 13th St., Paso Robles, 805/238-7432, www.pasokids.org, Mon., Thurs.–Sat. 11 A.M.–5 P.M., adults $7, children $6). As much a playground as a museum, the space offers themed interactive exhibits with a slight educational bent for toddlers and elementary school-aged children. Kids can draw, paint, climb, jump, play, and learn in one of the few spots in Paso Robles dedicated entirely to the younger set.

The **Paso Robles Pioneer Museum** (2010 Riverside Ave., 805/239-4556, www.paso roblespioneermuseum.org, Thurs.–Sun. 1–4 P.M.) celebrates the settlement of San Luis Obispo County. Exhibits have a distinctly Western Americana flavor and includes some larger displays of carriages, farm equipment, and even an old one-room schoolhouse.

## SPORTS AND RECREATION

**Harris Stage Lines** (5995 N. River Rd., 805/237-1860, www.harrisstagelines.com) doesn't offer the typical sedate trail rides. Instead of climbing up onto the back of a horse, you'll get into a refurbished historic coach or wagon and go for a ride like they did in the 19th century. Harris has a restored stagecoach, a chuck wagon, and even a couple of Hollywood-built Roman-style chariots. Call in advance to arrange the perfect outing for your party. If you're really into the historic vehicle scene, you can even book a private driving lesson. Riding lessons are also available.

The craze for floating above vineyards in a balloon basket has made it as far as Paso Robles. This wine region sits in a pretty valley that's perfect for a romantic ballooning jaunt. **Let's Go Ballooning!** (4295 Union Rd., 805/458-1530, http://sloballoon.com, $189/person) can take you on a one-hour ride up over the Paso wine country any day of the week. You'll meet early at the Rio Seco Winery and spend 2–3 hours with your pilot, preparing and learning about how to ride safely.

Several minutes' drive from downtown Paso, the **River Oaks Hot Springs & Spa** (800 Clubhouse Dr., Paso Robles, 805/238-4600, www.river oakshotsprings.com, Sun.–Thurs. 9 A.M.–9 P.M., Fri.–Sat. 9 A.M.–10 P.M., $12–16/hour) sits on country club land over one of the local sulfur-heavy mineral springs. You'll smell the sulfur even as you drive up and walk from the parking lot to the spacious lobby. An attendant will show you the facilities and guide you to your room. A popular and reasonably priced option here is an hour of relaxation and healing in one of the outdoor or indoor-open-air hot tubs. You can use the faucets to set your own perfect temperature, and gaze out into the thick gardens that screen the spas from the adjacent golf course. For a more thoroughly relaxing experience, pick a massage or facial treatment to go with your hot tub (or alone, if you don't care for sulfur water). Check the website for package specials (many of which include wine served in the privacy of your hot tub room) and aesthetic treatment options.

## ACCOMMODATIONS

Accommodations around Paso Robles tend toward upscale wine-themed B&Bs. **Le Domaine at Moss Ridge Vineyard** (1855 Twelve Oaks Dr., 805/227-4372, www.ledomainebb.com, $217, no smoking, no children under 16) sits on the Moss Ridge Vineyard, giving guests an up-close and personal view of the vines from each of the three French country style rooms. Serenity, privacy, luscious wine-country food, and luxurious amenities mark your stay at this tiny boutique inn.

The **Orchard Hill Farm Bed & Breakfast** (5415 Fairhills Rd., 805/239-9604, www .orchardhillbb.com, $220) has a more English country feel. The attractive manor house offers luxurious rooms with top-tier amenities, a gourmet breakfast, and attractive grounds for walking and lounging.

Out in the wooded region between Paso and the coast, the **Chanticleer Vineyard Bed and Breakfast** (1250 Paint Horse Pl., 805/226-0600, www.chanticleervineyard bb.com, $217, no smoking, no children) offers relaxed vacationing and fun pets. Each of the three rooms includes an iPod dock, organic spa toiletries, a fresh seasonal breakfast, and access to the house stock of cute fuzzy animals.

Rounding out the B&B offerings, **The Canyon Villa** (1455 Kiler Canyon Rd., 805/238-3362, www.thecanyonvilla.com, $224) is built in the Mediterranean style that suits this area so well. The decor of the four guest rooms continues the Italianate theme, while the oversized spa tubs, posh linens, and gas fireplace create a feeling of lush comfort.

## FOOD

**Gaetanos** (1646 Spring St., 805/239-1070, Mon.–Sat. 11:30 A.M.–2 P.M. and 5:30 P.M.–close, $10–30) serves traditional Italian fare with friendly flare. Order the handmade pizza and a glass of the house wine (the restaurant's own label), all accompanied by above-average service.

Getting back to the heavily Mexican influence of Paso's agricultural roots, grab a taco or two at **Papi's** (840 13th St., 805/239-3720, daily 11 A.M.–9 P.M., $10). Prices may be a bit higher than some taquerias, in honor of Paso's new tourist status, but the casual atmosphere and tasty enchiladas make up for it.

It's not the fanciest place in town, but the food at **( Panolivo** (1344 Park St, 805/239-3366, www.panolivo.com, Mon.–Thurs. 8–3 P.M., Fri.–Sat. 8–3:30 P.M., Sun. 9 A.M.–3:30 P.M., dinner Fri.–Sat. nights $17–28) might be the tastiest truly traditional French cuisine in town. Panolivo serves breakfast and lunch on the weekdays, adding dinner on the weekends. The casual dining room makes it easy to linger over a croque monsieur and dark coffee, though visitors just passing through can grab a luscious pastry from the display case up front.

At **Artisan** (1401 Park St., 805/237-8084, www.artisanpasorobles.com, daily 11 A.M.–10 P.M., $10–30) old school American cookery gets a California wine country makeover. The white tablecloths and numerous wine glasses hint at the fancy cuisine to come—unusual soups and sandwiches at lunch and high-end entrées at dinner.

## PRACTICALITIES

The closest thing to a visitors center is the **Paso Robles Chamber of Commerce** (1225 Park St., 805/238-0506, www.pasorobles chamber.com, Mon.–Fri. 8 A.M.–5 P.M., Sat.–Sun. 10 A.M.–2 P.M.). Pick up a guide to Paso Robles, or specific dining, lodging, and winery information.

For medical attention, the nearest hospital

is **Twin Cities Hospital** (see *Cambria* for more information).

The two best ways to get to Paso Robles are by car and by train. Drivers can take Highway 101 from the north or the south to directly to town. Once in Paso Robles, take Highway 46 east for the main wine road.

On the rails, the **Amtrak** Coast Starlight (www.amtrak.com) stops right in Paso. Avoid driving altogether by taking the train into town, then renting a limo or getting on with a wine tour.

# Santa Barbara

It's called the American Riviera, with weather, community, and sun-drenched beaches reminiscent to some of the European coast of the Mediterranean Sea. In truth, Santa Barbara is all California. Culturally, Santa Barbara sits in Southern California but the pace of life slows down just enough to make for a comfortable vacation. Many of the visitors to Santa Barbara do in fact come from elsewhere in California, and the town is known to residents as one of the best "local" beach resorts. In the town proper, you'll find lots of museums, outdoor shopping areas, and great restaurants. Inland a bit, a growing young wine region thrives. Along the soft, flat sandy beaches cluster fabulous four-star beach resorts.

## SIGHTS
### Santa Barbara Maritime Museum

It's only fitting that the Santa Barbara Maritime Museum (113 Harbor Way, 805/962-8404, www.sbmm.org, Thurs.–Tues. 10 A.M.–5 P.M., until 6 P.M. Memorial Day–Labor Day, adults $7, children/seniors $4, free for military personnel in uniform) sits right on the working harbor. It began as a Government Works Project during the Depression. For more than 50 years, the station was used by the U.S. Navy as a training facility. After being sold back to the city of Santa Barbara in 1995, construction

began on the museum, which opened in 2000. Over a dozen different exhibits show off the history of the California coast's relationship to the high seas. The Munger Theater screens high- definition educational films each day. The Children's Area features hands-on exhibits that make learning about the sea lots of fun for younger visitors. Many other galleries tell the maritime history of California, beginning with the local Chumash Native Americans, running through the whaling and fur-hunting eras, up through the modern oil drilling and commercial fishing industries. You can also learn a bit about sailing and yachting, safety on the Pacific, and how you can help preserve the ocean's environment.

### ◖ Santa Barbara Museum of Natural History

Continuing the outdoors theme that pervades Santa Barbara, the Santa Barbara Museum of Natural History (2559 Puesta del Sol, 805/682-4711, www.sbnature.org, daily 10 A.M.–5 P.M., adults $10, youth $7, children $6) has exhibits to delight visitors of all ages. Inside, visit the large galleries that display stories of the life and times of insects, mammals, birds, and dinosaurs. Learn a little about the human history of the Santa Barbara area at the Chumash exhibit. Head outdoors to circle the immense skeleton of a blue whale, and to hike the Mission

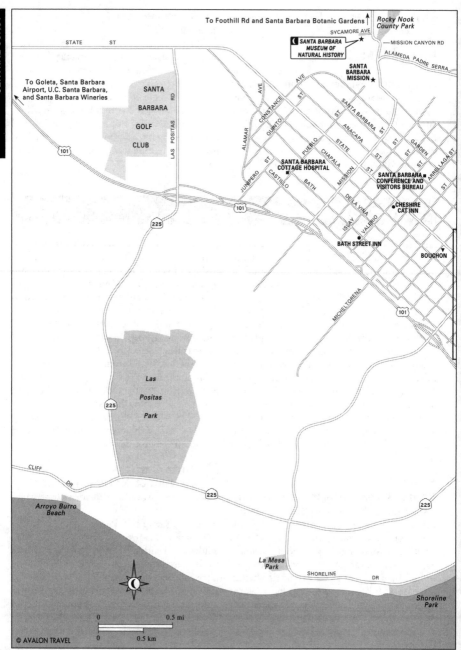

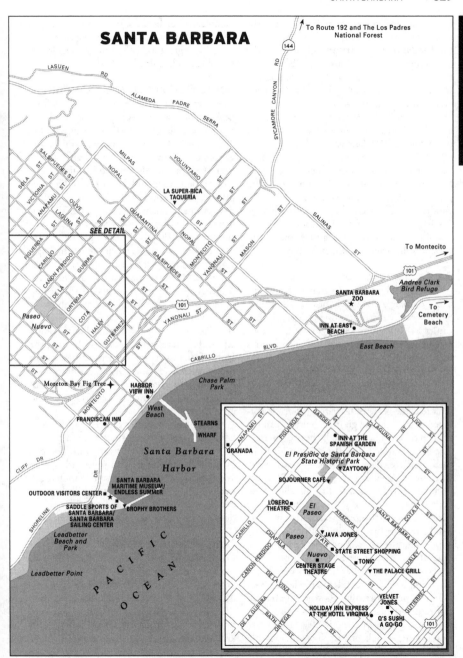

# SANTA BARBARA

To Route 192 and The Los Padres
National Forest

144

LASUEN RD

ALAMEDA PADRE SERRA

SYCAMORE CANYON RD

MILPAS

VOLUNTARIO

SOLA ST
VICTORIA ST
ANAPAMU ST
LAGUNA ST
OLIVE ST
NOPAL
QUARANTINA ST
SALSIPUEDES ST

LA SUPER-RICA
TAQUERIA

SEE DETAIL

FIGUEROA
CARRILLO
CANON PERDIDO
DE LA
ORTEGA
COTA
HALEY
GUTIERREZ
GUERRA

NOPAL
SALSIPUEDES ST
MONTECITO ST
YANONALI ST
MASON ST
SALINAS ST

To Montecito

101

Andree Clark
Bird Refuge

SANTA BARBARA
ZOO

To
Cemetery
Beach

Paseo
Nuevo

YANONALI ST

INN AT EAST
BEACH

CABRILLO BLVD

East Beach

Moreton Bay Fig Tree

MONTECITO

HARBOR
VIEW INN

Chase Palm
Park

FRANCISCAN INN

West
Beach

STEARNS
WHARF

CLIFF DR

Santa Barbara

Harbor

SHORELINE DR

OUTDOOR VISITORS CENTER

SANTA BARBARA
MARITIME MUSEUM/
ENDLESS SUMMER

SADDLE SPORTS OF
SANTA BARBARA/
SANTA BARBARA
SAILING CENTER

BROPHY BROTHERS

Leadbetter
Beach and
Park

Leadbetter Point

PACIFIC OCEAN

## Detail

GRANADA

ANAPAMU ST
FIGUEROA ST
GARDEN ST
ST LAGUNA
OLIVE ST

INN AT THE
SPANISH GARDEN

El Presidio de Santa Barbara
State Historic Park

ZAYTOON

SOJOURNER CAFÉ

LOBERO
THEATRE

El
Paseo

Paseo

CARRILLO
CHAPALA ST
STATE ST
ANACAPA ST
SANTA BARBARA ST
COTA ST
HALEY
GUTIERREZ ST

JAVA JONES

Nuevo

CENTER STAGE
THEATRE

STATE STREET SHOPPING

TONIC

THE PALACE GRILL

CANON PERDIDO
DE LA VINA
ORTEGA
BATH

VELVET
JONES

HOLIDAY INN EXPRESS
AT THE HOTEL VIRGINIA

Q'S SUSHI
A GO-GO

101

Creek Nature Trail. If you're interested in the nature of worlds other than this one, go into the **Gladwin Planetarium** and wander the Astronomy Center exhibits. The Planetarium hosts daily shows portraying the moon and stars, plus monthly Star Parties and special events throughout the year.

If you're more interested in the Earth's array of sea life, head down to Stearns Wharf and visit the **Ty Warner Sea Center** (211 Stearns Wharf, 805/962-2526, www.sbnature.org/seacenter, daily 10 A.M.–5 P.M.), which is operated by the Museum of Natural History (multi-museum passes at either location, adults $8, youth $7, children $5) Check out the tunnel through the 1,500-gallon surge tank, touch a sea cucumber, examine microscopic sea creatures, and get involved in the science of oceanography.

## Santa Barbara Zoo

It's not the biggest zoo in the state, but the Santa Barbara Zoo (500 Ninos Dr., 805/962-5339, www.sbzoo.org, daily 10 A.M.–5 P.M., adults $11, children $8). is a cool little municipal zoo. It shelters its critters in enclosures that resemble those of the San Diego Zoo, including a multi-species habitat that mimics an African savannah with giraffes, tortoises, cranes, and rodents all hanging out together. Granted, the pride of lions next door are corralled away from the giraffes, but you can get close to them and occasionally hear them roar. The Santa Barbara Zoo also takes pride in its local, endangered species—the Channel Island foxes are indigenous to an area only 20 miles from the zoo. The new California condor exhibit shows off one of the rarest birds in the state, still an endangered species. As you slowly stroll along the paths, you'll also see cute lemurs, huge elephants, monkeys, and gibbons. One of the best-named kids' exhibits ever, "Eewww!" showcases reptiles and wonderful slimy amphibians at children's eye level.

If you need a stroller or wheelchair, you can rent one just inside the zoo. Also close to the gate you'll find the Ridley-Tree House Restaurant, which offers plenty of outside tables and a walk-up arrangement that sells

sandwiches and burgers. In season, small carts ply the pathways, selling coffee, popsicles, and more. The gift shop offers cute souvenirs for both kids and adults.

## Santa Barbara Botanic Gardens

The year-round perfect weather makes for a perfect spot to grow the gorgeous Santa Barbara Botanic Gardens (1212 Mission Canyon Rd., 805/682-4726, www.santabarbarabotanic garden.org, daily 9 A.M.–5 P.M., until 6 P.M. Mar.–Oct., adults $8, youth $6, children $4). The gardens focus solely on the indigenous plants of California, with plantings from the deserts, chaparral, arroyo, and more. The gardens spread out over many acres, and crosses several hiking trails. Check out the coastal redwood forest, the centerpiece of the park, which remains shaded and cool even when the sun beats down in the heat of summertime. Another proud garden shows off the beauty of native California lilacs. The mission of the gardens encompasses conservation of not only the California wilderness areas, but the water and soil in developed areas as well. Visit the Home Demonstration Garden for an example of beautiful landscaping using California natives that are suited to the climate and conditions, and thus need less irrigation and chemical fertilizers.

Guided tours are offered each day with your admission ticket—join the standard tour or call ahead to arrange a private tour. You can take your own self-guided tour with a map and the advice of the docents. The shop offers books and garden-themed gifts, while the nursery sells native Californian plants. The garden does not include a restaurant or snack bar.

## Santa Barbara Mission

Often referred to as "Queen of the Missions," the Santa Barbara Mission (2201 Laguna St., 805/682-4713, http://santabarbaramission.org, daily 9 A.M.–4:30 P.M., tours $5 adults, $4 senior, $1 youth, children 6 and under free) is second to none for its art displays of art and graceful architecture, all of which are complemented by the serene local climate and scenery. Unlike

© ROBERT HOLMES / CALTOUR

**Santa Barbara Mission, Queen of the Missions**

many of the California Missions, the church at Santa Barbara remained in service after the secularization of the Mission chain in the 19th century. When you visit, you'll find the collection of buildings, art work, and even the ruins of the water system in better shape than at many other Missions in the state. The self-guided tour through the Mission complex gives visitors a sense of the Mission's story, its church and Native American history, and the lives of the people who lived and worked within it.

## WINERIES

Few people outside of the wine world or the state of California realize that Santa Barbara is a budding wine region. The grandfather of Santa Barbara wineries is the **Firestone Winery** (5000 Zaca Station Rd., 805/688-3940, www .firestonewine.com, $10). You'll enter a grand, elegant Napa-style tasting room with a trapezoidal tasting bar and various souvenirs and cases scattered around the room. The tones of the room and the lighting are warm, as are the manners of the staff up at the bar.

**Zaca Mesa Winery** (6905 Foxen Canyon Rd., Los Olivos, 805/688-9339, www.zaca mesa.com, daily 10 A.M.–4 P.M.) is the kind of winery tasters love to discover. A mid-sized producer with a mid-sized facility and tasting room, Zaca quietly makes some of the best Central Coast wines to be found anywhere in the region. The first vineyards on the property were planted in the early 1970s, long before anyone else saw Santa Barbara as a place with potential for great winemaking. The casual tasting room has been tempting customers new and old for almost 30 years. The bar sits at the back of the room, and the procedure to pay your tasting fee is a little convoluted. But once you're at the bar with your glass…oh my. A five-wine tasting can quickly become a 12-wine tasting if you chat up your pourer and express an interest in the vintages. The staff has amazing knowledge of the wines they're pouring, and will enthusiastically tell you the story of each wine, the history of the grapes, and anything else you want to know. Zaca makes many of the Rhone varietals that grow so well in the climate of the Central Coast, such as Viognier, Grenache, Roussanne, and Syrah. Classics lovers will enjoy the Chardonnay, and adventurous types shouldn't skip the Syrahs and the Z Cuvee.

## ENTERTAINMENT AND EVENTS

A wealthy town with close ties to cosmopolitan Los Angeles, Santa Barbara offers visitors a wealth of live cultural displays, from a symphony and opera to a near-endless parade of festivals. The students of UCSB add a lively bit of zest to the town's after-dark scene.

### Bars and Clubs

The proximity of UCSB to downtown Santa Barbara guarantees a more lively nighttime scene than you'll find elsewhere on the Central Coast. Check with the locals to discover the ever-changing hot spots du jour. Bars cluster on State Street and beyond, and plenty of hip clubs dot the landscape here.

For a uniquely California experience, head for **Q's Sushi a Go Go** (409 State St.,

805/966-9177, www.qsbilliards.com/santa barbara, Mon.–Sat. 4 P.M.–2 A.M.). Shoot a game of pool, get your dance on to local DJs, or sit down to a high-quality sushi dinner. Or do all three in the same night at the same spot! With four bars, a full sushi menu, and a lovely SOS (stands for Sick of Sushi) entrée menu, you can eat and drink the night away at Q's, or fuel up for an energetic session on the dance floor. Q's has three levels to suit a variety of entertainments. At the bar, order any mixed drink you can dream up, or one of the tasty on-tap beers.

Only two blocks up, **Tonic** (634 State St., 805/897-1800, www.tonicsb.com) has a hipster feel, complete with exposed brick walls and a long glass bar. Top-flight DJs spin h a mostly hip hop or house groove, with the occasional mash-up for variety. Check Tonic's Myspace page for a list of upcoming DJs. Two lounges provide a respite from the partiers at the main bar and on the dance floor. To cool down, go outside to the huge outdoor patio, which has its own funky octagonal bar.

If you prefer to dance and drink to live bands, head over to **Velvet Jones** (423 State St., 805/965-8676, www.velvet-jones.com, daily 9 P.M.–2 A.M.). Artists ranging from rapper KRS-One to goth-rock Evanesce to Alien Ant Farm have played Velvet Jones. Thursday through Saturday, bands take the stage for the dancing, yelling crowds. On other nights of the week, you might find karaoke, live comedy, or a DJ spinning. Check the calendar at the website for upcoming events and shows. Even if you're not into the scene, this bar is worth walking into just for the funky giant murals on the walls and the handblown glass ornaments (in a rock club!!) adorning the bar.

## Live Music

The **Lobero Theater** (33 E. Canon Perdido St., 805/966-4946, www.lobero.com) plays host to national and international jazz acts, folk and soft rock groups and singers, an annual percussion festival, and more. Everyone from the SFJazz Collective to Ani DiFranco

has performed here. The medium-sized theater has only one level, and it's filled with cushy red velvet seats—perfect for a music-filled night out on the town or a romantic date with your sweetie. Check the website for the shows coming up during your visit. Also be sure to look into the annual film festival. You can buy tickets online, by phone, or at the box office during your stay.

## Classical Music

The **Santa Barbara Symphony** (805/898-9626, www.thesymphony.org) aspires to compete with its brethren in Los Angeles and San Francisco. The symphony orchestra puts up seasons that pay homage to the greatest composers the world has ever seen, plus the works of less-known but equally talented artists. Whether you prefer Mozart or Mahler, you can listen to it at the Granada (1214 State St.) concert hall. Every seat has a great view of the stage, and the acoustics were designed with music in mind, making for an overall great symphony experience.

**Opera Santa Barbara** (www.operasb.com) has put up such classics as *Tosca, Rigoletto,* and *Madama Butterfly.* The festival format OSB has used for the last few years lets you take in two operas in a single weekend, if that's your choice. In fine tradition, OSB enjoys a focus on the classics and little-known works of the Italian masters. Operas are staged at the Lobero Theater (33 E. Canon Perdido St., 805/963-0761, www.lobero.com), a mid-sized space that allows for a more intimate operatic experience than those you find in larger cities.

## Dance

At the **Center Stage Theater** (751 Paseo Nuevo, 805/963-0408, www.centerstage theater.org, $22–50 depending on show), look for everything from Pulitzer Prize–winning dramas to traveling nouveau ballet companies. Center Stage focuses on dance, offering more ballet and modern dance performances than it does plays. But the plays, some of which are staged by the Santa Barbara Theater

Company, tend to be some of the newest and best in the country. You won't see much Shakespeare or too many classics—instead you're likely to see *Doubt* or *The Pillowman* or something else that's fresh from Broadway and the Tony Awards.

## SHOPPING

If you're looking for a fairly standard shopping expedition in Santa Barbara, go to **State Street**. From end to end, this busy main drag hosts a near-unbelievable array of mall-style stores, plus a few independent boutiques for variety. You'll find lots of lovely women's apparel, plenty of housewares stores, and all the usual stuff you'd expect to find in a major urban shopping center. In truth, there's little that's truly special on State Street—it's a sprawled-out, mid-to-upper tier mall.

## SPORTS AND RECREATION

With the year-round balmy weather, it's nearly impossible to resist the temptation to get outside and do something energetic and fun in Santa Barbara. From golf to sea kayaking, you've got plenty of options for recreation here.

### Beaches

There's nothing easier than finding a beach in Santa Barbara. Just follow State Street to its end, and you'll be at the coastline. Municipal beaches flank Stearns Wharf on either side—rather uncreatively named **East Beach** (1400 Cabrillo Blvd., www.santabarbaraca.gov, daily sunrise–10 P.M.) and **West Beach** (West Cabrillo Blvd., www.santabarbaraca.gov, daily sunrise–10 P.M.). In fine SoCal tradition, these beaches are broad and flat and sandy, lending themselves to Frisbee and ball games, beach volleyball, and lots of lounging about in the sunshine.

To the north of town, **Arroyo Burro Beach** (Cliff Dr., 805/687-3714, www.sbparks.org, daily 8 A.M.–sunset) is a favorite for dog-owning locals. To the right as you face the water, dogs are allowed off-leash to dash across the packed sand and frolic and fetch out in the gentle surf. Arroyo Burro is rockier than the downtown beaches, making it less friendly to games and sunbathers. But the rocks and shells make for great beachcombing, and you might find a slightly smaller crowd on sunny weekend days. You'll find a snack bar, restrooms, outdoor showers, and a medium-sized pay parking lot for your convenience.

### Surfing

It's not one of the legendary California surfing locales, but there are waves to be caught in Santa Barbara, if you don't mind surfing in the shadow of the ever-present oil derricks.

A great spot for newbies to both surfing and the area is **Leadbetter Point** (Cabrillo past Stearns Wharf). The locals are reasonably welcoming, and the small right break makes for easy and fun rides. Another small-wave spot sits right in front of the east edge of **UC Santa Barbara at Isla Vista** (bordered by El Colegio Rd., Ocean Rd., and Camino Majorca). You'll find a big crowd of college students here (UCSB even has a surf team!), but the point break similar to that at Leadbetter is friendly to longboarders and newer surfers. Do watch out for the naturally occurring tar that mars the water and the beach sands.

For a bit more of a challenge, paddle out to the barrels at **Sand Spit** (Santa Barbara harbor). This break only really works in the wintertime when a big western swell comes in, and the water can be unpleasantly dirty. But its location within sight of the Harbor and Stearns Wharf makes it convenient.

If there's such a thing as One True Break in Santa Barbara, it's **Rincon** (U.S. 101 at Bates Rd. on the Ventura County line). If you start at the right spot, you can catch a ride over a mile long here. The sets are reliable and the waves are bigger than most other Santa Barbara breaks. For obvious reasons, locals flock to Rincon so you'll definitely be part of a crowd when you surf here.

Looking for surfing lessons? Check out the **Santa Barbara Surf School** (www.santa barbarasurfschool.com). The instructors have decades of surfing experience and pride themselves on being able to get beginners up and riding in a single lesson.

CENTRAL COAST

© LANCE SCOTT

surfers paddling

## Kayaking and Sailing

One of the best ways to see the Santa Barbara harbor and bay is under your own power in a kayak. A number of rental and touring companies offer lessons, guided paddles, and good advice for exploring the region. **Paddle Sports of Santa Barbara** (117B Harbor Way, 805/899-4046, www.kayaksb.com, Thurs.–Tues. 10 A.M.–6 P.M., $10–20/hour, tours $50–215) has everything you need to paddle the waters of Santa Barbara and Ventura. You can rent a sit-on-top or closed-deck sea kayak to take your own ride around the harbor or out into the bay. If you want to hit the Channel Islands, you must take a guided tour. Paddle Sports offers all-day trips around Santa Cruz Island, Anacapa Island, and Santa Barbara Island, as well as more sedate two- to four-hour trips around the harbor and down the Santa Barbara waterfront. Most trips are suitable for paddlers of all experience and ability levels, but be sure to tell the staff when you book if you've never been in a kayak before. If that's the case and you prefer to get some

experience before you take one of the longer tours, Paddle Sports offers lessons in both sit-on-top and closed-deck kayaking. Whether you choose a lesson or a tour, reservations in advance are recommended, especially for summer weekend days.

The **Santa Barbara Sailing Center** (133 Harbor Way, 805/350-9090, http://sbsail.com, tours $65) offers a full range of kayaking options, from rentals to tours to classes, plus some great trips for more advanced paddlers. The basic excursion takes you to the Mesa Coast via one of the company's yachts, then drops you off onto a single- or double-seat sit-on-top kayak. You might see dolphins, seals, sea lions, or even migrating whales as you paddle along towards your destination: the harbor docks. For something more intense, call the SBSC to arrange a private intermediate or advanced tour.

SBSC also offers sailing excursions aboard the 50-foot *Double Dolphin* sailing catamaran.

## Fishing and Whale-Watching

Santa Barbara's prime location on the coast

makes it a great spot for deep-sea fishing and whale-watching. With its proximity to the feeding grounds of the blue and humpback whales, Santa Barbara is one of the best spots to go whale-watching in the state.

If you're looking for a whale-watching expedition or a dinner cruise, check out the **Condor Express** (Harbor Way, 805/882-0088, www.condorcruises.com, adults $50–100, children $30–50). In the summertime, they can take you out to the Channel Islands to see the blue and humpback whales feed; in the winter, the captain sails into the path of migrating gray whales. The boat is a sleek modern speed demon with posh amenities and lots of outdoor deck space that can seat almost 70 people. Whale-watching cruises depart almost daily all year long; call to purchase tickets in advance.

**Captain Don's** (219 Stearns Wharf, Ste. G, 805/969-5217, www.captdon.com) offers whale-watching and pleasure cruises with a fun pirate theme. Pleasure trips include a quick 30-minute ride around the Santa Barbara Harbor that's geared toward fun for the kids or a 90-minute sunset cocktail cruise that includes rum drinks with your ticket. Whale-watching cruises leave several times each day, heading out to the Channel Islands in the summertime and the Channel itself in winter.

If you want to go fishing, give **WaveWalker Charters** (691 Camino Campana, 805/964-2046, www.wavewalker.com) a call. This private six-passenger charter boat rents for $700 for a three-quarter day—expensive unless you bring five friends along to split the cost! Bait and all tackle are included with the charter, but a fishing license is not. Call for more information about what you can fish for when.

## Golf

It might not get the most press of the many golf destinations in California, but with its year-round mild weather and resort atmosphere, Santa Barbara is a great place to play a few holes. There are six public courses within an hour of downtown Santa Barbara—everything from a popular municipal course to championship courses with views of the ocean from the greens.

It's still a golf course, but **Glen Annie** (405 Glen Annie Rd., 805/968-6400, www .glenanniegolf.com, $60–75, carts $6–11) has worked with Audubon International to create wildlife habitats on its land. Who knows what you might see when you're out walking the lush, green, 18-hole, par-72 course? Well, you'll definitely get great views of the town of Santa Barbara, the ocean, and the Channel Islands on this hilly course. The Frog Bar & Grill, the on-site restaurant, draws any number of non-golfers up to Glen Annie for lunch. Set in a castle-like structure, the Frog serves California cuisine dishes that are a far cry from most clubhouse fare. So come for the golf, stay for the unusual and delicious fare.

If you're already interested in exploring Santa Barbara's wine country, consider reserving a tee time at **La Purisima Golf Course** (3455 Hwy. 246, 805/735-8395, $30–80). This golf course, built in 1986, gets high praise for its design and difficulty level—even if you're an expert golfer, "La Piranha" will test your skills. The par 72 course is a 45-minute drive from downtown Santa Barbara, but many locals think it's worth the trip. In addition to the 18 holes, you can access the grass driving range, the short-game practice area, and the pro shop. A number of PGA and LPGA golf pros are on hand to help you improve your game.

The **Sandpiper** (7925 Hollister Ave., 805/968-1541, www.sandpipergolf.com, $60–140, cart $16) boasts some of the most amazing views you'll find in all of Santa Barbara. They're so great because they're right up close, and on several holes your ball is in danger of falling into the world's largest water trap. And hey, there's a great championship rated 74.5, 18-hole, par 72 golf course out there on that picturesque beach too! Take advantage of the pro shop and on-site restaurant, but do be aware of the semi-formal, denim-free dress code Sandpiper enforces. It's not cheap, but a long walk on the beach with a great golf game in the middle of it seems well worth it to an endless stream of golfers who rank Sandpiper as one of their favorite courses.

## Spas

Folks who can afford to live in Santa Barbara tend to be able to afford many of the finer things in life, including massages, facials, and luxe skin treatments. You'll find a wide array of day spas and medical spas in town.

**Beleza Skin Care Center** (219 Gray Ave., 805/966-2373, www.belezaskincare.com) sits in the Studio E Healing Arts center. This high-end spa specializes in the best skin care money can buy, with a focus on anti-aging and acne treatments. Choose from an array of luxurious facials, chemical and herbal peels, microdermabrasion, makeup consultation, and permanent makeup application. You'll walk into the charming spa with its live plants and Eastern decor, check in, and be led back into your treatment room. Most facials and treatments last an hour or more. Beleza also offers a full menu of waxing services.

If you prefer a slightly more natural spa experience, book a treatment at **Le Reve** (21 W. Gutierrez, 805/564-2977, www.le-reve.com). Using biodynamic skin care products and pure essential oils, Le Reve makes good on the advertising billing it as an "aromatherapy spa." Choose from an original array of body treatments, massage, hand and foot pampering, facials, and various aesthetic treatments. If you're up for several hours of relaxation, check out the spa packages that combine facials with massage and body treatments.

**Cielo Spa and Boutique** (1725 State St., Ste. C, 805/687-8979, www.cielospasb.com) prides itself on its warm, nurturing environment. Step inside and admire the scents and the soft lighting and the natural, new agey decor. Contemplate the colorful live orchids, feel soothed by the flickering candlelight, and get lost in the tranquil atmosphere. The menu of services has an almost Northern Californian flare, with signature Champagne treatments and a focus on organics and natural lotions and potions. Check into the luxury packages that combine massages, facials, and more for a full day in the spa.

## ACCOMMODATIONS

If you want a posh beachside room in Santa Barbara, you'd better be prepared to pay for it. All the seaside resorts charge a premium rate. On the other hand, Santa Barbara offers several charming and reasonably priced accommodations near downtown and other attractions.

### $100-150

A lovely little boutique hotel in a quiet residential neighborhood near the beach, the **Franciscan Inn** (109 Bath St., 805/963-8845, www.franciscaninn.com, $125–160) looks just like a Spanish Colonial Revival hacienda, with pale adobe-style walls and a traditional red-tiled roof. Guest rooms offer everything from cute, economical, double-bed rooms to luxurious multiple-room suites. The decor tends toward the flowery, with designer wallpaper and comforters. The largest suite sleeps six comfortably; smaller rooms can sleep four if they're friendly. The amenities add to the charm of the place; you can grab a complimentary fresh croissant and a cup of coffee for breakfast, or a warm cookie in the afternoon. Take a swim in the heated pool, check your email with the free Wi-Fi, or even throw in a load of laundry at the on-site coin-op machines. Stearns Wharf and downtown are a short walk away.

The **Bath Street Inn** (1720 Bath St., 805/682-9680, www.bathstreetinn.com, $140–315) specializes in small-town charm and hospitality. It's large for a B&B, with eight rooms in the Queen Anne main house and another four in the more modern summer house. Each room has its own unique color scheme and style. Certainly you'll find some traditional floral Victorian decor, but many of the rooms are done up with elegant stripes rather than cloying blooms. Some rooms have king beds, others queens, and several have two-person whirlpool tubs. Despite the vintage trappings, the Bath Street Inn features modern amenities such as flat-screen TVs and free Wi-Fi. Early each morning, a sumptuous home-cooked breakfast is served downstairs. Choose between sharing your meal with your fellow guests in the dining room, or escaping to the sunny garden patio for a bit of privacy.

If you're in Santa Barbara to soak up the sun on the sandy beaches, book a room at the **Inn at East Beach** (1029 Orilla Del Mar, 805/965-0546, www.innateastbeach.com, $140–400). Unsurprisingly, it's just across the road from East Beach, and a nice walk along the waterfront boardwalk will take you to Stearns Wharf and to downtown. This smallish motor lodge gained notoriety when President Ronald Regan was in office, and his staff stayed at the inn while he spent time at his Santa Barbara ranch. Today, guests find sizeable rooms done up in blue carpets and comforters with pine furniture and a strange plethora of telephones. The inn prides itself on its attractive swimming pool and courtyard area, and you can feel free to bring down a bottle of wine and enjoy the balmy evenings with fellow guests. If you're planning a longer stay, get a kitchen suite so you can cook your own meals and take advantage of the inn's guest laundry facilities.

## $150-250

If you're willing to pay a premium rate for your room, the **Cheshire Cat Inn** (36 W. Valerio St., 805/569-1610, www.cheshirecat .com) can provide you with true luxury B&B accommodations. Each room has an *Alice in Wonderland* name, but the decor doesn't really match the theme—instead of whimsical and childish, you'll find Victorian floral elegance. Guest rooms are spread out through two Victorian homes ($199–299), the coach house ($279–379), and two private cottages ($369–399). Some rooms have suite-level space and amenities, including spa tubs and private balconies. Relax in the evening in the spacious octagonal outdoor spa, or order a massage in the privacy of your own room. Each morning, come downstairs and enjoy a light breakfast.

It's a chain now, but the **Holiday Inn Express at the Hotel Virginia** (17 W. Haley St., 805/963-9757, www.hotelvirginia.com, $170–275) has lots of history in Santa Barbara. Sitting right on the corner of the main drag, the Hotel Virginia welcomed guests come to take the waters and enjoy the scenery of Santa Barbara starting in 1925. Ten years ago it was renovated to bring it up to code and to spiff up the older guest rooms. Today it is run by the folks at Holiday Inn Express, but they elected not to eradicate the historic charm and atmosphere of the Virginia. When you walk into the lobby, you'll step onto a red-tiled floor and gaze upon a bright, multihued blue fountain. Upstairs, your room will feature antique-looking furnishings, exuberant floral bedspreads and curtains, and swirly green carpets. The smallish bathrooms feature prized showerheads, and the beds have both cotton and feather pillows to choose from. If you choose to stay in your room for a while, you can make yourself coffee to sip while watching your LCD flat-screen. The restaurants and shops of State Street are steps from the lobby, and the beach isn't too much farther.

## Over $250

For a taste of Santa Barbara's posh side, stay at the **Inn at the Spanish Garden** (915 Garden St., 805/564-4700, www.spanishgardeninn .com, $280–575). This small boutique hotel gets it right from the first glimpse; the building in the historic Presidio neighborhood has the characteristic whitewashed adobe exterior with a red-tiled roof, arched doorways, and wooden balconies. Courtyards seem filled with lush greenery and tiled fountains, while the swimming pool promises relief from the heat. Inside, guest rooms and suites whisper luxury with their white linens, earth-toned accents, and rich, dark wooden furniture. Enjoy the benefits of your own gas fireplace, deep soaking bathtub, French press coffee maker, plush bathrobes, and honor bar. The complimentary continental breakfast can be delivered right to your door upon request. Also upon appointment, you can arrange for a massage or facial in the comfort of your room. The Spanish Inn sits only three blocks from State Street, and within walking distance of a number of theaters and historic Santa Barbara attractions.

Are you ready and willing to pay premium prices for a luxury beachfront resort hotel room? If so, check out the **Harbor View Inn** (28 W. Cabrillo Blvd., 805/963-0780, www .harborviewinnsb.com, $352). This stunning Spanish Colonial–style property sits right across the street from the flat white sands of West Beach and steps from Stearns Wharf. Blooming flowers and bright ceramic tiles create beautiful outdoor spaces everywhere on the property. The pool is a focal point of the resort, with long hours and food and beverage service. Inside your lovely guest room, soft lighting and orange-and-red tones create a feeling of warmth. Suites offer palatial spaces and extra amenities. If you want to enjoy a tasty meal without leaving the resort property, choose between room service and the on-site oceanfront restaurant **Eladio's.** Eladio's is best known for its breakfasts, but serves three meals each day and has a good list of wines that's heavy on the local vintages.

## FOOD
### American

Yes, they do mean *that* 🎬 **The Endless Summer** (113 Harbor Way, 805/564-4666, www.endlesssummerbarcafe.net, daily 11 A.M.– close, $10). When they decided to create a new restaurant out on the pier, the owners went to Bruce Johnson, a Santa Barbara resident and acknowledged creator of the "real" surfing movie genre, and asked him if he would mind having a restaurant named for his most famous film. Bruce thought it was a fine idea, and not only gave the project his blessing, he quickly became a regular in the dining room. Photos of Bruce, other famous surfers, and lots of surfing paraphernalia from the historic to the modern deck the walls of this seaside bar and café. The menu has plenty of salads and sandwiches, includes some intriguing daily specials, and serves from the menu of the Waterfront Grill downstairs. Service is friendly, and the atmosphere tends towards casual local hangout. Many patrons know each other and the staff, and the bar gets crowded as the evening wears on. Live music— sometimes just a talented solo player—provides pleasant background and occasionally a dance track for the more energetic patrons.

### Café

Whether you're a vegetarian or not, you'll find something delicious at the **Sojourner Café** (134 E. Canon Perdido St., 805/965-7922, www .sojournercafe.com, Mon.–Sat. 11 A.M.–11 P.M., Sun. 11 A.M.–10 P.M., $20). In fact, a select few dishes include a bit of lean poultry or fish in amongst the veggies. Sojourner features healthful dishes made with ingredients that showcase local organic and sustainable farms. Lots of the cuisine has ethnic flavors, from familiar Mexico to exotic India. Daily specials use ingredients that are fresh and in-season, including some seafood. Then again, Sojourner also serves a classic root beer float and chocolate milkshakes as well as a big selection of house-baked confections to go along with their health food. Sojourner displays the work of local artists on a rotating schedule. If you fall in love with the wall art over your table, inquire with your server about purchasing it.

### California

Of the many and varied high-end California cuisine restaurants that crowd Santa Barbara, **Bouchon** (9 W. Victoria St., 805/730-1160, www.bouchonsantabarbara.com, daily 5:30 P.M.–close, $30) might be the best. Though it's no relation to the bistro of the same name in Yountville, Bouchon prides itself on both creative cuisine and top-notch service every night. You'll pay a premium to dine here, but it's worth it for a special night out. Your server will be your guide, helping you make selections from the menu, recommending wine pairings with each course, and answering any questions you might have about the restaurant or the food. California-style dishes are prepared with local and organic ingredients whenever possible, and the menu changes often based on what's available. The wine list is a special treat. It consists almost entirely of local wines—really local—from the Santa Barbara and Paso Robles regions. Servers have favorites and they're generally great. The presentation of the food matches its quality. The dining room features romantic low lighting, smallish tables, interesting artwork, and an outdoor patio that's perfect for balmy summer nights.

## Creole

**The Palace Grill** (8 E. Cota St., 805/963-5000, www.palacegrill.com, daily 11 A.M.–3 P.M., 5:30–11 P.M., Fri.–Sat. until midnight, $20–40) boasts of being one of Santa Barbara's most popular restaurants and a little piece of old New Orleans in sunny California. The atmosphere gets lively in the evenings, so this isn't the place to come for a quiet meal. Live entertainers delight the crowds several nights each week, and every once in awhile a restaurant-wide sing-along breaks out. The food is pure Louisiana bayou; look for classically prepared etouffes, jambalaya, and gumbo ya-ya. Most of the seafood is flown in fresh daily, the steaks are aged to perfection, and much of the fresh finned fish and meat is served blackened and spiced in Cajun style. Even the appetizers and desserts drip Creole and Cajun flavors. Start off with a house specialty cocktail or a glass of California wine. While you dine, be sure to take a moment to appreciate the particularly fine service that is a staple of the Palace's reputation.

## Mexican

Have you ever wanted to know what true, authentic Mexican food might taste like? **La Super-Rica Taqueria** (622 N. Milpas St., 805/963-4940, Thurs.–Tues. 11 A.M.–9 P.M., Fri.–Sat. 11 A.M.–9:30 P.M., $10) can hook you up. Of course, you must be prepared to stand in line with dozens of locals and even commuters up from Los Angeles and the occasional Hollywood celeb who think La Super-Rica's got some of the best down-home Mexican cuisine in all of SoCal. This was Julia Child's favorite taco stand, and it's been reviewed by the *New York Times*.

Folks don't come for the ambiance—expect paper plates, plastic chairs, and shorts and sandals on the diners in a genuine shack of a building. You also need to adjust your concept of Mexican food; if you're looking for a fast-food burrito supreme with chips and salsa, you'll definitely be disappointed. But if you're ready for the real deal, you've found it. The corn tortillas are made fresh each day, the meat is slow cooked and seasoned to perfection, and the house special is a grilled pork-stuffed pasilla chile. Vegetarians can choose from a few delicious meat-free dishes, while carnivores will leave satisfied with their pork-, chicken-, or steak-based entrées.

## Middle Eastern

For a Middle Eastern feast, go to **Zaytoon** (209 E. Canon Perdido St., 805/963-1293, www.cafezaytoon.com, Mon.–Sat. 11:30 A.M.–9 P.M., Sun. 4–9 P.M., $10–30). This restaurant and hookah bar appeals to a crowd that wants to enjoy an evening out with a group of friends, to share a hookah around the table, and to ogle talented belly dancers shimmying amongst the tables. While the interior dining room is attractive, with potted palms and gauzy fabric draped from the ceiling, it's not the best place to sit at Zaytoon. Instead, try to get a table out on the garden patio, a large, softly lit space almost completely enveloped by a living green jungle. It is out here that you can order up your own hookah. The menu has most standard Middle Eastern favorites, such as baba ghannouj, hummus, falafel, Greek salad, shawarma, and kebabs of many kinds.

## Seafood

It takes something special to make Santa Barbara residents take notice of a seafood restaurant, and **Brophy Brothers** (119 Harbor Way, 805/966-4418, www.brophybros.com, Sun.–Thurs. 11 A.M.–10 P.M. Fri.–Sat. 11 A.M.–11 P.M., $10–30) has it. Look for a small list of fresh fish done up California style with upscale preparations. The delectable menu goes heavy on locally caught seafood. At the clam bar, you can order some fresh raw clams (duh!) or oysters, a bowl of the house clam chowder, or a tasty seafood salad. With a prime location looking out over the masts of the sailboats in the harbor, it's no surprise that Brophy Brothers gets crowded at both lunch and dinnertime, especially on weekends in the summertime.

## Coffee

Skip the big chains and head for **Java Jones** (728 State St., 805/962-4721, daily 7 A.M.–11 P.M.), conveniently located in the middle of State Street. This local coffee house has brick walls, cushy couches in the upstairs loft seating area, and local art on the walls. It's also got a better-than-average selection of caffeinated go-juice, including Turkish coffee and Vietnamese coffee. In the morning, locals and visitors alike can order from the limited but tasty breakfast menu. Pastries and salads are available all day and late into the night. Go ahead and bring your laptop (yup, they've got Wi-Fi), grab a chair, and settle in.

## INFORMATION AND SERVICES

The **Santa Barbara Conference and Visitors Bureau** (1601 Anacapa St., 805/966-9222, www.santabarbaraca.com) maintains an **Outdoor Visitors Center** (113 Harbor Way, Waterfront Center, 4th Fl., 805/884-1475) for visitors who never want to leave sight of the beach.

As a major metropolitan city, Santa Barbara publishes its own daily newspaper, the *Santa Barbara News Press* (www.newspress.com). Look for it in shops, on newsstands, and in your hotel or inn. Check the *Scene and Life* sections for information about entertainment, events, and attractions.

The major hospital in town is **Santa Barbara Cottage Hospital** (320 W. Pueblo St., 805/682-7111, www.sbch.org), which includes a full-service emergency room.

## GETTING THERE AND AROUND

To reach Santa Barbara by air, fly into the **Santa Barbara Municipal Airport** (Moffet Rd., 805/967-7111, www.flysba.com). A number of major commercial airlines fly into Santa Barbara, including United, Alaska/Horizon, Delta, and American Airlines.

A more beautiful and peaceful way to get to Santa Barbara is by train. The **Amtrak** Coast Starlight (www.amtrak.com) runs into town daily. From Los Angeles or San Francisco's east bay, connect to other trains that run into California from points east.

Santa Barbara is located on Highway 101, also known as the Pacific Coast Highway and El Camino Real in this neck of the woods. To head out to the Santa Ynez Valley and other local wine regions, take CA Highway 154 east. If staying in Santa Barbara proper, expect fairly standard city driving, complete with traffic jams during weekday business hours and on beach access roads on the weekends. Parking can be challenging, especial at the beach on sunny summer weekends. Expect to pay a premium for a good-to-mediocre spot, or to walk for several blocks. If possible, take the local public streetcar from the downtown area to the beach and leave your car elsewhere.

Santa Barbara has its own transit authority. The **MTD Santa Barbara** (805/963-336, www.sbmtd.gov) runs both the local bus service ($1.25 regular fare) and the Waterfront Shuttle and Downtown-Waterfront lines ($0.25 regular fare). Have exact change to pay your fare when boarding the bus or shuttle; if transferring buses, ask the driver for a free transfer pass.

# BACKGROUND

## The Land

### GEOGRAPHY

California includes just about every geographical feature imaginable, from alpine lakes to parched and delicate deserts to active volcanoes and sun-swept Pacific beaches. The state is trisected vertically by mountain ranges, with valleys in between, and terminates west at the coast of the Pacific Ocean. Many rivers flow west as the ocean wears away at the land, creating coves, waterfalls, and immense bays.

To the east, the Sierra Nevada mountain range looms above all other geography, with craggy snowcapped peaks, alpine lakes and meadows, and gold-producing foothills. The northern mountains—Shasta and Lassen—are the southern tip of the Cascade Range that stretches far into the Pacific Northwest, all the way through Oregon and into Washington. This youthful volcanic chain is part of the Pacific Ring of Fire, contributing recent eruptions by Mount Lassen and Mount St. Helens. Though it's been a while since Shasta's fires last burbled to the surface, the mountain is classed as dormant, not extinct; if she ever blows again, the effects on the whole of the American West will be staggering.

At the foot of the Sierras sits a giant fertile valley that is the produce capital of the state, and much of the West. Maps and books refer to it as the San Joaquin Valley, but Californians usually call it the Central Valley, and much of the state's massive agriculture industry resides here.

To the south, deserts rule the landscape. California boasts two distinct desert regions: the northern and higher-elevation Mojave Desert, and the southern and low-elevation Colorado Desert (which encompasses Anza-Borrego State Park and the southern half of Joshua Tree National Monument).

The coastal region is bounded by a mountain range, famed in the north for forests filled with enormous coast redwood trees. The northern coastline winds along soaring craggy cliffs overlooking rocky beaches and coves, while the southern coastline tends toward the broad, sandy beaches that California is famous for.

## CLIMATE

Though California is known for the mild climate along its southern shores, the state can claim a number of distinct climate zones.

Mark Twain's famous 19th-century quote—"The coldest winter I ever spent was a summer in San Francisco!"—still stands. If you're visiting "the City" in July or August, don't bother bringing shorts—the weather is generally foggy and cool, with temperatures in the 50s and 60s. These cool temperatures persist along the Bay Area coastline as well. But if you head south to Silicon Valley or to the East Bay, expect temperatures to get up to 20–30° warmer and to see sun instead of fog.

Up along the North Coast, the weather stays about the same year-round: chilly, windy, and foggy. Temperatures can get up into the sunny 80s on rare hot summer days, and winter storms can pound the area with rain. These weather patterns turn milder toward coastal Sonoma in the southern Wine Country. Napa's scorching hot valley summers and mild-to-cool winters are perfect for the grapes growing everywhere—and the tourists who come to drink them.

Lake Tahoe, Mount Shasta, Mount Lassen, Yosemite, and the Eastern Sierras all experience harsh, snow-filled winters that can close roads and wreak havoc with travel plans, but present ideal conditions for a multitude of winter sports. The short, hot summers also draw tourists out in droves.

Sacramento and the Central Valley boast high heat in the summers—often over 100°F—and cool but usually clear winters. The surrounding Gold Country, however, often receives snow in winter and can make roads here impassible.

The Central Coast has somewhat warmer temperatures than the Bay Area beaches, but you can still expect average cool temperatures and plenty of fog in the summer, with chill winds and some rain in the winter. The inland Central Coast wine regions mimic the climate patterns of the Wine Country and are more mild.

From the Los Angeles Basin down to San Diego and up the coast to Santa Barbara, temperatures are mild all year long. Expect fog on the beaches during the summer, cool days in the wintertime, and hotter temperatures in the inland valleys and Disneyland. For the best summertime beach weather in the state, head for San Diego.

The central and eastern deserts in the southern end of the state experience typical desert climates. That means mild, comfortable winters perfect for hiking and outdoor sports, but with nighttime temperatures in the 30s and 40s. The deserts' dangerously hot summers can easily reach 110–120°F.

## ENVIRONMENTAL ISSUES

Environmental issues are California's political bread-and-butter. Los Angeles is rightly famous for its smog, though the San Francisco Bay Area is rapidly catching up in this unattractive race. If you're sensitive to airborne pollution, take special precautions on days that local air quality officials designate "Spare the Air." These are days, mostly in the summer, when pollution levels are especially high. Stay indoors or, when going out, use public transportation.

Water pollution is also an issue in California;

plenty of sensational news stories crucify the state's drinking water, while others laud it. Most tap water is safe to drink, but swimming in California's plentiful rivers and ocean requires more caution. Sadly, water pollution from dumping into the ocean affects beach goers. Dirt and pollution are common in the waters and on the beaches of Los Angeles and Orange Counties, while fishing is no longer permitted in the San Francisco Bay due to the long-standing pollution problems and high mercury levels in the bay's fish.

There are major restrictions on the types of power boats you can launch at Lake Tahoe, due to protections instituted to keep the azure-blue waters of this huge alpine lake pristine. Similar restrictions can also be found for waterways across the state; check the regulations for any lake or river before planning a boating trip.

The good news is that environmental conservation and protection are taken very seriously in California. Recycling, public transit growth, and water cleanup programs proliferate throughout the state. Even as a short-time visitor, you can help California's efforts to get and stay clean: Use any recycling bins you see on the street; minimize your use of plastic bags; and don't leave litter on the beach or out in wilderness areas—either throw it away or pack it out with you.

## FLORA AND FAUNA

California's diverse geography gives rise to dozens of different ecosystems, each of which has its own unique native plants and animals. Botanical gardens, zoos, and wildlife preserves abound throughout the state, giving visitors ample opportunities to smell the flowers, pet the animals, and learn about the complex and varied life that abounds all through the Golden State.

### Redwoods

The most famous trees native to California are undoubtedly the redwoods. The **coast redwood** *(Sequoia sempervirens)* grows on the North Coast and down through the Bay Area all the way to Big Sur. Coast redwood trees perch on cliffs overlooking the sea, but most of the best groves are inland, in the mountains. The Redwood National and State Parks do

© LIZ HAMILL SCOTT

**redwoods in the sky**

the best job of showcasing these grand trees, though any hiker in the Santa Cruz Mountains can reach out and touch soft redwood bark.

The truly immense redwood trees don't grow along the coast—they're much farther inland. The **giant sequoia** *(Sequoiadendron giganteum)* grow in the Sierra Nevada mountains. These redwoods can live for thousands of years and grow to unimaginable heights. The museum at Sequoia-Kings Canyon National Park includes a wonderful interpretive display describing the life cycle of the giant sequoia, including information about the importance of fire to the health and propagation of these trees. Sequoia groves grow aplenty in Yosemite National Park, Calaveras Big Trees, and a few other select spots in the Sierras.

## Joshua Trees

One famous California tree isn't a tree at all. The desert-dwelling **Joshua tree** *(Yucca brevifolia)* is actually a member of the yucca family. You can't miss a Joshua tree—from a distance, it almost resembles an honest-to-goodness deciduous tree. But when you get up close, the scaly "bark" starts to look strange and the "leaves" even odder—spiky and big. Larger Joshua trees can get up to 15 feet tall with dozens of leafy "branches" at their tops. While the best place to see forests of Joshua trees is, of course, in Joshua Tree National Monument, Joshua trees thrive in the Mojave Desert ecosystem—they're all over the Mojave Preserve and can even be found alongside the desert's highways.

## Wildflowers

California's state flower is the **California poppy** *(Eschscholzia californica)*. The pretty little orange blossom grows just about everywhere, even on the sides of the busiest highways. Though most California poppies are bright orange, they also appear occasionally in white, cream, and even deeper red-orange.

## Reptiles

If you spot California's most infamous native reptile, keep your distance. Several varieties of **rattlesnakes** are indigenous to the state. The Pacific Northwest rattler makes its home in Northern California, while more than half

a funky Joshua tree

© LANCE SCOTT

a dozen different rattlesnake varieties live in Southern California, including the Western diamondback and the Mojave rattlesnake.

All rattlesnakes are venomous, though death by snakebite is extremely rare in California. Most parks with known rattlesnakes in residence post signs alerting hikers; your best bet to keep safe is to stay on trails and avoid tromping off into meadows or brush. Pay attention when hiking, especially when negotiating rocks and woodpiles, and never put a foot or a hand down in a spot you can't see first. Wear long pants and heavy hiking boots for protection (from snakes, plus insects, other critters, and unfriendly plants you might encounter).

## Butterflies

California isn't the tropics, but its vast population of wildflowers attract an array of gorgeous butterflies. The **Monarch butterfly** has become an emblem of the state. These large orange-and-black butterflies have a migratory pattern that's reminiscent of birds. Each winter, the butterflies fly south from their summertime wanderings to cluster in several groves of eucalyptus trees throughout the temperate coastal zone. As they close up their wings to hibernate for the winter, their crowding and dull outer wing color makes them resemble clumps of dried leaves, thus protecting them from predators. In spring, the butterflies begin to wake up, fluttering lazily in the groves a bit before flying north to seek out milkweed on which to lay their eggs. Santa Cruz and Cambria are two great places to visit the California "butterfly trees."

# History and Economy

California boasts a rich history, filled with great stories and fascinating characters. The state's timeline flows from the Native Americans through the first European explorations to the building of the Spanish missions, then the Gold Rush, and on into the millennium.

Today, California takes an active role in the economy and culture of the United States and indeed the world. The Internet began, took off, boomed, busted, and settled into its current iteration as a worldwide communication and commerce web in the Bay Area. Central Valley agriculture remains the state's economic mainstay, while the motion picture industry continues to dominate the Los Angeles landscape. Movie stars keep getting into politics; actors Ronald Regan and Arnold Schwarzenegger have claimed residence in the Governor's Mansion and Clint Eastwood's credits include a stint as mayor of Carmel-by-the-Sea.

California has had good times and bad, triumphs and shame, but one thing has remained constant—the story of California is never, ever boring.

## THE MISSION PERIOD

California's earliest explorers and European colonists were mostly from Spain—hence the proliferation of Spanish-named streets, towns, and even colleges that persist to this day. Monuments to many of these men can be found in various parts of the state.

No single man is credited with as much influence on the early development of California than Father Junípero Serra. The Franciscan monk took an active role in bringing Christianity (and, unfortunately, the corollary syphilis, measles, and smallpox) to native peoples from San Diego all the way up to Sonoma. To that end, the Franciscan order built a string of missions, each of which was meant to be a self-sufficient parish that grew its own food, kept up its own buildings, and took care of its own people. The monks also created a road between the missions—El Camino Real—with the idea that a pilgrim could travel the length of El Camino Real and find a bed at the next mission after only one day's journey. Today, El Camino Real remains a vital part of the state and much of the original path still exists; just look for the mission bells mounted on curved poles posted along the sides of the road. In the Bay Area, El Camino Real isn't a highway—it's a business street running the length of the Peninsula. To the south, El Camino Real and U.S. 101 sometimes merge into one; at other points El Camino rambles away from any main roads.

The missions prospered in the early 1800s, then gradually deteriorated until they were ordered to secularize in the middle of the 19th century. Some took on new uses; others fell into disrepair and outright abandonment. It was only in the 20th century that interest in the history of the missions was rekindled and money was invested into restoring many of the churches and complexes. Today, many (but not all) of the missions have been restored as Catholic parishes, with visitors centers and museum displays of various levels of quality and polish.

## THE GOLD RUSH

In 1849, a worker discovered nuggets of gold in the machinery at Sutter's Mill. The news that chunks of gold were just sitting there on

Sutter's Mill, the birthplace of California's Gold Rush

the riverbeds for the taking spread like wildfire. The Gold Rush was on. People from the East Coast and all over the world streamed into California by land and by sea, seeking a fortune in gold—or a fortune in serving or selling to the gold-seekers. Thousands of men panned every available stream for nuggets, then water-blasted hillsides away seeking the elusive precious metal. Even then, the wanton destruction caused by the blasting was quickly seen to be a problem. And so the famous hard-rock mines of California began construction. Though panning continued (hope springs eternal, after all), by the 1860s most of the rough men had taken jobs working in the deep, dangerous mines.

With the influx of gold seekers, new cities sprang up almost overnight. The previously small town of San Francisco became the major port of entry for immigrants. Sacramento's river location made it a perfect transportation hub and waypoint between San Francisco and the gold fields. Mining towns like Sonora, Volcano, Placerville, Sutter's Creek, and Nevada City swelled to huge proportions, only to shrink back into obscurity as the mines closed one by one in the 20th century.

As American and European men came to California to seek their fortunes in gold, a few wives and children joined them, but the number of families in the average mining town was small. Yet a few lone women did join in the rush to the gold fields. These ladies took up "the oldest profession," servicing the population of single male miners and laborers in desperate need of (ahem) female companionship.

The other major group of immigrants at this time came to California from a land distant in both distance and culture: China. Thousands of Chinese men came, not to mine, but to labor and serve the white miners. Most were forced to pass through the wretched immigration facilities on Angel Island in the middle of San Francisco Bay—sometimes being essentially imprisoned for months before either being allowed onto the mainland or summarily shipped back to China. San Francisco's Chinatown became a hub for the immigrants,

to honor the "Ladies of the Evening"

a place where their language was spoken and their culture comprehended. But thousands headed east, becoming low-level laborers in the industry surrounding the mines, or workers on the railroads endlessly spooling out to connect Gold Country to the rest of the state and eventually to the East Coast by way of the Transcontinental Railroad.

## THE 1960S

Few places in the country felt the impact of the radical 1960s more than California. In fact, it's arguable that the peace and free love movements began right here, probably on the campus of the infamous and indomitable University of California at Berkeley. Certainly Berkeley helped to shape and grow the culture of hippies, peaceniks, and radical politics. The college campus was the home of the Black Panthers, anti-Vietnam War sit-ins, and numerous protests for all sorts of liberal causes.

If Berkeley was the de facto home of 1960s political movements, then San Francisco was the base of its social and cultural phenomena. Free concerts in Golden Gate Park and the growing fame of the hippie community taking over an area called Haight-Ashbury drew teenagers from across the country. Many found themselves living on Haight Street for months, experimenting with the most popular mind-altering chemicals of the era. The music scene became the stuff of legend and song (sorry). The Grateful Dead—one of the most famous and longest lasting of the 1960s rock bands—hailed from the Bay Area.

## ECONOMY

The state of California boasts the eighth-largest economy in the *world*. California's contribution to the United States outpaces even its immense size and population.

### Agriculture

Many people guess incorrectly when asked what California's number one economic sector is. It's not high tech. It's not films. It's farming! California's agricultural juggernaut supplies much of the world with crops of almost all kinds, from grapefruit to grass-fed beef.

In warm Southern California, citrus trees rule much of the landscape; you can even find grapefruit groves in the harsh climate of the

Anza-Borrego Desert. The Central Valley's flat, fertile fields produce everything from rice to corn to tomatoes. In the summertime, tomato trucks drive routes all around Sacramento to processing plants that create that all-important American staple food: ketchup. The cooler Central Coast region grows sweet strawberries and spiky artichokes in abundance. As the fog gets colder and drippier in Marin, ranchers take advantage of the naturally growing grasses to ranch herds of cattle destined for the growing sustainable-food market. In truth, cattle are ranched all over the state, from the far-north reaches down to the southern deserts.

Today, as awareness grows about the harmful affects of pesticides and petrochemical fertilizers on both the land and consumers, organic farms and ranches are proliferating across California. In addition to the giant factory farms so prevalent in the Central Valley, you'll also see an increasing number of small farms and ranches growing a variety of crops using organic, sustainable, and even biodynamic practices. Most of these farmers sell directly to consumers by way of farmers markets and farm stands—almost every town or county in the state has a weekly farmer's market in the summertime, and many last year-round.

And then there's the wine. It seems like every square inch of free agricultural land in the state now has a grapevine growing on it. The vineyards that were once primarily seen in Napa and Sonoma Counties can now be found on the slopes of the Sierra Foothills, down south in Santa Barbara, and even close to coastside in Mendocino and Carmel. Surprising to some, it's actually the wine industry that's leading the charge beyond mere organic and into biodynamic growing practices, such as using sheep to keep the weeds down in the vineyards and provide natural fertilizer, or harvesting grapes and pruning vines according to the moon's cycles to promote optimum wine quality. (In truth, it makes sense, and serious wine drinkers are willing to pay premium prices for top-quality vintages.)

## Industry

The motion picture industry draws the most publicity to California. Though little filming takes place in and around Hollywood today, it's still the home of the major studios and their prominent executives.

© LIZ HAMILL SCOTT

Agriculture is California's major economic sector.

In Northern California, Silicon Valley has made a name for itself as the epicenter of the technology industry. Despite the expense of property in the Bay Area, nearly every major high-tech company maintains a presence somewhere near Silicon Valley, as many were founded and are still headquartered there. Major tech legends include Hewlett-Packard in Palo Alto, Apple Computer in Cupertino, and Intel on the border of Santa Clara and San Jose. Google remains loyal to its hometown of Mountain View, and Microsoft has opened offices throughout Silicon Valley. During the "dot-com boom" of the early 1990s, nearly everyone in the region seemed to somehow be employed by the tech industry, and when the bust came it hit the region like a ton of outdated CRT monitors.

Today, the tech industry still provides hundreds of thousands of top-paying jobs in Silicon Valley and throughout the greater Bay Area and most residents of the region tend towards the tech-savvy.

# People and Culture

## RELIGION

A wide variety of religions and belief systems have come to characterize California. The state is home to large populations of Catholics, Protestants, Jews, Muslims, Buddhists, and even Wiccan religions and Scientologists. Many urban centers, especially San Francisco and Los Angeles, provide houses of worship or religious centers for practitioners of these and many other faiths.

Many Californians cherish the religious tolerance found here, and the right and ability of all to practice their desired form of worship is widely protected. So expect to see everything from rigorous observance of Lent to traditional Chinese New Year to pagan solstice rituals in the park.

## LANGUAGE

As in the rest of the United States, English is the official language in California. However, the state's large immigrant population has resulted in equally large non-English speaking communities. Due to the state's proximity to Mexico, Spanish is the most widely spoken foreign language. Other major spoken and written languages include Chinese, Cantonese, Korean, Vietnamese, Japanese, and various East Indian dialects. Throughout the state, this multilingualism often results in a colorful blend of cultures, creating a multiethnic tapestry of California residents. However, in both Los Angeles and the Bay Area, tightly knit Asian and Hispanic communities sometimes feature little-to-no signs or menus in English, and few proprietors speak standard English. Exploring the culture of California means exploring the backgrounds of those who live here, so be prepared to learn more about the world even as you learn more about the state.

Signs in Chinatown reflect a mix of languages.

# ESSENTIALS

## Getting There

### BY AIR

It's easy to fly in to California, particularly if you're heading for one of the major metropolitan areas. Reaching the more rural or outlying regions of the state is a bit trickier and you'll probably find yourself driving—possibly for hours—from one of the major airports.

### Los Angeles

The greater Los Angeles area is thick with airports. **Los Angeles International Airport** (LAX, www.lawa.org) serves the greater Los Angeles area, and is located about 10 miles south of the city of Santa Monica. If you're coming in from another country or from across the continent, you're likely to find your flight coming into this endlessly crowded hub. If you're flying home from LAX, plan plenty of time to get through security and the check-in lines—up to three hours for a domestic flight on a holiday weekend.

To miss the major crowds, consider flying into one of the many suburban airports. **John Wayne International** (www.ocair.com) services Disneyland perfectly, and the **Long Beach** airport (www.longbeach.gov/airport) is convenient to the beaches. Ontario Airport is farther out but a good option for travelers

planning to divide their time between Los Angeles, Palm Springs, and the deserts.

In Los Angeles, free shuttle buses provide service to the Los Angeles County **Metropolitan Transportation Authority Metro Rail** (800/266-6883), accessible at the Green Line Aviation Station. Metro Rail trains connect into Long Beach, Hollywood, North Hollywood, downtown Los Angeles, and Pasadena. Passengers should wait under the "LAX Shuttle Airline Connection" signs outside the lower-level terminals and board the "G" shuttle. Passengers may also take the "C" shuttle to the **Metro Bus Center** (800/266-6883), which connects to buses that serve the entire L.A. area. Information about bus service is provided via telephones on the Information Display Board inside each terminal.

Shuttle services are also available if you wish to share a ride. **Prime Time Shuttle** (800/733-8267, www.primetimeshuttle.com) and SuperShuttle (800/258-3826, www.super shuttle.com) are authorized to serve the entire Los Angeles area out of LAX. These vans can be found on the lower/arrivals deck in front of each terminal, under the orange "Shared Ride Vans" signs. Average fares for two people are about $32 into downtown Los Angeles, $34 into West Hollywood, and $30 into Santa Monica.

**Taxis** can be found on the lower/arrivals level islands in front of each terminal, below the yellow "Taxi" signs. Only licensed taxis are allowed into the airport; they have standard rates of about $40 to downtown and $30 to West Los Angeles.

### San Diego

Three terminals at **San Diego International Airport** (N. Harbor Dr., San Diego, www.san .org) provide easy access to Southern California. (They somehow managed to squeeze the runways in right downtown by the ocean, making it incredibly convenient for visitors to the seaside city.) Long- and short-term parking is available by the hour or day. The airport is serviced daily by **Amtrak** (800/872-7245, www .amtrak.com) and by **Coaster** (www.gonctd .com, 800/262-7837, Mon.–Sat., $4) trains via

the Santa Fe Deport train station downtown. The Flyer Route No. 992 metro **bus** (http:// transit.511sd.com, 5 A.M.–12:50 A.M., $2.25) stops downtown and connects with the San Diego Trolley, Coaster, and Amtrak. Note that the Trolley does not connect directly to the airport.

## BY TRAIN

Several cross-country **Amtrak** (www.amtrak .com) trains rumble into California each day. If you're arriving from another part of the country, the train can be a relaxing way to make the journey to the Golden State; long-distance train routes usually include dining and lounge cars. There are eight train routes that service California: The California Zephyr travels to Chicago, Denver, and Emervyille; the Capitol Corridor services Auburn, Sacramento, Emeryville, Oakland, and San Jose, and a popular route with local communters; the Coast Starlight travel down the west coast, from Seattle to Portland and ending in Los Angeles; the Pacific Surfliner will get you to the Central Coast and southern California, while the San Joaquins services the Central Valley; the Southwest Chief, Sunset Limited, and Texas Eagle brings travelers from the south and midwest into California.

## BY CAR

Many Americans get to visit California by driving here. A number of interstate highways run into the state from points east and north. From the Pacific Northwest, I-5 runs north and south through the state and will get you here quickly. The coastal routes along Highway 1 and Highway 101 are longer, but prettier. I-10 and I-15 allow access from the southeastern regions.

### Car Rental

Most major car rental companies are located in one central area at the major airports. To reserve a car in advance, contact **Budget Rent A Car** (800/527-0700), **Dollar Rent A Car** (866/434-2226), **Enterprise** (www.enterprise .com), or **Hertz** (www.hertz.com).

# Getting Around

## BY AIR

When traversing major cities within the state, flying can be an economical (and faster) option.

**Los Angeles International Airport** (LAX,www.lawa.org) serves the greater Los Angeles, offers a wealth of airline options, and can connect with flights both to San Francisco and Los Angeles. But it can be a hectic and time-consuming maze to navigate. Other options in the area include the **Bob Hope Airport** (2627 N. Hollywod Way, Burbank, 818/840-8840, www.burbankairport.com) and the **Long Beach Airport** (4100 Donald Douglas Dr., 562/570-2600, www.longbeach .gov/airport).

The **San Diego International Airport** (N. Harbor Dr., San Diego, www.san.org) provides easy access to southern California and Mexico, if your travelers take you further south.

## BY TRAIN

**Amtrak** (www.amtrak.com) trains run several corridors through the state. The California Zephyr, Capitol Corridor, Coast Starlight, and San Joaquins routes offer services to Auburn, Sacramento, Emeryville, Oakland, San Jose, Los Angeles, the Central Coast, and the Central Valley. Train are roomy, comfortable, and offer a dining car for affordable snacks and meals.

## BY CAR

California is great for road-tripping. Scenic coastal routes such as Highway 1 and Highway 101 are often destinations in themselves, while inland I-5 is the most direct route north and south through the state. However, traffic jams, accidents, mudslides, fires, and snow can affect highways and interstates at any time. Before heading out on your adventure, check road conditions online at the Calfiornia Department of Transportation (Caltrans, www.dot.ca.gov). Note that mountain passes such as I-80 into Tahoe, I-5 at the Grapevine, and the Shasta and Lassen regions may require snow tires and/ or chains. In rural areas and in the deserts, gas stations may be few and far between.

# Visas and Officialdom

## PASSPORTS AND VISAS

If you're visiting California from another country, you must present a valid passport upon entry into the United States. You must also hold a return plane or cruise ticket to your country of origin dated less than 90 days from your date of entry (Canada excepted).

If you hold a passport from one of the following countries, you do not need a visa to enter California: Andorra, Australia, Austria, Belgium, Brunei, Denmark, Finland, France, Germany, Iceland, Ireland, Italy, Japan, Liechtenstein, Luxembourg, Monaco, the Netherlands, New Zealand, Norway, Portugal, San Marino, Singapore, Slovenia, Spain, Sweden, Switzerland, and the United Kingdom.

In most other countries, the local U.S. embassy should be able to provide a free tourist visa, often within 24 hours of request. Do plan more time for visa processing if you're requesting travel in the high summer season (June–Aug.).

## EMBASSIES

San Francisco and Los Angeles both shelter embassies and consulates from many countries around the globe. If you should lose your passport or find yourself in some other trouble while visiting California, contact your country's offices for assistance. To find an embassy, check www.travel.state.gov for a list of embassies within the state.

## CUSTOMS

Before you enter California from another country by sea or by air, you'll be required to fill out a customs form. Check with the U.S. embassy in your country or the Customs Bureau website (www.cbp.gov) for an updated list of items you must declare.

If you require medication administered by injection, you must pack your syringes in a checked bag; syringes are not permitted in carry-ons coming into the United States.

Also pack documentation describing your need for any narcotic medications you've brought with you. Failure to produce documentation for narcotics upon request can result in severe penalties in the United States.

If you're driving into California along I-5 or another major freeway, prepare to stop at Agricultural Inspection stations few miles inside the state line. You don't need to present a passport, a visa, or even a driver's license. Instead, you must be prepared to present all your fruits and vegetables.

California's largest economic segment lies in agriculture, and a number of the major crops grown here are sensitive to pests and diseases. In an effort to prevent known pests from entering the state and endangering the crops, travelers are asked to identify all produce they're carrying in from other states or from Mexico. If you've got produce, especially homegrown or from a farm stand, that might be infected by a known problem pest or disease, expect it to be confiscated on the spot.

You'll also be asked about fruits and veggies on your customs form, which you'll be asked to fill out on the airplane or ship before you reach the United States.

# Tips for Travelers

## CONDUCT AND CUSTOMS

The legal drinking age in California is 21. Expect to have your ID checked if you look under 30, especially in bars and clubs, but also in restaurants and wineries.

Most California bars and clubs close at 2 A.M.; you'll find the occasional after-hours nightspot in Los Angeles, San Francisco, and Palm Springs.

Cigarette smoking has been all but criminalized throughout the state of California. Don't expect to find a smoking section in any restaurant or an ashtray in the bars. Smoking is illegal in all bars and clubs, but your new favorite watering hole might have an outdoor patio where smokers can huddle. Taking the ban one step further, many hotels, motels, and inns throughout the state are strictly non-smoking, and you'll be subject to fees of several hundred dollars if your room smells of smoke when you leave.

There's no smoking in any public building, and even some of the state parks don't allow cigarettes. There's often good reason for this; fire danger in California is extreme in the summertime, and one carelessly thrown lit butt can cause a genuine catastrophe.

## TRAVELING WITH CHILDREN

Many spots in California are ideal destinations for families with children of all ages. In both the San Francisco Bay Area and the Los Angeles region, amusement parks, interactive museums, zoos, parks, beaches, and playgrounds all make for family-friendly fun. Even some of the upscale hotels offer great programs for young people, and many Southern California resorts designate at least one swimming pool as "family" or "loud" to accommodate rambunctious fun and outside voices.

You know your children best, so you can plan a great trip they'll love based on their special interests. Would they prefer Disneyland or the San Diego Zoo? Surf lessons at Huntington Beach or rock climbing school at Joshua Tree? Redwood trees or youth nightclubs?

On the other hand, there are a few spots in the Golden State that beckon more to adults than to children. Frankly, there aren't many family activities in Wine Country. This adult playground is all about alcoholic beverages and high-end dining. Similarly, romantic B&Bs bring out couples looking for weekend getaways rather than families. In fact, before you book a room at a B&B that you expect to share with your kids, check to be sure that the inn can accommodate extra people in their guest rooms and allows guests under 16 years old.

## WOMEN TRAVELERS

California's a pretty friendly place for women traveling alone. Most of the major outdoor attractions are incredibly safe, and even many of the urban areas boast pleasant neighborhoods that welcome lone female travelers.

But you'll need to take some basic precautions and pay attention to your surroundings just as you would in any unfamiliar place. Carry your car keys in your hand when walking out to your car. Don't sit in your parked car in a lonely parking lot at night; just get in, turn on the engine, and drive away. When you're walking down a city street, be alert and keep an eye on your surroundings and on anyone who might be following you. In rural areas, don't go tromping into unlit wooded areas or out into grassy fields alone at night without a flashlight; many of California's critters are nocturnal. (Actually, this caution applies to men traveling alone as well. Mountain lions and rattlesnakes don't tend to discriminate.)

Some neighborhoods in the big cities are best avoided by lone women, especially at night. Besides the obvious—the Tenderloin in San Francisco and the Compton, Watts, and Inglewood neighborhoods of Los Angeles—some other streets and neighborhoods can turn distinctly hostile after dark.

## SENIOR TRAVELERS

California makes an ideal destination for retired folks looking to relax and have a great time. You'll find senior discounts nearly every place you go, from restaurants to golf courses to major attractions, and even at some hotels, though the minimum age can vary from 50–65. Just ask, and be prepared to produce ID if you look young or are requesting an AARP discount.

For landlubbers, RV parks abound throughout the state, and even many of the state and national parks can accommodate RVs and trailers. The Southern California deserts are particularly popular with snowbirds. Check with the parks you want to visit for size and location restrictions, hookup and dump station information, and RV slot prices.

## GAY AND LESBIAN TRAVELERS

California is known for its thriving gay and lesbian communities. In fact, the Golden State is a golden place for gay travel—especially in the bigger cities, and even some of the smaller towns both in the north and the south parts of the state. As with much of the country, the further you venture into more rural and agricultural regions, the less likely you're to experience the liberal acceptance the state is known for.

In Northern California, San Francisco has the biggest and arguably best Gay Pride Festival (www.sfpride.org) in the nation, usually held down Market Street the last weekend in June. All year-round, the Castro District offers fun of all kinds, from theater to clubs to shopping, mostly targeted for gay men but with a few places sprinkled in for lesbians. If the Castro is your primary destination, you can even find a place to stay right in the midst of the action.

Both gay men and women flock to Santa Cruz on the coastline, though the quirky town is specially known for its lesbian-friendly culture. A relaxed vibe informs everything from underground clubs to unofficial nude beaches to live-action role playing games in the middle of downtown. Even the lingerie and adult toy shops tend to be female-owned and -operated.

So where do gay and lesbian San Francisco residents go to get away for the weekend? Many flock to Guerneville—an outdoorsy town on the Russian River. Rustic lodges offer cabins down by the river, rafting and kayaking companies offer summertime adventures, and nearby wineries offer and relaxation. The short but colorful Main Street is home to queer-friendly bars and festivals. (See *Moon Northern California* for full coverage.)

Down south, the most gay-friendly town has to be Palm Springs. Gay bars and clubs proliferate here in a relaxed and friendly atmosphere that welcomes men, women, and even straight senior citizens. The White Party and Gay Pride (www.pspride.org, first weekend in November) are huge events that draw tens of thousands of visitors to the desert city. Perhaps best of all, more than a dozen gay resorts cluster in the sun-drenched town, offering swimming pools, hot tubs, and clothing-optional common spaces.

West Hollywood in the Los Angeles Basin has its own upscale gay culture. Just like the rest of L.A.'s clubs, the gay clubs are havens of the see-and-be-seen crowd. The famous Barney's Beanery offers beans and boys, and now has a second location on the Promenade in Santa Monica.

The oh-so-fabulous California vibe has even made it to the interior of the state—Sacramento's newly revitalized Midtown neighborhood offers a more low-key but visible gay evening scene.

# Information and Services

When visiting California, you might be tempted to stop in at one of several Golden State Welcome Centers scattered throughout the state. In all honesty, these visitors centers aren't that great. If you're in an area that doesn't have its own visitors venter or tourist bureau, the State Welcome Center might be a useful place to pick up maps and brochures. Check www.visitcwc.com to find a local Welcome Center wherever you're visiting. Otherwise, stick with local, regional, state, and national park visitors centers (see *Internet Resources*), which tend to be staffed by volunteers or rangers who feel a real passion for their locale.

## MAPS AND TOURIST INFORMATION

Almost all gas stations and drugstores sell maps both of the locale you're traversing and of the whole state. California State Automobile Association (CSAA, www.csaa.com) offices offer maps to members for free.

Many local and regional visitors centers also offer maps, but you'll need to pay a few dollars for the bigger and better ones. But if all you need is a wine-tasting map in a known wine region, you can probably get one for free (plus a few tasting coupons) at the nearest regional visitors center. Basic national park maps come with your admission fee. State park maps can be free, or can cost a few dollars at the visitors centers.

## HEALTH AND SAFETY

Have an emergency anywhere in California? Dial 911. Inside hotels and resorts, check your emergency number as soon as you get into your room. In urban and suburban areas, full-service hospitals and medical centers abound. But in the more remote regions, help can be more than an hour away.

If you're planning a backcountry expedition, follow all rules and guidelines for obtaining wilderness permits and for self-registration at trailheads. These are for your safety, letting the rangers know roughly where you plan to be and when to expect you back. National and state park visitors centers can advise in more detail as to any health or wilderness alerts in the area.

### Poison Oak

There is only one major variety of plant in California that can cause an adverse reaction in humans merely upon touching the leaves or stems. That is poison oak, a common shrub that inhabits forests up and down the state. Poison oak has a characteristic three-leaf configuration, with scalloped leaves that are shiny green in the spring and then turn yellow, orange, and red in late summer and fall. In fall the leaves drop, leaving a cluster of innocuous-looking branches. The oil in poison oak is present all year long in both the leaves and branches. Your best protection is to wear long sleeves and long pants when hiking, no matter how hot it is. A product called Tecnu is available at most California drugstores—slather it on *before* you go hiking to protect yourself from poison oak. If your skin comes in contact with poison oak, expect a nasty rash well known for its itchiness and irritation. Poison oak is also extremely contagious, so avoid touching your eyes, face, or other parts of your body to prevent spreading the rash. Calamine lotion can help, and in extreme cases a doctor can administer cortisone to help decrease the inflammation.

## MONEY

California businesses accept the U.S. dollar ($). Most businesses also accept major credit cards: Visa, MasterCard, Discover, Diner's Club, and American Express. ATM and check-cards work at many stores and restaurants, and you're likely to find ATMs in most every town of any size.

You can change currency in any international airport in the state. Currency exchange points also crop up in downtown San Francisco and Los Angeles and at some of the major business hotels in the urban areas.

# RESOURCES

## Internet Resources

It should come as no surprise that California travel leads the way in use of the Internet as a marketing, communications, and sales tool. The overwhelming majority of destinations have their own websites—even tiny towns in the middle of nowhere proudly tout their attractions on the Web.

### CALIFORNIA
**California Department of Transportation**
**www.dot.ca.gov/hq/roadinfo/statemap.htm**
This website contains state map and highway information.

**Visit California**
**www.visitcalifornia.com**
The official tourism site of the state of California.

### REGIONAL SITES
**Central Coast Regional Tourism**
**www.centralcoast-tourism.com**
A guide to the Central Coast region, including Santa Cruz, Monterey, and Santa Barbara.

**LATourist.com**
**www.latourist.com**
An informative Los Angeles tourist website.

**Los Angeles County Visitors Bureau**
**www.lacvb.com**
The official website of the Los Angeles Convention and Visitors Bureau.

**San Diego Visitors Bureau**
**www.sandiego.org/nav/visitors**
The official website of the San Diego Visitors Bureau.

### PARKS AND OUTDOORS
**California Outdoor and Recreational Information**
**www.caoutdoors.com**
This recreation-focused website includes links to maps, local newspapers, festivals and events, as well as a wide variety of recreational activities throughout the state.

**California State Parks**
**www.parks.ca.gov**
The official website lists hours, accessibility, activities, camping areas, fees, and more information for all parks in the state system.

**Death Valley National Park**
**www.nps.gov/deva**
The official website for Death Valley National Park.

**Disneyland**
**http:/disneyland.disney.go.com**
The official website for Disneyland and all Disney attractions.

### Joshua Tree National Park
**www.nps.gov/jotr**
The official website for Joshua Tree National Park.

### Sequoia and Kings Canyon National Parks
**www.nps.gov/seki**
The official website for Sequoia and Kings Canyon.

### State of California
**www.ca.gov/tourism/ greatoutdoors.html**
Outdoor resources for California state and government organizations. Check for information about fishing and hunting licenses, backcountry permits, boating regulations, and more.

### Yosemite National Park
**www.nps.gov/yose**
The National Park Service website for Yosemite National Park.

### Yosemite National Park Vacation and Lodging Information
**www.yosemitepark.com**
The concessionaire website for Yosemite National Park lodging, dining, and reservations.

# Index

# List of Maps

# www.moon.com

DESTINATIONS | ACTIVITIES | BLOGS | MAPS | BOOKS

**MOON.COM** is all new, and ready to help plan your next trip! Filled with fresh trip ideas and strategies, author interviews, informative blogs, a detailed map library, and descriptions of all the Moon guidebooks, Moon.com is all you need to get out and explore the world—or even places in your own backyard. As always, when you travel with Moon, expect an experience that is uncommon and truly unique.